Trends in Linguistics

Studies and Monographs 23

Editor

Werner Winter

Mouton Publishers
Berlin · New York · Amsterdam

Historical Syntax

edited by

Jacek Fisiak

Mouton Publishers
Berlin · New York · Amsterdam

Professor Jacek Fisiak
Institute of English
Adam Mickiewicz University
Poznań, Poland

Papers presented for the
International Conference on Historical Syntax
held at Błażejewko, Poland,
31 March – 3 April 1981

Library of Congress Cataloging in Publication Data

Historical syntax.

(Trends in linguistics. Studies and monographs; 23)
Includes index.
1. Grammar, Comparative and general Syntax Congresses. 2. Historical linguistics
Congresses.
I. Fisiak, Jacek.   II. Series.
P291.H56 1984   415   84–8208
ISBN 90–279–3250–6

Typesetting: COPO Typesetting, Bangkok, Thailand. – Printing: Druckerei Hildebrand,
Berlin. – Binding: Lüderitz & Bauer Buchgewerbe GmbH, Berlin.

Printed in Germany

Preface

The third international conference on historical linguistics organized by the Institute of English, Adam Mickiewicz University, at Błażejewko near Poznań, was devoted to historical syntax. It aroused a lot of interest and enthusiasm among linguists and forced the organizers to increase the number of invited scholars to over a hundred from the originally planned sixty. Alas, the political unrest in Poland in March 1981 reduced the ranks of participants finally to the number of 46 courageous ones, who came to the conference to present and defend their own ideas and debate the ideas of their colleagues thereby contributing to a further development of their field of interest. To all of them go our sincerest words of thanks. Their lively participation, endless discussions in the conference room and outside allowed many to clarify their views and revise the final versions of papers printed in this volume.

The present volume contains a selection of twenty-nine papers and two comments on papers (Martinet and Vennemann). Out of those twenty-nine, thirteen papers were not presented and discussed at the conference (i.e. Akiba-Reynolds, Birnbaum, Hamp, Harris, Mitchell, Mithun, Pilch, Ramat, Rissanen, Romaine, Rudes, Seefranz-Montag, Stockwell and Winter) but have been included here with the permission of their authors.

The papers cover a wide range of issues within different theoretical paradigms from traditional to advanced transformational-generative. Among the more central theoretical problems confronting a historical syntactician appear, for example, syntactic change, syntactic reconstruction and typology in historical syntax. All these issues found an appropriate place at the conference and consequently in the present volume.

Numerous contributions in the volume refer to particular developments in the history of syntax of various languages. Among them several papers are concerned with non-Indo-European languages.

The Błażejewko conference has not solved or even attempted to solve any particular problems of historical syntax. It seems that the prevailing atmosphere there as well as the tenor of the papers included in the present volume adequately characterize the situation in historical syntax today, a search for

theoretical solutions in the atmosphere of general confusion in syntactic
theory parallelled by data-oriented research concerning various details of
syntax.

We hope that in this situation the conference and the present volume contain at least some elements which can be considered a step forward, even if a
small one, towards a better understanding of some fundamental and several
perhaps less fundamental but still important aspects of historical syntax.

The Błażejewko conference could not have materialized without the support of the Adam Mickiewicz University Vice Rector for Research and
Foreign Exchanges, Professor Stefan Kozarski, to whom we owe our deep
gratitude.

The efficiency and administrative skills of Barbara Płocińska, M.A., have,
as usual, guaranteed the smooth progress of the conference and have contributed to its success.

Poznań, July 1981   Jacek Fisiak

Table of contents

List of conference participants

at the International Conference on Historical Syntax held at Błażejewko, Poland, March 31 – April 3, 1981.

Director

Professor Jacek Fisiak	Adam Mickiewicz University, Poznań

Participants

Professor Werner Abraham	State University of Groningen
Mrs. Arleta Adamska-Sałaciak	Adam Mickiewicz University, Poznań
Dr. Khalil Amaireh	Yarmouk University, Jordan
Professor Henning Andersen	University of Copenhagen
Docent Wiesław Awedyk	Adam Mickiewicz University, Poznań
Professor Jerzy Bańczerowski	Adam Mickiewicz University, Poznań
Dr. Donna Christian	Adam Mickiewicz University, Poznań
Professor Sandra Chung	University of California, San Diego
Docent Andrei Danchev	Institute for Foreign Students, Sofia
Professor Xavier Dekeyser	University of Antwerp and University of Leuven
Professor Dorothy Disterheft	University of South Carolina, Columbia
Dr. Grzegorz Dogil	Adam Mickiewicz University, Poznań
Professor Peter Erdmann	University of Saarbrücken
Professor Detlev Fehling	University of Kiel
Professor Udo Fries	University of Zurich
Ms. Claudia Gdaniec	Technical University of Berlin, West Berlin
Ms. Marinel Gerritsen	Royal Netherlands Academy of Arts and Sciences, Amsterdam
Professor Robert K. Herbert	SUNY at Binghamton
Dr. Raymond Hickey	University of Bonn
Professor David Huntley	University of Toronto
Professor Dieter Kastovsky	University of Vienna
Mr. Roman Kopytko	Adam Mickiewicz University, Poznań
Professor F.H.H. Kortlandt	University of Leiden

Professor Karen C. Kossuth	Free University, West Berlin, and Pomona College, Claremont, California
Docent Mira Kovatcheva	University of Sofia
Ms. Angelika Lutz	University of Munich
Professor Witold Mańczak	The Jagiellonian University of Cracow
Dr. Lynell Marchese	University of Ilorin, Nigeria
Professor Hanne Martinet	The Copenhagen School of Economics
Professor Pamela Munro	UCLA, Los Angeles
Dr. Ernst-August Müller	Free University, West Berlin
Dr. Mirosław Nowakowski	Adam Mickiewicz University, Poznań
Ms. Barbara Płocinska	Adam Mickiewicz University, Poznań
Dr. Teresa Retelewska	Adam Mickiewicz University, Poznań
Professor Sandor Rót	Lorand Eötvös University, Budapest
Professor Mats Rydén	University of Stockholm
Professor Carmen Silva-Corvalan	University of Southern California, Los Angeles
Docent Aleksander Szwedek	Pedagogical University, Bydgoszcz
Ms. Małgorzata Tecław	Adam Mickiewicz University, Poznań
Professor Alan Timberlake	UCLA, Los Angeles
Mr. Jerzy Tomaszczyk	University of Łódź
Professor Theo Vennemann	University of Munich
Dr. Alicja Wegner	Adam Mickiewicz University, Poznań
Dr. Jerzy Wełna	University of Warsaw
Dr. Ronald Zwanziger	University of Vienna

KATSUE AKIBA-REYNOLDS

Internal reconstruction in pre-Japanese syntax*

In this paper, I will propose a reconstruction of part of the pre-Japanese[1] syntax based on synchronic data from Old Japanese (approx. 8–10th century) and will discuss some consequences of the proposed reconstruction for the theory of internal reconstruction and the question of the genetic affinities of the Japanese language.

1. There are a number of problems in Old Japanese grammar that defy synchronic solutions and thus call for historical explanations. The problems relevant for the present reconstruction all involve *ni*.

1.1 Case particle *ni*

In Old Japanese sentences, oblique nominals including locatives, datives, directionals and temporals were marked with the same particle *ni* as illustrated in the examples below.[2]

(1) Okina ... toguti *ni* wor=i.
Okina   door OBL be=*U*
'Okina was at the door.'   (T, 61)

(2) kano ihe   *ni* yuk=i-te ...
that house OBL go=*I*-SS
'(he) went to that house, and ...'   (T, 31)

(3) kono tuki no zyuugo-niti *ni* ... hito-bito maudeko-n- zu.
this month ASS fifteen-day OBL people come=*A*-FUT-EMPH
'The people will surely come ... on the fifteenth day of this month.'   (T, 59–60)

(4) onna   *ni* kahar=i- te ...
woman   OBL substitute=*I*-SS
'(I) substitute for the woman, and ...'   (Ise, 174)

One can notice that the semantic range of the case marked with *ni* was much wider than any known oblique case. A more curious fact about this case particle is that it was followed by *te*, a conjunctive particle, when the oblique nominal was not an argument (i.e. complement) nominal as seen in the following examples.

> (5) Mukasi   yama   *ni-te* mituk=e-tar=u.
>   long+ago mountain OBL-SS find =*I*-PERF-*URU*
>   '(She) (is) the one that (I) found on a mountain long ago.'
>
> (T, 56)

> (6) Mine   *ni-te*   su-   be=ki   yau osih=e-
>   mountain+peak OBL-SS do=*URU* must=*KI* way teach=*I*-
>   tamah=u.
>   HON=*U*
>   '(He) taught (them) the way (they) must do at the moun-
>   tain peak.'   (T, 67)

The conjunctive particle *te* was used more typically to conjoin clauses, being suffixed to the Conjunctive Form (to be discussed shortly) of a verb or auxiliary at the end of the first clause to be conjoined. It also had the function of indicating that the subjects of the clauses on both sides are the same in reference.[3] For example:

> (7) kore wo mi-   *te*, hune yori or=i- *te*, "..." to toh=u.
>   this DO see=*I*-SS boat from alight=*I*-SS   COMP ask=*U*
>   '(He) saw this, alighted from the boat, and asked, "..."
>
> (T, 38)

The *te* in examples like (5) and (6), therefore, must be treated as an exception in the synchronic grammar of Old Japanese if *te* is analyzed as a conjunctive particle, as is generally accepted among Japanese grammarians. And the question "Why did it exceptionally occur with the case particle *ni*?" remains to be answered.

1.2 Copula *ni*

In Old Japanese, a verb assumed slightly different forms largely depending on the syntactic or semantic context where it occured. This phenomenon has traditionally been treated as conjugation by Japanese grammarians. Major conjugational forms and their contexts are as follows.[4]

Unrealized Form: Followed by an auxiliary of negation, futurity
(Stem=A)   or voice (passive and causative).

Conjunctive Form: a. In the final position of nonfinal conjunct
(Stem=I)   clauses $S_1 \ldots S_{n-1}$ of a conjunction
                     construction $[S_1 \& S_2 \ldots \& S_n]$.
                     b. Followed by an auxiliary of honorification,
                     aspect or tense.

Final Form: In the sentence final position.
(Stem=U)

Nominal Form: In the final position of a nominal clause.
(Stem=URU)

Realized Form: Followed by different-subject marking con-
(Stem=E)   junctive particle *ba*.

Table 1 shows the verb types and the conjugation pattern of each type.

Table 1: Verb conjugation. Most of the Old Japanese verbs were regular, conjugating in either of the four patterns.

FORM	Type-I	Type-II	Type-III	Type-IV
Unrealized (A)	Stem=a-	Stem=e-	Stem=i-	Stem=ϕ
Conjunctive (I)	Stem=i-	Stem=e-	Stem=i-	Stem=ϕ
Final (U)	Stem=u	Stem=u	Stem=u	Stem=ru
Nominal (URU)	Stem=u	Stem=uru	Stem=uru	Stem=ru
Realized (E)	Stem=e-	Stem=ure-	Stem=ure-	Stem=re-

Most of the Old Japanese verbs belonged to Type-I, -II or -III. Type-IV verbs, the stem of which consists of a single consonant and *i*, were limited in number.[5] In addition to these regular verbs, there were several irregular verbs.

Curious was the fact that not only main verbs but also auxiliary suffixes expressing voice, honorification and tense-aspect conjugated exactly in the same manner except that some of them did not fully conjugate. The predicate consisting of a main verb and one or more auxiliary suffixes, therefore, had a dual structure as illustrated in Figure 1.

The similarity in the conjugational pattern between the verb and the auxiliary suffic may very well be taken as tue to the verbal origin of the auxiliary suffixes.[6] In fact, most of the auxiliary suffixes are identical with or similar to some main verbs in the phonological form. (E.g., *ki*:PAST is identical with *ki*, the Conjunctive Form of *ku* 'to come,' and *tamahu*:HONORIFIC with *tamahu* 'to give.') The conjugational suffixes are, on the other hand, ex-

MAIN VERB – AUXILIARY SUFFIX – AUXILIARY SUFFIX – AUXILIARY SUFFIX
　　'write'　　　　　(CAUSATIVE)　　　　(HONORIFIC)　　　　(PERFECT)

Stem=Suffix(*A*) – Stem=Suffix(*I*)　–　Stem=Suffix(*I*)　–　Stem=Suffix(*U*)

　kak=a-　　　　　*s=　　e-*　　　　*tamah=i-*　　　　　　*n=u*

'(he) has made (her) write'

Figure 1: Verb with auxiliary suffixes

tremely difficult to associate with any lexical categories. The most we can say about conjugational suffixes is that they must have been independent ele‐ ments (presumably particles) which had definable grammatical functions. It is common that the basic form of the verb plus an auxiliary element re‐ sults in a conjugated form by losing the morpheme boundary.[7]

The copula *nari* 'to be' was peculiar: It conjugated very much like the existential verb *ari* 'to be/exist,' which was also anomalous in the Final Form, but it had, unlike *ari,* two Conjunctive Forms, which were complementary in distribution. Compare the two BE verbs in Table 2.

Table 2: Conjugation of BE verbs. Old Japanese BE verbs, existential 'to be' and copula 'to be' were irregular in the Final Form. Copula had two Conjunc‐ tive Forms: the regular *nari* and suppletive *ni.*

Form	Existential	Copula
Unrealized	ar=a-	nar=a-
Conjunctive	ar=i-	nar=i-/ni-
Final	ar=i	nar=i
Nominal	ar=u	nar=u
Realized	ar=e-	nar=e-

Notice that both verbs take *i* in the Final Form instead of the regular Final Form suffix *u*. Here are a couple of examples of the copula *nari* in the Final Form.

(8)　ito　kata=ki　　akinahi nar=i.
　　very difficult=*KI* trade　COP=*U*
　　'(it) is a very difficult trade.'　　　　　　　　　　　　　　　(T, 42)

(9) kehahi   ahare   nar=i.
     appearance pitiful   COP=*U*
     'the appearance was pitiful (i.e.,
     It appeared to be pitiful).'   (G, 43)

It is well established that the copula *nari* was derived from *ni-ari* through a standard fusional process *ia→a*. This is evidenced by the fact that *ni* appeared unchanged in honorific copular sentences or in emphatic sentences in which the condition for the fusion was not met. The following sentences illustrate this point.

(10) Sama   mo yo=ki   hito   *ni* ohas=u.
     appearance also good=*KI* person *NI* be+HON=*U*
     '(he) is a person whose appearance also is good.'   (T, 37)

(11) Tama   no eda   *ni* zo ar=i-ker=u.
     jewel   ASS spray *NI* EMPH be=*I*-PAST=*URU*
     '(it) was a jewel spray, indeed.'   (T, 40)

There is no doubt about the change *ni-ari→nari*. What is more curious is the *ni*. What was it? Where did it come from?

A clue to these questions seems to come from the fact that *ni* alone appeared as the copula in the Conjunctive position and the conjunctive particle *te* directly followed it as seen in the following sentence.

(12) tuki   no   miyako   no   hito   *ni-te*
     moon ASS   City+Royal ASS   person *NI-SS*
     titi   haha   ar=i.
     father mother be=*U*
     '(I) am a person from the City Royal of Moonland, and have a father and a mother.'   (T, 60)

This is one of the two major positions in which the Conjunctive Form of the verb or auxiliary suffix occurred. In the other position, i.e., the position followed by an auxiliary suffix, the copula *nari* exhibited its regular conjugational pattern as in the following example.

(13) mi-   si-   hito   nar=i-*ker*=i.
     see=*I*-PAST=*URU* person COP=*I*-PAST=*U*
     '(it) was a person (I) had seen.'   (Ise, 116)

This distributional irregularity gives rise to another question: Why did *ni* alone occur in the conjunctive position while the regular Conjunctive Form *nari* was available in the pre-auxiliary position?

Some Japanese grammarians contend that the *ni* in these examples was the case particle *ni*. Such analysis, however, does not answer the above questions and it is rather difficult to understand why the predicate nominal was regularly marked as an oblique nominal. The formal identity between the *ni* in question and the case particle *ni* certainly needs to be explained, if it was not accidental, but the explanation must also answer the above questions concerning the *ni* in copular sentences.

1.3 Auxiliary *nu*

Another morpheme which should be taken into account together with the oblique case particle *ni* and the copula particle *ni* is the perfect auxiliary *nu*, which is often compared with *tu*, another Old Japanese perfect auxiliary. Here are examples of *nu* and *tu* in the Conjunctive and Final Form.

Conjunctive

(14) ito yowa=ku nar=i- tamah=i-*n*=i- ker=i.
very weak=*KU* become=*I*-Hon=*I*- PERF=*I*-PAST=*U*
'(he) had become very weak.'   (T, 53)

(15) Ohoku no hito   koros=i-*t*=e- ker=u   kokoro ...
many   ASS person kill=*I*-PERF=*I*-PAST=*URU* mind
'... the mind (with which) (she) had killed many people.'   (T, 55)

Final

(16) Yatuhasi to   ih=u   tokoro ni itar=i-*n*=*u*.
Yatuhasi COMP call=*URU* place OBL arrive=*I*-PERF=*U*
'(He) has arrived at a place called Yatuhasi'.   (Ise, 116)

(17) Akita Nayotake=no=Kaguyahime to   tuk=e- *t*=*u*.
Akita Nayotake=no=Kaguyahime COMP name=*I*-PERF=*U*
'Akita named (her) Nayotake=no=Kaguyahime.'   (T, 30)

Although the functional differences between the two auxiliaries are not clearly summarizable, they were not interchangeable in Old Japanese. The following discrepancies in distribution are observed among other things.

(i)   Causative predicates (derived or lexical) took only *tu* and passives only *nu* with some exceptions.

(ii) Typical action verbs (e.g. *kudaku* 'to crash,' *huru* 'to shake,' and *musubu* 'to tie') took only *tu* and nonaction verbs (e.g.

aku 'to dawn,' *aru* 'to become devastated' and *saku* 'to bloom') only *nu*.

It seems that *tu* was used when an animate subject, i.e. agent, was involved, emphasizing completion of an action by the agent, while *nu* was less restricted as to the animacy of the subject and it was perhaps used to focus on the state resulting from a completed action.

The etymology of these auxiliaries is far from being clear. It is generally contended among Japanese grammarians (e.g., Matsumura 1971) that *nu* and *tu* had come from verbs *inu* 'to go away' and *utu* 'to throw away,' respectively. Ide (1969) objects to this and suggests that there were main verbs *nu* 'to go away' and *tu* 'to throw away' to begin with which often occurred with prefixes *i* and *u*, respectively, and that it was this main verb *nu* that changed into the Old Japanese auxiliary *nu*. However, these conjectures have no support except for the formal and semantic resemblances.

I would like to call attention to a fact that has so far been completely overlooked, i.e., the formal identity of the Conjunctive Form of the auxiliary *nu* with the two particles we have just discussed. This may be crucial for the history of this perfect auxiliary suffix as well as that of the copula particle *ni* and the case particle *ni*. Furthermore, the fact that the Conjunctive Form of the auxiliary *tu* and the same-subject marking conjunctive particle *te* had the same form may not be accidental.

2. In order to answer the questions raised above, I stipulate that there was a locative BE **nu* at a certain stage of pre-Japanese. By "locative BE" I mean a verb which takes an unmarked locative nominal as one of the arguments. The following Twi sentence depicts a locative sentence with such a BE-verb.[8]

(18) sukuu wɔ Kumase.
     school be+at Kumase.
     'The school is at Kumase'.

The locative nominal *Kumase* is not particularly marked as such but the meaning of the verb *wɔ* signals that Kumase is a locative nominal. Locative verbs like *wɔ* are not rare in world languages. Clark (1970) mentions several languages including Syrian Arabic, Eskimo and Kurukh as having such verbs.[9]

If we assume that the perfect auxiliary *nu*, the copula particle *ni* and the case particle *ni* were all derived from this locative verb, we can account for all the attested forms as in Table 3.

Table 3: Old Japanese reflexes of **nu*

	PERFECT AUXILIARY	COPULA	OBLIQUE CASE
Unrealized	na		
Conjunctive	ni	ni	ni
Final	nu		
Nominal	nuru		
Realized	nure		

Although the conjugation of the perfect auxiliary *nu* was irregular, most of the forms were the same as those of the Type-I verb. It is likely that the auxiliary *nu* was originally conjugated as a Type-I verb but underwent some minor changes in the Nominal and Realized Forms. There are two factors that possibly implemented the modification of the conjugational pattern of *nu*. Compare the conjugation of the reconstructed locative BE-verb **nu* with those of the auxiliary *nu* and the negative suffix *zu* in Table 4.[10]

Table 4: Conjugation of **nu, tu, nu* and *zu*

	*nu	*tu*	*nu*	*zu*
Unrealized	**na*	te	na	---
Conjunctive	**ni*	te	ni	zu
Final	**nu*	tu	nu	zu
Nominal	**nu*	ture	nuru	nu
Realized	**ne*	ture	nure	ne

Note that the perfect auxiliary *nu* would have merged with the negative suffix in the two forms in question if it had remained unchanged. Thus, there was a good motivation for these two forms to change. The choice of the new forms, however, must have been made by analogy to the conjugational pattern of *tu*, the already existing perfect auxiliary.

Below I will show how naturally the case particle *ni*, the copula particle *ni* and the perfect auxiliary *nu* could be derived from the main verb **nu* 'to be at'.

2.1 From locative verb to locative case particle

A number of examples of the change from verbs to case markers via serialization have been presented in recent studies (e.g., Lord 1973, 1976, Li &

Thompson 1973 and 1974 and Givon 1975). Given the main verb **nu* 'to be at', the development of the case particle *ni* can be understood along the same line as suggested in these studies. Using sentence (1) as an example, the reanalysis of the main verb **nu* as a perfect auxiliary will be schematized as in Figure 2. (I assume for the sake of simplicity that other things than *ni* remained equal).

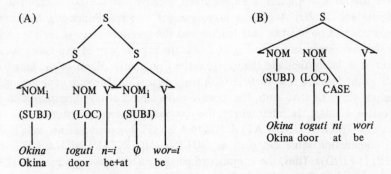

Figure 2: From main verb to case marker

n=i
be+at

The case particle *ni* may have had the specification [+Location] at first and may have been used only for the purpose of marking locative nominals, but it must have gradually become a more general oblique case marker by losing this specification. Thus, it appeared in Old Japanese marking almost any oblique nominals as well as locative nominals from subject and direct object nominals.

Understanding the development of the oblique case particle *ni* this way, the occurrence of the conjunctive particle *te* immediately after the case particle would not be surprising. When the conjunctive particle *te* came into existence in Japanese, *ni* must still have been the Conjunctive Form of the locative BE verb. The reason that the *te* could suffix to *ni* only when the *ni* was marking a non-argument nominal would be the following. Verbs such as 'to be/exist' and 'to live' have a strong implication of a location where the 'being' or 'living' takes place and they are rarely used without expressing or implying a locative nominal. The locative nominal occurring with such a verb often has more semantic prominence than the verb itself. It is very rare that being or living itself is asserted. Verbs such as 'to cry' and 'to kick', on the other hand, have more focus on the action of 'crying' and 'kicking' itself or the object that is affected by such an action than the place where it takes place although it does occur somewhere. Let us distinguish these two types of verbs for our purposes and refer to the former as "locative verbs" and to the latter as "non-locative verbs". Argument and nonargument locative nominals will then be defined as locative nominals that are in construction with a locative verb or a non-locative verb, respectively. Thus, the *Los Angeles* in *I live in Los Angeles* is an argument locative but the *Los Angeles* in *I played golf in Los Angeles* a non-argument locative. Supposing that pre-Japanese had no locative case marker and the conjunction construction such as the one shown in (A) in Figure 2 was the regular way of expressing location, it is likely that the change from the Conjunctive Form of the locative BE to the locative case particle took place first where the verb of the second clause was a locative verb, for locative verbs almost always occurred with a locative nominal. In other words, the compression of conjunction sentences such as ((OKINA DOOR AT) & (OKINA EXIST)) occurred earlier than that of conjunction sentences such as ((OKINA MOUNTAIN AT) & (OKINA CHILD FIND)). Thus, the conjunctive particle, which developed around this time, could suffix to the *ni* marking the location of a nonlocative verb because it was still verbal, but it could not suffix to the *ni* marking the location of a locative verb because it was no longer a verb. Some time later, after the Old Japanese period, however, the *ni-te* together was reanalyzed as the marker for the nonargument oblique case and underwent a series of phonological changes: *nite* > *nte* > *nde* > ^{n}*de* > *de*. Thus, modern Japanese distinguishes the argument oblique and the nonargument oblique by marking the former with *ni* and the latter with *de*.

The development of the case particle *ni* from **nu* and the changes related to it could then be ordered as follows:

- i.   The reanalysis of the Conjunctive Form of the locative verb as the argument locative marker.
- ii. The appearance of the conjunctive particle *te*.
- iii. The reanalysis of the Conjunctive Form of the locative BE verb *ni* plus the conjunctive particle *te* as the nonargument locative case marker.
- iv. The phonological changes: *nite* → *de*.

2.2 From locative BE to copula

Given that the **nu* was a two-place predicate taking a subject and a locative, the change from locative BE verb 'to be at' to copula BE 'to be' is quite easy to understand: by bleaching out its locative sense, its most specific semantic feature that one of the arguments is locative, **nu* should have been able to become a copula with little difficulty since the semantic distinction between the locative sentence 'NOM$_1$ is at NOM$_2$' and the copula sentence 'NOM$_1$ is NOM$_2$' is sometimes very slight. A copula sentence like:

(19) Mr. Jones is the chairman of the department.

can be paraphrased with a locative sentence like:

(20) Mr. Jones is in the position of the chairman of the department.

It is possible that the locative sentence pattern was used for certain copula expressions first and the locative verb in such sentences gradually lost the feature [+Locative]. Such a bleaching process is one of the most common channels for semantic change.

The reason this copula is found only in the Conjunctive Form is not clear for the moment. It may have developed only in the conjunctive position from the outset because predicate nominal sentences did not require a copula in the sentence final position in Old Japanese.[11]

2.3 From main verb BE to auxiliary BE

Serial constructions have provided Japanese with historical sources for auxiliary verbs, verb affixes and adverbs throughout the history of the language.[12]

There were two kinds of conjunctions in Old Japanese that developed into serial constructions, which I call zero-conjunction and *te*-conjunction. In a zero-conjunction sentence, nonfinal conjunct clauses ended with a verbal element in the Conjunctive Form and there was no conjunctive morpheme between conjunct clauses. In a *te*-conjunction sentence, nonfinal clauses were marked by the conjunctive particle *te* suffixed to the Conjunctive Form of the clause-final verb element. Compare the following zero-conjunction sentence with the *te*-conjunction sentence (7).

(21) kono hito-bito . . . mono wo omoh=i, inori wo s=i,
      this people   thing DO think=*I* pray DO do=*I*

      gan wo tat=u.
      wish DO make=*U*

      'these people . . . thought of things, did praying, and made
      wishes'.   (T, 31)

Although there are several differences between the two conjunctions in detail, of direct relevance for the present discussion is the fact that the zero-conjunction was historically earlier than the *te*-conjunction. Most of the serial constructions found in Old Japanese were from zero-conjunctions. That is, the nonfinal verbs in a series were in the Conjunctive Form and there was no conjunctive morpheme between verbs. The serial constructions with *te* between serialized verbs are never or very rarely found in Old Japanese though they are common in modern Japanese.[13]

The fact that the Old Japanese perfect auxiliary *nu* required the preceding verbal element to be in the Conjunctive Form (Stem=*I*) suggests that this auxiliary had a serial verb origin. Taking into account all the facts about this auxiliary discussed in previous sections together with this possibility, one can reasonably infer that auxiliary *nu* came from the serialized **nu* as two-clause conjunction sentences collapsed into single-clause sentences as schematized in Figure 3.

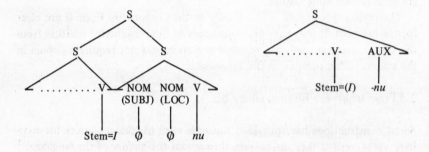

Figure 3: From main verb BE to auxiliary BE

A sentence like (16), for instance, would have been analyzed before the reanalysis as a two-clause conjunction sentence meaning '(He) arrived at a place called Yatuhasi and (he) is (there)'. In Old Japanese, in which *nu* no longer occurred in the main verb position, sentences like this were always given single-clause interpretations such as '(He) has arrived at a place called Yatuhasi'.

2.4 From perfect auxiliary to conjunctive particle

It has been implied in previous sections that the conjunctive particle *te* came into existence in Japanese at a certain point in the period when **nu* 'to be at' was getting reanalyzed as the oblique case particle and so forth. The question of where it came from has some bearing on the changes that we have been discussing.

Some grammarians relate the conjunctive particle *te* to the Conjunctive Form of the perfect auxiliary *tu*, which was briefly discussed in 1.3. This is in fact the most plausible hypothesis in every respect. The Conjunctive Form of *tu* was used in the pre-auxiliary position as seen from the way it is used in sentence (15). Recall that the Conjunctive Form of verbs and most auxiliaries occurred in two positions: in the pre-auxiliary position and in the conjunctive position. Therefore, if we analyzed the Old Japanese conjunctive particle *te*, which was always in the conjunctive position, as having come from the Conjunctive Form of the perfect auxiliary *tu*, we would obtain the regular distributional pattern for the auxiliary *tu* at least in the historical context. But why did it become a conjunctive particle? The change seems to have been triggered by a change in the system of tense-aspect.

As mentioned earlier, the conjugational suffixes provide an important clue to the prehistoric state of the language. The contexts in which the Unrealized suffix *A* and the Realized suffix *E* occurred in Old Japanese suggest that these suffixes were aspect markers. *A* perhaps indicated irrealis aspect and *E* realis (or anterior) aspect. In conjunction sentences with different-subject marking conjunctive particle *ba*, the conjugation of the final element of the clause to which *ba* was suffixed was fully responsible for a conditional clause interpretation (e.g. (22)) and an anterior reading (e.g. (23)).

> (22) sihite   tukau=matur=a-s=e-   tamah=a-ba,
>   forcibly serve+HON=*A*- CAUS=*I*-HON=*A*- DS
>
>   kiye=us=e- n=a-   n-   zu.
>   disappear=*I*-PERF=*A*-FUT-EMPH
>   'if you forcibly make me serve (him), (I) will be gone'.
>
>   (T, 55)
>
> (23) sode wo torah=e-tamah=e-ba,
>   sleeve DO catch=*I*-HON=*E*- DS
>
>   omote wo hutag=i-te- ...
>   face   DO cover=*I*-SS
>   '(he) caught (her) sleeve, and (then) she covered
>   (her) face ... '   (T, 56)

The final suffix *U* seems to fit perfectly in the aspectual category which Bickerton (1975) calls "nonpunctual". It indicated durative or iterative aspect for action verbs, and it was indifferent to the past-nonpast distinction. The fact that the existential *ari* and its derivatives, which were the only stative verbs in Old Japanese, did not take the regular Final suffix *u* is also in accordance with the observation that nonpunctual aspect markers cannot normally co-occur with stative verbs. Since no suffix is relatable to past tense, one may infer that the tense-aspect marked by the conjugational suffixes was different from that expressed with auxiliary suffixes. There was probably a shift in the tense-aspect system in Japanese, from the system without the past-nonpast distinction to the one with it. In the older system, events were perhaps measured and marked in relation to each other. For example, in a conjunction sentence (S_1 & S_2 ... & S_n) describing a series of events (E_1 & E_2 ... & E_n), the final clause S_n may have been marked with the nonpunctual aspect marker, and all others S_1 ... S_{n-1} with the realis/ anterior marker to indicate that E_1 preceded in occurrence E_2, E_2 preceded E_3, ..., and E_{n-1} preceded E_n. Such aspect markers are subject to attrition, loss of neighboring morpheme boundaries and phonological fusion, and eventually become defunct and give way to a new set of devices with the same or similar functions. It is quite possible that *te,* the Conjunctive Form of a perfect auxiliary of the new generation, was used with anterior clauses to enforce the old tense-aspect system during the transition period from the system of conjugational suffixes to that of auxiliary suffixes. This conjecture is well supported by the fact that the conjunctive particle *te* did not occur in conjunction sentences describing simultaneously occurring events and the fact that there are many cases of *te* which are analyzable as the Conjunctive Form of *tu.* Sentence (7), for example, can be given an equally plausible interpretation if the *te* at the end of the two nonfinal clauses is regarded as the perfect auxiliary as shown in (24).

(24) kore wo mi- *te,*   hune yori ori=i- *te,*

" ... " to   toh=u.
COMP ask=*U*
'(he) saw this, (and then) (he) alighted from the boat, (and then) (he) asked, " ... " '   (T, 38)

The reason the *te* in the conjunctive position came to be reinterpreted as the marker of the conjunctive position may be because it was used in this position more and more frequently ans the older system lost its functional transparency. It must be after the reanalysis of *te* as a conjunctive morpheme that *te* became almost obligatory in the position after the locative BE and the copula of nonfinal clauses because these predicates are inherently stative and normally do not take an auxiliary of "completion".

The changes that have been discussed in the present paper must have taken place, then, in the following order.

		$\nearrow$ *nu*	(Perfect Auxiliary)
i.	**nu*	$\rightarrow$ *ni*	(Copula: Conjunctive Form)
		$\searrow$ *ni*	(Argument Oblique Case Marker)
ii.	*ni-ari* $\rightarrow$ *nari* (Copula)		
iii.	**te* (Auxiliary) $\rightarrow$ *te* (Conjunctive Particle)		
iv.	(*)*ni-te* (Locative BE − Conjunctive Particle) $\rightarrow$ *nite* (Nonargument Oblique Case Marker)		
v.	*nite* $\rightarrow$ *de*		

(Items with * may have existed only in pre-Japanese.)

Even this much of reconstruction may give some idea about the characteristics of pre-Japanese. In the earliest period of the pre-Japanese history, a sentence may have consisted of coordinately conjoined clauses each of which had a main verb with or without an auxiliary element and at most two nominals semantically associated with the verb.

3. At the very beginning of the reconstruction of **nu*, I took notice of three morphemes which were distinct in meaning/function but the same in form. The formal resemblance, however, can be accidental and has little evidential value by itself. What is more important is the range of the irregularity in the synchronic grammar of Old Japanese that this reconstruction can account for and the naturalness of the postulated syntactic changes. The changes are considered to be natural in the following three respects.

First, the changes conform to the condition which Timberlake (1977) convincingly argued for, the condition that the given output must be sufficiently ambiguous with respect to syntactic analysis for reanalysis to take place. For example, the two analyses (A) and (B) in Figure 2 are equally plausible for the output *Okina toguti ni wori*. That is, the output is ambiguous between the two analyses and the reanalysis of (A) as (B) could occur without affecting the meaning.

Second, syntactic changes similar to those that I have postulated have been observed in so many other languages that one can reasonably suspect that such changes are motivated by some universal factors although it is difficult to discuss them in formal terms.

Third, the changes are all consistent with the general tendency that Japanese has been increasing surface differentiation, adding new grammatical devices.

The third point will be most clearly seen in the development of the case markers. As one may have already noticed, nominals were not as distinctively marked for case in Old Japanese as in modern Japanese: the subject was regularly left unmarked unless it was marked as the topic with *ha;* the direct object was only optionally marked by *wo;* and all other cases were almost indiscriminately marked with the general oblique case marker *ni* except associatives (nominals linked with other nominals rather than with verbs, e.g. *Okina* in *Okina no ihe:* Okina ASS house 'Okina's house' and *tuki* in *tuki no miyako:* moon ASS city royal 'the city royal of the moon') and peripheral oblique cases such as ablatives and illatives. There is some evidence that *wo* used to be an emphatic particle, the use of which came to be limited to the direct object. If this is the case and if the reconstruction I am proposing here is accepted, we would be able to say that associatives were the only major case markers that existed since the earliest time of the history of Japanese and that oblique case particle *ni* and direct object marker *wo* were added to the grammar in the course of time prior to the Old Japanese period. During the period between Old Japanese and modern Japanese, *ga,* one of the associative particles, was reanalyzed as the subject marker, *ni-te* (which I have analyzed as the Conjunctive Form of the locative BE plus the conjunctive particle *te*) became the nonargument oblique case marker and underwent a series of phonological changes to yield *de* in modern Japanese, and *to,* which was used mostly to conjoin nominals and occasionally to mark comitatives in Old Japanese, established its status as the comitative marker.

The case system of Old Japanese and that of modern Japanese will be summarized as in (A) and (B) in Figure 4, respectively.

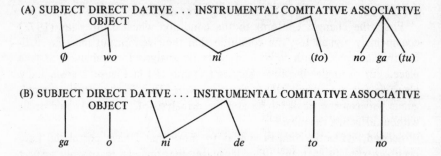

Figure 4: Change in case marking

It is clear that modern Japanese reflects the underlying meanings in a much more one-to-one fashion than Old Japanese. That is, Japanese has been moving towards a language with a richer case marking system. It would be unnatural to think that the drift started all of a sudden in Old Japanese. It is more likely that the language had been changing in the same direction before the Old Japanese time. Thus, the reconstruction of **nu,* which virtually makes the claim that pre-Japanese had no oblique case marker, is quite compatible with the direction of the drift that the language has been undergoing throughout its history.

The tendency towards more surface differentiation is not restricted to the case system alone, but it is observed in conjunction, in subordination and in the auxiliary system as well. It seems that the direction in which the language has been changing as a whole suggests where the language came from.

4. In this section I will discuss several hypotheses advanced for the origin of Japanese and will argue that comparative data alone are not sufficient in choosing a correct hypothesis.

4.1 The hypotheses that have been proposed as explanations for the genetic relationship of Japanese to other languages are basically of two categories, the Altaic hypothesis and the mixed language hypothesis.

The proponents of the Altaic hypothesis — the hypothesis that Japanese was derived from proto-Altaic like Mongolian, Tungus and Korean — point out (i) that Japanese resembles Altaic languages in syntax, (ii) that there is a considerable amount of lexical correspondence between Japanese and Altaic languages, especially Korean, and (iii) that Japanese had vowel harmony, which is characteristic of Altaic languages. However, these arguments are not convincing enough. The lexical correspondence is too scanty and there are other languages, as will be mentioned later, which seem to share a greater part of the vocabulary with Japanese. Vowel harmony applies only for a very limited number of items and it has been pointed out by Murayama (1969) that the vowel harmony is not necessarily ascribed to the genetic relationship of Japanese with Altaic languages. The syntactic argument that Japanese has the same basic word order, Subject-Object-Verb, and has case markers placed after nominals much in the same way as Altaic languages is not tenable given the theory of typological universals as of Greenberg's (1972). The common syntactic features such as Modified-Modifying order and Main Verb-Auxiliary may be due to the fact that Japanese and Altaic languages belong to the same type, SOV language, rather than to the genetic relationship between these languages. Moreover, Japanese did not have as rich a case system as it is generally believed to have had as we have already seen. Thus, syntactic arguments also fail to support the genetic relationship between Japanese and Altaic languages.

The main arguments for the mixed language hypothesis are as follows. First, as Ono (1970) points out, the mixed language hypothesis is more consistent with the findings in archeological and anthropological studies about the evolution of the Japanese. It is almost established that the first inhabitants on the island of Japan were related to oceanic people but some northern (Altaic) people with a more advanced culture migrated to the island and began to live with the aborigines. Second, Old Japanese had a considerable number of Malayo-Polynesian elements. For example, Murayama (1969) has presented data to show (i) that Old Japanese had prefixes like Malayo-Polynesian in addition to suffixes (Altaic languages are consistently suffixal), (ii) that the CVCV syllable structure is characteristic of Malayo-Polynesian, (iii) iteration/reduplication, a characteristic mechanism for word formation in Japanese, is more commonly utilized in Malayo-Polynesian than in Altaic and (iv) that prenasalization of certain consonants, another characteristic feature of Malayo-Polynesian, did exist in Japanese also. Murayama concludes from these facts that Japanese is a hybrid language whose most important components are Altaic and Austronesian.[14] Kawamoto (1974) added to the data in favor of the mixed language hypothesis and made a more specific claim than Murayama that Japanese developed from a pidgin whose main source language was a Melanesian one. Although it is not totally clear what kind of process Murayama meant by "hybrid", I assume the claim made by Murayama does not crucially differ from Kawamoto's pidgin hypothesis. Whinom (1971), who makes a clear distinction between hybridization and pidginization, claims that a hybrid language does not become stabilized to the extent it can be used as a common vernacular unless it undergoes pidginization.

It is undeniable that there were two or more languages in close contact in the early history of Japanese which contributed in one way or other to the formation of Japanese. This fact alone, however, does not immediately lead us to a pidgin hypothesis, for it is still possible that the process involved could be borrowing rather than mixing, i.e., pidginization. In order for a pidgin hypothesis to be more fully justified, it must show that the language had grammatical features which are sufficiently characteristic of pidgins. Pidginization simplifies the grammar of the source languages to such an extent that the grammar of the resultant pidgin would be no longer comparable with the grammar of the source languages. Thus, internal reconstruction of pre-Japanese grammar and comparison between the reconstruction and pidgins would play a crucial role in establishing the pidgin hypothesis.

4.2 As implied in the present reconstruction, pre-Japanese grammar seems to resemble pidgin-creole languages in a significant number of respects.[15]

First of all, the fact that Old Japanese had very few case markers found in pre-Japanese corresponds perfectly to the observation that pidgin-creoles have very limited noun inflections.

Second, I have previously suggested that the zero-conjunction was the oldest device for conjoining clauses that developed in the history of Japanese and the *te*-conjunction followed it. I have shown elsewhere (Akiba (1977) and (1978)) that Old Japanese was developing several conjunctive particles in addition to *te* and that modern Japanese abounds in subordinate conjunctions which can specify various relationships between conjoined clauses. It is certain that Japanese has been changing as a whole towards more surface differentiation in the conjunction system. Paratactic conjunction as found in pre-Japanese is another characteristic feature of pidgin-creoles.

Third, Old Japanese did not distinguish nominalization, relativization and complementation. All the subordinate clauses except direct quotations were uniformly marked by the same morphology, i.e., by the Nominal Form of the clause final verbal element. It was after the period of Old Japanese that the language came to possess different devices for different types of subordinate clause messages. There are some indications that the conjugational suffix used for the Nominal Form was once an associative particle. If it is really the case, pre-Japanese perhaps had no productive method for subordination, either. This is, again, the situation that is commonly found in pidgins and creoles.

Fourth, the pre-Japanese tense-aspect system that I suggested in 2.4 strikingly resembles the system that Bickerton (1975) has claimed to be that of creoles. If further examinations do not disprove the suggestion, this feature will be taken as another piece of evidence for the pidgin-creole origin of Japanese.

Finally, to mention a phenomenon which is not directly related to the reconstruction of **nu*, reduplication was an important mechanism in Old Japanese for word formation, pluralization and intensification. Old Japanese abounds in iterative adverbs which seem to be onomatopoetic or mimetic in origin: the *yo=yo=to* in *yo=yo=to nak=i-tamah=i-n=u* (... cry=*I*-HON=*I*-PERF-*U*) describes a woman's bitter crying and the *ture=dure=to* (*ture+ ture+to*) in *ture=dure=to komor=i-wor=i-ker=i* (... remain+indoor=*I*-be= *I*-PAST=*U*) a languid and lonely state of being. Certain nouns were reduplicated for pluralization: *yama-yama*: mountain-mountain 'mountains', *hito-bito*: (< *hito+hito*): person-person 'people', *kuni-guni* (< *kuni+kuni*): country-country 'countries', *ki-gi* (< *ki+ki*): tree-tree 'trees'. Reduplication of the Final Form of a verb expressed an iterative or durative action accompanying another action.

> (25) Taketori *nak=u-nak=u* maus=u.
> Taketori cry=*U*-cry=*U* say+HON=*U*
> 'Taketori said (while) crying'. (T, 61)

Reduplication of the Conjunctive Form of a verb indicated iterative/durative aspect of the verb.

> (26) *yuk=i-yuk=i-te* Suruga no kuni
>   go=*I*- go=*I*- SS Suruga ASS country
>
>   ni   itar=i-n=u.
>   OBL arrive=*I*-PERF=*U*
>   '(He) went on and on and arrived in the country of
>   Suruga'.   (Ise, 117)

If these processes utilizing reduplication were no longer productive in Old Japanese, these examples should be taken as residues of pre-Japanese rules. Reduplication is said to be one of the conspicuous features of many pidgins and creoles.

Pidgin and creole studies are still in their adolescence, although their recent progress is remarkable in quantity and quality, and pidgin-creole characteristics have not yet been defined to the extent that they can be used as criteria for recognizing all pidgins and creoles. Future studies may reveal inadequacies of these crude criteria, but this line of investigation of language development is basically correct and it is especially important for the genetic question of Japanese.

5. To summarize, I have attempted to show that there was a locative BE verb **nu* in pre-Japanese and that the verb was reanalyzed as a case marker, a copula and a perfect auxiliary in subsequent periods. The reconstruction is evaluated as highly plausible in terms of the number and value of synchronic facts (especially anomalies) of Old Japanese grammar which are explained by it and the naturalness of the postulated syntactic changes. I have also suggested that the reconstruction has important bearings on the genetic question of the language, supporting the hypothesis that the language evolved from a pidgin-creole largely based on Altaic and Malayo-Polynesian.

Notes

* I must indicate my gratitude to Prof. Sandra A. Thompson, UCLA, for her generous assistance and constant encouragement, to Prof. Susumu Ono, Gakushuin University, Tokyo, for inspiring comments, and to Prof. Takeo Kawamoto, Joetsu University of Education, Japan, for sharing valuable information with me.
1. The term "pre-Japanese" does not refer to a single stage in the history of Japanese, but to the time preceding the earliest records in the language.
2. In transliterating Japanese examples, I have employed the system of romanization used in *Intensive Course in Japanese,* Japanese Language Promotion Center, with

some minor deviations, which seems to be more convenient for our purposes of discussing historical changes than the Hepburn system.

Since the conjugational suffixes vary from type to type, I have indicated the conjugational form in which verbs and auxiliaries are actually used in sample sentences with italic capital letters, *A, I,* etc. As to which letter represents which conjugational form, refer to Table I. Conjugational suffixes of the adjective (e. g. *KI*) are quite different from those of the verb but they are not our present concern. In examples, the following conventions are used.

Symbols

−: between bound morphemes

=: between the stem and the conjugational suffix

+: to show that the elements connected by this sign correspond to a single Japanese element.

Abbreviations

DO: Direct Object
ASS: Associative Particle
OBL: Oblique Case Particle
SS: Same-Subject Marking Conjunctive Particle
DS: Different-Subject Marking Conjunctive Particle
COP: Copula
HON: Honorific
EMPH: Emphatic
FUT: Future
PAST: Past Tense
PERF: Perfect

The examples used in this study are from *Taketori Monogatari* (T) 'Tale of a Bamboo-Collector,' *Genji Monogatari* (G) 'Tale of Genji' and *Ise Monogatari* (Ise) 'Tale of Ise.' The page number indicated in parentheses at the end of each example is based on the texts of the *Iwanami Koten Bungaku Taikei* 'The Iwanami Series of Japanese Classics.'

3. Akiba (1977) discusses the same-subject-marking conjunctive particle and different-subject-marking conjunctive particles in Old Japanese.

4. The list of the contexts is not exhaustive but rather skeletal.

5. These verbs were problematic, because if they conjugated like Type-I verbs, they would have had only one consonant segment constant in all the conjugated forms, which is extremely undesirable from the conceptual point of view.

6. There were some suffixes which seemed to have been derived from adjectives. E.g. *-besi* 'must,' ending with *si* like most Old Japanese adjectives, followed the conjugational pattern of adjectives.

7. Kawamoto (1979) postulates the following forms as the elements that developed into the Old Japanese conjugational suffixes.

*a	Unrealized Suffix	(the irrealist-imperative)
*i	Conjunctive Suffix	(the infinitive)
*wori	Nominal/Final Suffix	(the attributive-predicative)
*ai	Realized Suffix	(causal)

The names in parentheses are Kawamoto's and they suggest what Kawamoto thinks to be their original functions.

8. This Twi sentence was taken from Ellis and Boadi (1969).

9. S. A. Thompson (UCLA) reminded me of the Mandarin locative verb *zai,* as another example. Also *se* in SiSwate, *le* in Ewe.

10. The negative must have come from two different sources, one of which was *nu.* Whether this *nu* was related to the perfect auxiliary *nu* is not known.

11. Ferguson (1971) states that there are some languages in which copula shows up only in independent clauses. Pre-Japanese may have been such a language.
12. There were a number of verb prefixes which had the function of adding some subtle connotations to the meaning of the stem. For example, *uti-naku:* HIT-cry 'to cry bitterly,' *sasi-agu:* PIERCE-raise 'to raise high,' etc. There were some other verbs which were suffixed to the main verb and modified the meaning of the main verb. For example, *hahi-iru:* crawl-ENTER 'to crawl in,' *kaki-yaru:* write-SEND 'to write to,' etc.
13. There are several auxiliary-like verbs with some discourse or aspectual function: *tabe-te-miru:* eat-SS-SEE 'to eat for taste,' *it-te-oku:* say-SS-LEAVE 'to say for future reference,' *tabe-te-simau:* eat-SS-FINISH 'to have eaten.'
14. According to Murayama, this hypothesis was first advanced by E. D. Polivanov half a century ago.
15. Since the distinction between pidgins and creoles is irrelevant here, the terms "pidgin," "creole" and "pidgin-creole" are used rather loosely.

List of figures

References

Akiba, Katsue
    1977   "Switch reference in Old Japanese", *Proceedings of the Third Annual Meeting of the Berkeley Linguistics Society,* 610–619.
    1978   *A historical study of Old Japanese syntax.* Unpublished Ph.D. dissertation, University of California, Los Angeles.
Bickerton, Derek
    1974   "Creolization, linguistic universals, natural semantax and the brain", *Working papers in linguistics* (University of Hawaii) 6.3:125–141.
Clark, Eve Vivienne
    1970   "Locationals: a study of the relations between 'existential', 'locative', and 'possessive' constructions", *Working papers in language universals* (Stanford University) 3:1–36.
Ferguson, Charles A.
    1971   "Absence of copula and the notion of simplicity: a study of normal speech, baby talk, foreigner talk, and pidgins", *Pidginization* and *creolization of languages,* edited by Dell Hymes (Cambridge: Cambridge University Press), 141–150.
Givón, Talmy
    1975   "Serial verbs and syntactic change: Niger-Congo", *Word order and word order change,* edited by Ch. Li (Austin: University of Texas Press), 47–112.
Greenberg, Joseph
    1972   "Some universals of grammar with particular reference to the order of meaningful elements", *A reader in historical and comparative linguistics,* edited by A. R. Keiler (New York: Holt, Rinehart and Winston), 306–337.

Ide, Itaru
　1966　"Kodai Nihongo Dooshi no Imi Ruikei to Jodooshi tsu . nu no Tsukai-wake [Semantic Categories of Old Japanese verbs and auxiliaries: The use of *tu* and *nu*]", *Kokogo Kokubun* (Kyoto University) 381:25–47.

Kawamoto, Takao
　1974　"Nihongo to naNtoogo (shutoshite meranesia shogo) to no gokukoosei-joo no idoo ni tsuite [A comparative study of Japanese and southern languages – mainly Melanesian languages – in word formation]", *Minzokugaku Kenkyuu* 39.2:113–129.
　1979　"Toward a comparative Japanese-Austronesian III", *Bulletin of Nara University of Education* (Nara, Japan), 1–20.

Li, Charles N. – S. A. Thompson
　1973　"Serial verb construction in Mandarin Chinese: subordination or co-ordination", *Papers from the Ninth Regional Meeting, Parasession volume* (University of Chicago Linguistics Society), 96–103.
　1974　"Co-verbs in Mandarin Chinese: Verbs or prepositions?" *Journal of Chinese linguistics* 2.4:257–278.

Lord, Carol
　1973　"Serial verbs in transition", *Studies in African linguistics* 4.3:269–296.
　1976　"Evidence for syntactic reanalysis: from verb to complementizer in Kwa", *Papers from the parasession on diachronic syntax* (Chicago Linguistics Society), 179–192.

Matsumura, Akira (ed.)
　1971　*Nihon Bumpoo Daijiten* (Tokyo: Meiji Shoin).

Murayama, Shichiro
　1969　"The origin of the Japanese language", *Minzokugaku Kenkyuu* 35.4: 249–261.

Timberlake, Alan
　1977　"Reanalysis and actualization", *Mechanisms of syntactic change*, edited by Ch. Li (Texas: Texas Press), 141–177.

Whinom, Keith
　1971　"Linguistic hybridization and the 'special case' of pidgins and creoles", *Pidginization and creolization of languages*, edited by Dell Hymes (Cambridge: Cambridge University Press), 91–115.

HENRIK BIRNBAUM

Notes on syntactic change: Cooccurrence vs. substitution, stability vs. permeability

1 Preliminaries: Definitional framework; focus; data base

The following remarks address themselves to some controversial or, at any rate, much-debated issues regarding linguistic change as they pertain to the domain of syntax. While there exist a number of definitions and delimitations of the field of syntax, to avoid possible misinterpretations this traditional term will be taken here to denote any and all facets of the theory of the sentence and, in particular, of sentential semantics, i.e., the study of the grammatical meanings (functions) of individual sentences and their constituent members (as opposed to the study of lexical meanings of individual items, or words). In addition, syntax will be understood to refer to the principles and mechanics of sentence structure, ranging from the minimal phrase or word combination (also known as syntagm, R *slovosočetanie*, G *Wortgefüge*) to the compound and complex sentence, or period, with the latter consisting of two or more clauses linked by coordination and/or subordination; for an incisive discussion of the structure of the phrase ("syntactic group") and that of the sentence, their relationship and the parallelism obtaining between them, see, Kuryłowicz 1948: 60–71. Thus, syntax is used here to cover both the sub-theory of grammatical meanings (or functions proper) and that of sentence structure. However, this division is admittedly somewhat fuzzy and artificial; grammatical meanings, and their sum total within one sentence or, even beyond that, the overall semantic gestalt of the sentence — the sentential meaning as a whole — form an integral part of, and are defined by, the general patterning of sentence structure. On grammatical meaning and its place in sentence structure, see also Admoni 1979. By the same token, what will remain outside the purview of the present considerations are larger syntagmatic structures, entire paragraphs as well as texts (or, in spoken form, utterances). These are properly the domain of the communication-theoretically based branch of the study of language (as a semiotic system) usually, at least in American parlance, referred to as functional sentence perspective (FSP, R *aktual'noe členenie predloženija*, the Russian term echoing the original Czech designation). As is well known, FSP views such contrasts as theme/rheme, topic/comment, new/old information, actualization (or foregrounding)/automatization — the latter with significant implications for poetics — in the framework of the overall organization of speech (and its graphic rendition). These as well as related topics fall into the broader field of discourse analysis or text grammar (G *Textlinguistik*), again with important ramifications in stylistics.

Thus conceived and defined, syntax (sentence theory) constitutes an independent component of linguistic structure which operates on an autonomous level (or, to be precise, on two interrelated, specifically syntactic levels). Syntax, though separate, interacts and correlates with other components of the linguistic system, or (if viewed in the purely theoretical terms of a construct) of the linguistic model. The syntactic component is regarded, then, to be directly related to and informed by lexical semantics, on the one hand, and, on the other, by morphology, i.e., the theory of the formation and variation of minimal meaning carriers (morphemes).

Even though I cannot espouse some of the major tenets of transformational-generative (TG) theory, in its various formulations, I do subscribe to one of its basic premises, namely, that of distinguishing between a prelinear semantic deep structure (DS) and a linear surface structure (SS), the latter readily identifiable both at the syntactic and the phonological levels. For some forceful overall critiques of Chomskyan linguistics, see Collinder 1970, Robinson 1975, Hudson 1976, Gross 1979; for a view of the DS-SS relationship and interaction roughly equivalent to mine, cf. Hetzron 1975. Elsewhere I have suggested that the DS concept of TG theory be substantially modified. Thus I have proposed that several layers of DS be identified and distinguished: (1) profound structure, which is truly language-universal; (2) shallow structure, which is always language-specific, and as such can be conceived of as the structural common denominator of syntactic synonymy (for a slightly different, yet also transformational, view of syntactic synonymy, see Korel'skaja 1975); and, (3) medial structure, which consists of a set of structural layers of varying depth whose precise place and nature is contingent on the definition of a particular linguistic type, representing one of the many classes into which the languages of the world can be grouped. It follows that, while the profound structure contains relatively few elements representing dependency constellations, the shallow structure, by contrast, is comparatively rich and complex when it comes to its integral categories and the relational configurations obtaining among them. The several typologically defined deep-structural layers vary, obviously, as to their degree of complexity in terms of the functional entities which constitute them as well as their inherent relations, depending on the scope of a given language type. For discussion, cf. esp. Birnbaum 1968a, 1968b, 1970, 1975, 1976, and 1977a; see also Ineichen 1979: 124–6.

Regarding the specific mechanisms of syntactic change, I will be primarily concerned here with two sets of problems: (1) Does syntactic change take place abruptly (discretely) or gradually (continuously), and is the question of sudden vs. progressive change in syntax a matter of objective reality or merely one of imperfect perception or even distorted analysis and opinionated construction on the part of the linguist? In this context, what are the precise conditions or, at least, the general prerequisites for cooccurrence of synonymous, or near-synonymous, syntactic categories (and their overt manifestation) in one language, as opposed to the substitution of one category (or, rather, its corresponding morphological expression) by another, and of one dependency-relational configuration of categories (and their correlates at the level of morphology) by a different one? (2) Is (a) the syntactic component of linguistic structure more susceptible to modification and adaptation under the impact of foreign models than other parts of language, in other words, is syntax particularly permeable to foreign syntactic influences? Or (b) is it, on the contrary, more stable and hence resistant to such penetration, at least at some level of depth or covertness on the scale ranging from syntactic SS to the profound level of semantic structure? Or (c) is it perhaps even conceivable somehow to combine these two seemingly opposite views?

Reference will be made here, for purposes of illustration, to a number of instances of syntactic change and overall development in syntax, all taken from the history of recorded languages, without it being possible, within the limited scope of a conference paper, to enter into a detailed discussion of their sometimes controversial nature and particulars. Though syntactic reconstruction, including the recovery of syntactic change, poses a number of intriguing and challenging methodological problems (some of which I have considered elsewhere; cf. Birnbaum 1977b: 30–41, and 1980b), I will not discuss here any of these intricate questions. Let me merely remark that I am somewhat skeptical of recent attempts to reduce the inquiry into syntactic reconstruction to issues of word-order typology (of the kind proposed by J. Greenberg and symbolized by the formulas VSO, SVO, SOV, etc.) or, at any rate, to place almost exclusive emphasis on matters of word order especially with regard to such an archaic, highly inflected language type as Proto-Indo-European (or preliterate and early recorded Ancient Indo-European); cf. Greenberg 1963/66 and 1964; Lakoff 1972: 195–7 (n. 16); Lehmann 1974: esp. 30–9 and 238–51, Friedrich 1975; generally on word-order typology, see further Ineichen 1979: 130–48.

2 Gradualness of syntactic change: Cooccurrence and substitution

Turning now to the issues themselves, it is my contention that syntactic change most definitely is gradual, not abrupt or discrete. I therefore fully agree with the view expressed by S. Chung (1977) and supported by a formalized analysis of pertinent data. Using Polynesian and other Austronesian (Malayo-Polynesian) evidence, Chung suggested that the hierarchical order of syntactic change which she was able to establish is borne out by the change being implemented progressively, viz., so that the change is first reflected in superficial rules and only subsequently in major cyclic rules; furthermore, it interacts with simple sentences before interacting with any superficial rules at all. Among the latter (taken as a whole), syntactic change will first affect the more superficial and only then the less superficial rules. As Chung also pointed out, this interpretation, though remaining within the overall framework of generative theory, represents a major departure from the standard view of generative historical linguistics which, at best, has recognized general trends ("drift") in syntactic modification (cf., e.g., Lakoff 1972), but has assumed that such trends could be broken up and isolated into a series of discrete shifts analyzable and describable in terms of the well-known TG mechanisms of rule addition, rule deletion ("rule loss"), simplification, and reanalysis; for more details concerning this line of reasoning, see Chung 1977. While R. D. King (1969:115) has perhaps most unambiguously and explicitly stated the view that any nonphonological change by its very nature precludes gradualness, other generativists have echoed similar opinions (Klima 1964, Traugott 1965, Lakoff 1970).

For a somewhat refined TG approach to syntactic change (within the framework of the "Extended Standard Theory"), see now also Lightfoot 1979. Concerned, in particular, with "radical" reanalysis of such portions of grammar which, over a period of time, have grown more marked, this approach incorporates a new "Transparency Principle", requiring that derivations be minimally complex and that SS therefore not deviate considerably from DS. It is claimed that this principle has the double advantage of both making diachronic data inform the theory of grammar, and having the latter yield new (and, presumably, better) explanations for syntactic change. Though probably applicable to some instances of English historical syntax discussed in the book, the principle introduced by Lightfoot cannot, to my mind, claim universal validity − least of all when it comes to the correspondences obtaining between typological (i.e., medial) DS and syntactic SS. While the author must be commended for exercising due caution in discussing the conceivable causes of linguistic innovation, he, too, seems generally more preoccupied with theory building (and rule formulation) than with achieving what ought to be the primary goal in any attempt at historical analysis (including, obviously, such conceptualization as can be derived from it): to let the diachronic data itself inform and shape the theory.

Here the parallelism with phonological change (or lack thereof) deserves a brief comment, as it illustrates particularly well the difference, or rather, discrepancy existing between linguistic reality and observational perception of the processes at hand. It goes almost without saying that change at the phonetic (subphonemic and, in this instance, also sub-distinctive-feature) level occurs gradually: the actual articulation of an individual sound segment may – and, in fact, does usually – shift slightly and almost unnoticeably long before a sound change in the functional-semiotic sense, i.e., on the (distinctive) feature and phonemic levels, takes place. It is precisely this realization that underlies, for example, H. Andersen's much acclaimed and, in my view, generally compelling abductive model of phonological change. Here the assumption is that a grammar 2 replaces a previous grammar 1 only when an ongoing, progressively more pronounced sound change is reinterpreted by a following generation (or, as I have tried to clarify, otherwise emulating population segment) as constituting a definite and completed shift from (producing and perceiving) one speech sound to (articulating and hearing) another, distinct one; cf. Andersen 1973, 1974, and 1978; Birnbaum 1979.

In a roughly analogous vein, it should be noted that the gradual nature of linguistic change on the surface-syntactic level is not merely a matter of our perception (and analysis) of how a syntactic innovation is introduced, enters into competition with earlier existing forms and sequences, spreads, and, eventually, may entirely supersede any previous ones. It can be ascertained that this gradual sequence of actual modifications does occur, but it is not only our perception and internalization of these modifications that need registering. In fact, this gradual nature of evolution on the level(s) of syntax is usually even underscored by a considerable time lag that can be observed (or, in less clear instances, assumed) between the implementation of a specific syntactic change and its being reflected in the recorded evolution of a language and thus, as it were, acknowledged. But over and above that, the innovation itself, even if not yet manifest in writing, usually occurs not at once, but over a certain time span, often reflected in long periods of syntactic synonymy in the history of a language. Syntactic synonymy, that is to say, the occurrence and virtual interchangeability of functionally identical or nearly identical formal means, in part conditioned and qualified only by stylistic and other not strictly grammatical considerations, is thus the norm rather than the exception at any given stage in the diachronic variation of a linguistic system. It is precisely the syntactic synonymy that constitutes the overt manifestation of the underlying, shallow semantic-syntactic infrastructure of an individual language, as was mentioned above.

The point of the time lapse separating the actual syntactic change (in the spoken language) and its reflection in the written records was eloquently, if informally, argued by C. I. Ståhle over two decades ago, in connection with his investigating syntactic and stylistic characteristics of Old Scandinavian, notably Old Swedish, legal language. Thus, Ståhle (1958:121–2) pointed out, among other things, that

> by contrast to the majority of the phonological and morphological historical varia-
> tions the syntactic ones do not need to imply that a newly introduced construction
> renders an older one superfluous – old and new syntactic phenomena coexist and
> are resorted to to a various extent depending on the speaker's or writer's need of ex-
> pression and stylistic ability. The period when several of the syntactic features – e.g.,
> various degrees of subordination (hypotaxis) – which for a variety of reasons have
> been considered more recent, actually were an innovation of language, in many in-
> stances probably considerably antedates the earliest written records. – It should
> further be noted . . . that several traits which are usually regarded as primitive, e.g.,
> coordination (parataxis), are natural in written languages without a tradition. The
> less sophisticated writer will form simpler sentences, even if the language in itself
> should offer possibilities for a more complex, variegated, and expressive sentence
> structure. These possibilities are increasingly resorted to as a writing tradition grows
> stronger and is supported by an educated class accustomed to writing. If the oldest
> written sources reveal a simple, paratactic language, one can, nonetheless after even
> a century or two, note longer periods with flexible use of expressions for various
> kinds and degrees of hypotaxis; this does not have to mean that these hypotactic
> means of expression constitute innovations in the language, but merely that a higher
> degree of mastering the possibilities available to the language has been achieved – it
> is quite conceivable that the very same development could have been observed had
> writing been introduced a few centuries earlier.

I have deliberately quoted this passage in extenso (translated from the Swedish) since it is not readily accessible and, in my opinion, captures the essence of a major facet of syntactic change in languages with a long tradition of literacy. A statement largely to the same effect was made by me some years ago (Birnbaum 1971:37; see also Birnbaum 1977c:14, n. 7). As for the assertion of an initially or early only partial utilization of the repertoire of formal devices for expressing grammatical meanings, its full employment not coming into play until later (and often triggered by external factors), this point will be pursued a bit further in the next section, in the context of loan syntax. Along similar lines as those suggested by Ståhle, the notion of the "historical process of the fading of elements of an old kind and of the accu-mulation of elements of a new kind", introduced and amply illustrated with Russian syntactic data by T. P. Lomtev (1956:esp. 16–33), can no doubt prove useful; cf. also Staniševa 1958.

Admittedly, the ultimate forces determining linguistic evolution will in all probability remain forever concealed, as is the primary motivation for the phylogenetic origin of language itself. Yet we can speculate about the causes for both, viewing the development of language as subject either to a teleological dynamics (cf. R. Jakobson's means-ends model; see esp. Jakobson 1963) or to a continuous striving for restoring the equilibrium of a semiotic system in one way or another permanently out of balance with itself, that is, incessantly engaged in the process of compensating, at one level or another, for the ongoing decay or, in other terms, the increasingly inadequate measure of efficiency in transmitting information; this latter notion could properly also be labeled the entropic view of linguistic evolution. Yet there are certain communication-theoretical factors which, even though the exact share of their respective, conflicting impact cannot easily be gauged or otherwise determined, obviously influence the direction and pace of this evolution, among other things, on the level(s) of syntax as well. The competing factors that I am referring to are a striving for economy (in the last analysis tending toward a high degree of ellipsis), on the one hand, and a need for explicitness (implying always a certain measure of redundancy), on the other. While one tendency is naturally oriented toward preserving energy, that is, minimizing the effort expended in the process of communication (notably, in the speech act), the other one is, on the contrary, designed to safeguard the unimpeded (or rather, only minimally reduced) flow of information between speaker and hearer, writer and reader; it thus provides a set of built-in safety valves, should the primary means of communication fail. At the phonological (subphonemic) level of language, this interplay can be readily observed in the distribution and interaction of distinctive vs. redundant features, along the paradigmatic axis, with the redundant features ready to take over where the distinctive features are rendered nonfunctional, so that a shift in functional load of feature oppositions (e.g., from voiced/voiceless to lax/tense) is fairly common, with a corollary redundant-to-distinctive shift if the change is more than merely occasional or temporary. Whereas these conflicting tendencies of economizing vs. amplifying the means of expression have long been recognized and to some extent elucidated when it comes to the phonological component and its modification over a period of time (cf. esp. Martinet 1955), much less is known about their role and significance in grammar and especially in syntax. In fact very little work has, to the best of my knowledge, gone into studying syntactic change specifically from this point of view. As an example of the few applications of the principle of economy also to syntactic change one could mention the relevant sections in Koenraads 1953: 92–118 and 168–76, conceiving the evolution of German primarily from the angle of economy and efficiency.

This, however, is not the place to explore this approach to syntactic change in any detail. Suffice it to say that I am satisfied that more attention paid to this specific aspect, particularly if applied in a formalized, rigorous fashion (resorting to findings and techniques of contemporary communication theory), is bound to yield new and revealing insights also regarding the factors responsible for the cooccurrence of diverse formal means to denote the same or very close grammatical meanings, or serving as constituent elements in building distinct syntactic structures and constructing differently fashioned sentences with essentially identical meaning – in other words, syntactic synonymy. A proper consideration of the intrinsic workings of the economy vs. redundancy factors in language would thus allow us to better understand some of the reasons for the preservation of syntactic cooccurrence as well as for the substitution of one set of formal means by another one and its particular pace beyond the more easily ascertained and understood extraneous parameters of cultural change (with its frequent repercussions particularly on the stylistic level of language).

As merely one case in point reference can be made here to the development of relative constructions in Indo-European. There can be little doubt that relativity (in the grammatical sense) could be and was in fact expressed, also by formal means, in preliterate Indo-European and in all likelihood in the common proto-language as well (cf. Lehmann 1974:61–8, 243–5). Yet the evolution and continuous refinement of the means for denoting this particular kind of subordination of one clause to another, or rather, to a word or word group within another clause, can be studied throughout the course of the attested history of Indo-European. For one thing, the lack of any formal marking of relativity (obviously an archaic feature) can be found even in some contemporary Germanic languages, notably in English and, to a somewhat lesser extent, Scandianavian; cf. E *She is the woman I love*, Sw *Hon är den kvinna/kvinnan jag älskar* as against G *Sie ist die Frau, die* (or *welche*) *ich liebe*, the use of a relative pronoun being mandatory in German. (Notice that while in Swedish both variants cited are possible, there is a slight stylistic and semantic difference: *den kvinna*, with the determinative pronoun *den* but without the postposed definite article, is slightly more formal and emphasizes the particular woman as being singled out; *kvinnan*, marked only for definiteness, as its English counterpart, is now also fully acceptable but still somewhat colloquial and carries the generalizing implication 'of all women'.) More frequent than not marking relativity in the relevant constructions (or marking it only minimally as in the case of the use of the Swedish determinative pronoun), is of course formal subordination by means of a relative pronoun or relative adverb. Leaving aside the second possibility (of the type: *the town where I was born*) for the purpose of the present discussion, the relative pronoun normally used to establish relative subordination is then either an original relative pronoun, goes back to a demonstrative-anaphoric pronoun (or is homonymous with a still existing one), or betrays its origin in an interrogative pronoun, which itself may well continue to be used in the language. In addition, relative pronouns can sometimes be traced to an original and frequently still used comparative conjunction. Thus, for example, classical Greek *hós, hḗ, hó,* is, as indicated by its Sanskrit parallel *yás, yā́, yā́d,* to be derived from a relative pronoun PIE **yos *yā *yod.* In Latin, by contrast, it is the original interrogative *qui, quae, quod* that has taken on the additional function of a relative pronoun. In Germanic, the relative pronoun either reflects its demonstrative provenience (E *that,* G *der, die, das,* Da *der* — the last an adverb, also used as a relative pronoun, but only in subject function) or its interrogative origin (E *who, which,* G *welcher, welche, welches,* Sw *vilken, vilket*), partly with clear semantic and/or stylistic constraints. The generalized Swedish *som* (stylistically neutral and without semantic restrictions) goes back to a comparative conjunction (cf. the homonymous *som* as well as its synonym, *såsom*). Old Swedish had three different particles for establishing relative subordination: *är* (Runic Sw *is,* Icelandic *es, er* = Gothic *is,* corresponding to G *er* 'he', originally a demonstrative pronoun, subsequently, as is often the case, faded into a personal pronoun — cf. Slavic *on* — but in Old Nordic reinterpreted as an uninflected particle), *sum* (modern *som*), and *þär* (originally of course a demonstrative-deictic adverb, modern *där* 'there'; however, in addition OSw *þär* seems also to point to contamination with *þät* 'that, it' as well as being the result of contraction from *þän, þe, þät + är* 'is'); for details, see Wessén 1956:227—54. In Slavic, finally, the development known from Germanic has gone one step further: the original demonstrative or anaphoric pronoun has systematically been replaced by an original interrogative pronoun. Thus, while in Early Slavic (e.g., Old Church Slavic, Russian Church Slavic, Old Polish) forms like *iže, jen, jenže* predominate in relative function, they are gradually replaced by forms of the type *kotoryj, ktory* (modern *który*) as well as *kto, čto/co,* with the last pronoun (in the neuter) assuming the function of a *relativum generale* (functionally comparable to Sw *som*). The relevant development in Polish, from the earliest texts of the 14th and 15th centuries (earlier fragments, glosses, and names yielding no significant data) through the present, thoroughly charted and investigated, provides particularly telling evidence both of cooccurrence and substitution in this respect. For further discussion, see esp. Urbańczyk 1935 and 1939:4—33 and 50—62; Nieminen 1939 and 1950: 7—23 and 65—164; for pertinent data, cf. also, e.g., Klemensiewicz 1961/ 65/72:129/120—1 and 236—7/154, Klemensiewicz *et al.* 1966:24—30, 37— 8, and 46—7.

3 Loan syntax: Receptiveness vs. resistance to foreign influence; differences in surface vs. typological deep syntax

Moving on, now, to the other main problem mentioned above, that of the permeability and susceptibility of syntax to foreign influence, that is, to the impact of another set of syntactic features and structures, it should be noted at the outset that the most commonly held view is that syntax is indeed highly permeable as compared to, at any rate, phonology and morphology. By the same token, the vocabulary of a language, like syntax, frequently absorbs, in the course of its evolution, a great many foreign lexical elements (borrowed words turning into grammatically more or less integrated loanwords). Consequently, the total word stock of a language oftentimes is made up of more lexemes which have entered it, at some point in time, from without than there are genuinely inherited items (G *Erbwörter*) still in use (excluding also preliterate borrowings). For some explicit assertions considering the high permeability of syntax (given certain qualifications), see, e.g., Bauer 1958:73—4, Kurz 1963:6, Birnbaum 1963. Examples of a substantially refashioned syntactic component owing to foreign influence are provided by such instances as the impact of Greek syntax on Early Slavic, especially Old Church Slavic (OCS), phrase and sentence structure, of Latin on Czech and Polish syntax, of Russian Church Slavic (RChS), Polish, and French on the shape and complexity of the sentence structure of Contemporary Standard Russian (CSR), to mention just a few instances where Slavic syntax has been affected. For details and further discussion, see esp. Bauer 1958 (Greek → OCS, and Latin → Czech); Růžička 1958, 1966; Kurz 1963; Večerka 1968, 1971; Birnbaum 1958, 1968a, 1968b (Greek → OCS); Wierzbicka 1966; Birnbaum 1977 (Latin → Polish); Stender-Petersen & Jordal 1957:201—18; Bräuer 1959; Dvořaková 1959; Meščerskij 1962 (Greek → OCS/RChS → CSR); Isačenko 1974b:270—2 (French → CSR); 1974a:24 and 27—39 (Greek → OCS/RChs → CSR, and French → CSR), forthcoming: esp. 16.3.3. (Greek → RChS → CSR, and Polish → CSR, with French → CSR being essentially a development of the 18th—19th cc., not considered here); Buttler 1976:93—101 (CSR → Polish).

On other occasions, where the prerequisites for foreign impact on the syntactic component of a particular stylistic sphere or genre would seem to have been present, minimal, if any, cross-language influence in syntax can be noted. Such is the case, for example, with the Old Russian legal language of the *Russkaja Pravda* for which little foreign influence can be shown to have existed. Otherwise, one might have expected here the style and syntax of Old Scandinavian legal practice, notably, those of the medieval Swedish provincial law codes (which recorded the originally recited customary law, as did the

Old Russian legal text, at least in its earliest portion), to have served as one of the models; cf. Birnbaum 1962, for some more information on the peculiarities of Scandinavian, especially (Old) Swedish, legal language, see Ståhle 1958 and Wessén 1968.

Even if we accept, for the time being, the view that syntax is essentially a component of linguistic structure particularly receptive to foreign influence, this opinion is in need of some significant qualification. First, one has to distinguish at least two kinds of outside interference in the field of syntax, live or spoken, and literary or written. Second, one must differentiate between such influence which constitutes a purely mechanic transfer of altogether alien syntactic elements (functions, structures) to a language not in any way previously known to it, and the impact that merely implies the activation and enhancement of already existing or potentially developable formal means (word forms, constructions, clause and sentence patterns) found within the grammatical system of the influenced language itself. Needless to say, both types of qualification concerning external influence in syntax — spoken vs. written language and mechanic transfer vs. activating effect — have previously been noted and discussed to some extent; cf., among others, Jarceva 1956; Birnbaum 1958, 1963; Buttler 1976:93–101, esp. 98–101.

As for the first distinction, that between live and literary, it should further be remarked that the former can be divided into two subtypes: (1) syntactic interference due to earlier contacts with a non-extant population speaking a different language, and (2) syntactic influence which is the consequence of a prolonged, well-attested, and, in some instances, still ongoing symbiosis and bilingualism or, as the case may be, multilingualism. True, the borderline between these two types of live contacts and syntactic influences is occasionally somewhat less than distinct: a "foreign" — or even an originally indigenous — population can have cohabited in the same area with a second one, before disappearing or moving away.

A third consideration concerns the question whether the influence and penetration occurs between two closely related languages (such as the Slavic, Scandinavian, or Romance languages) or between two more or less distantly cognate languages (say, between two languages belonging to different branches of Indo-European, e.g., Greek and Old Church Slavic or Russian, Latin and Polish or English; between member languages of Slavic and Baltic, e.g., Polish and Lithuanian; or even between two not particularly closely kindred Germanic languages, like German and English). Finally, such interference can take place between two completely unrelated languages in one and the same *Sprachbund* or linguistic convergence area with live-contact conditions as a result of political developments and/or overall cultural integration (e.g., the impact of Turkish on Bulgarian and Macedonian). Further exemplification of the distinction between live and literary syntactic influences is provided by the vernacular Byzantinisms of the Macedo-Bulgarian "first" and "third" homeland of Old Church Slavic (given that the "creators" of the first literary language of the Slavs, Constantine and Methodius, were themselves bilingual, and considering the fact of the subsequent flowering of Old Church Slavic writing in late-9th and 10th-century Bulgaria). This impact of the spoken language of the bilingual Greek-Slavic milieu may thus be viewed in contrast to the purely literary influence on Old Church Slavic writing exerted by the syntactic patterns of *koinē* and Byzantine Greek (of the New Testament, the Septuagint, and the patristic literature). In addition, a number of pseudo-Hellenisms actually turn out to be Semitisms (in the text of the Psalter as well as in some of the sayings attributed to Jesus, echoing the Hebrew original of the Septuagint and the spoken Aramaic of the times of Christ, respectively). The live syntactic Byzantinisms of Old Church Slavic, reflecting the usage of the spoken Middle Greek language, foreshadow, to some extent, the Balkanisms of a significant (and still increasing) portion of South Slavic; cf. Sedláček 1963, Birnbaum 1965:esp. 31–8. Another example of literary syntactic influence is that of French on Russian in the 18th and 19th centuries. By contrast, the Polish impact on Russian syntax paralleling an analogous influence in the lexicon and dating back to the 15th through the 18th centuries (culminating in the 17th and early 18th centuries), was both literary – partly through the vehicle of Ukrainian – and spoken, given the Polish-Lithuanian administration of vast parts of the so-called *Jugozapadnaja Rus'*; for an influence in the opposite direction, from Russian to Polish, in more recent times, see Buttler 1976:93–101. Primarily literary was, of course, the impact of Latin on Polish, Czech, and the Croatian variant of Serbo-Croatian, as well as on Hungarian, German and Swedish (in various phases of their evolution). The influence of German on Polish syntax was possibly both literary and live, considering the large-scale influx of a German-speaking population to many Polish towns during the later Middle Ages. Similar factors were at work with regard to German syntactic influence noticeable in Swedish, a comprehensive study of which has yet to be written.

A telling example of syntactic influence resulting from an underlying linguistic substratum is the possible impact of Finnic on the syntax of Russian, both the standard language and, even more so, some of its dialects. I am referring here, in particular, to the so-called nominal or 'be' sentence of Contemporary Standard Russian (with the zero form of the copula in the present) and to what has been termed the nominative object (occurring with nouns in *-a* only and in conjunction with the infinitive; type: *voda pit'*), known from North Russian dialects and recorded, with some frequency, in official, especially legal, documents of the 12th through 18th centuries from the same area. This puzzling syntactic phrase has left no traces in the literary language, however. Moreover, an analogous construction is attested in East Baltic and West (or Baltic) Finnic.

With regard to the construction of the standard language, at least three competing views have been advanced: (1) that we are dealing here with an archaism of Indo-European origin (cf. such Latin parallels as *vox populi vox dei, cuius regio eius religio*, largely limited to gnomic usage, however); (2) that this is a characteristic of Russian (and, with some qualifications, East Slavic in general) explicable in terms of internal structural modifications of Russian (and its closest cognate languages); or (3) that this phenomenon is due to the impact of a Finnic substratum, a trace of the speech of the aboriginal population of vast parts of northern Russia conquered and assimilated by the invading Eastern Slavs in the second half of the first millennium A. D. Naturally, some combination of these explanations has also been considered. Discussing previous relevant research, V. Kiparsky in 1969 expressed some serious doubts as to the likelihood that the Finnic construction (fully equivalent to that of Russian, incidentally, only in some, not all, Finnic languages, and slightly different also in the Ugric linguistic branch as represented particularly by Hungarian) is the direct source of this peculiarity of Russian syntax; cf. Kiparsky 1969a:16—18. Isačenko (forthcoming: 16.1.4) adopts a compromise position: noting Kiparsky's rejection of Veenker's (and his predecessors') hypothesis and referring also to his own characterization of Russian as a 'be' language, he points to the more precise localization of the phenomenon in question by L'Hermitte as reflected in the early evidence, which in fact would rather favor the substratum theory. And, finally, L'Hermitte himself, in his recent major work on the nominal sentence in Russian, primarily Old Russian (and Russian Church Slavic), not yet available to Isačenko, arrives again at the cautiously phrased conclusion that the substratum explanation probably is the relatively most satisfactory one, certain difficulties notwithstanding; cf. L'Hermitte 1978 esp. 287—310; for an assessment of L'Hermitte's findings, see also Birnbaum 1980a. To my mind, a solution to this thorny problem may perhaps be sought along slightly different lines. At a typological deep-structural level of syntax, the Russian 'be' sentence corresponds to a specific type of predication to which Russian, with its peripheral and archaic character, eminently belongs. In terms of the more superficial restructuring of the syntactic pattern of the language, however, the impact of a Finnic substratum — here as a conservative force, preventing a development more in line with that of other European languages — may well have played a decisive role. Cf. also the relatively late emergence of genuine 'have' constructions in Russian; for more discussion, see Isačenko 1974a.

As regards the other construction mentioned, that of the so-called nominative object in *-a*, Kiparsky (1967, 1969a:19–20, 1969b, amply quoting previous relevant research, both his own and that of others) again does not accept the notion of a direct influence from underlying Finnic but concedes that the substratum here may have played an important part in terms of preserving (or, "refrigerating", following a coinage of G. Jacobsson) an earlier syntactic structure. Isačenko (forthcoming: 16.4) does not offer a solution of his own but seems generally less critical of Larin's explanation (who assumed substratum influence) while remaining unconvinced by the case-semantic explanation proposed by Timberlake (1974). Both appreciative and critical about Timberlake's ingenious (though, no doubt, somewhat strained) explanation – operating as it does with case theory, markedness, rule ordering, and language typology – is Sappok (1979) in reviewing his work. For my own part, I see considerable merit in Timberlake's argument, especially as his approach combines a semantic-structural analysis (in broad and unorthodox generative terms) with the historically plausible consideration that the so-called nominative object in early North Russian dialects as well as in East Baltic (Lithuanian and Latvian) arose as a result of borrowing from some part of West Finnic. At any rate, Timberlake makes a valid point for arguing that the structural differences (of environment and inventory) found in the languages concerned are, in fact, illusory; cf. Timberlake 1974:220–1. It is with his case specification – of the nominative not necessarily originally being the case of the subject in Indo-European – that I confess to have some difficulty, though. For while it is true that the logical (or 'deep') subject does not usually "surface" in the nominative in instances where the infinitive functions as predicate (cf. however the type *on – bežat'*) but in the dative (type *emu ničego ne skazat'*, with modal connotations, cf. Birnbaum 1967; Veyrenc 1979), it does not necessarily follow that the Indo-European nominative could ever be used for the direct object. I would rather, therefore, consider the construction *voda pit', zemlja paxat'* another instance of a nominal sentence without copula (cf. E *he is easy to please*) and as such a transform, or paraphrase, of an impersonal phrase with a direct object (*[emu] pit' vodu, paxat' zemlju*; cf. E *it is easy to please him* – this comparison having been made previously).

If it is sometimes difficult to draw a sharp line between what must be considered live and literary influences in syntax, the same is probably true to an even higher degree of the suggested distinction between a mere mechanical transfer of foreign syntactic patterns and the activation and intensification of pre-existent indigenous syntactic models or formal-functional means, inherent in the affected language but triggered by foreign influence. Yet this distinction is crucial. The mixed Greek-Slavic syntax of Old Church Slavic (and the evolving Slavic literary languages patterned, to a varying extent, on it) is both a rewarding and, in some respects, frustrating field of inquiry when it comes to establishing the criteria for ascertaining what is genuinely alien and truly imposed, and what is simply at first latent or undeveloped but potentially capable of being developed and utilized to full strength as regards the language's own intrinsic means (cf., e.g., the rich participial system of OCS and, patterned on RChS, also of CSR).

The realization of the availability of certain formal devices and structural possibilities for subsequent increased syntactic use has led some linguists to deny altogether, or at least seriously to question, the alleged high permeability of the syntactic component to foreign prototypes by comparison to other parts of linguistic structure. Thus it has been suggested that such influences from the outside at most affect the pace and particular direction of the relevant evolution; cf. Lomtev 1956:17–19; Sprinčak 1960:18–20 and 30. This guarded (and, to my mind, both overcautious and at the same time self-assertive) view ought not to be confused, however, with that of other scholars who, at least for some syntactic phenomena, are inclined to play down the role of any foreign model primarily because of a perceived substantial difference in the permeability/penetrability vs. stability/resistibility relationship when applied to the surface-syntactic as opposed to the deep-syntactic levels of language. This reasoning underlies, it would seem, H. Andersen's interpretation of the origin of the dative absolute construction in Baltic and Slavic, and similar considerations may also have prompted R. Růžička's approach to this controversial phenomenon in Slavic; cf. Andersen 1970, Růžička 1961; for an assessment of Andersen's approach, see Birnbaum 1970:45, in n. 40; on Růžička's point of view, cf. Birnbaum 1968b:58. My own conception of the absolute case constructions of Ancient (and archaic) Indo-European, including the Slavic dative absolute, was spelled out in Birnbaum 1970:43–5.

The third consideration mentioned above, interrelated with the two previous ones, namely, as to whether the language extending certain syntactic loans is closely or distantly related or perhaps altogether unrelated to the receiving linguistic system, hardly needs to be commented upon any further in order to prove its significance. Obviously, the kind of syntactic borrowing that may have occurred between, say, Latin (especially, Late or Vulgar Latin) and Early French or Italian, or between Old Church Slavic and Russian, or even between Middle Low German and Swedish or Danish must, qualitatively and quantitatively, be of a different kind than, e.g., that between Turkish and Bulgarian or some Finnic language (or dialect) and Russian. The impact of Latin on the syntax of both Spanish and English would seem to fall somewhere in between these two extremes; cf. Lakoff 1968; see also Birnbaum 1970:46.

The question of the degree of permeability of syntax has come into a new light, as was already indicated, with the introduction of a TG viewpoint also regarding the comparative (and contrastive) study of syntax. Thus, in particular, with the identification of clear-cut language families (in the genetic sense) as constituting at the same time specific language types (regardless of how these particular language groups evolved), so that, to cite a few examples, Ancient Indo-European, Romance, or Slavic can be regarded as linguistic types with their own — typological — pecularities in addition to being genetically definable language classes; and, further, with the identification and isolation of specific typological intermediate layers of DS (cf. above), it has become clear that the (typological) DSs of Ancient Indo-European, Romance, or Slavic each share a considerable number of syntactic characteristics found in the member languages of these respective groups. It is thus quite appropriate to speak of a certain stability of syntactic DS, a stability which transcends the specific limitations of individual languages belonging to one and the same type. As I have put it earlier, therefore, "superficially seen, syntax has correctly been assigned a high degree of 'penetrability' (by comparison with phonology and morphology). It can, however, in its typological deep structure aspect, actually be considered a fairly stable component of language also when viewed in the context of bilingualism and language interference". Cf. further Birnbaum 1968a:21–31, esp. 22–3; 1968b:60–2; 1970:42–7, esp. 42–3.

4 Conclusions

In closing these remarks, the following general, tentative inferences seem to suggest themselves as emerging from the line of reasoning adopted here:

(1) Syntactic change is gradual. Any notion of abrupt (discrete) innovation in syntax is based on a mistaken identification of the descriptive analysis of a diachronic process (including the formulation and manipulation of rules designed to capture such processes) with the process itself. In this respect a parallelism can be ascertained between the mechanism (and description) of phonological and syntactic change. However, while in phonology (except in stylistically conditioned free variations), once a gradual shift is completed, one entity perceived as distinctive (a feature, a phoneme) fully replaces an earlier one so that on the perceptional (acoustic) level an either/or situation obtains, in syntax a both/and situation (syntactic synonymy) may prevail for a considerable period of time. In fact, to some degree this is the rule,

not the exception: language at all times avails itself of a variety of formal (structural) means to convey one and the same grammatical meaning (separate function or sentential meaning). Syntactic change, having taken place in the spoken language, is normally not immediately reflected in writing. The recorded history of most, if not all, languages therefore is marked by a time discrepancy between the actual occurrence (or rather, introduction) of a syntactic innovation in speech and its subsequent graphic manifestation. Even though synonymous syntactic constructions — one (or some) older or even archaic, the other one(s) more recent — cooccur at a given period, frequently allowing for stylistic differentiation and/or subtle semantic fine-tuning (so that near-synonymy often might be more accurate a designation than plain synonymy), one syntactic change, when completed, frequently will trigger further modifications in the syntax of a language.

(2) On the surface, the syntactic component is highly susceptible to foreign influence. The impact of foreign models may either imply a mechanical transfer of syntactic features or structures altogether alien to the receiving language, or it may activate and enhance previously less developed or latent formal means available to the influenced language. The impact of a foreign syntactic pattern can further occur in the spoken and/or written (literary) language. The former influence is usually prompted by a situation — reconstructible or attested, long past or continuing — of bilingualism (or multilingualism) and attendant language interference; the latter is normally the result of cultural influence (or even domination) finding its expression in literature. The susceptibility of syntax to foreign influence at the surface level is comparable to the "mobility" of foreignisms in the lexical sphere: here, too, we can distinguish between a mechanical transfer of foreign words (G *Fremdwörter*) and the integration of foreign elements with the vocabulary of the recipient language, either by formal adaptation of loan words (G *Lehnwörter*) to the morphological paradigms of the language concerned or by reproducing the semantic elements (and, in the case of compound words, their combination) with indigenous lexical means (lexical calques, loan translation). At a deeper level of linguistic structure — that of typological DS — syntax is more resistant to foreign influence and may thus be considered more stable, less permeable. Basically, however, this is not so much a matter of any inherent difference in the degree of stability or permeability of syntax at various levels of syntactic structure, as it is one of a far-reaching structural coincidence or identity in the patterning of the deep-structural, i.e., prelinear, dependency relations among languages belonging to one and the same typological class (granted the remaining difficulties in defining the exact criteria for establishing linguistic types). This therefore renders superfluous a potential adaptation

of the underlying sentence structure of one language to the deep-seated syntactic patterning of another.

References

Admoni, V. G.
1979   "Struktura grammatičeskogo značenija i ego status v sisteme jazyka", *Struktura predloženija i slovosočetanija v indoevropejskix jazykax*, edited by V. G. Admoni (Leningrad: "Nauka"), 6–36.
Andersen, H.
1970   "The dative of subordination in Baltic and Slavic", *Baltic linguistics*, edited by T. F. Magner and W. R. Schmalstieg (University Park and London: The Pennsylvania State University Press), 1–9.
1973   "Abductive and deductive change", *Lg* 49:765–93.
1974   "Towards a typology of change: Bifurcating changes and binary relations", *Proceedings of the First International Conference on Historical Linguistics*, edited by J. M. Anderson and C. Jones (Amsterdam: North Holland), II, 17–60.
1978   "Perceptual and conceptual factors in abductive innovations", *Recent developments in historical phonology*, edited by J. Fisiak (The Hague: Mouton), 1–22.
Bauer, J.
1958   "Vliv řečtiny a latiny na vývoj syntaktické stavby slovanských jazyků", *Československé přednášky pro IV. Mezinárodní sjezd slavistů v Moskvě* (Prague: Nakladelství ČSAV), 73–95.
Birnbaum, H.
1958   "Zur Aussonderung der syntaktischen Gräzismen im Altkirchenslavischen", *ScSl* 4:239–57.
1962   "On Old Russian and Old Scandinavian legal language: Some comparative notes on style and syntax", *ScSl* 8:115–40.
1963   "Reply to the question "Kakvi sa genezisăt i xarakterăt na čuždite sintaktični vlijanija v slavjanskite ezici?", *Slavjanska filologija* I: *Otgovori na văprosite za naučnata anketa po ezikoznanie* (Sofia: BAN), 126–8.
1965   "Balkanslavisch und Südslavisch. Zur Reichweite der Balkanismen im südslavischen Sprachraum", *ZfBalk* 3: 12–63.
1967   "Predication and the Russian infinitive", *To Honor Roman Jakobson* (The Hague: Mouton), 271–94.
1968a   "On deep structure and loan syntax", *Studies in Slavic linguistics and poetics in honor of Boris O. Unbegaun*, edited by R. Magidoff et al. (New York and London: New York University Press and University of London Press), 21–31.
1968b   "Obščeslavjanskoe nasledie i inojazyčnye obrazcy v strukturnyx raznovidnostjax staroslavjanskogo predloženija", *American contributions to the Sixth International Congress of Slavists* I: *Linguistic Contributions*, edited by H. Kučera (The Hague: Mouton), 29–63.
1970   "Deep structure and typological linguistics", *Problems of typological and genetic linguistics viewed in a generative framework* (The Hague: Mouton), 9–70.
1971   "Zum infiniten Ausdruck der Prädikation bei Johannes dem Exarchen", *Studia palaeoslovenica* [= Fs. J. Kurz] (Prague: Academia, Nakladelství ČSAV), 37–47.

1975 "How deep is deep structure?", *Proceedings of the Eleventh International Congress of Linguistics* II, edited by L. Heilmann (Bologna: Il Mulino), 459–79.

1976 "Il componente semantico e le stratificazioni della struttura profonda", *La tipologia linguistica*, edited by P. Ramat (Bologna: Il Mulino), 263–301.

1977a "Toward a stratified view of deep structure", *Linguistics at the crossroads*, edited by A. Makkai et al. (Padua and Lake Bluff, Ill.: Liviana Editrice and Jupiter Press), 104–19.

1977b *Linguistic reconstruction: Its potentials and limitations in new perspective* (Washington, D. C.: Institute for the Study of Man).

1977c "On the vernacular and Latin syntactic subcomponents in Polish prose of the Renaissance period", *Papers in Slavic Philology* I: *In Honor of James Ferrell*, edited by B. A. Stolz (Ann Arbor: Dept. of Slavic Languages and Literatures, University of Michigan), 1–17.

1979 "Ongoing sound change and the abductive model: Some social constraints and implications", *Proceedings of the Ninth International Congress of Phonetic Sciences* II (Copenhagen: Institute of Phonetics, University of Copenhagen), 185–95.

1980a "Review of L'Hermitte 1978", *RL* 5:99–102.

1980b "On protolanguages, diachrony, and 'preprotolanguages' ", *Ezikovedski proučavanija v čest na akad. V. I. Georgiev* (Sofia: BAN), 121–9.

Bräuer, H.
1959 "Zur Frage der altrussischen Übersetzungsliteratur", *ZfslPh* 27:322–47.

Buttler, D.
1976 *Innowacje składniowe współczesnej polszczyzny* (Warsaw: PWN).

Chung, S.
1977 "On the gradual nature of syntactic change", *Mechanisms of syntactic change*, edited by C. N. Li (Austin: University of Texas Press), 3–55.

Collinder, B.
1970 *Noam Chomsky und die generative Grammatik. Eine kritische Betrachtung* (Uppsala: Almqvist and Wiksell).

Dvořaková, E.
1959 "Syntaktické grecismy v cirkevné slovanštině a ve staré ruštině", *Československá Rusistika*, 2:115–20.

Greenberg, J. H.
1963/1966 "Some universals of grammar with particular reference to the order of meaningful elements", *Universals of language*, 2nd ed., edited by J. H. Greenberg (Cambridge, Mass.: The MIT Press), 73–113.

1964 "Some universals of word order", *Proceedings of the Ninth International Congress of Linguists*, edited by H. G. Lunt (The Hague: Mouton), 418–20.

Gross, M.
1979 "On the failure of generative grammar", *Lg* 55:859–85.

Hetzron, R.
1975 *Surfacing: from dependency relations to linearity* (Padua: Liviana Editrice).

Hudson, R. A.
1976 *Arguments for a non-transformational grammar* (Chicago: University of Chicago).

Ineichen, G.
1979 *Allgemeine Sprachtypologie* (Darmstadt: Wissenschaftliche Buchgesellschaft).

Isačenko, A. V.
1974a "On 'have' and 'be' languages A. typological sketch", *Slavic forum: Essays in linguistics and literatures*, edited by M. S. Flier (The Hague: Mouton), 43–77.

1974b   "Vorgeschichte und Entstehung der modernen russischen Literatursprache", *ZfslPh* 37:235–74.

forthcoming "Zur syntaktischen Problematik bis etwa 1700", chapter 16 in: *Geschichte der russischen Sprache* II (Heidelberg: C. Winter).

Jakobson, R.

1963   "Efforts toward a means-ends model of language in interwar continental linguistics", *Trends in European and American Linguistics 1930–1960*, II (Utrecht: Spectrum), 104–8.

Jarceva, V. N.

1956   "Problema vydelenija zaimstvovannyx èlementov pri rekonstrukcii sravnitel'- no-istoričeskogo sintaksisa rodstvennyx jazykov", *VJa* 1956:6:3–14.

King, R. D.

1969   *Historical linguistics and generative grammar* (Englewood Cliffs, N. J.: Prentice Hall, Inc.).

Kiparsky, V.

1967   "Nochmals über das Nominativobjekt des Infinitivs", *ZfslPh* 33:263–6.

1969a   *Gibt es ein finnougrisches Substrat im Slavischen?* (Helsinki: Suomalainen Tiedeakatemia).

1969b   "Das Nominativobjekt des Infinitivs im Slavischen, Baltischen und Ostseefinnischen", *Baltistica* 5:141–8.

Klemensiewicz, Z.

1961   *Historia języka polskiego*, I: *Doba staropolska*, II: *Doba średniopolska*, III: *Doba nowopolska* (Warsaw: PWN).

Klemensiewicz, Z., et al. (eds.)

1966   *Zapomniane konstrukcje składni staropolskiej* (Wrocław-Warsaw-Cracow: Ossolineum).

Klima, E. S.

1964   *Studies in diachronic transformational grammar* (Unpublished Ph. D. dissertation, Harvard University).

Koenraads, W. H. A.

1953   *Studien über sprachökonomische Entwicklungen im Deutschen* (Amsterdam: Meulenhoff).

Korel'skaja, T. D.

1975   *O formal'nom opisanii sintaksičeskoj sinonimii* (Moscow: "Nauka").

Kuryłowicz, J.

1948   "Les structures fondamentales de la langue: groupe et proposition", *Studia philosophica* 3:203–9 (reprinted in: *Esquisses Linguistiques*, Wrocław-Cracow: Ossolineum: 35–41). Polish version: "Podstawowe struktury języka: grupa i zdanie", *Problemy składni polskiej. Studia, dyskusje, polemiki z lat 1945–1970*, edited by A. M. Lewicki (Warsaw: PWN), 37–44.

Kurz, J.

1963   "Problematika issledovanija sintaksisa staroslavjanskogo jazyka", *Issledovanija po sintaksisu staroslavjanskogo jazyka. Sbornik statej.* (Prague: Nakladelství ČSAV), 5–14.

Lakoff, G.

1970   *Irregularity in syntax* (New York: Holt).

Lakoff, R.

1968   *Abstract syntax and Latin complementation* (Cambridge, Mass.: The MIT Press).

1972   "Another look at drift", *Linguistic change and generative theory*, edited by R. P. Stockwell and R. K. S. Macaulay (Bloomington: University of Indiana Press), 172–98

L'Hermitte, R.

1978   *La phrase nominale en russe* (Paris: Institut d'études slaves).

Lightfoot. D. W.
1979   *Principles of diachronic syntax* Cambridge University Press).
Lomtev, T. P.
1956   *Očerki po istoričeskomu sintaksisu russkogo jazyka* (Moscow: Izdatel'stvo Moskovskogo Universiteta).
Martinet, A.
1955   *Économie des changements phonétiques. Traité de phonologie diachronique* (Berne: Francke).
Meščerskij, N. A.
1962   "O sintaksise drevnix slavjano-russkix perevodnyx proizvedenij", *Teorija i kritika perevoda*, edited by B. A. Larin (Leningrad: Izdatel'stvo Leningradskogo Universiteta), 83–103.
Nieminen, E.
1939   *Beiträge zur altpolnischen Syntax*, I (Helsinki: Suomalainen Tiedeakatemia).
1950   *Beiträge zur altpolnischen Syntax*, II (Helsinki: Suomalainen Tiedeakatemia).
Robinson, I.
1975   *The new grammarians' funeral: a critique of Noam Chomsky's linguistics* (Cambridge: Cambridge University Press).
Růžička, R.
1958   "Griechische Lehnsyntax im Altslavischen", *ZfSl* 3:173–85.
1961   "Struktur und Echtheit des altslavischen dativus absolutus", *ZfSl* 6:588–96.
1966   "O ponjatii 'zaimstvovannyj sintaksis' v svete teorii transformacionnoj grammatiki", *VJa* 1966:4:80–96.
Sappok, C.
1979   Review of Timberlake 1974, *RL* 4:175–9.
Sedláček, J.
1963   "Sintaksis staroslavjanskogo jazyka v svete balkanistiki", *Slavia* 32:385–94.
Staniševa, D. S.
1958   "Nekotorye voprosy istoričeskogo sintaksisa padežej slavjanskix jazykov (na materiale tvoritel'nogo padeža)", *Slavističen sbornik*, I: *Ezikoznanie* (Sofia: BAN), 13–34.
Ståhle, C. I.
1958   *Syntaktiska och stilistiska studier i fornnordiskt lagspråk* (Lund: Carl Bloms Boktryckeri).
Stender-Petersen, A., and Jordal, K.
1957   "Das griechisch-byzantinische Erbe im Russischen", *Acta Congressus Madvigiani. Proceedings of the Second International Congress of Classical Studies*, V (Copenhagen: Munksgaard), 163–218.
Sprinčak, Ja. A.
1960   *Očerk russkogo istoričeskogo sintaksisa. Prostoe predloženie* (Kiev: "Radjans'ka škola").
Timberlake, A.
1974   *The nominative object in Slavic, Baltic and West Finnic* (Munich: Sagner).
Traugott, E. C.
1965   "Diachronic syntax and generative grammar", *Lg* 41:402–15.
Urbańczyk, S.
1935   *Wyparcie staropolskiego względnego jen, jenże przez pierwotnie pytajne który* (Cracow: PAN).
1939   *Zdania rozpoczynane wyrazem co w języku polskim* (Cracow: Nakładem PAN).
Večerka, R.
1968   "Otnositel'no problematiki vlijanija grečeskogo na staroslavjanskij", *Actes du Premier congrès international des études balkaniques et sud-est européennes*, VI (Sofia: BAN), 753–62.

1971   "Vliv řečtiny na staroslověnštinu", *LF* 94:129–51.
Veyrenc, J.
1979   *Les propositions infinitives en russe* (Paris: Institut d'études slaves).
Wessén, E.
1956   *Svensk språkhistoria,* III: *Grundlinjer till en historisk syntax* (Stockholm: Almqvist & Wiksell).
1968   *Svenskt lagspråk*, 2nd ed. (Lund: Gleerups).
Wierzbicka, A.
1966   *System składniowo-stylistyczny prozy polskiego Renesansu* (Warsaw: PIW).

ANDREI DANCHEV

Translation and syntactic change*

Syntactic change undoubtedly continues to command wide interest today, but although a number of new ideas have recently been advanced, some of the important issues are evidently still unclear. It has even been claimed that much of the work "has resulted in inadequate, and sometimes even untenable theories of syntactic change" (Parker & Macari 1978:5). New suggestions are to be expected therefore, but rather than presenting a new proposal I would simply like to draw further attention to the role played in various instances of syntactic change by translation.

The reference to translation obviously implies a closer look at bilingualism in situations of language contact. It must be pointed out here that whereas the effect of bilingualism on language change has long been recognized, it was only in relatively recent years that its real impact began to be appreciated more fully. This increased awareness is probably also due, among other things, to the continuing intensive development of contrastive linguistics (including error analysis) over the past ten years or so and the vast amount of new data that has thus come to light. The suggestion that many instances of interference in situations of natural and/or artificial language contact can be viewed in terms of partial or complete translation (cf. also Ivir 1979:91) is thus a further elaboration of the view that bilingualism is a major factor of language change in general and of syntactic change in particular.

In a number of publications dealing with various aspects of bilingualism (e.g. Bally 1932/1965; Weinreich 1953; Haugen 1953; Havránek 1966; Overbeke 1972; Rozencvejg 1972; Dešeriev 1976; Costello 1978. a.o.) translation is mentioned in passing only or not at all. In fact, no explicit theoretical connection between the problems of bilingualism and interlingual interference on the one hand and translation theory on the other would seem so far to have been established. This is probably due to the circumstance that by the time the main aspects of bilingualism and interlingual interference had already been extensively researched and reported, translation theory had still not been given sufficient attention. As a matter of fact, certain sections of what may loosely be described as the linguistic community still do not seem to be wholly cognizant of translation theory and the implications it holds for various fields of language research.

Before proceeding it must be specified that as used in this paper the term 'bilingualism' covers both natural bilingualism in situations of historical language contact and artificial bilingualism in situations of foreign language teaching and acquisition.[1] Since a considerable proportion of the data on both types of bilingualism displays striking similarities it appears expedient to investigate them in parallel. Though by no means new, this approach seems to be gaining ground again today (cf. e.g. Richards 1974; Baron 1977; Corder & Roulet 1977, a.o.).

It may be recalled now that although a number of points are still at issue, the contributions of R. Jakobson, A. Fjodorov, E. Nida, G. Mounen, A. Ljudskanov, I. Revzin, J. Catford, A.D. Švejcer, L.S. Barxudarov and many others (for a survey and bibliography of recent work see e.g. Rado 1977; Komisarov 1980; Vaseva 1980) have resulted in a fairly well-developed translation theory (as this relatively new discipline is commonly termed now),[2] which, with certain qualifications, can be described as 'standard' today. Allowing, of course, for differences in individual approaches, the main features of the so called 'standard' theory of translation can be summed up as follows.

To begin with, it is firmly rooted in linguistics. The translation process is modelled with an increasingly refined description of the relationship between isomorphic and allomorphic features, mapped out in the surface and deep structures of the respective languages. One of the central points is the consideration of translation as a set of interlingual transformations, the basic information content remaining invariant. In addition to purely linguistic constraints, the choice between various possible functional equivalents depends on extralinguistic factors too, this introducing a distinct and very important macrolinguistic dimension into the discipline. Another point, which is of some importance too, concerns the mainly descriptive and only partially prescriptive nature of the standard theory. All this being common knowledge today, at least among the linguists working with and on translation, a brief outline seems sufficient.

With respect to the synchronic and diachronic aspects of the problem it is evident that since language contact can be approached both synchronically and diachronically, the same also holds true of translation. Although it is developed today mainly by linguists who have little affiliation with historical linguistics, translation theory is one of those areas of linguistic research that throw into bold relief the sterility of the still surviving antinomy between synchrony and diachrony. Indeed, J. Catford reminds us that "from the point of view of translation theory the distinction between synchronic and diachronic comparison becomes irrelevant. Translation equivalents may be set up,

and translation performed, between any pair of languages or dialects – 'related' or 'unrelated' and with any kind of spatial, temporal, social or other relationship between them" (Catford 1965:20). It might be added that the use
of translation theory makes class-room work on old texts, where translation
is the basic tool of analysis, more rigorous and amenable to theoretical generalization. When translating a text from, say, Old English into Modern English, the translator performs operations that coincide at least partly with some
of the processes of historical change. The explicitation of these operations will
obviously contribute to the overall clarity of presentation. The theory of language contact, supplemented with translation theory, thus helps to reduce further the residual post-Saussurian antinomy between synchrony and diachrony
(cf. also Danchev 1974). The standard theory can therefore be expanded so
as to cover the diachronic angle as well.

For obvious reasons the standard theory is concerned with the study of
translation as a conscious activity only. And while translation as a conscious
process has been envisaged in language change before, for example in tracing
the influence of bible translation and generally of the classical and other languages on the written languages of Europe (see e.g. the bibliography in Zvegincev 1962; Birnbaum this volume; Fehling 1980), the existence of unconscious translation, whose effects seem to be more far-reaching, has largely been
neglected till now.[3] In the standard theory interlingual interference is considered merely insofar as it is the cause for poor translation, for instance in
translation criticism when referring to clumsy word for word translation, to
the 'false friends' and various other instances of a translator's or interpreter's
failures. However, recent research having confirmed the impression that many
cases of interlingual interference are due to unconscious or 'hidden', so to
speak, translation from the first into the second language (and frequently the
other way about)[4], translation theory could also be profitably applied to this
kind of process. It must be admitted, of course, that it is sometimes difficult
to distinguish between conscious and unconscious translation. On the whole
it appears that while lexical and morphological calquing are often a conscious
activity, the borrowing and translation of syntactic patterns is mostly unconscious (Darbelnet 1980; cf. also Danchev 1980).

It is evident, therefore, that in order usefully to serve historical linguistics,
the synchronically and prescriptively orientated standard theory will have to
be enlarged so as to include both the diachronic aspect and the various types
of unconscious translation. The notion of 'translation' in such an expanded
version of the theory is obviously conceived rather broadly, as it includes both
lexical and grammatical calquing, as well as 'structural' translation and 'transformulation' (Bolinger 1966). And since no hard and fast line can be drawn
between interlingual and intralingual translation such an 'expanded' theory of

translation (cf. also Danchev 1980) will necessarily also include 'code' and 'style' switching. It might furthermore be necessary to specify more distinctly the difference between 'transfer' and 'translation' here, as the two terms are not infrequently used together (cf. e.g. Harris 1954). What is often called 'negative' transfer usually amounts only to partial translation, affecting the structure of the receiving language and distorting it in a way that leads to temporary or permanent change. Compared to ordinary translation, which is a much wider notion than 'transfer' and actually encompasses it, transfer is mostly unconscious. Whereas in a number of cases transfer is equivalent to calquing,[5] translation usually involves more than one language level and requires a whole set of transformations including the semantic component, too.

The proposition that many instances of syntactic change should be linked more specifically with translation received further confirmation after studying the evidence contained in numerous publications, as well as in an extensive corpus of speech performance of Bulgarian learners of English (students of English at Sofia University and adult learners on intensive language courses at the Institute for Foreign Students in Sofia). It was found that a substantial percentage of the deviations and errors in the learners' corpus were due to unconscious translation from the native into the foreign language,[6] irrespective of whether conscious translation had been part of the teaching method or not. And the fact that many of the errors in the corpus coincide with attested historical changes supports the assumption that a significant proportion of allegedly autonomous syntactic change, ascribed to internal development, may in fact also stem from unconscious translation.

Various types of faulty translation that lead first to temporary syntactic change in a single idiolect only may have a cumulative effect in the direction of permanent change, allowing, of course, for natural variability. One way or another, there is ample evidence to suggest that unconscious translation emerges as a universal feature of most kinds of bilingualism.

The available linguistic data illustrate a wide variety of translation types. It is generally recognized today that interlingual interference operates on all language levels and that the syntactic component is particularly susceptible to foreign influence, in its permeability coming second only to the lexicon. Some of the evidence was already known to scholars such as H. Schuchardt, O. Jespersen and C. Bally and has naturally been added to significantly since then, but as it still tends to be ignored by a good many historical linguists, who are firmly committed to the 'one language' approach, it might be useful to quote and discuss a few examples.

Although it does not come under the heading of 'syntactic change' proper, in order to provide an overall picture of the impact of translation on the language as a whole and proceeding from shorter to longer speech units, one might begin by mentioning calquing on the morphemic and compound word levels. Calquing probably underlies the emergence of a number of common features of the languages of the so called 'Balkan Sprachbund', such as the development of the post-posited definite article in Albanian, Bulgarian and Roumanian, of analytical forms of the future tense, etc. (it should be recalled, of course, that the majority of Balkanisms are of a syntactic nature and that the most striking and dynamic convergence processes have been on the syntactic level — cf. e.g. Civjan 1977). Much has already been said on lexical calques, and yet one feels tempted to refer to the numerous popular calques of compound words such as *gratte-ciel* in French, *Wolkenkratzer* in German, *neboskrjob* in Russian, *nebostargac* in Bulgarian, etc., all of them from English *skyscraper.*[7]

Translation on the phrase level is abundantly attested too and this is where a large body of idiomatic expressions and turns of speech, common to many languages, e.g. *an der Nase herumführen* in German from French *mener par le but du nez* (Bally 1965:304), cf. also the Bulgarian equivalent *vodja njakogo za nosa*, are undoubtedly to be dealt with. As pointed out by O. Jespersen, a great many idioms and turns of phrases have been introduced into English, German and the Scandinavian languages from French and Latin, and into Danish and Swedish from German (Jespersen 1922:215). The more recent examples illustrate mainly the present-day spreading influence of English on a world-wide scale, e.g. *das Beste aus etwas machen* in German from English *to make the best of something* (Carstensen 1979:74), Canadian French *au-delà de notre contrôle* (Darbelnet 1980:320), etc. A wide variety of syntagmatic Anglicisms is to be found in a large number of languages all over the world. Phraseological innovations of this type naturally do not affect the core of the syntactic structure of the language (Carstensen 1979:74–75), but they show very clearly the ease with which foreign patterns are often borrowed.

The most interesting examples are doubtlessly on the sentence level. However, since they illustrate very well the all-pervading nature of interlingual interference, I shall dwell first briefly on several instances of changes in prepositional phrases. Although prepositions are rarely borrowed (Jespersen 1922: 211), the data show that in situations of language interference they can change their distribution, functions and meanings.

Beginning again with the Balkan languages, it is worth noting that both Modern Bulgarian and Modern Greek have a prepositional construction of the type *I study 'for' (so as to become) a teacher*, which cannot be derived from the inner development of the two languages. According to N. Kočev in both Bulgarian and Greek this phrase was translated from the phrase *estudio para profesor* in the Spanish based 'Judezmo' speech of the once numerous Jewish population in Salonika and other Greek and Bulgarian cities (Kočev 1980; for more examples of common prepositional usage in the Balkan languages see Asenova 1972).

Another instance of a preposition insertion rule is seen in the Swiss French prepositional phrase *attendre sur quelqu'un* due to interference from the German *auf jemanden warten* (Marouzeau 1951), and similarly *für eine Woche* in German from English *for a week* (Carstensen 1979:67).

The substitution of one preposition for another is illustrated in the Pennsylvanian German example *Der Pitscher waar verbroche bei der Anna*, which has *bei* instead of *von*, due to English influence, quoted in Costello 1978. The author speaks here of calques that were introduced as an additional expansion of rules already present in the base component. Regardless now of whether one will follow the standard Chomskyan approach to this particular case, the interesting point is that the reference is obviously to translation (cf. the mention of 'calques'), without, however, naming it. Such a discussion of translation processes without explicitly recognizing them as such is characteristic of much of the work on bilingualism, interference and language change. J.R. Costello admittedly speaks of foreign transformations borrowed into the transformational component and used differently from the way they are used in the language of their origin. But by not mentioning translation explicitly the analysis is not related to relevant theoretical generalizations that are already available in the existing theory of translation, for example the description and typology of interlingual transformations, etc.

Partial or temporary change is illustrated by the phrase *in anderen Worten*, occurring occasionally in German, presumably translated from English *in other words*, although according to B. Carstensen most speakers of German still prefer to say *mit anderen Worten* (Carstensen 1979:67).

Examples of the type discussed above remind us of H. Bradley's speculation (disputed by later authors) that prepositional phrases of the *son of David* type may have attained general currency due to some degree of French influence (Bradley 1904/1968). Incidentally, D. Baron too envisages the possibility of French influence in the *like + of* construction (from *se plaire de*) in Middle English, e.g. *Of this message me liked yll* (Baron 1974:94). Prepositional usage in written Old English was occasionally affected by foreign (Latin) influence too (cf. Hendricksen 1948 and also Danchev 1969).

It has been pointed out repeatedly indeed that the influence of a foreign pattern may also be indirect, activating a previously less developed or latent construction in the receiving language (see e.g. Havers 1931; Moser 1962; Birnbaum this volume).

A substitution similar to some of the ones discussed above, but from the first to the second language, is evidenced in the frequent error made by Bulgarian learners of English when they say *we talked for the book* instead of *we talked about the book*, due to overgeneralization of the correlation between Bulgarian *za* and English *for*. This is a typical case of erroneous reduction to the '1 : 1' isomorphism pattern, characteristic of interlanguages (Danchev 1979).

Among other things, these and other similar examples of spontaneous translation confirm the view that in the competence of speakers many prepositions are coded with autonomous meanings of their own and not simply as 'empty' form words.

The proliferation of various prepositional phrases is naturally one of those manifestations of the common Indo-European 'drift' that are usually triggered off or accelerated in situations of language contact. Indeed, the historical drift towards analytical sentence structure seems to be sustained mainly by the trend towards more explicit surface structure with a higher degree of redundancy, needed for maintaining the efficiency of communication.

Notwithstanding the considerable amount of research so far, in the history of English there still are unsolved problems that can receive more or less plausible solutions in terms of language contact. This obviously applies to the Middle English period in particular, when numerous speakers of English were exposed to Scandinavian and French and, especially towards the end of the period, when there was also intensified contact among the speakers of the various regional dialects. This must have conditioned the emergence and development of a variety of interlanguages (in the sense this term is used in Selinker 1972 and generally in the already vast literature on error analysis today), or at least of elements of interlanguages.

Many of the examples in the corpus and the literature on areal linguistics can thus be explained as being due to various types of translations involving interlingual and intralingual transformations with incorrect rule addition, deletion, substitution, reordering, etc. The difficulty often consists in pinpointing the exact place(s) in a derivational string where such faulty identifications and transformations occur.

Most of the examples discussed so far illustrate various types of calquing and were chosen specifically to render the occurrence of translation in situations of language contact more conspicuous. The assumption is that if intensive calquing has taken place, this should be an indication that there must also have been many instances of other translation types.

The role of translation ought not to be exaggerated, of course, nor should it be regarded as excluding explanations in terms of internal development. But especially in cases where there are identical or similar developments in geographically contiguous or otherwise contacting languages the investigator should at least be prepared to examine the likelihood of possible foreign influence, rather than rejecting it in advance.

A case in point is the late Middle English and early Modern English personalization of impersonal constructions, which is obviously continuing to attract interest today. A similar process having taken place in both Scandinavian and French, two languages with attested influence on English in other spheres, the question arises naturally whether there could not have been any influence at work in that quarter too. The counterargument that is usually advanced in this case is that since the details and timing of the development in French and Scandinavian were different from those in English, there could not have been any significant influence. In this way the problem is often studied in isolation within the framework of one language only, without considering more seriously the possibility of foreign influence.

The circumstance that there exist differences in details and in chronology does not amount to much and shows insufficient awareness of the mechanisms of language contact and interference. It is already well-known today that interlanguages exhibit features that differ from either of the two (or more, as the case may be) contacting languages, and that the communicative strategy of bilingual speakers often results in the deletion of difficult foreign structures and the generation of new structures. And as every foreign language teacher knows only too well, a structure may be difficult not only if it is unfamiliar to the speaker of the receiving language, but also when it is close to similar structures in it. The learner's strategy in such cases often leads to the abandonment of such structures in his native language too and this is exemplified by O. Jespersen's popular account of the loss of noun inflections during the Middle English period.

No final conclusions as to any kind of language change in Middle English should thus be drawn before having examined attentively the possibility of foreign influence in situations of likely bilingualism. In practical terms this would imply giving more attention to translation corpora of French (and some Latin) texts translated into English. It might be rewarding to establish, for example, how French impersonal constructions were rendered in late Middle English and early Modern English, whether they were regularly translated by means of similar impersonal constructions of Anglo-Saxon origin, or wether there were any signs of a trend towards avoiding impersonal equivalents and using personal ones instead. In case the evidence adds up to a pattern this would certainly provide valuable pointers as to the communicative strategy of Middle English bilingual (and trilingual) speakers in situations of language contact. So as to capture also all the instances of intralingual translation the various diachronic and diatopic versions of the same text must evidently be studied very closely too.

The personalization process can also be represented in terms of verbal valency, which in turn can be shown to change easily in the course of erroneous translation, e.g. when Bulgarian learners of English sometimes slip into errors of the type *this book likes me* instead of *I like this book*. The reverse process in this case, that is, the impersonalization of the Modern English personal construction is obviously due to structural translation from the Bulgarian impersonal construction *tazi kniga mi xaresva*. Needless to say, it would be well worth trying to find similar examples in Middle English (and later) texts translated from French. As regards Scandinavian, its influence must of course have been stronger, although it is obviously more difficult to find attested evidence. Nevertheless, despite the lack of direct documentation, the process could be simulated up to a point by using additional evidence from Middle English and other creolized languages. The incorrect identification of the agent and recipient of the action is seen in examples of the type *this woman loves the man* instead of *this man loves the woman* under the influence of the underlying German sentence *Diese Frau liebt der Mann* (in U.S. immigrant speech and with almost exact parallels in the utterances of Bulgarian learners of English), provided in Weinreich 1953.

Speaking of verb valency change, there is an interesting example of an ongoing change of a somewhat similar type in Modern Bulgarian. Until fairly recently the verb *kasae* 'concern' was used only reflexively and only with a prepositional object. However, over the past years there has been a marked trend, steadily gaining ground despite the objections of purists, for this verb to be used with a direct object and without the reflexive particle *se*. This change has demonstrably come about in the course of frequent translation from Russian into Bulgarian.

Similar examples can naturally be found in other languages too, including English. A great number of innovations in the lexicon, morphology and phonology of Middle English having been accounted for as creolization phenomena, the same possibility should be considered very carefully for syntax, including the personalization of the Middle English impersonal constructions. It could tentatively be assumed then that the late Middle English and early Modern English personalization of impersonal verb constructions was an interlanguage feature. Future research will either bear out or disprove this hypothesis, but in the meantime it could be taken into account as a possibility.

The introduction of translation theory into historical linguistics makes it possible to answer more adequately than most other approaches to syntactic change the five questions of 'actuation', 'constraints', 'transition', 'embedding' and 'evaluation' which, as U. Weinreich, W. Labov and M. Herzog maintain, a theory of change must be able to handle (Weinreich et al.1968). In most cases the approach briefly outlined here enables the investigator to provide a fairly adequate answer to the 'actuation' problem in particular, the most difficult of all five, as it involves the question of why changes take place in a particular language at a given time, but not in other languages with the same feature, or in the same language at other times.

Concerning the nature of the syntactic change due to translation it seems obvious that while from the point of view of a single idiolect it is abrupt, when viewed as spreading to other idiolects it is gradual.

A further important point in connection with translation is that of deep structure. Although the recognition of both surface and deep structure is almost universal today, there is obviously still no uniform view of what exactly the latter term should be taken to mean and no conclusive answer to this question is yet in sight. The use of translation theory makes it possible to obviate to a certain extent this difficulty without, of course, abandoning the notion of 'deep structure'. On the contrary, by adopting a model of interlingual transformations, which do not affect the basic information of the message, and generally the translatability principle, one adopts automatically the view that there exists a universal cognitive structure common to all languages. But since some interlingual transformations sometimes seem to proceed on lower levels, short-cutting, as it were, the deeper layers (cf. E. Nida's well-known comparison of the translator to a traveller seeking the easiest place for crossing a river), the derivational history can occasionally be mapped out without having to indicate explicitly the deep structure. Given the circumstance that what in one language is in the deep structure often turns out to be in the surface structure of another language and vice versa (Danchev 1976), the process can sometimes be formalized without necessarily having to postulate hypothetical deep structure forms. In this way the distance between the starting point and the outcome of a series of transformations is shortened and consequently made more accessible to empirical verification. The optimal model seems to be one with a multilayered deep semantic component (cf. also Birnbaum 1977) and a shallower syntactic component.

Of special interest for the theory is the further specification of interlingual transformations. Generally speaking one might say that the transformations of translation theory are more 'realistic' than the transformations of standard generative grammar, although some of the latter may at first sight seem more economical. The way the transformational history of interlingual transformations is developed will often not coincide with the way it is developed in ordinary transformations in one language only. Of particular importance too is the study of the various types of text explicitation, compression and decompression in translation, of the balancing and compensating function of the broader context, and the dependence of transformations and functional equivalents on extra-linguistic factors.

More work along these lines is obviously needed, yet the fact remains that translation theory has developed a methodology which to all intents and purposes is still not put fully to advantage in theoretical and especially in historical linguistics. The application of translation theory to historical linguistics can contribute effectively to the further 'decompartmentalization' of the latter, making historical linguists more keenly aware of the findings and methods used in other branches of linguistics, including applied linguistics. Instead of frequently overcomplex and highly elaborate theoretical explanations in terms of microlinguistic internal development in one language only, an interdisciplinary apporach can often prove more productive.

Rather than being a concrete case study, this paper touches on points of a more general nature, some of which undoubtedly require elaboration, but if it can stimulate further discussions of the connection between translation and syntactic change it will have served its purpose.

Notes

* For enabling me to attend the 1981 Historical Syntax Conference at Błażejewko where I presented a preliminary version of this paper, I am grateful to the Bulgarian Translators Union.

1. The evidence showing that there is always some degree of interlingual interference the distinction between so called 'subordinative' and 'co-ordinative' bilingualism, maintained by many authors, is not kept up here.
2. Since translation theory draws on contrastive linguistics, text linguistics, psycholinguistics, sociolinguistics and some other branches of theoretical and applied linguistics, the broader term 'translation studies' has been used by some authors (suggested by J. Holmes in 1972 and quoted in Toury 1979).
3. In Catford 1965 there is a section on 'involuntary' phonological translation.
4. Worth noting is O. Jespersen's remark that "it is doubtful whether the syntactical influences which occur from native language interference have the same permanent effect on any language as those exerted on one's own language by the habit of translating foreign works into it" (Jespersen 1922: 215). As pointed out by V. A. Zvegincev, this echoes a postulate by W. Windisch, formulated in his "*Zur Theorie der Mischsprachen und Lehnwörter*", published in 1897. This observation is certainly very interesting and insightful, but the data available today show that it is rather difficult to generalize. Depending on the specific historical, social, cultural and other attending circumstances either of two contacting languages may gain the upper hand.
5. Trivial as this may sound, the way in which the term 'calque' is rendered in some languages, e.g. 'loan translation' in English and 'Übersetzunglehnwort' in German is indicative of its nature.
6. The presence of 'hidden' translation can be inferred not only from the instances of negative transfer, which distorts the formal and/or semantic structure, but also from positive transfer. Thus in cases when there is an option between two equally correct constructions in the target language, the bilingual speaker is likely to use the one which is isomorphic with the equivalent construction in the source language. This is often seen, for example, in the preference of Bulgarian (and other) speakers of English for sentences of the type *the book which I'm reading* rather than the asyndetic *the book I'm reading*.

58   Andrei Danchev

7. In order to be precise one should note the different ways in which *sky* is translated in German *Wolkenkratzer* and French *gratte-ciel*; as is known, the European languages follow either the German or French way of calquing *skyscraper* (for details and bibliography see Akulenko 1972). The possibility of partial deviations in calquing has been indicated by C. Bally.

References

Akulenko, V. V.
  1972   *Voprosy internacionalizacii slovarnogo sostava jazyka* [Problems of the internationalization of the lexicon] (Xar'kov: Izdatel'stvo Xar'kovskogo universiteta).
Asenova, P.
  1972   "Unité dans l'emploi des prépositions dans les langues balkaniques", *Annuaire de l'université de Sofia: Faculté des lettres* lxvii, 1:179–250.
Bally, C.
  1932   *Linguistique générale et linguistique française*, 4th ed. rev. by S. Heinemann 1965 (Bern: A. Francke).
Baron, D. E.
  1974   *Case grammar and diachronic English syntax* (The Hague: Mouton).
Baron, N. S.
  1977   *Language acquisition and historical change* (Amsterdam: North Holland).
Birnbaum, H.
  1977   "Toward a stratified view of deep structure", in: *Linguistics at the crossroads*, ed. by A. Makkai et al (Padua & Lake Bluff, Ill. : Jupiter Press), 104–119. this volume "Notes on syntactic change: cooccurrence vs. substitution, stability vs. permeability".
Bolinger, D.
  1966   "Transformulation: Structural translation", *Acta Linguistica Hafniensia* 9: 130–144.
Bradley, H.
  1904   *The making of English*, rev. ed. by S. Potter 1968 (London: Macmillan).
Carstensen, B.
  1979   "The influence of English on German – syntactic problems", *Studia Anglica Posnaniensia* 11:65–77.
Catford, J. C.
  1965   *A linguistic theory of translation* (London: Oxford University Press).
Civjan, T. V.
  1977   "O postroenii sintaksisa v gramatike balkanskogo jazykovogo sojuza" [On the structure of syntax in the grammar of the Balkan Sprachbund], *Balkanskij lingvističeskij sbornik*, edited by T. V. Civjan (Moskva: Nauka), 312–323.
Corder, S.P. – E. Roulet (eds.)
  1977   "The notions of simplification, interlanguages and pidgins and their relation to second language pedagogy", *Actes du 5ème colloque de linguistique appliquée de Neuchâtel 20–22 mai 1976* (Neuchâtel: Université de Neuchâtel).
Costello, J. R.
  1978   "Syntactic change and second language acquisition: The case for Pennsylvania German", *Linguistics* 213: 29–50.
Danchev, A.
  1969   "The parallel use of the synthetic dative instrumental and periphrasic prep-

ositional constructions in Old English", *Annuaire de l'univerité de Sofia: Faculté des lettres* lxiii, 2:39–99.

1974 "Za saotnošenieto na sinxronijata i diaxronijata" [On the relationship of synchrony and diachrony], *Ruski i zapadni ezici* 2/3:1–13.

1976 "Za njakoi strani na sapostavitelnite isledvanija" [On certain aspects of contrastive studies], *Bjuletin za sapostavitelno isledvane na balgarskija ezik s drugi ezitsi* 1:7–26.

1979 "Kontrastivna lingvistika, analiz na greškite i čuzdoezikovo obučenie" [Contrastive linguistics, error analysis and foreign language teaching] in: *Sapostavitelno ezikoznanie i čuzdoezikovo obučenie*, edited by A. Danchev et al (Veliko Tarnovo: Veliko Tarnovo University Press), 11–31.

1980 "Za razširen obseg na teorijata na prevoda" [For a wider range of the theory of translation] in: *Izkustvoto na prevoda* 4, edited by F. Ginev et al (Sofia: Nauka i izkustvo), 56–69.

Darbelnet, J.
1980 "Bilinguisme et traduction", *Le francais moderne: Revue de linguistique française* 4: 319–326.

Dešeriev, J. D. (ed.)
1976 *Razvitie nacional'no-russkogo dvujazycija* [The development of national-Russian bilingualism] (Moskva: Nauka).

Fehling, D.
1980 "The origins of European syntax", *Folia Linguistica Historica* 5.1/2: 353–387.

Harris, Z. S.
1954 "Transfer grammar", *International journal of American linguistics* 4:259–270.

Haugen, E.
1953 *The Norwegian language in America* (Philadelphia: University of Pennsylvania Press).

Havers, W.
1931 *Handbuch der erklärenden Syntax* (Heidelberg: Winter).

Havránek, B.
1966 "Zur Problematik der Sprachmischung" in *Travaux linguistiques de Prague* 2:81–95.

Hendrickson, J. R.
1948 "Old English prepositional compounds in relationship to their Latin originals", *Language* XXIV (Supplement).

Ivir, V.
1979 "Remarks on contrastive analysis and translation" in: *Trends in kontrastiver Linguistik* I (2nd. rev. ed.), edited by H. Raabe (Tübingen: Gunter Narr), 93–104.

Jespersen, O.
1922 *Language: Its nature, development and origin* (London: George Allen & Unwin).

Kočev, N.
1980 "Edna ispanska sintaktična sxema v novogratski i bulgarski" [A Spanish syntactic pattern in modern Greek and Bulgarian], *Ezik i literatura* 2:119–120.

Komisarov, V. N.
1980 *Lingvistika perevoda* [The linguistics of translation] (Moskva: Meždunarodnye otnošenija).

Marouzeau, J.
1951 *Lexique de la terminologie linguistique*, translated into Russian by N. D. Andreeva 1960 (Moskva: Izdatel'stvo inostrannoj literatury).

60   *Andrei Danchev*

Moser, H.
1962   "Sprachliche Folgen der politischen Teilung Deutschlands" (= *Beihefte zur Zeitschrift Wirkendes Wort* 3) (Düsseldorf: Schwann), 62pp.
van Overbeke, M.
1972   *Introduction au problème du bilinguisme* (Bruxelles: Editions Labor; Paris: Fernand Nathan).
Parker, F. – N. Macari,
1978   "On syntactic change", *Linguistics* 209:5–41.
Rado, G.
1977   "An international bibliography on translation", *Babel* 2:88–96.
Richards, J. (ed.)
1974   *Error analysis* (London: Longman).
Rozencvejg, V. J.
1972   *Jazykovye kontakty* [Language contacts] (Leningrad: Nauka).
Selinker, L.
1972   "Interlanguage", *International review of applied linguistics* 3:209–231.
Toury, G.
1979   "Interlanguage and its manifestation in translation", *META* 2:223–231.
Vaseva, I.
1980   *Teoria i praktika perevoda* [The theory and practice of translation] (Sofia: Nauka i izkustvo).
Weinreich, U.
1953   *Languages in contact: Findings and problems* (New York: Publications of the Linguistic Circle of New York 1).
Weinreich, U. – W. Labov – M. Herzog,
1968   "Empirical foundations for a theory of language change", *Directions for historical linguistics*, edited by W. P. Lehman and Y. Malkiel (Austin & London: University of Texas Press), 95–188.
Zvegincev, V. A.
1962   *Očerki po obščemu jazykoznaniju* [Outlines of general linguistics] (Moskva: Izdatel'stvo moskovskogo universiteta).

XAVIER DEKEYSER

Relativicers in early Modern English:
A dynamic quantitative study

There is no reason to suppose that quantitative models incorporating variable rules
are incapable of handling the dynamic aspects of language change.
Ralph W. Fasold (1975): 54

0 Introduction

0.1 Scope of the paper

OE* relative clauses were introduced by the invariable marker þe or by the deictics se, seo, þaet; the latter strategy of relativization involved number and gender agreement between the relativizer and its antecedent. A third possibility was a conflation of se, seo, þaet and invariable þe.[1] Though still frequent in EME, invariable the disappeared in the course of the 13th century. That, partly the reflex of OE þaet, became the most important relative marker in EME, and could be used with +H and -H antecedents, both in restrictive and non-restrictive clauses. However, the universal spread of that was checked by the introduction of WH-pronouns, supposedly due to Latin and/or French influence. Which, oblique whom and genitive whose were used as relative pronouns from the 12th century onwards, while who was, apart from a few earlier sporadic occurrences, first recorded in 15th century letters. It was possible for any of the ME WH-forms to be freely combined with that : who that, which that, etc.[2] In addition, relativizers could be deleted under certain conditions.[3]

No new elements have been added to the set of relativizers since the 15th century. The crucial difference between ME and PE is not the number of relatives, but the system that governs their distribution. Prima facie EMODE was a continuation of LME. However, on closer inspection syntactic changes showed up which unmistakably foreshadowed the PE grammar of relativizers. It is the aim of the present paper to highlight some aspects of relativization in (more or less) standardized EMODE.

The evidence has been primarily drawn from a corpus of 17th century discourse (see 0.2); for diachronic purposes this has been supplemented by M. Rydén's extensive data covering the first half of the 16th century (currently referred to as "1520–1560" in this paper), and also Toshio Saito's material, which bears on Modern Colloquial English (from 1566 to 1958). In a few cases I have also used the findings derived from a late 16th century corpus: 1560–1599 (with a coverage of circa 450,000 running words), which was processed by some of my students a few years ago. Whenever possible, this EMODE evidence is set against PE as represented in Quirk's (1968) well-known material of relative clauses. Of course, a caveat has to be entered as to the use of PE: Quirk's survey covers spoken discourse in the full sense of the word, whereas the EMODE material represents varied kinds of written English. Nevertheless, I believe that a critical and judicious comparison of the PE and EMODE samples can be indicative of syntactic change in view of the high absolute values involved.

0.2 Survey of the corpus

The EMODE corpus consists of 40 units of ca. 6,000 running words each, all of them published between 1600 and 1649. I have attempted to distinguish between 'formal' and 'informal' language by dividing the corpus into two major strata, a D stratum and a P stratum, each ca. 96,000 running words long and basically reflecting written-to-be-spoken and written discourse. In addition, I have distinguished two minor strata, each ca. 24,000 words long: the E stratum and the V stratum.

The *P stratum* is made up of narrative/descriptive and informative prose. Since novels are all but absent in the early 17th century, narrative prose occupies a minor place in this substratum. Informative prose is found in scientific and quasiscientific writings, such as biography, essay, writings on religion, philosophy, history, etc.

The *D stratum* represents the (mostly informal) written-to-be-spoken segment of language and is composed of dramatical works. As the EMODE plays are all, for the greater part, in verse, a distinction between prose drama and verse drama has not proved useful. The *E stratum* consists of epistolary prose; it happens to have a more or less official character and does not reflect the informal (written) language of the time. As we shall see later, this stratum approximates the P stratum rather than the D stratum. The *V stratum* corresponds to poetry.

The corpus includes the following units, arranged per stratum:

P stratum
1600 Cawdrey, R.: *A Treasury or Store-house of Similies.*
1602 Campion, Th.: *Observations in the Art of English Poesie.*
1603 Daniel, S.: *A Defence of Ryme.*

1605 Bacon, F.: *The Advancement of Learning.*
1607 Anonymous: *The Pleasant Conceits of Old Hobson, the Merry Londoner.*
1610 Selden, J.: *The Duello or Single Combat.*
1614 Overbury, Th.: *The Miscellaneous Works in prose and verse of Sir Thomas Overbury.*
1621 Burton, R.: *Anatomy of Melancholy.*
1625 Glanville, J.: *The Voyage to Cadiz in 1625.*
1626 Moryson, F.: *Shakespeare's Europe.*
1628 Earle, J.: *Micro-cosmography.*
1631 Stow, J.: *Annales or A Generall Chronicle of England.*
1640 Walton, I.: *The Life of Dr. Donne.*
1641 Milton, J.: *Of Reformation.*
1642 Browne, Th.: *Religio Medici.*
1642 Fuller, Th.: *The Holy State and the Profane State.*

D stratum
1604 Marston, J.: *The Malcontent.*
1607 Chapman, G.: *Bussy d'Ambois.*
1607 Heywood, Th.: *A Woman Killed with Kindness.*
1609 Beaumont, F. and Fletcher, J.: *The Knight of the Burning Pestle.*
1611 Barry, L.: *Ram-Alley or Merrie-Trickes.*
1611 Brome, R.: *The City Wit.*
1611 Tourneur, C.: *The Atheist's Tragedy, or, The Honest Man's Revenge.*
1612 Webster, J.: *The White Devil.*
1615 Tomkis, Th.: *Albumazar.*
1630 Middleton, Th.: *A Chaste Maid in Cheapside.*
1631 Dekker, Th.: *Match me in London.*
1632 Hausted, P.: *The Rival Friends.*
1633 Ford, J.: *'Tis Pity She's a Whore.*
1633 Massinger, P.: *A New Way to Pay Old Debts.*
1637 Shirley, J.: *The Lady of Pleasure.*
1649 D'Avenant, W.: *Love and Honour.*

E stratum[4]
1601–27 Donne, J.: *The Life and Letters of John Donne.*
1622–39 *Letters and Papers of the Verney Family.*
1635–48 Cromwell, O.: *The Letters and Speeches of Oliver Cromwell.*
1642–46 *Letters and Papers relating to the Irish Rebellion between 1642 and 46.*

V stratum

1623   Wither, G.: *Hymns and Songs of the Church.*
1633   Herbert, G.: *The Poetical Works of George Herbert.*
1640–41 Jonson, B.: *The Complete Poetry of Ben Jonson.*
1647–48 Herrick, R.: *The Poetical Works of Robert Herrick.*

0.3 Acknowledgements

The present paper on relativizers in EMODE is only 'the top of the iceberg': it rests on the work of many. I want to thank lic. J. Cumps, who was responsible for the composition of the EMODE corpus (including the 1560–1599 period). I am particularly indebted to lic. M. Van Craeyevelt, who processed the 17th century material with the utmost care, and who gave me the permission to use some of the quantitative data in her unpublished memoir (see References). My thanks are also due to the students who participated in the Leuven seminars on the *History of English Syntax* about five years ago, and who worked on the 1560–1599 corpus: their researches were meant as a link between Rydén's early 16th century material and the 17th century. Following the *English Historical Linguistics Conference*, Durham, Sept. 1979, Dr. Suzanne Romaine sent me two insightful papers which treat relativization in Early Modern Scots; Prof. Rydén provided me with a xerox copy of Toshio Saito's article on relative pronouns in Modern Colloquial English (again see References)

1 Overall survey of relativizers in Modern English

Table I

	WHO (M)/ WHOSE	(THE) WHICH	THAT	Ø	Totals
1520–1560[5]	2,442 (8.09%)	13,253 (43.90%)	14,038 (46.50%)	456 (1.51%)	30,189
1600–1649	588 (17.43%)	1,191 (35.31%)	1,152 (34.15%)	442 (13.11%)	3,373
PE (Quirk)	255 (19.67%)	440 (33.96%)	373 (28.78%)	228 (17.59%)	1,296

This table reveals the expansion of WHO and a sizeable increase of pronoun deletion in EMODE, while both (THE) WHICH and THAT are on the decrease. Actually, the 1600–1649 sample comes a great deal closer to PE than to the first half of the 16th century. Each of the recorded shifts is carried through in PE, which is also borne out by the numerical evidence collected by Toshio Saito 1961:72 (Table I).

In the following table three relativization strategies are set out diachronically: WH-, THAT and Zero:

Table II

	WH-	THAT	Ø	Totals
1520–1560	15,695 (51.99%)	14,038 (46.50%)	456 (1.51%)	30,189
1600–1649	1,779 (52.74%)	1,152 (34.15%)	442 (13.11%)	3,373
PE (Quirk)	695 (53.63%)	373 28.78%)	228 (17.59%)	1,296

The total share of WH- is remarkably steady in the three samples of discourse; the decline of the long-standing THAT strategy is entirely counterbalanced by an almost identical rise of Ø. As we shall see later, the increase of Ø is due to deletion being increasingly applied on object and prepositional relativizers, while deletion of subject relativizers falls into disuse in Standard English.

The above evidence pertains to +R/−R clauses alike; as in PE the three strategies occur side by side only in +R clauses, it is interesting to split up frequencies according to clause type, which is done in Tables IIIa and b. I give Rydén's data with some restriction (hence the brackets), because they only cover relativizers in subject function and involving +H/−H antecedents, and object function, but only with +H antecedents; in addition, Rydén has only included nominal antecedents in his frequency counts as regards +R/−R. In −R clauses WH- is virtually the only strategy applied in PE; on the temporary increase of −R THAT in the 1600–1649 segment see 2.4. As regards +R clauses, WH- has been expanding, together with Ø, and now accounts for almost 50% of all relativizations[6]; see also section 5: *AH and syntactic change*. The overall figures in Table II are somewhat biassed owing to the fact that −R clauses, and consequently also the WH- strategy, are rather unusual in present-day *spoken* English, as compared with the written EMODE samples I

Table IIIa: +R clauses

	WH-	THAT	Ø	Totals
1520–1560	(2,286)	(6,362)	(456)	(9,104)
	(25.11%)	(69.88%)	(5%)	
1600–1649	544	913	442	1,899
	(28.65%)	(48.08%)	(23.27%)	
PE (Quirk)	522	372	228	1,122
	(46.52%)	(33.16%)	(20.32%)	

Table IIIb: −R clauses

	WH-	THAT	Ø	Totals
1520–1560	(5,350)	(480)	–	(5,830)
	(91.77%)	(8.23%)		
1600–1649	1,235	239	–	1,474
	(83.78%)	(16.21%)		
PE (Quirk)	173	1	–	174
	(99.43%)	(0.57%)		

have analysed; see Tables VIII and IX. This shift accounts for the WH- strategy being seemingly stable; actually this strategy has gained in frequency for both types of clause.

2 Type of clause: restrictive vs. non-restrictive[7]

2.1 E. C. Traugott: 103 rightly observes that the contrast between what she calls 'appositive' and restrictive relatives must have existed from the earliest times "since the distinction is in essence that of fundamental semantic relationships. There is no evidence, however, that the two constructions were overtly differentiated, that is, the surface structures for both are the same (note: in OE and ME)". In present-day Standard English there is a sharp distinction with THAT virtually confined to +R clauses, while the WH- forms are not at all constrained on that score.[8]

2.2 WHO in +R/−R clauses

In the 17th century corpus I have analysed the distribution +R and −R for WHO-WHOM-WHOSE is as follows: +R: 163 (27.72%), −R: 425 (72.28%), Total: 588. In the early 16th century WHO is used non-restrictively in the great majority of the cases, as appears from Table IV.

Table IV: Nominative WHO with noun antecedents

	+R	−R	Totals
1520−1560	24 (3.02%)	770 (96.98%)	794
1600−1649	19 (17.27%)	91 (82.73%)	110
Totals	43	861	904

X^2 = ca. 43 P < .001

Note: As Rydén only has numerical evidence for nominative WHO with noun antecedents, I have adapted the figures to this restriction.

We can infer from Table IV that WHO, still an innovation in the early 16th century, was first introduced in a −R context. One century later +R WHO was already well established; the same trend, but over a longer period of time, appears from Tables III and V in Toshio Saito's article (1961:77−78). It must be added that there is no significant difference between nominative WHO and oblique WHOM:

Table V: WHO and WHOM in the 1600−1649 corpus

	+R	−R	Totals
WHO	71 (24.57%)	218 (75.43%)	289
WHOM	47 (32.87%)	96 (67.13%)	143
Totals	118	314	432

X^2 = 3.36 P > .05 (not significant)

2.3 (THE) WHICH in +R/−R clauses

Unlike WHO, (THE) WHICH does not show a shift in either direction:

Table VI: Subjective and objective (THE) WHICH (with nom. antecedents)

	+R	−R	Totals
1520–1560	1,784 (36.06%)	3,163 (63.94%)	4,947
1600–1649	203 (35.87%)	363 (64.13%)	566
Totals	1,987	3,526	5,513

X^2 = .0084 (not significant)

Note: Since Rydén gives no figures for the distribution of objective personal (THE) WHICH as regards clause type, the figures only include non-personal (THE) WHICH.

2.4 THAT in +R/−R clauses

According to Mustanoja (1960:197) "the beginnings of the Mod.E. practice to limit the use of *that* to defining (restrictive) relative clauses make themselves felt to some extent in later ME, although no definite rule concerning this point can be said to exist". In Rydén's material +R THAT was already very preponderant; however, this trend was discontinued in the following decades, as shown in Table VII:

Table VII: Subjective and objective THAT (nom. antecedents) in +R/−R clauses

	+R	−R	Totals
1520–1560	6,362 (92.85%)	490 (7.15%)	6,852
1600–1649	536 (79.06%)	142 (20.94%)	678
Totals	6,898	632	7,530

X^2 = ca. 152 P < .001

The change revealed in the above table is also present in the Leuven corpus: 1560–1599: here the percentage for +R THAT is 76.41%, which is very close to what I have found for 1600–49. It appears from Toshio Saito's table on p. 78 that the decrease of −R THAT sets in after 1650, and very sharply so, at least as far as colloquial written English is concerned.

2.5 Overall survey of restrictiveness and non-restrictiveness

Table VIII: early 17th century WHO-WHICH-THAT and +R/−R

	+R	−R	Totals
WHO	163 (27.72%)	425 (72.28%)	588
WHICH	381 (40.57%)	558 (59.43%)	939
THAT	913 (79.25%)	239 (20.75%)	1,152
Totals	1,457 (54.39%)	1,222 (45.61%)	2,679

Table IX: PE WHO-WHICH-THAT and +R/−R[9]

	+R	−R	Totals
WH-human	224 (87.84%)	31 (12.16%)	255
WH-non-human	298 (67.73%)	142 (32.27%)	440
THAT	372 (99.73%)	1 (0.27%)	373
Totals	894 (83.71%)	174 (16.29%)	1,068

In EMODE WHO is mainly used in non-restrictive clauses and THAT in restrictive ones, while WHICH is 'neutral' on that score, but the division is a great deal more outspoken in Rydén's material than in my own. There is a striking difference between Tables VIII and IX as regards the scope of the two types of clause.[10] Two parameters seem to account for this: the different kinds of corpora (i.e. written vs. spoken discourse) and probably also the time discrepancy. Anyway, the frequent use of the −R clause (i.e. the deliberate inclusion of parenthetic information within the sentence) seems to be a feature of EMODE syntax.

3 Type of antecedent: human vs. non-human

3.1 In LME and EMODE non-human WHO(M) is attested, but examples are so scarce[11], that it cannot be regarded as part of the relative system; the occurrence of −H WHO(M) is quantitatively interesting, but not qualitatively. In nearly all of the cases the use of −H WHO(M) can be put down to personification, or the antecedent NP refers to an animal.

3.2 WHOSE compatible with +H/−H antecedents

Unlike the nominative and the oblique forms, there has never been a constraint on WHOSE in terms of +H/−H antecedents. Mustanoja: 200 observes that in ME the genitive "occurs with reference to persons and things, though its use for inanimate objects is infrequent and first recorded in the latter half of the 14th century". It appears from the table below that −H WHOSE is not very frequent in EMODE, though obviously much more firmly established than −H WHO(M), and that the +H/−H ratio remains stable throughout this period (X^2 proves the recorded differences to be non-significant).

Table X: +H/−H WHOSE

	+H	−H	Totals
Elyot[12]	95 (85.59%)	16 (14.41%)	111
1560−1599	260 (81.25%)	60 (18.75%)	320
1600−1649	127 (81.41%)	29 (18.59%)	156
Totals	482	105	587

$X^2 = 1.15$ $P > .50$ (not significant)

The 4% difference between Elyot and the two other segments is situated at the .3 level of probability, and so is not significant either. In the colloquial corpus excerpted by Saito –H WHOSE, and in fact the WHOSE relativization throughout, is rather rare; Quirk's (1968) data include only six instances of WHOSE, all of which relate to a +H antecedent. Roggero (1967:408–409), who has analysed a varied corpus of recent works published between 1955 and 1966, has demonstrated that relativization in the genitive slot, including the use of OF WHICH, and the occurrence of –H WHOSE are a mark of more complex registers; see also Steinki 1932:33–34.[13]

3.3 The 'de-humanization' of (THE) WHICH

Table XI: +H/–H parameter

	+H	–H	Totals
1520–1560	4,402 (33.22%)	8,851 (66.78%)	13,253
1560–1599	371 (18.18%)	1,670 (81.82%)	2,041
1600–1649	97 (10.34%)	841 (89.60%)	938
Totals	4,870	11,362	16,232

X^2 = ca. 373 (highly significant: for 2dfs P = .001 with X^2 = 13.815). X^2 calculated for the first two segments and the last two segments separately yields values as high as resp. ca. 186 and 30; again P = .001 for 1df is far exceeded.

The above table crucially reveals the implementation phase[14] of the 'de-humanization' of WHICH. This change is virtually completed by 1700, as evinced by Toshio Saito's figures (1961: 84).

3.4 THAT and the +H/–H parameter

It appears from Quirk (1968:104) that there is a considerable restriction on +H THAT in present-day (spoken) English ("far greater than has been generally supposed", Q. writes on p. 103): in fact there is a 1/9 ratio for +H/–H. Does the small shift towards –H recorded for 1600–49 mark the inceptive phase of a process of de-humanization of THAT in MODE? This may be the

case, but we should beware of jumping to conclusions in view of the fact that
the discrepancy is statistically not significant. Saito's percentages, pp. 84—85,
reveal a sharp drop of +H THAT in the 19th and 20th centuries, which is in
substantial agreement with Quirk's survey of PE.

Table XII: +H/–H THAT

	+H	–H	Totals
1520—1560	8,006 (57.03%)	6,032 (42.97%)	14,038
1600—1649	619 (55.52%)	496 (44.48%)	1,115
Totals	8,625	6,528	15,153

$X^2 = 0.96 \ .50 > P > .30$ (not significant)

4 Accessibility Hierarchy and EMODE relativization

4.1 Keenan and Comrie (1977) have tried to determine the universal properties of relative clause formation strategies. On the basis of data from no fewer
than about 50 languages they have set up an *Accessibility Hierarchy* (or AH),
which looks like this: SU > DO > IO > Oblique > Genitive > Object of
Comp. They have convincingly demonstrated that subjects are more accessible to relativization than DO's, DO's more than IO's, etc.; in other words, the
left-hand positions on the AH scale are the easiest to relativize, and *vice versa*.
Keenan (1975) has shown that AH can also be stated in terms of frequency.
His first prediction (p. 139) runs as follows: "The frequency with which
people relativize in discourse conforms to the CH (note: i.e. Case Hierarchy),
subjects being the most frequent, then direct objects, etc." A second prediction (p. 141) pertains to syntactic complexity: the frequency with which
certain NPs are relativized correlates with syntactic complexity: authors or
speakers who use a simple syntax tend to have a greater proportion of relativizations near the 'easy' end of the scale than authors or speakers using a
more complex style.

4.2 Romaine (1980) has amply demonstrated that Keenan and Comrie's AH
predictions work nicely for Middle Scots (i.e. ca. 1450—1650). In the following sections I shall examine whether and how they work for the EMODE
corpus I have analysed. I shall use a somewhat adapted AH scale: Subject >

Objects > PC > ADV > Genitive, Objects cover both direct and indirect objects; PC: prepositional complement, i.e. any preposition-initiated NP. There are no examples of Object of Comparison, which is at the bottom of Keenan and Comrie's AH. Locatives like *the place where*, and temporals like *the time when* have been included under ADV, which also comprises adverbial *that* in e.g. *the time that*.[15]

4.3 In Table XIII I present the AH data for the 1600–49 corpus:

Table XIII.

	S	O	PC	ADV	GEN	Totals
WH-	765	339	210	229	156	1,699
	(45.03%)	(19.95%)	(12.36%)	(13.48%)	(9.18%)	
THAT	992	108	17	7	–	1,124
	(88.25%)	(9.61%)	(1.51%)	(0.62%)		
Ø	111	268	48	12	–	439
	(25.28%)	(61.05%)	(10.93%)	(2.73%)		
Totals	1,868	715	275	248	156	3,262
	(57.27%)	(21.92%)	(8.43%)	(7.60%)	(4.78%)	

It is interesting to point out that the 1560–99 corpus, which is composed of roughly the same registers as the 1600–49 corpus, exhibits an almost identical AH: S = 56.79%, O = 21.99%, PC = 7.73%, ADV = 7.24% and GEN = 6.25%; total N = 5,124. As far as essentials go, the above distributions agree with Keenan's (1975:146) AH for PE. Though the ADV position is not represented on the figure, it appears from the percentages Keenan gives in his additional comment that this would rank between what I regard as PC and GEN. However, subject relativization only accounts for 46.16%, which is a great deal lower than what I have calculated for EMODE; X^2 reaches a highly significant value, viz. ca. 74. Very typically, Quirk's (1968:104) material also shows such a low frequency for S, viz. ca. 46.60%, while Romaine (1980: 228) arrives at 65% for Middle Scots (restrictive) relative clauses. Both Romaine, 229ff. and Keenan (1975:141ff.) have convincingly demonstrated that AH is an index of syntactic complexity, and that more complex registers are characterized by a smaller proportion for S, and *vice versa*. From the diachronic point of view this seems to justify the conclusion that PE is syntactically more sophisticated than, say, EMODE and Middle Scots. Finally, GEN is the least accessible position on the AH (Object of COMP is absent); in agreement with what I have just said about AH and syntactic complexity its frequency is register-sensitive; see Keenan 1975:143, or Roggero 1967:408: " ... la fréquence de WHOSE et de OF WHICH croît pour l'un comme pour l'autre en raison directe du registre de langue".

4.4 We now proceed with a semantic arrangement of the data on the basis of the +H/-H difference. In Table XIV I have correlated this parameter with subject and non-subject positions, which produces a statistically very signifi cant result; indeed, X^2 is so high that the possibility of a deviating distribution is virtually excluded.

Table XIV: AH and the +H/−H parameter

	Subject	Non-subject	Totals
+Human	1,026 (72.25%)	394 (27.75%)	1,420
−Human	842 (45.71%)	1,000 (54.29%)	1,842
Totals	1,868 (57.27%)	1,394 (42.73%)	3,262

X^2 = ca. 232 (for 1df and X^2 = 10,827, P = .001)

I have also examined this correlation for WHICH in the 1560–1599 corpus, the results of which are substantially in agreement with the evidence of the above Table; detailed data are to be found in note 16. In the following graphs the +H/−H is spelled out per syntactic position.

Graph I: AH and +H antecedents

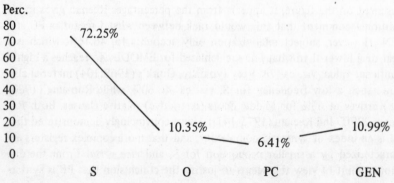

Graph II: AH and −H antecedents

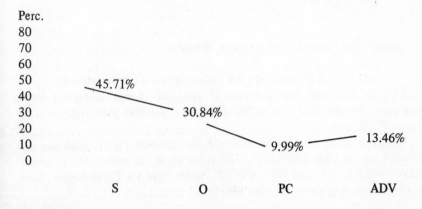

These figures demonstrate that −H subjects are less liable to be relativized than +H ones, and *vice versa* for the non-subject positions. A first conclusion we can draw from this is that the AH scale is not only affected by register (syntactic complexity), but also correlates with the semantics of the relativized NPs (and so indirectly with the semantics of the antecedents). Next, the +H/−H discrepancy further substantiates Keenan's first prediction (see my section 4.1), viz. that frequency of relativization reflects or is related to NP accessibility. One could object that e.g. S's show the highest frequency of relativization simply because they occur in almost every English clause; in other words, frequency of relativization would be determined by the general distribution of NPs in English. Keenan (1975) argues against this objection by pointing out that subjects are more often relativized in simple than in complex syntax, for which we cannot account if AH were only a matter of NP distribution in English discourse. *Mutatis mutandis*, the +H/−H difference I have established for EMODE lends further support to Keenan's prediction. Actually, my two graphs and Keenan's graphs (1975:143) about AH and register remarkably coincide as far as their paths in general are concerned.

Now we can attempt to answer the question why the +H/−H dichotomy of NPs is a parameter affecting AH. As +H subject NPs generally refer to an agent or an experiencer (I have not examined passive clauses separately), it can be reasonably assumed that they are the semantically most important parts of the clause, which would promote the relativization process. Thus, both position (coupled with syntactic complexity) and semantic prominence determine AH. In other words, subjects, irrespective of their frame of reference, are more often relativized than any other slot in the sentence; this is particularly the case with NPs having human reference; conversely, when non-human reference is involved, it is the non-subject positions which are comparatively more weighted.

5 Accessibility Hierarchy and syntactic change

5.1 A processing of the available AH data in terms of relativization strategies enables us to detect the direction of syntactic change as regards these strategies. We shall first look at WH- and THAT, and then turn to the issue of pronoun deletion.

When we set up an AH that differentiates WH- and THAT, there is a significant gap in their distribution. This is shown in the next Table, in which ADV WHERE, etc. and GEN WHOSE, which have no TH-analogues, have been left out so as not to bias the WH-/THAT ratio.

Table XV: AH and WH- vs. THAT

	S	O	PC	Totals
WH-	765 (58.22%)	339 (25.80%)	210 (15.98%)	1,314
THAT	992 (88.81%)	108 (9.67%)	17 (1,25%)	1,117
Totals	1,757	447	227	2,431

X^2 = ca. 300 (with 2dfs and X^2 = 13.815, P = .001)

The 1560–1599 corpus reveals a WH-/THAT distribution which comes very close to the above Table, while also Romaine's (1980) data for Middle Scots point in the same direction. We can infer from these figures that WH- is significantly more frequent in the less accessible parts of the AH scale than THAT, and *vice versa*.

Following Romaine (1980) I am inclined to believe that the introduction of the partly extraneous WH- strategy (prompted by French and/or Latin QU-forms) is a change from above, or a non-natural change. According to Bailey (1973) the direction of such a change is from the lightest environment to the heaviest; in terms of AH, this is from right to left. That this was actually the case in the history of MODE relativizers is corroborated by the evidence in Table XVI. The directionality of change could also explain the time lag of relative WHO in the nominative: the easiest position is the last to be affected by the WH- strategy.

Table XVI.

		WH-	THAT	Ø	
SUBJECT	1600–49	765 (40.95%)	992 (53.10%)	111 (5.94%)	1,868
	PE (Quirk)	451 (72.28%)	171 (27.40%)	2 (0.32%)	624
O/PC	1600–49	549 (54.79%)	125 (12.48%)	328 (32.73%)	1,002
	PE (Quirk)	231 (36.49%)	184 (29.07%)	218 (34.44%)	633

Romaine (again 1980:234) also shows that the WH- infiltration is more out-spoken in complex registers than in simple ones: "The data I have presented here show that the WH strategy entered the written language and worked its way down a stylistic continuum ranging from the most to the least complex styles". This, of course, is a strong argument in favour of the change-from-above-hypothesis. I have not been able to implement refined register-based calculations comparable with Romaine's, but I have overall data per register (see 0.2) in Table XVII, which show that THAT (together with Ø) is partic-ularly frequent in drama, while WH- is mainly to be found in the more com-plex registers: narrative/descriptive and informative prose (P), letters (E) and verse (V).[17]

Table XVII: Relativization strategies and register

	WH-	THAT	Ø	Totals
E	260 (71.43%)	51 (14.01%)	53 (14.56%)	364
P	939 (65.57%)	418 (29.19%)	75 (5.24%)	1,432
V	236 (55.66%)	152 (35.85%)	36 (8.49%)	424
D	344 (29.84%)	531 (46.05%)	278 (24.11%)	1,153
Totals	1,779 (52.74%)	1,152 (34.15%)	442 (13.11%)	3,373

I think that these inevitably rough data are in agreement with Romaine's findings. Clearly, in order to have full certainty about the directionality of syntactic change as regards THAT and the infiltration of WH-, ME relativization strategies should be examined in some detail. In any case, it appears from the available data (Tables IIIa and b, Tables XV and XVI) that WH- has been expanding in (standard) MODE, and that the direction of this expansion is from right to left on the AH scale; in -R clauses this change is now complete. This is manifestly not (yet) the case in Modern Scots (Romaine 1980) and other regional varieties of English (e.g. Trudgill and Ihalainen).

5.2 I have tried to demonstrate that the introduction and expansion of the WH- strategy is probably an instance of change from above, i.e. one that operates from right to left on the AH. The directionality of pronoun deletion seems to be the opposite. It is generally accepted that in OE and ME the deletion or reduction strategy mainly affects the subject, while deletion of objects, etc. is rather rare; see e.g. Traugott 1972:105 and 159, Visser 1963: 536ff.; Caldwell 1974:63, who examined relative pronouns in Early Scots (ca. 1375–ca. 1500) comes to a 6/4 ratio for resp. subjects and nonsubjects.

In (standardized) EMODE (and perhaps also in LME) there is a diachronic shifting from subject deletion to other slots, which is clearly shown in Table XVIII:

Table XVIII: Pronoun deletion in EMODE

	Subject	O/PC	Totals
1520–1560	136 (33.17%)	274 (66.83%)	410
1600–1649	111 (25.28%)	328 (74.72%)	439
Totals	247	602	849

$X^2 = 6.61$, P = .01 (very significant)

Toshio Saito's evidence (Tables VI and VII, pp. 79–80) fully discloses the implementation phase of this syntactic change, at least as far as EMODE (and Modern) drama is concerned. Quirk (1968) has virtually recorded no instances for standard spoken PE. However, this change is not completed (if there is any change at all) in the regional varieties of English; see e.g. Romaine 1979 for Middle and Modern Scots, Ihalainen 1980:189 or Hughes and Trudgill 1979:17–18. Romaine (1979:26) observes, and rightly so, that Bever and Langendoen have not satisfactorily accounted for the recession of subject deletion in Modern English. B. and L. argue that it is the danger of faulty segmentation that eventually ousts this construction in PE. If this assumption is correct, why does it not apply to non-standardized English as well? I hope to have an opportunity to go into this matter in some detail in another paper.

Meanwhile one point seems to stand out: diachronically relativizer deletion has moved down the AH. Its directionality is thus an instance of what Bailey calls natural change. Again, more detailed researches for ME, particularly LME, are called for in order to lay bare fully conclusive evidence.

6 Conclusions

6.1 The history of relativization in more or less standardized English is characterized by two major syntactic changes: a) The development of coexisting relativization strategies in ME: Ø (from OE), THAT (partly a reflex of an OE relativizer) and extraneous WH-. As compared with PE, the application of these strategies is generally not constrained by the type of clause or antecedent involved (apart perhaps from +H WHO (M) and +R Ø), although some "tendencies" are discernible; see Mustanoja 1960:196. b). Since LME the set of available relativizers has remained virtually intact: the second important syntactic change consists in the introduction of constraints on the selection of pronouns in MODE, coupled with distributional shifts between members of the set (Tables I, II, III). Very interestingly, EMODE shows the 'implementation' phase of *some* of these changes; in other words, EMODE foreshadows the present-day grammar of relativization.

6.2 These changes can be diagrammatically presented as follows (brackets indicate very sporadic occurrence, while ? is used to signal a change that tends to reach completion):

LME	WHO	WHICH	THAT	Ø
↓	+H/(−H)	+H/−H	+H/−H	
	+R/−R	+R/−R	+R/−R	+R(−R)
↓	↓	↓	↓	All slots (exc. GEN)
PE	+H	−H	−H/+H?	+R ↓
	+R/−R	+R/−R	−H	Non-subject slots (exc. GEN)

6.3 The implementation phase of the constraint on WHICH in terms of +H/−H, coupled with a considerable increase of WHO, is amply substantiated in the EMODE corpora. With WHO being increasingly used for +H antecedents, also +H THAT begins to give way gradually; however, this development has not (yet) reached its final stage in PE. The tendency towards —H THAT seems to be modestly at work in EMODE, but the recorded difference of ca. 1.5% is statistically not significant. See Tables XI and XII.

6.4 Unlike WH- relativizers, both THAT and $\emptyset$ are now blocked from —R clauses in PE. As regards $\emptyset$, this constraint is already present in (L)ME and EMODE, but not absolutely so. The change towards —R THAT is not unidirectional: —R THAT is rather rare in the 16th century, but then it temporarily gains in frequency in the first half of the 17th century (Table VII).

6.5 The THAT strategy is obviously on the decrease in Standard MODE, whatever some grammars may have said to the contrary (Table II). This change has to be put down to various factors: the expansion of $\emptyset$, the constraint or —R THAT and the near constraint on +H THAT. Extraneous WH- is firmly established in —R clauses, while it has gained full currency in +R clauses (Tables IIIa and b). As pointed out before, its *prima facie* stability is due to the high rate for —R clauses as compared with PE; the split tables reveal an actual increase of WH- for both types of clause.

6.6 Whatever the details of these changes may have been, it is obvious that MODE has built semantic constraints into the available strategies. It is tempting to compare this systematization with what happened in Standard Dutch. We have no early evidence for Dutch comparable to that of OE. In Middle Dutch, i.e. from ca. 1200, there are three strategies: zero, deictic words and interrogatives; zero-marking later fell into disuse. The important thing to note is that, from Middle Dutch on, there has always been a *paradigmatic* selection between two available strategies, which we still find in present-day Standard Dutch:

	Singular		Plural
	Masculine/Feminine	Neuter	
Nom./Acc.	*DIE*	*DAT*(WAT)	*DIE*
Gen.	VAN WIE(WAARVAN)	WAARVAN	VAN WIE(WAARVAN)
	WIENS(formal)/WIER(id.)		WIER(formal)
PP	Prep. + WIE	WAAR–	Prep. + WIE
	(WAAR–)		(WAAR–)

The *italicized* items (in Nom. Acc.) are historically deictics; *waarvan* and *waar–* are pronominal adverbs (cfr. English *whereof*, etc.). Now I wonder whether, on the basis of this evidence, we cannot put forward the claim that a language which develops two or more relativization strategies, will also introduce selectional constraints. Of course, such a claim should be based on more than two languages in order to be more widely valid.

6.7 The present paper has also demonstrated the relevance of Keenan and Comrie's AH for EMODE. Along with register, the +H/−H dichotomy is found to be a parameter with which one should reckon when setting up an AH scale: +H subjects are semantically more prominent than −H ones, which has an incidence on the accessibility scale (Table XIV). What Romaine (1980) has discovered for Middle Scots also applies to EMODE in general: the (more or less) extraneous WH- strategy is comparatively more frequent in the difficult positions and is generally a mark of more complex English. As such it seems to be an instance of change-from-above. See Tables XV, XVI and XVII.

6.8 Relativizer deletion is not very common in OE and ME, and is virtually confined to the subject slot. During EMODE this process gains in frequency, whereas it begins to be increasingly restricted in the subject slot (this restriction has now reached its completion in Standard PE). The directionality of change is reverse to that of the WH-strategy: it moves down the AH and can as such be accounted for as an instance of natural change. The history of MODE relativizers in general is thus characterized by two important changes: an expansion of WH- *up* the AH scale, matched by an expansion of pronoun deletion *down* this scale. I am not claiming that this holds for each element of the Keenan-Comrie hierarchy, but as a generalization it is certainly valid for a condensed scale of subject and non-subject positions.

Appendix: EMODE (1600–49) sample sentences

WHO (M)/WHOSE

+H/+R S   *Earle* 47: and is like *a desperate soldier, who* will assault any thing where he is sure not to enter.

      O   *Donne*, II 41: as to *a person whom* God had made so great an instrument of his providence . . .

      G   *Dekker* 298–299: 'tis not well to strike *A man whose* knowledge I have made A witness . . .

+H/−R S   *Herbert* 29: *Mine own Apostle, who* the bag did beare . . .

    PC   *Old Hobson* 18: *A poore beggar man*, . . . , *to whom* Maister Hobson said . . .

      G   *Tourneur* 86: Shall *man, to whose* command and use all creatures Were made subject . . .

−H   G   *Daniel* 364: *their excellent conceits, whose* scattered limbs we are faine to looke out . . .

PC   *Cawdrey* 238: gnaweth and consument *the tree, of whom* it hath his beginning . . .

(THE) WHICH

+H/−R S   *Walton* 368: I have been enabled to requite most of *those friends which* showed me kindness . . .

+H/−R S   *Herbert* 224: For when *My Master, which* alone is sweet . . .

−H/+R S   *Donne*, II 156: I waited upon you heretofore when *a cause which* concerned me was brought before you . . .

O   *Daniel* 358: at *Wilton, which* I must euer acknowledge to haue beene my best Schoole . . .

−H/−R PC   *Beaumont and Fletcher* 234: I have but *one horse, (up) on which* shall ride This fair lady . . .

THAT

−H/+R S   *Jonson* 43: We need *a man that* know the severall graces of historie . . .

+H/−R S   *Bacon* 184: or life unto *my brother, that* was sent hither . . .

−H/+R S   *Tourneur* 73: I behold *the object that* Mine eye affects.

PC   *Heywood* 362: I can tell you sir, *the game that* Master Wendoll is best at.

−H/−R S   *Chapman*   359−360: But *D'Ambois sword (that* lightned as it flew) Shot like a pointed Comet . . .

PC   *Tourneur* 29: Heaven give *your marriage that* I am deprived of, joy.

Ø

+R   S   *Brome* 346: Have you *any Pleasures in the Court*, can make a man forget he has a Wife?

S   *Ford* 44−45: I met   *a swaggering fellow* would needs take the wall of me . . .

O   *Heywood* 352: *The love* I bear my husband is as precious As . . .

O   *Ford* 9: And yet is here *the comfort* I shall have . . .

PC   *Dekker* 271: I am not *the roaring girle* you take me for.

PC   *Verney Papers* 240: they will make use of *the advantage* they have us att . . .

ADV *Overbury* 185: That greatnesse comes not down *by the way* it
went up . . .

−R O *Hausted* 67: Does *your first son's* name You shall beget . . .

List of abbreviations used

ADV	adverbial slot
AH	Accessibility Hierarchy (see section 4)
df	degree of freedom (see X^2 in this list)
DO	direct object
D stratum	drama (see previous section)
E stratum	epistolary prose (again, see previous section)
EME	Early Middle English (ca. 1100–ca.1300)
EMODE	Early Modern English (ca. 1500–ca.1800)
H	human (as a semantic feature)
IO	indirect object
LME	Late Middle English (ca.1300–ca.1500)
ME	Middle English (ca.1100–ca.1500)
O	direct and indirect object
OE	Old English (roughly 700–1100)
P	probability of occurrence of a deviation (see X^2 in this list)
P stratum	narrative/descriptive and informative prose (see 0.2)
PC	preposition complement (i.e. any preposition-initiated NP)
PE	present-day English
R	restrictive (as a semantic feature of relative clauses)
S	subject
V stratum	poetry (see 0.2)
WH-	a *wh*-relativizer like *who* or *which*
Ø	this symbol marks a deleted relativizer as in: Is *Lord of the Flies* a novel Ø you can read in one evening?
X^2	or Chi-square. The X^2-test is a simple device to find out whether the discrepancy between two or more sample frequencies is statistically significant or not. This is not the proper place to explain how X^2 is calculated. Suffice it to say that Chi-square is the squared deviation of actual frequency from theoretical frequency, divided by the theoretical frequency; this value has to be calculated for each cell of a given table. For more details see Herdan 1956:88–99 or Muller 1968, chapter 15; a simple description of the test can also be found in Dekeyser 1975:325–327. In order to understand how this test is applied (also in the present paper) a word should now be said about the so-called *degrees of*

freedom and the *probability of occurrence of a deviation* or P. Let us first look at df: in a 2x2 or a 4-cell table, there is 1df: this means that, if one value is known, the other ones are not free, the totals being known. In a 6-cell table there are 2dfs. The tables in the present paper are mostly of the 1df type. The significance or non-significance of computed X^2-values, coupled with the number of dfs, can be read from *ad hoc* distribution tables, which can be found in e.g. Muller 1968:241, or Herdan 1956:341. An example: if Chi-square reaches 3.841, and with 1df, we speak of a .05 significance, or P = .05. This means that the probability of a deviating distribution is only 5%, or 5 in 100; with X^2 (and 1df) = 6.635, P = .01, etc. The .05 level is generally accepted as the border value of statistical significance: the observed discrepancy is not due to chance. If Chi-square is smaller than 3.841 (again with 1df), the difference may be the result of mere chance. Most of the tables in this paper contain highly significant values for X^2.

Notes

1. See Mitchell 1968:73–74, or Andrew 1966:35–47.
2. On this so-called pleonastic *that* see Kivimaa 1966.
3. The ME survey is based on Mustanoja 1960:187–208. In addition there is also relativizer *what*, and the adverbials *when, where*, etc.
4. I have excerpted only the epistolary parts of these works.
5. In this table, and in the following ones, "1520–1560" refers to the numerical data found in Rydén's *Frequency Surveys* at the end of his book.
6. This wide-spread infiltration of WH- into the relative system is a feature of the standard language; in other varieties of English THAT and $\emptyset$ are generally preferred to WH-. See Romaine 1980, more particularly pp.229 ff.
7. Three criteria are commonly used to distinguish between +R/−R clauses: phonetic (intonation), graphical and semantic. It is clear that the first criterion is of no use here. The graphical criterion must also be put aside, because the haphazard EMODE punctuation is often not reliable at all (see e.g. Rydén: xlvi). This means that only the traditional semantic contrast between +R and −R clauses is left (see e.g. Dekeyser 1979:9.5–9.6). Though I have attempted to apply this parameter as consistently as possible in the context given, I may have made a wrong decision every now and then. However, in view of the great number of clauses which we have worked on the overall analysis of the available data is no doubt more than approximately correct.
8. See Quirk 1972:871–872.
9. Based on Quirk 1968:104.
10. Inclusive of the cases of deletion, the rates are:
    EMODE: +R 1,613 (56.76%) −R 1,229 (43.24%); total: 2,842
    PE: +R 1,112 (86.47%) −R 174 (13.53%); total: 1,286
11. I have recorded only 7 instances of −H antecedents against 425 +H ones. See also Rydén, 1966: e.g. 12, 21, 33, 46; and Saito 1961:86–87.

12. As far as WHOSE is concerned, Rydén gives numerical evidence only for Sir Thomas Elyot's work (1966:47ff.); in order to cover the 16th century more fully I have made use of the 1560–1599 data.
13. The infrequency of genitival relativization will be further commented on in section 4.3.
14. I have borrowed this term from Romaine 1980:237.
15. For reasons of time I have not differentiated +R and –R clauses. Romaine (1980), notes 13 and 14 observes that the AH scales are different for the two types of clause, but she gives no further evidence.
16. +H/–H WHICH in subject, object and other positions:

	S	O	Other pos.	Totals
+Human	311 (83.83%)	34 (9.16%)	26 (7%)	371
–Human	780 (46.71%)	561 (33.59%)	329 (19.70%)	1,670
Totals	1,091	595	355	2,041

X^2 = ca. 169

17. The four epistolary units investigated happen to have a more or less formal character and do not seem to reflect the colloquial language of the time.

References

Andrew, S. O.
1966 *Syntax and style in Old English* (New York: Russell and Russell).
Bailey, Charles-James N.
1973 *Variation and linguistic theory* (Arlington, Virginia: Center for Applied Linguistics).
Bailey, Charles-James N. – Roger W. Shuy (eds.)
1973 *New ways of analyzing variation in English* (Washington, D. C.: Georgetown University Press).
Bever, T. G. – D. T. Langendoen
1972 "The interaction of speech perception and grammatical structure in the evolution of language", *Linguistic change and generative theory*, edited by R. P. Stockwell and R.K.S. Macaulay (Bloomington and London: Indiana University Press), 32–95.
Caldwell, Sarah J. G.
1974 *The relative pronoun in Early Scots*. (=*Mémoires de la Société Néophilologique de Helsinki*, xlii), (Helsinki: Société Néophilologique).
Craeyevelt (van), Magda
1977 *Relative pronouns in Early Modern English* (1600–1649) (Unpublished memoir of the K. U. Leuven).
Dekeyser, Xavier
1975 *Number and case relations in 19th century British English: a comparative study of grammar and usage.* (=*Bibliotheca Linguistica: series theoretica*), (Antwerpen-Amsterdam: Uitgeverij De Nederlandsche Boekhandel).
Dekeyser, Xavier – Betty Devriendt – Guy Tops – Steven Geukens
1979 *Foundations of English grammar: for university students and advanced*

learners. (=*Bibliotheca Anglistica: series practica, title no. 3*), (Antwerpen-Amsterdam: Uitgeverij De Nederlandsche Boekhandel).

Fasold, Ralph W.
1975 "The Bailey wave model: a dynamic quantitative paradigm", *Analyzing variation in language. Papers from the Second Colloquium on New Ways of Analyzing Variation*, edited by R. W. Fasold and R. W. Shuy (Washington, D. C.: Georgetown University Press), 27–58.

Herdan, G.
1956 *Language as choice and chance.* (Groningen: Nordhoff).

Hughes, Arthur – Peter Trudgill
1979 *English accents and dialects: an introduction to social and regional varieties of British English* (London: Edward Arnold).

Ihalainen, Ossi
1980 "Relative clauses in the dialect of Somerset", *Neuphilologische Mitteilungen* 81:187–196.

Keenan, Edward L.
1975 "Variation in universal grammar", *Analyzing variation in language. Papers from the Second Colloquium on New Ways of Analyzing Variation*, edited by R. W. Fasold and R. W. Shuy (Washington, D. C.: Georgetown University Press), 136–148.

Keenan, Edward L. – Bernard Comrie
1977 "Noun phrase accessibility and universal grammar", *Linguistic Inquiry 8*: 63–99.
[*Note:* This article is an expanded version of a paper presented at the *Linguistic Society of America* Winter Meeting, 1972.]

Kivimaa, Kirsti
1966 *The pleonastic that in relative and interrogative constructions in Chaucer's verse.* (=*Commentationes Humanarum Litterarum* 39:3), (Helsinki: Societas Scientiarum Fennica).

Mitchell, Bruce
1968 *A guide to Old English* (Oxford: Basil Blackwell).

Muller, Charles
1968 *Initiation à la statistique linguistique. Langue et langage* (Paris: Larousse).

Mustanoja, Tauno F.
1960 *A Middle English syntax. Part I: Parts of speech.* (=*Mémoires de la Société Néophilologique de Helsinki* xxiii), (Helsinki: Société Néophilologique).

New Cambridge Bibliography of English Literature (1974). Vol. I: 600–1160 (Cambridge: University Press).

O'Neil, Wayne
1976 "Clause adjunction in Old English", *General linguistics* 17: 199–211.

Quirk, R.
1968 "Relative clauses in educated spoken English", *Essays on the English language, Medieval and Modern* by R. Quirk (London: Longmans), 94–108.
[*Note*: This article is a reprint of an article in *English Studies* 38 (1957): 97 ff.]

Quirk, R. – S. Greenbaum – G. Leech – J. Svartvik
1972 *A Grammar of contemporary English* (London: Longman).

Roggero, J.
1967 "WHOSE et OF WHICH. Recherche en vue d'une application à l'enseignement", *Les langues modernes* 61:29–40.

Romaine, Suzanne
1979 *Syntactic complexity, relativization and stylistic levels in Middle Scots* (University of Birmingham: Department of Linguistics).
1980 "The relative clause marker in Scots English: Diffusion, complexity, and style as dimensions of syntactic change", *Language in society* 9:221–247.

this volume "Towards a typology of relative clause formation strategies in Germanic",

Rydén, Mats
1966   *Relative constructions in Early Sixteenth Century English, with special reference to Sir Thomas Elyot.* (*Acta Universitatis Upsaliensis: Studia Anglistica Upsaliensia* 3) (Diss. Uppsala; Uppsala/Stockholm: Almqvist & Wiksell).
1974   "On notional relations in the relative clause complex", *English studies* 55:542–545.

Saito, Toshio
1961   "The development of relative pronouns in Modern Colloquial English. A statistical survey of the development of their usage seen in British prose plays from the 16th century to the present time", *The scientific reports of Mukogawa Women's University* 8: 67–89.

Steinki, J.
1932   *Die Entwicklung der englischen Relativpronomina in spätmittelenglischer und frühneuenglischer Zeit,* Breslau Dissertation, (Ohlau: Eschenhagen).

Traugott, Elizabeth Closs
1972   *A history of English syntax: a transformational approach to the history of English sentence structure* (New York: Holt, Rinehart and Winston, Inc.).

Trudgill, P.
1975   *Sociolinguistics: an introduction* (Harmondsworth: Penguin).

Visser, F. Th.
1963   *An historical syntax of the English language. Part I* (Leiden: E. J. Brill).

DOROTHY DISTERHEFT

Irish complementation:
A case study in two types of syntactic change

1 Introduction

Old Irish (OIr) patterns of nonfinite complementation are a valuable source for observing the kinds of change possible and the manner in which new rules are incorporated in this part of the grammar. In the earliest texts, which are glosses on the Latin bible and date from the eighth and ninth centuries A.D., major changes in verb complementation had previously occurred. These in turn opened the way for innovations — still in progress in this period — which produced a system drastically different from the inherited one.

The nonfinite form of the predicate, called verbal noun (VN) in traditional Celtic grammars,[1] is a nominalization of a verb (e.g., to the root *lec'* — 'leave' is added a nominalizing suffix which yields *leciud* 'leaving') and a member of productive nominal paradigms. At some point prior to the OIr period this nominalization had been reanalyzed as the nonfinite predicate in subordinate clauses. Such a process is paralleled in the rest of Indo-European (IE); doubtless its beginnings can be traced to Proto-Indo-European (PIE). Morphological reconstruction unequivocally shows that, with few exceptions,[2] all IE infinitives were inflected verbal nominalizations which have established one case ending for the infinitive marker as a consequence of shifting to verbal status. Latin and Greek infinitives have become so completely verbal that their infinitives are morphologically marked for tense and voice, e.g. Gk *pepaideu+sthai* (perfect verbal root of 'educate' + medio-passive infinitive desinence).

The developments in the OIr verb complements which will be treated below are essentially of two types. The first involves the initial reanalysis of the nominalization as nonfinite predicate. Complements produced by this innovation are indeterminately direct object NPs or sentential objects with mandatory subject coreference. As a result of the reanalysis of the VN's surface features, several changes took place which yielded many unambiguous complements so that prior to the earliest texts the VN must have already been a distinct nonfinite predicate. Consequently in these sources a new syntactic rule operates on the underlying structure which produced the first complements with mandatory subject coreference. This one, however, produced a radically different sentence pattern by raising embedded object to main clause object. I will argue that, although at first glance this looks like a straightforward case of rule addition, this was actually added as a result of the generalization of another complement pattern which raised both subject and object from the embedded clause to main clause object.

The model of change which I assume here is one implicitly followed by many people, but most clearly defined and elaborated by Andersen (1973, 1974). In first language learning, grammatical rules can only be formulated on the basis of the output of older speakers' grammars, that is, abductively. Since it is only necessary that the language learner produce utterances – not rules – identical to his model, a certain amount of rule diversity with no immediate consequences is normally quite common, even in a homogeneous speech community (Andersen 1974:24). This kind of innovation is possible when the output of the older generation is ambiguous and can be accounted for by two different sets of rules. Abductive innovation cannot be observed directly from the output of the new grammar, but must instead be inferred when the new rules are applied to produce surface forms which are at variance with those of the model. The manifestation of new rules is always a deductive process: any overt change in a grammar is a sign that a separate abductive innovation has occurred at a prior stage. Both kinds of innovation are clearly responsible for the changes in the OIr complement system: the initial reanalysis of the VN as a nonfinite predicate and the addition of new syntactic processes are classic cases of abduction while the addition of verbal features which yield a distinct verbal complement are deductive.

2.1 The accusative VN complement

In the early glosses the VN has syntactic properties of both a NP and a nonfinite predicate. I have argued elsewhere (1980:190–2) that this ambivalence was not new to Irish, but had been inherited from a late stage of PIE. The major evidence for this claim lies in the fact that Indo-Iranian, the only other branch of IE with morphologically archaic, nominal infinitives, shared this pattern. The reanalysis of the nominalized verb as nonfinite predicate (i.e. an infinitive) resulted from surface patterns which could be interpreted in more than one way. Sequences like

> (1) (NP) NP V
>   nom acc

(where the nominative NP was optional when the subject of the sentence was pronominalized) could represent either the underlying structure:

(2a) (S) O V

where object was any kind of NP, including the deverbal noun. On the other hand, the accusative NP might be a sentential object:

(2b) (S_1) $[S_1$ $V]_{\bar{s}}$ V

if it was a nominalized verb and subject coreference was inferrable. Vedic Sanskrit preserved indeterminate surface sequences very close to this earliest verb complement type:

(3) *ayan*   *ā́po*   *'yanam*
   they-came the-waters(nom) way/flow (acc)

   icchámānāḥ   (RV III.33.7)
   wishing(nom pl)
   (i) object: 'the waters came, wishing a way (out)'
   (ii) complement: 'The waters came, wishing to flow (forth)'

The reanalysis of the nominalized verb as nonfinite predicate must have taken place a good while before the Vedic period, for the indeterminacy remaining in the complement system was not at all widespread. As embedded predicates, about half of the forms attested were a nonobject case (dative, locative), and hence distinct from the pattern which produced (2):

(4) *sám anyámanyam arthayanty* étave   (RV V.44.11)
   together each-other(acc) they-strive come(dat inf)
   'They strive to come together with each other'

2.2 Since the period of IE unity, OIr has shifted to VSO order, but still retained more indeterminacy than found in Indo-Iranian. The surface sequence

(5) V (NP) NP
      nom   acc

(again with optional subject NP) might represent a simple sentence:

(6a) V (S) O

or one with a verb complement in object position where both subjects were mandatorily coreferent:

(6b) V (S_1) $[V$ $S_1]_{\bar{s}}$

The majority of verb complements in the OIr biblical glosses employed an accusative VN phrase which could be interpreted nominally (7a-i) or clausally (7a-ii) with coreferential deletion of subordinate subject:

> (7a) *conn- gestais   huili   taidchor*
>   so-that they-would-pray all(nom) release(acc VN)
>
>   *as   indoiri*   (Ml 131 d 13)
>   from captivity
> (i) object: 'so that they would all pray for release from captivity'
> (ii) complement: , . . . to be released from captivity'

Deletion of lower subject, however, was optional; a genitive pronominal clitic often copied the higher subject in the VN clause:

> (7b) *ni   rufrescachtar* a   *n-íc*   (Ml 26b 25)
>   NEG they-expected   their save(acc VN)
> (i) object: 'they did not expect their salvation'
> (ii) complement: 'they did not expect to be saved'

Nominal modifiers of the VN were also genitive: (7c) is such an example. The genitive was a possessive if the VN was nominal, but the direct object if a complement clause:

> (7c) . . . *adcobra ícc*   omnium   (Wb 28 b 2)
>   he-desires save(acc VN) all(gen)
> (i) object: 'He desires the salvation of all (people)'
> (ii) complement: 'He desires to save all (people)'

In order to obtain the ambivalent structures of (6), the main clause verb must obviously have had semantic properties which allowed it to select either a simple NP or an embedded sentence as object. *Wishes, desires, expects* were the most common verbs which did so during this period.

Sequences of the type found in (7) provided the source for the original abductive innovation. In many sentences like these, it is impossible to analyze the accusative VN either one way or the other. Only passages that translate or paraphrase Latin nonfinite complements can be treated as such with any degree of certainty.

2.3 When surface sequences that could not possibly be given a nominal interpretation were produced, we have good evidence that further grammatical change had taken place. In the case at hand, this was provided by an extension of the classes of main clause verbs allowed. Whereas those which provided indeterminate readings had to allow either NP or embedded sentences in object position, a later type only selected subordinate clauses. The same texts that allowed patterns like (6) had a newer type, with which no indeterminacy was possible since the main verb normally did not take a nominal object. Most of these were modals and attitude predicates, e.g. *is able* (8a), *intends* (8b), *thinks* (8c), and formerly had taken finite complements.

> (8a) ... *arní cumgat   comallad   inna-firinnesin*
>   for-not they-are-able fulfill(acc VN)   that justice(gen)
>
>   *inógai*   (Ml 94 b 3)
>   completely'
>   'for they are not able to fulfill that justice completely'

> (8b) *arromertussa buith   and   angaimredsa* (Wb 31 d 14)
>   I-intended   be(acc VN) there   this-winter
>   'I intended to be there this winter'

> (8c) ... *air ní   tormenatar som etir   an   ditin*
>   for NEG they-thought   at-all their protect(acc VN)
>
>   *⁊ an ícc*   (Ml 106 d 11)
>   and their save(acc VN)
>   '... for they did not at all think that they would be protected
>   and saved'

2.4 Once the VN was reanalyzed as a nonfinite predicate, other properties of complements were extended to it. The first innovation from the stage represented in (6) was the inclusion of predicates (8) which selected only sentential objects. A second one allowed a noncoreferent subject in the complement; the pattern which had produced the reanalysis admitted only coreferential subjects. The accusative VN held the same position as in (7) and (8), the only difference being the addition of a postposed subject in a prepositional phrase (always after *do* 'to'; the prepositional phrase with *do* was a common agent in OIr).

> (9) *asrochoili   inna chridiu buid   dond- ingin*
>   he-decides in-his heart be(acc VN) for-the daughter(dat)
>
>   *in-ógi*   (Wb 10 b 20)
>   in celibacy
>   'He decides in his heart that his daughter will be in celibacy'

Though this accusative VN-prepositional phrase pattern may incorporate all constituents found in nonreduced, finite clauses, it remained a minor one in the glosses. It might have enjoyed wider use in pre-OIr, but it certainly gained no ground in OIr and indeed appears to be on the wane in Middle Irish (MIr).

3.1 The dative VN complement

In the same period in which the accusative VN with postposed genitive object was the nonfinite complement when subject coreference obtained, an innovative type with dative VN (always preceded by preposition *do* 'to') began to emerge. In addition to the new form of the VN, other differences are that the subordinate object was now accusative and preposed:

> (10) V   (NP)   NP   *do*-VN
>   nom   acc

This new construction is found twice only in the oldest glosses (Würzburg, c. 750):

> (11a) *ciad-   cobrinn móidim   do-dénum* ...   (Wb 17 d 17)
>   though I-desired boast(acc VN) to do(dat VN)
>   'though I desired to do boasting (i.e. 'to boast')'

It appears twice in those from St. Gall of approximately a century later:

> (11b) ... *ar-indí nád cumaiṅg maith*
>   because NEG he-can   good(acc)
>
>   *do-dénom*   (Sg 50 a 14)
>   to do(dat VN)
>   'because he cannot do good'

and about ten times from the contemporaneous Milan glosses:

> (11c) *co-   carad   chaingnimu   du-denum*   (Ml 14 a 8)
>   so-that he-loved good-deeds(acc) to do(dat VN)
>   'so that he loved to do good deeds'

In all, I have found only about twenty passages with this pattern in the OIr corpus, which spans approximately 250 years (750–1000). This was indeed a minor construction in comparison with the accusative VN (7) which was the standard nonfinite predicate in object position during the same timespan.

3.2 The innovative accusative NP-*do*-VN pattern has always been something of an anomaly in OIr grammatical tradition. Thurneysen(1946:445) noted that it was probably the only use of the VN which approximated the infinitive constructions in other languages because it had a 'true' object in the accusative and the VN itself was a nonobject case. We have seen, however, that

VNs with genitive object were just as 'verbal' as infinitives in other IE langua-ges that have a separate infinitive category with accusative object. Their syn-tactic properties reveal that they had already been reanalyzed as nonfinite predicates in OIr. Witness the lack of indeterminacy of (8) and (9).

Thurneysen's admittance of these as infinitives in his *Grammar of Old Irish* may be ascribed to the fact that dative VN with preposed accusative object was a construction entirely different from that with accusative VN. The appearance of this new pattern was not simply a matter of the VN having become less nominal in its case marking or even developing more verbal characteristics such as accusative object selection. If this were the situation, we would expect that VN-object order be maintained, just as it was in other new constructions that were developing roughly during the same period, for example, Subject-to-Object raising (Disterheft, 1982). Here the VN was dative, but the genitive direct object followed just as in the older accusative patterns:

(12) *ma-ni- fessed comdidnad du-thiarmoracht*
if NEG it-knew consolation(acc) to follow(dat VN)

ind-uilc (Ml 87 d 4)
the evil(gen)
'if it did not know that consolation follows evil'

However, sentences with object (either genitive or accusative) *following* the VN were inadmissible for these dative complements with coreferential subject deletion. The accusative object was clearly in the 'wrong' position — before its VN — if we compare it with other subordinate structures.

On the other hand, it may be argued that the variant features of the dative VN object indicate that it is not a member of the complement clause, but is a constituent of the matrix. Three kinds of evidence, from case marking, word order, and passivization, show that the accusative NP is subject to rules that normally apply to main clause objects.

First, the canonical object case of finite verbs was accusative, of VNs, genitive. But in (11) the VN object was accusative. This is the only clause type with object so exceptionally marked. If its case were still determined by the dative VN, it would have genitive, as in the Subject-to-Object Raising structure of (12). More evidence comes from sentences where the verb con-trolling case assignment of the VN object took a case other than accusative. In (13) the higher predicate is itself a VN. Since VNs assign genitive to their objects, the object of the rightmost clause carries that case:

(13) ... *imgabail uilc do-denum* (Ml 14 c 12)
avoid(VN) evil(gen) to do(dat VN)
'to avoid doing evil'

Second, word order is VSO; hence direct object was the last argument of a clause (unless an indirect object was present). The internal structure of the matrix was evidently very tight: only a nominative NP, if subject was not pronominalized, was allowed in addition to the accusative NP. If the object were still syntactically a member of the subordinate clause, it would have to be postposed, as in (8a) and (12). Therefore, it is obvious that the logical VN object has been moved out of the subordinate clause and holds object position in the higher clause.

Third, when subordinate object is passivized to subject of the main clause, it is marked with nominative case and controls subject-verb agreement in that clause:

(14a) *trenailce* . . .   *na*   *cuimgidthur*
strong-foundations(nom) REL-NEG they-are-able(pass)

do cumscudugh   (O'Don 15)
to move(dat VN)
'the strong foundations . . . which cannot be moved'

(14a) is derived by passivizing 'one is not able to move the strong foundations', whereby the logical object of the VN, 'foundations', is directly promoted to main clause subject and then relativized. Another sentence shows a similar promotion to main clause subject under passivization:

(14b) *cesu   meinciu aranecar* verbum *do epirt*
though-it-is oftener it-is-found (nom)   to call(dat VN)

donaib huilib rannaib. . .   (Sg 137 b 2)
to-the all   parts(of-speech)
'though it is oftener found that all the parts of speech are called *verbum.* . . '

It is not possible, however, to make a case for clause membership of the VN subject on case marking alone because *verbum* is a Latin neuter noun whose nominative and accusative have the same form. The two examples in (14) are the only passages in my collection with passivized main clause predicates; that this is the case is not surprising, given the small data base.

The syntactic properties of the logical VN object, therefore, lead to the conclusion that it is superficially the main clause direct object due to its movement to the matrix and participation in main clause processes. Such phenomena can only be explained by the addition of a new rule, Object-to-Object Raising (OOR) in eight-century Irish.

3.3 During the MIr period (tenth to fourteenth centuries), the dative VN complement acquired a much greater frequency in texts. Whereas in the eighth to tenth centuries OOR can be found in texts less than twenty times, in the later period it became truly competitive with the accusative complements. An expansion in the lexical items which trigger OOR accompanied the increase in numerical incidence; furthermore, this process became less typical of modals and desideratives and more the domain of utterance predicates.

(15a) *ni   ro-ataim   in   topur   d' fagbail*   (EMEM 198.11)
NEG he-admitted the well(acc) to find(dat VN)
'He did not admit that he had found the well'

(15b) *tarngairit   curpu   do chrádh*   (Acallamh 7593)
they-promised bodies(acc) to torment
'they promised to torment (their) bodies'

(15c) ... *corobáig-si   frie   a   cend   do béim*
then-she-vowed to-her her head(acc) to strike(dat VN)

di   acht mani aprad   (FR 29–30)
from her unless   she-spoke
'then she vowed to her to strike off her head unless she spoke'

3.4 Let us return briefly to the late OIr period. In the glosses on native texts (end ninth century), a complement of the form accusative object-*do*-VN made its first appearance after a different syntactic class of predicates. The only distinction between this and (11) is that main clause indirect object (instead of subject) controlled coreference.

(16a) *co   nerbairt fria   na   lina   do chor*
and he-told to-her the nets(acc) to cast(dat VN)

isin   usce   (BH 345.21–22)
into-the water
'and he told her to cast the nets into the water'

(16b) *atrubairt Brenaind   fria   gilla   a   chochull*
he-told Brendan(nom) to-the servant(dat) his cloak(acc)

do chur   forro   (BH 335.27)
to put(dat VN) upon-them
'Brendan told his servant to put his cloak upon them'

The expansion from subject-o indirect-object-controlled coreference entailed the addition of new semantic classes of complement-taking predicates. The native texts of "Broccán's hymn" (from the "Liber hymnorum") (16) offer the first attestations of causative predicates. Otherwise, syntactic properties of these complements exactly match the pattern of (10) and, as such, should likewise be analyzed as OOR.

According to the textual evidence, verbs whose indirect objects control coreference were added to OOR structures about 150 years after those whose subjects do. At the time when OOR was introduced, causative predicates almost always admitted only finite complements. In the OIr glosses a very few nonfinite ones are attested, though, but always with the nonraised, accusative structure:

(17) *ní- relic   dia   doib   orcuin*
      NEG he-allowed God(nom) to-them slay(acc VN)

      nduaid   (Ml 23 b 4)
      David(gen)
      'God did not allow them to slay David'

Clearly any nonfinite complement to predicates whose indirect objects controlled coreference were rare in OIr. The accusative VN construction appeared less than ten times in the glosses from Würzburg and Milan, and remained rare in late OIr. In MIr, however, OOR with indirect-object equi verbs gained ground, just as it did after subject equi.

3.5 At first glance the appearance of OOR in the mid-eighth century appears to be a case of simple rule addition. However, when we look elsewhere in the complement system, we find that NP-Raising structures are common. In the Würzburg glosses, the following pattern is well-entrenched in the grammar:[3]

(18) *be* NP ... NP *do*-VN
           nom   nom

Here a copular sentence, consisting of a form of *be* and predicate noun (nominative) could take a sentential subject whose own subject was a nominative NP followed by a dative VN.

(19a) ... *ní-   amre   limsa   didiu   aís*
          it-is-not wonder(nom) with-me therefore people(nom)

      lobor do-dénum   diibsi   (Wb 17b 29)
      weak to   do(dat VN) from-you(pl)
      'therefore, I do not wonder (that) weak people were made from you (lit.: 'it is not a wonder with me. . . ')'

(19b) *is- bés   leosom   in- daim*
it-is custom(nom) with-them the oxen(nom)

do-thúarcuin   ind-arbe   (Wb 10 d 6)
to tread-out(dat VN) the corn(gen)
'It is a custom with them (that) the oxen tread out the corn'

(19c) *is- dóire   duibsi   inso uile*
it-is baseness(nom) to-you(pl) this all(nom)

do-foditin   (Wb 17 c 17)
to endure(dat VN)
'It is baseness to you to endure all this'

I have argued elsewhere that, on the basis of case marking and word order, the NP immediately preceding the dative VN has been moved from subordinate to main clause subject (Disterheft, 1982). This rule, Raising-to-Subject (RS), moved to subject the first NP to the right of the VN in the underlying structure: either an original subject (19a), one derived by passivization (19b), or a direct object if there was no subject in the embedded clause (19c).

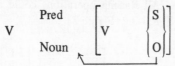

Figure 1. Raising-to-Subject

About the same time that OOR first appeared, another rule which I have identified as Subject-to-Object Raising (SOR) did also (Disterheft, 1982). The surface constituents that result from its application are identical to those for OOR (cf. (10)):

(20) V (NP) NP *do*-VN
       nom   acc

The verbs which triggered SOR were most often utterance predicates (21) (but cf. *know* in (12)).

(21) *huare   nad-rogaid   huisce*
because NEG he-prayed water(acc)

do-thinnaccul   (Ml 124 c 10)
to give(VN)
'because he did not pray that water be given'

The surface features of SOR were apparently patterned on ambiguous constituents of RS. Indistinctly marked sequences had developed with the latter when most (two-thirds) of the NPs immediately preceding the VN were ambiguously nominative or accusative. Because of the indistinct case marking of forms like *uile* (nom/acc) in (19c), the surface relationship of that NP to the rest of the main clause was usually unclear. Such ambiguity eventually allowed surface patterns wherein the NP in its raised position could be identified as having an object relation to the main clause verb: hence SOR. Since the NP in RS's subordinate clause could also be moved from object as well as subject position — whichever was immediately to the right of the embedded predicate (Figure 1) — the way was also open for OOR. Raising from object fulfilled the requirement that the NP immediately following the VN be moved (just as in (19c)). Since the lower subject had been deleted by coreference, only the object remained to be moved.

By the eighth century, then, adaptation in Raising had increased the number of sentence types this process operated on. The main clause verb was no longer limited to copula (for discussion see Disterheft, 1982), and the raised NP could hold either subject or object slot. If the matrix verb were *be*, the raised NP was nominative, but if it were a complement-taking predicate, the NP was accusative. All Raising operations could at this point be accounted for by one rule, NP-Raising (Figure 2).

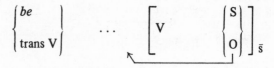

Figure 2. NP-Raising

The developments which resulted in NP-Raising must have taken several centuries to evolve and must have done so in discrete stages, as the difference between Figures 1 and 2 suggests. The first version of the Raising rule (Figure 1) was probably introduced before the loss of final syllables (fourth-fifth centuries A.D.), which obscured the case marking of the moved NP.[4] At any rate it was well-established in Würzburg, to judge by its frequent use. There is no direct evidence as to which of the subordinate NPs was raised first to subject, but in such circumstances it is tempting to invoke the NP Hierarchy developed by Keenan and Comrie (1977) and to argue that the direct object could not have been raised unless the subject were also. The question of whether Raising to object from subject/object was added together as one rule or in separate stages is impossible to determine: both are incipient in the earliest texts and could easily have been simultaneous developments since RS had already operated on both subordinate subject and object. It cannot be disputed, though, that at least two separate abductive innovations contributed to the single synchronic rule of NP-Raising in OIr.

4 Conclusions

The changes in the Irish complement system outlined here took at least two and a half millennia to evolve — if one accepts the PIE date for reanalysis — and entailed three major stages (Figure 3). The innovation initiating the process which culminated in NP-Raising was an abductive reanalysis of the nominalized verb as a nonfinite predicate. As a result of this category shift, the new complement clause dropped several of the early constraints, for example, that the complement subject be coreferent with the matrix subject and that the main verb be transitive. During the pre-OIr period the VN was introduced as the predicate in sentential subject (RS) directly as a result of its new status. (Details of its inception cannot be discussed here, but will be dealt with in a future publication.) The loss of final syllables, probably a subsequent development, obscured the case of the raised NP. When nouns with indistinct case marking commonly appeared in this position, it came to be interpreted as either a subject or object. In early OIr subordinate objects now occupied this matrix slot and the early rule of RS had become a more general NP-Raising process.

> Stage I   (PIE):   NP reanalyzed as nonfinite predicate
> Stage II   (pre-OIr): Raising-to-Subject introduced
> Stage III (OIr):   Raising-to-Subject extended to NP-Raising
>
> Figure 3.

Concomitant with the lessening of clause structure restrictions was the expansion of lexical triggers and the selectional properties admitted for them. The first OOR trigger was a desiderative (*desires*); in the ninth century modals (*is able*) and achievement (*succeeds,* (neg) *avoids*) predicates appear, and in the late ninth, utterance predicates first come into the texts, with the latter dominant in MIr. When indirect objects control coreference, causatives make their appearance and are the major triggers of this kind of OOR in MIr.

The pattern of abductive reanalysis seen in Irish is by now well-documented in the literature. In all cases, indeterminate surface sequences very slowly change an existing category into a new one. For example, Li and Thompson (1974) show how the Archaic Chinese pattern SVO has changed under some circumstances to SOV in Modern Chinese by reanalyzing the verb *bǎ* 'to take hold of' as an objective case marker when the next verb is polysyllabic

(200f.). This process began in the ninth century A.D. and has yielded many sentences today where the only grammatical order is verb final. Likewise, *bèi* 'receive' was reanalyzed as a passive agent marker in the fourth-fifth century A.D., but only became common in the late-nineteenth and early twentieth century (202f.). Li and Thompson emphasized the slow period of transition and cite *bǎ* — O — V sequences which are indeterminately serial constructions or object-marked NP and verb in a simple sentence (1976:485). In a similar manner, Lightfoot 1979:98–115 has chronicled the restructuring of the English VP by reanalysis of the Old English preterite-presents as modals, the reassignment of certain English adjectives to a separate class of quantifiers (168–186) and African serial verbs to prepositions (213–228).

Abductive innovations which produce new rules like Raising to object position in Irish have also been reported elsewhere. For instance, Hahn 1950 proposed that the accusative with infinitive in Latin after *see, hear, remember,* etc. (i.e., the type derived by subject deletion under identity with matrix object) developed from surface sequences when the verb took an object followed by a participle:

(22) *vidi et illam   et hospitem complexam*
I-saw and her(acc) and guest(acc) hug(ptc-acc)

osculantem   (Mil 533–4)
kiss(ptc-acc)
'I saw her and the guest hugging and kissing'

Since the infinitive in nonpresent tenses was formed periphrastically by a combination of a participle and *to be,* with the copula often being deleted, the participle was sometimes ambiguous:

(23) *meminestin   me   gravidam?*   (HT 626)
you-remember me(acc) pregnant(ptc-acc)

Gravidam here is either attributive ('Do you remember me (being) pregnant?') or predicative ('Do you remember that I was pregnant?'). Some sentences could only be analyzed as having a sentential object in which the participle was an elliptical past tense infinitive with *to be* deleted:

(24) *faenus   creditum   audio*   (Most 629)
interest(acc) credit(ptc-acc) I-hear
'I hear that it has been credited for the interest'

That the old NP(acc) — participle(acc) had been reanalyzed as NP(acc) — infinitive(perfect) with the application of Equi-NP Deletion is conclusively shown only when a deductive change admitted a present tense infinitive:

(25) *sed tu   enumquam piscatorem   vidisti* . . .
    but you ever   fisherman(acc) you-saw

piscem   cepisse?   (Rud 987ᵣ8)
fish(acc) catch(inf)
'But did you ever see a fisherman catch a fish?'

On the other hand, there are, as far as I am aware, no reported cases of deductive innovations which are responsible for syntactic class changes or rule addition of the types discussed here. This mode of inference typically extends to new environments a rule previously added by surface reanalysis, as in (25). Timberlake (1977:147) reported the loss of SOR in Finnish, following Anttila's (1972:103–4) description of the phonological merger of final nasals which yielded some nouns ambiguously accusative or genitive. When the verb in a main clause was active and the subject of a following participial predicate was a singular noun, the latter would carry an *-n* ending (the old genitive), which could be analyzed as either an accusative resulting from application of SOR or a genitive in a nonraised construction. The original grammar had possessed a SOR rule which, because of this ambiguity, was gradually lost. Though the locus of the innovation was with singular nouns which were derived objects after positive, active SOR triggers, the rule was subsequently dropped with underlying pronominal subjects, then with plural agentive nouns, and most recently with plural nonagentive nouns (Timberlake 1977:156). In contemporary Finnish SOR no longer exists and genitive is assigned to the subject of all these embedded clauses.

Joseph (1978), using Greek, likewise charted the loss of syntactic rules which resulted in the virtual disappearance of the infinitive. Though he could not explain why the infinitive was lost in the first place, Joseph did reject the traditional explanation (Anttila 1972:102–3) that homophony between the infinitive and the third singular indicative present verb caused the latter to assume the former's function: this phonological change took place too late (tenth-twelfth centuries A.D.). At any rate, the finite constructions started to replace infinitives in late Classical Greek and continued to do so until the fifteenth-sixteenth centuries. This development involved both the step-by-step loss of rules which required infinitives and the loss of lexical triggers. The first overt change is documented when a subjunctive with complementizer replaced the infinitive in purpose clauses after verbs of motion (Joseph 1978: 28) in biblical texts. In later Christian writers the infinitive was replaced by the inflected verb after Subject-equi verbs which formerly took either an infinitive or finite complement (e. g. *thelō* 'want'; 1978:29). During the Byzantine period infinitive complements which had been obligatory with certain verbs became optional (1978:31). Just as in the Finnish rule loss, restrictions on the appearance of the new construction disappeared in specific lexical and syntactic environments.

Li and Thompson (1976:480f.) have similarly detailed the shift from peripheral to central status of the compound causative in Mandarin Chinese. This construction, which consists of two morphemes, 'cause' and 'result' (e.g. *lǎ-chǎng* 'pull-long' = 'lengthen') was introduced in the first century A.D. By the time it was established as a separate category in the seventh-ninth centuries, the number of possible constituents had increased. For instance, the first one, 'cause' in the beginning had only been transitive verbs denoting action; in contemporary Chinese it even allows intransitives here, e.g. *zuò-tā* 'sit-collapse'.

By comparison with most syntactic change reported during the last decade, it becomes obvious that the OIr developments in nonfinite complementation are typical of what is possible in such innovation. It is also evident that deduction cannot produce new rules or cause shifts in syntactic categories, but is the vehicle by which new rules become productive in a grammar. New syntactic rules and categories are instead created out of old patterns and directly motivated by surface ambiguity. The old assumption that synchronic rules are the result of the direct addition of identical (or at least similar) diachronic rules is by now moribund.[5]

The following textual abbreviations were used:

Acallamh	"Acallamh na senórach", ed. Stokes 1900
BH	"Broccán's hymn" from the "Liber hymnorum", ed. Stokes and Strachan 1903:327–349
EMEM	"Echtra mac Echach muigmedoin", ed. Stokes 1903
FR	"Fingal Rónáin", ed. Greene 1955:1–12
Ml	"The Milan glosses and scholia on the psalms", ed. Stokes and Strachan 1901:7–483
O'Don	O'Donovan's law transcripts in the Royal Irish Academy, Dublin
Sg	"Glosses on Priscian (St. Gall)", ed. Stokes and Strachan 1903:49–224
Wb	"The Würzburg glosses and scholia on the Pauline Epistals", ed. Stokes and Strachan 1901:499–712

Notes

1. McCloskey (1980) has recently used the term infinitive in a discussion of a similar clause type in Modern Irish, where he argued for a rule of Infinitive Preposing rather

than Subject Raising. The data he presented have different syntactic properties from what is found in OIr; I would, therefore, ascribe the differences in our analyses to syntactic changes which have taken place since the Middle Irish period.

2. I allude here to Indo-Iranian *-*dhyāi*; for discussion of the morphological problems and bibliography, see Disterheft 1980:13.
3. The first constituent following *be* can also be an adjective; I have, however, simplified my description here by excluding this variant. See Disterheft, 1982, for examples with adjective.
4. If the NP were not moved out of its phrase, its case would still in many environments be indicated by nasalization or lenition (spirantization) of the initial segment of the following word. The NP, however, only rarely affects the *do* in these constructions.
5. This research was partially supported by a grant from the Committee on Productive Research of the University of South Carolina.

References

Andersen, Henning
1973   "Abductive and deductive change", *Lg* 49:765–793.
1974   "Towards a typology of change: bifurcating changes and binary relationships", *Historical linguistics*, edited by J. Anderson and C. Jones (Amsterdam: North Holland), II, 17–60.
Anderson, John M. – Charles Jones (eds.)
1974   *Historical linguistics* I, II (Amsterdam: North Holland).
Anttila, Raimo
1972   *An introduction to historical and comparative linguistics* (New York: Macmillan).
Disterheft, Dorothy
1980   *The syntactic development of the infinitive in Indo-European* (Columbus, Ohio: Slavica).
1982   "Subject Raising in Old Irish", *Current issues in linguistic theory*, edited by Anders Ahlqvist (Amsterdam: Benjamins), 44–53.
Greene, David (ed.)
1955   *Fingal Rónáin and other stories* (Dublin: Institute for Advanced Studies).
Hahn, E. Adelaide
1950   "Genesis of the infinitive with subject accusative", *TAPA* 81:117–129.
Joseph, Brian D.
1978   *Morphology and universals in syntactic change: evidence from Medieval and Modern Greek* (Bloomington, Indiana: Indiana University Linguistics Club).
Keenan, Edward L. – Bernard Comrie
1977   "Noun phrase accessibility and universal grammar", *LI* 8:63–99.
Li, Charles N. (ed.)
1977   *Mechanisms of syntactic change* (Austin: University of Texas Press).
Li, Charles N. – Sandra A. Thompson
1974   "Historical change of word order: a case study in Chinese and its implications", *Historical linguistics*, edited by J. Anderson and C. Jones (Amsterdam: North Holland), I, 199–217.
1976   "Development of the causative in Mandarin Chinese: interaction of diachro-

nic processes in syntax", *The grammar of causative constructions,* ed. by M. Shibatani (New York: Academic Press), 477–492.

Lightfoot, David W.
1979   *Principles of diachronic syntax* (= *Cambridge studies in linguistics* 23) (Cambridge: University Press).

McCloskey, James
1980   "Raising in Modern Irish", *Ériu* 31: 59–99.

Shibatani, Masayoshi (ed.)
1976   *The grammar of causative constructions* (= *Syntax and semantics* 6) (New York: Academic Press).

Stokes, Whitley (ed.)
1900   "Acallamh na senórach", *Irische Texte* 4.1 (Leipzig: Hirzel).
1903   "Echtra mac Echach muigmedoin", *RC* 24:190–203.

Stokes, Whitley – John Strachan (eds.)
1901, 1903 *Thesaurus palaeohibernicus* I, II (Cambridge: University Press) (Reprinted by the Dublin Institute for Advanced Studies: 1975).

Thurneysen, Rudolf
1946   *A grammar of Old Irish* (Dublin: Institute for Advanced Studies).

Timberlake, Alan
1977   "Reanalysis and actualization in syntactic change", *Mechanisms of syntactic change,* edited by C. N. Li (Austin: University of Texas Press), 141–177.

MARINEL GERRITSEN

Divergent word order developments in Germanic languages:
A description and a tentative explanation

0 Introduction

Historical linguists dealing with surface word order at sentence level in the Germanic languages have mostly concerned themselves with reconstruction: establishing the word order of Proto-Germanic was generally attempted on the basis of the syntactic and morphological patterns that were found in the earliest records of the various daughter languages.* Word order reconstruction is no easy matter, though, and this certainly holds for Proto-Germanic, as is clearly shown by the different Proto-Germanic word orders proposed by various scholars.[1] Considering this difficulty, it is remarkable that so few historical linguists have shifted their intention from the reconstruction of Proto-Germanic to a more accessible area of diachronic Germanic syntax: the development of word order from the earliest records to the present.

I am not sure why so many historical linguists have preferred to speculate on the word order in which prehistoric Germans might have communicated. Perhaps the different possibilities for investigating Germanic word order have never even been considered. Whatever the case may be, it is not the purpose of this paper to discuss and speculate on the reasons for this bias towards reconstruction. I will only attempt to show that it might be equally interesting to study Germanic word order change from another point of view: the verb-position changes in surface word order at the sentence level that may be traced from the earliest sources up to the present in each of the Germanic languages.

Such an approach might not only be equally interesting, it might even give us a better insight into the mechanisms of word order change than reconstruction, since it does not only allow us to check word order changes on real data, but also to discover other language phenomena that co-occur with the ones under observation. As a result, this method will provide us with the tools to find possible reasons for the observed changes (cf. Lightfoot 1979:16).

In the first part of this paper I will give a description of two typologically important phenomena in the word order development of sentences in the

Germanic languages: embraciation and inversion (1.). I will then try to explain why the Germanic languages developed differently from one another in these two respects (2.). Finally I will discuss briefly what these findings might mean for reconstruction and theories on syntactic change (3.).

1 Embraciation and inversion in the Germanic languages

1.1 The phenomena of embraciation and inversion

When native speakers of English learn Modern German, they will soon discover that there are some striking differences in the position of finite and non-finite verb in English and German.

a. In the surface word order of German declarative main clauses, the verbal elements do not all show up as one constituent: the finite verb occupies the second position, and all other verbal elements the last position. Nominal objects, for example, occur in between the finite and the non-finite verb.

> (1) *Ich* habe *Peter* gesehen
> I   *have* Peter *seen*
> 'I *have seen* Peter'

b. In German dependent clauses all verbal elements show up at the end of the clause. Nominal objects, for example, appear obligatorily before the verb or verbal complex.

> (2) *dass ich Peter* gesehen habe
> that I Peter *seen have*
> 'that I *have seen* Peter'

c. Inversion of subject and finite verb is obligatory in German declarative main clauses beginning with any other constituent than the subject.

> (3) *Morgen* werde *ich Peter* sehen
> Tomorrow *will* I Peter *see*
> 'Tomorrow I *will see* Peter'

The phenomena mentioned under a. und b. are traditionally regarded as one and the same and are both labeled *Embraciation* (Einklammerung or Umklammerung in the German literature). Under special conditions, for example in afterthoughts and with long constituents, the brace can be broken up in German by Prepositional Phrases and Adverbials. Those constituents then occur to the right of the non-finite verb in declarative main clauses and to the right of the verbal complex in dependent clauses (see Lambert 1976). In view of this phenomenon and the fact that the position of the nominal object in relation to the subject and the verbs is usually regarded as a decisive factor in typological word order studies, I have only considered the position of nominal objects for determining whether a language is embraciating or exbraciating.

The phenomenon under c. is called *Inversion* (or Verb Second rule). Both Embraciation and Inversion play an important role in current theories on word order typology, because their occurrence or non-occurrence is a factor in characterizing a language as SOV (+ embraciation, − inversion), (X)VSO (− embraciation, + inversion) or (X)SVO (− embraciation, − inversion).

1.2 The Standard Modern Germanic languages

My study of embraciation and inversion in the Modern Germanic languages is restricted in two respects. In the first place I have left out of consideration those Germanic languages which have only come into existence relatively recently and which have been strongly influenced by members of other language families: Afrikaans and Yiddish. In my opinion, these two qualities make them less useful for discovering general internal linguistic factors behind word order change in the Germanic languages. The restriction as to recent origin needs no further argumentation in a real-time investigation while, as a result of the strong influence from other Germanic languages, the syntax of Afrikaans and Yiddish could also have been modified by non-linguistic factors, which are even more difficult to determine than linguistic ones.[2] The second limitation lies in the fact that I have only taken into consideration the Standard Germanic languages. As far as I have been able to determine, the word order phenomena discussed here do not deviate from those in the dialects. Most dialect atlases provide little information on syntax, though, so that I have not been able to investigate this thoroughly.[3]

According to the standard grammars of the Modern Germanic languages embraciation of nominal objects occurs in German, Frisian and Dutch dependent and declarative main clauses only.[4] Inversion is obligatory in all the Germanic languages, except in English[5], in declarative main clauses beginning with *any* other constituent than the subject. In Modern English some constituents may trigger verb second order optionally, to serve some special pragmatic functions (Green 1980), when they occur in front position (Stockwell: this volume). A few other constituents trigger Inversion obligatorily (Stockwell: this volume).

Although inversion is obligatory in all Germanic languages other than English, this does not mean that fronting of other constituents than subjects is subject to the same syntactic and pragmatic conditions for all the Germanic inversion languages. This is of importance because the fewer conditions on fronting an inversion language has, the more it deviates from a non-inversion language (e.g. English). I have not been able to determine the conditions on fronting for all the languages concerned in detail, but it seems to me that there are not many differences between the various languages. This idea is supported by the fact that counts for spoken Norwegian, German and Dutch show that about 40% of all declarative main clauses have some other constituent than the subject in front position in all three languages (Faarlund 1981, Jansen 1978, 1981), making it plausible that, with respect to inversion, all Germanic languages deviate from English to the same extent.

It appears that, with respect to Embraciation and Inversion, Modern Germanic languages can be divided into three groups:

a. English (− Embraciation, − obligatory Inversion)
b. Scandinavian Languages (− Embraciation, + obligatory Inversion)
c. German, Frisian, and Dutch (+ Embraciation and + obligatory Inversion).

These findings are summarized in Table 1, column a, b, and c. In the next section I will show that this tripartition can only partly be recovered in the earliest records of the languages.

1.3 The findings in the earliest records of the Germanic languages

Before dealing with the results of my survey on embraciation and inversion in the earliest sources of the Germanic languages, I will point out two problematic aspects of this investigation which might complicate the comparison between the various languages: the differences in the character and age of the earliest records. It is frequently pointed out that syntax could have been seriously affected by factors such as genre, style, rhyme, metre etc. (e.g. Werth 1970:28−29, Watkins 1976:314−315). Since the earliest sources of the Germanic languages consist of texts which differ in these respects (see Table 1, column h), this could hamper the comparison. I do agree with this point of view in general, but, for the phenomena under consideration here, I do not consider these problems very serious. I do not believe, for example, that a language that never embraciates will suddenly start doing so in a certain style. The second problem is that the earliest sources do not all date from the same period (see Table 1, column g). This complicates the comparison because the further back in time a comparison between the various Germanic

Table 1. *Embraciation* and *inversion* in the Germanic languages according to the Standard Grammars and the oldest records ²)⁴)⁵)⁶)

Germanic languages	CURRENT NORMS			OLDEST RECORDS				
	a Embraciation in declarative main clauses SVfOV	b in dependent clauses SOVf	c Obligatory Inversion in declarative main clauses XVfS	d Embraciation in declarative main clauses SVfOV	e in dependent clauses SOVf	f Obligatory Inversion in declarative main clauses XVfS	g Date of oldest record	h Name
English	–	–	∓	∓	±	∓	741	Anglo Saxon Chronicle
Icelandic	–	–	+	–	∓	+	±1000	Edda Saga's Runes
Norwegian	–	–	+	∓	∓	+	±1000	
Swedish	–	–	+	∓	∓	+	±1200	Laws
Danish	–	–	+			+	±1300	–
Faroese	–	–	+	?	?	?	–	–
German	+	+	+	±	±	±	±800	Isidor
Frisian	+	+	+	±	±	?	±1470	Letters
Dutch	+	+	+	±	±	±	±1275	Limburgse leven van Jezus

– never occurs
+ always occurs
? no data available

± mostly occurs
∓ seldom occurs

languages is attempted, the less likely is it that records will be available to compare all the Germanic languages of one particular period. This problem can partly be remedied by studying the word order changes for all the languages concerned up to 1475, the date of the earliest source for Frisian. The available Frisian sources happen to be the youngest, compared to those for the other Germanic languages, so we will unfortunately never know anything about Frisian word order at the time of, for example, the first part of the Anglo Saxon Chronicle, simply because no data are available on the Frisian of that particular period.

A summary of the occurrence and non-occurrence of Embraciation and Inversion in the oldest sources of the respective Germanic languages is given in Table 1, column d, e, and f.[6] This table shows that for all Germanic languages other than English the word orders which are obligatory in the Modern Standard languages are either very frequent or also obligatory in the earliest sources of these languages. The difference between the Modern Scandinavian languages and German, Frisian and Dutch with regard to embraciation are already present in the earliest sources. The way in which the differences appear varies, though: we encounter absolute differences between the standard languages, but gradual differences between the languages in their earliest sources. Inversion, the phenomenon that distinguishes Modern English from the other Modern Germanic languages, also sets apart Old English from the other Old and Middle Germanic languages. The tripartition found in the Modern languages (see 1.2) is apparently also present in the earliest sources, though it is expressed partly in a different manner. Old English and Modern English differ strongly as regards embraciation. In Old English it occurs frequently in dependent clauses and sometimes in declarative main clauses, while Modern English shows no embraciation at all. In this respect Old English in fact resembles Old German, Middle Dutch and Middle Frisian to a certain extent.

The next section discusses the changes in embraciation and inversion that have taken place in each of the Germanic languages from their oldest sources to the present.

1.4 The changes over time

In all Germanic languages, other than English, deviations from the standard word order disappear gradually over time.[7] Variation is more and more restricted by syntactic and pragmatic factors and, by the time the various Standard languages are established, the few remaining exceptions are overridden by the normalizing influence of the Standard. The disappearance of embraciation in English also proceeds gradually. Exbraciation, on the other hand, seems to have already been well established before the standard language comes into existence. It appears from the study by Bean (1976:146, 173, 180) that embraciation and true verb final constructions hardly ever occur in the main clauses of the Anglo Saxon Chronicle after 884, while in dependent clauses it disappears after 1122.

For inversion the changes in English are more complex. It might appear from Table 1 that no changes have taken place at all, but this is not the case. In all periods inversion may occur in English under certain conditions, but the conditions change over time. Stockwell (this volume) has made a first attempt to trace the changes in these conditions factors. On the basis of Bean's data (1976:145), summarized in Table 2, he claims that in late Old English inversion was far less constrained than it is in Early Old English and Modern English. Inversion is apparently sufficiently frequent for Stockwell to call it the prose word order norm for late Old English. Table 2 shows that the frequency of inversion increases up to 1001 and then gradually declines. By the end of the 14th century it occurs only rarely. The few constituents that trigger verb second optionally or obligatorily when occurring in front position in Modern English are in part reflexives of the Old English structures and in part innovations of Early Modern English (Stockwell, this volume).

Table 2. The word order of declarative main clauses beginning with another constituent than the subject in the Anglo Saxon Chronicle (based on Bean (1976:145))

	XVS N		XSV N		T
Before 755	38	29%	93	71%	131
755–860	41	52%	38	48%	79
865–884	59	97%	2	3%	61
885–891	22	73%	8	17%	30
892–900	39	93%	3	7%	42
958–1001	21	100%	0	0%	21
1049–1066	64	82%	14	18%	78
1122–1124	37	88%	5	12%	42
1132–1140	29	76%	9	24%	38

The changes in the use of embraciation and inversion in the Germanic languages may be summarized as follows.

Inversion showed the following changes:

a. It disappeared in English;
b. It became obligatory in German and Dutch.

In Embraciation the following changes took place:

a. It disappeared in English and in the Scandinavian languages;
b. It became obligatory in German, Frisian and Dutch.

A tentative explanation for these changes will be given in the next section.

2 Tentative explanation of the tripartition of the Germanic languages

This is not the first time the observation has been made that the Germanic languages developed from one group of languages with more or less the same word order possibilities to three different language groups. At the end of his outstanding work on word order change from Proto-Germanic to Early Germanic, Fourquet (1938:223) makes the same observation. He does not venture much of an explanation, though, and indicates the complexity of the issue when he writes: "Ce sont des causes infimes qui ont pu faire pencher la balance" ("Infinitely small causes could have tipped the balance") (Fourquet 1938:233). Nearly half a century of continued research later we still find ourselves in the same, or maybe even worse situation, for nowadays it is often questioned whether explanation of linguistic change, and particularly syntactic change (see Harris this volume and 1981), is possible at all. In spite of the problematic aspects of explaining language change, I will try to point out some possible causes for the divergent word order developments in the Germanic languages. I will first deal with the separation related to inversion and then with the divergence connected with embraciation.

2.1 Inversion and the creole character of English[8]

I have shown that inversion has disappeared almost completely in English, has become obligatory in German and Dutch and has already become obligatory in the earliest sources of the other Germanic languages. The disappearance of inversion in English seems to be the exception and demands explanation.

Some linguists have argued that the frequent occurrence of inversion in late Old English does not constitute evidence for an ongoing word order change, but that it is due to the style in which this part of the Anglo Saxon

Chronicle has been written. Bean (1976:149) views it as a consequence of the Chronicle's vivid style which would lend itself particularly for XVS order. Fourquet (1938:90) accounts for it by referring to Aelfred's efforts to establish a literary tradition during his reign. I believe, though, that we have to look at the problem from a different angle, in view of the developments in the other Germanic languages. Instead of attempting to explain why inversion was so frequent in late Old English we must explain why it did not become obligatory in English, as it did in the other Germanic languages.

I do agree with Givón (1977), Stockwell (1977) and Vennemann (1974b) that a natural word order drift may follow the paradigm SOV → (X)VSO → SVO. From that point of view the English development is quite normal, but the really interesting questions concern the short time-span in which verb third order was stabilized in English. It is a short time-span, at least, in comparison with the long-lasting intermediate stage between XVS and SV in which the other Germanic languages still find themselves after many centuries and which they do not seem to be on the verge of abandoning, as far as I know.

Several internal linguistic factors have been cited to account for the quick regularization of verb third order in English.[9] For few of these factors it has been determined whether or not they were also present in the other Germanic languages. Givón (1977:175) is an important exception. He argues that the more often languages have subject agreement conjugation, the less likely they will have regularized SV order. In this way he connects inversion with the viable subject agreement paradigm in German and Old English, while he relates the infrequency or complete absence of inversion in Modern English and the Scandinavian languages to the largely eroded subject agreement conjugation in those languages. I find this explanation unconvincing since it relies partly on incorrect data, so that counterexamples are easy to find. In Modern Norwegian and Modern Dutch, for example, 40% of the declarative main clauses have inversion (see 1.2), but both languages have a similar subject agreement paradigm as English does. We apparently need other explanations for the fast development to verb third order in English.

Explanations ascribing this development explicitly to factors present in no other Germanic language than English have in common that they often refer to the changes resulting from the Scandinavian Invasions and settlements (± 787–1042) and the Norman Conquest (1066–1200). The early Scandinavian invaders in England were motivated largely by the desire to plunder. They did not have much contact with the Anglo Saxons, so they had little influence on their language. The Danes and Norwegians who came in the last quarter of the 9th century and the 10th century settled in England and did have continuous contact with the original population. They were socially not very different from the Anglo Saxons and willing to assimilate and consequently they felt a need for communication. Fisiak (1977:249) describes the development of a kind of interlanguage as a result of this contact. Since Anglo Saxon and Old Norse were cognate languages, they already resembled each other to a great extent and were probably even mutually intelligible, but in both languages additional changes were introduced that made them converge still more. This process may have resembled pidginization, but since the use of the interlanguage seems to have been restricted to special domains, it is doubtful whether it ever reached creolization. It is beyond dispute, though, that the alternate use of the interlanguage and English can be considered one of the factors which have caused a development in English that differed from developments in the other Germanic languages. The alternation between languages brought about both special changes and accelerated the normal processes of change.

The quick disappearance of inversion is apparently not a direct result of the Scandinavian invasions and settlements, because it only declined after the year 1001 (cf. Table 2). Various scholars have suggested that the Scandinavian invasion might have caused this word order change indirectly. The loss of inflexions that came about as a result of the Scandinavian invasions is thought by some linguists to have affected the fixing of English word order in the 12th, 13th and 14th century. This causal relationship is open to question (cf. Fisiak 1977:254, Steele 1978:609), but other reasons can be given to view the fast development of verb third order in English as an indirect result of Scandinavian interference. According to Bailey and Maroldt (1977: 26) it caused a linguistic instability that paved the way for substantial changes during and after the Norman Conquest. Bailey and Maroldt as well as Domingue (1977) maintain that although the number of French-speaking Anglo-Norman immigrants in England was probably rather small and only the influential part of the population used French, the Norman Conquest contributed to possible creolization of Old English. The authors of both articles describe an enormous quantity of innovations in English on a lexical, morphological and phonological level, which all came about during and after the Conquest and which may be considered characteristic of creoles. However, neither of these articles mention word order. This is not surprising since the general syntactic characteristics of creoles have not yet been formulated thoroughly.[11] Still, I believe that the stabilization of verb third order in Middle English should also be considered a direct result of its creole character, if it is indeed plausible that Middle English is to some extent a creole.

According to Voorhoeve (personal communication) verb third order is a hard and fast rule in creoles for sentences beginning with a constituent other than the subject. My own survey of about twenty creole languages confirms this observation: without exception all of them use the XSV-order, even those few creoles based on languages that do not have XSV order at all. Moreover, it appears from other studies that in cases of interference or pidginization of two or more languages of which only one or none has XSV-order, a development of verb third order still takes place (Bickerton and Givón 1976, Clyne 1980:30, Voskuil 1956). These facts support the hypothesis that the fast development of verb third order in English might be due to its creole character. This is all the more plausible, since XSV-order had already been almost completely regularized in Norman French, one of the languages on which this 'creole' English is based.[12]

The question may arise whether the rapid grammaticalization of verb third order in English could be considered a direct influence from French. This has been suggested for example by Fisiak (1977:255–256), who ascribes the influence of French to its prestigious position in Middle English society: speakers of French formed the most influential stratum of society and, during the whole Middle English period, French was the language of written documents and correspondence. This prestigious position of French may have faciliated its influence on English.

Fisiak's article appeared in the same year as the articles by Bailey and Maroldt (1977) and Domingue (1977) and could, therefore, not have been a reaction to their viewing Middle English as a language with creole characteristics. It is implicit in Fisiak's study, though, that he considers the sociolinguistic context of Middle English less appropriate for creolization than the Old English context, and he even doubts whether Old English is actually a creolized language (Fisiak 1977:249). He shows that the French-English communicative community was completely different from the Scandinavian-English one: French and English were mutually unintelligible, no more than 10% of the population used both English and French, throughout the Middle Ages, and a great social distance existed between French and English-speaking populations.

I cannot decide here whether the fast stabilization of verb third order in Middle English is due to a creolization process involving Scandinavian and French or to direct influence from French. In order to make such a decision, we first of all need more complete knowledge of the sociolinguistic context of French and English in the Middle English society, because the descriptions in the articles mentioned here contradict each other in some important respects. For example, the authors hold different views about the degree of social distance between the English and French speaking populations. In my opinion, only a scholar with a thorough knowledge of the history of Medieval England, as well as of sociolinguistic issues, is qualified to judge whether the sociolinguistic context in Medieval England supports a creole hypothesis or a hypothesis positing influence from French. To decide on the most plausible hypothesis, we especially need answers to two important questions: what is the position of word order among the linguistic changes under influence of creolization and what are the constraints on borrowing of word order at the sentence level. Borrowing is generally regarded as a weak tool for explanation. This certainly holds for borrowing at the sentence level, since, to my knowledge, no convincing example has ever been presented (cf. Moravcsik 1978: 102). This would seem to lead us to prefer the creole hypothesis, but in the case of Middle English there has been such ample opportunity for borrowing that its influence can hardly be refuted. Be this as it may, it does seem plausible that the rapid disappearance of Inversion in Middle English — at least in comparison with the other Germanic languages — is a direct consequence of the fact that William the Conqueror decided to cast covetous eyes on England rather than on one of the other Germanic countries.

2.2 Embraciation and the development of an analytical verb system

It has been pointed out in 1.4 that we must try to account for the disappearance of embraciation in English and the Scandinavian languages and for its grammaticalization in German, Frisian and Dutch. Finding explanations for the divergence in the Germanic languages with respect to embraciation is even more difficult, though, than explaining the differences concerning inversion, since for all Germanic languages except the English, the absolute differences between the Modern Standard languages reflect the gradual ones that were found between the languages of the earliest sources. Therefore, it seems likely that for all the Germanic languages, except English, the motivations for the divergence were already present before the period from which we have data. It is evident that this lack of access to factors determining the divergence complicates its explanation.

Fortunately, the disappearance of Embraciation in English has taken place in a period for which data are available, so that it is possible to trace the process. Stockwell (1977:296) has suggested the following sequence of word order changes from Germanic to Modern English:

(4) (a) SO(V)v → vSO(V) by Comment Focusing
    (b) vSO(V) → xvSO(V) by Linkage or Topicalization
    (c) TvX(V) → SvX(V) by Subject = Topic
    (d) SvX(V) → SvVX by Exbraciation
    (e) Subordinate Order → Main Order by Generalization (or, at least, elimination of whatever difference existed.)

According to this sequence of changes, embraciation in English disappeared after inversion, but in 1.4 we have seen that in the other Germanic languages the disappearance seems to occur in the reversed order, stage (c) after (d) and (e). The Scandinavian languages pass through all changes except (c). The output of stage (b) reflects the word order of Modern German, Dutch and Frisian. In the remaining part of this paper I will only deal with the phenomenon under (d) and (e): exbraciation.

Stockwell suggests that embraciation in English disappeared because a number of phenomena in Old English, the so-called 'motivations for exbraciation', destroyed the verb-final appearance of the language and led to a reinterpretation of English as a non-embraciating language (Stockwell 1977:310). He presents the following 'motivations for exbraciation'

a) Simple verbs occur far more frequently than complex ones in Old English and consequently all objects and adverbial material appear in those sentences after the main verb.
b) Extraposition of relative clauses, conjuncts and appositives.
c) Postdeposition of adverbs and afterthoughts.
d) Rightward movement of sentential objects and subjects.

I believe that the first 'motivation for exbraciation' is more important in the change from embraciation to exbraciation than the others, first of all, for the simple reason that every sentence has a verb and therefore verbs occur far more frequently than the parts of speech mentioned in Stockwell's other motivations. Secondly, because the occurrence to the right of the non-finite verb or verbal complex of afterthoughts, relative clauses, sentential subjects and objects is also found in accepted verb final languages and does not seem to have resulted in reinterpretation as a non verb final language in these cases.

If we assume that the frequent occurrence of simple verbs in Old English is indeed the principal cause for the appearance of exbraciation, it may also be assumed that the divergent development in the Germanic languages is due to the fact that this motivation for exbraciation has not been sufficiently present in German, Frisian and Dutch to lead to reinterpretation at the time when these languages were in the exbraciating stage of their development (cf. Gerritsen 1980:133). In other words, the divergence might be explained by the fact that the English and Scandinavian verb systems were more synthetic when those languages entered the exbraciation stage than the verb systems of German, Frisian and Dutch when they began to exbraciate. Since we do not know when each of the respective languages reached the exbraciation stage or to what extent their verb systems were analytic at the time they entered it, this hypothesis is difficult to prove. Despite these inevitable missing links in the argumentation, I will try and trace whether the history of the periphrastic verb system in the Germanic languages supports the hypothesis, assuming that all the languages entered the exbraciation stage at the same time.

2.2.1 The development of a periphrastic tense system in the Germanic languages

It is generally accepted that the Germanic tense system developed from synthetic to analytic. For Proto-Germanic only two tenses have been reconstructed, which were both inflected: present and preterit. Gothic, the earliest of the derivate languages, also works with only these two tenses, but in the earliest sources of the Nordic and Westgermanic languages, analytic tenses for the past (perfect and pluperfect) do already occur. These periphrastic constructions are formed with the verbs 'to have' or 'to be', the original situation being that in the active voice transitive verbs normally selected the former and intransitives the latter.[13] Since the periphrastic formations with 'to be' occur even in the earliest sources, they are considered an indigenous development. It has been suggested, though, that the existence of similar constructions in Romance could have stimulated their use (Lockwood 1969:115). The constructions with 'to have' originated from reinterpretation of the verb *have* as an auxiliary in constructions such as Old German (5) in which the participle was constructed as an adjective modifying the accusative object of the main verb *have*.

(5)   *ir*   *den*   *christianum*   *namun*   *intfangan*   *eigut*
      PRO ACC m sg   ACC m sg   ACC m sg   PA-PRT   PRES 2pl
      you   the   Christian   name   accepted   have/own
(Exhortatio)

Since the reflexes of this change are still found in the oldest sources of the Germanic languages, it is thought to be relatively recent: it probably did not arise until just before the documented period. A similar development has taken place in the evolution from Latin to Romance (cf. Benveniste 1968:86, Bynon 1979³:61) and the genesis of a periphrastic tense with 'to have' in Germanic is assumed to be the result of imitation from the Romance languages. The evolution of an analytic future tense mainly took place during the documented period. Previous to that development the present tense was sufficient to express futurity. Again, the development of future tense is thought to have been encouraged by its existence in Latin and French (Lockwood 1968:113). The development of an analytic present and preterit in English is only found in the do-periphrasis used to construct the present and preterit of negative, emphatic and interrogative sentences in the active voice. Since such periphrastic constructions do not appear until the thirteenth century and since even in the fifteenth century they were only a peripheral category (Samuels 1972:173), they are not important for the argumentation here, because embraciation in English had already disappeared before that time (cf. 1.4).

It is clear from the above that Romance is believed to have played a prominent part in the development of the periphrastic tenses in the Germanic languages: Romance is thought to have stimulated the use of the periphrastic perfect with 'to be' and the periphrastic future, and to have been a model for the periphrastic perfect with 'to have'. Although several eminent linguists have advanced and adhered to this theory (Brinkmann 1931:25, Lockwood 1969:75, Meillet 1917:129), others have their doubts about it. Especially the hypothesis that the development of the periphrastic tenses with 'to have' is due to borrowing from Romance has been criticized. Ebert (1978:59) argues that Old Icelandic, which certainly cannot have been influenced by Romance, does have a periphrastic perfect with 'to have', albeit rarely (Heusler 1913:144). To me, this only seems an apparent counterargument, because the development of a novel complex tense system in Icelandic is said to be due to Irish influence (Haugen 1976:307). Other opponents of the Romance influence theory are Kern (1912:8) and Zieglschmid (1929:57), who both consider the development of the periphrastic perfect with 'to have' an indigenous Germanic development. They argue that somewhat parallel developments are found in certain modern Indo-European languages outside the area in question and they do not believe that borrowing of Romance lexical elements in Germanic has occurred. Their argumentation is all the more convincing, since it is in line with Moravcsik's (1978:110) first constraint on borrowing: "No non-lexical language property can be borrowed unless the borrowing language already includes borrowed lexical items from the same source language". It appears from the study of Frings (1966, maps), though, that borrowing of lexical items from Romance did in fact take place and that weakens the argument against borrowing of the periphrastic perfect. Zieglschmid (1929:59) does not completely reject possible influence from Romance, maintaining that the occurrence of the periphrastic tense with 'to have' in Romance could have favored its development in Germanic. This is exactly Bynon's (1979[3]:250) line of reasoning: the inbuilt tendency towards analytic structures in Germanic does not exclude the possibility of such innovations having developed in a contact situation.

In any event, whether the origin of periphrastic tenses is ascribed to direct influence from Romance or — as for the other periphrastic active tense formations — to an inbuilt tendency accelerated by Romance influence, both hypotheses support the theory that a relationship exists between the grammaticalization of embraciation and the speed with which the periphrastic tense system spread across the Germanic language area. Lockwood (1969:75) maintains that most likely the periphrastic tenses established themselves first in West Germanic, in the area where the Romance influence was the greatest, gradually spreading subsequently to Scandinavia, the area where Romance had little or no influence. Unfortunately, he does not give evidence for this hypothesis and I have not been able to trace when the periphrastic tenses were grammaticalized in each of the languages concerned. If this hypothesis is indeed correct, it might explain the disappearance of exbraciation in the Scandinavian languages as opposed to its grammaticalization in German, Frisian and Dutch, since the Scandinavian languages used periphrastic tenses to a lesser extent than the other three languages when they entered the exbraciation phase. This does not explain the disappearance of embraciation in English, but there are reasons to believe that the English tense system developed from synthetic to analytic at a later stage than the tense system of the other West Germanic languages. First of all, this is plausible from a historical point of view: during the period in which the periphrastic tenses developed in the Romance languages — between the third and the seventh century AD (Benveniste 1968:88) — there was less of a relationship between England and the area where the Romance languages were spoken than between the German, Frisian and Dutch area and the Romance area. Secondly, there also is linguistic evidence that the tense system of English developed from synthetic to analytic at a later date than that of German and Dutch. Unfortunately, I have not been able to find data about the development of periphrastic tenses in Frisian, so, the English development of periphrastic tenses could only be compared with developments in German and Dutch.

With respect to the future tense, no great differences can be traced between the languages in question, since the idea of futurity is most commonly expressed by the present tense and periphrastic forms developed relatively late in the course of the Middle Ages.[14] The future-like periphrasis, especially with 'shall' and sometimes with 'will', seems to have occurred more frequently in Old German than in Old English: Mustanoja (1960:483) discusses its rare occurrence in Old English, while Paul (1920:147) states that it is found 'öfters' (rather often) in Old German translations from Latin.

With respect to the development of the periphrastic past tenses remarkable differences may be noticed between English, on the one hand, and German and Dutch on the other. In Old English, perfect or pluperfect was expressed very often by means of the preterit. According to Mustanoja (1960:499), many linguists believe that it is not until the early middle English period that participial constructions with 'to be' and 'to have' can be regarded as true perfects and pluperfects. Before that time, the past participles are considered to be predicate adjectives. Both Mustanoja and Jespersen (1938:193) locate the gradual development of the periphrastic past tense system in English in the latter part of the Middle Ages. Visser (1966:751) places it even later, stating that it took place in the Early Modern English period. The earliest sources of Dutch show an abundant use of perfects and pluperfects, according to Weijnen (1971:88). He even points out that there is a perfect periphrase with 'to have' in the only Old Dutch sentence that has been handed down to us:

> (6) *Hebban olla vogalas nestas bigunnan hinase hi(c) enda thu*
>   Have   all   birds   nests   begun   except I   and you

The German periphrastic past tense does not yet occur in the earliest sources of Old German, but it does appear in the beginning of the 9th century and in Notker (922–1022) it is already grammaticalized to a certain extent, according to Ebert (1978:58), Koch (1974:78) and Lockwood (1968:115). In subsequent periods periphrastic past tenses became more and more common usage and by the 12th century the perfect must have almost taken over from the preterit (Lockwood 1969:121). It seems, therefore, that English did not only develop periphrastic tenses more slowly than German and Dutch did, there is also a difference in the number of functions of the perfect, at least between English and German. The perfect in English has retained the one function it originally had in all the Germanic languages: completion of an action. In German, on the other hand, it has become the general tense to express past, and it has taken over the functions of both perfect and preterit (Mustanoja 1960:505).

In short, the different developments of the periphrastic tense system in English, on the one hand, and German and Dutch, on the other, corroborate the hypotheses that exbraciation might be grammaticalized in English and not in German and Dutch because there was less of a change in the English tense system from synthetic to analytic.

There is also other evidence for a relationship between the development of periphrastic tenses and the grammaticalization of embraciation. Lockwood (1968:121) describes the competition between German preterit and perfect. During the 12th century the perfect tense largely took over from the preterit and the use of the perfect for preterit spread from the South of Germany to the North. If the occurrence of periphrastic tenses has indeed contributed to the grammaticalization of embraciation, we would expect it to have appeared first in the parts of Germany where the use of perfect for preterit was first regularized, namely first in Southern Germany and later in the other parts. These are precisely the findings of Maurer (1926). According to him, the grammaticalization of embraciation did in fact gradually spread from the Southern part of Germany to the North.

It is clear from the above that the different developments of the periphrastic tenses in the Germanic languages, which other historical linguists have assumed and which I have only partly been able to trace, lend support to the hypothesis that the slower development of the tense system from synthetic to analytic in English and the Scandinavian languages in comparison with German, Frisian and Dutch, contributed to the disappearance of embraciation in English and the Scandinavian languages and, on the other hand, to its grammaticalization in German, Frisian and Dutch.

2.2.2 The development of a periphrastic and a synthetic passive in the Germanic languages

Although remnants of the Indo-European inflected passive have been preserved in the present tense of Gothic only, it is generally assumed that the periphrastic Germanic passive developed from a synthetic one. The genesis of the periphrastic passive probably took place in the period of Common Germanic and it is considered to be an indigenous Germanic development (Ebert 1978:61; Kossuth 1981:2; Lockwood 1968:142; Zieglschmid 1929: 29). Since periphrastic passives occur in all the Germanic languages, even in the earliest sources, we cannot trace the change from synthetic to analytic to determine whether it ocurred at an earlier date in the 'embraciating' languages than in the others.

Still, a difference did arise in the way passivity was expressed in the Nordic and Western Germanic languages: a novel synthetic medio-passive originated between 600 and 1000 in the Scandinavian languages. This development caused the verb system of Scandinavian to become less analytic than that of the other Germanic languages. The mark of the synthetic medio-passive was an enclitic derived from the reflexive pronoun. As a suffix (*s/st*) added to the active forms it could have reflexive, reciprocal, medial, active or passive meaning, competing in most of these meanings with other devices. Thus, for expressing the passive, the Old Swedish form (7) could also be expressed by (8) and after 1400 also by (9).

(7) *Klaedhas* 'be dressed', 'clothe oneself', 'get dressed'

(8) *Varda klaedd* 'be dressed'

(9) *Bliva klaedd* 'be dressed'

In the oldest sources of Swedish the use of the synthetic passive is frequent, though. The different meanings of forms like (7) disappeared in the course of time and their meaning became limited to the expression of passivity. In modern times periphrastic passives became increasingly productive (Haugen 1976:309, 378; Wessén 1970:198).

The occurrence of synthetic and periphrastic passives side by side, even in the oldest sources of Scandinavian, is more evidence that the verb system of Scandinavian was more synthetic than that of the other Germanic languages, and this evidence supports the hypothesis that exbraciation continued to exist in those languages because their verb systems were more synthetic than in the 'embraciating languages'.

2.2.3   The development of periphrastic durative aspect in the Germanic languages

It is generally assumed that in Proto and Early Germanic aspect oppositions were more elaborate than they are nowadays and that they used to be expressed synthetically, by means of prefixes. In the course of time the aspect distinctions either disappeared or were expressed by other means. One of the most important developments was the genesis of the periphrasis with a present participle to express the durative aspect. According to Mossé (1938: I, 37), the development of these periphrastic forms was infinitely richer in the West Germanic languages than in the others. He shows that the constructions with a present participle were especially frequent in the language of scholars and this leads him to ascribe their origin to borrowing from Latin, which might explain, at the same time, why this construction hardly occurs in the Scandinavian languages. Other linguists have proposed that this development must be indigenous, though perhaps favored by Latin influence, since the construction also occurs in other Indo-European languages (cf. Visser 1973: 1988).

In any event, the geographic distribution of this construction in the oldest sources of the Germanic languages corroborates the hypothesis that the grammaticalization of exbraciation in the Scandinavian languages, as opposed to German, Frisian and Dutch, might be related to the more synthetic character of the verb system in the Nordic Germanic languages. The fact that embraciation disappeared in English and not in the other West Germanic languages does not seem to be related to divergent developments in the periphrasis with a present participle. In all the languages concerned, it occurred with more or less the same frequency in the oldest sources, but in the latter part of the

Middle Ages it disappeared in all languages, except German and English. The periphrases with 'werden' evolved into the future tense in German in the course of the Middle Ages. In English, the periphrastic constructions with the present participle developed into the expanded form (*He was/is going*), but it was not until 1500 that it became frequent. Visser (1973:1997) quotes Leah Dennis (1940:860) and agrees when she states that at present, English uses five to ten times as many progressive forms as it did in 1600 and ten to twenty times as many as in 1500. In other words, the full development of this construction, which made the English verb system more analytic in this respect than that of the other West Germanic languages, took place after the period when embraciation had disappeared in English and therefore it cannot be viewed as a counterexample to my hypothesis.

2.2.4 The development of periphrastic mood in the Germanic languages

In all the Germanic languages the morphological mood distinctions on the verbs were either replaced by a periphrasis with modals or the mood disappeared completely. This change seems to be far more complex than the ones I have described above. So far I have not been able to trace its development in all the Germanic languages. I do have the impression, though, that in the whole Germanic language area the change from a synthetic to an analytic mood-system took place relatively late.

Maybe this change came about even later than the stabilization of the standard word order patterns and, consequently, it might not have had any influence at all. This should obviously be investigated more thoroughly.

2.2.5 Concluding remarks on the connection between the grammaticalization of embraciation and the genesis of a periphrastic verb-system

The data presented in this section support my hypothesis that the divergent development of the Germanic languages with respect to Embraciation are related to differences in the analytic character of the verb-system at the time these languages entered the Exbraciation stage. The differences between English and the Scandinavian languages on the one hand and German, Frisian and Dutch on the other, may be due to differences in the development of periphrastic tenses. Besides, the development of a synthetic passive next to a periphrastic passive in the Scandinavian languages and the divergent developments regarding to the periphrasis with a present participle could be attributed to the differences between the Nordic languages and German,

Frisian and Dutch. However, the relationship between the grammaticalization of embraciation and the rise of an analytic verb-system definitely needs to be investigated more thoroughly. It is evident that the divergent developments with regard to Embraciation are not necessarily caused by the difference in analycity of the verb systems in the languages concerned. Other factors may also have contributed to this change (cf. Vennemann, this volume). The disappearance of embraciation in English, for example, may also be due partly to its creole character or to influences from French (cf. 2.1), since the brace is one of the first syntactic phenomena that disappear under influence of language contact (cf. Clyne 1980:30).

3 Concluding remarks

Assuming that my description of the divergent word order developments in the various Germanic languages and my tentative explanations are correct — at least to some extent — they seem to inspire some notes of caution for historical syntacticians.

In the first place, it should not be presumed without question that the syntactic development of one particular language is representative for that of all members of a language family. Curiously enough, the word order development of English has, nonetheless, been taken to be representative for that of the other Germanic languages (e.g. Vennemann, 1974, a, b), although English word order development is in fact the most deviant.

In the second place, it is not possible to reconstruct or predict which word order change would have taken place in the past or will take place in the future when we have data for one stage of a language only. This is clearly illustrated by my observation that the word order in all the Germanic languages was more or less the same initially, while three distinctly different types developed in later stages.

In the third place, the social, cultural, and historical setting of a language is of major importance in questions of language change. In this paper I have suggested that word order developments in the Germanic languages are closely connected with such non-linguistic factors and I believe that they should not be taken lightly, since they may play an important role in syntactic change.

It is evident from these remarks that the prospects for word order reconstruction are not encouraging, given our present state of knowledge. So many factors involved in syntactic change are difficult to trace, that an attempt to reconstruct word order changes that may have taken place in the past seems to be a precarious undertaking.

As far as the formulation of theories of word order change are concerned, I am somewhat more optimistic than, for example, Lass (1980), who believes that word order change is as unpredictable as clothing fashions. As I have been at least partially successful in explaining why the Germanic languages underwent divergent word order changes, I believe that it will eventually be possible to develop a theory of word order change. I do agree with Harris (1981), though, that many more problems need to be solved, before such a theory of word order change can be fully formulated.

Notes

* This paper reports on research in progress on syntactic change in the Germanic languages. The Dutch version of this paper was presented at the Twelfth Annual Meeting of the Linguistic Society of the Netherlands. I am grateful to the participants in the meeting, particularly to Simon Dik, Frank Jansen and Jan Kooij, and to the participants of the Historical Syntax Conference, especially Jacek Fisiak, Xavier Dekeyser, Karen Kossuth and Theo Vennemann, for fruitful discussion concerning the matters dealt with in this paper. I also thank Henriëtte Schatz for polishing style and content of this paper.

1. For example, Lehmann (1972) and Ries (1908) SOV; Schneider (1938) VSO; Wakkernagel (1920) Verb-second; Delbrück (1911), Koch (1974), Hopper (1975) SOV under way to SVO; Braune (1894), Fourquet (1938), Hirt (1929), Meillet (1917) free word order.

2. Obviously, Afrikaans and Yiddish are interesting objects of study, particularly with respect to the question whether such 'mixed languages' show similar word order development as their 'pure' Germanic counterparts. With regard to embraciation and inversion this seems to be the case for Afrikaans, which has the same order as Modern Dutch (+ embraciation, + inversion), but not for Yiddish which has inversion as German has, but not the German embraciation (Ponelis 1979:495, Weinreich 1980:32, 532).

3. Questions on Inversion and Embraciation have been inserted in the second questionnaire for the survey of the Atlas Linguarum Europae (Weijnen, 1979:27–34), which will take place in the eighties all over Europe. I hope that the results of this survey will provide more insight in the phenomena of Inversion and Embraciation as they occur in the dialects of the Germanic standard languages.

4. See for English Quirk (1972), and Hornby (1976[2]); for Icelandic Kossuth (1978), and Thráinsson (1979); for Norwegian Haugen (1976:311–312), and Faarlund (1981); for Faroese Krenn (1941), and Lockwood (1955:156); for Danish Maling (1979); for Swedish Wessén (1970:223–238), and Ten Cate (1973:96); for Frisian Anglade (1966), Fokkema (1948:85–89), and Sipma (1949); for German Duden (1973:623–630); and for Dutch Jansen (1978), Gerritsen (1980), and the references cited there.

Regarding embraciation of other constituents than nominal objects the comments in 1.1 on German are also valid for Frisian and Dutch (Fokkema 1948:85–86 and Jansen 1979).

In the language in which embraciation of nominal objects is unacceptable, this also holds for prepositional phrases. Some sentential adverbials occur obligatorily before the non-finite verb in declarative main clauses and before the finite verb in dependent clauses in English and the Scandinavian languages. Different sentential adverbials in the various languages follow this rule. A Swedish example might clarify the matter here:

    (a) *Han har* tyvär   *varit sjuk*
        He has *unfortunately* been ill
    (b) *Hon sägar, att han* tyvär   *har varit sjuk*
        She says that he *unfortunately* has been ill

Some sentential adverbials may occur in English main clauses in between subject and finite verb:

    (c) He *often* goes there
    (d) They *still* want to go

This "OV" order is – as far as I know – unacceptable in the Scandinavian languages. Gerritsen (forthcoming) deals with the differences and similarities of the conditions on the occurrence of sentential adverbials before finite or non-finite verb in the various exbraciating Germanic languages.

5. There are some exceptions of minor importance. In Frisian inversion is not obligatory when the main clause is preceded by a dependent clause. In the Scandinavian languages it is not obligatory for sentences beginning with *kanska/i/e* 'perhaps'.

6. Data for Old English are based on Bean (1976:149), Canale (1976), and Fourquet (1938:90–93, 120); for Old Icelandic on Fourquet (1938), Heusler (1913), Kossuth (1978a and b), and Ureland (1978); for Old Norse on Christoffersen (1980); for Old Swedish on Ureland (1978), and Wessén (1970); for Old Danish on Ureland (1978); for Old Faroese I have not been able to find data; for Old German the data are based on Ebert (1978:39–43), Fourquet (1938), and Lockwood (1968); for Middle Frisian on Bor (1982); and for Middle Dutch on Gerritsen (1980 and forthcoming).

7. See for the Scandinavian languages Haugen (1976), Kossuth (1978a and b), Ureland (1978), and Wessén (1970); for German Ebert (1978), Ebert (1980), Lehmann (1974), and Lockwood (1968); for Frisian Bor (1982); for Dutch Gerritsen (1980), and Gerritsen (forthcoming).

8. In this section I worked out ideas that Frank Jansen and I developed while working on a paper about the differences and similarities in syntactic development between English and Dutch, presented at the department of Modern Languages of the University of Salford in March 1980.

9. See, for example, the summary in Koch (1974:67).

10. See, for example, Baugh and Cable (1978[3]), Bailey and Maroldt (1977), Domingue (1977) and Fisiak (1977) for the historical aspects and their linguistic consequences and Jespersen (1938), Kellner (1905), Koch (1974), Strang (1970) for the linguistic aspects.

11. See, for example, Mühlhäusler (1974:92) and Valdman (1977).

12. Dees (1980:300) has shown that in the 13th Century French of Normandy inversion occurred in only 3% of the declarative main clauses that have a pronominal subject and begin with any constituent other than the subject.

13. Perfect and pluperfect formations in the passive voice are left out of consideration here, since passives are periphrastic anyway in all the Germanic languages, except Scandinavian (cf. 2.2.2), so that they are not important for the argumentation.

14. See Fisiak (1977:75), Mustanoja (1960:480, 483), Visser (1966:669) for English; Ebert (1978:60), Koch (1974:78) and Lockwood (1968:107) for German and Weijnen (1971:88) for Dutch.

130   *Marinel Gerritsen*

References

Anglade, I.
1966   *Petit manuel de Frison Moderne de l'Ouest* (Groningen: J. B. Wolters).
Bailey, C.-J. N. – Karl Maroldt
1977   "The French lineage of English", *Langues en contact/Languages in contact. Pidgins – Creoles,* edited by Jürgen M. Meisel (Tübingen: Verlag Gunter Narr), 21–53.
Baugh, Albert C. – Thomas Cable
1978[3]   A history of the English language (London, Henley and Boston: Routledge and Kegan Paul).
Bean, Marian Callaway
1976   *A study of the development of word order patterns in Old English in relation to theories of word order change,* unpublished Ph. D. diss., UCLA.
Benveniste, Émile
1968   "Mutations of linguistic categories", *Directions for historical linguistics,* edited by W. P. Lehmann and Yakov Malkiel (Austin and London: University of Texas Press), 85–95.
Bickerton, Derek – Talmy Givón
1976   "Pidginization and syntactic change. From SXV and VSX to SVX", *Papers from the parasession on diachronic syntax, April 22,* edited by P. Ebert (Chicago: Chicago Linguistic Society), 9–39.
Braune, Wilhelm
1894   "Zur Lehre von der deutschen Wortstellung", *Forschungen zur deutschen Philologie. Festgabe für R. Hildebrand* (Leipzig: Verlag von Veit und Comp.)
Brinkmann, Hennig
1931   *Sprachwandel und Sprachbewegungen in althochdeutscher Zeit* (Jena: Verlag der Frommannschen Buchhandlung).
Bor, A.
1982   *An aspect of word order in Frisian* (= *Carefrissel* foar prof. dr. E. G. A. Galama ta syn santichste jierdei) (Grins: S. F. Frysk Ynstitút oan de Ryksuniversiteit).
Bynon, Theodora
1979[3]   *Historical linguistics* (Cambridge, London, New York, Melbourne: Cambridge University Press).
Canale, M.
1976   "Implicational hierarchies of word order relationships", *Current progress in historical linguistics,* edited by William M. Christie, Jr. (Amsterdam: North-Holland), 39–71.
Christoffersen, Marit
1980   "Marked and unmarked word order in Old Norse", *Papers from the 4th International Conference on Historical Linguistics,* edited by Elizabeth C. Traugott et al. (Amsterdam: John Benjamins B. V.), 115–123.
Closs Traugott, Elizabeth
1972   *The history of English syntax* (New York: Holt, Rinehart and Winston Inc.).
Clyne, Michael
1972   *Perspectives on language contact* (Melbourne: The Hawthorne Press).
1980   "Typology and grammatical convergence among related languages in contact", *ITL* 49–50:23–37.

Dees, Anthonij
1980   "Variations temporelles et spatiales de l'ordre des mots en ancien et en moyen français", *Sémantique lexicale et sémantique grammaticale en moyen français*, edited by Marc Wilmet (Brussel: V.U.B. Centrum voor Taal- en literatuurwetenschap), 293–304.
Delbrück, B.
1911   *Germanische Syntax II. Zur Stellung des Verbums (= Band 28 der Abhandlung der Philologisch-historischen Klasse der Königl. Sächsischen Gesellschaft der Wissenschaften, No. 7)* (Leipzig: Trübner).
Domingue, Nicole Z.
1977   "Middle English: another creole?", *Journal of Creole Studies* 1:89–100.
Duden
1973   *Duden Grammatik der deutschen Gegenwartssprache* (Mannheim/Wien/Zürich: Bibliographisches Institut, Dudenverlag).
Ebert, Robert Peter
1978   *Historische Syntax des Deutschen* (Stuttgart: Sammlung Metzler).
1981   "Social and stylistic variation in Early New High German word order: the sentence frame", *Beiträge zur Geschichte der deutschen Sprache und Literatur* 103:204–238.
Faarlund, Jan Terje
1981   "Obligatory fronting in a verb initial language: an attempt at pragmatic syntax", *Paper presented at the seventeenth meeting of the Chicago Linguistic Society*.
Fisiak, Jacek
1977   "Sociolinguistics and Middle English: some socially motivated changes in the history of English", *Kwartalnik Neofilologiczny* 24:247–259.
Fokkema, K.
1948   *Beknopte Friese Spraakkunst* (Groningen-Batavia: J. B. Wolters' Uitgeversmaatschappij N. V.).
Fourquet, J.
1938   *L'ordre des éléments de la phrase en germanique ancien. Études de syntaxe de position* (Strasbourg: Publications de la faculté des lettres).
Frings, Th.
1966   *Germania Romana* (Halle (Saale): VEB Max Niemeyer Verlag).
Gerritsen, Marinel
1980   "An analysis of the rise of SOV patterns in Dutch", *Papers from the fourth international conference on historical linguistics*, edited by Elizabeth C. Traugott et al (Amsterdam: John Benjamins B. V.), 123–136.
(forthcoming) *Veranderingen van de plaatsing van de zinsdelen ten opzichte van de werkwoorden in het Nederlands: vergelijking met de andere Germaanse talen en verklaring voor de verschillen en overeenkomsten* (Dissertation).
Givón, Talmy
1976   "On the VS word order in Israeli Hebrew: Pragmatics and typological change", *Papers in Hebrew syntax*, edited by P. Cole (Amsterdam: North-Holland), 153–181.
Green, Georgia M.
1980   "Some wherefores of English inversions", *Language* 56: 582–603.
Gutenbrunner, Siegfried
1951   *Historische Laut- und Formenlehre des Altisländischen* (Heidelberg: Carl Winter Universitätsverlag).
Harris, Martin B.
1978   *The evolution of French syntax. A comparative approach* (London and New York: Longman).

1981   "On explaining language change", *Paper presented at the fifth International Conference on Historical Linguistics* (Galway).

this volume   "On the strength and weaknesses of a typological approach to historical syntax".

Haugen, Einar
1976   *The Scandinavian languages: an introduction to their history* (London: Faber & Faber Ltd.).

Heusler, A.
1913   *Altisländisches Elementarbuch* (Heidelberg: Carl Winter Universitätsbuchhandlung).

Hirt, Hermann
1929   *Indogermanische Grammatik, Teil V: der Akzent* (Heidelberg: Indogermanische Bibliothek)
1931   *Handbuch des Urgermanischen. Teil I: Laut und Akzentlehre* (Heidelberg: Carl Winter Universitätsbuchhandlung).
1932   *Handbuch des Urgermanischen. Teil II: Stammbildungs- und Flexionslehre* (Heidelberg: Carl Winter Universitätsbuchhandlung).
1934   *Handbuch des Urgermanischen. Teil III: Abriss der Syntax* (Heidelberg: Carl Winter Universitätsbuchhandlung).

Hopper, Paul I.
1975   *The syntax of the simple sentence in Proto-Germanic* (The Hague/Paris: Mouton).

Hornby, A. S.
1976²   *Guide to patterns and usage in English* (London: Oxford University Press).

Jansen, Frank
1978   "Sentence initial elements in spoken Dutch", *Linguistics in the Netherlands 1974–1976*, edited by Wim Zonneveld (Lisse: The Peter de Ridder Press), 102–109.
1979   "On tracing conditioning factors of movement rules: Extraposition of PP in spoken Dutch", *Sprachstruktur, Individuum und Gesellschaft*, edited by Marc Van de Velde and Willy Vandeweghe (Tübingen: Niemeyer), 83–93.
1981   *Syntaktische konstrukties in gesproken taal* (Amsterdam: Huis aan de drie grachten).

Jespersen, Otto
1938   *Growth and structure of the English language* (Stuttgart: Teubner Verlag).

Kay, Paul – Gillian Sankoff
1974   "A language universals approach to pidgins and creoles", *Pidgins and creoles*, edited by David DeCamp and Jan F. Hancock (Washington: Georgetown University Press), 61–73.

Kellner, Leon
1905   *Historical outlines of English syntax* (New York: Macmillan and Co. Ltd.).

Kern, J. H.
1912   *De met het Participium Praeteriti omschreven Werkwoordsvormen in het Nederlands* (Amsterdam: Muller).

Koch, Monica
1974   "A demystification of Syntactic Drift", *Montreal working papers in linguistics* 13:63–114.

Kossuth, Karen C.
1978a   "Typological contributions to Old Icelandic word order under particular consideration of the position of the verb", *Acta Philologica Scandinavica* 32, 1:37–53.

1978b   "Icelandic word order: In support of drift as a diachronic principle specific to language families", *Proceedings of the 4th Annual Meeting of the Berkeley Linguistic Society*, edited by Jeri Jaeger, Anthony Woodburg, Farrell Ackerman et al, 446–457.
1981   *A history of the auxiliary verb in German* (MS).
Krenn, Ernst
1940   *Färoyische Sprachlehre* (Heidelberg: Carl Winter Universitätsbuchhandlung).
Lambert, P. J.
1976   *Ausklammerung in Modern Standard German* (Hamburg: Helmut Buske Verlag).
Lass, Roger
1980   *On explaining language change* (Cambridge: Cambridge University Press).
Lehmann, W. P.
1971   "On the rise of SOV patterns in New High German", *Grammatik, Kybernetik, Kommunikation, Festschrift für Alfred Hoppe*, edited by K. G. Schweistal (Bonn: Ferd. Dümmlers Verlag), 19–24.
1972   "Proto-Germanic syntax", *Toward a grammar of Proto-Germanic*, edited by F. van Coetsem and H. L. Kufner (Tübingen: Max Niemeyer Verlag), 239–268.
Lightfoot, David
1979   Review of *Mechanisms of syntactic change*, edited by Charles N. Li, *Language* 55:381–396.
Lockwood, W. B.
1955   *An introduction to modern Faroese* (København: Ejnar Munksgaard).
1968   *Historical German syntax* (Oxford: At the Clarendon Press).
1969   *Indo-European philology, historical and comparative* (London: Hutchinson).
Maling, Ales
1979   *Deense spraakkunst voor iedereen* (Utrecht/Antwerpen: Uitgeverij Het Spectrum).
Maurer, F.
1926   *Untersuchungen über die deutsche Verbstellung in ihrer geschichtlichen Entwicklung* (Heidelberg: Carl Winter's Universitätsbuchhandlung).
Moravcsik, E. A.
1978   "Universals of language contact", *Universals of human language*, edited by J. H. Greenberg, C. A. Ferguson and E. A. Moravcsik (Stanford C. A.: Stanford University Press), Vol. I, 93–122.
Mossé, F.
1938   *Histoire de la forme périphrastique être + participe présent en germanique* (Paris: Librairie C. Klincksieck).
Mühlhäusler, P.
1974   *Pidginization and simplification of language* (Pacific linguistics Series B. No. 26).
Mustanoja, Tauno F.
1960   *A Middle English syntax* (Helsinki: Société Néophilologique).
Ponelis, F. A.
1979   *Afrikaanse Sintaksis* (Pretoria: J. L. van Schaik).
Quirk, Randolph – Sidney Greenbaum – Geoffrey Leech – Jan Svartvik
1972   *A grammar of contemporary English* (London: Longman).
Ries, John
1907   *Die Wortstellung im Beowulf* (Halle: Niemeyer).

Samuels, M.
1972   *Linguistic evolution with special reference to English* (London: Cambridge University Press).
Schneider, Karl
1938   *Die Stellung des finiten Verbs im urgermanischen Haupt- und Nebensatz* (Giessen: Carl Winter).
Sipma, P.
1949   *Ta it Frysk III* (Ljouwert: R. van der Velde).
Steele, Susan
1978   "Word order variation: a typological study", *Universals of human language*, edited by J. H. Greenberg, C. A. Ferguson and E. A. Moravcsik (Stanford (CA): Stanford University Press), vol. 4, 585–624.
Stockwell, Robert P.
1977   "Motivations for exbraciation in Old English", *Mechanisms of syntactic change,* edited by Charles N. Li (Austin: University of Texas Press), 291–314.
this volume   "On the history of the verb-second rule in English".
Strang, Barbara M. H.
1970   *A history of English* (London: Methuen and Co. Ltd.).
Ten Cate-Sifwerbrand, R. B.
1973   *Zweedse grammatica* (Utrecht/Antwerpen: Het Spectrum).
Thráinsson, Höskuldur
1979   *On complementation in Icelandic* (New York/London: Garland Publishing Inc.).
Trnka, B.
1930   *On the syntax of the English verb from Caxton to Dryden* (Prague: Jednota československých matematiků a fysiků).
Ureland, P. Sture
1978   "Typological, diachronic and area linguistic perspectives of North Germanic syntax", *Proceedings of the Third International Conference of Nordic Languages and Modern Linguistics 3,* edited by J. Weinstock (Austin: University of Texas Press).
Valdman, Albert (ed.)
1977   *Pidgin and creole linguistics* (Bloomington and London: Indiana University Press).
Vennemann, Theo
1974a   "Analogy in generative grammar; the origin of word order", *Proceedings of the Eleventh International Congress of Linguists,* edited by Luigi Heilmann (Bologna: Il Mulino), 79–83.
1974b   "Theoretical word order studies. Results and problems", *Papiere zur Linguistik 7:5–25.*
Visser, F. Th.
1966   *An historical syntax of the English language* (Leiden: E. J. Brill).
Voskuil, J. J.
1956   *Het Nederlands van Hindoestaanse kinderen in Suriname* (Amsterdam: N. V. Noord-Hollandsche Uitgeversmaatschappij).
Wackernagel, J.
1920   *Vorlesungen über Syntax mit besonderer Berücksichtigung von Griechisch, Lateinisch und Deutsch* (Basel: Kommissionsverlag von Emil Birkhäuser und Cie).
Watkins, Calvert
1976   "Towards Proto-Indo-European syntax: Problems and pseudoproblems", *Papers from the parasession on diachronic syntax* (Chicago: Chicago Linguistic Society), 291–305.

Weinreich, Max
    1980   *History of the Yiddish language* (Chicago and London: The University of Chicago Press).

Werth, R. N.
    1970   "The problem of a Germanic sentence prototype", *Lingua* 26:25–34.

Wessén, Elias
    1970   *Schwedische Sprachgeschichte III* (Berlin: Walter de Gruyter and Co.).

Weijnen, A. A.
    1971   *Schets van de geschiedenis van de Nederlandse Syntaxis* (Assen: Van Gorcum & Comp. N. V.).

Weijnen, A., et al.
    1979   *Atlas Linguarum Europae, second questionnaire* (Assen: Van Gorcum).

Zieglschmid, A.J.F.
    1929   *Zur Entwicklung der Perfektumschreibung im Deutschen* (Baltimore: Linguistic Society of America).

HUBERT HAIDER AND RONALD ZWANZIGER

Relatively attributive:
The 'ezāfe'-construction from Old Iranian to
Modern Persian

0 Introduction

0.1 What is *ezāfe*?

The term *ezāfe* (Arabic *iḍāfat* 'connection') in traditional grammar of Persian comprises a variety of constructions that consist of a noun followed by an attribute, i.e. a noun, a pronoun, an adjective, a participle, or an infinitive. In an *ezāfe*-construction the first constitutent (the determined) is linked to the second constitutent (the determiner) by means of an unstressed particle 'i'.

0.2 Its ancestry

The particle 'i', in Modern Persian confined exclusively to NP-attribution, has partly assumed this function already in Middle Persian. Its etymological predecessor *cy* (Manichaean Middle Persian, s. below) also occurs as a relative pronominal stem in Old Iranian (cf. Avestan *ya-*; in Old Persian extended to *haya-*). The following table gives an overview of the particular syntactic inventory, which we are to discuss, in four subsequent cross-cuts:

Table:

	Gatha-Avest.		Young Avest.		Middle Pers.		Mod.Pers.	
	ka-	*ya-*	*ka-*	*ya-*	*ka-*	*ya-*	*ka-*	*ya-*
Relative	−	+	−	+	+	+	+	−
Ezāfe	−	−	−	+	−	+	−	+
Interrogative	+	−	+	−	+	−	+	−
Complementizer	*yaṯ*		*yaṯ*		*kw*		*ki*	

The remarkable features are the balance between the syntactic structures of noun phrase and sentential complementation, on the one hand, and on the other hand, the properties of the class of sentence-introducing elements.

Gatha Avestan and Modern Persian, as opposed to Young Avestan and Middle Persian, are characterized by clear cut distinctions in their respective syntactic inventories. Young Avestan and Middle Persian offer insight into the intermediary stages in a diachronic perspective. As it will become clear in the subsequent discussion, the developments have to be interpreted within a theory of complementizers, i.e. the system of sentence-initially placed elements and their specific syntactic functions. It is therefore important to note that with respect to the complementizer *yaṯ* there is a partial homonymy with the relative pronouns, i.e. the relative pronoun nom.acc.sg.n., which is *yaṯ*. It is this element which is the cue for the rise of the *ezāfe*.

0.3 Its fascination

The *ezāfe* construction is the temporary outcome of a development, whose origins can be traced back to the particular syntactic properties of Old Iranian. Its intermediary stages are well documented. As indicated in the table above the *ezāfe*-construction fits into a fairly stable syntactic patterning, which can be construed as a consolidation after a long standing reconstruction process.

The relative clause construction of Old Iranian developed into a device for nominal attribution and a new type of relative clause emerges. Parallel to this process and partly due to the same triggering influences Modern Persian ends up with a far more rigid serialization compared to its 'great-grand parents'.

0.4 Its explanation

We attempt to reconstruct the historical development in terms of a general theory of grammar: In relating the properties of a particular grammar to the general principles of the theory of grammar we derive the cues for the latter development. In section 2 the onset of the 'decay' of the relative clause construction is isolated: Its main features are the existence of two types of relative attributes, i.e. the ordinary relative clause and a verbless one. Case agreement between head and relative pronoun is the prime evidence for the beginning of a separate development, the main lines of which can be derived from the theory of sentence-introducers (Comp-universals, cf. 1) and the theory of case agreement. Section 3 is a characterization of the instable system which is the preliminary output of an ongoing process of reshaping the grammar. Its new consolidation in Modern Persian is discussed in section 4. Section 5 contains metatheoretical reflections in support of the explanatory ambition of this paper.

1 Theoretical background: The structure of embedded clauses

We assume that (1) is the basic structure for languages with sentence-initial placement of subordinating particles, relative pronouns, and interrogative pronouns (cf. Bresnan 1972, Emonds 1976).

(1)

(2) a) *I know [[who][Bill met −]]*
  b) *I know [[that][Bill was late]]*
  c) *the fact [[which][Bill mentioned −]]*
  d) *the fact [[that][Bill mentioned −]]*
  e) *the fact [[that][Bill is ill]]*
  f) *[[who] [− has left]]*

As the examples in (2) illustrate, 'comp' identifies the sentence-initial position. It contains those elements that introduce sentence, e.g. constant elements like conjunctions (e.g. that, as, than, etc.) or sentence-initial pronominal elements like relative or interrogative pronouns. For a syntactic justification we refer to the literature cited above.

The pronominal sentence introducers perform a double function: They are able to introduce a subordinate clause (the conjunction function) and they are also able to convey a semantic relation (the anaphoric function of pronominals). In generative treatments the combination is brought about by a movement rule: Wh-elements are moved into 'comp', leaving behind a gap (cf. Chomsky 1977).

In the case of questions, direct or indirect, as well as in relative clauses the pronouns allow the identification of the syntactic position and consequently the semantic role of the element that is 'in question'.

(3) a) *Which house did John buy −?*
  b) *I know which house John has bought −.*
  c) *the house, which John bought −.*

The identification is possible by means of case marking or marking on dimensions like humanness in English. In languages with richer inflectional devices, marking for gender, number etc. is common.

With regard to (3) c) it has to be noted that there is an additional realization: Not only is the pronoun related to the syntactic position it has been moved from, but there is also a predicative relation to the nominal head of the relative nominal phrase which is established by the anaphoric function of the relative pronoun. It is important for the following discussion of the Persian data to keep these two functions distinct. (4) is ungrammatical due to the violation of the predicative requirement of agreement:

> (4) *the fact, who Bill mentioned*

As we can observe in English, the condition that requires matching of features is inoperable in certain cases of neutralization: As Culicover (1976: 198) notes, the distribution of 'that' is similar to the distribution of 'which' in dialects that do not restrict 'which' to non-humans.

> (5) a) *Mary is the only person that John likes.*
> b) *This is the only book that was on the table.*
> c) *I met the children that you had told me about.*
>   (Examples taken from Culicover; (8.49) in his numbering)

It is a typological commonplace to point out that relative pronouns are morphologically identical either with interrogative or demonstrative pronouns (cf. Downing 1978:385). Since 'that' is clearly a demonstrative pronoun, sentences as in (5) are likely to be analyzed along these lines. There are, however, cases where 'that' is not permitted to replace a relative pronoun:

> (6) a)   *This is the book whose cover is missing*
>   *This is the book that's cover is missing*
> b)   *New York is the place to which Mary is heading*
>   *New York is the place to that Mary is heading*
> c)   *The person/whom I gave the book to was very thankful*
>   *The person to that I gave the book was very thankful*

It is hard to see how the starred sentences in (6) can be ruled out if we consider 'that' to be a pronoun. A comparison of the examples in (2), especially d) and f), point to an alternative analysis: 'that' is the complementizer constant rather than the demonstrative pronoun as in (7).

> (7) a) *that is what I want*
> b) *that book I want*

On this assumption the ungrammatical sentences in (6) are ruled out simply by the fact that a complementizer constant cannot be part of a phrase in the way a pronoun can: the only position where it can occur is 'comp'. Consequently it cannot be part of another phrase that has reached comp-position by wh-movement as e.g. in (8).

(8) *This is the book* [[   ] [[*whose cover*] *is missing*

comp

$\longrightarrow$

This is the book [[*whose cover*] [– *is missing*]]

Thus relative NPs with 'that' have to be analyzed as consisting of the head noun followed by an embedded sentence, introduced by the complementizer constant 'that'. It is the anaphoric function of the pronoun that has been dropped, the conjunctive function is fulfilled by the complementizer 'that'. Nevertheless a relative clause can be identified by the gap, which gives the cue for relating head noun and clause. (2) d) differs from e) in exactly this respect: d) shows a gap while e) is a complete clause (cf. also Bresnan 1972 for an exhaustive analysis of related problems).

2 Avestan

2.1 The onset of the latter 'ezāfe'-construction has to be sought in the development of the nominal relative clauses, as we shall try to demonstrate in the following interpretation of Avestan data. For an excellent survey of the properties of the Avestan relative attribute we refer to Seiler (1960). The relative attributes are usually classified as verbal or nominal depending on the presence or absence of a verbal item, i.e. the nominal attribute is the equivalent (with some important restrictions to be added below) of a relative clause without a verb. The following examples are to illustrate the main distinctions we want to make:

(9) Verbal relative attributes:
     a) correlative
        V.3.31.   *Yō yaom kāraiieiti hō aṣ̌əm kāraiieiti*
                  'who tills corn, this one tills truth'
     b) clause final:
        Yt 6.2   *buuaṯ dąma aṣ̌auua yaoždāϑrəm yā̊ hənti*
                 spəntahe mainiiə̄uš
                 'there happens purification of the righteous
                 beings, which adhere to the holy spirit'

In the correlative relative construction, the relative clause precedes the entire clause which contains the modified noun. Typically, the relative NP and the head are both marked by correlative morphemes: In Avestan a demonstrative is attached to or represents the head NP.

Clause final relative clauses occur at the end of, or follow, the clause containing the modified nominal.

Nominal relative attributes:

    (10) a) correlative

                Y. 36.3 hiiat *vā. tōi nāmanam vāziśtəm ātarə mazdā̊ ahu-*
                rahiiā tā. *ϑβa pairijasāmaidē*
                'which of your names is the best, o Atar, of Mazda Ahura,
                with which we approach you'

    (10) b) clause final

                Yt 13.61 *yā̊ auuąm kəhrpəm aiβiiā̊xšaiieinti yąm sāmahe*
                kərəsāspahe
                'the ones who guard the body, which (is) of
                the Samid Krsaspa'

It is a longstanding view, that the nominal relatives are to be analyzed as derived from a verbal relative clause by copula ellipsis (cf. Reichelt 1909: §§734ff.), Bartholomae (1979c:1197ff.).

The ellipsis-hypothesis has to face critical attacks: Seiler (1960:67) notes that relative clauses containing the copula *asti* still exist in the corpus. He takes this as counterevidence: If it were true that all relatives containing a copula have become nominal relatives, sentences like (11) should not exist any longer:

(11) shows that *asti* is still productive.

    (11) Yt 19.9   *x^varənō mazdaδātəm yazamaide . . .*
                    yat̰ asti ahurahe mazdā̊
                    'the mazda-created glory we worship . . .
                    which belongs to Ahura Mazda'

This conclusion, however, is not cogent.

The question is whether Avestan nominal relatives can be analyzed as a special case of relative clauses, whose properties an be derived from verbal relatives, containting a copula or whether they should be taken as a construction in its own right.

His observation on the productivity of *asti* does not bear directly on this issue: Since copula ellipsis is a rule of Avestan syntax, it may apply in relative clauses as well. Being an optional rule in general, it may be constrained in some cases, as in (11).

Asti in predicative contexts functions as a dummy verb (in the absence of a lexical verb) and carries the tense and agreement markes, but it is semantically empty. Not so in (11): Here *asti* + Genitive is a possessive expression, i.e. has semantic content different from the ordinary predicative occurrence, and thus may forego ellipsis.

A second and more serious problem for the ellipsis hypothesis are nominal relatives which do not allow to add a copula as in (12), contrasted with (13):

(12) Yt 5.38   *gandarəβəm yim zairi. pāṣnim*
'Gandarva (acc.), the golden heeled'

(13) Yt 10.17   *miϑrəm . . . yō nōiṯ kahmāi aiβi. draoxδō*
'Mithra (acc.) . . . , who (nom.) is not
deceived by anyone'

An analysis of these cases will crucially depend on this very difference: The absence of the verbal element triggers case agreement, and that entails an analysis which assigns a different syntactic structure to the agreement cases and the nominal relative without agreement. Copulative clauses are nominative, i.e. the subject and the predicative noun or adjective agree in case. Thus in a copulative predicative relative clause, the only case the relative pronoun can get assigned is nominative. In (12), however, the relative pronoun is marked with accusative.

It is the absence of a verb which leads to case agreement with the head of the relative clause. This entails an analysis which assigns a different syntactic structure to the constructions which show agreement on the one hand and to the nominal relatives on the other. The latter still are of a sentential structure while the former are non-sentential attributes.

As Seiler (1960:128—130) has found out, all except two of the nominal relatives which show agreement (Yt. 13.1, V.13.2), have a structural property in common: Adjacency of head-noun and relative pronoun.

This is a remarkable feature, since adnominal verbal relatives are rare in Avestan, due to extraposition.

Given the theory of grammar we sketched above (1) with regard to the structure of complementizers and relative clauses, this very property follows.

The relative pronoun in 'comp' is marked for the case assigned to it in the syntactic position from which it has been fronted.

(14) Yt 10.20

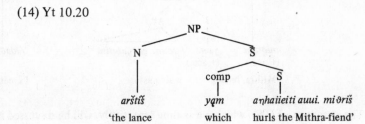

S̄ is the domain of case-assignment, i.e. it is impossible for a governing element which is not contained in the respective S̄ to assign case to a noun contained in this S̄. In every S̄ the verb governs the respective cases. Especially
the nominative depends on the presence of a finite verb. Thus if there is no
finite verb it is the nominative case which is affected. This seems to be the
correct approach, since otherwise we would expect to find case agreement
with the head in the verbal relatives too (cf. (14)).

Examples like (12) show that in nominal relatives the relative pronoun
may be marked with a case for which there is no governing verb in the relative
'clause'. As there is agreement with the head noun it is reasonable to assume
that the governor of the case of the head also governs the case of the relative
pronoun, which in turn, as is the normal situation in predicative copula constructions, is in case-congruence with the predicative noun or adjective. Since
S̄ is a barrier for governing we are forced to conclude that nominal relatives
with head-pronoun congruence are liable to have no S̄ boundary cf. (15) vs.
(16):

(15) Yt 10.65 (adapted)

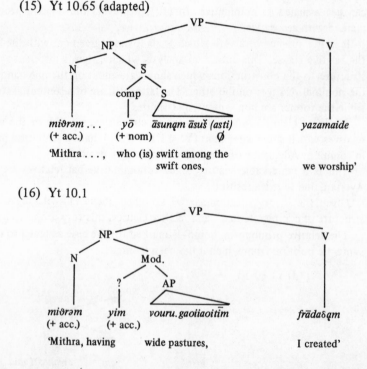

miϑrəm . . .   yō   āsuṇąm āsuš (asti)   yazamaide
(+ acc.)   (+ nom)   Ø

'Mithra . . . ,   who (is) swift among the   we worship'
                         swift ones,

(16) Yt 10.1

miϑrəm   yim   vouru.gaoiiaoitīm   frādaδąm
(+ acc.)   (+ acc.)

'Mithra, having   wide pastures,   I created'

The structure of (16), which we assume tentatively, will be discussed in detail below. What is important, however, is the lack of an S̄ constituent. Thus (16) becomes similar to an adjective attribute as in (17).

(17) Yt 10.7

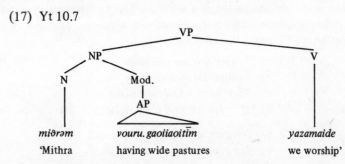

| miϑrəm | vouru. gaoiiaoitīm | yazamaide |
| 'Mithra | having wide pastures | we worship' |

For a collection of constructions of these types we refer to Seiler (1960:105). It is worth noting that the adjectives may precede or follow the noun:

(18) a) Yt 10.19 *miϑrō graṇtō upa. ṭbištō*
'the   angry offended Mithra'

b) Yt 10.31 *sauuišta miϑra*
'most powerful Mithra'

Since there are two syntactically different though semantically equivalent — both are attributive — constructions for attributive modification, i.e. (16) and (17), it is reasonable to ask why they have not been collapsed. In other words, if nominal relatives are reduced relative clauses, why are they not reduced completely and the relative pronoun elided as well? As there is a functional motivation for the reduction of relative clauses (as discussed above), is there also one which forbids complete reduction? A comparison of (18) a) and b) will illustrate the point:

(18) a) is ambiguous between noun phrase reading (19) a') and a sentential reading (19) a"):

(19) a')   the offended Mithra
a")   Mithra is offended

The presence of a relative pronoun clearly precludes the sentential reading.

(20) *azəm yō ahurō mazdå̄*

(20) is a noun phrase. If the relative pronoun were missing (20) could be glossed either with (20)' or (20)":

(20)' I, the Ahura Mazda
(20)" I am Ahura Mazda

It is well known (cf. Kuno 1974, Bever 1970) that there are processing strategies to the effect that a sequence which might be interpreted as a sentence is in fact interpreted as a sentence. Due to this strategy it is impossible to delete sentence initial complementizers, which are deletable in non-initial position (cf. Chomsky/Lasnik 1977).

(21) a) *I think that he will come*
    b) *I think Ø he will come*
    c) *That he is a fool is obvious*
    d) **Ø   He is a fool is obvious*

(22) a) *Ich glaube, daß er kommen will*
    b) *Ich glaube   er will kommen*
    c) *Daß er kommen will, freut uns*
    d) **   Er will kommen freut uns* (German)

Before we will start a detailed analysis on the lines sketched above we have to justify our assumption with regard to the structural position of the relative clause in Avestan.

Since the bulk of the corpus contains relative clauses of the type illustrated in (9) the structure proposed for (15) needs justification. The analysis of the agreement-facts requires that the head NP and the pronoun which agrees in case are part of an NP constitutent (cf. (16)). As a consequence we have to analyze clause-final relatives as derived, e.g. by a rule of extraposition. This calls for an explanation why only verbal relatives are extraposed in an almost obligatory way. Before we venture an answer on this issue, two observations in support of the NP-constituency of relative clauses. First of all, the distribution of nominal relatives needs explanation: Assuming for the moment that they are non-sentential, it has to be explained why they occur postnominally whereas other attributes, e.g. adjectives, genetives may occur pre- or postnominally. If on the other hand nominal relatives are derived from relative clauses, the distributional properties can be inferred. Secondly, embedded relative clauses, rare though they are, occur:

(23) Y 9.22   *haomō aēibiš yōi auruuantō hita taxšənti arənāum zāuuarə aojå̄sca baxšaiti*
                 'Haoma offers to those, who hurry harnessed to their destination (?), power and strength'

The low frequency might be due to a functional constraint: We note that the ellipsis-hypothesis correlates with a (dys-) functional property of postnominal relative clauses in a verb-final language:

Center-embedding is circumvented frequently either by extraposition or by a correlative construction, i.e. fronting.

First we would like to claim that the absence of the copula is due to necessity more than to chance: Kuno (1974) drew attention to the fact that in
verb-final languages every relative clause will occur in center-embedded position, a configuration which reduces the comprehensibility of sentences because of perceptual difficulties. In SOV-languages with postnominal relative
clauses every relative clause leads to a center-embedded structure as indicated
in (3), where a) contains an intransitive verb, b) a transitive verb with a relative clause on the subject, and c) a transitive verb with a relative clause on the
object.

(24) a) *Boy [Mary loved] died*
     b) *Boy [Mary loved] Jane hated*
     c) *Jane boy [Mary loved] hated*
                              (Newmeyer 1980:222)

This situation can be improved in two respects:
   a) reduction of the embedded clause,
   b) removal of the embedded clause (extraposition or fronting).
   Kuno (1974:132) observed "that nonrigid SOV languages such as Persian,
Bengali, and Georgian, which place relative clauses postnominally and which
place conjunctions at clause-initial position, utilize rightward extraposition to
avoid center-embedding and conjunction juxtaposition". Extraposition places
an embedded sentence at the end of the matrix clause, and consequently after
the matrix verb. Although this reduces the perceptual difficulties with respect
to center-embedding it leads to new problems.
   a) In OV languages the verb signals the end of the clause; but the final verb
of a complex sentence is also always the main verb. The extraposed relative
clause destroys this pattern.
   b) The need for extraposition systematically violates the tendency to group
together syntactically items which belong together semantically (Behaghel's
first law, cf. Behaghel 1923:IV).
   It is noted by Keenan that there is a general functional principle which is
violated in our case when the relative clause is extraposed: "A language is
cognitively dissonant to the extent that principles of semantic interpretation
which apply to basic sentences of the language must be modified to yield the
correct interpretation for complex sentences." (Lehmann ed. 1979:310) In
this situation we expect at least one therapeutive move: The reduction of
the relative clause whenever it is possible. The deletion of the verbal item
restores the general pattern where the last verbal item in a sequence is the
main verb. Copula structures are the most prominent candidates for reduction,
which indeed can be observed frequently:
   The relevant examples are of the type illustrated in (10) a)—c). It is clear

that given the possibility of reduction, this is not confined to the extraposed clause. Since it is impossible to reduce every extraposed relative clause without violation of recoverability constraints, i.e. there are extraposed relative clauses with a full verb, which cannot be deleted, copula deletion is compatible with, but not contingent on, extraposition. It is the reduction of the embedded clause which solves the problem posed by center-embedding most effectively.

2.2 Summary

There are two types of nominal relative attributes, differing in case agreement

$$(25) \quad A: \quad [N \quad [R \quad X]]_{NP}$$
$$[case\ \alpha] \quad [case\ \beta]$$

$$B: \quad [N \quad [R \quad X]]_{NP}$$
$$[case\ \alpha] \quad [case\ \alpha]$$

The structures represented in (B) show, according to Seiler's (1960:138) findings the following property:

  — non-extraposed, non-fronted, i.e. adjacency between head and relative pronoun

We have argued that it is the embedded sentence structure which leads either to reduction or displacement of the embedded sentence. On the other hand case agreement precludes any sentence boundary between the congruent items. Thus it is no coincidence, but an entailment of our analysis that precisely the reduced relatives which show case agreement are adjacent to the head. Case agreement entails that the head noun and the relative pronoun belong to the same constituent and are thus governed by the same case-assigning element. Appositives, on the other hand, need not be part of the same constituents (cf. Emonds 1979); they act like parentheses and are therefore not candidates for reduction.

2.3 A comparison from Gatha Avestan to Young Avestan

In the language of the Gathas, the oldest Avestan documents, case agreement of head and relative pronoun is confined to the Accusative (and allegedly instrumental), cf. (26).

(26) Y 32.5   *vå̊ yə̄ng daēuuə̄ng*
              'you, the Daēvas'

If the head is nominative it is undecidable, clearly, whether there is agreement or not. Accusative and instrumental also go together in Young Avestan with regard to agreement. But in these documents the relative pronoun in the other cases (dative, locative, ablative, vocative) is replaced by *'yat'*. This situation is characterized by Reichelt (1909:749) as follows: "Das Ende der Entwicklung dieser Relativsätze im Aw. ist also, dass Pron. rel. und Prädikatsnomen auch im Kasus mit ihrem Bezugsworte kongruieren. Im gAw. ist die Kongruenz auf Akk. und Instr. beschränkt. Im Y.Hapt. und im jAw. nehmen alle Kasus daran teil; für die zweisilbigen Formen des Relatives tritt jedoch das Neutrum *hyat̰, yat̰* ein."

Seiler's (1960:68) qualification of this comment with the term 'nonsensical' seems to indicate that Reichelt is pursuing a spurious generalization. First of all there is no motivation for invoking agreement if it has obviously been neutralized. Secondly Reichelt's characterization cannot be meant as an explanation. Why should a second syllable be a barrier (a phonologically based syntactic constraint!)? Seiler seeks an explanation for the clustering of the cases along the following lines: Nominative, accusative and instrumental are in Seiler's term cases of quotation (Nennkasus), whereas the others are not. This property might be invoked to justify this grouping as a syntactically supported division but it does not explain a) why it is precisely these cases that induce agreement, b) why it is *yat̰*, which appears in the other cases. It is obvious that an answer to these questions has to be sought in a theory of case assignment, which we will try to sketch below. Before turning to that problem we must add a few details about *yat̰* support. *Yat̰* is generally taken to be a form of the relative pronoun *ya-*, i.e. neuter singular. The following examples (27) a)–c) show that there is no agreement whatsoever, not even in number, which should make anyone suspicious who claims that *yat̰* is a pronoun, since there is also a plural form *yā*.

(27) a) Yt 10.95 *karana aiṅhā̊ zəmō yat̰ paϑanaiiā̊* (gen.sing.fem.)
                        'the two boundaries of the Earth, the spacious (one)'

   b) Vr 9.4   *aēibiiō yazataēibiiō yat̰ aməṧaēibiiō spəntaēibiiō* (dat.plur.masc.)
                        'these deities, the Aməša Spəntas'

   c) V 5.39   *ahmi aṅhuuō yat̰ astuuainti* (loc.sing.masc.)
                        'in this life, the material (one)'

It seems that Seiler fell into the same trap which he believed Reichelt to have stepped into. He claims in the face of the evidence of (27), which he himself cites, that *yaṯ* is a pronoun. If *yaṯ* were a 'neutral' pronoun, its neutrality would not be endangered by number-agreement. At the very least this is a fact which calls for an explanation.

Let us recall the illustrative examples (1)–(6) for English. The impossibility of 'that' being marked by case-assigners (i.e. prepositions, etc.) could be deduced from the fact that 'that' is not a pronoun but a sentence-initial complementizer.

If *yaṯ* is indeed a complementizer particle then it is no surprise at all that we do not find any agreement — a property of pronouns (cf. Reichelt 1909, § 759). Taking this for granted, we will try to relate these facts, i.e. the agreement in nominative, accusative and instrumental and *yaṯ* support, within a coherent framework based on the properties of case assignment. In our view the nominal attributes are partitioned in three classes:

(28) a)   N   R   Pred
         a case   nom

    b)   N   R   Pred
         a case   *yaṯ*

    c)   N   R   Pred
    acc./instr.   acc./instr.

Examples for (28):

    a) Yt 10.20 *arštiš yąm aṅhaiieiti auui.miðriš*
                 'the lance which hurts the Mithra-fiend'

      Yt 10.93 *aheca aṅhōuš yō astuuatō*
                 'this existence which is material'

      Yt 10.65 *miϑrəm yō āsunąm asuš*
                 'Mithra, who is fast among the fast'
                              (Gershevitch 1959)

    b) V 7.44 *təm iϑra hamjaså̄nta yaṯ mąϑrəm spəntəm baēšazəm*
                 'they should turn to that one, namely to
                         the holy healing word'

      Yt 5.18 *puϑrəm yaṯ pourušaspahe*
                 'the son of Pourušaspa'

c) Y 35.4   *adāiš tāiš šiiaoϑanāiš yāiš vahištāiš*
'as a revenge for the best of all deeds'

Y 65.5   *vīspāiš auui karšuuąn yāiš hapta*
'upon all seven continents'

Yt 10.1   *miϑrəm yim vouru.gaoiiaoitīm*
'Mithra with wide pastures'

Y 71.10   *vīspe tē ahurō mazdā̊ huuapō vanuhīš dāmąn
ašaonīš yazamaide yāiš dadāϑa pouruca vohuca
yōi tē hənti yasniiāca*
'all your brave righteous beings, ... we
worship, which you ... have created, which
are venerable for you'

In the above arrangement the only case to be termed 'agreeing' proper is
c) as we shall demonstrate. Before we can do this some preliminaries to case
assignment: Case assignment requires a governing element:
— Nominative normally depends on the presence of a finite verbal element.
— Accusative requires a transitive verb in the simplest case.
The above cases constitute a structural relation, without assigning also a semantic qualification in addition, which is typical for the other cases — locative, ablative, dative, genitive — as can be most clearly seen in languages where
these relations are expressed by prepositions for instance. Instrumental is exceptional since, at least in the Avestan corpus, it seems to have the properties
of the inherent cases, i.e. a thematic quality, but also structural properties,
similar to the accusative. Thus we may distinguish nominative, accusative and
instrumental as cases which are assigned structurally, whereas genitive, locative, dative and true instrumental are assigned according to their inherent
semantic properties.

Although the exact details are not yet clear, it is important to note that in
a special declension class (n-stems, neuter) the modifier may be marked instrumental while the head is neuter, a fact, that will be of importance for the
examples in c), cf. (29):

(29) a) Y 57.17   *vīspāis aiiąnca xšafnasca*
'all days and nights'
[Mod. (+ Inst.) [$_{NP}$ N N+Conj (+Acc)]

(30) is an example for conjoined NPs, which, though governed by the same
verb differ in case, again accusative and instrumental.

(30) Y 55.1   *tanuuasca azdəbĩsca*
                    [acc.] & [instr.]
                    'the bodies and the bones'

We should like to interpret this as indication that the instrumental shifts from an inherent to a structural case. Even this very informal characterization is sufficient for the interpretation of the patterning in (28). In (2.1) we assigned structure (31) to the nominal relatives:

(31)

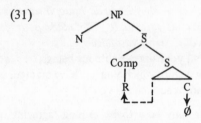

(28) a) requires that the copula, which is elided, assigns case to the relative pronoun, i.e. the nominative, since the only property of the copula is to carry tense and agreement features.

(28) b) is already the beginning of a reanalysis. Clearly in copulative predicate construction case has no distinctive function, i.e. the pronoun will invariably occur in nominative case, unlike verbal relatives, where the case of the pronoun is a cue for its syntactic position (i.e. subject, object, etc.). In this situation one of the two syntactic functions, i.e. clause subordination and encoding of the syntactic relation, is redundant. It is only the subordinating property which is relevant in nominal relatives. But this very function is the only function of a complementizer, the complementizer *yat̯*.

(28) c) is the only true case of agreement, or case attraction. Although it seems marginal it plays an important role for the development. If we want to account for (c) we are forced to conclude that the structure of (c) differs from that of (a) and (b):

(32)

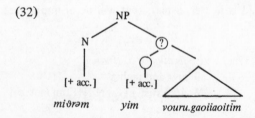

Since the head and the pronoun agree in case the obvious explanation for this is, that they are both governed by the same case assigning element, a transitive verb perhaps. What is important, however, is that a sentential attribute blocks case assignment as has become clear from examples in (2.1).

This leads straightforward into a conflict: Relative pronouns are allowed only in complementizer-position, but a complementizer-node requires a sentential structure, i.e. a barrier for case assignment. Either the pronoun stays in 'comp', then it cannot receive case, or it receives case, then it cannot sit in 'comp'. The latter development shows that it is the first option that has been given up, which is the cue for the *ezāfe*-construction since it made it impossible for *yaṯ* to act as a (sentential) complementizer. The transitory stages are easy to reconstruct. Structure (33) is the result of reanalysis, i.e. there is no elision of a copula any more, thus S does not contain a verbal element. If we interpret S̄ as the case domain of the verb contained in S, which makes S therefore 'immune' against case assignment from outside, it becomes clear that the absence of a verb is the precondition for assigning case from outside. Since there are only structural properties involved it is no surprise that the structural case par excellence − the accusative − crosses the barrier. The only other case that is possible is the instrumental, since it requires no governing element and thus is not subject to barriers. The properties of case assignment clearly require that there be no verb in the embedded clause. But this is in conflict with general structural properties of sentences: Sentences are projections of the verbal elements (cf. Jackendoff 1977, Chomsky 1970, Hornstein 1977), i.e. they are to contain a verb. Thus if there no verb ever appears in a constituent, this constituent cannot be a sentence. It was the absence of a constant verbal element (i.e. the copula) which made it possible to replace the relative pronoun by a complementizer, which ends up in a structure that is not a structurally well formed sentence.

(33)

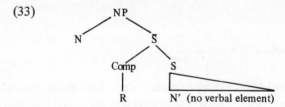

2.3.1 Summary

1) Nominal relatives have to be analyzed as originally copulative predicative clauses. The verbal element, being contextually determined and thus recoverable, was elidable:

a) there is a general option for copula elision in main clauses
b) copula elision improves the perception of otherwise perceptually difficult embedded clauses.

2) The absence of a verbal element obscured the government relation with regard to the case of the relative pronoun, which, as a consequence leads to a)
reanalysis by which a verb-less relative clause is reanalyzed as an attributive
non-sentential phrase which is part of the NP containing the head, b) the replacement of the pronominal sentence-introducer by a complementizer particle (*yat*) and c) a reanalysis resulting in so-called case-attraction.

It is important to emphasize the hybrid status of *yat* with respect to
options a) and c). The emergence of *yat* in nominal relatives is clearly de-
ducible from the theoretical framework, i.e. the properties of complementizers.

The actual breakthrough, however, has to be construed as a case of abduction (cf. Andersen 1973). There was a set of constructions which allowed
two different, incompatible, but equivalent analyses:

(34)   [N   [[$_{Comp}$yat] . . . . . .]$_S$]$_{NP}$
        [+ neuter] S

Yt 17.18   *staota ašəm yat vahištəm*
            'praised righteousness, which the highest value'

yat may be either analyzed as the pronoun or as the complementizer constant. Both analyses fit equally in the case of nominal relatives. If it is interpreted as pronoun, it is open for reanalysis: *yat* is analyzeable both, as the
original nominative or – after reanalysis – as accusative by agreement with
the head!

3 Middle Persian

The (Manichaean) Middle Persian corpus that we have at our disposal allows a
fascinating insight into how the problematic heritage of Old Iranian is tackled.
There is one fact to be mentioned that had a catalytic influence on the development: In Western Middle Iranian, due to a strong initial stress in the fore-
going period, the inflectional endings are gradually reduced and finally cause
the complete restructuring of the inherited Old Iranian syntax. – Since we
possess a complete computerized corpus of Manichaean Middle Persian, we
confine ourselves to this particular text corpus, which is relatively compact
in chronology and offers no problems of scribal and text tradition (all references are given according to Boyce 1975).

While *ya-* is the only relative pronoun in Old Iranian, the Middle Persian language has three of them. These are (in descending frequency): (35) *ky*, originating from an oblique form of the Old Iranian *ka-* interrogative pronoun, (36) *ᶜy*, from Old Iranian *ya-*, and finally (37) *cy*, a phonological variant of *ka-*. We give one example for each:

> (35) *ᶜyn zn, kyš yk pws ᵓst* (Sundermann 1975:90)
> 'this woman who has a son of her own'

> (36) *kwp ᶜy sdyg, ᶜy pwr xᵓr ᵓwd tšk bwd* (dh 3)
> 'the third hill which is full of thorns and scrubs'

> (37) *ᵓwd hrw cy bwd ᵓwd bwᵓd* (c 2)
> 'and all that was and will be'

So much for the relative clauses. *ᶜy* as descendant of *ya-* is rather inconspicuous as a relative pronoun, however, it combines with agent and pronominal suffix. Of particular interest in our context however are *ᶜy* and *ᶜyg* (the latter being an extended form from *ᶜy* without differentiation in usage), which are the continuants of the Avestan *yat̬-* construction (which, in a direct line, leads to the Modern Persian *ezāfe*-construction).

With respect to the properties of the complementizer system there are various options available for the implementation of clausal attributes (i.e. relative clauses).

Schwartz (1971:142) provided a classification of post-nominal relative clauses with respect to

a) presence or absence of an introducing particle (complementizer), symbolized below by *that*
b) presence vs. absence of a clause-initial relative pronoun, symbolized by *wh*
c) presence or absence of a non-relative pronoun (PRO) within the clause:

(in our terminology:)

$$(38) \quad a) \ N \ [_s \ldots \emptyset \ldots] \qquad\qquad [N \ [_s \ [\ \emptyset \ ]$$
$$\quad\quad\ \ b) \ N \ that[_s \ldots \emptyset \ldots] \qquad [N \ [_s that[_s - \emptyset -]$$
$$\quad\quad\ \ c) \ N \ that[_s \ldots PRO \ldots] \qquad [N \ [_s that[\ldots PRO \ldots]$$
$$\quad\quad\ \ d) \ N \ [_s wh. \ldots] \qquad\qquad [N \ [_s wh.[\ldots \ldots]$$
$$\quad\quad\ \ e) \ N \ that[wh. \ldots \ldots] \qquad [N \ [_s that \ wh.[\ldots \ldots]$$

The type we find in Old Iranian is clearly d). Due to the extension of the function of the relative pronoun as an introductory particle for attributes d) was reanalyzed as b). Evidence with a resumptive pronoun introduces the further possibility c).

(39) a) N [s̄ wh. . . . . .]
    bᵓ mᵓ byc hᵓd ks ky gwᵓd
    'But there should not be a person who would say'
                   (Brunner 1977:83)

   b) N [s̄ that . . .]
    ᵓfryd by̱h kw frzwfsᵓnd pd ᶜspwₗgᵓryy xwᵓryn
    'Blessed be the sisters that/which may become perfected
              in fullness' (Brunner 1977:237)

   c) N [s̄ that . . . PRO . . .]
    tw hy . . . dyᵓg ᶜy wyspᵓn qyrbgyhᵓn ᵓw frzyndᵓn kyt
    ᵓwyš pywsynd
    'You are the giver of all pious things to the children who
    long for you'   (Brunner 1977:113)

The appearance of (39) c) is a clear indication that the former relative pronoun is analysed as a complementizer particle. Since there is no longer a clearly identifiable *relative* pronoun to occupy the *wh* position in (39) a) it is no surprise that the interrogative pronoun, a *wh* − element, takes on this function and occupies the same position in relative clauses which it occupies in direct questions. In the following we want to stress two aspects:

a) the properties of the clausal attributes, which are conditioned by the two factors
   i) the degenerating inflectional system
   ii) the heritage of Old Iranian nominal attributes
b) the rise of the *ezāfe*-construction, which
   i) becomes the only exclusively attributive construction, and
   ii) shows rigid serialization.

The first question that calls for attention is the retreat of the old *ya*-type relatives in favor of the relative clauses introduced by interrogatives. As we noted in the summary above (2.3.2), there are two different syntactic positions, i.e. clause-introducers and nominal modifiers, which may be occupied by morphologically related though distinguishable (due to inflection) items. If the discriminatory function of inflection gets lost this leads to a merger of two entirely different syntactic systems. It does not come as a surprise that, given that there is a competing non-conflicting variant, this variant wins: In particular, a verb-final language has processing difficulties, since every sequence of a NP followed by the 'ambiguous' particle becomes ambiguous. being either a) a noun followed by a non-sentential attribute, or b) a noun followed by a sentential attribute, or c), in the worst case, a NP followed by an embedded clause.

We note that the Avestan conjunction *yaṭ* has no successor in Middle Persian, which on the one hand supports our analysis of Avestan – the conjunction is now confined to nominal attribution – and on the other gets rid of option c).

Yet the ambiguity of a) and b) is still problematic, since the disambiguating element, the verb, is clause-final, which implies the well-known difficulties of center embedding. All these problems disappear if $^c y$ is restricted to its *ezāfe*-use as an attributive marker. The Middle Persian evidence shows considerable uncertainty in applying the syntactic facilities offered by a system in transition from the inflectional type of Old Iranian with free word order to the strictly ordered, at least as far as the *ezāfe*-construction is concerned, Modern Persian type. To show this is one of the main purposes of the following notes. Let us start with the appositional type. With proper names the usage of *ezāfe* is possible (41) but not obligatory (40), otherwise it is generalized (42):

(40) *whmn šhryʾr* (cu 39)
  'Wahman the ruler'

(41) *nwhzʾdg* $^c yg$ *trkwmʾn* (n 1)
  'Nuhzadag the interpreter'

(42) *nwg* $^c spsg$ $^c y$ *nyw frzynd* $^c y$ *whmn* (cq 4)
  'the new bishop, the worthy son of Wahman'

As far as attributive usage is concerned, the material shows many different pattern. A genitive attribute, for instance, may be either in prenominal position without (43) or in postnominal position with *ezāfe* (44):

(43) *drxt* $^c yw$ *nyw* $^ʾ wd$ *bʾrwr twhm* (b 3)
  'a good and fruitful tree's seed'

(44) *sr* $^c y$ *wyspʾn wyhyhʾn* (c 1)
  'the head of all wisdoms'

Regarding personal pronouns there are two types of construction without relative particle, i.e. contact position (45) ore enclitic connection with preceding conjunctions (46):

(45) *pd tw nʾm* (bt 4)
  'in thy name'

(46) *ʾwtʾn pd ṭwhmgʾn* (n 3)
  'and to your (*ʾw-tʾn pd*) family'

The *ezāfe*, however, in anticipating the Modern Persian type, becomes more frequent:

(47) *dyl ᶜyg ᵓmᵓḥ* (cu 36)
'our heart (heart PART our)'

Adverbial phrases with preposition always occur in postnominal position (48).

(48) *prystg ᶜy ᵓbr rᵓmyšn* (bt 2)
'messenger PART for peace'

The Middle Persian relative particle, in contrast to Modern Persian usage, links with enclitic pronouns, e.g.

(49) *bwzᵓg ᶜym ᵓcptyᵓr* (be 18)
'my savior (*bwzᵓg ᶜy-m*) from adversity'

The prevailing instability in regard to the position of attributes is best shown in a context which includes several attributive adjectives. They may either precede the head noun

(50) *ᵓnwšg rwšn whyšt* (cu 9)
'eternal radiant paradise (*whyšt*)',

or stand on both sides

(51) *nwg xwrxšyd rwšnygr* (cu 42)
'new lightspending sun (*xwrxšyd*)',

or follow entirely in one of the four ways shown beneath:
i) Each adjective is linked with an *ezāfe* particle, e.g.

(52) *hᵓn rwšnyy ᵓwd xwšn ᶜy xwyš ᶜy nxwstyn* (y 20)
'that first (*nxwstyn*) light and beauty of theirs (*xwyš*)'

ii) No adjective attribute is linked by *ezāfe*, but the last one in the chain receives the conjunction *ᵓwd* ('and'):

(53) *prysp prᵓwhryn wᵓdyn rwšnyn ᵓdwryn ᵓwd ᵓbyn* (y 2)
'walls of ether, air, light, fire and water'

iii)The whole chain is linked to the regent noun by *ezāfe*, inside the chain, however, *ᵓwd* ('and') is used:

(54) *pyd ᶜy dwšᵓrmygr ᵓwd pryhrwd* (cb 2)
'beloved and sympathetic father'

iv) In an early text *ᵓwd* and *ᶜy* are even linked together:

(55) *ʾwrzwg ᶜy nr ʾwd ᶜy mʾyg* (u 3).
'male and female desire'

Finally, two cases of more complexity, which also show that congruence of number is the common usage, though exceptions do exist:

(56) *bwyst̲ʾn ʾfrydg ᶜyg ʾsprhmʾn xwmbwynʾn* (cm 10)
'blessed garden (*bwyst̲ʾn*) of fragrant (*xwmbwynʾn*) flowers'

(57) *prwxʾn przyndʾn ᶜy wʾxš ywjdhr* (cr 3)
'happy (*prwxʾn*) children of the Holy Spirit (*wʾxš*)'

3.1 Summary

In Middle Persian the whole syntactic system is on the move. Several solutions are applied, and the uncertainty which prevails is particularly evident in the older texts. The late texts, however, show signs of transition towards a new order in a syntactic system as it is found in Modern Persian.

One of its remarkable features is the strict postnominal serialization properties of the *ezāfe*-construction. In contrast with the freedom observed in Middle Persian attribution is confined to the *ezāfe*-construction which imposes rigid serialization. This strictly rigid serialization is due to the origin as a relative clause like construction, which was postnominal as has been discussed above. Prenominal occurrences are secondary, being of the correlative type.

Especially the existence of this type in a SOV language supports this assumption:

"As far as can be determined from available description of languages that utilize definite correlative constructions, all have basic SOV word-order. Surprisingly perhaps, none of these languages appears to use prenominal ad-relative clauses. Instead, some allow replacive or postnominal RC's or right-extraposed RC's as alternatives to the correlative construction. These facts suggest the following generalizations:
Y. Correlative relative constructions with a definite Rel NP and unreduced nominal heads are found only in languages in which verbs follow their objects in the basic word-order. (IU)
Z. If a language has correlative relative constructions, it does not have prenominal ad-relative clauses. (IU)" (Downing 1978:400)

It should be noted that according to Seiler's findings there are not any prenominal relatives introduced by *yat̲* found in Avestan, i.e. the predecessor of the postnominal property of *ezāfe*:

"Die Anfangsstellung der Relativgruppe innerhalb des attributiven Typus unterliegt einer wichtigen Beschränkung: Es gibt sie nur dann, wenn das Relativum in einer nach Genus, Numerus und Kasus veränderten Form auftritt; während der Typus N R^{yat}N' (vgl. Übersicht C.A.c.a.) sehr geläufig ist, ist R^{yat}N'N so gut wie gar nicht vertreten". (Seiler 1960:125)

4 Modern Persian

ezāfe is a term employed by grammarians to describe a variety of constructions in this language that consist of a noun followed by an enclitic particle *-i* followed by a noun, or adjective, or adverb, or infinitive, or a pronoun. These adjuncts are interpreted as attributive.

> (58) a) *āb-i garm* (adj.)   (water-i hot)   'hot water'
>   b) *rūz-i gu*dh*ashta* (part.)   (day-i passed)   'the previous day'
>   c) dj*awānān-i imrūz* (adv.)   (youth-i today)   'modern youth'
>   d) *mughi^c-i raftan* (inf.) (time-i to go) 'time for going'
>   e) *lab-i la^{ɔ}l* (noun)   (lip-i ruby)   'a ruby lip'
>   f) *la^{ɔ}l-i lab* (noun)   (ruby-i lip)   'the ruby of the lip'
>   g) *kitāb-i ḥasan* (pr.noun)   (book-i Hasan) 'Hassan's book'
>   h) *rūz-i ba^{ɔ}d az ān atafāḳ*   (day-i after that incident)
>   'the day after the incident'

As the above examples and the following ones show, *ezāfe* is the general attributive construction, i.e. any noun modifier is placed after the noun, preceded by the enclitic particle. Although there have been proposed analyses which try to derive this construction from an underlying relative clause (Tabaian 1975, Palmer 1971) with deletion of *budan* in (59) a) or *daštan* as in (59) b), these analyses are bound to fail, since it is only a limited sub-class of the whole paradigm which lends itself to such an analysis. Since relative clauses serve the same function it is no surprise that there is an overlap. But that cannot be taken as justification.

> (59) a) *kitāb-i girān* (book-i expensive) 'expensive book'
>   ⇒ *kitāb-i ki girān ast* 'book which is expensive'
>
>   b) *kitāb-i ḥasan* (book-i hasan) 'Hassan's book'
>   ⇒ *kitāb-i ki ḥasan dārad* 'book which Hassan has'

This approach fails in two respects, discussed by Windfuhr (1979:58–61): There are *ezāfes* whose underlying structure implies a deviant semantic interpretation as in (60) where a) is interpreted as inalienable possession, whereas the relative clause is compatible only with alienable possession:

(60) a) *dast-i ḥasan*   (hand-i hasan)   'Hassan's hand'
    b) ⇒ **dast-i ki ḥasan dārad*   'the hand which Hassan
                                       has i.e. not his own'

The difference in the presuppositional content of a) and b) follows from their
different syntactic status. The second case can be illustrated with *ezāfe* attributes which cannot be derived by copula-deletion, since their underlying
structure does not contain one:

(61) *(ḥasan) ba tihrān raft*   'Hassan to Teheran went'
    ⇒ *raftan-(i ḥasan) ba tihrān* 'Hassan's going to Teheran'

Clearly there is a nominalized infinitive independent from the occurrence of
ezāfe indicated by bracketing in (61). There is no need for additional devices:
The nominalized infinitive will be treated just like any noun with regard to
attribution. Anyone advocating a transformational derivation is forced to
allow for the transformations a format which exceeds the limits for possible
transformations, which in addition, are not allowed to change category labels
(cf. Wasow 1977: 331). What is the biggest disadvantage of such an approach,
however, is the fact, that it appears to be a matter of pure chance, that the
application of a range of different rules all result in the same innocuous construction. There is no need for a transformational derivation and no generalization it would capture. It is a triviality that there are paraphrases for an attributive construction like *ezāfe* if there is another attributive construction,
in this case a relative clause. It is far from trivial, however, to see how noun
phrases like those in (63) could be derived transformationally. The examples
can be derived simply in the base by means of rules (62):

(62) N″   →   N′   M
    M   →   m   X′ (or X″, s. below)

    N′   → $\begin{cases} N' M \\ N \end{cases}$

(63) a)   b)

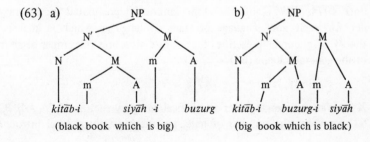

(black book which is big)   (big book which is black)

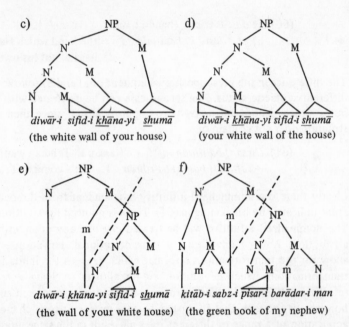

c) *diwār-i sifid-i khāna-yi shumā*
(the white wall of your house)

d) *diwār-i khāna-yi sifid-i shumā*
(your white wall of the house)

e) *diwār-i khāna-yi sifid-i shumā*
(the wall of your white house)

f) *kitāb-i sabz-i pisar-i barādar-i man*
(the green book of my nephew)

If the sentences in (63) are generated in the structures sketched above by phrase structure rules of the base-component of the grammar we are in a position to deduce various consequences for the application of general principles of the theory of the base component.

4.1 Excursus: X̄-convention

It is assumed that the theory of grammar is to define a highly restricted class of grammars for natural languages. For the categorial part of the base component this is realized by the requirement that phrase structure rules are subject to a version of the X̄-convention (cf. Chomsky 1970, Emonds 1976, Jackendoff 1974, 1977) and therefore cannot be postulated in arbitrary manner for each new language or stage of language which is analyzed. The theory of grammar prescribes that phrase structure rules must be an instance of the general scheme (64):

$$(64)\ X^i\ \rightarrow\ \ldots\ X^{i-1}\ \ldots$$

X is a variable ranging over any lexical category such as N, V, Adj, P. 'i' and 'i-l' represent the number of bars, i.e. the hierarchical level introduced by phrase structure rules. X is referred to as the head of the phrase. Scheme (64) yields structures like (65).

(65)   :

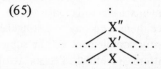

The path from X via X′ to X″ is called the main projection line. Scheme (64) defines the available phrase structure rules of a grammar and will permit a particular grammar to contain the rules (66):

(66) a) N″ → Det N′
     b) N′ → N′ (M)
     c) M → m X″

m abbreviates for the position of modifiers. In case of *ezāfe* 'i' is inserted by lexical insertion under m. 'Det' stands for the class of determiners and other specificatory elements as e.g. the article 'an'. Thus the proposed rules in (62) are properly represented as (66) b) and c). A comparison of the structural pattern in (63) reveals that they induce left-branching recursion: This seems to be an optimal structure for the processing of phrases whose degree of embedding is higher than three as e.g. (63) d) and f), since in these linearly branching structures the main projection line coincides with the iterative application of a simple bottom-up parsing principle (cf. Kimball 1974). The exceptionless head-modifier serialization thus facilitates parsing, a task relevant for processing. But there is no need to invoke processing strategies as an account for the remarkable serialization properties of the Modern Persian *ezāfe* in comparison with Middle Persian. There is a purely syntactical reason for the clear up:

As we have noted above Middle Persian shows three patterns for e.g. adjectival attributes: .

(67) a) Adj − N
        nwg ᶜ*spsg*   'the new bishop'

     b) N ezāfe Adj
        pyd ᶜ*y dwšᵓrmygr*   'beloved father'

     c) N Adj
        bwystᵓn ᵓ*frydg*   'blessed garden'

This patterning needs base rules that are exceptions from the principles of the X̄-convention. These principles require a unique serialization, as indicated in (11):

$$(68) \quad N^n \quad \rightarrow \quad \ldots N^{n-1} \ldots$$

The '. . ٪ .' is fixed through all categories. That is to say if a specifier precedes the noun and specifiers and complements have to be adjacent to the head, then complements are to follow. Since there is no way to distinguish categorically between various complements any complement will be subject to this serialization. If the distributional patterns of Middle Persian attributes are filtered through the principles of base their unstable status is recognizable immediately. We take it for granted that every exception from general principles needs special marking devices. An illustrative example is the serialization of adjectives with regard to their head. Due to the emergence of the *ezāfe* the noun-modifier serialization is to be interpreted as primary. First of all its position is fixed, being the successor of a relative clause. Secondly, since the inflectional system lost its functioning it is optimally encoded, marked by a particle. (67) a) therefore will be subsumed under b) which leaves a) as the exception from the general pattern. As a deviation it needs special marking. Inflection, which could fulfill this task, is inoperable. Since the inflectional system cannot be used the only possibility would be to bring a completely new device. Without discussion we assume that the appearance of new functions are always interpretable as assigning a new function to already existing elements, a shift in function (cf. the reanalysis of *yat̲*).

Since there are no clear options, we are driven to the conclusion that the exceptional pattern will be given up. It goes without saying that this change is also preferred on functional grounds, as to ease of perception. If there were an unmarked Adj-N order on a par with N-Adj any sequence (Adj)-N-Adj-N would be ambiguous between the alternative bracketings (N-A)-N and N(A-N).

Thus the resulting patterns are generated by the rules (66) which turn out to be in line with the $\bar{X}$-requirements. An analysis in terms of $\bar{X}$ reveals another remarkable and hitherto unregistered feature: (66) c) expresses the fact that any major category may occur in the modifier position of a noun phrase, i.e. NP, AP, PP. All these instantiations of X'' are attested, but the list is not complete: The V-projection is missing, since NP, AP, PP are the maximal projections of N, Adj, P, respectively. The principles of the base then require, provided that the analysis in (66) is correct, that the maximal projection of V should be able to occur as X'' in the expansion of (66) c). The maximal projection of V is $\bar{S}$ (cf. Jackendoff 1977:46). As a consequence we are prepared to find structures as (68).

(69)

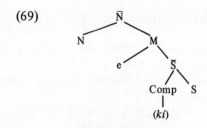

The appearance of the complementizer *ki* is predictable since it is the most common subordination particle. "The apparent multitude of functions of *ki* is quite easily explained by the observation that *ki* in contemporary Persian is a 'dummy' which is inserted in the surface string in case of subordinate clause embedding." (Windfuhr 1979:69). Instances of (69) are listed in (70):

> (70) a) *(ān) mard-e musinn-i ki kif dast-ash būd*
> b) *(yik) mard-e musinn-i ki kif dast-ash būd*

If we take into consideration that the difference between /i/ and /e/ is non-phonemic in contemporary Persian (cf. Windfuhr 1979:133–35, Lentz 1958: 183) although in some transcriptions 'i' is used for the ezāfe-particle and 'e' for the particle introducing a relative clause — then sentences (70) are identical with (70'), which Windfuhr (1979:65) cites as standard examples of restrictive relative clauses in Modern Persian:

> (70') a) *(an) mard-i musinn*   *-i ki kif dast-ash būd*
> (the older man   that had a briefcase)
>
> b) *(yik) mard-i musinn*   *-i ki kif dast-ash būd*
> (an older man   who had a briefcase)

The question why it is the relative clause introduced by the so-called 'demonstrative *i*' which is the restrictive relative clause, simply reduces to the fact that every instance of an *ezāfe* is attributive and thus restrictive. We would like to interpret this finding, which has not found clear interpretation in standard literature, as support for a properly constrained and explicit theory of grammar. It is the prognostic quality of a theory that helps to avoid wild guesses, as e.g.: "It would be important to investigate the possibility that all subordinate clauses in Persian are to be derived from underlying relative clauses." (Windfuhr 1979:69).

5   Afterthoughts – or what has been explained?

If we were to give a one-sentence answer to the above question several statements come into mind. What has been explained is
a) the development of an attributive construction, from its beginning in
    Avestan to contemporary Persian
b) a typological difference in the syntactic patterns of two historically re-
    lated languages
c) a difference in the grammars of two historically related languages
d) the mechanisms that lead to the emergence of different grammars for
    historically related stages of a language.
The list should reflect the ranking with regard to the ambitiousness of the
explanatory standards. The explanations we have offered rest on two sub-
theories of a general theory of grammar: i) the theory of the categorial component (i.e. base) of a grammar and ii) (a sketch of) the theory of case assignment. Given the specific conditions at the various stages of the languages in
question, we tried to deduce the respective grammars from the general theory
of grammar. It seems to us that the attempt was successful, and that it could
be worthwhile therefore to take a stand on the claim that there is no explanatory theory of language change, as defended by Lass (1980, 1981). He is right,
in an uninteresting interpretation of his claim though: If there is no theory of
language change, there is no explanatory one, obviously. Metatheoretically
uninteresting as this interpretation is, Lass seems to stick to it. What his position implicitly seems to aim at is a criticism of the attempt to devise a 'diachronic grammar' as a theory of diachronic change. The unfruitfulness of
such an attempt has been discussed at length in Lightfoot (1979:Ch. 3), who,
unlike Lass, offers another perspective:

> "In the light of the formal diversity of possible changes, I hypothesize that there are
> no formal constraints on possible changes beyond those imposed by the theory of
> grammar. (. . .). A restricted theory of grammar can be seen to impose severe limits
> on possible changes, even though this approach to diachrony has by no means been
> successfully explored" (Lightfoot 1979:147).

Lass (1980) discusses three strategies of explanation and comes to the conclusion that
a) deductive-nomological explanations cannot be invoked for language change,
    because laws of the appropriate kind do not yet exist
b) probabilistic, as well as
c) functional models are able to provide neither necessary nor sufficient con-
    ditions for explaining and predicting (instances of) language change (cf.
    Lightfoot 1980:143).

Since we have referred occasionally to functional concepts, c) deserves closer inspection.

After Lass (1980:198) functional models are inadequate for at least two reasons:
i) the paradox of individualism (Lass 1981:§3)
ii) the concept of function has no coherent definition, and a principled definition of 'dysfunction' is missing (Lass 1980:86)
As for i) functionalism entails pace Lass two commitments:
1) The speech community is nothing more than the sum of its members, i.e. there are no emergent properties
2) Language does not exist in the collectivity in any mode different from that of its existence in any particular individual speaker.
For Lass it is paradoxical that the locus of change is a language, spoken by the collectivity of members of a speech community while the 'motivations' for change are more generally described in terms of the psychology of a single speaker. He tries to push 2) to the consequence that change in terms of functionalism should be pan-societal and instantaneous: "If language resides wholly in the individual and the underlying 'competence' of all individuals is substantially the same this predicts that a functional motivation will make itself felt by all members at the same time" (1981:§3). Taking this as a reductio ad absurdum he concludes that "the psychology of the individual is not our proper concern. As diachronic linguists we ought to be genuinely *dia*-chronic, our subject matter is pattern and evolution over time. (. . .) The subject of our discipline is radically trans- or metaindividual: the historian is involved with language *qua* language i.e. as it transcends and outlives its speakers" (1981:§3).

It is this very last statement that indicates where Lass is fundamentally mistaken. Although a historical linguist might characterize his activity as being involved with language, he should be more precise and better say that he is involved with grammar. Language as a social institution is an epiphenomenon, a derivative concept: It is the result of the interaction of various cognitive systems with grammar (cf. Chomsky 1980:90). Taking into consideration the way in which a language is learned, there is no reason to expect a priori that language cannot exist in the collectivity in a different mode from that of any particular speakers, i.e. there need not be a complete congruence, only an overlap.

It is this very fact which is the basis of language change as can be illustrated elegantly in Andersen's (1973) concept of language change: A particular language is based on a particular grammar. Grammars are discontinous objects transmitted via language. For an illustration we refer to Andersen's (1973: 767) diagramme:

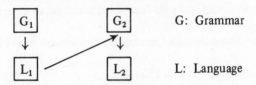

It is due to a *functional* requirement that language seems to exist in the collectivity in a mode different from that of its existence in any particular individual speaker. It is a functional necessity that communicability must be preserved between the speakers of speech community. Since grammars have to be created anew by each speaker in the course of language acquisition we expect that the individual grammars differ with respect to non-universal and peripheral properties of a specific language, since there is no one-to-one relation between languages and grammars. These differences have to be kept within limits, which can be viewed as an effect of the use of adaptive rules, with a slight modification of Andersen's (1973) notion. This self-regulatory property of the grammatical system is the cue for language change. It is a functional requirement again that the set of adaptive rules must be as small as possible.

Finally, what we have referred to as a cybernetic property of self regulation can be reconstructed in terms of the principles of UG (Universal Grammar): Since any grammar is constructed by filtering a particular language through the principles of UG, we expect restructuring whenever it is possible to choose a grammar G_i, different from G_j, where G_i is less marked for deviances from UG, i.e. G_i is the preferred projection of L onto a set of possible grammars for L. There is a trade-off relation between different grammars. It is this relation which Andersen tries to account for by the concept of adaptive rules.

According to Chomsky (1981) the relation between a particular grammar and UG is the following:

> "The grammar is a characterization of the steady state (reached in language acquisition. Z. & H.); the term universal grammar is now often used as a characterization of the initial state S_0. With systematic ambiguity, the same terms are used for the steady state and initial state themselves.
>
> Both terms — 'grammar' and 'universal grammar' — are modified from traditional usage, in accordance with the shift of focus from language to grammar that I outlined. Universal Grammar may be thought of as some system of principles, common to the species and available to each individual prior to experience, that determines the basic character of the particular grammars that develop at the steady state, that is, that determines the basic properties of the state of knowledge attained. The principles of universal grammar may be thought of as a function that maps experience into grammar." (Chomsky 1981:5)

It is now easy to see how Lass's paradox dissolves: Since language is the vehicle for transmitting grammar it is trivially the locus of language change, because every grammar is constructed upon a language. The restructuring, however, has to be described in terms of the principles which enable the individual speaker to acquire the grammar. Thus it is clear that it is an important goal for functional explanations to determine the tolerance level for initial structure opacity (cf. Lightfoot 1979:192f), since this is the onset for restructuring. Secondly, given that language change is in effect a restructuring process on the level of grammar it is obvious the language change is non-deterministic, since grammars practise therapy (rather than prophylaxis, pace Lightfoot (1979:147)).

5.1 On the charm of functional reasoning

Let us suppose for a moment that functional analysis will never meet the standards of an explanatory paradigm. Why, then, are linguists so fond of functional reasoning and so unwilling to adopt the scientific standards of 'hard science' for their purportedly explanatory arguments?

It seems that this has to be interpreted in relation with the particular objects of research. Linguists, not unlike biologists, try to gain insight into a dynamic system which is highly interactive, at least to a significant degree compared to the systems of physics. We would like to emphasize, therefore, that the study of generative grammar was marked by a significant shift in focus, from 'language' to 'grammar'.

> 'The language now becomes an epiphenomenon; it is whatever is characterized by the rules of grammar (perhaps, in conjunction with other systems of mind, or even other factors, depending on how we choose to conceive of the notion of 'language'). The grammar in a person's mind is real; it is one of the real things in the world. The language (whatever it may be) is not.' (Chomsky 1981:3)

The approach of generative grammar chosen for research into the systems of grammar is characterized as 'modular' (cf. Chomsky 1980:ch.2). For a similar approach cf. Dressler (1981).

The modular organization of grammar, i.e. a system of distinct though interacting systems, is not merely an analytic strategy but seems to reflect relevant properties of the way the system of grammar is structured cognitively. The interaction of the systems (modules) is analyzeable in functional terms, e.g. 'it is the function of morphology to encode syntactic relations which themselves function in semantic interpretation'. On the other hand, the interactional properties can be analyzed by means of functions as well: Language change, understood as a grammar change, can be construed as a consequence of the limitations on the ways the modules are able to interact. Whenever the proper interaction gets impaired, e.g. due to a change in the structure of a specific module, this may lead to a chain of restructuring processes in other modules, cf. e.g. the influence of stress shift (phonology-module) on syntax and morphology in Middle Persian.

Since the structures of the subsystems and their variability as well as the modes of interaction are determined by general principles of the theory of grammar, these principles can be taken as the general laws in a deductive nomological explanation. Thus any functional analysis, provided that it is based on a theory in terms of which these functions are expressible, can be framed as a deductive nomological explanation. There is no deductive explanation without a deductive theory. The study of grammar(s) – as exemplified in generative studies – provides a general theory. It is this line of reasoning which makes us feel that explanations are not banned from the realm of linguistics.

Note

* The authors wish to thank Arnold Evers, Jochem Schindler and Chlodwig Werba for valuable discussion. They assume, however, sole responsibility for the content and the shortcomings of this paper.

References

Andersen, Henning
    1973   "Abductive and deductive change", *Language* 49:765–793.
Bartholomae, Christian
    1979   *Altiranisches Wörterbuch, zusammen mit den Nacharbeiten und Vorarbeiten* (Berlin: de Gruyter).
Behaghel, Otto
    1932   *Deutsche Syntax. Eine geschichtliche Darstellung.* Vol. IV: *Wortstellung. Periodenbau* (Heidelberg: Winter).
Bever, Thomas G.
    1970   "The cognition basis for linguistic structure", *Cognition and the development of language,* edited by S. R. Hayes (New York: Wiley), 279–362.
Boyce, Mary
    1964   "The use of relative particles in Western Middle Iranian", *Indo-Iranica. Mélanges . . . Georg Morgenstierne* (Wiesbaden: Harrassowitz), 28–47.
    1975   *A Reader in Manichaean Middle Persian and Parthian.* (= Acta Iranica 9 = Sér. 3,2) (Leiden: Brill; Téhéran – Liège: Bibl. Pahlavi).
Bresnan, Joan W.
    1980   *Theory of complementation in English* (= MIT-doctoral dissertation) (New York: Garland).

Brunner, Christopher J.
1977   *A Syntax of Western Middle Iranian* (= *Persian Studies Series* 3) (Delmar, N. Y.: Caravan).
Chomsky, Noam
1970   "Remarks on nominalization", *Readings in English transformational grammar*, edited by R. A. Jacobs and P. S. Rosenbaum (Waltham Mass.: Ginn), 184–222.
1977   "On wh-movement", *Formal Syntax*, edited by P. Culicover and T. Wasow and A. Akmajian, (New York: Academic Press), 71–133.
1980   *Rules and representations* (New York: Columbia Univ.).
1981   "On the representation of form and function", *Linguistic review* 1:3–40.

Chomsky, Noam – H. Lasnik
1977   "Filters and control", *Linguistic inquiry* 8:425–504.
Culicover, Peter W.
1976   *Syntax* (New York: Academic Press).
Downing, B. T.
1978   "Some universals of relative clause structure", *Universals of human language*, vol. 4: *Syntax*, edited by J. H. Greenberg (Stanford: Univ. Press), 375–418.
Dressler, Wolfgang
1981   "Outlines of a model of morphonology", *Phonologica 1980*, edited by W. Dressler et alii (Innsbrucker Beiträge zur Sprachwissenschaft 36) (Innsbruck: Institut für Sprachwissenschaft). 113–123.
Emonds, Joseph E.
1976   *A transformational approach to English syntax* (New York: Academic Press).
1979   "Appositive relatives have no properties", *Linguistic inquiry* 10:211–243.
Geldner, Karl F.
1896   *Avesta. The sacred books of the Parsis.* Vol. 1–3 (Stuttgart: Kohlhammer).
Gershevitch, Ilya
1959   *The Avestan hymn to Mithra* (= *University of Cambridge oriental publications* 4) (Cambridge: Univ. Press)
Hornstein, N.
1977   "S and the X̄-convention", *Linguistic analysis* 3:137–176.
Insler, Stanley
1975   *The Gāthās of Zarathustra* (= *Acta Iranica* 8 = sér. 3,1) (Leiden: Brill; Téhéran – Liège: Bibl. Pahlavi)
Jackendoff, Ray
1974   *Introduction to the X̄-convention* (Bloomington: Indiana Univ. Linguistics Club).
1977   *X̄-syntax: a study of phrase structure* (Cambridge Massachusetts: MIT Press).
Keenan, Edward L.
1979   "The syntax of subject-final languages", *Syntactic typology*, edited by W. P. Lehmann (= *Harvester studies in cognitive science 10*) (Hassocks: Harvester Press), 267–327.
Kent, Roland G.
1944   "The Old Persian relative and article", *Language* 20:1–10.
Kimball, John
1973   "Seven principles of surface structure parsing in natural language", *Cognition* 2:15–47.
Kuno, Susumo
1973   "Constraints on internal clauses and sentential subjects", *Linguistic inquiry* 4:363–385.
1974   "The position of relative clauses and conjunctions", *Linguistic inquiry* 5: 117–136.

Lass, Roger
  1980   *On explaining language change* (= *Cambridge studies in linguistics* 27) (Cambridge: Univ. Press).
  1981   "Explaining sound change: the future of an illusion", *Phonologica 1980*, edited by W. Dressler et alii (Innsbrucker Beiträge zur Sprachwissenschaft 36) (Innsbruck: Institut für Sprachwissenschaft). 257–275.
Lehmann, Christian
  1979   *Der Relativsatz. Typologie seiner Strukturen. Theorie seiner Funktionen. Kompendium seiner Grammatik* (= Arbeiten des Kölner Universalien-Projekts 36) (Köln: Institut für Sprachwissenschaft der Universität Köln).
Lentz, Wolfgang
  1958   "Das Neupersische", *Handbuch der Orientalistik* I/iv/1 (Leiden-Köln: Brill), 179–221.
Lightfoot, David W.
  1979   *Principles of diachronic syntax* (= *Cambridge studies in linguistics* 23) (Cambridge: Univ. Press).
Monna, Maria C.
  1978   *The Gathas of Zarathustra. A reconstruction of the text* (Amsterdam: Rodopi)
Newmeyer, F. J.
  1980   *Linguistic theory in America* (New York: Academic Press).
Palmer, Adrian S.
  1971   *The ezafe construction in Modern Standard Persian.* (= unpubl. doctoral dissertation, University of Michigan).
Reichelt, Hans
  1909   *Awestisches Elementarbuch* (= *Indogermanische Bibliothek* I/i/5) (Heidelberg: Winter)
Schwartz, A.
  1971   "General aspects of relative clause formation", *Working papers on language universals (Stanford Univ.)* 6:139–171.
Seiler, Hansjakob
  1960   *Relativsatz, Attribut und Apposition* (Wiesbaden: Harrassowitz)
Sundermann, Werner
  1973   *Mittelpersische und parthische kosmogonische und Parabeltexte der Manichäer* (= *Berliner Turfantexte 4*) (Berlin: Akademieverlag).
Tabaian, Hessam
  1975   "Conjunction, relativization, and complementation in Persian", *Colorado research in linguistics (Univ. of Colorado)* 5:1–182.
Wasow, Tom
  1977   "Transformations and the lexicon", *Formal syntax*, edited by P. W. Culicover, T. Wasow and Adrian Akmajian (New York: Academic Press)
Windfuhr, Gernot L.
  1979   *Persian grammar. History and state of its study* (= *Trends in linguistics. State-of-the-art-reports* 12) (The Hague: Mouton)

ERIC P. HAMP

The reconstruction of particles and syntax

I insist that we cannot arrive at satisfactory (indeed, any) phonetic reconstructions without taking adequate account of the morpho-syntactic and semantic aspects of the construction(s). Likewise, we cannot reconstruct syntax without making the relevant morpho(pho)nological identifications. Apart from the fact that syntax is much more than word order, the simple manipulation of such symbols, and their presumed but ill defined classes, as OV and VO will not suffice; nor will the counting of instances; nor will the use of texts without elaborate allowance for their style or register characteristics, for their poetic formulae etc. I prefer for the present to concentrate on structures of modest scope, where our already acquired traditional knowledge reaches proportionately far. By "modest" I here mean two notions of scope: Either shortness of the average instance, i.e. "phrasal" status, i.e. small number of lower PS nodes; or small membership in the characterizing word class. In the latter case we can consider finite problems with great confidence, inspecting all crucial elements in detail. This choice is a matter of taste; I do not imply that other approaches and emphases should be rejected or avoided. To the contrary, without exploration from all valid vantage points we will fail to discover the limits and properties of our method. I choose here two problems of this latter sort, from Indo-European material. I offer, to each of these, solutions which have not before been proposed, and which I hope will find favour.

1 Slavic *i*, Lithuanian *ĩr* 'and'

I have written on 'and' in IE more than once recently; see, as the latest, my article in the *Kerns Memorial* (Hamp 1981). In that article I discussed *i* and *ĩr* briefly, on the basis of the scholarship which comes down to us, but my discussion was inconclusive and, I think, partly wrong. Let us inspect what has come down to us.

Lithuanian *ĩr* has been equated with Latvian *ir* now replaced by *un* and

Old Prussian *ir*. These in turn have been placed in relation to Lith. *ař* 'ob, order, interrogative', *arbà*, Latv. *ar* 'also, with', and again to Baltic *er* 'even, interrogative'. Baltic *ir* is then usually equated with Greek ἄρ, ῥα, ἄρα; this would reflect an IE *$r̥$*. Prior work is to be found in the material assembled in Fraenkel 1962; Frisk (1960:127) adds nothing substantial to the IE side.

On the other hand Slavic *i* tends to be traced to *$i̯ei$* or *ei*, of pronominal origin; for informative reference to earlier work see Sławski (1952–56: 442–3). Now if one were to start from a thematic stem *$i̯o$-*, a normal locative formation would indeed be *$i̯e-i$* (Hamp 1971:104–5; 1975:64). But such a stem, which might best be a relative pronoun, would scarcely be appropriate here. That is to say, explicitly, the phonetics proposed suggest a formative typical of relative syntax (not necessarily semantics!), and therefore not apt for generalized descent from conjoining(s). Surely we will do better here with the anaphora *ei- i-*; for its morphology see Hamp (1975–6: 68–9), and for the semantax see the Kerns Volume *loc.cit*. But then in that case *ei* is not the correct form for the locative singular, since this case formation was not based on the oblique stem *e-* in the original paradigm. In fact, the correct old locative sing. was *$i̥$* (Hamp 1976a:20–1).

Now there is no reason to deny that an IE particle *$r̥$* may have contributed at least in part to the genesis of Baltic *ir*. This is particularly true so long as we cannot accurately reconstruct the exact force and value of IE *$r̥$*. Let us therefore digress momentarily to consider some aspects of the probable nature of a particle *$r̥$*, and in this fashion clarify our grasp of the problem properly concerning us. Anders Ahlqvist (1975: 162–7) has recently paved the way for our understanding of some important dimensions of the particle *$r̥$* when he wrote about the different manifestations of the Old Irish preverb *ro*. Ahlqvist commendably dealt carefully with the phonology of his proposed particle *$r̥$*, but in the context of the present discussion there is room for some additional comment. In Celtic a sequence *ra* is impossible as a direct output of *$r̥$*; Kuryłowicz has labelled this a "morphological zero" grade, but that falls short of explaining – although I think there is in fact for Celtic and Latin (differently from Greek) a morphonological explanation. For the present, let us not complicate things but simply note that by strict phonetic change *$r̥$* may give contextually Celtic *ar* and *ri*, and from the latter next to labio-velar also *ru*, and subsequently from the last two by affection we can get *re* and *ro*. The rich possibilities of these beside *$pro > ro$* give an excellent lesson in care and caution with the phonetics in syntactic problems. Add to this the fact that *$r̥$* + *ro* in succession could appear either to be a Sievers variant *$r̥ro$* of *ro* after heavy syllable or *rHo* > Celtic *aro*, which latter would then be open to gobbling of the vowel by contraction, and the choices can rapidly become alarming unless very stern constraints are observed. Moreover, by historic Old Irish time *rr* is taken as "strong" *r*, which is what any unmutated initial *r-* is. Once these phonetic complexities are controlled, Ahlqvist gives a fine account of the recovery of Old Irish traces of the enclitic particle **ŗ* buried in the complex and dual syntactic (and also, I would add, semantic!) behaviour of the (non-enclitic!) preverb *ro*.

Additional to Ahlqvist, I suggest some more traces of **ŗ* in Celtic. First consider OIr. *etir . . . 7 . . . 7 . . .* (Thurneysen 1946:881), used for conjoining multiple strings; this has never been satisfactorily explained; see Hamp (1973: 239). This could be **anti-r,* with **ŗ* in the correct position enclitic to the cognate (or one of the merged cognates) of Eng. *and* and Germ. *und.* The internal structure (always an important aspect of syntactic problems) as well as the external function is then exactly parallel to OIr. *se-ch* (Thurneysen 1946:882), since *-r* is enclitic like *-ch.* Secondly, we seem to have an excellent trace in Welsh in the so-called "contracted" form of *ry* as *-r;* see Simon Evans (1964 # 185 and 272a, p. 241). After all, except for mild cases of elision before *following* vowel, Welsh simply does not lose or syncopate vowels at an early date, save in a very few well understood forms; see Hamp (1979: 343ff). Cf. also Welsh *o'r kyuarffei* 'if it might have met', and Roberts (1975: 9, note to 34). Moreover there are examples in Welsh where *ry* seems not to be semantically needed. Note the matching syntax in the following example, where we may easily imagine a "resumptive" *-r* for the second clause: *ny duc neb kyrch waeth no'r dugum ymma* 'no one has made a worse sally than I have made here [not made somebody sally worse than-*r* I-made here]'. Finally there is the Welsh prefix *cyfr-* 'utterly, very', for which I have never seen a satisfactory explanation; we cannot accept the thesis of alleged losses of syllables in a preverb/prefix such as *ry-* without further strong motivation (e.g. clear contexts of vowel absorption, vel sim); cf. Hamp (1979:343ff). Now the fact that this prefix semantically approaches *ro* 'very' (originally, but not later, semantically and syntactically the same as perfective *ro*) seems to me particularly important for the present topic, which would draw these elements together on quite separate grounds. Drawing in my reconstruction (Hamp 1973:243–4) of the syntax of OIr. consecutive $co^N <$ **kom,* I therefore suggest the origin of *cyfr-* $<$ **kom-ri+* $<$ **kom-r+* '*and-furthermore'. Through this collocation we see the possible meaning of **ŗ* in deeper and enriched focus.

When these deeply embedded and old Celtic reflexes — non-productive fossils and debris are always the most diagnostic, as Meillet pointed out, provided we can motivate their former status — are ranged parallel to the known Greek and Tocharian enclitic sentence particles there can scarcely be any doubt of the reconstruction for the phonetic and gross syntactic aspects. This weak concatenator, of difficult semantics but perhaps even bound up with verbal diathesis or deixis (if Watkins' suggestions on the *-r* endings of verbs lead anywhere), notably took second, or Wackernagel's, position, and appears able to co-occur with and reinforce a clearly conjoining connective. In short its syntax points to its being not a conjunction 'and', but a suitable companion to such a connective. This does not seem to be what we are looking for in Baltic *ir*.

Now if we are to search for a different origin for Baltic *ir*, we shall invoke two principles to govern our search. One of these principles is historically specific: we will favour a solution that conforms to our emerging picture of IE dialectology; this principle is a restricted and applied form of Occam's razor. The second principle dictates that for such an element with such a semantactic function (in this case, a major, and sentence-, conjoining connective) we seek an origin with an internal morphology and semantics which is found elsewhere, at least in the same linguistic family or culture area or Sprachbund. The second principle, again a specimen of Occam's razor, may be called a pseudouniversal in a good sense: i.e. while historical specifics will be taken into account, the structure favoured will belong to a small number forming a set believed to characterize human languages generally.

Now to the specifics of our proposal, based on these criteria. We believe Baltic and Slavic (and, less closely, Albanian) to be closely related dialects of IE. Therefore we shall seek a common solution. Now I have already argued (Kerns volume, loc. cit.) that among IE expressions for 'and' we find a notable set of locatives; so it is with Armenian *ew* and English *and* as well as Albanian *e-dhe* in all likelihood. I have also pointed to the fact that several IE words for 'and' have a pronoun as their original base. We are looking for a structure, then, that could be glossed 'there(up)on, in that(case)' and the like. Latin, a well explored language, provides a set of models. Turning to Kühner-Stegmann and Thierfelder (1955), we find as 'consecutives' (176 a and b, p. 146) *eō, ideō*, (176 f,g,h, p. 147) *hinc, inde, proin(de)*, and (153.4, p. 17) *atque adeo* as a reinforcement of *atque*. All these Latin elements contain locative-ablative forms of the anaphora.

I have said above that the true locative singular of the IE anaphora in my view was **i*. This will immediately yield Slavic *i* by known phonetic, allegro, and clitic (Ashby 1981) conditions: **i* gives *i* which initially must always take pro(s)thetic *j-;* then *ji > i.*

On the other hand **i* gives Baltic and Lith. *i*. But now we must note that Lith. 'where' is *kur̃*, i.e. the ancient locative **ku + -r*. I have discussed this morphological formation for these ancient pronominals, (Hamp 1974a: 7–8). Therefore we should expect the locative of the anaphora to yield Lith. *i-r̃*.

All our criteria are now satisfied.

2 Albanian negatives

The *Fonetika dhe gramatika e gjuhës së sotme letrare shqipe* II (Tiranë 1976) lists (370) as negative particles *jo, nuk, s', mos, jo që jo, asqë* (adding a protective "etc."). To these should be added the non-finite form of the verb with *pa,* otherwise meaning 'without' (ibid. 289–91). There are also negative adverbs, e.g. (ibid. 317, 318) *kurrë* etc., *asgjë-kundi, (kurr-) kund.* Our discussion here embraces only *nuk, s* (and its combinations), *mos,* and *kurrë.*

We begin with Eqrem Çabej's most recent account (*Studime etimologjike* 92) s.v. *as* (there is no need to dwell for the moment on the uses of this concatenation): < *a* interrogative + *s* negative, which string is, however, wrongly equated in constituency with *mos.* This string could in fact be composed of a conflation with the Latin *aut* + the element NEG, i.e. *s.* With this value for *s,* as we shall see, the string must be recently formed. It is, however, at least as old as Buzuku (1555); *as iγ dini seh muo meh duhete meh clene ende caphset teh atit tim?* [A s ju dini se mua më duhetë me klenë (qenë) ndë kafshët të Atit tim?] 'Don't you know that I must be about my Father's matters (business)?'[1]

kurrë 'never', in which there is no need for us to notice dialect variants, is partly clear, but not completely so to me: We must have *kur* 'when' + NEG, perhaps **ne,* but I am not sure what else terminated the word so that a final *-ë* was left. From this the etymologically pleonastic *as- mos-kurrë* were formed; these are surely not old, and we may compare *as- mos-kush* 'no one', *as- mos-kund* etc. In any event, we find in *kurrë* the IE **ne* somehow buried.

We must now stop to take note of the presence of IE **k^w id* 'what, something, at-all' in Albanian. *si* 'how' is probably **k^w id* as an adverbial accusative, but it could imaginably also be **k^w ei(-)*; cf. Slovene *či*, Pol. *czy.* 'What' in Albanian, in its simplest form, is *ç(ë).* This must have developed early from **tod-k^w id* > **të-či* > **t(ë)ǯë* > [č]. For the pronominal construction cf. *tânë* 'all' < **tod-óinom* 'that-one', and Slavic *čito* 'what' < **k^w id+tod.*

In Albanian there are two simple predicate/sentence negatives, shown above as *nuk* and *s.* Their distribution is very difficult to describe or predict, and is at present largely undescribed in detail in explicit terms. Some dialects nearly lack *s;* it is heavily governed by prosody, following consonantism, identity and "centrality" of verb and phrase, etc., and may be avoided before vocalic object pronoun. Some examples; I choose these from a casual reading of Buzuku: *e γ nuche genohe* [E u nukë e njoh], 'And I don't know him'; LI verso b (II Kings IV, 6) *Mā nukë kā anë* (slavishly) 'There is no vessel more'; XLVII end . . . *aj di se u bukë nukë kam. Tjetërë nukë kam* . . . 'he knows that I do not have bread. Other have I not . . .'; XII verso (*Psalm. 20–1*) *E kështu s kā bām gjithë fare, e atyne nukë u kallëzoi gjyqetë e tī.* 'And he has not done thus to any race, and to them his judgements are not told'. We see that as early as 1555 both *nukë* and *s* could occur before, e.g. *kā* 'has'; my notes from outlying enclaves reveal similar subtleties which I have not learnt to predict. But I must confess that I have not worked systematically on this problem, nor have I studied the incidence with tense in Buzuku. I think however that these spots of ignorance will not be damaging to our current findings.

   nuk(ë) is least well analyzed in the scholarly literature. Jokl (reproduced in Tagliavini 1937:207) had it **ne + kë,* but we can be much more precise and broadly explanatory. The dialects show a fair number of variants for *nuk(ë)*, which I shall introduce from my fieldnotes without documenting them in detail. *nuk(ë)* must be an early conflation of *nëkë* and Latin *nunquam.* The presence of the latter is demonstrated by the survival of the alternant *nëngë* in some dialects. If instead of being reduced by a "French e-muet" rule to *nëng* both *nëkë* and *nëngë* suffered the reduction in the first syllable, both these latter merged as *ngë* (> *ng*). Moreover *nëkë* could have been aided in its survival by Latin *nec* and *neque;* cf. my remarks on Romanian *nici* (Hamp 1976b:36). Here we appeal to known Sprachbund facts to help explain the competition of multiple variants, a multiplicity we cannot blink at and which gives us valuable data for the total explanation. Our basic inherited form, without outside source, is then seen to be *nëkë.* This is indeed parallel to Greek οὐκί, but the exact reconstruction must be **ne-k^{w}od* or **ne-k^{w}ō(i).* Such a predicate as *nuk u-dogj* 'it didn't get burnt up' must be reconstructed as **ne-k^{w}o- e-ue dhēg^{w}h-.*

   It is now possible for us to consider *s.* We may dismiss without discussion G. Meyer's Latin *dis-* (wrong morpho-syntax, unnecessary borrowing, inexact phonology) and Pedersen's equation with Armenian *č* and *oč* (see Tagliavini 1937:242). We shall also improve upon Jokl's attempt to explain *mos* (see Tagliavini 1937:197) in the process. We have reviewed above the evidence for the presence of IE **k^{w}id* in Albanian. I have proposed (Hamp 1974b: II, 156) that *s* be derived from **k^{w}i* < **(ne)k^{w}id* with loss of **ne* by a deletion rule; I should be reprimanded for such a suggestion, since I had no idea how such a deletion syntax, not inherently beyond belief in itself, arose. I suggested (Hamp 1975–6:67) that the loss of **ne* be compared to French (*ne*) . . . *pas*; but we have no direct evidence that the phonetic and allegro and clitic (Ashby 1981) conditions that obtain in French applied in early Albanian. Nevertheless, I submit that *s* is indeed the descendent of **k^{w}id*, and that the present account should supersede that of Çabej (1976: II, 104–5).

   Our strongest argument that *s* continues **k^{w}id* and not some kind of **NEG lies in the structure which we must reconstruct for *mos*, the prohibitive and subordinate NEG in Albanian. It is agreed by all scholars, and obvious, that *mo-* is cognate with Greek μή, Armenian *mi*, etc. and goes back to **mē* or *meH$_e$*. It is this portion of the structure that must contain the lexicalization of NEG. We therefore cannot assign NEG to *-s* without violating a principle of reconstruction: The same semantic element cannot be reconstructed for a single structure twice without the reconstruction also of a suitably motivated copying, or concord, rule. Hence, *-s* must be **-k^Wid*. The precise comparandum for *-s* < **-k^Wid*, and hence also for *s* 'not' as we shall see, is therefore the 'emphasizing' Indic (RgVeda +) *-cid*, Avestan *-čit̲*, OPersian *-čiy*, and the 'generalizing' *-cid* used with relatives, conjunctions, and *mâ* (RV 621.1). We may also structurally relate to *mo-s* < **meH$_e$-k^Wid* the adverbial *mâ-kis* and *mâ-kîm* = Avestan *mā(δa)čim*, and Greek μήτι 'lest by any means, that by no means; whether perchance'. Finally, it is clear to us that **mē* was not likely to get detached in *mo-s* when we recall that in a number of Greek constructions with μή this particle occurred initial in the clause; thus the nexus **mé̄-k^Wid* was natural and not likely to be subject to movement or tmesis. Albanian *mos* is therefore guaranteed as continuing a specific IE collocation consisting schematically of the formants **[-FACT] [NEG] [EMPHASIS]* (or [CATEGORICAL] or [ALL]) and the rule **EMPH-k^W* → Qualifying-enclisis, vel sim.

We are now in a position to return to *s*, which we have derived from **k^Wid*, or rather **-k^Wid*. I propose now to rehabilitate my first proposal of **(ne)-k^Wid* by recovering the necessary syntax and conditions for loss of **ne*. First of all, we may justify the nexus by identifying in Indo-Iranian the syndrome of comparanda. These comparanda are seen to be simply additional members of the selfsame class of forms, i.e. further tokens of identically the same structure, that we have appealed to above in the equation of Indo-Iranian *mā* with Alb. *mo-*. We are thus occupied again with the collocation **[± FACT] [NEG] [EMPHASIS]* and the rule **EMPH-PRONOM* → Qualifying-enclisis. A close match is Vedic *ná-kis* and *ná-kîm* 'nimmer, nicht', and a highly similar parallel is Vedic *néd* 'nicht' = Avestan *nōit̲*. OPersian *naiy* < IE **né-id* 'NEG+anaphora-EMPH'.[1] The last has then been extended in Iranian to collocations with **ne* preposed: Avestan *naē-kay-* 'nemo, nihil' and *naē-ča*, *naēdā(čit̲)* (*-čim*) 'neque, Umbrian *neip*'. But it is Avestan that shows the most suggestively close structure to Alb. *s* < **(ne) -k^Wid*, with *naē-čĭm naē-čiš* 'nòn'. Thus we may juxtapose (V. 18.56f) *čiš aiṅhe asti uzvarəzəm* 'quid eius est piaculum?' and *naēčiš aiṅhe asti uzvarəzəm* 'non eius est piaculum'. We might put these into mock-Albanian: *Ç'është të dhënëtë të tī? Atī(në) s i është të dhënëtë* (Only some dialects would use the extended form of the pronoun *atinë* 'to him, his'; this pair of sentences is neither expected nor properly topicalized Albanian). Finally, we find the precise equivalent, but with **ne* relexified, in Ionic Greek οὐκί and Attic οὐκ + V 'not', which reflect pre-Mycenaean **ou-k^{W}i(d)*.

The way is now prepared for the crucial question: If *s* is derived from **(ne)-k^{W}id* and *nëkë* from **ne-k^{W}o-*, why does *s* lose **ne* but not *nëkë*? The answer must be that the two had, or participated in, different syntaxes; i.e. the behaviour of **-k^{W}id* was quite different from that of **k^{W}o-*. Since **-k^{W}id* was enclitic it could be detached from **ne* and cliticized elsewhere, at least within the phrase. Thus we have *s kam* 'I don't have' < **né-k^{W}id kapmi*, but also **né x́-k^{W}id kapmi* and **x́-k^{W}id né kapmi*. On the other hand, as I have shown elsewhere, the vocalism seen in **k^{W}o-* is that of the pronominal suffixed, or combining, form; we might imagine a formation in the order of Greek πῶς 'How, in any way'. Thus we have at bottom here a NEG-prefixed (compounded) indefinite pronoun in some adverbial inflexion or derivation corresponding to Ionic οὔκως 'by no means'; compounded **ne-*, which had been prefixed by a NEG-attachment rule, could not subsequently be detached and moved. The constituency of these two different bipartite structures explains completely their varying potential for separation of their components in their subsequent history.

In contemporary English we might gloss **né-k^{W}id* 'not at all' and **ne-k^{W}o-* 'no-way'.

If, as we have just argued, the order and attachment of **né . . . k^{W}id* was open to different possibilities we might easily expect different fates and roles, and even semantactic reflexes for the collocations of these two components. So for example we find different results in Modern English for NEG in *not, none, aught, un-, fuck-all, (I could care,) less forget-it*. But we must now enquire into the mechanism whereby **ne* was lost without trace in the modern language. I suggest that the crucial element is to be found in the structure of optional and contextual forms of the personals of Albanian. It should first be noted that personal pronouns may occur as emphasizing or topicalizing forms in subject and object relation in close syntactic association with the verb nucleus. It seems in fact that throughout the Balkan Sprachbund it was common, and regular in certain case relations, for a personal form which was called forth in addition to the expected unstressed adverbal form and which served to topicalize etc. to be both stressed and suffixed. The shape of this suffixal areal feature was *-nV;* see my discussion (Hamp 1976b: 35–6). Thus, as a result of this suffixation, which has become partly optional and partly dialectal (and now selectively standardized), we find in Albanian *u* and *unë* 'I' (the latter is the standard), *ti* and *tinë* 'thou' (the former is the standard), etc.

With these elements and optionalities (originally stylistic?) in mind, let us reconstruct some probable sample sequences: *u s kam 'I* don't have' < *ég-k^W id né kapmi = unë s kam* < **ég-ne-k^W id né kapmi* ⇒ *ég-ne-k^W id kapmi* 'ég né-k^W id kapmi = u s/nuk kam' > *ég-ne k^W id-kapmi* 'unë s-kam'. What has occurred here is of course an instance of syntactic misdivision and morphonemic misassignment. It is a very harmless instance of the principle that I have called "derring-do" (Hamp 1976c:348ff.).

In this syntactic reassignment there was no semantic loss in the basic sentence structure. At most there was loss in stylistic force.

Note

1. The OPers. *mātya* (prohibitive), which is *mā+tya* (Kent §292b), could lead us to consider analyzing Alb. *mos* as **mē + tị̄V* instead of **mē + k^W id*. This is seemingly, though not particularly relevantly, supported by the fact that the forms of the Albanian "article" (or concord particle in NPs) in *s-* must be derived from the same conflation of pronouns, i.e. **t-ị̄V-*, as that found in Old Persian. However the Albanian syntactic conditions relating to the rise of the concord particle are restricted to NPs, whereas we see that Iranian had a pattern which could generate new collocations of pronouns, such as *tya,* with negatives.

References

Ahlqvist, A.
  1975 "A note on Old Irish *ro*," *Ériu* 26:162–167.
Ashby, William J.
  1981 "The loss of the negative particle *ne* in French", *Lg.* 57:674–687.
Çabej, E.
  1976a *Studime Gjuhësore* (Prishtine:Rilindja).
  1976b *Studime etimologjike në fushë të shqipes,* II, A-B (Tiranë: Akademia e Shkencave).
Evans, D. Simon
  1964 *A Grammar of Middle Welsh* (Dublin: Institute for Advanced Studies).
Fraenkel, E.
  1962 *Litauisches etymologisches Wörterbuch,* 2 Bde (Heidelberg: Carl Winter Verlag), xxiii, 1560 pp.
Frisk, Hj.
  1960 *Griechisches etymologisches Wörterbuch,* Bd I (Heidelberg: Carl Winter Verlag), xxx, 938 pp.
  1970 *Griechisches etymologisches Wörterbuch,* Bd II (Heidelberg: Carl Winter Verlag), 1154 pp.
  1972 *Griechisches etymologisches Wörterbuch,* Bd III (Heidelberg: Carl Winter Verlag), 312 pp.

Hamp, E.P.
1970   "Locative singular in -ει", *IF* 75:105–106.
1973   "Inordinate clauses in Celtic", *Papers from the Comparative Syntax Festival* (Chicago Linguistic Society), 229–251.
1974a   *"Yrà"*, *IJSLP* 17:7–8.
1974b   "The major focus in reconstruction and change", *Historical linguistics* II, edited by J. Anderson and C. Jones (Amsterdam: North Holland), 141–167.
1975a   "Latin *sīdus, sīdera"*, *AJP* 96: 64–66.
1975b   "Miscellanea Celtica", *Studia Celtica* 10–11:54–73.
1976a   "Lat. *inde"*, *AJP* 97:20–21.
1976b   "Some Romanian areal etymologies", *SCL* 27:33–36.
1976c   "Why syntax needs phonology", *Papers from the Parasession on Diachronic Syntax,* edited by S. Steever et al. (Chicago: CLS), 348–364.
1979   "On syllabic reduction and syntax", *Festschrift Szemerényi,* edited by Bela Brogyanyi (Amsterdam: Benjamins), 343–50.
1981   "Albanian *edhe* 'and' ", *Bono homini donum: Essays in historical linguistics in memory of J. Alexander Kerns,* edited by Y. L. Arbeitman, A. R. Bomhard (Amsterdam: Benjamins), 127–131.
Kent, Roland G.
1950   *Old Persian* (New Haven: The American Oriental Society).
Kühner, R. – C. Stegmann – A. Thierfelder
1955   *Ausführliche Grammatik der lat. Sprache* (Leverkusen: Gottschalksche Verlagsbuchhandlung).
Roberts, B. F., ed.
1975   *Cyfranc Lludd a Llefelys* (Dublin: Institute for Advanced Studies).
Sławski, F.
1952-56 *Słownik etymologiczny języka polskiego* I (Kraków: Tow. Miłośników Języka Polskiego).
Tagliavini, C.
1937   *L'Albanese di Dalmazia* (Firenze: Olschki).
Thurneysen, R.
1946   *A Grammar of Old Irish* (Dublin: Institute for Advanced Studies).

MARTIN B. HARRIS

On the strengths and weaknesses of a typological approach to historical syntax*

During the last decade or so, numerous scholars, starting from the (synchronic) implicational universals associated primarily with the work of Joseph Greenberg, have suggested that the frequent correlation of various morphological and syntactic features in diverse languages may be of interest to the diachronic linguist. In particular, it has been proposed that languages will tend to evolve towards greater 'consistency' in terms of a typology based on sets of features which frequently co-occur, and that the historical grammarian can make use of this fact in his analyses. Within such a framework, the known history of certain languages has been examined to see to what extent this confirms the typological hypothesis and, more controversially, attempts have been made to engage in syntactic reconstruction, particularly of Indo-European, on the assumption that the hypothesis is correct.

More recently, the value of a typological approach to historical syntax has been called into question. The present paper will examine in particular observations made by David Lightfoot (see especially Lightfoot 1979a, 1979b) and Neil Smith (Smith 1981) with a view to seeing to what extent their criticisms are valid, will consider recent work by John Hawkins (see especially Hawkins 1979, 1980), and will conclude with the view that, while some of the more extreme claims made in favour of the utility of a typological approach to historical syntax cannot be upheld, it is nevertheless the case that any theory which ignores the insights gained by such an approach is substantially impoverished by so doing.

By way of introduction, let us consider the theoretical framework within which Lightfoot operates, noting as we do so substantial areas where disagreement may be more apparent than real. Central to Lightfoot's work is the distinction between a 'theory of grammar' and a 'theory of change'. Lightfoot asserts, surely without fear of contradiction, that given an adequate synchronic theory of grammar, there would be two constraints providing 'the upper bound to possible diachronic changes' (1979a:141): one would be that no change could occur, the result of which could not be generated by a possible grammar of natural language, and the other is that mutual intelligibility must be maintained between generations. ('Both grammars [i.e. that of the earlier and later generation] must satisfy the limits on a possible grammar of a natural language. The grammars must also generate outputs which permit mutual comprehensibility' 1979b:385.) The first of these conditions must be true if, like Lightfoot, we 'take the theory of grammar to specify what counts as a possible grammar of a natural language' (1979a:141); the second is a pragmatic necessity. One goal of grammatical theory is therefore to specify the absolute limits of historical change, another to indicate the maximal permissible differences between the grammars of succeeding generations. It is also in Lightfoot's view a central question for grammarians to ask *why* syntactic change occurs in a language, a question to which he proposes various answers, answers which do not include a 'drift towards consistency' as advanced by typologists. It seems important to note at this stage that it is also a legitimate object of study to consider the 'manner' in which a language changes, that is to ask *how* a language moves from one *état de langue* to another, whether there are patterns discernible in this area, and if so whether any possible explanations can be advanced for the observed phenomena. While fully accepting Lightfoot's own goals, therefore, and sharing his distaste for the fact that some recent work appears to be set within no theory of grammar of any kind, it is not *prima facie* evident that other goals and other methods have nothing to offer.

Let us now turn to the distinction between a 'theory of grammar' and a 'theory of change'. Lightfoot's two principal axioms are (i) that the second is logically dependent on the first − which is not in dispute − and (ii) that 'possible changes cannot be *formally* distinguished from impossible ones' (1979a:141). ('There appear to be no formal constraints on the ways in which a grammar may differ from that of the preceding generation, beyond constraints imposed by the theory of grammar . . .' 1979b:385). The fact that the goals prescribed for a theory of grammar as described above, though eminently desirable, are at present unattainable, coupled with the inability to formalize in a watertight fashion any other patterns and regularities apparent in diachronic data, causes Lightfoot to adopt an extremely cautious attitude towards a possible theory of change. This is perhaps typified in his discussion of analogy (1979a:343−72). Within a (synchronic) theory of grammar, Lightfoot observes, analogy has no role; within a possible theory of change, it would be excessively powerful, and in any case cannot be formalized.[1] In sum, 'the fact that many reanalyses can be interpreted as analogical extensions does not make analogy a principle of change or anything more than a *pre-theoretical concept*' (1979a:373, italics added). This rather dismissive attitude is immediately somewhat softened: the role of analogy in governing language acquisition and therefore historical change should not be 'belittled'.

Furthermore, 'surface analogies clearly play an important role in syntactic analysis' (*loc.cit.*). Despite the fact, therefore, that for Lightfoot analogy has no place within a theory of change as such, it is nevertheless clear that a theory of historical grammar which, seen in its entirety, has no place within it for the notion of analogical change is poorer than one which has.

So there is in fact a place within Lightfoot's total approach to language change for a factor or process which is neither represented in the grammar nor can be stated as a formal principle within a theory of change. This factor does not have explanatory power, in the sense of explaining why a change takes place – something which is often misunderstood – but rather indicates the type of change which may well occur once some other circumstance has rendered a change inevitable. One reaction to intolerable opacity, for instance, may be to extend the use of some already occurring surface pattern: analogy is thus one form of therapy available to the language in times of need. If one such factor can be accorded such a role – to indicate the manner in which a change took place – it is surely conceivable at least that other factors might play a similar role. We shall return to this point later in connection with 'typological change', the principal topic of the present paper.

Lightfoot's theoretical position has been outlined in some detail so that in due course it will be possible to examine more clearly the extent to which it can be reconciled with some at least of the insights of a typological approach to diachronic syntax. First of all, however, we should look briefly at one issue which is in a sense rather tangential to the main topic of this paper, namely syntactic reconstruction. It is perfectly possible to claim, as I shall be doing, that the insights gained by a typological approach are valuable and must be incorporated at some point within an overall linguistic theory, without in any sense necessarily accepting that the application of such an approach to a particular task, specifically syntactic reconstruction, will prove to be satisfactory in practice. Not only are the problems of syntactic reconstruction in general very far from a universally accepted solution (cf. Lightfoot 1979b:386/7), but the typological method in particular, given that, as we shall see, it can normally make only probabilistic rather than absolute statements and that the central notion 'consistent language' has to be treated with great caution, encounters particular difficulties. In view of the fact that languages need not be – and rarely are – fully consistent, and that changes which occur only tend towards consistency as one favoured developmental pathway, one is justified in being extremely sceptical about attempts to apply the method 'in reverse', as it were, in order to establish some hypothetical earlier stage of a language or language family. Of course, the data provided by the observable tendency towards increased consistency when changes occur is of interest to those concerned with syntactic reconstruction – but of neither more nor less interest than data concerning other likely 'manners' in which languages may move from one synchronic stage to another. To use syntactic typology as an 'intellectual straitjacket' (Watkins 1976:306) in this field is surely not desirable; nevertheless, one should be careful not to equate doubts about the application of a theory to one particular task with doubts about the theory itself.

We are now in a position to turn to the central theme of our paper, the strengths and weaknesses of a typological approach to historical syntax, the preceding paragraph having no doubt given an inkling at least of the line to be adopted here. By far the main difficulties facing what I will call the 'classical' model of diachronic typological syntax – i.e. the model associated primarily with such scholars are Lehmann and Vennemann and applied by many others (such as myself to the evolution of Romance: Harris (1978)), lie in the notion 'consistent language'. The truth is, as Smith (1981:39) observes, that 'unless one chooses to pick on the particular constellation of properties of a specific language and define consistency in terms of them, so that that language is consistent by definition, there is virtually no typological implicational statement that does not have exceptions'. (Cf. also Lightfoot 1978:57). And indeed the 'classical' model of typological change actually posits the introduction of inconsistency into a language, for whatever reason, as the first step in a cycle which leads eventually to a newly consistent language of some other type. Thus for instance, a (more or less) consistent SOV language may become inconsistent as a result of the progressive innovation of one or more features not primarily associated with SOV languages, after which further changes in the same direction gradually restore consistency, but now as, for example, an SVO language. Almost all languages are therefore 'in transition' from another, a point which has relevance throughout the discussion which follows. (It should be noted that many authors have posited cyclical changes from one language type to another; this claim is irrelevant to the matters under consideration here and is not considered further.)

One fact emerges very clearly from what has gone before, namely that typology as generally understood is dealing with *tendencies* rather than absolutes. Languages tend to conform to certain patterns, changes from one synchronic stage to another tend to follow certain pathways. That this is descriptively true seems beyond dispute. It follows that these tendencies can enable us to predict, with some degree of accuracy, the type of change likely to occur if, in a given language at a given time, a particular existing structure is, for whatever reason, found to be inadequate. Note that, at this stage, we are talking about the response which a language makes to an independently motivated need, and claiming that a solution consistent or harmonic, in definable ways, with a number of other specifiable structures in the language is likely to prove the favoured response. We shall discuss later why this might be; suffice it to say at this point that useful statements at the descriptive level can be made about the manner in which languages normally change — namely that they tend to change in the direction of greater consistency, defined in terms of synchronic, statistical universals — without in any way imputing a causal role to the notion 'consistent language'. It is not necessary — though we shall return to this statement briefly later — to see a language striving towards the goal of consistency in order to accept that there may still be considerable interest in demonstrating preferred ways in which language may undergo change. Surely it is preferable, in the light of current knowledge, to have a probabilistic model, one which tells you with some considerable likelihood of accuracy how a language is likely to react to a particular need for change, than no model at all, pending the establishment of a wholly formalizable, absolutist model at some unspecified future date. Given this perspective, one would agree with those, from Watkins (1976) to Smith (1981), who deny to the notion 'consistent language' the ability to explain why change takes place, and accept, with Lass (1980:21), that 'statistical laws' can never be falsified, while still observing that many attested changes do in fact lead to greater consistency in the sense in which that term is used here.

If, then, one denies explanatory power to the notion 'consistent language' and if one accepts that 'syntactic drift' does not have predictive value, what can be claimed in support of a typological approach to historical syntax? To answer this question, we need to develop further the positive points which have been outlined in what has gone before, continuing for the time being to use the 'classical' model of typological change alluded to earlier. What is indisputably attested is a series of parallel changes occurring in many languages at various times, which tend to increase the extent to which the language conforms to a particular type. One has then a series of partial but not absolute generalizations. The problem of the value of generalizations which do not hold 100% of the time is by no means limited to linguistics, but is endemic in various other disciplines, in particular the social sciences. Such generalizations will, by their very nature, lack predictive force and cannot be seen as having a general explanatory value. It is nevertheless not normal practice to reject such generalizations out of hand but rather to attempt progressively to establish the relevant conditioning factors, thereby constraining the generalization in question and increasing its utility to the discipline involved.

Let us then at this point recall Lightfoot's conclusion about analogy, a process far too well attested in the annals of historical linguistics to be summarily rejected. After noting, as we saw earlier, that 'Analogy is too general a notion and cannot be used as the basis for a predictive theory,' Lightfoot nevertheless feels that 'the appropriate response to this is not to reject the notion out of hand but . . . to seek to constrain its application' (1979a:361). Surely a similar approach should be adopted with regard to a tendency towards consistency. We have already noted that typological drift does not need to be seen as explaining change in the sense of causing it; Lightfoot is right, therefore, in claiming (1979a:391) that 'positing a typological shift does not constitute an explanation for the various changes'. But this does not justify the extreme scepticism of the role of typological drift evinced by recent critics. Elsewhere, I have written (Harris 1978:7): 'Inasmuch as a language evolves, we may now assert that it will normally exhibit a series of changes which, taken together, will tend to move that language from being of one type to another' and, later, that it is possible 'to demonstrate that the major grammatical changes in Romance [my own particular interest] are very much in accord with an ongoing typological shift from (S)OV to (S)VO . . .' This is a far cry indeed from claiming that typological change 'explains' in the sense of 'causes' linguistic change – although as so often part of the problem lies in insufficiently explicit uses of the word 'explain' by various authors, 'explain why' often being inadequately differentiated from 'explain how'. Equally, however, it seems wholly fair to see syntactic drift as being on a par with, for example, analogy as providing a preferred pathway for change once that change has been independently motivated: to use one of Lightfoot's favourite phrases (1979a:396; 1979b:390), borrowed from Kuryłowicz (1945–9), 'gutters are prescribed for historical changes'.

In effect, then, we are arguing for a middle position between the view that typological drift is responsible for 'goal-oriented clusters of changes' (Lightfoot 1979a:390) – what Watkins (1976:306) calls 'a superficial "explanatory" teleological theory of syntactic change' – and the view that such widely distributed moves towards consistency as are attested are largely the result of external factors, as strongly urged by Smith (1981:51). What we are claiming is that there is indeed what Smith calls an 'external principle' involved here, very much on a par with analogy: let us call both analogy and typological drift 'psycholinguistic tendencies'. It is surely not controversial to assert, quite simply, that when a language is to change, whether the initial impetus for this change is entirely internal – such as the necessity to avoid excessive opacity, so clearly illustrated by Lightfoot – or external, as in language contact, the manner in which the change takes place will probably – though not necessarily – be of a predictable kind. In other words: 'we are in a strong position to predict the *sort* of changes – though not necessarily the actual *form* these changes will take – which will happen in the future' (Harris 1978: 7). These 'psycholinguistic tendencies' are not rules of the grammar; indeed, they are not rules at all. Neither can they be formalized – at present, at least – within a theory of change; there are simply too many variables to be built in to the equation. Nevertheless, it seems to be clear, empirically, that there are indeed 'gutters' prescribed by our own internal mental apparatus which lead us to prefer to effect linguistic change in certain ways rather than others: one important such gutter is a preference for typological consistency. And to agree with Anttila (1972:181) that 'the mind shuns purposeless variety' does not entail the view that a desire for consistency is somehow mystical or inherent in the spirit of the language; it is merely a fairly uncontroversial statement about the nature of human beings.

Gutters are, of course, not pipes; diversion from a preferred pathway, given some other intruding factor, is not only possible but by no means infrequent; at the very least, we need to consider 'the indeterministic element introduced by the fact that language is spoken by human beings in society' (Lass 1980:61). Preferred manners of change, however, there clearly are, and the evidence in favour of the tendency towards consistency — Lehmann's 'structural principle of language', Vennemann's 'principle of natural serialization', Hawkins' 'principle of Cross-Category Harmony' — is far too strong to be dismissed as Smith does (1981:52): 'While . . . the internal coherence of consistency might conceivably effect some structural pressure for language change, such explanations are not only *post hoc* but also of negligible importance in comparison with change due to language contact'. We shall return later to the first part of this statement; as regards the second, the overwhelming evidence from Romance, for example, where the role of language contact, while not wholly excluded, surely cannot be seen as the primary motivating factor towards consistency, casts doubt on ascribing a necessarily fundamental role to this factor. In any event, while language contact may well lead to convergence between various languages — as Masica (1976) so convincingly shows — why should contact of itself lead to *consistency* in a typological sense? As for being *post hoc*, typological drift shares with analogy the feature of being at present too unconstrained to be predictive. To doubt its existence, however, as a preferred gutter for historical change seems perverse.

What we have, then, is an external factor which seems to resemble on the diachronic plane perceptual facility on the synchronic plane. Like analogy, drift towards consistency provides a preferred manner of change when a change becomes — in general — independently necessary. But just as there is not yet an all-embracing statement as to exactly the point at which perceptual difficulties must be remedied, or at which opacity becomes intolerable, so we cannot yet indicate incontrovertibly when a change will be effected through analogy or through a drift towards consistency. Vincent (1976:55) suggests that the statistical nature of the universals outlined by Greenberg may in some sense be *due* to limitations on the human perceptual mechanism. 'Perceptual factors are of necessity "fuzzy" . . . Hence any constraints on languages deriving from limitations on the perceptual system would only make themselves felt gradually over a period of time, thereby allowing for the existence of intermediate stages and mixed types'. To this we may add that certain of these constraints can be positively ignored, a point taken up again below.

It seems likely, in fact, that analogical extension and the drift towards consistency, whether or not these are ultimately attributable to the human perceptual mechanism, are actually two different aspects of one psycholinguistic tendency; indeed, recent work within the X-bar convention suggests, as Hawkins rightly notes (1979:646), 'an analogical preference for like semantic elements — operators and operands — to be treated in like manner'. My own recent work on noun phrases and verb phrases in Romance (Harris 1980) highlights just such a set of parallel developments. Clearly, there is a powerful 'external factor' at work here, even if we cannot yet incorporate it formally within our theory.

And this brings us to a consideration of John Hawkins' own recent work (1979, 1980). We have assumed throughout the 'classical' statements of universals, — those of Greenberg as adopted and adapted by such scholars as Lehmann, Vennemann and Li — which are almost all relative or statistical. They cannot, therefore, for the reasons stated by Smith, be incorporated in a theory of grammar. If however certain universals could be restated in such a way as to be absolute (*i.e.* exceptionless), then it could be argued that knowledge of these universals would be part of our linguistic competence and as such necessarily part of any theory of grammar. It would also be axiomatic that syntactic change could only occur within the parameters permitted by these synchronic universals.

This is the goal which Hawkins has set himself. He attempts to establish synchronically certain exceptionless 'implicational universals', which have been checked against all the data in Greenberg's Appendix II: many of these are listed in both Hawkins (1979) and Hawkins (1980). Assuming the successful establishment of such universals, it would presumably follow that the constraints they embody applied also in the past; and Hawkins indeed concludes (1979:633) that 'impossible word order co-occurrence types, on current synchronic evidence, are impossible also in diachrony', and again (1979: 634) 'Evidently, languages will change historically only within the parameters of synchronically attested variation types'. Note how close this is, inevitably, to Lightfoot's position, that no change could occur the result of which could not be generated by a possible grammar of natural language.

Hawkins' claim, if upheld by checking against diachronic data from a wide variety of languages, has two principal consequences for a typological approach to diachronic syntax. First of all, it restricts the applicability of the 'classical' view of typologically inspired diachronic syntax, insofar as a key element in this approach, called by Hawkins the Universal Violation Hypothesis, sees the elimination of inconsistency of whatever kind – introduced for whatever reason – as the *primum mobile* for syntactic drift, whereas only those types of inconsistency not incompatible with properly formulated universals would be permissible under Hawkins' own Universal Consistency Hypothesis. Change could occur only between one permitted type and another. On the other hand, it greatly strengthens the view advocated here that consistency is apparently a major desideratum for a language; although the language types permitted by Hawkins' universals do not exclude – and could not, empirically, exclude – combinations of characteristics shown to be statistically infrequent by Greenberg's original relative universals, nevertheless, 'the more similar the balance in operator preposing and postposing across the different operand categories, the greater the number of languages – and the more dissimilar, the fewer the languages' (1979:646). What Hawkins calls the principle of Cross-Category Harmony is simply the most recent formulation of the view that language change tends, once initiated, to lead to greater consistency on many occasions, just as the analogical reorganization of surface structure is often in evidence in comparable situations.

The perspective adopted to this point has been very clear: that syntactic drift, like analogy, constitutes a pathway for change, a manner of change, and not a cause. By adopting such a perspective, the dangers inherent in a teleological approach can be avoided, and one is not compelled to see a language, under the influence of some 'metacondition' (Lakoff, 1972:192), as conspiring relentlessly towards the target of typological consistency. Equally important, one is not driven to Lakoff's alternative, 'an overwhelming series of coincidences' (*loc.cit.*), since the principle of natural serialization/Cross-Category Harmony may be seen as explaining the preference for certain types of instantiation of change over other conceivable changes.[2] As Hawkins puts it (1979:646): 'If there is an independently motivated need for, e.g. the verb to shift position, it is expected [but not certain: M. H.] that this verb shift will be matched by cross-categorial word order re-adjustments to the extent predicted by C.C.H., in order to simplify the grammar'. On this basis, it seems to me, one can mount a perfectly respectable defence of the utility of typological studies for diachronic linguistics. Let me now, however, stick my neck out just a little and ask: is it really inconceivable that factors such as those which have been discussed here ever have a causal role in linguistic change?

Consider first analogical change, looking at one French example and a perhaps more controversial example from the same grammatical area of contemporary spoken English. One of the main markers of past time in French, the past simple (*fit*), has ceased to be used in the contemporary spoken language, and has been replaced by the present perfect (*a fait*). One of the consequences of this has been the replacement of the past anterior (*eut fait*) by the so-called double compound perfect (*a eu fait*), by means of a perfectly simple analogical extension (*fit: a fait :: eut: a eu*). So far, so good; analogy is here providing a gutter for change in response to an independently motivated need. But this new paradigm, *a eu fait*, has provided a model on which a whole series of new paradigms has been formed, used by different speakers in different ways and by some speakers not at all, which have been attested for centuries but which are still not normally recognised as part of the standard language. (See Foulet 1925; some discussion appears in Harris 1978: 155–6). Is the analogical extension here a response to some need? Or is it not at least equally plausible to suggest that the psycholinguistic tendency discussed earlier, frequently to innovate on the basis of analogical extension, has actually led to the creation of new forms to which, by some speakers at least, a use is then attributed?

The spoken English example may be more contentious. In my idiolect, the following sentence would be (orally at least) not at all uncommon: 'He really should've done that, but even if he had've, it wouldn't've made any difference'. The sentence contains the element *had've* (consistently written 'had of' by my younger son), a sequence which can be generated by no known rule of English syntax. The development of *had've* by virtue of an analogical extension to the series *could've, would've, should've, might've* etc. is clear − yet it meets no perceptible syntactic or semantic need and cannot really therefore be said to be responding to some externally motivated pressure for change. Let us note in passing that it seems therefore to be an instance of 'pure syntactic change', a not uncontroversial notion; c.f. Lightfoot, 1979a:153. If this structure succeeds in gaining admission to the language, what is the most likely *cause* of that change? Could this be an instance of 'the *explanatory* power of surface factors in syntactic change' (Naro 1976; italics added), a notion treated with great scepticism by Lightfoot (1979a:358)?

And could syntactic drift *never* have a causal role comparable to that just suggested, in certain circumstances, for analogy? I just put forward one rather tentative suggestion, drawn again from my own work on Romance. French inherited from Latin a system of verbal inflections to mark person and number, subject personal pronouns normally being omitted. In Spanish and Italian, the position is essentially unchanged to this day. In French, however, subject pronouns came to be generally used long before the erosion of the inherited suffixes, traditionally said to have caused the change in question (Harris 1978:113). We know now, however, that Old French passed through a TVX (verb second) phase, during which the subject pronoun, while continuing to be almost always omitted if some other element filled the pre-verbal slot, came to be almost invariably present if the verb would otherwise have appeared in first rather than second place in the sentence. (Foulet 1919 paras. 446–80 describes the situation in detail; see Harris 1978:111–2 for some discussion.) Now, an overall tendency to prefer verb second order may well have been motivated in this instance, partly at least, be language contact, specifically the interaction of Germanic and Gallo-Romance after the end of the Roman Empire. But the preferred order could not readily by imple-mented in sentences where the subject was an unemphatic subject pronoun and no other element was topicalized or used anaphorically. We are therefore surely entitled to see the introduction of personal pronouns in this context – from which they later spread gradually throughout the language – as being motivated, in some sense at least, by a pressure within the language to con-form more consistently to its currently preferred type. Recall here Smith's earlier concession (1981:52): 'the internal coherence of consistency might conceivably effect some structural pressure for language change'.

Note once again that ascribing a causal role to analogical extension or typological consistency in certain circumstances does not enable us to develop a predictive theory, in the sense of predicting that a particular change will occur in a particular situation on a particular occasion;[3] we therefore still cannot incorporate these notions within a theory of grammar or a (formal-ized) theory of change. And note also how 'consistency as a phenomenon to be explained' (Smith 1981:51) is, though logically distinct, in fact inextri-cably bound up with 'consistency (or a tendency towards consistency) as an explanatory principle in its own right'.

What then, in sum, are the strengths and weaknesses of typological work in the area of historical syntax? First of all, while not denying absolutely the possibility of structural pressure within language itself helping to bring about linguistic change, we must be wary of attempting to ascribe a primarily causal role in linguistic change to the concept of drift towards consistency. The risk of such an approach becoming hopelessly teleological is clear. Furthermore, because drift is not in any sense predictive, we must be very cautious of engaging in syntactic reconstruction, since the method works only by as-suming in the past a very much higher degree of predictability than seems to be the case today. On the other hand, we equally must resist the temptation to throw out the baby with the bathwater.[4] The fact that consistency cannot be shown to be a principle invariably holding in language and therefore neces-sarily part of a theory of grammar, and that a tendency to change in the direction of greater consistency cannot be formalized as part of a theory of change does not entitle us to deny the fact that many languages over many millenia have changed in the way typologists have predicted.[5] (Hopefully, this is exactly what Harris 1978 shows in respect of French.) Languages *do* tend to drift towards greater consistency; like analogy, this is one of the gutters down which linguistic change flows. And the manner in which historical change is instantiated forms a significant part of the material in which the diachronic linguist is interested.

It is clear then that the initial causes of change, be they intra- or extra-linguistic, are normally responded to in general terms in one of a restricted set of predictable ways. As far as consistency is concerned, it is clear that the general tendencies — statistical universals — outlined by Greenberg and exploited by many of us since, do throw considerable light on the ways in which languages change; they do not, however, *prescribe* a particular change, nor, in general, are they to be seen as causing or explaining change. It may be that, in addition, as Hawkins has argued, there are certain combinations of characteristics which are ruled out *a priori*, in effect by our linguistic competence. Since the combinations proposed are those which are maximally disharmonic, this merely strengthens the position adopted here. We might argue that the tendency towards consistency is best represented as a kind of spectrum, certain types of inconsistency being tolerated, or even introduced to solve some other problem or as a result of simplification elsewhere in the grammar, while other types are generally avoided and yet others apparently wholly excluded. Support for such a view of consistency as a kind of external principle comes not only from its clear association with the traditional notion of analogy but also from the wealth of recent work within the X-bar theory: as Hawkins (1979:646) puts it: 'a language with a comparable balance of operators to operands across the different operand categories permits the formulation of more cross-categorial rules of grammar than one with disharmonic orderings'. Cross-categorial rules are valued — but not at any price!

Work done in the field of historical linguistics within the typological tradition can and does yield valuable insights into the way in which languages change. This approach does not normally provide an explanation for the changes but the existence of a psycholinguistic principle favouring consistency in operator-operand order can in one sense 'explain' why changes, once necessitated, often take the form they do, and may even, we have suggested, bring about changes in its own right in certain circumstances. It is wholly unconvincing to ascribe virtually the entire movement towards consistency to language contact, as Smith does ('consistency, where it exists, must be explained by external factors' 1981:51); nor can we ignore the evidence because it cannot be formalized within a theory of change, as Lightfoot at times seems to suggest. Rather, we must adopt the view Lightfoot himself adopts in the case of analogy and seek to clarify and constrain as far as possible the operation of the principle in question. In short, the data unearthed by diachronic syntacticians working within this paradigm 'demand explanation and constitute challenges for existing theories' (Lightfoot 1979b:393); indeed, they 'are of enormous importance for a theory of grammar' (*op.cit.*:391). The evidence is that, given a proper understanding of what the nature of the drift towards consistency really is, it can play an invaluable supportive role to an approach to diachronic syntax such as that expounded in Lightfoot 1979a; the work reported in Hawkins (1979, 1980) further strengthens such a conclusion. Only when the approach attempts to exceed its own limitations will it deserve some at least of the criticisms which it has recently received.

Notes

* An earlier version of this paper was read at the LAGB Autumn Meeting, University of Surrey, September 1980. I am grateful to Susan Price, Neil Smith and Nigel Vincent for their suggestions and comments.
1. Lass (1980:148), citing the views of Polanyi, explicitly rejects the idea that only what is formalizable is worth studying. This thus contradicts Lightfoot's ostensible position though not, as the present discussion should be in the course of making clear, his actual view of language change in totality.
2. A parallel dichotomy presented in Lightfoot (1978:62–3) appears to suggest that the linguist must choose between 'relentless' syntactic drag-chains and 'chance' in seeking to account for the observed data. Both alternatives are unacceptable for the reasons already stated. In fact, Lightfoot himself does not really mean 'chance', but rather a series of changes unamenable to formalization. This latter position, if explicitly formulated, could easily be reconciled with the line followed in the present paper. As he himself says (*op.cit.*:68) 'one must distinguish the causes of a historical reanalysis from its effects and from its formal characterization'. The recurrent patterns within the instantiation of change which we have been discussing are in fact equivalent to the 'effects' of a reanalysis, in Lightfoot's terms. (Note in passing that what has been said does not involve dissent from Lightfoot's view (*op.cit.*:71) that chance has *some* role to play in historical change: it is simply defeatist to use it to 'explain' the data unearthed by typologists.)
3. Note that, as Neil Smith has pointed out (personal communication) *prediction* and *explanation* are independent (though hopefully correlated) notions. If my analysis of the changes outlined above is accepted, then one has hopefully arrived at an *explanation* of them; but one still cannot *predict* changes of this type in a given situation. Equally, we can predict all kinds of changes without explaining them. We thus dissent from the view of Lass (1980:13) that 'any (correct) explanation involves correct prediction'. (All are agreed that prediction does not involve explanation.)
4. Our view of the appropriate way to treat babies can thus be seen to differ from that of Lass, who writes (1980:4): 'If a totally negative assessment causes the babies to be thrown out with the bathwater, this is no great loss: if the babies are really worth keeping and raising to maturity, someone is bound to fish them out again'. Such a procedure seems both unnecessarily cumbersome and open to the charge of cruelty to children!
5. It will be clear from what precedes that our sympathies lie more with the 'epistemo-

logical pluralism' advocated in Chapter V of Lass (1980) ('even second-best is not the same as universal darkness' *op.cit.*:147) than in the more absolutist – and consequently more pessimistic – position elaborated in the main body of that work, for example (p.31) 'there seem to be no laws of any interest... in a domain... like language change' and again (p.75) 'we haven't a clue as to what (if anything) causes or constrains linguistic change'. It simply is not true that 'linguistic change should... in principle be no more predictable than change in art styles' (*op.cit.*:132) – and this should give food for thought to those tempted to espouse Lass's extreme pessimism.

References

Anttila, R.
    1972   *An introduction to historical and comparative linguistics* (New York: Macmillan).
Foulet, L.
    1919   Petite syntaxe de l'ancien français (Paris: Champion).
    1925   "Le développement des formes surcomposées", *Romania* 51:203–52.
Greenberg, J.
    1963   "Some universals of grammar with particular reference to the order of meaningful elements", *Universals of language*, edited by J. Greenberg (Cambridge: M.I.T. Press), 73–113.
Harris, M. B.
    1978   *The evolution of French syntax: a comparative approach* (London: Longman).
    1980   "NPs and VPs in Romance", *Transactions of the Philological Society*: 62–80.
Hawkins, J.
    1979   "Implicational universals as predictors of word order change", *Language* 55: 618–48.
    1980   "Two types of word order universals: implicational and distributional", *Journal of linguistics* 16:193–235.
Kuryłowicz, J.
    1945–9 "La nature des procès dits 'analogiques' ", *Readings in linguistics* II, edited by E. P. Hamp (Chicago: Chicago U. P. 1966), 158–174.
Lakoff, R.
    1972   "Another look at drift", *Linguistic change and generative theory*, edited by R. P. Stockwell and R. Macauley (Bloomington: Indiana U. P.), 172–198.
Lass, R.
    1980   *On explaining language change* (Cambridge: C.U.P.).
Lehmann, W. P.
    1973   "A structural principle of language and its implications", *Language* 49:47–66.
    1974   *Proto-Indo-European syntax* (Austin: University of Texas Press).
    1978   *Syntactic typology: studies in the phenomenology of language* (Austin: University of Texas Press).
Li, C. N. (ed.)
    1975   *Word order and word order change* (Austin: University of Texas Press).
    1977   *Mechanisms of syntactic change* (Austin: University of Texas Press).
Lightfoot, D. W.
    1978   "Explaining syntactic change", *Montreal working papers in linguistics* 11:55–91.
    1979a   *Principles of diachronic syntax* (Cambridge: C.U.P.)

1979b   Review of Li 1977, *Language* 55:381–95.
Masica, C. P.
1976   *Defining a linguistic area: South Asia* (Chicago and London: Chicago U. P.)
Naro, A.
1976   "The genesis of the impersonal reflexive in Portuguese", *Language* 52:779–810.
Smith, N. V.
1981   "Consistency, markedness and language change: on the notion 'consistent language' ", *Journal of linguistics* 17:39–54.
Vennemann, T.
1974   "Topics, subjects and word order: from SXV to SVX via TVX", *Historical linguistics*, edited by J. Anderson and C. Jones (Amsterdam: North Holland), 339–76.
1975   "An explanation of drift", *Word order and word order change*, edited by C. Li (Austin: University of Texas Press), 269–305.
Vincent, N.
1976   "Perceptual factors and word order change in Latin", *Romance syntax: synchronic and diachronic perspectives*, edited by M. B. Harris (Salford: Salford University).
Watkins, C.
1976   "Towards Proto-Indo-European syntax: problems and pseudo-problems", *Papers from the parasession on diachronic syntax*, edited by S. Steever, C. Walker and S. Mufenwe (Chicago: CLS), 305–326.

RAYMOND HICKEY

A valency framework for the Old English verb

The purpose of the present paper is to offer tentatively a description of OE verbs, as they occur in attested sentences,[1] in terms of the valencies[2] which can be established for them. The term OE verb as it occurs in the title refers to the set of independent verbs which have specific and differentiated valency frameworks:

$$(1) \quad \{V\} \quad = \quad \{ V_{\langle i \rangle}, \quad V_{\langle j \rangle} \ldots V_{\langle n \rangle} \}$$

where i, j . . . n represent one or more valencies and where i ≠ j. I specify that the set consists of independent verbs (notated as V_i) as two further sets also exist: that of modals, V_m, and that of auxiliaries, V_a. While these have complements (two and two only: CO, the subject complement and C9, the verbative complement, a non-finite verb form, i.e. an infinitive or past participle) they are not capable of forming a sentence of their own. In dependency analysis the sentence is the basic unit and consists of any syntactic sequence which contains a finite form of an independent verb (or a modal/auxiliary with a non-finite form of an independent verb) accompanied by the complements demanded by its valency framework. In elliptical circumstances some (though never all) of these complements may not be realised.[3]

The effectivity of applying dependency formalisms to (Modern) English has been shown to be considerable (see Emons, 1974; Emons, 1978; and Hickey, 1980) if the formalism is adapted to deal specifically with the contingencies of English syntax. The basic principle of elaborating a system of complementation[4] categories which cover the totality of possible valencies for the verbs of a language is maintained although the actual valencies may differ considerably from one language to another. The most exhaustive frameworks developed thus far are those for German (see Engel, 1977; Engel/Schumacher, [2] 1978; and Helbig/Schenkel, 1969 for typical examples).

In a language such as Modern English position within a syntagm is used as a cue for the recognition of complementation categories. With OE, however, categories can be identified on the grounds of morphological marking and/or government by prepositions and conjunctions, this last also fulfilling an identifying function in Modern English. In the valency framework presented here no attempt is made to determine deep structures[5] for OE verbal constructions: what is of relevance (given the theoretical basis I affiliate myself with) is the manifestation of actual verbal constructions.[6] However a valency description goes beyond a mere taxonomy of verbal forms: in assigning valencies to these it attains an element of prediction:[7] if the valencies are correct then we know that a verb x with the valency y will always occur in a syntagm of a given type (in nature and number of complementation categories).

Central to any valency description is the system of complementation which obtains. Most sentence elements apart from the verb itself can be a complement to the verb. With OE a tenfold division of complement types seems appropriate. This division allows a discriminating analysis of those elements which appear in a sentence due to the demands (or possibilities) given by the main verb. They include not only the normal four categories[8] of surface case in OE but also a further six divisions which rely more on a notional interpretation of complementation. It should not, however, be imagined that these are case categories in a Fillmore sense,[9] they may coincide in some instances but that is merely coincidental. The basic orientation of the system of complementation offered here is towards surface forms. These will of course also reflect semantic relations with the verb and to that extent they also betray a partial origin outside of the requirements of surface syntax.

1 Complementation categories

The numbering of the categories of complementation is in itself arbitrary[10] but has the advantage of mirroring (in most cases) the frequency of occurence of such categories. Thus the subject of the sentence has the designation CO as in

(2) He cwæþ soðlice.   cwæþ$_{\langle 07 \rangle}$
     'He spoke truly'.

which can be represented stemmatically as

(3)

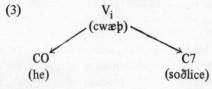

With each sentence I also give a valency description of its main verb which is quoted in the finite form in which it occurs. Adjuncts (marked simply as 'A') will be placed outside valency brackets. If an infinitive is quoted then the valency brackets contain the set of complements possible with that verb. For reasons of practicality these are indicated by a series of dots so that if I begin with the above sentence I may write

(4) cweðan$_{\langle 07 \ldots \rangle}$

which I may procede to expand on collecting attestations of larger valencies such as

(5) He cwæþ soðlice to his leorningcnihtum.   cwæþ$_{\langle 047 \rangle}$
'He spoke truly to his disciples'.

(6)

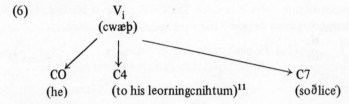

$$V_i$$
$$(cwæþ)$$

CO   C4   C7
(he)   (to his leorningcnihtum)[11]   (soðlice)

which allows me to write

(7) cweðan$_{\langle 074 \ldots \rangle}$

and so forth.[12] The ordering of complements in the stemma usually places the complements from left to right in numerical order and is not supposed to correspond to the linear sequence of the actual sentence; again it may do so by coincidence. A subscript $_c$ is used after a complement to denote that it is complex, i.e. that it contains more than one occurrence of the element which is minimally required to represent this category (additive complexity) or that it itself governs further elements (dependent complexity, for examples see below). This, with an instance of CO should it consist of two nouns, obtains the notation CO_c. This is frequently so with disjuncted complements in OE such as

(8) Petrus eode ut and se oðer leorningcniht . . .   eode$_{\langle O_c \rangle}$
'Peter and the other disciple went out'.

The category CO does not always require to be realised in OE, as for example, in coordinated sentences. In such cases the coordinated sentence, seen in dependency terms, is connected of necessity with the first one:

(9) And hi him lustlice tiʒðodon and him biscop sendon.
tiʒðoden $_{\langle 037 \rangle}$; sendon$_{\langle \emptyset 13 \rangle}$

'And they granted (it) to him willingly and sent a bishop to him'.

(10) N_c (and)————V_i———— N_c(and)———— V_i
             (tiʒðodon)   (sendon)

         ↙   ↓   ↘   ↙   ↓   ↘
        CO   C3   C7   CØ   C1   C3
        (hi) (him) (lustlice) ☐ (biscop) (him)
        └ – – – – – – – – – – – – – – – – – ⬏

The broken-lined arrow indicates the reference identity of the CO in the first sentence with the non-realised $CØ^{13}$ of the second coordinated sentence while the square indicates the position at a dependency node which the subject would occupy were it realised. The direct object is marked as C1 and is either morphologically or positionally recognizable in a sentence:

(11) Hi þeah micle fierd ʒeʒadrodon.   ʒeʒadrodon$_{\langle 01 \rangle}$
      'Nonetheless they gathered a great army'.

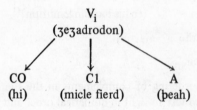

V_i
(ʒeʒadrodon)

CO   C1   A
(hi)   (micle fierd) (þeah)

In agreement with the morphological form of the pronoun which they re-quire reflexive verbs have the minimal valency CO1 as in

(12) Hiene bestæl se here.   bestæl$_{\langle 01 \rangle}$
      'The army stole away'.

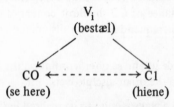

V_i
(bestæl)

CO ←– – – – – – –→ C1
(se here)   (hiene)

Furthermore a sub-group of verbs takes two non reference identical C1s, such as the verb *ascian*:

(13) þa acsode man hine hwylcne cræft he cuðe.   acsode$_{\langle 0118 \rangle}$
      'Then he was asked what his trade was'.

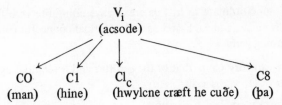

This fact is of importance in an attempt to define the category 'complement' and demarcate it from that of 'adjunct'. A formal criterion which is generally valid (precisely with the exception of a double C1) is that a complement does not occur twice in the same sentence whereas an adjunct may do so at will. However, even if we had no instances of double C1 then this would simply be an incidental formal concomitant to the valency determination of complement categories.[14]

With some verbs we encounter a particular kind of complementation where the complement is not a member of a word class but a clause in itself:

> (14) ... ; bæd he þæt hi him biscop onsenden.   bæd$_{\langle O\ SLC\rangle}$
> 'He requested that they send him a bishop'.

This I refer to as a sentence-like complement (SLC)[15] which can occur not only in place of C1 but of a number of other complements as well. Formally we may notate the above sentence as

> (15) bæd$_{\langle O\ SLC[þAET]\rangle}$ '[þAET]   onsenden$_{\langle 013\rangle}$

and represent it stemmatically as

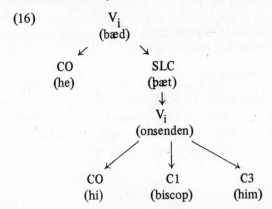

Sentence-like complements should be clearly differentiated from instances of C9, the verbative complement. The former involve a shift in sentence rank, i.e. they contain an embedded sentence which is a valency satellite of a verb which is superordinate to it. C9s are always non-finite verb forms which do not involve a shift in rank and as such a formal connector (such as *þæt*) with the governing verb.

The next category C2 is that of the genitive and is required by the valency of a number of OE verbs as in

(17) Sawla moton lifes brucan.   brucan$_{\langle 02 \rangle}$
      'Souls are able to partake of life'.

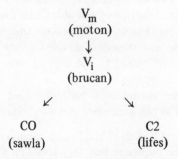

This sentence shows the use of a modal verb which always governs the independent verb which occupies the node below it. The designation independent is nonetheless appropriate for the verb in this stemma because it can appear on its own; a modal verb is not independent in this sense as its occurrence is concomitant with the non-finite form of an independent verb (whether realised or not).

Although its application in the nominal area is complicated, as a complementation category of the verb the genitive presents little difficulty. When specifying the valency of OE verbs which take a genitive complement alternatives must be given with certain verbs:

(18) fægnian$_{\langle 02/4 \rangle}$[16]

      $\langle 02 \rangle$: Ðeah he þæs fægnige.
               'Although he rejoice in that'.
      $\langle 04 \rangle$: Fægnode min cild on minum innoþe.
               'My child rejoiced on my womb'.

      ehtan$_{\langle 02/1 \rangle}$

      $\langle 02 \rangle$: Ne eht he nanre wuhte.
               'He does not attack anything'.
      $\langle 0158 \rangle$: Ðonne hi eow ehtaþ on ðysse byrig.
               'When they attack you in this stonghold'.

Such verbs are to be held distinct from those which take C2 and another complement simultaneously, e.g. biddan$_{\langle 021 \rangle}$, sceamian$_{\langle 021 \rangle}$; forwyrnan$_{\langle 023 \rangle}$, þancian$_{\langle 023 \rangle}$.

Even more than the genitive the dative complement occurs not only with verbs but with prepositions and certain adjectives[17] which require a relational object, e.g.

> (19) þu eart rihtwis and me ȝecweme.   eart$_{\langle 07_c \rangle}$
> 'You are righteous and pleasing to me'.
>
> Wirc ðe twa stænene tabulan ðam oðrum gelice.   wirc$_{\langle 01_c \rangle}$
> 'Make two stone tablets like the others'.

The notion of relation, however, is not contained in those occurrences of the dative with verbs which have only a CO as the remaining complement:

> (20) derian$_{\langle 03 \rangle}$
>
> Him þa stormas derian ne mahan.
> 'Storms cannot harm him'.
>
> þeowan$_{\langle 03 \rangle}$
>
> He Drihtne ðeowde.
> 'He served the Lord'.

The occurence of the dative in the valency frameworks of these and other verbs is not semantically motivated and shows the arbitrariness of syntactic case requirements. With such verbs as take both dative and accusative this is not so, there being a definite relational feature attached to the occurrence of the dative:

> (21) Hit him Romane alyfdon.   alyfdon$_{\langle 013 \rangle}$
> 'The Romans granted it to him'.

Formal argumentation for the occurrence of this relation, that is, when a C1 co-occurs, is not tenable as it is also present with other complements, e.g. with C9:

> (22) Alyfe me to farenne.
> 'Allow me to go'.

However, as both the semantically vacuous and the relational datives have the same formal manifestation they are both subsumed here under the category C3. This also applies to that type of relational dative called pertinence dative[18], i.e. where it is semantically equivalent to a possessive pronoun:

(23)   he ... sette his ... hond him on þæt heafod.   sette$_{(013)}$
       'He placed his hand on his head'.

       dyde him of healse hring gyldenne.   dyde$_{(\emptyset13)}$
       'He took (the) gold ring from his neck'.

C3 is often the category of the subject with a subset of verbs in OE which are traditionally designated impersonal verbs with reference to their lack of a CO in their framework. With such verbs the frequently occurring valency is ⟨23⟩:

(24)   ofþyncan$_{(23)}$

       ... þæt him ðæs slæpes ofþuhte.
       'that he was displeased with this sleep'.

In many cases the C2 can be replaced by a sentence-like complement:

(25)   ... þæt him ofþuhte þæt he æfre manncynn
       ȝesceop.   ofþuhte$_{(3\ SLC)}$
       'that he regretted ever having created mankind'.

In such a case we cannot say that we have a C2 in the form of a SLC but merely that the SLC fills the position in the valency framework of this verb which is otherwise occupied by a nominal C2. A different situation sometimes obtains where the SLC has a correlate in the sentence. This correlate (usually a demonstrative pronoun) is inflected and occupies a preverbal position with the SLC occuring post-verbally. An example with an ordinary (not impersonal) verb is

(26)   Ælc man ðæs tiolaþ, hu he on ecnesse swincan mæge.
       'Every man endeavours (to see) how he can strive after eternity'.

When specifying the valency of the verb in this sentence C2 is included as it is present with the correlate *ðæs* (contrast the case with *bæd* above)

(27)   tiolaþ$_{(02>SLC\ [HU\ ])}$

With those impersonal verbs which take C1 for the subject we may also have the C2 realised by a nominal or replaced by a SLC, SLC with correlate or C9:

(28)   Ðam men ðe hine ne lyst his metes.   lyst$_{(12)}$
       '(to) that man who does not want his food'.

       Nænne mon ne tweoþ, ðæt God sy swa mihtig. tweo þ$_{(O\ SLC)}$
       'Nobody doubts that God is so mighty'.

       Nane monðæs tweogan ne þearf, ðæt ealle men geendiaþ

on ðam deaþe.   tweogan $_{\langle 02\ SLC\rangle}$
'Nobody need doubt that all men die'. (lit.:end in death)

Hine ne lyst his willan wyrcean.   lyst $_{\langle 19_c\rangle}$
'He did not wish to do his will'.

The category C4 is that of prepositional complementation and refers to those instances where an object of a verb is governed by a preposition which is in collocation with that verb. If it varies then it belongs to a small set which may or may not operate a semantic distinction. Prepositional complements are distinct from the categories C5 to C8 which may involve a preposition but which are clearly identifiable in terms of their distinguishing characteristic (location, direction, etc.). But with most complements, needless to say, border line cases exist as for example in

(29) Comon hiz of þrim folcum ðam stranzestan Germanie.
       V$_i$ CO   C3e
       'They came from the three strongest peoples of Germany'.

where the dative complement could perhaps be interpreted as an instance of C6 (see below).

The particular preposition which the complement C4 takes can be specified in the valency description; this is advisable considering the range of prepositions which may occur. Thus the verbs in

(30) ... hwearf eft on þæt weorc (Zodes word to lærenne ...)
       '(he) threw himself on that task of teaching God's word'.

and

(31) ... þa wæs zestrangod Azustinus mid trymnesse...
       'then Augustine was strengthened with firmness'.

can be specified as

(32) hweorfan $_{\langle 04\ [on]\rangle}$:   strangian $_{\langle 014\ [mid]\rangle}$

The C4s in such constructions may be complex, indeed they frequently are, something which occurs of necessity in sentences which are more than minimal. The inclusion of such complex complements in the valency description of the main verb of the sentence is not necessary as here only those elements of the sentence which are of primary rank (i.e. that closest to the main verb) need to be specified. A description of complex complements can be made of course with regard to the nucleus of the complement. An example will illustrate this.

(33) ... hwearf eft on þæt weorc Zodes word to lærenne.

Here the preposition on of the C4 governs the NP *þæt weorc* which in its turn governs the verbative complement *ʒodes word to lærenne,* in itself complex. The governing nucleus is in this case the NP with preposition:

$$(34) \quad C4 \text{ [on]} \overset{\Delta}{\rightarrow} C9_c$$
$$ C9_c \quad = C9 \overset{\Delta}{\rightarrow} C1$$

thus *ʒodes word to lærenne* is governed by *on þæt weorc.* The arrow with a delta above it indicates that the element it points away from governs that it points towards. The phrase *ʒodes word to lærenne* is an element of secondary rank as it is not directly governed by the verb and complex as it consists of a C9 (*to lærenne*) which governs the C1 (*ʒodes word*).

The necessity of a complementation category of location, C5, can be deduced from those verbs where it is an obligatory requirement in the valency framework. An example of such a verb is *licʒan* ⟨05⟩

(35) . . . his lic liþ æt Winburnan.   liþ ⟨05⟩
      'His body lies at Winburn'.

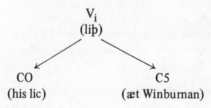

Along with such instances C5 is found with verbs where it is not obligatory but nonetheless is possible and appropriate in an expansion of valency, e.g. with *secan:*

(36) ⁊ þone here sohton æt Eoforwicceastre.   sohton ⟨Ø15⟩
      'and (they) sought the army at York'.

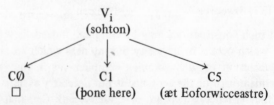

As was the case above it is necessary to distinguish ranks within valency frameworks so as to avoid classifying an element incorrectly. In the following sentence for example

(37) . . . sealde he him stowe and biscopseðl in Lindesfarena ea.

> 'he granted him a site and bishop's seat on the island of Lindesfarne'.

the elements marked are not seen as constituting a C5 in the valency framework of *sealde* but are governed by *stowe* and *biscopseðl* so that the verb's framework is then $\langle 01_c 3\rangle$ with $C1_c$ = C1 + C1 $\overset{\triangle}{\rightarrow}$ C5.

Closely connected with the category of location is that of direction C6; it is very frequently a complex complement, which when not including instances of repetition can have the following three subtypes:

$$(38) \quad \text{origin} \quad : \quad C6_a$$
$$\text{transition} \quad : \quad C6_\beta$$
$$\text{destination} \quad : \quad C6_\gamma$$

For purposes of illustration I have exclusively chosen examples from the *Anglo-Saxon Chronicle* (Parker Manuscript) which at the head of almost every entry contains an instance of C6. The examples show the combinatory possiblities of the subtypes.

> (39) Her for se here from Lindesse to Hreopedune.
> 'Then the army journeyed from Lindsee to Reptow'.
> $C6_c$ = $C6_a$, $C6_\gamma$
> ɤ he for to Rome.
> 'and he journeyed to Rome'.
> $C6$ = $C6_\gamma$
> Her rad se here ofer Mierce innan East-Engle.
> 'Then the army rode through Mercia into East Anglia'.
> $C6_c$ = $C6_\beta$, $C6_\gamma$

The most common subtype is $C6_\gamma$; with the verb *faran* it is always present though the occurrence of $C6_a$ is facultative. This can be shown formally as

$$(40) \quad \text{faran}_{\langle 06_c \rangle} = C6_a \quad \overset{\triangle}{\rightarrow} \quad C6_\gamma$$

where the dependency arrow shows that $C6_a$ implies $C6_\gamma$ though the converse does not hold. The occurence of $C6_a$ on its own is unusual, an example (in a relative clause) being though:

> (41) and ymb ii ȝear þæs ðe he of Francum com he gefor . . .
> 'and about two years after he had come from France he died'.

Note that the verb is *cuman,* which can, however, occur with both $C6_a$ and $C6_\gamma$. The simple complement $C6_\beta$ is likewise rare but can be seen in

(42) ꝥhi fluӡon ofer Temese buton ælcum forda . . .
'and they fled across the Thames where there is no ford'.

Her for se here up þurh þa brycӡe æt Paris . . .
'Then the army travelled up through the bridge at Paris'.

It is the equivalent with verbs of motion of C5 with those of rest (e.g. *Wæs halig leoht ofer westenne*, 'There was (a) holy light over the wilderness'). Finally the occurrence of an additive C6 should be mentioned; this is very common and entails the use of different prepositions:

(43) Her cuom se here to Readingum on West-Seaxe.
'Then the army came to Reading in West Saxony'.
$C6_c = C6_\gamma$ [to] + $C6_\gamma$ [on]

The seventh complementation category has been labelled 'equational' as it involves the adordinate linking of two elements. These normally belong to the same word class, that of nominals, as in

(44) Ðu ana bist eallra dema.
'You alone are the judge of all'.

The same category is used when a nominal is linked to an adjective. In such instances the determining characteristic of C7 is the attribution of a quality to an object (animate or inanimate). Unlike Engel 1977 or Engel/Schumacher [2] 1978 I see no compelling reason to create an additional category to cover such instances. The basic relation is still that of equation. Thus in

(45) Ðonne ic stille beom.
'When I am calm'.

an equation is made between the subject, *ic,* and the class of objects with the quality *stille.*

On first glance many occurrences of C7 may look like C4 as in

(46) Of Ӡeata fruman syndon Cantware and Wihtsæton.
'The inhabitants of Kent and of the Isle of Wight are
of Geatish origin'.

inasmuch as they have a preposition at their head, but again it is a question of an equation between the subject CO and those who show the quality expressed in the C7 prepositional phrase. Lastly I should remark that *beon/ wesan* is not the only verb which may have a C7 in its valency framework. Another verb with which this is possible is *hatan* as in

(47) Ða deor hi hataþ hrānas.
'The animals they call reindeer'.

Among the possible complements in the valency frameworks of OE is also the temporal complement, C8. Its surface realization can vary considerably from a simple adverbial to an involved prepositional construction. Furthermore we can distinguish different meanings of formally similar verbs by the occurrence of C8 with certain other complements. Thus when the verb *gefaran* occurs with only CO and C8 its meaning is 'to die':

(48) Her gefor Ælfred.
'Then Alfred died'.

Where the C8 co-occurs with a C6 or where it is not present at all the meaning is 'to travel, journey':[19]

(49) Swa feor swa man on anum gefara
'As far as man may travel alone'.

Examples of more complex C8 constructions are:

(50) On þy ilcan ȝeare worhte se foresprecena here geweorc . . .
'During that same year the above-mentioned army did . . .'

þa þæs on sumera on þysum ȝeare tofor se here.
'Then in the summer of that year the army dispersed'.

As with other complements C8 can also occur in a disjuncted form:

(51) Her hine bestæl se here on midne wintre ofer twelfan niht
to Cippanhame.   bestæl ⟨0168$_c$⟩
'Then the army stole away in the middle of winter after
(the) twelfth night to Chippenham'.

A subclassification of temporal complements is advisable as these vary among themselves. As space does not permit it I can not offer anything like a comprehensive classification but can at least attempt an initial one. For example the C8 of the last sentence may be broken down into

(52) C8$_c$ = C8 [INDEF] + C8 [SPEC:DEF] + C8 [REL:DEF]

where [SPEC:DEF] stands for the definite specification of the point in time (*on midne wintre*) and [REL:DEF] for the definite specification of the duration (*ofer twelfan niht*). [INDEF] refers to the use of the indefinite temporal adverbial *her*. Such a tentative classification must also distinguish degrees of definite specification so that we obtain different labelling for *on sumera* and *on þysum ȝeare* in

(53) þa þæs on sumera on þysum ʒeare . . .

This may be achieved by indexing, where numerals refer to the degree of the quality they are attached to, increasing in number corresponding to an increase in degree so that we have

(54) C8 [SPEC:DEF, 1] = on þysum ʒeare
      C8 [SPEC:DEF, 2] = on sumera

There may be some doubt about the necessity or at least about the precise nature of the last complementation category, the verbative C9. It is necessary, however, as it denotes a category which is part of the valency of a number of verbs and which furthermore is of equal rank with other possible complements. Thus in the sentence

(55) . . . ða sædon hi þæt ðæs hearperes wif sceolde acwelan . . .
      'then they said that the harper's wife should die'

we do not have a C9 but a C1 which is realised as a relative clause (sentence-like complementation, see above) connected to the main verb by þæt but containing a finite verb form with a CO (here: a modal with an independent verb) which is however on a rank lower than that of the main verb. The stemma for this sentence is then

(56)

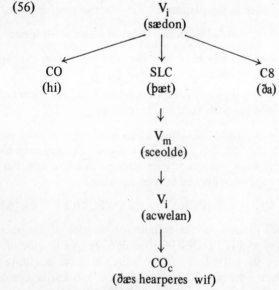

However in the following sentence

(57) He heht englas him to coman.   heht ⟨019c⟩
'He commanded angels to come to him'.

we have a verbal element (*coman*) which is directly coupled (not rank-shifted) to the main verb. This verbative complement is furthermore complex in that it contains a C4 of its own. Stemmatically I represent the sentence as

(58)

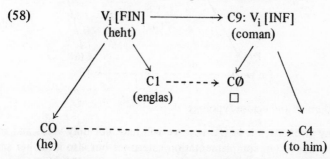

The broken arrows indicate reference identity of complements and the bracketing behind the V$_i$ forms indicates that the main verb is finite and the C9 non-finite. This is always the case. No two finite verb forms can co-exist on the same rank within a sentence unless they share their CO and are used additively.

The complements contained in a complex C9 are independent of the valency framework of the main verb and vice versa. A further characteristic of C9s is that the CO of their verbs is always unrealised as it is present as a complement of the main verb. Those verbs which may take a C9 are not numerous but of high frequency; as with Modern English they include verbs of perception and the verb *let*. Typical examples are:

(59) Ic þæt londbuend . . . secgan hyrde . . .   hyrde ⟨019⟩
'I have heard country dwellers . . . say'.

Ic seah turf tredan .vi. gebroður   seah ⟨019c⟩
'I saw six brothers traverse a field'.

God let hi habban agenne cyre.   let ⟨019c⟩
'God let them have their own choice'.

Note that in the above examples the C1 of each sentence is reference identical with the non-realised CO of the subsequent C9. This need not be the case as the CO of the main verb can also be that of the C9 (here also unrealised):

(60) þa begann se wer dreorig wepon
'Then the man began sadly to weep'.

which I represent as follows:

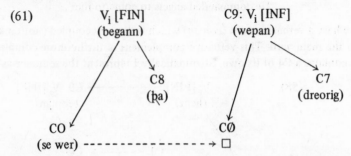

(61)

2 Adjuncts and clause typology

In any given stretch of OE text we will have not only verbs and some or all of the above ten complementation categories but also a further small set of non-classified elements (some of which have occurred in the sentences above) and which I designate adjuncts. If the complements are determined by the valency frameworks of particular verbs then adjuncts are determined by the textual framework in which the verb with its complements resides. The textual framework derives ultimately from the expressional intention of the author. Thus a typical adjunct such as negation cannot be dependent on the verb affected but stems from the wish of the author to make a negated statement. Equally we obtain a set of attitudinal adjuncts (see the two examples in the text above). Other adjuncts refer to attendant aspects of a verbal action, e.g. *eac* (concomitance), *eft* (repetition).

The syntagms in which a verb with its complements occurs stand in relationship to each other in a text. This relationship can be of various kinds (declarative, interrogative, causative, adversative, concessive, etc.) and its classification results in a clause typology. However for a valency framework of the verb, such a typology is not a pertinent desideratum. For a text dependency grammar it certainly is, but that has not been intended here.

Notes

1. By far the larger number of example sentences given here are from OE prose texts, the remainder are from poetical texts. I have dispensed with giving sources as they are of little relevance for the theme of the paper. As an aid I add a Modern English gloss to each sentence.
2. I use the term valency in the classical sense of Tesnière, 1959, that is, the demands for certain complements placed by specific verbs. For refinements of the use of this term, see Engel, 1972.

3. Thus for example the long sequences in the *Anglo-Saxon Chronicle* consisting of syntagms connected by 'and' would be subdivided into smaller units (normally corresponding to what is contained between two occurrences of 'Ꝣ') each of which from the point of view of dependency analysis constitutes a sentence.

4. The term complement refers to those elements of a sentence which are present due to the demands of the main verb of the sentence. They may range from the (traditional) subject to a verbative construction and include all elements which are governed directly by the main verb. On adjuncts, see below.

5. On the relationship of valency to deep structure, see Helbig, 1969.

6. Such manifestations are also the main subject of interest in the historical development of English: it is precisely the differences in the surface structure in English verbal constructions on the time axis which renders a diachronic study of them rewarding.

7. Prediction is vital where dealing with a living language: by establishing it we can account for all possible occurrences of a certain verb.

8. Dative and instrumental are taken together here as C3.

9. Neither in the classical exposition, Fillmore 1968, nor in that of subsequent modifications, Fillmore 1971; Fillmore 1977.

10. My system of complementation is similar but by no means identical with that presented in Engel/Schumacher, [2]1978:26. Among the more important differences are the reduction of C7 ('Einordnungsergänzung') and C8 ('Artergänzung') to one, C7 ('equational'), the expansion of their C9 ('Ergänzungssatz'), my 'verbative', and the introduction of a temporal complement, my C8.

11. The stemmas in this paper are all on the level of complements, i.e. they show the entire complement at the corresponding node. Complements which consist of more than one lexical item could be given more detailed representation; here this would be

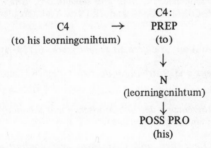

12. I should remark that in this treatment of OE I am not going to attempt to distinguish between obligatory and facultative complements as this cannot be done conclusively for an extinct language. Thus I satisfy myself with the twofold distinction complement:adjunct.

13. A complement which is not realised superficially is shown with a stroke through it in a valency description.

14. A procedure for differentiating complements and adjuncts is offered in Andresen, 1973.

15. See Engel/Schumacher, [2]1978:79 ff. where a similar category is described.

16. A stroke indicates that the complements immediately before and after it are alternatives of one another.

17. A formalization of adjectival valencies (for German) is found in Sommerfeldt/Schreiber, 1974.

18. This type of construction, common in Modern German, is dealt with in Polenz, 1969.

19. It should be mentioned that with this meaning the verb more frequently occurs without the prefix ʒ *e*.

References

Andersen, H.
1973   "Ein methodischer Vorschlag zur Unterscheidung von Ergänzung und Angabe im Rahmen der Valenztheorie", *Deutsche Sprache* 1:49–63.
Emons, R.
1974   *Valenzen englischer Prädikatsverben* (Tübingen: Niemeyer).
1978   *Eine Valenzgrammatik für das Englische* (Tübingen: Niemeyer).
Engel, U.
1972   "Bemerkungen zur Dependenzgrammatik", *Neue Grammatiktheorien und ihre Anwendung auf das heutige Deutsch,* edited by H. Moser (Düsseldorf: Schwann), 111–115.
1977   *Syntax der deutschen Gegenwartssprache* (Berlin: Eric Schmidt).
Engel, U. – H. Schumacher
1978   *Kleines Valenzlexikon deutscher Verben* (Tübingen: Narr).
Fillmore, C.
1968   "The case for case", *Universals in linguistic theory,* edited by E. Bach and R. T. Harms (New York: Holt), 1–88.
1971   "Some problems of case grammar", *Monograph series on languages and linguistics* 24:35–56 (Washington: Georgetown University Press).
1977   "The case for case reopened", *Syntax and semantics 8: Grammatical relations,* edited by P. Cole and G. M. Sadock (New York: Academic Press), 59–82.
Helbig, G.
1969   "Valenz und Tiefenstruktur", *Deutsch als Fremdsprache* 6:159–169.
Helbig, G. – W. Schenkel
1969   *Wörterbuch zur Valenz und Distribution deutscher Verben* (Leipzig: Bibliographisches Institut).
Heuer, K.
1977   *Untersuchung zur Abgrenzung der obligatorischen und fakultativen Valenz des Verbs* (Frankfurt am Main: Athenäum).
Hickey, R.
1980   *Satzstrukturen des Deutschen und Englischen, eine kontrastive Analyse im Rahmen der Dependenzgrammatik.* Diss. Kiel.
Polenz, P. von
1969   "Der Pertinenzdativ und seine Satzbaupläne", *Festschrift für Hugo Moser zum 60. Geburtstag,* edited by U. Engel, P. Grebe, H. Rupp (Düsseldorf: Schwann), 146–171.
Sommerfeldt, K. E. – H. Schreiber
1974   *Wörterbuch zur Valenz und Distribution deutscher Adjektive* (Leipzig: Bibliographisches Institut).
Tesnière, L.
1959   *Éléments de syntaxe structurale* (Paris: Klincksieck).

DAVID HUNTLEY

The distribution of the denominative adjective and the adnominal genitive in Old Church Slavonic

This paper examines some of the syntactic and semantic conditions governing the distribution of the denominative adjective and the adnominal genitive in Old Church Slavonic.[1] Under certain syntactic conditions, the denominative adjective is obligatory, while under other syntactic conditions the adnominal genitive is obligatory. Under yet other syntactic conditions, the choice of adjective or adnominal genitive is optional. Under some of these conditions the choice between adjective and adnominal genitive is governed by a semantic hierarchy. Competing with both denominative adjective and adnominal genitive in Old Church Slavonic, there also occurs the adnominal dative. The use of the adnominal dative is governed by semantic conditions which I shall not touch upon in this paper.[2]

The denominative adjective is obligatory when used as a single unmodified item in a discourse where no overt head noun is present:

(1) Supr. 370.9–11 . . . 22–4 Ty pritľ čę podobišę věřnaago› roba i nerazumľ naago i *gospodňe* (ta despotika) rastrošivǔšaago . . . On de bo bijąštaago i pijanaago i *gospodьsko* (ta despotika) trošęštaago i pogubľ jająštaago mąčitǔ. 'Those parables compared the faithful servant and the ignorant one who wasted *his master's property* . . . For there he torments the one who beats and is drunk and who squanders and destroys *his master's property*.'

In several rubrics marking feast days on which texts are to be read, in the *Savvina kniga* and the *Kiev Missal,* unmodified adnominal genitives occur without head nouns. These are not reliable counterexamples to the rule exemplified in (1) above, since they may well be scribal abbreviations of adnominal genitives with modifiers.[3] Examples of type (1) are attested only when the referent of the adjective is singular. In general, the denominative adjectives discussed here have only singular referents. For plural referents, the genitive plural of the noun is used for such nominal stems. Thus in the examples examined below the referents of either the adjectives or the adnominal genitives will always be singular, and never dual, or plural (except in Example (21), below).

Even with a singular referent, though, the adnominal genitive is obligatory for an item that is modified by an adjective other than a denominative adjective, or by a pronoun other than a personal pronoun:

(2) Supr. 508.11–12 Svętaago *otĭca* našego Ioana arxiepiskopa konstanı tinja grada zlatoustaago. 'Of our holy *father* John Chrysostom, archbishop of Constantinople.'

The adnominal genitive singular *otĭca* 'father' is used in (2) because this item is modified by the non-derived adjective *svętaago* 'holy', and by the possessive pronoun *našego* 'our'.

Indeed, there are only two examples attested where a denominative adjective is modified by another adjective, and in both of these examples the modifier happens to be a denominative adjective:

(3) Supr. 192.27–8 ... 193.7 ... 8–10 ... 194.6–7 I im za uzda *koňě jego*[4] (tou hippou autou) stavĭjasě i ... i jedva ... vŭzmogošę otŭ trŭgnąti rącě jego otŭ uzdy *koňĭnylę cěsarę* (tou hippou tou basileōs) ... i paky imŭ za uzdą *konja cěsara* (tou hippou tou basileōs) ... 'And taking hold of the bridle *of his horse*, he tried to stop him ... and scarcely ... could they drag his hands away from the bridle *of the Emperor's horse* ... and again taking hold of the bridle *of the Emperor's horse* ...'

In this example, the adnominal genitive *koňě/konja* 'horse' (two alternative ways of spelling the same item) is modified by *jego* 'his', and then by a denominative adjective *cěsara* 'of the Emperor'. These are very typical Old Church Slavonic constructions. The untypical construction here is *uzdy koňĭnyję cěsarę* 'of the bridle of the Emperor's horse', where *koňĭnyję*, the denominative adjective, occurs in spite of the fact that it is modified by another (denominative) adjective *cěsarę*. Syntactically, in fact, *cěsarę* modifies *uzdy*, rather than *koňĭnyję*. Here the message of the passage is signalled pragmatically, rather than syntactically, since the reader knows that it is the horse, rather than the bridle, which is presented as belonging to the Emperor.

A similar pragmatic, rather than syntactic cohesion occurs in the only other attested example where a denominative adjective is modified by another adjective:

(4) Supr. 5.18–19 Prěkrŭstista ici svoi obrazomŭ *krestŭnyimŭ xristosovomŭ* (tou staurou tou Khristou). 'They crossed their faces with the sign *of the Cross of Christ.*'[5]

Here the reader knows pragmatically that the reference is to the sign of the Cross rather than to the sign of Christ, even though syntactically *xristosovomŭ* 'Christ's' modifies *obrazomŭ* 'sign' rather than *krestŭnyimŭ* 'of the Cross'.

This type of pragmatic, rather than syntactic cohesion emerges even more strikingly in the only attested example where a denominative adjective is modified by a pronoun:

(5) Supr. 349.27–8 Moje bo brašíno, reče, jestŭ da sŭtvorǫ volǫ *otĭčǫ si* (tou patros mou). "For my food", he said, "is that I should do the will *of my Father."*

Here the dative enclitic personal pronoun *si* 'one's own' modifies the denominative adjective *otĭčǫ* 'father's'. There are two possible syntactic interpretations of this passage. Either *si* syntactically modifies *volǫ* 'will', or else the passage is syntactically ambiguous. It is a matter of pragmatic knowledge, however, that Jesus must here be referring to his father's will, rather than to his own will as well as his father's.

Even when the modifier of the head noun is itself modified by a dative enclitic pronoun, the modifier typically takes the form of the adnominal genitive as in (6), rather than of the denominative adjective as in (5):

(6) Supr. 505.14–15 Uvědě vŭ tę *otca ti* božĭstvo. 'I recognize in you the divinity *of your father.'*

Thus, when the modifier is itself modified by an adjective other than a denominative adjective, or by a pronoun other than a dative enclitic pronoun, the modifier of the head noun takes the form of the adnominal genitive. When modified by a denominative adjective or a dative enclitic pronoun, it is marginally possible for the modifier of the head noun to take the form of the denominative adjective where the semantic cohesion is pragmatically unambiguous.

There are attested fourteen examples in which the modifier of the head noun is itself modified by a subordinate clause. In all of these examples, the modifier of the head noun takes the form of the denominative adjective.[6] Thirteen of these examples are semantically unambiguous:

(7) Lk. 22.61 Zo. Mar. I poměnǫ Petrŭ slovo *gospodĭne* ěkože reče emu . . . (tou kuriou, hōs eipen autōi) 'And Peter remembered the word *of the Lord*, how he said to him . . .'

(8) Supr. 395.25–7 Eliko vas *iliini* (tou Ēlia) učenici jeste ježe ubogyjǫ trepezy vŭdovičę ne poxuli, (tou . . . mē exouthenēsantos) u nasŭ vitaite. 'Whoever of you are the disciples *of Elijah*, who did not scorn the meagre table of the widow, dwell with us.'

(9) Supr. 245.25–6 I tŭ bo *isajevy* (Ēsaiou) glasy slyšaaše ježe reče . . . 'For he, too, heard the words *of Isaiah*, who said . . .'

(10) Supr. 424.10–12 Pristǫpaimŭ kŭ trepezě *xristosově* (tou Khristou), sŭ ńimže otcu slava . . . 'Let us come to the table *of Christ*, to whom with the

Father there is glory . . .'

(11) Ps. 3.1 Sin. Psalmŭ *davydovŭ* (tōi Dauid) egda běgaše otŭ lica aveseluma, syna svoego. 'A psalm *of David*, when he was fleeing from the face of Absolom, his son.'

There are seven more examples in the Psalter similar to (11), all containing the denominative adjective *davydov-* 'of David', translating the Greek adnominal dative *tōi Dauid*. [7]

(12) Supr. 533.3–5 Samo že to slovo syna *božija*, imže vĭsa byšę ... 'For this is itself the word of the son *of God*, through whom all things came to be . . .'

Example (12) is rather different from (7) – (10) and from (11) and the examples analogous with (11). In (7) – (11) the antecedents of the subordinate clauses must be, the Lord, Elijah, Isaiah, Christ, and David, respectively, even though these participants are expressed by denominative adjectives. In (7) and (11), the verb in the subordinate clause is third singular and grammatically could have the head noun as the antecedent. Lexically, though, these verbs require animate subjects, so their antecedents must be the denominative adjectives. In (8) and (9), the subordinate clauses also have third singular verbs, but clearly have the denominative adjectives as their antecedents, since the adjectives have singular referents, whereas the head nouns have plural referents. In (10), the relative pronoun is masculine, with an adjective derived from a masculine stem as its antecedent, whereas the head noun is feminine. Thus, in (7) – (11) the cohesion is either lexical or morphological, rather than syntactic.

In (12), however, there is both lexical and morphological ambiguity, and in this example the cohesion is purely pragmatic. On both morphological and lexical grounds, the antecedent in (12) could be either God or his son, but it is a part of the pragmatic beliefs of the translator and his audience that the Creator was not God the Son, but God the Father.

In (13), however, the ambiguity would appear to be unsolvable:

(13) Mt. 26.75 Mar. Ass. Sav. I poměnǫ Petrŭ glagolŭ isusovŭ iže (Zo. i) reče emu ... (tou rhēmatos Iēsou eirēkotos autōi) 'And Peter remembered the word *of Jesus*, who said to him . . .'

From the Slavonic alone, it is not clear whether the relative pronoun *iže* 'who, which' is nominative with the antecedent 'Jesus', or accusative with the antecedent 'word' since this pronoun is homonymous in nominative and accusative singular masculine. The passage could mean 'the word of Jesus, which he said to him'. The translator could have produced a completely unambiguous version with a literal, and perfectly good Slavic translation of the participial phrase as was done in (14) and (15) below. Example (13) was not ambiguous to the translator since he was working from the Greek text, but he may not have realized that his version would be ambiguous to his audience. However, since in all the attested examples in which the modifier of the head noun is modified by a subordinate clause the modifier of the head noun always takes the form of the denominative adjective and never that of the adnominal genitive, the adjective may have been obligatory in this type of construction.

Whereas it appears from the pattern of attestation that the denominative adjective was obligatory with a subordinate clause modifier, the adjective appears to be the highly preferred form when the modifier of the head noun is in its turn modified by a participial phrase. There are three examples attested where the head noun is modified by an adnominal genitive which is itself modified by a participial phrase:

(14) Lk. 11.51 Zo. Mar. ... otŭ krŭve Avelě pravĭ dŭnaago do krŭve *Zaxariję pogybŭšaago* (Zakhariou tou apolomenou) meždju oltaremĭ i xramomĭ.
'... from the blood of Abel the just man to the blood *of Zachariah, who perished* between the altar and the sanctuary.'

(15) Supr. 106.1–3 Rabŭ azŭ *Xristosa rekŭšaago* ... (Khristou tou eirēkotos) 'I am the servant *of Christ, who said* ...'

(16) Supr. 456.21–2 ... i otŭkryti tělo *boga sĭměrĭšaago* sę voleją. '... to uncover the body *of God, who humbled himself* of his own free will.'

The syntax of these three examples is perfectly good Slavic, and in (14) and (15), and presumably in (16) is identical with the Greek, since the head noun is modified by a genitive singular masculine noun modified by a participle which is also in the genitive singular masculine.

The syntax of the eight examples contained in (17) – (21) is equally transparent, but in these examples the syntax of the Slavonic differs from that of the Greek:

(17) Ps. 28.5 ... 7–8 ... 9 Glasŭ *gospodĭnĭ sŭkrušająštaago* (kuriou suntribontos) kedry ... Glasŭ *gospodĭnĭ prosěkająšta* (kuriou diakoptontos) plamenŭ ogna. Glasŭ *gospodĭnĭ sŭtręsająštago* (kuriou susseiontos) pustyną ... Glasŭ *gospodĭnĭ sŭvrŭšająštago* (kuriou katartizomenou) eleni. 'The voice *of the Lord who breaks* the cedars ... The voice *of the Lord who cuts through* the flame of fire. The voice *of the Lord who shakes* the wilderness ... The voice *of the Lord who creates* the deer.'

(18) Ps. 123.9, Supr. 80.6–8 Pomoštĭ naša vŭ imę *gospodĭne sŭtvoršaego* (kuriou tou poiēsantos) nebo i zemlją. 'Our help is in the name *of the Lord, who made* heaven and earth.'

(19) Supr. 454.9–10 Daždĭ mi tĕlo *isusovo omračĭšaago* (tou Iēsou tou ...
skotisantos) slĭnce prĕžde mala vrĕmene. 'Give me the body *of Jesus, who
darkened* the sun a little while ago.'

(20) Supr. 457.9–11 Vole ubo i vodojǫ omyvaješi tĕlo *božije izmyvŭšaago*
(theou tou ... ekplunantos) vĭsę? 'Do you then also wash with water the
body *of God who* washed everyone?'[8]

(21) Supr. 396.16–17 Ole nečuvŭstvo *židovŭsko ne razumĕjǫštiixŭ* (Ioudaiōn
tōn mēnoountōn) ... 'Oh the unfeeling *of the Jews, who did not understand* ...'

The syntax of the Greek in (17) – (21) is the ʏame as in (14) and (15).
In the Slavonic version, however, the participle does not modify the denominative adjective, but, rather, is governed by the head noun. A literal translation of the Slavonic version of these examples would be:- 'The voice of the
Lord, of the one who breaks ...', and so on. Although the adjective in (21)
has a plural referent, the example has been included here because the Greek
sources of the Slavonic happen to contain relatively few examples of this type
of construction.

There are two examples of this type of construction with a passive participle:

(22) Mt. 26.3 Zo. Mar. Ass. Sav. Tŭgda sŭbŭrašę sę arxierei i kŭnižĭ nici i
starci ljudĭscii na dvorŭ *arxiereovŭ naricaemago* (tou arkhiereōs tou lego-
menou) Kaiĕfa. 'Then the high priests and scribes and the elders of the people
gathered at the court of the high priest named Caiaphas.'

(23) Supr. 279.2–3 ... vŭ četvrŭtoje lĕto *markianja* (Markianou) cĕsarĭstva
bogomŭ *ljubimago* (tou theophilous) ... '... in the fourth year of the reign
of Marcianus, who was loved by God ...'

In (23) the participle could syntactically either be governed by or agree
with 'reign'; that this is an instance of government, and not agreement, is
clear on lexical, but not on syntactical grounds.

In the Greek sources there are some fifty examples where a head noun is
modified by two adnominal genitive singular nouns in apposition one with
another. Since in (17) – (23) the Slavonic versions have the head noun modified by a denominative adjective and a participle in apposition one with another, it is of interest to compare the Slavonic versions in (17) – (23) with
the Slavonic versions where there occurs apposition of two adnominal genitives in the Greek. In over forty of the examples, the Slavonic follows the
Greek by having both modifiers take the form of the adnominal genitive, for
example:

(24) Lk. 1.32. Zo. Mar. Ass. Sav. ... prestolǔ *Davyda otǐca* ego ... (Dauid tou patros) ... '... the throne *of David, his father* ...'

There are six examples where the first of the modifiers, however, takes the form of the denominative adjective. These are analogous with the examples having a denominative adjective and a participle in the genitive in (17) – (23). One of these examples, where the Greek text is similar to that of (24), is attested in Old Church Slavonic only in the two extant *tetraevangelia*. In this example, (25) below, the *Zographensis* has the adjective, while the Marianus has the adnominal genitive. However, it is the difficult *Zographensis* reading which is supported by all of the younger Church Slavonic witnesses available to me, and which therefore probably stems back to the original translation:

(25) Lk. 1.69 Zo. ... vǔ domu *davydově* otroka svoego (Dauid paidos) ... Mar. Davyda. '... in the house of *David, his servant.*'

The other examples similar to (25) are cited under (26)   (30) below:

(26) Mt. 1.1 Ass. Sav. Kǐnigy rodǐstva *isuxristova syna davydova syna avraamlě.* (Iēsou Khristou huiou Dauid, huiou Abraam). 'The book of the genealogy *of Jesus Christ, son of David, son of Abraham.*'

(27) Mk. 1.1 Zo. Mar. Ass. Sav. Začęlo evanǵelič *isuxristova syna božič.* (Iēsou Khristou huiou theou). 'The beginning of the Gospel *of Jesus Christ, son of God.*'

(28) Lk. 8.3 Mar. Ioanna žena *xuzaně pristavǔnika irodova* (Khouza epitropou Hērōidou) i susana i iny mnogy. Zo. žena *xuzěanina* iny mnogy. 'Joanna, the wife *of Chuza, Herod's steward,* and Susanna and many others ...'

The *Marianus* reading is supported by younger witnesses, while the *Zographensis* reading is a case of haplography.[9] Example (29) is cited from a younger witness which has the best reading for the form *xusiiněx* , which could mean either 'of Chusi', or 'of the Cushite':

(29) Ps. 7.1 Pog. Psalomǔ davydovǔ iže pětǔ gospodǔ o slovesexǔ *xusiiněxǔ, syna iemsnina.* (Khusi huiou Iemeni) Sin. *susiiněxǔ,* Bon. xusiją, Sin. Bon. *iemeniina.* 'A Psalm of David which he sang to the Lord, concerning the words *of Chusi, the son of Benjamin.*'

(30) Ps. 89.1 Molitva *moseova člověka božič.* (tou Mōusē anthropōu theou). 'A prayer *of Moses, the man of God.*'

The denominative adjectives which I have discussed under examples (7) – (13), (17) – (20), (22), (23), and (25) – (30) above contain several lexical features in common. They refer either to unique human beings, or else are derived from noun stems which have a strong lexical tendency to refer to unique beings. The only exception occurs in (21) where the adjective referring to Jews has plural reference. However, even here the reference is to a specific group of Jews, namely those who were supposed to have witnessed Christ's miracles, and yet still did not understand, rather than to the whole lexical class of Jews or to random representatives of that class. Nevertheless, the adnominal genitive could be used with such reference, as can be seen from (14) — (16), and from the large number of examples analogous with (24). Much more frequently attested than the constructions examined under (1), (3) — (30) above is the construction where a head noun is modified by a bare, unmodified adnominal genitive, or denominative adjective. In this type of construction, the stronger the tendency of the lexical item to refer to a unique being, the stronger is the tendency for the denominative adjective to be used, rather than the adnominal genitive.

The stems with the strongest predisposition to refer to unique beings are, of course, those which bear unambiguous lexical reference to unique beings. For the stem *soton-* 'Satan' there are nine examples attested of the bare denominative adjective, but none of the bare adnominal genitive. For the stems *xristos-/xr st-* 'Christ', and *isuxristos-/isuxr st-* 'Jesus Christ', there are over 140 examples of the bare denominative adjective, but only two of the bare adnominal genitive.

Other stems with a strong, but not unambiguous lexical reference to unique beings, *bog-* 'God', *Isus-* 'Jesus', *dijavol-* 'the Devil', *neprijazn-* 'the Evil One', *gospod-* 'the Lord', nearly always have unique reference in the Old Church Slavonic texts, and are attested with over 800 examples of the bare denominative adjective, but none of the bare adnominal genitive singular. The stem *s pas-* 'Saviour' is exceptional with two examples of the bare adnominal genitive, Supr. 392.29, 396.28, and three of the bare denominative adjective, Supr. 325.13, 487.11, and 513.17.[10]

Noun stems denoting given names, because of their lexical properties, nearly always refer to unique persons, and in the Old Church Slavonic texts always do so. For such stems there are attested in Old Church Slavonic nearly 300 examples of the bare denominative adjective, but only four examples of the bare adnominal genitive. Noun stems denoting social ranks and professions are also strongly lexically predisposed to refer to unique beings, and in Old Church Slavonic these stems have 85 examples of the bare denominative adjective, versus five of the bare adnominal genitive.

Common human noun stems, however, in Old Church Slavonic are attested with a much higher ratio of bare adnominal genitive to bare denominative adjective than is the case for any of the lexical classes of noun stem mentioned in the previous three paragraphs. Common noun stems are not strongly lexically predisposed to refer to unique entities, but in Old Church Slavonic the bare adnominal genitive singular of such stems tends to refer to a unique individual, whereas the bare denominative adjective modifier tends to refer to a random member of the lexical class. This pattern is not observed in noun stems mentioned in the previous three paragraphs because the noun stems themselves carry specific reference lexically. There is thus a strong tendency in Old Church Slavonic for the bare noun modifier to take the form of the denominative adjective when the modifier refers to a single entity. However for stems which do not carry a high degree of inherent specific reference, such specific reference tends to be signalled by the adnominal genitive singular.

This point is best illustrated by examining those common human noun stems which are attested with both denominative adjective and adnominal genitive bare modifiers of a head noun. In this group of examples, which will be discussed in detail below, there are twenty-five occurrences of the adnominal genitive, and twenty-three of the denominative adjective. Thus, whereas for stems denoting rational beings the adnominal genitive singular accounts for less than one per cent of the examples for stems with a high degree of specific lexical reference, for common noun stems denoting rational beings for which both bare adnominal genitive and denominative adjective are attested, the genitive singular accounts for just over a half of the attested examples. Further, for these common noun stems, nineteen examples of the adnominal genitive refer to specific individuals, and six examples have generic reference, whereas seventeen examples of the adjective have generic, or in some cases vague reference, whereas six examples of the adjective refer to specific individuals. In order to establish this point, all the examples containing stems with both the denominative adjective and the adnominal genitive singular of common rational nominals as bare modifiers of a head noun will be examined in detail below.

First of all, I shall discuss examples where the adjective has generic reference, but where the genitive has specific reference:

(31) Supr. 78.23–5 Poběždenŭ že byvŭ dijavolŭ prěměni sę vŭ *mǫžeskŭ* obraz . (eis andra) 'Being defeated, the devil changed himself into the form *of a man*.'

(32) Supr. 299.10–11 Pomysli oděti sę vŭ *mǫžĭskyi* (andrikon) obrazŭ. 'She decided to dress herself in the style *of a man*.'

(33) Supr. 546.13–14 Ne blagovolitŭ gospodĭ vŭ kŭkŭnju *mǫžĭsku*. 'The Lord does not take pleasure in the legs *of a man*.'

The adjectives in (31) – (33) unambiguously refer to the generic class 'man', not to particular individuals who happen to be members of that class. However, the adnominal genitives in (34) – (40) refer to specific men who have been mentioned previously in the narratives from which these examples are excerpted:-

(34) Supr. 364.30 Vidě li krotostí i vŭzdrǔžanije *mǫža*? (andros) 'Did you see the gentleness and reserve *of the man*?

(35) Supr. 514.13–14 Vĭsi že *mǫža* (tou andros) žitiju divęšte sę kŭ nemu sĭbiraaxǫ sę. 'Now all marvelling at the life *of the man*, gathered to him.'

(36) Supr. 522.23–4 Tako i priležĭnoje pokaanĭje *mǫža* (tou andros) uvěděvǔšě ne na sę nadějemŭ sę. 'As we have learnt of the sincere repentance *of the man*, let us not rely upon ourselves.'

(37) Supr. 520.23–5 Nŭ jakože velikyję i istinǔnyję blagyję nravy *mǫža* (tou andros) sǔkazaaxomŭ ... 'But as we have related the great and true virtue *of the man* ...'

(38) Supr. 523.16–17 Izvoĺenĭja bo *mǫža* (tou andros) ni viděti mogy dijavolŭ... 'But the devil, not even being able to see *the man's* resolve ...'

(39) Supr. 564.4–6 Moljaaše boga pobĕditi svoimŭ člověkoljubiimŭ zŭlobǫ *mǫža*. 'He begged God, through his love for mankind, to overcome the spite *of the man*.'

(40) Supr. 567.6–7 Posŭlašę na mǫža duxŭ vŭ obrazě zmiině iže vĭlĕzŭ vŭ lonǫ *mǫža* mǫčaaše. 'They sent against the man a spirit in the form of a snake, which, getting into *the man's* breast, tormented him.'

The adjective in (41) is used in a way similar to that in (31) – (33):

(41) Supr. 96.5–9 Sama svoima rǫkama vĭzem'ši na rama, vŭzloži na kola, na ńixŭže pročii iže ležęšte na ogńĭ vezomi beaxǫ, po istině mati *mǫčeniča*. (marturos) 'Lifting him up with her own hands onto her shoulders, she put him on the cart, on which the others were lying and being taken to the fire, in truth the mother *of a martyr*.'

The sense of the passage is not that the woman showed herself to be the mother of this particular martyr, but rather that she showed herself worthy of being the mother of such a person. Hence the adjective itself refers to the class of persons to which the referent belongs, rather than to a specific person.

In (42) and (43), however, the adnominal genitive singular refers to martyrs who have been mentioned previously in the narratives, and therefore presents the referents as specific individuals:

(42) Supr. 62–6–8 Jed'ĭnače jemu gněvomŭ dušǫštu o prětrŭpěnii *mǫčenika* (tou marturos), reče ... 'Still breathing with anger over the endurance *ot the martyr*, he said ...'

(43) Supr. 228.7–9 Približająštu sę mąčeniku kŭ crĭkvištu ne sŭtrŭpęšte zvěrije tii sily *mąčenika* . . . 'As the martyr was approaching the temple, the beasts not being able to withstand the power *of the martyr* . . .

Examples (44) – (49) contain occurrences of the denominative adjective and of the adnominal genitive of the stem *prav d nik-* 'just man', with the same distinction between these two forms that was observed in (31) – (43) above:

(44) Mt. 10.41–2 Mar. Ass. Priemlęi proroka vŭ imę *proroče* (profētou) mĭzdą *proročą* (profētou) priemletŭ i priemlęi pravedĭnika vu imę *pravedĭniče* (dikaiou) mĭzdą *pravedĭničą* (dikaiou) priimetŭ. I iže koližĭ do napoitŭ edinogo ot malyxŭ sixŭ čąsą studeny vodytŭkmo vŭ imę *učenika* (mathētou), aminĭ glagolją vamŭ ne pogubitŭ mĭzdy svojeję. Zo. *učeniče*, Sav. *učeniku*. 'Whoever receives a prophet in the name *of a prophet* will receive *a prophet's* reward, and whoever receives a just man in the name *of a just man* will receive *a just man's* reward. And whoever gives one of these little ones even only a cup of cold water to drink in the name *of a disciple*, truly I tell you, will not lose his reward.'

In (44) the accusative singular nouns *proroka* 'prophet' and *pravedĭnika* 'just man' refer to any random member of the class. The adjectives *proroč-* and *pravedĭnič-* have an even more abstract reference than their nouns do in this passage, since these adjectives refer, not to random members of a class, but to the idea of their lexical classes in general. The bare adnominal genitive of *prorok-* is not attested in Old Church Slavonic.

Where the *Marianus* and the *Assemanianus* in (44) have the adnominal genitive *učenika* 'disciple', the *Zographensis* has the denominative adjective *učeniče*, while the *Savvina kniga* has the adnominal dative *učeniku*. The difficult reading of the *Marianus* and the *Assemanianus* is supported by a number of younger witnesses and probably represents the original version. Whereas for 'prophet' and 'just man' the adjective is used to express a greater degree of abstraction than that expressed by the corresponding nouns in this passage, the item 'disciple' occurs only once. It is clear from this passage that the bare adnominal genitive, as well as the denominative adjective could refer to the lexical class, rather than to a specific individual.

In (45), the adjective refers to any random member of the class, rather than to any particular just man:

(45) Ps. 93.21 Ulovętŭ na dušą *pravedĭničą*. (dikaiou) 'They will prey upon the soul *of a just man*.'

The adnominal genitives in (46) – (48), however, just like those in (34) – (40), (42), (43), refer to specific individuals who have already been mentioned in the respective narratives:

(46) Supr. 166.24–5 I lizaaše potŭ *pravedĭnika* i vĭziraaše na n̅ĭ̅. 'And it was licking the sweat *of the just man* and looking at him.'

(47) Supr. 219.24–5 Se jestŭ svętaago Dometija žitije, se jestŭ *pravedĭnika* (tou dikaiou) mǫčenije. 'This is the life of the holy Dometius, this is the suffering *of the just man*.'

(48) Supr. 229.14–16 Izlězošę že zvěrije vŭnŭ crŭkŭve povelěniimĭ *pravĭdnika*. 'Then the beasts came out of the temple at the order *of the just man*.'

In (49), on the other hand, it is the noun, rather than the denominative adjective, which refers to random members of the lexical class:

(49) Ps. 57.11 Vŭzveselitŭ sę pravedĭnikŭ egda viditŭ mestĭ rǫcě svoi umyetŭ vo krŭvi *grěšĭnika*. (tou hamartōlou) I rečetŭ člověkŭ, "Ašte ubo estŭ plodŭ *pravedĭnika*." (tōi dikaiōi) 'A just man will rejoice when he sees vengeance, he will wash his hands in the blood *of the sinner*. And a man will say, "Perhaps there is a reward *for the just man*."

This is a statement of general validity in which all the nouns, whether or not they are in the genitive, and whether or not they require the definite article in either Greek or English, refer to representatives of the lexical class. Whereas in (44) the adjectives were used for a degree of abstraction greater than that signalled by the noun, here all the nouns, beginning with the nominative *pravedĭnikŭ*, express an equal degree of abstraction. This example, like (44), shows that the noun, as well as the adjective, could refer to a random member of a lexical class.

In particular, the adjective *pravedĭničǫ* in (45) and the adnominal genitive *pravedĭnika* in (49) express equal degrees of abstraction, just as do the genitive *grěšĭnika* 'sinner' in (49) and the adjective *grěšĭniča* in (50):

(50) Ps. 54.3–4 Vŭskrŭběxŭ pečaľijǫ moejǫ i sŭmęsŭ sę otŭ glasa vražĭě i otŭ sŭtǫžanĭě *grěšĭniča*. (hamartōlou) 'I grieved in my sadness and was disturbed by the voice of an enemy and the oppression *of a sinner*.'

Here the reference is to random individuals who happen to be enemies and sinners, rather than to particular identifiable enemies and sinners.

A similar degree of abstraction occurs with the adjective from the stem *rab-/rob-* 'servant' in (51)–(54) and the genitive of the noun in (55):

(51) Euch. 3b.1–4 Togo poslušaite nevidimaago vidima ziždite lě vŭ *rabĭ i* obrazě. 'Heed him, the visible architect of the unseen, in the form *of a servant*.'

(52) Supr. 345.1–2 Nŭ vŭzalka *robijemŭ* obrazomŭ. (tou doulou) 'But he thirsted in the form *of a servant*.'

(53) Supr. 480.8–9 Vŭ *rabii* (doulou) obrazŭ sę oblěče angelïskyi vladyka. 'The Lord of the angels dressed himself in the form *of a servant*.'

(54) Supr. 533.5–6 ... vŭobrazivŭša že sebe vŭ *rabii obrazŭ* '... forming himself in the image *of a servant*.'

(55) Euch. 4a.24–4b.2 Pride na zemlja obrazŭ *raba* (doulou) priemŭ vŭ podobïi člověči (anthrōpōn) byvŭ. 'You came to earth having taken on the form *of a servant*, having become the likeness of men.'

Example (55) would not be ambigous either for the translator or for his audience, since it was part of their pragmatic beliefs that Jesus took on the form of a servant in general, and not that of a particular servant.

In (56), however, the denominative adjective of the stem *rab-* is used where both translator and audience know pragmatically that the reference is to a specific individual:

(56) Euch 3a.14–17 Ierŭdanŭ vŭzvrati sę vïspętï viděvŭ dlanï *rabiją* prě-cistěmï tvoemï vrŭsě prikasająštją sę. 'The Jordan turned back, seeing the palm *of a servant* touching your pure head.'

The servant in question happens to be John the Baptist, but the point is being made that it was a servant who baptized Christ, so that the adjective presents its referent as belonging to a certain class of persons.

There are several other examples in which the denominative adjective refers to a person whose identity is known pragmatically. In (57), the reference is to Joseph's master, Potiphar:

(57) Supr. 365.24–5 Nagŭ izběže da *gospodinja* (despotikēn) ne oskvr nit města. 'He fled naked, so that he would not defile *his master's* place.'

This passage is somewhat ambiguous, however, since the point of the passage is to illustrate Joseph's loyalty, implying that he would be loyal not just to this particular master, but to any master in general. In the English translation 'a master's place' could be substituted for 'his master's place'. This is not the case in (58) where the adnominal genitive *gospodina* 'of the master's is coreferential with the pronoun *emu* 'to him' and unambiguously refers to a particular master:

(58) Mt. 13.27 Mar. Ass. Prišedŭše že rabi *gospodina* (tou oikodespotou) rěšę emu, "Gospodi ..." Zo. rabi *gospodinu* rěšę, "Gospodi ..." 'The servants of the master came and said to him, "Lord ..." '

The *Zographensis* reading is almost certainly secondary here.

In (59), the identity of the adjective's referent is known not only pragmatically, but the referent, Judas Iscariot, has been mentioned by name previously in the sermon:

(59) Cloz. 3b.7–8 ... 30–31 Sŭmęte sę ubo zĭrę bezumĭě *učeniča* (tou mathētou) ... Člověkoljubecĭ gospodĭ zĭrę drŭzosti *učeničę* (tou mathētou) sŭmąštaaše sę. 'For he was troubled at seeing the folly *of the disciple* ... The philanthropic Lord, seeing the audacity *of the disciple*, was disturbed.'

The point of the passage is that Jesus was disturbed because it was a disciple, rather than someone else, who had betrayed him. Here the adjective does refer to a particular disciple, but is used in a context where it is stressed that the individual does belong to that class. Thus the adjective may have abstract as well as specific reference, at one and the same time.

In (60), however, the genitive of the noun is used with reference to a disciple who has been named earlier in the sermon:

(60) Supr. 499.6–7 Da i nevěrstvije *učenika* (tou mathētou) našei věrě mati bystŭ. 'So that the disbelief *of the disciple* became the mother of our faith.'

The point of this passage is that a stubborn disbeliever, who happened to be a disciple, came to be a firm believer, rather than that it was a disciple in particular who followed this course of action. When (59) and (60) are compared with (44) where the adnominal genitive *učenika* refers unambiguously to the lexical class and not at all to a particular individual, it is clear that the semantic distinction between adnominal genitive and denominative adjective lies in the tendencies governing the choice of the forms, rather than in any invariant meaning.

In (61), the adjective *blądĭničĭsk-* 'of a prostitute', like the adjective in (59) refers to a particular prostitute whose identity is known pragmatically, and who is mentioned earlier in the sermon, whereas the noun in (62), like the noun in (44) refers to the whole lexical class, rather than to a particular prostitute:

(61) Supr. 392.24–5 ... vidęšte i krotŭko trĭpęšta lobŭzanija *blądĭničĭska*. (pornika) '... seeing him meekly tolerating the kiss *of a prostitute*.'

(62) Supr. 351.10–11 Běgai *blądĭnicę* slasti sladŭko sĭ ńeją besědująšte. 'Shun the pleasure *of the prostitute*, as you sweetly converse with her.' As in (59), the adjective in (61), stresses the point that it was a particular class of person rather than a particular individual involved, while the choice of the noun in (62), rather than the adjective, is influenced by the fact that the sentence contains a coreferential pronoun.

In (8) above, the adjective *vŭdovič-* 'of a widow' refers to a particular widow whose story is related in 1 Kings 17.9–16. This is another example where the adjective is used when it is known pragmatically that the reference is to a specific individual. The adnominal genitive of this stem is also attested twice under similar conditions:

(63) Zo. 129b.2 Mar. 126a.22 O syně *vĭdovicę*. 'Concerning the widow's son.'

(64) Euch. 13b.8–10 Priemy vŭzmožĭno prinošenie *vŭdovicę* (tēs khēras) blagovoleno ... 'You who received with pleasure the offering *of the widow*, who brought what she could ...'

Example (63) occurs in the list of contents that precedes the Gospel according to Saint Luke, and refers to the widow mentioned in Luke 7.12–13. In (64), the reference is to the widow mentioned in Mark 12.42–3, Luke 21.2–4.

Similarly, both adjective and adnominal genitive from the stem *učiteĺ-* 'teacher' are attested with reference to a specific individual:

(65) Cloz. 4a.10–11 Vidě li ispytanĭe *učitelevo*? 'Did you see the diligence *of the teacher*?'

(66) Supr. 442.16–17 Nŭ oběštanii li *učiteĺevy*? (tou didaskalou) 'But through the promises *of the teacher*?'

The references are, respectively, to Saint Paul, and to Christ, each of whom has been mentioned previously in the respective sermons in which these examples of the adjective occur. In (67), the adnominal genitive of the noun refers twice to Christ:

(67) Supr. 408.16–21 I jegda blądĭnica pokaja sę, jegda vladyką pozna, tŭgda učenikŭ učitelja prěda. Sego dělma reče, "tŭgda", da ne okleveteši *učitelja* (tou didaskalou) nemoštĭ, jegda vidiši učenika prědająšte. Tolika sila běaše *učiteĺja* (tou didaskalou), da i blądnicę privlěšti na svoje poslušanie. 'And when the prostitute repented, when she came to know the Lord, then the disciple betrayed the teacher. Because of this the evangelist said, "Then", so that you should not slander *the teacher's* weakness when you see the disciple betraying him. For such was the power *of the teacher* that he attracted even prostitutes to obey him.'

There is one common noun stem denoting a human being which has three examples of the adjective attested with specific reference, and two examples of the adnominal genitive, one with specific reference, and the other with abstract reference:

(68) Supr. 298.30–299.2 To slyšavŭ onŭ, vĭ sčudi sę o *starči* (tou gerontos) prozorĭněěmĭ daru. 'He having heard this, marvelled at *the old man's* perspicacious gift.'

(69) Supr. 299.26–8 I prišŭdŭšu učeniku *starču* (tou gerontos) i obrazŭ lice pověda otče. 'And when *the old man's* pupil came, she described both the appearance and the face of the father.'

(70) Supr. 300.27–8 I se dǫbŭ vĭpijetŭ dobrotě *starči* (tou gerontos) sĭvědě-teĺĭstvuję. 'And so the tree cries out, bearing witness to *the old man's* goodness.'

In the *Vita* in which these three examples occur, it is quite clear from the contexts surrounding the examples that the adjective refers to a specific individual. Further, the reference is to a monk, and the translation could be 'elder', rather than 'old man', in which case the adjectives are used for a term of rank, a semantic type of stem which uses the denominative adjective more frequently than do other common human noun stems.

Of the two attested examples of the bare adnominal genitive of the noun from this stem, (71) has an unambiguous specific reference while (72) is unambiguously generic. Both examples refer to an old man, not to the rank of elder:

(71) Supr. 555.18–21 . . . ne vidęštumu tělesĭnyima očima, nŭ božestvĭnyima xotęšteje byti prišĭstvije na navěždenĭje *starca* prišĭdŭše. '. . . to one not seeing with bodily, but with godly eyes, the event that was about to occur for the visitation of the old man.'

(72) Supr. 192.1–4 Onŭ že viděvy i vŭ takomĭ ništi obrazě i vŭ prŭtištixŭ *starca* (gēraleon) přeobidě i i ne otvěšta jemu ni jednogo slovese. 'He, seeing him in such a beggarly appearance and in the rags *of an old man*, scorned him and did not answer him a single word.'

The relative frequency of occurrence of the bare adnominal genitive singular modifier is higher for common human noun stems than for stems with a higher degree of lexical specificity, as a result of the general distinction between adjective and noun, of the different lexical meanings of various noun stems, and of the freedom with which adjectives as well as nouns can be derived from nominal stems in Old Church Slavonic.

For stems denoting unique entities, both adjective and noun will always refer to such unique entities. For stems with a lesser degree of lexical specificity, either noun or adjective may refer either to a random member, or to a unique member of the lexical class. Since nouns tend to refer to entities, and adjectives to qualities, in Old Church Slavonic the adnominal genitive singular of common human nouns tends to refer to a common human entity, while the adjective tends to refer to the quality of belonging to the lexical class signalled by the nominal stem. Since the bare adnominal genitive singular is occasionally attested even for nouns with unique lexical reference, while the bare denominative adjective of common human stems may refer to a specific individual, the distribution of these forms in Old Church Slavonic is governed by a hierarchical tendency, rather than by a semantic invariant: the higher the degree of lexical specificity, the higher is the probability of occurrence of the denominative adjective; the lower the degree of lexical specificity, the higher is the probability that the adnominal genitive will refer to a unique individual, and that the denominative adjective will refer to the lexical class in general.

Such a hierarchical choice of forms has been described for a number of languages[11]. On such hierarchies Dixon (1976:8) comments, "In each case no fixed 'yes/no' rule can be given for which alternative to employ in any instance; *both* alternatives are *possible*, in most cases, but one of the choices becomes more frequent as one moves along a hierarchy." It is hoped that the present paper will have shown that such hierarchical tendencies can be discovered even in a small corpus of old texts, especially where one can examine the habits that native speakers adopted in the course of their activity as translators.

Notes

1. For previous discussions, including various aspects not touched upon in this paper see Miklosich (1883:7–17), Meillet (1905:330–32, 370–71, 375–7, 382, 440–42), Trubetzkoj (1937: passim), Večerka (1957: passim), (1963:193–9), Vaillant (1958: 595–602), (1964:132–4), (1974:429–30, 473–9, 441–2, 444, 448–9), Watkins (1967:2195), Flier (1974:81–101, 114–5, 165–6), and especially Cooper (1971: passim). I am very grateful to Dr. Cooper for the generous gift to me of a copy of his thesis.

2. For discussion of the adnominal dative, see Havers (1911: passim on Indo-European, 305–10 on Old Church Slavonic), Mrázek (1963:229, 240–42), Vaillant (1964:189), and on Indo-European, Watkins (1967: passim).

3. See Večerka (1957:32).

4. I cannot agree with the statement of Vaillant (1964:178) that *koňě* is here a genitive-like accusative.

5. Cooper (164–5) citing (4) and referring to (3), states that the construction occurs rarely. These are the only two examples that I have found in the Old Church Slavonic 'canon', including texts from which I have not cited examples.

6. Večerka (1957:28) cites one of these examples, my example (13), as if the adjective were exceptional in this construction. He makes no reference to other examples involving relative clauses.

7. Ps. 7.1 (my example (29) below), 33.1, 50.1, 53.1, 62.1, 96.1.

8. Večerka (1957:28) does not cite (19) and (20).

9. Meillet (1905:442) and the dictionaries Sadnik & Aitzetmüller (1955) and Lysaght (1978) cite *xužeanina* without commenting on the fact that this is a scribal error.

10. Večerka (1957:31–2) cites neither these examples, nor those I cite under (35) – (39), (47), (48), (62), (67), (71), (72), but does cite some examples which I have not discussed here, but for which denominative adjectives are not attested. He states correctly that most of the bare adnominal genitives are attested for stems which form their denominative adjectives with the *-j-* suffix. He states that this suffix did not so clearly denote individual entities as did the *-ov-* and *-in-* suffixes and that the *-j-* suffix

234   *David Huntley*

soon ceased to be productive. Thus the occurrence of the bare adnominal genitive singular is accounted for by Večerka on the basis of the synchronic patterning of the types of suffix, and on the diachronic fate of the *-j-* suffix. In my opinion, both the synchronic and diachronic data are better explained on the basis of the lexical features of noun stems, since stems with a higher degree of specific lexical reference replaced the *-j-* suffix with the *-ov-* suffix diachronically, rather than with the adnominal genitive, and amongst the data not cited by Večerka, the stems *sŭpas-* and *učitel-* derive their adjectives with the *-ov-* suffix, there being no evidence that these stems ever used the *-j-* suffix.

11. See for example, Dixon (1976:7–8), 1977:110–12, 181–5, 265–8, 362–3), Heath (1976: passim), McConvell (1976: passim), Silverstein (1976: passim).

References

Cooper, D. S.
    1971   *Studies in possessive adjectives in Old Church Slavonic*, unpublished Ph.D. diss. Harvard University.
Dixon, R. M. W.
    1972   *The Dyirbal language of North Queensland* (Cambridge: Cambridge University Press).
    1976   "Introduction", *Grammatical categories in Australian languages*, edited by R.M.W. Dixon (New York: Humanities Press), 1–15.
    1977   *A Grammar of Yidiɲ* (Cambridge: Cambridge University Press).
Dixon, R. M. W. (ed.)
    1976   *Grammatical categories in Australian languages* (New York: Humanities Press Inc.).
Dostál, A. (ed.)
    1959   *Codex palaeoslovenicus glagoliticus tridentinus et oeniponantus* (Prague: Nakladatelství Československé Akademie věd).
Flier, M. S.
    1974   *Aspects of nominal determination in Old Church Slavonic* (= *Slavistic printings and reprintings 172*) (The Hague: Mouton).
Havers, W.
    1911   *Untersuchungen zur Kasussyntax der indogermanischen Sprachen* (Strassburg: Trübner).
Heath, J.
    1976   "Substantival hierarchies: addendum to Silverstein", *Grammatical categories in Australian languages*, ed. by R.M.W. Dixon (New York: Humanities Press), 172–190.
Jagić, V. (ed.)
    1907   *Psalterium Bononiense* (Vienna: Gerold).
Jagić, V. (ed.)
    1954   *Quattuor evangelorium codex Glagoliticus olim Zographensis nunc Petropolitanus* (Berlin: Weidmann, 1879, reprint Graz, 1954).
Kurz, J. (ed.)
    1955   *Evangelarium Assemani 2* (Prague: Nakladatelství Československé Akademie věd).

Lysaght, T. A.
1978   *Material towards the compilation of a concise Old Church Slavonic-English dictionary* (Wellington: Victoria University Press with Price Milburn).
McConvell, P.
1976   "Nominal hierarchies in Yukulta", *Grammatical categories in Australian languages*, edited by R.M.W. Dixon (New York: Humanities Press), 191–200.
Meillet, A.
1905   *Etudes sur l'étymologie et le vocabulaire du vieux slave 2* (= *Bibliothèque de l'école des hautes études 139.2*) (Paris:Bouillon).
Miklosich, F.
1883   *Vergleichende Grammatik der slavischen Sprachen 4: Syntax* (2nd edition) (Vienna:Braumüller).
Mrázek, R.
1963   "Datel'nyj padež v staroslavjanskom jazyke" [The dative case in Old Church Slavonic], *Issledovanija po sintaksisu staroslavjanskogo jazyka* (Prague: Izdatel'stvo Československoj Akademii nauk),225–261.
Nahtigal, R. (ed.)
1942   *Euchologium sinaiticum* 2 (Ljubljana: Akademija znanosti in umetnosti).
Sadnik, L., R. Aitzetmüller
1955   *Handwörterbuch zu den altkirchenslavischen Texten* (The Hague: Mouton).
Sčepkin, V. (ed.)
1959   *Savvina kniga* [*Savva's book*] (St. Petersburg: Izdanie otdelenija russkogo jazyka i slovesnosti Imperatorskoj Akademii nauk, 1903, reprint Graz, 1959).
Sever'janov, S. (ed.)
1904   *Suprasl'skaja rukopis'* 1–2 [The Suprasliensis manuscript 1–2] (St. Petersburg: Izdanie otdelenija russkogo jazyka i slovesnosti Imperatorskoj Akademii nauk, 1904, reprint Graz, 1956).
Sever'janov, S. (ed.)
1922   *Sinajskaja psaltyr'* [The Sinai Psalter], edited by S. Sever'janov (Petrograd: Izdanie otdelenija russkogo jazyka i slovesnosti Rossijskoj Akademii Nauk, 1922, reprint Graz, 1954).
Silverstein, M.
1976   "Hierarchy of features and ergativity", *Grammatical categories in Australian languages*, edited by R.M.W. Dixon (New York: Humanities Press), 112–171.
Trubetzkoj, N.
1937   "O pritjažatel'nyx prilagatel'nyx (possesiva) starocerkovnoslavjanskogo jazyka" [On possessive adjectives in Old Church Slavonic], *Zbornik lingvi-stičkih i filoloških rasprava A. Beliću o četrdesetogodišnjici njegova naučnog rada posvećuju njegovi prijatelji i učenici* (Belgrade: Mlada Srbija), 15–20.
Vaillant, A.
1958   *Grammaire comparée des langues slaves 2 pt. 2 Morphologie* (Lyons: IAC).
1964   *Manuel du vieux slave* 1 (2nd edition) (Paris: Institut d'études slaves).
1974   *Grammaire comparée des langues slaves 4: La formation des noms* (Paris: Klincksieck).
Večerka, R.
1957   "Ke konkurenci adnominálního genitivu a adjektiva v staroslověnštině" [On the competition of adnominal genitive with adjective in Old Church Slavonic], *Sborník prací filosofické fakulty Brněnské University A5*, 25–38.
1963   "Sintaksis bespredložnogo roditel'nogo padeža v staroslavjanskom jazyke" [The syntax of the genitive without preposition in Old Church Slavonic], *Issledovanija po sintaksisu staroslavjanskogo jazyka* (Prague: Izdatel'stvo Československoj Akademii nauk),183–223.

Watkins, C.
  1967   "Remarks on the genitive", *To honor Roman Jakobson* 3: 2191–2198
         (The Hague: Mouton).

WITOLD MAŃCZAK

If I was instead of *if I were*

Constructions of the type *if I was* instead of *if I were*, i.e. constructions showing the substitution of the indicative for the subjunctive (or conditional) in conditional subordinate clauses, occur, on a smaller or larger scale, in many languages. As to the Germanic languages, one may mention Dutch *doch het zou ons te ver voeren, als wij alle biezonderheden gingen optekenen* or German *sprang ich nicht schnell über den Rhein, der Narr hätte mir mit seiner Peitsche das Haupt zerschlagen.* The same phenomenon occurs in the Romance languages, cf. French *s'il faisait beau, il viendrait*, Old Provençal *de totz conseils vos daria'l meillor, bella dompna, si vos n'en creziatz*, popular Spanish *si tenía dinero, se lo daba* (besides standard Spanish *si yo temiera* or *temiese, también temieras* or *temerías tú*), Portuguese *pelos modos, o Pedro soube-o, e ontem, se lho não tiravam das mãos, dava cabo dele* (Sten 1973: 104), Italian *se Lucia non faceva quel segno, la risposta sarebbe probabil-mente stata diversa*, Sardinian *si denía abba, deo dia buffare*, Rumanian *dacă nu erai tu, aş fi murit fără să cunosc partea asta dulce a vieţii* or Dalmatian *se pataite, kantaraite*. The same applies to the classical languages, cf. Greek *ei eschon – edōka (an)* or Late Latin *si jubebas . . . , accederemus ad prilium.*

It is worth noting that the same phenomenon, i.e. the substitution of the indicative for the subjunctive or conditional, occurs also in main clauses, cf. German *warf er das Schwert von sich, er war verloren*, Norwegian *var jeg ikke kavallerist, så ville jeg være hest* (this example and some others are borrowed from Wędkiewicz 1911) or Dutch *als ik dat geweten had, was ik niet gekomen.* As to the Romance languages, one can mention French *si Stanislas demeurait, il était perdu* (instead of *il serait perdu* or *il aurait été perdu*, cf. *Grammaire Larousse du XXe siècle*, 1936, p. 326), Spanish *si hubieras tardado un minuto más, perdías el tren*, Italian *ella non disse niente, ma cadeva, se non la sorreg-gevano le mani di lui*, Rumanian *dacă eram jurat, şi eu îl achitam* or Dalmatian *se-l veskui me pakua lo kal, ju andua a Rum.* Similar constructions may be found in some Slavonic languages, cf. Serbian *da sam imala svijeću u ruke, bješe mi građe* or dial. Bulgarian *az să ukă puvach, ako ne bese vodă tă tolkoz' studena*, and in the classical languages, cf. Greek *ei eschon – edōka (an)* or Late Latin *si Childerico potuissemus conperire . . . , eum recipebamus ad regem.*

The phenomenon in question is explained in a great many different ways. For instance, Visser (1966:882) writes as follows:

> The fact that in Old English both clauses with a modally marked and those with a modally zero form occur with extreme − in some writings with almost equal − frequency has led a number of grammarians to develop theories accounting for this divided usage. One of the most generally held views is that propounded by Prof. T. N. Toller: 'The indicative implies the certain occurrence of a state, etc. spoken in the clause, admits the truth of the statement contained in the clause'. A serious objection to this is that a study of the material reveals that in the majority of cases it is impossible to apply this criterion of certainty or incertainty without imposing a forced interpretation on the construction based on an unproven preconception. One gets an impression that here a rule was first formulated and that attempts were then made to find examples fitting this rule.

Visser himself (1966:885) thinks that

> in the existing Old English documents there was a tendency to consider the modality of the conditional clause already sufficiently expressed by the conjunction . . . and that consequently the additional signalling of this modality by a special form of the verb was felt redundant.

Quite a different view is to be found in *Duden, Grammatik der deutschen Gegenwartssprache* (1959:536):

> Wir können mit Gewißheit annehmen, daß der Indikativ nicht allein als bloßer formaler «Ersatz» für den Konjunktiv zu werten ist oder gar als Sprachnachlässigkeit, sondern daß sein Vordringen auf einer veränderten Sehweise beruht. Der heutige deutsche Mensch betrachtet viele Geschehnisse nicht mehr als bloß Gedachtes, Vorgestelltes, sondern bereits als vorgestellte Wirklichkeit, deren Aktualität ihm so nahe ist, daß er sich mit ihr wie mit einer «Tatsache» befaßt.

Probably the substitution of the indicative for the subjunctive or conditional has nowhere been studied so well as in French. This may be due to the fact that, in a sentence like *s'il faisait beau, il viendrait*, nowadays in the conditional clause beginning with *si*, there is no choice between the indicative and another mood. Therefore, it might be suitable to mention more opinions on the cause of this phenomenon.

Tobler (1862:49−50) thought that "für den eigenthümlichen französischen

Gebrauch des Imperf. Indic. im Nebensatz muß . . . ein dieser Sprache anhaf-
tendes lebendigeres Nachgefühl des im Conditionalis ursprünglich enthaltenen
Indicativ angenommen werden, der dann durch assimilierende Attraction
denselben Modus im Nebensatz hervorrief".

Meyer-Lübke (1899:736) was also convinced that the starting point of the
imperf. ind. in the clause beginning with *si* was in the conditional of the main
clause, a mood which arose from constructions of the type *cantare habebat*,
which show a form of the indicative. Two facts are against this hypothesis.
First, the Italian conditional arose from phrases with the perfect (*canterebbe*
'he would sing' < *cantare habuit*) and nevertheless the perfect does not appear in the conditional clause. Secondly, Gamillscheg proved that the imperfect appears in conditional clauses earlier than the conditional does in main
clauses, cf. Late Latin *se hoc facere potebat, de hac causa ipsi illi compascere
debirit.*

In the meantime, Burgatzcky (1885:10–11), following Koschwitz and
Foth, believed that "wie in dem Satze: *il dit qu'il a mangier li aportera*, dem
Substantivsatz als Bedingungshauptsatz ein bedingendes Glied hinzugefügt
werden kann, z.B. *se il vuelt*, ohne daß dadurch die Bedeutung des Futurs sich
ändert . . . , so auch in dem folgenden Satz: *Il li dist que il a mangier li apor-
teroit*, ein *se il voloit*".

The explanation of Bréal (1897: 225–226) is of a different sort:

> D'où vient l'idée conditionnelle qu'éveille en français et qu'éveillait
> déjà en latin la conjonction *si* ? Pour nous l'expliquer, il faut nous
> transporter beaucoup de siècles en arrière. La particule latine *si* était
> primitivement un adverbe signifiant «de cette façon, en cette manière».
> L'idée conditionnelle y est entrée par le voisinage du subjonctif ou de
> l'optatif. La vieille formule des invocations et des vœux: *Si haec, Dii,
> faxitis*, tire sa signification hypothétique du verbe. Le sens était
> d'abord le même que s'il y avait eu: *Sic, Dii, haec faxitis*. (L'adverbe *sic*
> n'est autre chose que *si* accompagné de l'enclitique que nous avons dans
> *nunc, tunc*.) La seconde proposition vient ensuite énoncer un second
> fait, conséquence du premier: *Aedem vobis constituam*. L'esprit a saisi
> un lien entre ces deux propositions, et comme des deux côtés l'action
> est présentée comme contingente, il a tout naturellement introduit dans
> le premier mot l'idée d'une supposition ou d'une condition. Déjà dans
> la formule précitée, quand elle était employée par les contemporains de
> Paul-Émile, *si* était une conjonction. Elle l'était devenue à tel point, elle
> avait tellement assumé en elle l'idée conditionnelle, qu'on pouvait la
> faire suivre d'un indicatif: *Si id facis, hodie postremum me vides*. Le

français est allé encore plus loin. Le conditionnel, après *si,* paraîtrait un pléonasme.

Bréal's explanation was approved by d'Harvé (1923: art. 122), who summed it up in the following manner: "La conditionnalité étant pleinement exprimée par *si,* il n'est plus besoin d'avoir recours au mode conditionnel, on emploie l'indicatif". It is worth noting that this explanation does not apply to the substitution of the indicative for another mood in the main clause.

According to Sechehaye (1906:348), "il y a un usage aussi ancien que la chute du futur latin qui veut qu'après *si* on emploie le présent et non le futur. On devait éprouver une certaine difficulté à employer le conditionnel après *si* et l'analogie devait nécessairement amener à choisir le temps qui est au conditionnel ce que le présent de l'indicatif est au futur, c.-à-d. l'imparfait de l'indicatif". Of course, he means the proportion *cantare habeo: canto = cantare habebam: cantabam.*

Lerch (1929:222 ff.) distinguished two causes for the appearance of the imperf. ind. after *si*:

1. The use of the imperfect in clauses of the type *s'il faisait* consists in a metaphorical use of a past tense in order to express incertitude at the moment of speaking. One presents the condition as a fact already accomplished to show better to the listener consequences which result. This is comparable to a German expression like *wenn du das getan hast,* where the German preterite expresses an action which will happen in the time to come.

2. The sentences such as *s'il vos plaisoit, o vos iroie* arose in the refined *milieu* of the courts, *s'il vos plaisoit* being considered more polite than *s'il vos plaist.* The relation between these two phrases is comparable to that one which exists between *je venais vous dire que . . .* and *je viens vous dire que . . .*

According to Gougenheim (1949: 103), Lerch somewhere else expressed the opinion that the substitution of the construction *s'il voulait, il pourrait* for the old one *s'il voulust, il peüst* is a linguistic manifestation of the medieval predilection for asymmetry, which is contradicted by the following statement by Lerch (1933: 24–25): "Man wollte Einheitlichkeit haben und man entschied sich für diejenige der beiden Ausdrucksweisen, deren Formen leichter zu bilden waren". Obviously, asymmetry and *Einheitlichkeit* exclude each other.

Martinon (1927: 362) considered the fact that the conjunction *si* does not occur with the conditional to be due "à ce que *si* se construisait à l'origine avec le subjonctif, qui servait pour le conditionnel comme en latin, et que ce subjonctif a été remplacé par l'indicatif", which is hardly an explanation.

Wagner's opinion (1939:307) on this subject is as follows:

Il se pose, en français, un problème de la détermination que notre langue résout en dosant avec soin tant le nombre que la qualité des déterminatifs pesant sur un thème donné; or si nous dissocions une forme verbale en ses éléments, nous reconnaîtrons dans la désinence tantôt un déterminatif orientant le radical (thème) vers une voie bien précise, tantôt un déterminatif indifférent qui, pour avoir un sens intelligible, doit être, comme une note de musique, transposée à l'aide d'une clef; le type des premiers est, si l'on veut, la désinence *-rais, -ras,* etc.; un bon exemple des seconds est fourni par la désinence *-ais* . . . Or dans une phrase telle que: *s'il travaillerait, je serais heureux*, la conjonction *si*, qui sert à transposer d'emblée la phrase sur le plan modal de l'éventualité, se voit doublée par la désinence *-rais*; il y a pléthore de déterminatifs, surcharge intolérable en français.

Wagner explains the phenomenon in question by a "loi d'équilibre . . . , à la fois nécessitante et *a-logique* au même titre que la plupart des règles essentielles de la syntaxe du français; aussi est-on conduit à reconnaître dans les tours — aujourd'hui populaires: *Se* + futur . . . futur et *Se* + forme en *-rais* . . . forme en *-rais* une sorte de réaction *logique* — et malheureuse de surcroît — contre la constance qui se marque par l'interdit signalé".

Gamillscheg's explanation (1957:720, 722) is different:

Das Eintreten des Indikativs des Imperfekts in den Bedingungssatz ist typisch für das Galloromanische. Es erklärt sich als Analogie zu der Entwicklung des abhängigen Fragesatzes, der mit *si* 'ob' eingeleitet wird . . . Hier ist gleichfalls schon im 6./7. Jh. statt des Konjunktivs, der in den anderen westromanischen Sprachen erhalten ist, auf der Zeitstufe der Gegenwart der Indikativ des Imperfekts, als Ersatzform für den untergehenden Konjunktiv des Imperfekts, eingetreten . . . Aus der Kreuzung der Typen *si j'avais, je donnerai,* (d. i. des rein potentialen Typus) und *si j'eusse, je donnerais,* (d. i. des irrealen Typus, der den Übergang zum Potentialis bildet . . .) entsteht der in den ältesten nordfranzösischen Denkmälern . . . noch fehlende Typus *si j'avais, je donnerais.*

Renchon (1967:52–53) in the construction of the type *s'il faisait* sees a norm which "s'est dégagée au cours de la période prégrammaticale de notre langue et qui doit donc être le reflet, dans l'expression linguistique, d'une tendance profonde de l'esprit français". This idea is several times repeated in his book, e. g.: "Historiquement, on est . . . fondé à voir dans le tour moderne une création spontanée répondant à une tendance foncière de ce que nous appellerions volontiers le «subconscient linguistique» de l'individu parlant français"

Guiter ascribes the substitution of the indicative for the subjunctive in

French to a Germanic influence:

> Ne semble-t-il pas symptomatique que l'imparfait de l'indicatif ait fait
> son apparition dans la subordonnée (pour y reconnaître par la suite un
> usage exclusif) au Nord de la Gaule et à l'époque mérovingienne, après
> plus de deux siècles de bilinguisme germano-roman, alors que toute
> distinction s'abolissait entre les imparfaits de l'indicatif et de l'optatif
> des verbes faibles germaniques, ceux dont le mécanisme était le plus
> accessible aux locuteurs romans . . . ? [1]

Rohlfs (1961:141–150) explains the construction *si avía accattava*, which
occurs at Salento and in different dialects of southern Italy, by the influence
of the Greek substratum. This view is criticized by Parlangèli, who thinks that
this phenomenon is not isolated "e quindi non deve essere necessariamente
posta in relazione con l'analoga costruzione greca, ché certo non sono stati i
Greci a portarla . . . in Sardegna e in Corsica (e in Puglia e in Lucania e, fatte
le debite riserve, in Francia e altrove)".

Finally, as to the use of the indicative in conditional clauses in Greek, Meillet and Vendryes (1924:296) write as follows: "Cet emploi est proprement
grec; il est né aux dépens de l'optatif et pour servir en quelque sorte d'optatif
dans le passé".

I do not think it necessary to present a detailed analysis of the quoted
opinions. However, it is worth observing that some explanations are contra-
dictory, while others are very complicated. But, the longer I deal with linguistics the more certain I am that language is a simple phenomenon and that all
true explanations of language phenomena are equally simple. In addition,
there is one alarming thing in the hypotheses concerning the origin of constructions of the type *if I was* (instead of *if I were*), namely the fact that
their authors, while deliberating on the origin of the phenomenon in question, treat it as an isolated phenomenon without considering other phenomena either in the analysed language or in other languages. However, the
elementary as well as fundamental principle of any scientific research (including linguistic) necessitates the discussion of each phenomenon against
the largest background.

Therefore, it is the aim of this paper to draw the reader's attention to the
fact that the substitution of the indicative for the subjunctive or conditional
may be explained by a law of analogical development. According to this law,
less frequently used forms are more often replaced by more frequently used
forms than vice versa (Mańczak 1958, 1963 and 1978). It is very easy to give
the reason for this. This is due to the simple fact that people can more easily
memorize what they say and hear more often than what they say and hear
less frequently. Therefore in historical grammars we can find hundreds of

examples confirming this law of analogical development (cf., e. g., Mańczak 1980, where the analogical changes have been counted). A few examples illustrating this law follow.

The singular is more often used than the plural and therefore singular forms sometimes substitute plural forms. The fact that in many Indo-European languages the nom. plur. of neuter nouns ends in *-a* (cf. Latin *oppid-a*, Greek *dōr-a*, Polish *okn-a* 'windows') is explained in the following manner: the ending of the nom.-acc.-voc. of neuter nouns is derived from the ending of singular feminine nouns of the type Latin *tabul-a* or Polish *kobiet-a* 'woman', which is proved, among others, by the Greek construction of the type *ta zōa trechei*, where a neuter noun in the plural is associated with a singular verb. In the Scandinavian languages, verbs in the pres. ind. show the same ending, e.g. Swedish *bind-er* corresponds to German *bind-e, -est, -et, -en, -et, -en*. The Scandinavian inflexion is a result of the generalization of an ending which originally was characteristic of a singular person on the whole paradigm, including the plural.

As to degrees, the positive degree is more often used than other degrees. Therefore forms of the positive supersede forms of other degrees. In the Romance languages, there are only remnants of the comparative and superlative, whereas in a majority of cases such forms as *clarior* and *clarissimus* have been replaced by phrases of the type *plus clair* and *le plus clair*, i. e. by phrases containing *clair*, which is derived from the positive degree *clarus*.

As to numerals, cardinals are more frequently used than ordinals, which results in the substitution of ordinals by cardinals. This phenomenon is so typical of modern European languages that it seems redundant to quote examples.

Among persons, the third person is used more often than others. Therefore, forms of the third person oust forms of other persons. For instance, in spoken French *on est* is often used instead of *nous sommes*.

As far as tenses are concerned, the present tense is more often used than other tenses, which results in the replacement of other tenses by the present tense. For example, in Gothic there was the preterite of the type *habaida*, whose equivalents in modern Germanic languages are not only forms of the type *he had* but also *he has had*, with a form of the present tense. The same applies to German *er ist gekommen* or French *il vient de faire*. Similarly in the Slavonic languages, e. g. Polish *pisałem* 'I have written' derives from *pisał jeśm*, a combination of the active past participle and the present of the verb *być* 'to be.' Latin forms of the future of the type *cantabo* did not remain in any Romance language but in all cases they were replaced by phrases containing the form of the present, cf. French *chanterai* < *cantare habeo* or Rumanian *voi cînta* < *volo cantare*. This process repeats itself as French *je chanterai* is often replaced by *je vais chanter*, where the present tense of the verb *aller* occurs. The same applies to the Germanic languages, cf. *I shall go, he will go* or German *er wird gehen*. A similar phenomenon is observed in Slavonic languages, where from the historical point of view e. g. Polish *napiszę* 'I shall write' is a form of the present tense, which used to mean 'I write'.

As to moods, the indicative is the most frequent, which explains why it supersedes other moods. The French conditional *chanterait* is derived from *cantare habebat* and the Italian conditional *canterebbe* from *cantare habuit*, i. e. that the forms of the indicative acquired the meaning of another mood. Cf. also Sp. *cantara* (subjunctive) < Lat. *cantaverat* (indicative). A similar phenomenon is found in the Slavonic languages, where e. g. Polish *pisałby* 'he would write' is a result of the combination of the active past participle and the aorist indicative of the verb *być* 'to be'.

Obviously, it cannot be denied that sometimes the analogical changes occur in an opposite direction, e. g. the singular French *feuille* is derived from the plural Latin *folia*. From the descriptive point of view nothing indicates that such adjectives as *extérieur* or *extrême* are derived from the forms of the comparative or superlative. The Slavonic cardinal as e. g. Polish *sześć* 'six' is a derivative from an Indo-European form from which Latin *sextus* and not *sex* arose. Latin *sunt* 'they are' was changed to Italian *sono*, in which *-o* is analogical to *sono* 'I am' < *sum* + *-o* (the first person singular ending). In spoken English, *I have* is replaced by *I've got*. The past perf. ind. Rumanian *cîntase* is derived from the subjunctive Latin *cantavisset*. All this is true, but it is worth indicating that these are exceptional cases whereas in a majority of cases an opposite process takes place, i. e. that more frequent forms oust less frequent forms.

Therefore, it should be concluded that there is nothing strange in the fact that in different languages of the world the following syntactic development takes place: either in subordinate clauses (as in English *if I was* instead of *if I were*) or in main clauses (as in French *si Stanislas demeurait, il était perdu* instead of *il serait perdu*) the indicative substitutes for other moods (the subjunctive or conditional). These are all particular cases of a universal law of analogical evolution according to which in all languages of the world and in all periods of their history it occurs more often that more frequently used forms replace less frequently used ones than vice versa.

Note

1. This quotation has been taken from an offprint of H. Guiter's review which appeared

in *Revue des Langues romanes* after 1970. Unfortunately, it is impossible for me to give a more precise reference.

References

Bréal, M.
1897   *Essai de sémantique* (Paris: Hachette).
Burgatzcky, O.
1885   *Das Imperfekt und Plusquamperfekt des Futurs im Altfranzösischen* (Greifswald).
D'Harvé, G.-O.
1923   *Parlons bien! Recherches et trouvailles grammaticales,* 2nd ed. (Bruxelles).
Duden
1959   *Grammatik der deutschen Gegenwartssprache* (Mannheim: Bibliographisches Institut).
Gamillscheg, E.
1957   *Historische französische Syntax* (Tübingen: Niemeyer).
Gougenheim, G.
1949   *Où en sont les études de français* (Paris: d'Artrey).
Lerch, E.
1929   *Historische französische Syntax* 2 (Leipzig: Reisland).
1933   *Französische Sprache und Wesensart* (Frankfurt a.M.).
Mańczak, W.
1958   "Tendances générales des changements analogiques", *Lingua* 7: 298–325 and 387–420.
1963   "Tendances générales du développement morphologique", *Lingua* 12: 19–38.
1978   "Les lois du développement analogique", *Linguistics* 205: 53–60.
1980   *Fonética y morfología histórica del español* (Kraków: Uniwersytet Jagielloński).
Martinon, Ph.
1927   *Comment on parle en français* (Paris: Larousse).
Meillet, A. – J. Vendryes
1924   *Traité de grammaire comparée des langues classiques* (Paris: Champion).
Meyer-Lübke, W.
1899   *Grammatik der romanischen Sprachen* 3 (Leipzig: Reisland).
Renchon, H.
1967   *Études de syntaxe descriptive* 1 (Bruxelles: Palais des Académies).
Rohlfs, G.
1961   "Su alcuni calchi sintattici dal greco nell'Italia meridionale", *Studi linguistici italiani* 2: 141–154.
Sechehaye, A.
1906   "L'imparfait du subjonctif et ses concurrents dans les hypothétiques normales du français", *Romanische Forschungen* 19.
Sten, H.
1973   *L'emploi des temps en portugais moderne* (Kφbenhavn: Munksgaard).
Tobler, L.
1862   "Übergang zwischen Tempus und Modus", *Zeitschrift für Völkerkunde und Sprachwissenschaft* 2.

Visser, F. Th.
  1966   *An historical syntax of the English language. Part II. Syntactical units with one verb* (Leiden: Brill).
Wagner, R.-L.
  1939   *Les phrases hypothétiques commençant par "si" dans la langue française* (Paris: Droz).
Wędkiewicz, S.
  1911   *Materialien zu einer Syntax der italienischen Bedingungssätze* (Halle: Niemeyer).

HANNE MARTINET

Comment on W. Mańczak's paper

First, I would like to mention that the French sentences given on pp. 237, 244 (1) *s'il faisait beau, il viendrait* and (2) *si Stanislas demeurait, il était perdu* are two different kinds of "irrealis". In (1), "irrealis" in the present, *both* clauses are considered contrary to a *de facto* reality, i.e. "it is not the fact that A then it cannot be the fact that B" (the sentence could be continued by *mais il pleut alors il ne viendra pas*). In (2), "irrealis" in the future, the indicative of the main clause indicates that *"if* A occurs then B will *inevitably* occur" (the sentence could be continued by *mais il partira alors il ne sera pas perdu*). I wonder then whether these two sentences are suitable to prove that the indicative may be substituted for the subjunctive or the conditional, or to prove analogical evolution. This also because the sentence (3) *si Stanislas demeurait, il serait perdu* given on p. 244 is not "irrealis" but "potentialis" in the future, and *both* clauses are considered possible in the future but not certain, i.e. *"if* A occurs then B might *probably* occur", which means that (1) is different from (3). I also wonder whether these different meanings were expressed previously, and how?

What is happening today is that the conditional is gaining ground, as in *s'il ferait beau, il viendrait* (equivalent to (1)), but this is another problem.

When considering why the *imparfait du subjonctif* has disappeared, it might be profitable to look also at the disappearance of other verbal flexions, not only in written language but also in spoken language. The *passé simple* for example cannot have disappeared because it was less frequent − if this was the case *passé composé*, its substitute in spoken everyday language, would not have become as frequent as it is today.

What we need to know also is why *imparfait du subjonctif* and *passé simple* have become less frequent.

It might be profitable to study the process that took place when the final consonants and the unstressed final *-e* began to disappear from Parisian French in the XVth century − a formal fact that gave rise to syncretism between *passé simple* and *imparfait du subjonctif* (*-a/-ât, -i/-ît*, etc.). (Today − May 1981 − I would refer you to André Martinet, 1975, *Evolution des langues et reconstruction*, Paris: P.U.F., p. 11 *et passim*).

LYNELL MARCHESE

Exbraciation in the Kru language family

1 Introduction

In all Kru languages,[1] there are two basic word orders: SVO and S AUX O V. Though it has been argued that the latter developed from the former (Marchese, 1978; 1979),[2] both constructions are presently attested. The dominant SVO structure is, however, exerting pressure on the innovative form, causing a breakdown in the verb-final S AUX (O) V construction. In this paper, evidence is given from over ten Kru languages, showing that elements such as temporal and manner adverbs, as well as oblique NPs designating reason and locatives are moving out of the verb brace S AUX X V. This has resulted in the emergence of a new construction S AUX V X. Factors motivating the word order change and the means by which the change is being realized are discussed. Similarities between Kru and other languages undergoing parallel phenomena are described. Alternative explanations are also explored.

There is little historical documentation on the Kru language family. The earliest work comes from the 1830's, but the bulk of linguistic description began only in the mid-sixties. The main evidence, then, for linguistic change in Kru is synchronic variation occurring between and within individual languages.

2 Synchronic variation: evidence for historical change

As mentioned above, the basic order throughout the Kru family is SVO, as seen in the following examples from Godié, an Eastern Kru language, and Wobé, a Western Kru language:

(1) Godié

ɔ	lɨ	sʉkʌ́	'He ate rice'
he	ate	rice	
S	V	O	

(2) Wobé

ɔ	di	dɛ		'He ate something'
he	ate	something		
S	V	O		

When an auxiliary[3] is present, however, another word order S AUX O V is attested:

(3) Godié

ɔ	yi	sʉkʌ́	lɨ	'He will eat rice'
he	FUT	rice	eat	
S	AUX	O	V	

(4) Wobé

ɔ	se	dɛ	di	'He didn't eat anything'
he	NEG	something	eat	
S	AUX	O	V	

In conformity with works on languages with similar structures (e.g. Stockwell, 1977), AUX. . . V will be called the *verb brace,* since the verbal elements AUX and V surround non-subjectival elements in the clause:

(5) Wobé

(a)

ɔ	se	Kei	ko	kpa
he	NEG	Kei	rice	bring
S	AUX	IO	DO	V
		└── verb	brace ──┘	

'He didn't bring rice to Kei'

(b)

ɔ	se	(e)dɔɔ	mu
he	NEG	market	go
S	AUX	LOC	V
		└── verb brace ──┘	

'He didn't go to the market'

In every Kru language, direct and indirect objects, including locatives functioning as objects,[4] must occur within the verb brace. Any occurrence outside the brace is completely unacceptable:

(6) Godié

*ɔ	yi	lɨ	sʉkʌ́	'He will eat rice'
he	FUT	eat	rice	
*S	AUX	V	O	

(7) Wobé

(a)
*ɔ	se	kpa	Kei	ko
he	NEG	bring	Kei	rice
*S	AUX	V	IO	DO

'He didn't bring Kei rice'

(b)
*ɔ	se	mu	edɔɔ
he	NEG	go	market
*S	AUX	V	LOC-OBJ

'He didn't go to the market'

However, other elements such as temporals, manner adverbs, peripheral locatives and reason clauses occur outside the brace. There is a considerable amount of variation from one Kru language to another. In some languages, these elements occur most often (and sometimes obligatorily) inside the brace, while in other languages, the same elements may occur optionally or obligatorily outside the brace. As an example, we can examine the placement of temporal adverbs and phrases. In Eastern Kru, most temporal adverbs occur within the verb brace,[5] if such a brace is present:

(8) Godié
ʌ̃	yʌ	*pʉpɛ*	sʉkʌ́	bóo	bia-a?
you	PERF	*just-now*	rice	bowl	finish-Q
S	AUX	ADV		O	V

'Have you just finished (eating) the bowl of rice?'

However, in many Western languages, such as Gbaeson Krahn, temporal adverbs can *never* occur in this position:

(9) Gbaeson Krahn
ɔ	mú	dɛ	di	*sia*
he	FUT	thing	eat	*today*
S	AUX	O	V	ADV
*ɔ	mú	*sia*	dɛ	di
*S	AUX	*ADV*	O	V

The variation present here between languages within the same family suggests that some historical change in word order has occurred.

Similar observations can be made about the placement of manner adverbs. In Eastern Kru, manner adverbs readily occur within the brace:

(10) Koyo   (Kokora 1976)
　　　donyi   yi   *kapakapasa*   lobee   no
　　　Donyi   FUT   *crazily*   work   do
　　　S   AUX   *ADV*   O   V
　　　'Donyi will do the work in a haphazard way'

In many Western languages, however, manner adverbs occur obligatorily outside the verb brace:

(11) Gbaeson Krahn
　　　ɔ   mú   dɛ   dí   *sùeí*
　　　he   FUT   thing   eat   *fast*
　　　S   AUX   O   V   *ADV*
　　　'He will eat fast'.
　　　*ɔ   mú   *sùeí*   dɛ   di
　　　*S   AUX   *ADV*   O   V

Peripheral locatives (i.e. those locatives which are not functioning as the object of the verb) and reason phrases exhibit similar behavior:

Locatives

(12) Godié   (locative inside the brace)
　　　a   kʉ   *mɔ́*   *dìɛ̀*   *mlɨ́*   ŋwíì
　　　he   CONDIT *there* *field*   *inside* cry
　　　S   AUX   *PER-LOC*   V
　　　'If he cries in the middle of that field. . . '

(13) Wobé (locative outside the brace)
　　　ɔ   se   na   *miabli*
　　　he   NEG   walk   *Kouibly*
　　　S   AUX   V   *PER-LOC*
　　　'He didn't walk to Kouibly'
　　　*ɔ   se   *miabli* na
　　　*S   AUX   *PER-LOC* walk

Reason phrases[6]

(14) Godié (reason phrase inside the brace)
　　　ɔ   ká   dú   *kòsùú*   *za*[7]   mʉ
　　　he   FUT   village *gun-DEF*   *sake*   go
　　　S   AUX   O   *REASON*   V
　　　'He will go to the village for (or because of) the gun.'

(15) Klao (reason phrase outside the brace)

dó	a	mu	cɛ́	kó	tꞷ	bò
Doe	INC	FUT	learn	*sake*	*Toe*	*sake*
S		AUX	V		*REASON*	

'Doe will learn for Toe.'

*dó	a	mu	kó	tꞷ	bò	cɛ́
*S		AUX	*REASON*			V

To summarize then, in Kru, object and indirect objects (i.e. non-subjectival 'terms'[8]) always occur within the verb brace, while 'non-terms' such as peripheral locatives and reason phrases, as well as temporal and manner adverbs show language-specific variation. In some languages, these elements may occur within the brace, while in others, such occurrence is ungrammatical. Thus, along with the SVO / S AUX O V alternation present in every Kru language, there are other word orders attested in the family, namely S AUX (O) V X (where X = non-term) and S AUX X (O) V. This language-specific variation is believed to indicate a word order change 'in progress'. There appears to be a rightward movement of elements outside the verb brace, a phenomenon which has been called *exbraciation* (Stockwell, 1977):

$$S \quad AUX \quad \overbrace{X \quad (O) \quad V \quad \vec{X}}$$

3 Factors motivating exbraciation

Exbraciation is believed to have occurred in at least two other language families in the world: Germanic (more specifically German and Old English (Stockwell, 1977)) and Hellenic (Lightfoot, 1979). Stockwell notes that the change was not unmotivated. He cites (1) the appearance of SVX word order, (2) rightward movement rules such as relative clause, conjunct, and appositive extraposition, (3) afterthought, and (4) the occurrence of sentential objects in sentence-final position as factors which led to the establishment of an SvVX word order.[9] This construction served as a 'pattern' on which exbraciation could be based, leading finally to the breakdown of the verb-final structure. Similar types of arguments have apparently been offered for a parallel phenomenon in Greek. Aitchison (in press, reported in Lightfoot 1979: 393–395) notes that "... a rightward operations conspiracy ... snowballed and destroyed the OV [order]".

I would now like to examine the factors which I believe are influencing the breakdown of the S AUX (O) V construction in Kru — factors which are indeed quite similar to those mentioned above.

3.1 SVX word order

Stockwell (1977:302—5) noted that though Old English was basically SXV, there was a verb-second rule which moved the finite verb into second position. When such sentences contained a simple verb, the resulting structure was SVX. This pattern led speakers to conclude that nominal and adverbial complements followed the main verb, leading eventually to the development of an SvVX construction. A similar motivation is present in Kru. As mentioned earlier, when auxiliaries are not present, all non-subjectival elements, whether terms (direct, indirect, or locative objects) or nonterms (instrumentals, peripheral locatives, reason phrases, as well as temporal and manner adverbs) normally appear in post verbal position:

(16) Wobé

ɔ	di-ɛ	kò	de	dɔɔ	sẽã
he	eat	rice	at	market	today
S	V	O	PER-LOC		ADV

'He ate rice at the market today'.

This SVX word order could lead speakers to make the following generalization: all non-subjectival elements follow the main verb. This generalization would enhance the acceptability of the word order S AUX V *X*.

3.2 Rightward movement rules

In Old English, certain stylistic rules including conjunct, appositive, and relative extraposition, apparently moved elements out of the verb brace into sentence-final position (Stockwell, 1977: 305—308):

(a) and also then he the boy (DO) returned
(gave back) *and the woman* (conjunct extraposition)

(b) and those men came into East Anglia *who*
on the ship were, extremely wounded (relative
clause extraposition)

Parallel types of surface variation also appear in Kru. Similarly, an S AUX V *X* pattern is established, which can serve as a model for a new word order. Elements which may occur outside the verb brace in Kru include expanded subject and object NPs, conjoined NPs, afterthoughts, and sentential objects.

Let us now examine in detail elements which may occur outside the verb brace. In Kru languages, there seems to be a general rule which permits a speaker to expand on something he has said by juxtaposing his comment onto the end of the sentence. In the following example from Neyo, the speaker 'spells out' or gives examples of the object NP "all the animals of the forest floor". This phenomenon could be described as a kind of verbal colon:

(17) Neyo   (Thomann, 1905)

ɔ	ule	kla	zɔ	a	mla	fɛ
he	call	forest	bottom	ASSOC	animals	all

sie   kwale ...
snails   turtles

'He called all the animals of the forest floor: snails, turtles . . .'

The preceding sentence does not contain an auxiliary, but if such a sentence does contain one, the verb is no longer in final position. In the following Godié example, where an auxiliary is present, the subject NP is expanded to the right of the verb brace:

(18) Godié

ιyʌ̀	wa	kʌ̀	síì	núu
and	they	FUT	also	understand
	S	AUX	ADV	V

kaadɛ	*papɷ*	*gbɔklιŋwlɔ*
Carol,	Lynell,	Sue
	X	

'And so they will also understand, Carol, Lynell, Sue . . .'

This results in the establishment of the S AUX (O) V X pattern — the same pattern obtained in exbraciation.

Similarly, in some languages, speakers 'spell out' a pronoun referent which is in view of both the hearer and the speaker. The construction could be described as a kind of reverse topicalization, i.e. 'comment-topic'.[10] When the sentence contains an auxiliary, the verb-final nature of the S AUX O V pattern is again violated:

(19) Nyabo

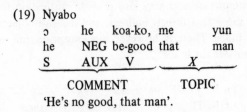

ɔ	he	koa-ko,	me	yun
he	NEG	be-good	that	man
S	AUX	V	X	

COMMENT   TOPIC

'He's no good, that man'.

Another stylistic device involves conjoined NPs. An NP subject may be expanded or added onto in postverbal position through conjunction and the introduction of new participants. Again, when an auxiliary is present, the verb-final nature of the clause is disrupted (note that this is a stylistic variation; normally full conjoined NPs may occur in either subject or object position):

    (20) Bété   (Werle and Gbalehi, 1976: 199)

n	làgɔ	yi-ɛ	glɔ	glɛ
then	God	SEQ	town	arrive
S	AUX	O	V	

ɔ̀	nyɛ̀	ɔ	yuə	á	sɔ́
he	and	his	children	ASSOC	two
X					

'Then God arrived at the village, along with his children'.

In Kru, new non-contrastive information typically occurs toward the end of the clause. It seems reasonable to assume that in the above example, *làgò* 'God', a frequent character in folktales, is known information, and thus occurs in subject position. 'His children' are undoubtedly new but secondary participants, occurring in sentence-final position.

    To sum up, in Kru, several expansion devices are at work which establish an S AUX (O) V *X* pattern – the pattern believed to serve as a model for exbraciation.

3.3 Afterthought

Afterthought, or the addition of forgotten elements onto the end of the clause may also serve to set up an S AUX (O) V *X* pattern. Hyman (1975: 126) noted that afterthought occurs in Klao, a Western Kru language, and suggested it could be a means of word order change:

    (21) Klao

ɔ́	sé	súa	tɛ̃́	*tái*	*kɔ̀*
he	NEG	fish	buy	*and*	*rice*
S	AUX	O	V		*X*

'He didn't buy fish. . . and rice'

3.4 Placement of sentential objects

The placement of sentential objects may also provide motivation for exbraciation. It was noted above that direct, indirect, and locative objects always occur within the verb brace. There is, however, one exception; full sentential objects always occur outside the brace:

    (22) Godié

wa	kʉ	ki	*mà*	*wa*	*yʌ*	*wá*
they	CONDIT	say	*that*	*they*	*PERF*	*their*
S	AUX	V		*X*		

lɩ	*gili*	*nʌ*	. . .
things	*steal*	*SUB*	
X			

'If they say that they have stolen their things. . .'

Stockwell notes that Old English sentential objects also always occurred outside the verb brace,[11] another process setting up an S AUX V X pattern.

3.5 Auxiliary-verb attraction

A principle known as Behaghel's First Law (Hyman, 1975) states that there is a general tendency for the auxiliary and verb to unite, thus forming one constituent. Just how much this tendency is playing a role in the S AUX V X shift in Kru is hard to determine. Nevertheless, it may be a contributing factor.[12]

3.6 Summary

To summarize, then, the factors which seem to motivate the S AUX (O) V X pattern in Kru are the following:

    (i) the basic SVX word order in clauses without auxiliaries;
    (ii) certain stylistic devices which allow elements to occur in postverbal position;
    (iii) afterthought;
    (iv) auxiliary-verb attraction.

Perhaps a comment is needed as to the relative importance of these factors. Stockwell notes (1977:299):

> "... while the 'afterthought' notion draws some explanatory force from the plausible psychological motivation it suggests, I think there are a number of structural motivations within the syntax of OE that considerably strengthen the tendency to exbraciate, and in general I find more persuasive than psychological generalizations *any* explanation that depends on prior existence of syntactic patterns as a basis for analogical extension ..."

It must be noted that the Kru facts confirm these claims. The basic SVX word order and the stylistic variations described as NP expansions are much more basic to the syntax of these languages than any form generated by afterthought. In other words, this historical change is not due to 'mistakes' (like forgetting some element); rather, rules which have been shown to break down the S AUX O V construction are deliberate and precise, based most likely on pragmatic considerations, forming sentences which are perfectly acceptable to the speaker.[13]

4 Actualization of the change

4.1 Stages of exbraciation

Exbraciation in Kru must be described as a change in progress since languages are at different stages of development. From examining the synchronic evidence, it would appear that there are essentially three stages in the process of exbraciation:

> (i) the element occurs obligatorily within the verb brace;
> (ii) the element occurs optionally inside or outside the verb brace;
> (iii) the element occurs obligatorily outside the brace.

Step (ii) may, in fact, be broken down into two sub-stages. Apparently at first, the inside position is preferred,[14] but eventually, the preference changes to the position outside the brace.

An example of how the stages actually are realized may be seen by examining temporal adverbs. In Godié, an Eastern Kru language, some temporal adverbs must appear within the verb brace (stage (i)):

> (23) Godié
>
> | ɔ | yi | *sisio* | yi |
> |----|-----|---------|------|
> | he | FUT | *soon* | come |
> | S | AUX | *ADV* | V |
>
> 'He will soon come'.
>
> | */? | ɔ | yi | yi | *sisio* |
> |-----|---|-----|----|---------|
> | */? | S | AUX | V | *ADV* |

Perhaps the majority of Eastern Kru languages, as well as a few Western ones, are presently at stage (ii), where temporal adverbs occur optionally inside or outside the verb brace:

> (24) Koyo (Eastern Kru; Kokora 1976)
>
> | dago | ta | *yeka* | du | mo |
> |------|-----|---------|------|----|
> | Dago | NEG | *today* | town | go |
> | S | AUX | *ADV* | O | V |
>
> or
>
> | dago | ta | du | mo | *yeka* |
> |------|-----|------|----|---------|
> | Dago | NEG | town | go | *today* |
> | S | AUX | O | V | *ADV* |

(25) Grand Bassa (Western Kru)

ɔ	se	pàniwá	kùà	nu
he	NEG	yesterday	word	do
S	AUX	*ADV*	O	V

or

ɔ	se	kùà	nu	pàniwá
S	AUX	O	V	*ADV*

Vogler (1976) notes that in Vata occurrence outside the brace is a kind of stylistic variant. Actually it seems that the initial placement outside the brace must serve some pragmatic function, such as highlighting the element (see section 4.3 for more discussion).

Finally, in several Western languages, stage (iii) has been reached. Temporal adverbs occur obligatorily outside the verb brace:

(26) Wobé

ɔ	se	ko	di	*sēā*
he	NEG	rice	eat	*today*
S	AUX	O	V	*ADV*
*ɔ	se	*sẽ̄ã*	ko	di
*S	AUX	*ADV*	O	V

(27) Nyabo

ɔ	he	kòà	nu	*pama*
he	NEG	work	do	*yesterday*
S	AUX	O	V	*ADV*
*ɔ	he	*pama*	kòà	nu
*S	AUX	*ADV*	O	V

Similar evidence can be given for manner adverbials, reason phrases and peripheral non-term locatives (Marchese, 1979b). It should be noted, however, that at present the majority of Kru languages are either fully into stage (ii) or at stage (iii).

4.2 Hierarchy of exbraciated elements

The ultimate result of exbraciation is the total breakdown of the verb brace. This is what apparently occurred in English, where verb-final word order has virtually been eliminated. In Kru, however, the process has not been as extensive, and is still going on today. Evidence shows that non-term elements have been or are being exbraciated. In contrast, non-subjectival terms (direct, indirect, and locative objects) normally maintain their position within the verb brace. This division is in keeping with what is known about exbraciation in other languages (Hyman, 1975; Stockwell, personal communication). Elements appear to be moving out of the verb brace according to a hierarchical scale, beginning with non-term or peripheral elements like adverbs and reason phrases, and ending finally with terms (i.e. direct and indirect objects).

In at least some Kru languages, the hierarchy discussed above interacts with transitivity and verb subcategorization. In Wobé, for example, it was seen that verbs such as 'go' take a locative NP which acts as the direct object of the clause. Proof of its status as an object is its occurrence within the verb brace:

(28) Wobé

ɔ	se	(de)	*dɔɔ*	.	mu
he	NEG		*market*		go
S	AUX		*LOC-OBJ*		V

'He didn't go to market'

The verb *mu* is apparently subcategorized for only one object. When a 'higher ranking' object is present (in this case, a nominalized goal NP), it takes the place of the locative, and the locative is 'demoted' or pushed out into post-verbal position, where it appears to assume the role of a peripheral locative (Bearth, personal communication):

(29) Wobé

ɔ	se	*ko*	*plea*	mu	*de*	*dɔɔ*
he	NEG	*rice*	*buy-NOM*	go		*market*
S	AUX		*O*	V		*LOC*

'He didn't go to buy rice at the market'

Thus, whether a locative occurs within or outside the verb brace depends not only on whether the locative is a term or non-term, but also on the verb itself, its subcategorization, and the number of NPs to be incorporated into the clause.

A similar phenomenon seems to affect exbraciation of non-term elements in some other languages. In Borobo and Sapo, both Western languages, the placement of manner adverbials inside or outside the verb brace seems to be closely connected to the transitivity of the verb. With transitive verbs, manner adverbs must occur outside the brace, as if the object were 'pushing' the non-term out:

(30) Borobo

ɔɔ	í	kùà	nu	*dɷɛdɷɛ*
he	NEG	work	do	*slowly*
S	AUX	O	V	*ADV*

'He didn't work slowly'.

	*ɔɔ	í	*dɷɛdɛ*	kùà	nu
*S		NEG	*ADV*	O	V

(31) Sapo

	ɔ	se	kò	di	*paapa*
	he	NEG	rice	eat	*fast*
	S	AUX	O	V	*ADV*

'He didn't eat rice fast'.

	*ɔ	se	*paapa*	ko	di
*S		AUX	*ADV*	O	V

However, when the verb in the clause is intransitive (for example, the verb 'walk' *na*), manner adverbs may not only occur within the brace — they are preferred there:

(32) Borobo

PREF:	ɔɔ	í	*dɷɛdɛ*	na
	he	NEG	*slowly*	walk
	S	AUX	*ADV*	V

'He didn't walk slowly'

OK:	ɔɔ	í	na	*dɷɛdɛ*
	S	AUX	V	*ADV*

(33) Sapo

PREF:	ɔ	se	*paapa*	na
	he	NEG	*fast*	walk
	S	AUX	*ADV*	V

'He didn't walk fast'

OK:	ɔ	se	na	*paapa*
	S	NEG	V	*ADV*

Sapo and Borobo, then, appear to favor one element within the verb brace, in seeming contradiction to the verb-auxiliary 'attraction' hypothesis discussed earlier. It can be noted that in Wobé, Sapo, and Borobo, one element too many 'pushes' the extra element outside the brace. Just how many languages exhibit this behavior is unknown; so is the reason behind it. However, it is worth mentioning that in Eastern languages where exbraciation is not so extensive and has not become obligatory, any number of elements of considerable length are incorporated into the verb brace with little difficulty.

It has been observed that subcategorization of verbs interacts with exbraciation. One interesting fact is that subcategorization of verbs may change, meaning that complements of the same verb may vary in position from one language to another. For example, it has already been noted that motion verbs usually take term or object locative complements. This is normally true of the verb 'arrive', as seen in the examples below:

(34) Borobo (Western Kru)

ɔ	di	*trubɔ*	ɲyinía
he	FUT	*Monrovia*	arrive
S	AUX	*Loc-OBJ*	V

'He will arrive at Monrovia'

*ɔ	di	nyinía	*trubɔ*
*S	AUX	V	*LOC*

(35) Lakota Dida (Eastern Kru)

ɔ	yi	*dáblé*	*né*	nyli
he	FUT	*market*	*at*	arrive
S	AUX	*LOC-OBJ*		V

'He will arrive at the market'

*ɔ	yi	nyli	*dáblé*	*né*
*S	AUX	V	*LOC*	

However, in at least three languages — Dewoin, Grand Bassa, and Vata — the verb has apparently changed subcategorization; instead of taking a term locative, it now takes a peripheral or non-term one. Thus, the locative occurs outside the verb brace:

(36) Dewoin

í	ji	ŋini	*ná*	*mǎ*	gbo
I	SEQ	arrive	*my*	*mother*	house
S	AUX	V		*LOC*	

'And then I arrived at my mother's house'.

For the moment, it is not known if closely related languages will 'copy' this innovation. The change in subcategorization does, however, set up a structure that looks very much like the S AUX V X pattern which has been seen to motivate, and which is the target of, exbraciation.

4.3 Exbraciation and individual lexical items

It has been claimed (Lightfoot 1979, among others) that linguistic change

tends to affect members of a lexical class one by one. As exception features
pile up on certain items, the system 'overloads', and a linguistic change results.
Data from exbraciation in Kru confirm this outlook. There is strong evidence
that exbraciation is realized by first affecting individual members of a syntactic class.

Manner adverbs in Tepo provide a good example of this process. In Tepo,
the stages which were seen to characterize different degrees of exbraciation
across languages can be applied to individual items in the language. The adverb 'slowly', for example, appears to be at stage (i), since it occurs obligatorily within the verb brace:

(37) Tepo

ɔ	dé	*gbέgbê*	na
he	NEG	*slowly*	walk
S	AUX	*ADV*	V

'He didn't walk slowly'.

*ɔ	dé	na	*gbέgbê*
*S	AUX	V	*ADV*

The adverb 'well', on the other hand, has begun to undergo exbraciation. It
occurs optionally inside or outside the verb brace. It is, then, at stage (ii):

(38) Tepo

ɔ	dé	na	*tê*
he	NEG	walk	*well*
S	AUX	V	*ADV*

'He didn't walk well'.

or

ɔ	dé	*tê*	na
S	AUX	*ADV*	V

The adverb 'quickly' however, has already reached stage (iii), i.e. it has been
exbraciated and must occur outside the brace:

(39) Tepo

ɔ	dé	ná	*tátâ*
he	NEG	walk	*quickly*
S	AUX	V	*ADV*

'He didn't walk quickly'

*ɔ	dé	*tátâ*	ná
*S	AUX	*ADV*	V

At this point, one would expect the grammar to re-organize itself in such a way that all manner adverbs are exbraciated. As yet, this has not happened. One obvious question is why one adverb (such as 'quickly') should be more susceptible to exbraciation than another. For the moment, no explanation is forthcoming.

Another case of an individual item being affected by exbraciation before others comes from Dewoin. It has already been pointed out that Dewoin is somewhat innovative, in that the verb 'arrive' has apparently undergone a change in subcategorization. There is one small piece of evidence from this language suggesting that objects may be beginning to be exbraciated. As in all other Kru languages, terms in Dewoin, whether simple or complex, occur within the verb brace:

(40) Dewoin

ɔ	nà	*kwiɛ*	*wɔ́lɔ̀*	6ɔ
he	PERF	*clothes*	*wash*	stop
S	AUX	O		V

'He has stopped washing clothes'
(where *kwiɛ-wɔ́lɔ̀* is a complex nominalized form)

However, with the verb 'finish', what one would normally interpret as the direct object occurs outside the verb brace:

(41) Dewoin

ɔ	nà	gwɛ̀	*kwiɛ*	*wɔ́lɔ̀*
he	PERF	finish	*clothes*	*wash*
S	AUX	V	O	

'He has finished washing clothes'.

A possible explanation is that 'finish', like the verb 'arrive', is changing subcategorization. In all other Kru languages observed, 'finish' takes a direct object. In this language, however, the complement may perhaps have changed its status from a term to a non-term. If this is the case, it would be roughly equivalent to the English expression 'He has finished with washing the clothes'. Another explanation, however, is that an object of one individual lexical item has been exbraciated. 'Finish' then would carry an exception feature. Other transitive verbs could be expected to follow suit, until a reshuffling of word order (as expressed, for example, in phrase structure rules) would be necessary. This could be the beginning of the final stage of exbraciation in Kru — exbraciation of term or object complements.[15]

4.4 Alternative proposals

There are two possible alternative proposals to account for the data presented in this paper. First, the claim could be made that 'embraciation' rather than 'exbraciation' has taken place. Second, one could propose that no change at all has occurred. This last claim seems extremely weak in light of the variation that exists between languages. All the evidence points to some kind of word order change. Let us, therefore, consider the possibility of 'embraciation'.

Documented cases of 'embraciation' are fairly rare. In at least one Niger-Congo language, however, there is some evidence that such a process occurs synchronically. Hyman (forthcoming) notes that in Aghem, a Grassfields Bantu language spoken in Cameroun, there are two variant orders: S AUX V O X and S AUX O V X. He suggests that some elements may be moved inside the brace as a result of a defocussing mechanism. Could the variant word orders in Kru be accounted for in the same way? There are several reasons for believing that this is not the case.

First, evidence has been given showing that exbraciation in Kru is a *motivated* change – that is, several processes were observed to be at work, setting up the S AUX (O) V X structure, which, in turn, serves a model for the change.

Second, the Kru facts parallel what is known about exbraciation in other language families. Given the universal nature of language change, it is not surprising that both the motivation and actualization of the change found in other languages are clearly reflected in Kru.

Third, and more specifically, there is evidence (Marchese 1979b and forthcoming) that some elements which moved out of the verb brace actually left remnants in this position. In several Kru languages, temporal adverbs developed into tense markers. For example, in Nyabo, most tense markers are shortened forms of temporal adverbs:

(42) | *Time adverb* | | *Tense marker* |
|---|---|---|
| 'today' kɛɛte | | kɛɛ |
| 'yesterday' pàma | | ma |
| 'a long time ago' | sekèe (ké) | e |

Time adverbs have undergone exbraciation (43), but reduced forms remained inside the brace (44):

(43) Nyabo

ɔ	hé	kúà	nu	$\begin{Bmatrix} kɛɛté \\ pàma \end{Bmatrix}$
he	NEG	work	do	$\begin{Bmatrix} today \\ yesterday \end{Bmatrix}$

'He didn't work $\begin{Bmatrix} \text{today} \\ \text{yesterday} \end{Bmatrix}$'.

(44) Nyabo

ɔ	hé	$\begin{Bmatrix} \text{kɛɛ} \\ \text{ma} \end{Bmatrix}$	kúa	nu
he	NEG	$\begin{Bmatrix} \text{today-T} \\ \text{yesterday-T} \end{Bmatrix}$	work	do
S	AUX	TENSE	O	V

'He didn't work $\begin{Bmatrix} \text{today} \\ \text{yesterday} \end{Bmatrix}$'.

*ɔ	hé	kúà	nu	$\begin{Bmatrix} \text{kɛɛ} \\ \text{ma} \end{Bmatrix}$
*S	AUX	O	V	TENSE

Exbraciation helps to explain how the shortened forms of adverbs and their full forms were differentiated (on the basis of distribution), resulting in the formation of a new syntactic category TENSE.

Exbraciation also explains why certain Kru languages have no tense suffixes at all. Languages such as Wobé and Gbaeson Krahn which have no tense suffixes are at the most advanced stages of exbraciation. Thus, it is claimed that, in such languages, the basic order was:

S AUX (ADV) (O) V

However, before the areal phenomenon of tense innovation began (Marchese 1979b: 471–473), temporal adverbs were apparently moved out of the brace through the process of exbraciation:

S AUX (O) V (ADV)

Thus, potential candidates for the category TENSE were moved out of an environment conducive to reanalysis before that reanalysis could take place.

Finally, coming back to the Aghem example, 'embraciation' occurs in order to de-focus certain elements. In contrast, Kru languages seem to be more susceptible to focussing mechanisms than to de-focussing ones. The rightward expansions discussed in section 3.2, while not indicating primary contrastive focus, do somehow (if only in a secondary way) highlight the postposed element. Relying on my own intuitions in the *ɟlʉkɔ* dialect of Godié (resulting from at least a few year's work in the language), the placement of some temporal adverbs outside the brace seems unusual or marked. In the examples below, there seems to be more emphasis on the adverb 'today' in sentence (45a) than in (45b):

(45) Godié

(a)

ɔɔ́	wɔ̀	*zukʌ́*	sʉkʌ́	lɨ
he-NEG	NEG	*today*	rice	eat
S	AUX	*ADV*	O	V

(b)

ɔɔ́	wɔ̀	sʉkʌ́	lɨ	*zukʌ́*
he-NEG	NEG	rice	eat	*today*
S	AUX	O	V	*ADV*

'He didn't eat rice today'

Given the background of Kru languages, it seems more plausible to me that a language would develop a rule to highlight an element rather than de-focus it.

For the reasons listed above, then, it seems fairly certain that we are really dealing with exbraciation, rather than embraciation.

5 Conclusion

In summary, the facts from Kru support a historical word order change that can be described as exbraciation. Both the nature of the change involved and the factors influencing the change closely parallel other known cases of exbraciation, suggesting that exbraciation is a cross-linguistic phenomenon which is motivated by common factors and realized in similar ways.

Notes

1. The Kru languages are spoken primarily in Liberia and southwest Ivory Coast. The family is divided into two main groups: Eastern and Western Kru, which are separated by a natural boundary, the Sassandra River. Languages referred to in this paper fall into the following groups (for a more detailed list, see Marchese 1979a):

Eastern	*Western*
Bété	Wobé
Godié	Gbaeson Krahn
Koyo	Sapo
Neyo	Grebo
Lakota Dida	Borobo
Vata	Nyabo
	River Cess Bassa
	Grand Bassa
	Dewoin˙
	Klao

Research for this paper was supported by a Fulbright-Hays research grant (1977–8: 441AH 70059). I would like to thank the following people for sharing their data: Thomas Bearth and Inge Egner (Wobé), John Duitsman (Gbaeson Krahn) and John

268   *Lynell Marchese*

Singler (Klao), as well as my language consultants for their cooperation and help: Bai
Boikai (Dewoin), Victor Chumbe (Borobo), Dago Truŋwɔ Hélène (Lakota Dida),
Daniel Myers (Grand Bassa), Peter Toby (Klao), 'Roger' (Tepo), Elizabeth Wah (Nyabo) and Zadi Sassi Michel (Godié). My thanks also go to Sandra Thompson, Pam
Munro, W. E. Welmers, R. P. Stockwell, A. Timberlake, and B. Chumbow, as well as
to members of the Conference and the Ilorin Seminar Group for comments on an
earlier version of this paper.

Abbreviations used in this paper include:

ADV	adverb	NEG	negative
ASSOC	associative	NP	noun phrase
AUX	auxiliary	O	object
CONDIT	conditional	PER-LOC	peripheral locative
DEF	definite	PERF	perfect
DO	direct object	PREF	preferred
FUT	future	Q	question
GEN	genitive	S	subject
INC	incompletive	SEQ	sequential
IO	indirect object	SUB	subordination
LOC	locative	T	tense marker
LOC-OBJ	locative object	V	verb

2. The origin of the S AUX O V construction does not directly concern this paper.
However, it can be noted that the construction apparently arose from a complex
structure SV_1 [OV_2] nominalizer where OV_2 functioned as the complex complement of V_1. V_1 underwent semantic bleaching and in most cases, the nominalizer
was lost. Hyman (1975) suggested that the S AUX O V construction is a result of
verb serialization (SV_1 OV_2), dating from a time when Kru was still SOV. While
there is some evidence that Kru was SOV at one time (postpositions, GEN N word
order), there is no evidence that serialization was responsible for the structure. Evidence points, rather, to a more recent development when the language was already
SVO. For a more detailed discussion see Marchese (1978, 1979b).
3. Auxiliaries express a variety of notions in Kru including futures, sequential actions,
obligation, negation, and conditionals.
4. In many west African languages, the complements of motion verbs act as objects of
those verbs. Awobuluyi (1974) notes the transitive nature of motion verbs in Yoruba.
A similar phenomenon is reported in Akan (Schachter, personal communication).
5. Temporal adverbs may, of course, occur in sentence-initial position, but this is part of
a focussing mechanism which fronts postverbal NPs. The rule applies to objects, indirect objects, instruments, etc. It is used primarily for contrastive focus or in an-
swering information-seeking questions.
6. Reason phrases are normally complex NPs consisting of an NP followed by a dependent postposition (example (14)). In a limited number of languages, the NP is surrounded by markers (example (15)). Such phrases have a wide semantic range, indicating both reason and benefactive.
7. The order S AUX O REASON V is itself a stylistic variant of S AUX REASON O V.
Elements within the verb brace, such as direct and indirect objects may optionally
shift positions in some languages.
8. The word 'term' is used to designate NPs which bear a relation of subject, object,
or indirect object to the verb. 'Non-terms' refer to NPs which bear another relation
(e.g. peripheral locatives). The terminology is a matter of convenience and does not
reflect an adherence to any particular school of linguistics.
9. SvVX in Stockwell's work corresponds to Kru S AUX V X.
10. All Kru languages typically use topic-comment strategy. Topics, which may or may
not be followed by a topic marker, occur in sentence-initial position. They are al-

ways replaced in the main clause by a recapitulative pronoun, as seen in the following example from Godié:

ŋwəniaa	wa	gʌ̀	yuə	ta
women-DEF	they	gave birth	children	three

topic	comment

(For more information on topics, see Marchese 1977, 1979a).

11. This behavior is certainly due to the difficulty in processing sentence-medial clauses (Kuno, 1974; Grosu and Thompson, 1977).

12. As a point of interest, in Ivorian French, a lingua franca spoken by many Kru speakers this is exactly what occurs. Instead of placing object pronouns between the auxiliary and the verb, the auxiliary and the verb are 'united': *Je vais te servir* (I will you serve) in Standard French becomes *Je vais servir toi* (I will serve you).

13. This can be seen in reactions by speakers of the various languages. Examples of expanded NPs were recorded in natural speech as well as elicited. Read back to the speaker, they are acceptable. Afterthoughts, however, evoke a desire to correct the 'mistake'. When confronted with an afterthought construction paralleling example (21), a speaker of River Cess Bassa kept insisting "you must say all before you say *dɔɔ*' (the main verb 'buy' occurring at the end of the sentence).

14. The term 'preferred' is used here to refer to sentences which are offered by the speaker without prodding. A sentence is marked as OK if it is accepted as grammatical by the speaker (this sentence may be one I offered myself).

15. Munro (personal communication) suggests another possibility. She notes that the placement of the verb 'finish' next to the AUX could be motivated by its inherent aspectual meaning. Thus,

ɔ	na	gwɛ̀	kwiɛ̀	wɔ̀lɔ
he	PERF	finish	clothes	wash

'He has finished washing clothes'

could be reanalyzed as:

ɔ	na-gwɛ̀	kwiɛ̀	wɔ̀lɔ
he	PERF	clothes	wash
S	AUX	O	V

'He has washed clothes'.

'Double' auxiliaries are attested in some Kru languages (Marchese 1979b: 242–252), so this analysis is certainly possible.

References

Aitchison, J.
(in press) "The order of word order change", *Transactions of the Philological Society*.

Awobuluyi, O.
1974   "Binary and Non-binary aspects of transitivity", paper presented at the West African Linguistic Society, Yaoundé, Cameroun.

Grosu, A. – S. Thompson
1977   "Constraints on the distribution of NP clauses", *Language* 53:104–151.

Hyman, L.
1975   "On the change from SOV to SVO: Evidence from Niger-Congo", *Word*

order and word order change, edited by Charles Li (Austin: University of Texas Press), 113–147.

(forthcoming) "Focus prominence in African languages", to appear in the proceedings of the 10th annual conference on African Linguistics (Champaign, Illinois, 1979).

Kokora, P.
1976   *Studies in the grammar of Koyo.* Unpublished PhD dissertation. University of Indiana, Bloomington.

Kuno, S.
1974   "The position of relative clauses and conjunctions", *Linguistic Inquiry* 51: 117–136.

Lightfoot, David
1979   *Principles of diachronic syntax* (Cambridge: Cambridge University Press).

Marchese, L.
1977   "Subordinate clauses as topics in Godié", *Studies in African Linguistics* (Supplement 7), 157–164.
1978   "Le développement des auxiliaries dans les langues kru", *Annales de l'Université d'Abidjan* série H, tome XI, 121–131.
1979a *Atlas linguistique kru – essai de typologie* (Université d'Abidjan, LXXII).
1979b *Tense/aspect and the development of auxiliaries in the Kru language family.* Unpublished PhD dissertation. University of California, Los Angeles.
(forth-
coming) "Tense innovation in the Kru language family".

Stockwell, R. P.
1977   "Motivations for exbraciation in Old English", *Mechanisms of syntactic change,* edited by Charles Li (Austin: University of Texas Press), 291–314.

Thomann, G.
1905   *Essai de manuel de la langue neoule.* (Paris).

Vogler, P.
1976   *Description synchronique d'un parler kru: le vata.* Thèse d'état. Paris.

Werle, J. M. – J. Gbalehi
1976   *Phonologie et Morphonologie du bété de la région de Guibéroua* (Abidjan: Publications conjointes: ILA/SIL, vol. 2).

BRUCE MITCHELL

The origin of Old English conjunctions:
Some problems

Summary

This paper does not offer a systematic treatment of the origin of Old English conjunctions, but is concerned only with certain problems which arise. Its starting point is the assumption that "it may be laid down as a general principle that in the progress of language parataxis precedes hypotaxis" (Small 1924:125), with a qualification which I made in Mitchell 1978a:393: "If parataxis preceded and developed into hypotaxis, there was probably − I am inclined to say certainly − an intermediate stage . . . There may indeed have been more than one." It goes on to suggest that the following types of conjunction were used adverbially before they were used conjunctionally:

(a) one word conjunctions whose demonstrative origin is either agreed, e. g. *þæs* and *þy*, or fairly widely accepted, e. g. *þær*, *þa*, and *þonne*;

(b) combinations which consist of an oblique case of the demonstrative *se* and a noun, to which may be added *þe* or *þæt*, e. g. the ancestor of MnE 'while' which appears as *þa hwile . . . þe* (so far recorded only in *Or* 212.25), *þa hwile þe*, *þa hwile*, (in later texts) *þa hwile þæt*, and (not until eME) *wile;*

(c) combinations which involve a preposition and the appropriate case of a demonstrative, to which may be added *þe* or *þæt*, e. g. *forþon*, *forþon . . . þe/þæt*, and *forþon þe/þæt*, or which may involve a preposition or be of comparative origin, viz. *siþþan* and formulae with *æfter* and *ær*.

The rest of the paper is primarily concerned with D. Carkeet's article (1976) and tries to explain why I disagree with many of his suggestions concerning the origin of Old English conjunctions and with many of the remarks about the Old English correlative system on which he bases his theory.

Topics discussed in passing include:

(a) types of conjunctions not already mentioned here;

(b) the distinguishing of conjunctions from adverbs of the same spelling by doubling, e. g. *swa swa*, or by the addition of *þe* or *þæt*, e. g. *forþon þe* and *forþon þæt;*

(c) the function of *þe* and *þæt* in such combinations;

(d) whether, when two words of the same spelling are used in what appear to be correlative pairs, one of them must be a conjunction;

(e) some of the conclusions reached by J. Erickson (1978) and S. G. Geoghegan (1975) in the articles listed in my References.

1. I begin by stressing that I intend to deal only with certain problems concerning the origin of some Old English conjunctions. I offer no systematic treatment of their origin; of such extensions of meaning as those by which *þonne* 'when' comes to express nuances of cause or concession or condition while still retaining its temporal senses; of the subsequent history of these conjunctions in English; or of the developments of their cognates in other Germanic languages.[1]

2. Looked at as they appear in the language, OE conjunctions can be divided into several groups. First, there are the 'one-word' conjunctions which have their origin in one word or which appear to be one word and are not immediately recognisable as combinations. These include what Braunmüller (1978: 104–5 and 107–9) call "genuine proto-Germanic conjunctions", "conjunctions directly derived from pronouns and other deictic items", and "conjunctions derived from enclitic particles plus other predications". His examples include respectively (the equivalents of) OE *and* and *gif*, *þa* and *þæt*, and *þeah*. The demonstrative origin of conjunctions such as *þæs* and *þy* is undoubted. That of *þær*, *þa*, *þonne*, and others, is fairly widely accepted; see such authorities as *OED*. A demonstrative origin would be in accordance with the conventional view that words like *þær*, *þæs*, *þeah*, and the like, were first used as adverbs and then developed into conjunctions, either alone, in doubled form, or with *þe* or *þæt*; see 4. We do not have to postulate a long period of time between parataxis and hypotaxis. But if, as seems beyond dispute (see **OES*), the conjunction *þæt* introducing noun clauses and the relative *se* introducing adjective clauses were originally demonstratives in simple sentences, it seems reasonable to believe that those conjunctions which were originally demonstratives passed through an intermediate stage in which they were adverbs which could introduce or be used within simple sentences.

3. I believe that in OE 'phonological differentiation' existed between demon-

strative *þæt* and conjunction *þæt*, despite Braunmüller (1978:112), between demonstrative *se* and relative *se*, and between adverbs such as *ær*, *nu*, *swa*, *þær*, *þanon*, *þider*, *þa*, *þeah*, and *þonne*, and conjunctions of the same spelling. But in the absence of intonation patterns and native informants, we are frequently unable to decide which we have. I have discussed the possibility that there may have been an intermediate stage, or intermediate stages, between the two (Mitchell, 1978a: 393–4 and forthcoming). Failure to recognise the existence of what I call ambiguous adverb/conjunctions and the ambiguous demonstrative/relative *se* in my opinion vitiates much modern work on Old English syntax. Thus, despite Andrew (1940:12 and 1948:12). there is no reason why the clause introduced by *Đa* in

> *Beo* 1600   Đa com non dæges.   Næs ofgeafon
>   hwate Scyldingas

"must be taken as subordinate" and, despite Erickson (1978:108), it is not certain that "*se* is a relative pronoun" in

> *Beo* 369   huru se aldor deah,
>   se þæm heaðorincum   hider wisade.[2]

4. Means of avoiding much, though not all, of this ambiguity arose. Some of these words appear in doubled form in the work of some writers. So, for example, *swa swa* is usually a conjunction. Some appear in combination with *þe*, e.g. *þæt þe* or *þætte*. Some are recorded with both. The forms *þa þa* and *þær þær* are much more common than *þa þe* and *þær þe*. But *þider þe* appears more often than *þider þider* in my collections and I have so far recorded *þanon þe* but not *þanon þanon*. Simple *þonne* is preferred to *þonne þe* and *þonne þonne*, but the latter two do appear. However, the presence of *þe* is not absolute proof that we have the conjunction rather than the adverb; see the comment by Baker quoted in 35, note 24. The addition of *þæt* sometimes denotes a difference in function; compare *swa*, which is primarily comparative when used as a conjunction, with *swa þæt*, which is primarily final or consecutive. But this is not always so. Thus *oþ* and *oþ þæt* can both be conjunctions and *gyf þæt* appears in *HomU* 44. 284.9, pre-dating *OED's 3iff þatt* from *Orrmulum*.

5. It is, of course, a syntactical commonplace that many of these adverb/conjunctions can be used in (what appear to be) correlative pairs. But even such an arrangement does not certify that one of the clauses must be subordinate to the other; consider the conventional, but not necessarily 'correct', punctuation of

Beo 126   Ða wæs on uhtan   mid ærdæge
                         Grendles guðcræft   gumum undyrne;
                         þa wæs æfter wiste   wop up ahafen,
                         micel morgensweg.

Erickson's statement (1978:102) that in the sequence *forþon* adv. . . . *forþon* conj. "it seems . . . suspicious . . . that the adverbial should have the same form as the subordinator" is however itself suspect and seems to be contradicted by his later statement (1978:106) that

> in addition to *forðon*, there are other OE main clause adverbials which may co-occur with homophonous subordinators. Among these, Andrew (1940:31) lists *ær* 'before', *nu* 'now', *siððan* 'after', *swa* 'so', *þeah* 'though', and *þær* 'there/where', and to the list one might also add *þa* 'then/when' and *þonne* 'then/when'.

There was no need, either, for Erickson to add *þa* and *þonne* to Andrew's list. He had already discussed these words at length and the sentence from which Erickson quotes actually contains both of them.

6. The second group of OE conjunctions comprises those which consist of an oblique case of the demonstrative *se* and a noun, to which may be added *þe* or *þæt*. The most interesting of these is the ancestor of the MnE conjunction 'while'. This has its origin in an accusative of duration of time, as in *ChronE* 129.16 (994) *⁊ man gislade þa hwile in to þam scipum*, to which is added a clause introduced by *þe*, e. g. *Or* 212.25 *Ic nat eac . . . hu nyt ic þa hwile beo þe ic þas word sprece* (the sole recorded example in which the two elements are separated) and *BlHom* 175.2 *⁊ þa, þa hwile þa he þær stod, he wearþ færinga geong cniht*. We occasionally find correlative *þa hwile þe . . . þa hwile*, e.g. *Or* 72.22 and *AeCHom* i.10.35. The form without *þe* is rarely recorded as a conjunction; examples include *Bede (Ca)* 188.4 *þa hwile*, where MS *O* has *þenden* and MS *T þendæn*. This latter is probably an older word. It is more common in the poetry than in the prose, but disappeared in late OE or early ME times and does not appear in *OED*; see Mitchell 1969:70–2. Forms with *þæt* instead of *þe* are late. Adams (1907: 86) records three examples: *Ch* 391, dated 'post-Conquest', and *ChronE* 252.34 and 253.1, both in the entry for 1123. The earliest example with the noun alone appears to be *wile* in *ChronE* 264.25 (1137). So Braunmüller's statement (1978:107) that 'ME *the while that* > ModE *while*' cannot be accepted as certain; the development may have been *þa hwile þe > þa hwile > wile*. The stage without *þe* appears in some later prose texts, e. g. *Lch* iii. 2.6 *þa hwile* and *Lch* iii.122.18 *ðe hwyle* and once in the poetry, viz. *JDay*

ii.83 *þa hwile*, and could well have been common in the spoken language in the eleventh century.

7. The formula *on þære hwile þe*, recorded in *Or* 130.9 and 170.12, is probably no more to be taken as a conjunction than MnE 'during the time that', but it provides a convenient means of transition to the third group of OE conjunctions, viz. combinations involving prepositions. These consist of a preposition followed by the appropriate case of the neuter demonstrative *þæt*, with the possible addition of *þe* or *þæt*, which may immediately follow the demonstrative (grouped formulae) or be separated from it (divided formulae). So we find (with the accusative) *oþ þæt* and *þurh þæt þe*; (with the genitive) *to þæs*, *to þæs þe/þæt*, and *to þæs . . . þe/þæt*; and (with the dative/instrumental *þæm*, *þam*, *þon*, *þy*, and other spellings) *forþon*, *forþon þe/þæt*, and *forþon . . . þe/þæt*. Combinations involving *æfter*, e. g. *æfter þæm (þe)* and *ær*, e. g. *ær þæm (þe)*, and the conjunction *siþþan* − *siþþan þe* has not yet been recorded − may belong here. But they may be comparative rather than prepositional formulae; see 26−28 and 30−31.

8. For purposes of this paper, it will suffice to mention a few other types of OE conjunctions. Formulae which certainly involve a comparative include *no ðy ær*, *þon ma þe*, and *þy læs (þe)*. Formulae with *loc(a)*, e. g. *loc(a) hwær* and *loc(a) hwonne*, and with *(swa . . .) swa*, e. g. *swa hwær swa* and *sona swa*, are also noteworthy. The list is not complete. But it does illustrate the variety of OE conjunctions − a variety which suggests to me that we are unlikely to find one sequence which will explain the origin of all, or even nearly all, of them. Yet the belief that conjunctions such as *þær*, *þa*, *þonne*, and *þeah*, *þa hwile (þe)*, and *forþon (þe)*, were originally adverbs introducing simple sentences is satisfying, and will not surprise those who, like me, accept Small's proposition (1924:125) that "it may be laid down as a general principle that in the progress of language parataxis precedes hypotaxis", or who, like Mann (1942:88), believe that

> wenn wir nach der Entstehung der Konjunktionen forschen, also nach den Hilfsmitteln, die einen Nebensatz dem Hauptsatz unterordnen, müssen wir von der Erkenntnis ausgehen, dass sich die moderne Sprachform der Unterordnung aus der der Beiordnung (Asyndese − verbundene Parataxe − Hypotaxe) entwickelt hat.

However, Carkeet (1976:49) is not content with the simple development set out at the beginning of my last sentence. The rest of this paper is primarily concerned with his attack on what he calls "a traditional view" of the origin of the OE correlative system, in the course of which he produces a new theory for the development of some OE conjunctions.

9. I begin with the correlative system. Carkeet (1976:56) states that "correlative adverbs systematically occur in main clauses which follow rather than precede subordinate clauses". (On 1976:52 it is "almost exclusively"). This statement requires qualification. It remains to be established for local and temporal clauses in the prose, but seems to me too sweeping; see *OES and consider the table below, which is based on Liggins's figures (1955:223, 228, 230, 252–3, and 259) for temporal/causal clauses introduced by *þa (þa)* with a correlative adverb *þa* and by *þonne (þonne)* with a correlative adverb *þonne*.

Conjunction	Principal clause precedes	Principal clause follows
þa	14	270
þa þa	8	116
þonne	50	197
þonne þonne	0	5
TOTAL	72 (11 per cent)	588 (89 per cent)

These figures do not in my opinion justify Carkeet's "almost exclusively" or indeed his "systematically". Those interested can cull further figures from Liggins 1955, passim. They will find (*inter al.*) that she lists thirty prose sentences with correlative *nu . . . nu* (1955:296–8 and 303). The principal clause precedes the subordinate in seventeen and follows it in thirteen.

10. Carkeet's statement is not valid for clauses of place introduced by *þær* or for clauses of time introduced by *þa* or *þonne* in the poetry if we accept the "curious superstition" referred to by Andrew (1948:vii–viii) which forbids "the subordination of a temporal clause . . . when the clause precedes the principal sentence". It is broadly true for clauses of concession, though Quirk's figures (1954:14–19) suggest that the difference is less clear cut in the poetry than, according to Burnham (1911:28), it is in the prose, and for clauses of condition. It does not hold for clauses of comparison like those in *ÆCHom* i. 4.14 *þonne cymð se Antecrist, se bið mennisc mann and soð deofol, swa swa ure Hælend is soðlice mann and God on anum hade*; *ÆCHom* i. 94.1 *And þæt tacn wæs ða swa micel on geleaffullum mannum, swa micel*

swa nu is þæt halige fulluht; and *ÆCHom* i. 84.10 *Ne mihte se manfulla ehtere mid nanre ðenunge þam lytlingum swa micclum fremian, swa micclum swa he him fremode mid ðære reðan ehtnysse hatunge*. It does not hold for the limited number of causal clauses in the prose in which *for* formulae are used as conjunctions with a correlative adverb in the principal clause. For, as a table in **OES* will show, the principal clause precedes the causal clause in two-thirds (67.7 per cent) of such examples; the usual patterns are those seen in *CP* 363.4 *Forðæm he cwæð ða word, forðæm ða Saducie antsacodon ðære æriste æfter deaðe ⁊ ða Farisseos geliefdon ðære æriste* and *CP* 353.15 *⁊ forðæm hit is awriten ðæt hiera honda wæren gehalgode Gode, forðæmðe hie ne sparodan ða synfullan ac slogon.*[3] Carkeet, who lists *Cura Pastoralis* among the texts he read (1976:63), asserts (1976:61–2, n. 9) on the basis of *John* 5.16, 10.17, and 12.18, that such constructions "are Latin-influenced and atypical of native OE prose". This enables him to dispose of a construction which runs contrary to his theory. But they seem to me a perfectly natural native development. There is nothing in the Latin of the two examples I quote from *CP* to support Carkeet's assertion. Van Dam (1957:42–3 and 48) gives references to more such examples and says (1957:84) that "the Latin does not appear to have influenced the use of causal conjunctions in the Old English texts under investigation". In this Liggins concurs; see **OES.*[4] All these are in effect exceptions to Carkeet's rule (1976:55) that "in fact no clause type which consistently follows the main clause, such as purpose and result clauses, can be paired with correlative adverbs occurring in the accompanying main clauses". There are even exceptions of a sort with clauses of purpose and result, e. g. *Bede* 392.23 *Wæs mid micle sare getogen, swa ic ær sæde, ⁊ se earm wæs swa swiðe great ⁊ aswollen, to ðon þæt he nænge begnisse in þæm elmbogan hæfde*; *Bede* 324.19–27 (where we also have *swa . . . to ðon þæt*); *AeCHom* i. 614.8 *To ðam he wext þæt he fealle*; *to ðy he sprytt þæt he mid cwyldum fornyme swa hwæt swa he ær sprytte*; and *WHom* 6.36 *And to ðam hy gesceop God ælmihtig, þæt hy ⁊ heora ofspring scoldan gefyllan ⁊ gemænigfyldan þæt on heofonum gewanad wæs*; cf. MnE 'To this end He came from Heaven and dwelt among men, that He might redeem mankind'.

11. Carkeet makes these statements about clause order as reasons for rejecting the proposition that adverbs were the source of conjunctions (1976: 52 and 55–6). But even if they could stand, arguments based on them would in my opinion be irrelevant. It is true that certain subordinate clauses tend to follow their principal clause while others tend to precede it; see **OES*. But there are no firm rules and nothing in the order in which OE clauses are arranged runs contrary to the proposition that parataxis preceded hypotaxis.

One can readily see that when sequences like the following became complex sentences, the principal clause followed the subordinate clause: 'There/then he waited by the ford. There/then he killed his enemy', 'But/Yet he waited by the ford. But/Yet he did not kill his enemy', 'O were I by the ford! Then I would kill my enemy', 'Who waited by the ford? He killed his enemy', and 'That (one) waited by the ford. That (one) killed his enemy'. But equally one can see that other sequences would produce a principal clause which came first, e. g. 'There/then he killed his enemy. There/then he waited by the ford', 'To that (end) he waited by the ford. Thus he killed/could kill his enemy', 'He was so clever. So clever was his teacher', 'For that he killed the man. For that the man killed his brother', '(But/Yet) he did not kill the man. But/Yet he had waited by the ford', 'I would avenge him. Were I free!', 'He said that. His enemy was dead', and 'That (one) is the man. That (one) is my enemy'. One can also see that correlation is likely to be more frequent in sentences of the first type than in those of the second. So, despite Carkeet (1976:56), the view that adverbs were "the historical starting point" *can* "explain the essential property of the correlative system, which is the very cooccurrence of the conjunctions and adverbs" and *can* account for the fact that correlative adverbs tend to occur in principal clauses which follow the subordinate clause.

12. The transition from two simple sentences to one complex sentence postulated by this view could have come about as the result of changes in stress and intonation affecting particularly the elements where the sentences met. On the possibility of an intermediate stage or stages being represented in extant OE texts, see *OES*. The syntactical (as opposed to phonetic) methods of distinguishing the principal from the subordinate clause – the use of *þe* or *þæt* with the conjunction, the doubling of the word when it was used as a conjunction, and the use of element order to distinguish the two clauses, on which see Campbell 1970:93–6, and *OES* – could have arisen simultaneously or subsequently. (I take up these points as they become relevant.)

13. Thus I have yet to be convinced that this "traditional view", as Carkeet (1976:49) calls it, is wrong. As I have pointed out in 38–40, I believe that it can account for all the phenomena which Carkeet uses as arguments against it. So I turn now to the theory which he evolved to explain the OE correlative system, viz. that most OE conjunctions can be traced back to a group consisting of a preposition + a noun phrase [= demonstrative + noun] in an oblique case [abbreviated by Carkeet to PP, even when there is no preposition (1976: 60, n. 5)] + *þe* or to a similar group without a preposition (1976:49). Only

those which cannot possibly be made to fit this theory are excluded – some specifically, e. g. *gif, nu, swa, swa hwær swa, swa hraþe swa, swa oft swa,* and *sona swa* (1976:54), others in almost silent desperation, e. g. *þanon* and *þider* (1976:54). This reinforces my belief that there is no need to assume (as Carkeet does) that all the conjunctions he lists apart from the first seven above must have been developed in the same way and that that method must explain not only the origin of the conjunctions concerned, but also the origin of the correlative system. It is a telling fact against his theory that the more likely it is that a particular conjunction was formed in accordance with his theory, the less likely it is to be used correlatively with itself. The reverse of this statement is also true. As we shall see, there are other arguments against his theory.

14. For prepositional conjunctions, Carkeet visualizes four stages: (1) *æfter þæm timum þe* (which on the evidence of his gloss "*on þam timum þe* 'at the time [*sic*] when' " (1976:50), he takes to mean 'after the time at which/ when'): prepositional phrase + relative pronoun; (2) *æfter þæm þe*: prepositional phrase + relative pronoun; (3) *æfter þæm þe*: conjunction; (4) *æfter þæm:* conjunction (1976:52–3). But he adds the comment (1976:53) that "there are, of course, plausible variations on this suggested chain of development. For example, there might be no stage 3 . . ."[5] and concludes "Similar series of rule changes can be set up for the other prepositional conjunctions as well." So *siþþan* goes back to some such sequence as *sib bæm timum be* [*sic*] (1976:53–4).

15. He then goes on (1976:53–4) to claim that most non-prepositional conjunctions 'can be historically traced back' to a noun phrase (demonstrative + noun) in the oblique case + *þe*, the development being similar to that for prepositional conjunctions. Thus *þæs þe* (and presumably *þæs* as a conjunction) are said to derive from *þæs geares þe* or some similar combination, *þa þe, þa,* and *þe,* from *þa hwile þe* or the like, and *þonne þe* and *þonne* from *þone fyrst þe* or the like. The local conjunction *þær,* however, is said to derive from *on þære stowe þe* or the like – a combination involving a preposition.[6]

16. The sequence proposed for prepositional conjunctions may well have some validity. Adams (1907:47) quotes *BlHom* 133.12 *Mid þon dæge wæs gefylled se dæg þe is nemned Pentecosten . . . , þa wæron ealle þa apostolas wunigende on anre stowe* as being "interesting chiefly for the light it throws on the origin and meaning of the *mid-* formulae in general" and as "probably another instance in which an earlier syntactical usage has been preserved" in

BlHom.[7] This suggests that here Adams had in mind some such sequence as that proposed by Carkeet. He suggests (1907:93) that *on þam þe* 'when, while' – which occurs twice in the late Chronicle viz. *ChronD* 169.28 (1050) and *ChronD* 179.16 (1052) – "probably ... arose from the omission of the substantive in such sentences as" *Or* 180.21 *On þæm dagum þe Titus Sempronius ⁊ Gratias Gaius wæron consulas on Rome* ... He also says (1907:94) of *onmang ðam ðe* 'when, while' that "doubtless the conjunctival use grew out of its employment as a preposition in cases such as this: *ChronE* 241.14 (1106) *⁊ onmang þam gewinnan se fæder forðferde.*" I can, however, find nothing else to justify Carkeet's assertion (1976:53) that "Adams generally favours the historical derivation of temporal conjunctions from sequences of PP + RELATIVE PRONOUN". Adams gives no such hints about sequences involving *æfter* (1907:105–6 and 109) – here indeed he comes close to suggesting the development which I outlined in *Guide*, §169, and which I discuss below – and advances quite different theories, not only for *siþþan* (which, as we have seen above, Carkeet (1976:53–4) tries to subsume) (1907:100–1), but also for sequences involving *ær* (1907:115–16 and 119–20) and *oð* (1907:127 and 130–1). Indeed, on 1907:94, he suggests that *betwux þam þe* 'when, while' may have developed from prepositional phrases like *betwyx þissum.* A comparison of this with his just-quoted comment on *onmang ðam ðe* suggests that here at any rate Adams was reacting to the material he had in front of him rather than formulating any coherent theory about the origin of prepositional conjunctions.

17. Carkeet's claim (1976:60–1, n. 6) that Shearin (1903:63) "offers an explanation along these same lines for OE clauses of purpose introduced by prepositional conjunctions like *to* + dat/inst + *þæt, for* + dat/inst + *þæt*, and many others" also seems ill-founded. What Shearin said on 1903:63 was that "in these formulae, the word immediately following the preposition is almost always in Old English a demonstrative pronominal ... However, rarely a noun may be in the place of the usual pronominal object ...", while on 1903:64 he observed that "it will be seen at once that these introductory formulae are merely the phrases already studied ... with the addition of a limiting *ðæt*-clause" – which he defined on 1903:63 as "a substantive clause explanatory of" the demonstrative object of the preposition. Neither here nor elsewhere did Shearin state or imply that the formula with a noun was an essential first stage. In view of this and of the fact that he sees the *þæt* clauses as originally noun clauses and not adjective clauses, his explanation is along very different lines from that of Carkeet. Since I am inclined to agree with Shearin, I do not pursue the *to* formulae further. The last element is *þæt*, not *þe* (*OES*), and in terms of the table in 24, they are recorded only in

phase 1 *to þam þingum þæt*, phase 2 *to þæm . . . þæt*, and phase 3 *to þæm þæt*; see the relevant sections in **OES*.

18. The question naturally arises whether a distinction can be drawn between *þe* and *þæt* in such combinations. It seems to me reasonable to postulate that originally the two were quite distinct and that *þæt* was a conjunction introducing what we would describe as a noun clause in apposition with a preceding object governed by a preposition. This object could be either a demonstrative used independently, as in *Or* 54.18 *ꝺ mid ungemetlicre pinunge he wæs þæt folc cwielmende, to ꝺon þæt hie him anbugen*, or a demonstrative + noun, as in *Or* 52.32 *ꝺ he Cirus Persea cyning hæfde þriddan dæl his firde beæftan him, on þæt gerad, gif ænig wære þe fyr fluge þe on ꝺæm gefeohte wæs þonne to þæm folce þe þær beæftan wæs, þæt hine mon sloge swa raꝺe swa mon hiora fiend wolde*. Here I differ from Benham (1908:218–19): "as in the case of purpose phrases, the word following the pronoun is *ꝺæt*, which, in the original composition of the phrase, was a demonstrative pronoun in relative function introducing an adjective clause".[8] For I cannot myself see how the *þæt* clauses in the two examples quoted above can be described as 'adjective clauses' in the sense in which I use the term. That the apparent agreement in *on þæt gerad . . . þæt* in *Or* 52.32 above is illusory is clear from the appearance of formulae like *AeCHom* ii. 534.35 *for ꝺam intingan þæt* and *WHom* 6.156 *to þam þingum þæt*.

19. The original function of *þe* is even less certain. In my *Guide* (1968:88), I wrote of the formulae *for þæm þe* 'because' that "we can call *þe* (if we wish) a subordinating particle. This is the general function of *þe* and its use as a relative pronoun is probably a special adaptation . . . We can perhaps get nearest to its original force by translating it as 'namely' "; on this, see Small (1924:148–52; 1926:312–13; and 1930:381–3). Carkeet (1976:56) objects that this "demands that we assign a brand new property to *þe*, that of 'subordinating particle' . . . , whereas the hypothesis proposed in this paper is based on the independently motivated and universally accepted view of *þe* as a relative pronoun". I do not accept the phrases "brand new" and "universally accepted" and still hold to my view that the general function of *þe* was that of a subordinating particle.[9] Even if we accept Carkeet's complicated hypothesis, it can explain only some prepositional formulae with *þe* and the appearance of *þe* 'relative pronoun' in a few non-prepositional formulae such as *þær þe*, *þa þe*, and *þonne þe*, in which *þe* is the exception rather than the rule (see **OES*) and is therefore more likely to be a later accretion than a fundamental and integral element. It cannot explain the prepositional formulae with *þæt* and cannot explain the appearance of *þe* in *þeah þe, þæt þe*

conj. – which Benham (1908:207) thinks may be "the parent form from which *ðæt* [conjunction] is descended" – (a doubtful proposition; see Kivimaa 1966:161) – *þætte, þy læs þe, þon ma þe*, and the like, or how *þe* in these groups can function as a 'relative pronoun'. But the hypothesis that *þe* was a subordinating particle explains this and also its use as a relative. As I suggested in *Guide* (1968, § 169), it also explains the presence of *þe* in prepositional formulae like *for þæm þe*, where it is hard to see how *þe* could ever have meant 'which' – either with or without a noun before it – but easy to see how it could have meant something like 'namely'. If we accept that the use of *þe* had its origin in formulae like *þa hwile þe* and **æfter þæm timan þe*, we can accept Kivimaa's proposition (1966:162 and 164–5) that it was originally of "relatival nature" and that its presence in formulae like *þeah þe* and *for þæm þe* was due to analogical use after "its full values" had "faded". But it seems more plausible to me to argue that in *þa hwile þe, for þæm þe*, and *þeah þe*, it was originally a subordinating particle and that in *þa hwile þe* it was subsequently interpreted as a relative '[during] the time in which'; see Mann, 1942:91–2 and the quotation from *Guide* (1968:88) with which I began this section.

20. But in either event, the formulae with *þæt* and those with *þe* would be different in origin. This is in fact suggested by Adams (1907:109) as a possible explanation for the solitary example he found of *æfter þæm þæt* conjunction 'after' (*Or* 212.28):

> The use of *ðæt* in this way is unusual, but may be regarded as one of the early stages in its progress toward its present regular relative use. Beside the more common *oð ðæt* we find *oððe*, so that in some connections the demonstrative and the relative were felt to be closely related, even in OE. Or *ðæt* may be regarded as the demonstrative introducing a substantive clause in apposition with *ðæm*.

But Adams's first explanation opens up another possibility, viz. that in all these formulae, *þe* – not *þæt* – was the original and that *þæt* came in only because the originally distinct *þe* and *þæt* became to some extent interchangeable, first perhaps by phonetic weakening of *þæt* to *þe*, as suggested for example by Adams for *oþþæt* and *oþþe*, and then by analogy.

21. This is undoubtedly a plausible and possible chain of events. But I do not accept it. The fact that Adams found so few temporal prepositional formulae with *þæt*[10] means that he was on firm ground when he put forward the idea that they were the result of later confusion. A similar preference for

þe is apparent in the figures for grouped formulae with *for* in causal clauses in early prose cited by van Dam (1957):166 with *for þæm/þam/þan þe* but four with *for þæm þæt(te)* (1957:44—5) and 335 with *for þon þe* but three with *for þon þæt(te)* (1957:52–3). The case for believing that in these two constructions the formula with *þe* was the original and the spasmodic examples with *þæt* are intruders is strong. But the reverse is true in clauses of purpose and result. *Þæt*, not *þe*, is the norm when formulae with *for* introduce clauses of purpose; see **OES* for details. Shearin (1903:63–8 and 78) notes only one example of a grouped *to* formula with dative/instrumental + *þe* in purpose clauses against 269 with *þæt* or (rarely) *þætte*. Even this has *þæt* on the testimony of Liebermann: *LawAfEl(EGH)* 13 `aluc ðu hine from minum weofode to þam þæt he deaðe swelte*. In clauses of result, Benham (1908:218 and 228) mentions none with *þe* against 202 with *þæt* or (rarely) *þætte*. Neither formula with *to* occurs in the poetry. Here the presumption must be that the formula with *þæt* was the original (*þæt* being an essential element) and that *þe* is the intruder. So the proposition that formulae with *þæt* and formulae with *þe* arose independently but later became confused as a result of phonetic reduction and analogy seems established.[1]

22. We must now ask whether Carkeet's theory is acceptable for prepositional formulae introducing clauses of time. On the evidence supplied by Adams (1907:242—5 and passim), we can divide the prepositions which appear in these formulae into three groups: first, those which never introduce a formula without a noun, e. g. *binnan, geond, in, of*, and *ymbe*; second, those which never introduce a formula containing a noun, e. g. *æfter* (Carkeet's initial **æfter þæm timum þe* is never recorded), *amang, betweoh, betwux, gemang, on(ge)mang*, and *under*; and third, those which introduce both, e. g. *ær* (only twice with a noun (Adams 1907:126) — *Matt(WSCp)* 26.29 and *HomU* 24. 123.5), *fram* (without a noun only in *ChronE* 258.26 (1127)), *fram þ* (Adams 1907:115), *mid* (with a noun only in *BlHom* 133.12 quoted in 16), *on* (only twice without a noun; see 16), *oð* (see 23), *to* (see 17), and *toforan/foran to* (both with and without a noun only in comparatively late texts (Adams 1907:126—7)). In general, it can be said of the third group that the less common formula occurs in comparatively late texts. These facts are not inconsistent with Carkeet's theory. In my opinion, however, they are most consistent with the proposition that some of the formulae without a noun developed from those with a noun, that some prepositions never governed a formula with a noun, and that with some prepositions the two formulae evolved independently. In other words, Carkeet's stage 1 was not essential, but was possible.

23. Gender provides us with what seems to me proof of the proposition that Carkeet's stage 1 is not essential. Most of the prepositional formulae involve the demonstrative *se* in the genitive, dative, or instrumental, in all of which the masculine and neuter forms are the same. So it is easy enough to insert masc. *timan* (rather than Carkeet's *timum*) in the formula *æfter þæm þe* and produce **æfter þæm timan þe*. Carkeet (1976:61, n. 8) ingeniously manages to derive *þær* from *on þære stowe þe* to avoid the difficulty of having to explain how *on þæm stede/staðole þe* became *þær*. He is able to avoid discussing *oð þæt (þe)* because it is not used correlatively. But it is impossible to use Carkeet's stages to derive *oð þæt (þe)* from attested formulae such as *ChronD* 99.29 (915) *oð ðone fyrst þe, Bede* 42.12 *oð ða tide þe,* and similar patterns cited by Adams (1907:139), or even from *Bo* 116.10 *oð ðone first þ,* which I see as the result of the intrusion of *þæt* into what was originally the sphere of *þe.* None of the nouns of time which Adams found in prepositional or non-prepositional formulae – *byre, dæg, fyrst, hwil, monaþ, niht, tid, tima* – is neuter except *æfen* (also masculine) and *gear.* We cannot insert these or any other neuter noun of time of which I can think in *oð þæt þe.* Carkeet's attempt to dispose of the problem of gender (1976:61, n. 8) does not meet this criticism. Benham (1908:217) suggests that *oð þæt* and *oðþe* "probably arose from the condensation of a phrase constructed with *oð* [such as *oð þone first ðæt* or *oð ðone first ðe*], while the *ðæt* or *ðe* is the introductory particle to the clause dependent upon the noun constructed with *oð*". This is different from Carkeet's proposal, for it involves the dropping of both the demonstrative and the noun. Benham goes on to claim that the likelihood of "such condensation of phrase ... is proved by the analogous cases of *to, wið,* or *embe* + *ðæt*" and refers us to Shearin. But Shearin (1903:76–7) cites no examples of these prepositions with formulae involving nouns and suggests two possible origins for the formulae cited by Benham:

> First, and far more probably, here we have two *ðæt*'s, the accusative object of the preposition and the *ðæt* introductory of the clause, blended into one. ... Second, it is conceivable that the *ðæt*-clause ... is the substantive object of the preceding prepositions ..., which govern it directly without an intervening pronominal. But this is hardly tenable ...

It is not clear which of these Adams was embracing when he wrote (1907: 127) that "logically, *ðæt* is the object of the preposition, and the subordinate clause is in apposition with it". Shearin (1903:76) does cite examples of *on ðæt gerad ðæt* 'on condition that', but **on ðæt (þe)* is not recorded; the formula is *on ðæm ðæt* (Shearin 1903:75), which (if we follow Carkeet) would have to go back to an unrecorded *on þæm gerade þæt*. Similarly, we cannot derive the solitary *fram þ* in *ChronE* 258.26 (1127) from the attested formulae *fram þam geare*(n)/*dæge*(m)/*timan*(m) *þe* (Adams 1907:114—15), in all of which *þe* has to be construed as dat./instr. Is it merely chance that while we find *of þære tide þe* (Adams 1907:114), *on þære hwile þe* (Adams 1907:87), and the phrase *for þære wiisan* (*Bede* 70.21), we do not find **of þære þe, *on þære þe,* or **for þære þe*? Are we to assume that these actually did once exist and were eliminated by analogy?[12] Or does their non-appearance support the proposition that in *æfter þæm þe, þæm* is the dative of the neuter demonstrative *þæt* used independently and that it never qualified a noun? I prefer to believe the latter.

24. So I conclude that Carkeet's stage 1 was not essential. Consideration of the table which follows may allow us to draw further conclusions. I use 'phase' instead of 'stage' to avoid confusion, since I include more patterns than Carkeet. 'No' means 'not recorded'[13]. Whether phases 1a and 1b had any meaningful independent existence is in my opinion doubtful. But see 14 fn. 5. Any form of the dative/instrumental may be represented by *þæm*. 'Prep' embraces postpositions (see Mitchell 1978b:240—56). I do not regard patterns such as *æfter/on/to þæt* as exemplifying phase 4. On *to* formulae see 17.

25. I have already demonstrated to my own satisfaction that phase 1 was not essential. There is little in the table to support the idea that it even played a part in the development of the prepositional conjunctions; the examples are too few in number and too spasmodic in appearance. Phase 2, in which the adverb phrase is separated from *þe* — as in *Or* 132.13 *He þa Alexander hit swiþost for þæm angann þe he wolde þæt his mærþa wæren maran þonne Ercoles* — is not found in temporal clauses; examples with tmesis occur only with a noun, i.e. in phase 1c — and then (as noted above) only twice.[19] So phase 2 — very common in causal clauses — can be eliminated from the development of the temporal formulae.

26. Where then do we begin? The fact that *ær* appears as a conjunction in the earliest texts, both prose and verse, and that **ær þe* is not recorded means, I think, that adv. *ær* became conj. *ær* without any intermediate steps involving a demonstrative and/or *þe*. But we still have to account for combinations like *ær þam (þe)* and *ær þon (þe)*. Adams (1907:119) writes: "In itself *ær* is a comparative, and, as such is followed by the dative. Naturally, then, when it came to be used as a preposition, it demanded the dative case. The addition of ðe gives this preposition with its object the force of a con-

Introductory word	Phase 1a Prep. noun Phrase + þe / Phase 1b Conjunction	Phase 1c Prep. noun Phrase + ...þe	Phase 2 Prep.phrase without noun + ...þe	Phase 3 Prep.phrase + þe > Conjunction	Phase 4 Prep.phrase alone = Conjunction	Phase 5 One word conjunction
æfter (adv., prep.)	No	No	No	*æfter þæm þe*	*æfter þæm*	No
ær (adv., prep.)	*ær þæm dæge þe*[14]	No	No	*ær þæm þe*	*ær þæm*	*ær*
mid (prep.)	No / *Mid þon dæge* occurs in BlHom 133.12	No	No	*mid þæm þe*	*mid þæm*	No
of (prep.)	*of þæm dæge þe*[15]	*of þæm dæge ...þe*[16]	No	No	No	No
on (prep.)	*on þæm dagum þe*[17]	No	No	*on þæm þe*	No	No
under (adv., prep.)	No	No	No	*under þæm þe*	No	No
for (prep.)	*for þæm intingan þe*[18]	No	*for þæm ...þe*	*for þæm þe*	*for þæm*	*for* (in late texts)

junction." This would seem to imply that phase 3 was essential in the development of *ær þam* – on this see 27–8 – and that formulae with the instrumental like *ær þon (þe)* were the result of dative/instrumental syncretism. (They occur too early to be due to phonetic weakening.) It is too exquisite to argue whether conj. *ær þam* ever produced conj. *ær* by shortening if conj. *ær* already existed through the first process described.

27. The fact that "the simple *ær* seems to be more common in early texts than in later; in general, the use of the relative in prepositional formulae of all kinds increases in later texts" (Adams 1907:120) supports the notion of a two-fold development. But it does not prove that *ær þam (þe)* and the like are in origin prepositional formulae. For Behaghel (1928, § 925) – followed by Möllmer (1937:76–7) – explains *þon* as a form of the temporal adv. *þonne* and suggests that there were originally two formulae – *er* (OE *ær*), used after a negative principal clause, and *er than* (OE *ær þonne/þon*) used after a positive principal clause. These two usages would spring from two original paratactic constructions which may be illustrated by the MnE sentences 'I do not go. Sooner he comes' and 'I go before. Then he may come'. This theory does account for the use of *ær* and *ær þon* in the earliest poetry. But if the distinction ever existed, it does not hold in OE poetry, where some twenty-three per cent (six out of twenty-six) negative principal clauses are followed by *ær þon* against some twenty-two per cent (fifteen out of sixty-nine) positive principal clauses. Both Behaghel and Möllmer agree that the alleged distinction broke down early. The figures they quote from the *Heliand* demonstrate its breakdown rather than confirm its existence and the fact that Adams (1907:220) found only four examples of *ær ðonne* – for a few more see *OES – must cast further doubt on it. Forms such as *ær ðam* (*Dan* 587) and *ær þy* (*GenA* 2766) would be due to an early feeling that *þon* was instrumental, a feeling which would be quite simply explained by analogy with *æfter þon*, *forþon*, and the like, while the forms with *þe* – according to Möllmer (1937:80–1) – are due perhaps to the influence of Lat. *antequam/priusquam* or possibly to that of combinations like *æfter þam/þon þe*. The acceptance of Behaghel's theory would mean that *ærþon* is different in nature and origin from combinations like *forþon* and *æfter þon* (if we agree that *æfter þon* is in origin a prepositional formula; see 31). But this in itself is not an argument against the theory.

28. Yet another different origin for *ærþon* is suggested by Small (1930: 389–91) – somewhat overconfidently, it must be said: "no one, it is believed, will differ with the writer upon the analysis of this subordinate conjunction". His theory is that in examples like

Phoen 377
Forgeaf him se meahta   moncynnes fruma
þæt he swa wrætlice   weorþan sceolde
eft þæt ilce   þæt he ær þon wæs,
feþrum bifongen,   þeah hine fyr nime

ær retains its comparative sense and *þon* is an instrumental of comparison. So we have an adverb phrase meaning 'earlier than that'. To this is added "the particle, *þe*, to convert the demonstrative phrase into a relative expression"; hence in

Jud 250
Hogedon aninga
hyra hlaforde   hilde bodian,
ærðon ðe him se egesa   on ufan sæte,
mægen Ebrea

"the basic meaning underlying the conjunction, *before*, is undoubtedly *'earlier than that, that* the terror was upon them' or, *'earlier than that, namely,* the terror was upon them'." Dative/instrumental syncretism would again account for forms like *ærðæmðe* in *CP* 5.8–10, which Small quotes. The weakness of this theory is Small's belief that "the usual forms [of the conjunctional] are *ær þon þe*, and *ær þam þe*" and his assumption that *ær þon þe* is the original one.[20] Behre's probably unknowing modification of Small's theory in part overcomes this weakness by showing how *ærþon* — as opposed to *ærþon þe* — could have become a conjunction, for Behre (1934:169) says that in

Max i. 109
wuda ond wætres nyttað þonne him biþ wic
alyfed,
mete bygeþ, gif he maran þearf,
ærþon he to meþe
weorþe

"the basic thought is: 'he buys meat if he needs more before (or: in preference to) this: he would become too faint (sc. if he did not buy meat)'." But the early use of *ær* alone as a conjunction remains a difficulty, despite Joly (1967:15).

29. Not unexpectedly, Johnsen (1916:117–18) adds yet another theory: to him, both *ær* and *þon* were originally "local demonstrative adverbs". I do not propose to adjudicate here. But I will repeat my belief that conj. *ær* arose directly from adv. *ær* and that formulae like *ær þam/þon (þe)* arose independently.

30. The possibility of a direct development from adverb to conjunction may

arise with *siþ*, which appears as a conjunction once – in *Ch* 1440 *Siŏ heora tuuege dæg agan sie, þonne agefe mon tuuenti hida* . . . But, as Adams (1907: 105) suggests, it may be a later reduction. Carkeet (1976:53–4) claims that "the absence of *þe* in conjunction with *siþþan* in attested Old English[21] does not at all falsify the claim that *siþþan* can be derived historically from some earlier sequence like *siþ þæm timum þe* . . .". If *siþþan* did indeed derive from such a sequence, it would be possible that phase 3 **siþ þæm þe* occurred early and is by chance not recorded. But Adams (1907:100) has a telling argument against this idea:

> This conjunction [*siŏŏan*] is, according to Sweet, *Student's Dictionary of Anglo-Saxon*, compounded of the preposition *siŏ* and its object in the dative. Others regard *ŏan* as being the instrumental in a phrase of comparison. I incline to the latter view; for *ŏæm* does not become *ŏan* until the later period of OE, and we have *siŏŏan* in the earliest texts.

Small (1930:389 fn. 21) lends his support to Adams:

> There is one other OE subordinate conjunction that is based upon a comparative adverb, and which in form and function exactly parallels the construction that is the subject of this article [viz. *þon ma þe*], namely, *siþ þan þe*, 'after', 'since'. The form, *siþ*, is a comparative meaning 'later', having developed regularly from Com. Gmc. **siþiz* (= Go. *seiþs*). The semantic base of the conjunction, *since*, is therefore 'later than that, namely, . . .' In ME this conjunction survived in the abbreviated form, *siþþen, sithen*, with later addition of the adverbial *-es*: *sithenes, sins, since*.

But in my opinion this particular formulation founders on the absence of **siþþan þe*.

31. Since *æfter* is not used alone as a conjunction in OE, the possibility of a direct development from adverb to conjunction does not arise. So we must postulate at least phase 3 and/or phase 4 if we assume that the formulae with *æfter* are in origin prepositional. It is interesting however to wonder why Small did not include these formulae along with those introduced by *ær* and *siþ* in view of the fact that *æfter* is in origin a comparative; see *OED*, s. v. *after* adv. and prep.

32. As far as I am aware, *mid* is not used as an adverb except in contexts where it can be taken as a postposition or separable prefix; see **OES*. Thus the possibility of a direct development is ruled out on two grounds – *mid*

was not an adverb and did not become a conjunction. The direct development must also be ruled out in the case of *for*, which is not used as an adverb in OE. So phase 3 and/or phase 4 are necessarily involved here. But in view of the many examples with tmesis, phase 2 may also be a necessary step, as van Dam (1957:45–6) suggests. It is, however, possible that phases 2 and 3 arose independently and that phase 2 is an alternative development rather than an essential one.

33. I must now attempt an answer to the question whether a phase with *þe* – phase 2 or 3 – is essential. Carkeet (1976:53) says that "there might be no [such] stage" and I have already given good reasons for believing that it did not occur with *siþþan*. The rarity of *oð þæt þe* and *oð þætte* (Adams 1907: 129–30) is suggestive rather than conclusive. Whether *forþæm . . . þe* and/or *for þæm þe* must have been part of their particular chain is a more difficult question. Despite Carkeet (1976:56), it does seem "plausible" to me to suggest either that *for þæm* prep. phrase developed into *forþæm (. . .) þe* conjunction – in other words, that at least one of phase 2 and phase 3 was essential – and that *þe* was subsequently dropped to give *for þæm* conjunction or that *for þæm* prep. phrase > adverb developed directly into a conjunction, the two being distinguished first by intonation and later by the addition of *þe* to the latter. (On this, cf. 41.) The same sequences – without phase 2 – might be postulated for those temporal conjunctions which are recorded both with and without *þe*, e. g. *æfter/ær/mid þæm (þe)*.[22] Anyone in doubt about the plausibility of the first development should see Adams 1907:119–20, van Dam 1957:xi-xii, 45–6, and 50, and Mann 1942:92–3.

34. Geoghegan (1975:42) writes:

> Also like *þæt*, *þe* could be deleted, so that *for þæm þe* 'because' on the surface looked like *for þæm* 'therefore'. This did not necessarily pose a problem for the speakers of Old English though because the accompanying change in word order in situations where *for þæm* meant 'because' offers support for the presence of *þe* at some point in the derivation, deleted after it had triggered the change in word order.

I am not sure that element order can be taken as proof that a phase involving *þe* was essential. Even if we concede – as in fact we cannot do – that the prepositional formulae always had the order S. V. when they were adverbs in initial position and S. ... V. when they were conjunctions,[23] it is not demonstrable that *þe* had to be present to produce this pattern. The change in intonation postulated in 33 could have been responsible. The same would be true of words like *þær*, *þa*, and *þonne*, where the conjunction regularly has S. (...) V. and the adverb V. S.; see Campbell 1970:93—6 and **OES*.

35. At the moment, then, while I am unable to demonstrate that a phase with *þe* was essential in the development of any of the prepositional formulae, I believe it to be likely in some, especially in the formulae involving *for*.[24] But, as I have shown, I also believe that there are some formulae, e. g. *oð þæt* and *siþþan*, in which it is unlikely to have played a part. I do not think that this is surprising. The marked variation in the patterns set out in the table in 24 does not suggest to me that there was any instinct — or whatever you care to call it — which demanded a uniform development.

36. Let us now turn to the non-prepositional conjunctions. Here I find it impossible to accept Carkeet's proposed derivations as in any way plausible. Even if we are willing to agree that *timan* in **æfter þæm timan þe* is a "semantically empty" noun which "can easily become an optional item" (Carkeet 1976:53), the same cannot be true of *geares* in *ÆCHom* i. 80.30 *þæs geares þe*, the only recorded formula with the genitive *þæs* expressing time and one which cannot be fitted into most of the uses of *þæs þe* conjunction 'when, after' — of which Carkeet sees it as the source. Why do we not find **þære þe* from such expressions as *Or* 226.17 *þære ilcan niht þe* or *þy þe* 'when' from *ChronE* 79.26 (885) *þy geare þe* or *þæs þe* 'where' from *Bede* 4.17 *þæs mynstres ðe*? I concede neither the need for, nor the likelihood of, the development postulated by Carkeet. See further **OES*.

37. His suggested sequence (1976:53) *þa hwile þe* > *þa þe* > *þa* and > *þe* is even more strange. It seems to me as unlikely as postulating the sequence *se mann þe* > *seþe* > *se* and > *þe*. It is significant that Carkeet is unable to produce any combination of *þone* + noun of time + *þe* to enable him to get to *þonne* (1976: 53) and has to fall back on the prepositional formula *on þære stowe þe* to produce *þær* (1976:54). His statement (1976:60, n. 5) that "henceforth we will be calling these oblique case NP's [*þa hwile þe* and the like] 'adverbial PP's', even though the preposition may not be present on the surface" seems to me an obvious but unsuccessful attempt to sweep very real difficulties under the carpet. If he is right, why is *þær* not **on þære þe*? What preposition does he imagine once appeared before *þæs geares þe* or before "*þæs dæges* 'on that day' " (1976:60, n. 5)? That confusion between what I regard as the original *þe* and the intruding *þæt* also occurred in non-prepositional temporal formulae is clear from late occurrences of *þa hwile þ* (see Adams 1907:86) — another pattern which Carkeet's theory cannot explain. Carkeet (1976:56) seems to admit that adverbs like *þær*, *þa*, and

þonne, and adverb phrases like *ær þæm* and *for þæm* were in existence before his hypothetical developments began. Indeed, this must be so unless he proposes to derive the adverbs *þær, þa*, and *þonne*, from the conjunctions which have developed from the demonstratives by his complicated process. He says (1976:52) that "almost all OE correlative adverbs are of the same root as the conjunctions with which they occur". In my opinion it is contrary to commonsense to claim that at a time when the adverbs were already in existence, the complicated processes suggested by Carkeet began and ultimately led to the appearance of conjunctions of exactly the same form. It would seem simpler to derive *þa* conjunction direct from *þa* adverb than from *þa hwile þe*. (Whether this necessarily involved an intermediate stage with *þe* is discussed in 41.) *Mutatis mutandis*, this is true of other correlative pairs like *þær* and *þonne* and of at least some of the prepositional formulae. I find it hard to believe that, if dem. *þæt* became conj. *þæt* and dem. *se* became rel. *se*, the adverbs mentioned above could not have developed directly into conjunctions.

38. It also remains a fact that Carkeet cannot really account for conj. *þeah* 'though' by his theory (1976:54) and admits that he cannot explain how *nu* and *swa* became conjunctions (1976:54). The "traditional view" can: they too underwent the direct development explained above. The great merit of the "traditional view" is that it admits the possibility of varying developments within the general thesis that parataxis preceded hypotaxis and is not tied to one particular theory. Some of these variations have just been illustrated. Others are discussed in **OES*; they include *hwonne* and the like, *swa (. . .) þæt, þonne* 'than', *þon ma þe* (here I am in basic agreement with Small, 1930), and *þy læs (þe)*.

39. It is impossible to reach certainty in any of these discussions. The same is true when we consider conjunctions like *butan, gif,* and *nefne. OED* s. v. *but* speaks of the OE adv. and prep. *be-utan, butan* functioning "as a conjunction, with uses arising immediately out of the prepositional sense" – I suppose this means a transition from *butan* (prep. + dat.) as in *ÆCHom* i. 8.26 *he is ende butan ælcere geendunge* to *butan* (prep. or conj.?) as in *ÆCHom* i. 174.4 *Hit is awriten on ðære ealdan æ, þæt nan man ne sceal hine gebiddan to nanum deofelgylde, ne to nanum ðinge, buton to Gode anum* to *butan* (conj., since it is followed by the nominative and not by the dative), as in *ÆCHom* i. 174.6 *forðon ðe nan gesceaft nys wyrðe þæs wurðmyntes, buton se ana seðe Scyppend is ealra ðinga* – and observes s. v. *if* that "it has not been certainly determined whether the conj. is thus derived from the sb. [represented by OHG *iba* (f), ON *if, ef* (n), and ON *ifi, efi* (m),

'doubt'], or the sb. founded on the conj." But I do not think that anything in their development runs contrary to the general thesis that parataxis preceded hypotaxis.

40. The notion of a direct transition from adverb to conjunction can account not only for the conjunctions discussed above but also for *swilce, þanon, þenden, þider, þy,* and so on.[25] In my opinion, this change of function was not necessarily dependent, as Carkeet (passim) seems to imply, on the presence of two adverbs in successive simple sentences which could be taken as correlatives – as in *Or* 14.26 *Nu hæbbe we scortlice gesæd ymbe Asia londgemæro; nu wille we ymbe Europe londgemære areccean* . . . and

Beo 126	Đa wæs on uhtan	mid ærdæge
	Grendles guðcræft	gumum undyrne;
	þa wæs æfter wiste	wop up ahafen,
	micel morgensweg –	

but could also have taken place when only one adverb was present – as in *Or* 58.21 *Nu we witan þæt ure Dryhten us gesceop; we witon eac þæt he ure reccend is* and

Beo 917		Đa wæs morgenleoht
	scofen ond scynded.	Eode scealc monig
	swiðhicgende	to sele þam hean
	searowundor seon;	

see Mitchell 1978a: 393–4.

41. Was an intermediate stage with *þe* essential in the development of any of the non-prepositional conjunctions discussed above? Some of them, e. g. *nu, swa, swilce,* and *þenden,* are never recorded with *þe;* see Kivimaa 1966: 165–6. So it seems reasonable to suggest that for them the answer is 'No'. *Þe* is not common with *þa* or *þonne* (see 4 and **OES*) and I have the feeling that *þe* is a later addition. But Adams (1907:23–4 and 25–6) is inclined to believe that the forms with *þe* were earlier and essential. *Þanon þe* and *þider þe* (both of which are restricted to the prose) are perhaps more common than *þær þe,* which occurs occasionally in early prose and twice in the poetry; see **OES*. But even when full statistics are available, the matter will probably remain one of opinion. Thus the comparative figures for *þeah (þe)* in the poetry (necessarily approximate) are *þeah* 135 and *þeah þe* 76 (Mitchell, *DPhil*, pp. 837–8). Burnham did not provide figures for the prose, but she observes (1911:14) that "in view of the adverbial use of *ðeah* . . . and in view of the obviously connective character of *ðe,* we may well infer the evolution:

ðeah adv. > *ðeah ðe* > *ðeah* conj.; though we cannot detect the process". Here, as with *þa*, *þonne*, *þær*, *þider*, and *þanon*, there are however two possibilities: viz. first, that envisaged by Burnham for *þeah*, in which the stage with *þe* was essential, and second, that in which *þeah* adverb became *þeah* conj. (as I believe happened with *nu* and *swa*) and that *þeah þe* represents a later stage. It is clear that various ways of distinguishing adverbs from conjunctions evolved to supplement or (in writing) replace intonation. Element order has been discussed in 34. Ælfric frequently distinguished *þa (. . .) þa* conj. from *þa* adv. and, according to Burnham (1911:13), "shows a very marked preference for *ðeah ðe* — desiring, perhaps, from his strong teaching instinct, to distinguish clearly between the adverb and the conjunction". It is possible that this exploitation of what I insist on calling "the subordinating particle *þe*" began in Alfredian times, though it has to be admitted that it was not carried out systematically in the early texts and, in the case of *þy læs*, had not even begun; see **OES*. There is room for more work here; see Kivimaa 1966:166–7. Meanwhile — although it is only fair to say that I have derived stimulus from Carkeet's article — I am content to leave it to the reader to judge whether his theory or the "traditional view" as expounded above involves the more "highly improbable" changes (Carkeet 1976:56).

Notes

1. The abbreviations for the names of texts are those proposed by Christopher Ball, Angus Cameron and myself (1975 and 1979). The quotations from OE texts are taken from the editions specified there with one exception: *Beowulf (Beo)* is quoted from Klaeber's Third Edition.
The name of the author serves as a cue-title for the works cited in the References.
For my own writings, I use the following:
D. Phil: 'Subordinate Clauses in Old English Poetry', unpublished D. Phil. dissertation, University of Oxford, 1959.
Guide: *A Guide to Old English*, Second Edition (Oxford: Basil Blackwell; New York: Barnes and Noble, 1968).
*OES: *Old English Syntax*, forthcoming
Some reference to this as an authority for statements which space does not permit me to elaborate here is unavoidable. It is hoped that the two-volume work will appear in 1984.
2. Erickson's paper elsewhere makes what seem to me unwarranted assumptions about OE "stylistic marking . . . the singling out of some sentence element or elements for emphasis" (1978:99). He appears to accept a distinction made by Bacquet. But see Mitchell (1966:86–97). Erickson (1978:99–100) offers six OE sentences in which he says we have "stylistic marking" — four from the prose, two from the poetry. Not one of these can be accepted unhesitatingly. The two verse examples Wan 12 and Wan 55 are typical of OE, a language in which the pattern 'That he was there is certainly true' has not yet been recorded, and in both of them initial *þæt* may be an unaccented element before the first stress; Kuhn's Law is relevant here. The influence of

Kuhn's Law too may account for initial *wæs* in *Or* 34.25. *Wæs se hunger on þæs cyninges dagum*; see Campbell 1970:93–5. But note the Latin *Fuit itaque haec fames magna sub rege Aegyptiorum. Æfter þæm wordum* in *Or* 244.2 could be resumptive rather than emphatic. Since *ac* as a clause introducer tends to produce the element order S. . . . V., *hit* could occupy an unemphatic position before the stressed subject *God* in *Or* 184.7. The most plausible example – especially out of context – is *Or* 18.10 *þa deor hi hataδ hranas*. But it could be read as resumptive in the somewhat clumsy passage in which it occurs. In my opinion, no general principle emerges from *this collection of examples*.

I disagree with what is said by O'Neil (1977:205, lines 18–30): *nu* and *þæs* can introduce causal clauses; for equivalents of *þenden* see 6 and 7; and on the functions of *þe*, see 19.

3. See the *Additional comment* which precedes the References.
4. His attempt to assign a Latin origin here and his failure to note the infrequency of the correlative use of the *for* formula are not the only ways in which Carkeet reveals an unfamiliarity with OE. Despite what he says on 1976:46, neither the repetition of a subject nor "inversion of subjects and verb phrases" nor the splitting of "conjoined subjects" is "normally" restricted to sentences containing an adjective clause. Documentation must await **OES*. Carkeet's statements number (1) and (2) at the bottom of 1976:49 and the top of p. 52 seem to assume what they help to "prove".
5. Another possible variation in the development proposed by Carkeet is hinted at by Adams (1907:32) when he speaks of the difficulty of deciding whether groups like *on þam daege þe* introduce "real temporal" clauses or remain combinations of a prepositional phrase + an adjective clause. He makes the same point about groups like *þaes geares þe* (1907:35). I take up the question whether stage 3 is essential in 33–5.
6. Why not from *on þære hwile þe* as well, since it sometimes means 'when'?
7. On syntactical archaisms in *BlHom* see further Benham (1908:216, 228, 229 and 230).
8. Shearin (1903:58) also uses the word "relative": "Old English *δæt* . . . [was] originally a pronominal neuter accusative used with relative force as a conjunction". But, as I note above, he defined the clause introduced by *þæt* as a substantive clause (1903:63).
9. The idea that *þe* is a particle which is not used solely in clauses which we think of as adjective clauses did not originate with me. For example, *OED* speaks of "† The, *particle (conj., adv.), relative pron.*"*OED* and I are not alone; see Kivimaa (1966: 160). But other writers, including Kivimaa, have taken the view that *þe* was in origin a relative; see Kivimaa (1966:160–7), who distinguishes an adverbial relative *þe* from a "pronominal" one (1966:162).
   Geoghegan (1975), who shows some unfamiliarity with Old English, takes a view contrary to that of Carkeet. She speaks of "the Old English subordinating particle *þe*" (1975:31 and 50) and says that "the word *þe* can in no way be considered a pronoun"(1975:43). We can, I believe, safely occupy the middle ground between these two extremes.
10. See his Appendixes I and V. Excluding *oþþæt* and its variants. there are only ten examples: two with *æfter*, one with *fram*, three with *mid*, and four with *to*. They are distributed thus: *Alex* (1), *Chron* 1127 (1), *Lch* iii (1), *LS* 10 *Guthlac* (4), and *Or* (3). The solitary *to* o in *ChronE* 264.13 (1137) is a ME ghost; Clark reads *it δ[at]*.
11. Further on the possibility of interchange of function between *þæt* and *þe*, see Kivimaa (1966:148–67). Her table on p. 161 is of special interest.
12. If Carkeet were to clutch at this straw, he would be in danger of having to eliminate *þa* as a conjunction because, since he derives it from the feminine demonstrative *þa* in *þa hwile þe*, it too could have been eliminated by analogy with *þonne*, which he derives from *þone* + noun of time + relative pronoun *þe*. See Carkeet (1976:53).
13. Neither Adams's collections nor mine are complete.

14. Adams (1907:126) records this in *Matt (WSCp)* 26. 29, along with *HomU* 24. 123.5 *ær þam byre þe*. I note *ÆCHom* i. 134.17 *ær ðam fyrste þe*.
15. Adams (1907:113–14 and 214) records five such examples, along with three with *of þære tide þe*.
16. Adams (1907:114) records two examples, viz. *ÆLS* 31. 1193 *of þam dæge æfre þe* and WHom 18. 78 *of þam timan ærest þe*.
17. Adams (1907:93) records this in *Or* 180.21, but implies that there are more. He also notes (p. 87) *on þære hwile þe* in *Or* 130.9 and *Or* 170.12.
18. I find this in *ÆCHom* i. 512.6. Further on causal conjunctions of this sort see **OES*. They too are rare.
19. Examples like *Bede* 46.19 ⁊ *hi wæron sona deade swa hi eorðan gesohtan* are not relevant here.
20. My figures for the poetry are *ær* 68, *ærþon/ðon* (written as one word or two) 21, *ærþan* 1, *ær þan* 1, *ærðæm* 1, *ær ðam* 1, *ær þy* 1, and *ærðon ðe* 1. For the prose, Adams (1907:215–20) lists the following (I give his spellings): *ær* 258, *ær ær* 3, *ær . . . ær* 37; *ær ðam ðe* 124, *ær ðan ðe* 133 (over 100 of these from Ælfric), *ær ðon ðe* 43 (less than one-third from 'Alfredian' texts); *ær ðam* 14, *ær ðan* 2, *ær ðon* 36; and *ær ðonne* 4.
21. As Adams (1907:104–5) says, the two possible examples of *siþþan . . . þe* are dubious. *Siþþan þe* has not been recorded.
22. The fact that both *ær* and *ærþon* appear as conjunctions in the earliest poetry and that *ærðon ðe* occurs only in *Jud* 252 may merely be due to the demands of metre, since formulae with *þe* occur in the earliest prose. So the fact that conj. *ærþon* is found in the earliest poetry does not show that it cannot be from *ærþon þe* – despite Möllmer 1937:81–2. For other theories about the development of these conjunctions see 26–9.
23. On this see Andrew (1940, §40), Campbell (1970:93–6), and **OES*.
24. Baker (1980:25–6 and 33) makes the valid point that conjunctions such as *for þæm (þe)* and *þeah (þe)* are subject to scribal omission or insertion of *þe* and are therefore not "very stable". This makes our task harder.
25. Erickson's presumption (1978:111) that '*þy . . .* is presumably a variation on *for þy* where the distinctive case marker (instrumental) allows the deletion of the preposition" is unlikely and unnecessary. It is the essence of an inflected language that a case form alone, without a preposition, can mark a distinction. The conjunctional use of *þy (þe)* could have arisen from an adverbial use of *þy* 'for that, by that', pointing either forward or back. Similarly, in my opinion, *þæs (þe)* 'when, after, since, because, as' is of separate origin from *to þæs (þe)* 'to the extent that, so that'. As far as I know, they remain distinct in OE. Erickson speaks of *to þæs* 'when'. Neither Adams nor I record any examples.

Additional comment

Erickson's discussion of causal clauses seems to me to be based on false premises. He says (Erickson 1978:100–1) that *forþon* "typically appears either in single main clauses, connecting the clause causally with what has preceded" – *forþon* means 'Thus, Therefore' – "or at the beginning of what is normally classed as a dependent clause, which provides justification for what has been stated in the preceding main clause" – *forþon (þe)* means 'because." But for him *BlHom* 3.10 *forþon heo fæmne cende, forðon heo wæs fæmne geeacnod* exemplifies "an unusual syntactic construction where a main clause adverbial (*forðon*) appears to anticipate the homophonous subordinator introducing a following subordinate clause". The exact reference of the word "unusual", which he repeats at p. 100, is not clear to me. But, for the reasons which follow, I do not find it appropriate.

Causal clauses frequently follow their principal clause in MnE, although correlation is employed less frequently than in OE; see my *Guide*, §§150–3. It is certainly not 'unusual' for a causal clause to follow its principal clause in OE; see the passage from van Dam (1957:82) referred to by Erickson (1978:111, n. 16) and his own comment there that "the normal expectation would be that a causal clause should belong to what precedes rather than to what follows".

Although Erickson (1978:111) refers to both van Dam and to my *Guide*, §169, he fails to take note of what van Dam and I have to say about correlative *forþon . . . forþon (þe)* 'for that [reason I am about to explain] . . . because'. In particular, he overlooks van Dam's comments (1957:79–80) about correlative causal clauses in early OE prose, which include this: "In approx. 70 % of the cases in which correlated groups were noted, the causal clause follows the main clause, which, indeed, is its *usual* position" [my italics]. Compare here my "67.7 per cent" (10), which is based on Liggins's figures for OE prose of all periods.

Erickson (1978:101) cites Andrew's comment (1940:32–3) that "when the principal sentence comes first, *forðon (forði)* shows that stress is laid not so much on the action predicated by the verb as on the reason for it . . ." but goes on: "Andrew's explanation accounts for the stress relationships between the two parts of the sentence, but it fails to give any justification for why the construction has the particular form that it has." I cannot see the need for more 'justification' than Andrew gives. Since the vast majority of OE causal clauses follow their principal clause, it is scarcely surprising that this is true when the two clauses are linked by correlatives. Erickson's argument that, because we have the sequence subordinate clause principal clause with *Gif . . . þonne* 'If . . . then', there is something 'unusual' in the sequence *Forþon . . . forþon (þe)* 'For that [reason I am about to explain] . . . because', overlooks the fact that in OE "the normal expectation would be that a causal clause should belong to what precedes rather than to what follows" (Erickson, 1978:111, n. 16).

It is true that a table in **OES* will show that only some six per cent of the causal sentences noted by Liggins involve correlation. So the construction described by Erickson as 'unusual' can perhaps be said to be uncommon. But this is not (it seems to me) what he meant. The fact that it is less common does not in my opinion make it less 'typically' Old English than the constructions in which *forþon (þe)* appears alone meaning either 'therefore' or 'because'. It merely reflects the fact that, of the three constructions under discussion, it was by its very nature the one most likely to be used least often.

References

Adams, A.
    1907   *The syntax of the temporal clause in Old English prose* (New York: Holt).
Andrew, S. O.
    1940   *Syntax and style in Old English* (Cambridge: CUP).
    1948   *Postscript on Beowulf* (Cambridge: CUP).
Bacquet, P.
    1962   *La structure de la phrase verbale à l'époque alfrédienne* (Paris: Les Belles Lettres).
Baker, P. S.
    1980   "The Old English Canon of Byrhtferth of Ramsey", *Speculum* 55:22–37.

Ball, C. – A. Cameron – B. Mitchell
1975   "Short titles of Old English texts", *ASE* 4:207–221;
1979   "Short titles of Old English texts", *ASE* 8:331–333.
Behaghel, O.
1928   *Deutsche Syntax*, Band III (Heidelberg: Winter).
Behre, F.
1934   *The subjunctive in Old English poetry* (Göteborg: Elander).
Benham, A. R.
1908   "The clause of result in Old English prose", *Anglia* 31:197–255.
Braunmüller, K.
1978   "Remarks on the formation of conjunctions in Germanic languages", *NJL* 1:99–120.
Burnham, J. M.
1911   *Concessive constructions in Old English prose* (New York: Holt).
Campbell, A.
1970   "Verse influences in Old English prose", *Philological essays studies in Old and Middle English language and literature in honour of Herbert Dean Meritt*, edited by James L. Rosier (The Hague: Mouton), 93–98.
Carkeet, D.
1976   "Old English correlatives: an exercise in internal syntactic reconstruction", *Glossa* 10:44–63.
van Dam, J.
1957   *The causal clause and causal prepositions in early Old English prose* (Groningen: Wolters).
Erickson, J.
1978 for   "Subordinator topicalization in Old English", *Archivum Linguisticum*
1977   8:99–111.
Geoghegan, S. G.
1975   "Relative clauses in Old, Middle, and New English", *Ohio State University working papers in linguistics* 18:30–71.
Johnsen, O.
1916   "More notes on Old English adverbs and conjunctions of time", *Anglia* 39:101–120.
Joly, A.
1967   *Negation and the comparative particle in English* (Québec: Les Presses de l'Université Laval)
Kivimaa, K.
1966   þe *and* þat *as clause-connectives in Early Middle English with especial consideration of the emergence of the pleonastic* þat (Helsinki: Societas Scientiarum Fennica).
Liggins, E. M.
1955   *The expression of causal relationship in Old English prose* (London: University of London, unpublished Ph. D. dissertation).
Mann, G.
1942   "Die Entstehung von nebensatzeinleitenden Konjunktionen im Englischen", *Archiv* 180:86–93.
Mitchell, B.
1966   Review of Bacquet, 'P. Bacquet *La Structure de la Phrase Verbale à l'Époque Alfrédienne*', *NM* 67:86–97.
1969   "Five Notes on Old English Syntax", *NM* 70:70–84.
1978a   "Old English oð þæt adverb ?", *NQ* 223:390–4.
1978b   "Prepositions, adverbs, prepositional adverbs, postpositions, separable prefixes, or inseparable prefixes, in Old English?", *NM* 79:240–57.

forthcoming "The dangers of disguise: Old English texts in modern punctuation",
 RES 31:385–413.
Möllmer, H.
 1937 *Konjunktionen und Modus im Temporalsatz des Altenglischen* (Breslau:
 Priebatsch).
O'Neil, W.
 1977 "Clause adjunction in Old English", *Linguistics* 17:199–211.
Quirk, R.
 1954 *The concessive relation in Old English poetry* (New Haven: Yale University
 Press).
Shearin, H. G.
 1903 *The expression of purpose in Old English prose* (New York: Holt).
Small, G. W.
 1924 *The comparison of inequality* (Baltimore: University Press).
 1926 "The syntax of *the* with the comparative", *MLN* 41:300–13.
 1930 "The syntax of *the* and OE. *þon ma þe*", *PMLA* 45:368–91.

MARIANNE MITHUN

Levels of linguistic structure and the rate of change

Until recently, most studies of language change have necessarily treated one area of language at a time: phonology, grammar, or the lexicon.[1] At present, however, we know relatively little about relationships between changes in different areas of language structure. We do know, for example, that certain types of vocabulary are more resistent to replacement than others, that certain morphological configurations are more susceptible to analogic leveling than others, and that certain combinations of syntactic rules are more stable than others, but we have as yet had little opportunity to compare functionally equivalent changes in different parts of the grammar.

Just such an opportunity exists among the Northern Iroquoian languages. Two sets of mechanisms interact pervasively throughout all levels of structure in all of these languages. One set reflects primarily the speaker's evaluation of the hearer's knowledge. Speakers exploit these mechanisms primarily to arrange information in such a way as to be most easily and readily understood. The other set, sometimes termed evidential, reflects the speaker's evaluation of his/her own knowledge, i.e., the reliability of the information communicated. Both types of distinctions, the assessment of hearers' and speakers' knowledge, are marked by syntactic, morphological, predicate, and particle devices in all of the Northern Iroquoian languages.

As can be seen from the diagram below, the nature of the genetic relationships among the Northern Iroquoian languages permits the reconstruction of five different stages in the development of the family: Proto-Northern-Iroquoian (PNI), Proto-Lake-Iroquoian (PLI), Proto-Inner-Iroquois (PII), proto-Western-Iroquois (PWI), and Proto-Eastern-Iroquois (PEI).[2]

In the sections which follow, the development of grammatical and lexical epistemological devices will be traced through the five reconstructable stages, then compared.

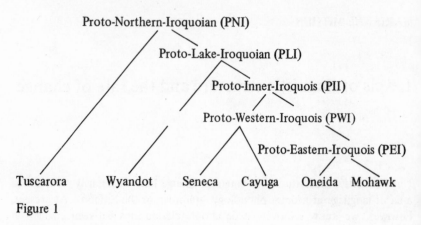

Figure 1

1 Syntactic devices

In all of the Northern Iroquoian languages, grammatical relations within clauses are generally clear from pronominal prefixes on verbs. Word order is therefore not needed to distinguish case relationships. Instead, ordering can be exploited to arrange constituents according to their importance to the discourse. Constituents can be highlighted, or put into focus, by being moved to the beginning of sentences. Given or predictable information, that which the hearer is expected to share, and/or be less interested in, appears later. All of the languages share this device of ordering constituents according to the knowledge expected in the hearer, as can be seen in the sample sentences throughout the paper.³ Note that such focus fronting often yields arrangements quite unlike English, where a more usual ordering is given-new.

(1) Cayuga: *Katsihwá' kiso:s . . To: ti'*
             hammer I-seek   How then

             nika:nǫ:'   *ne' katsihwa'*?
             so-it-is-expensive   the hammer

             'I am looking for a hammer . . . How
             much does this hammer cost?'

Another syntactic feature common to all of the Northern Iroquoian languages is an optional process of nominalization. All of the languages contain three morphological types of words: verbs, nouns, and particles. Morphological form does not necessarily match syntactic function, however. Since all verbs contain pronouns referring to their agents and/or patients, they can function as complete clauses in themselves. They can also function as syntactically nominal constituents. The syntactic status of formal verbs is thus often superficially ambiguous.

    (2) Seneca: *Honǫtka'te'   hatikęhtsishǫ́'ǫ*
    they-were numerous they-were-old

    ta: ne:' kę:s
    and it was used-to

    nę:kę: wa'ǫkhí:ǫnyę' hǫnǫtsyo:wi:
    this they-taught-us   they-told

    ne:nǫto:wæ:s kyǫ'ǫ   waęnǫtówætha'.
    the they-hunt it-was-said they-went-hunting
    'A lot of old people would explain to us what it was like when the hunters would go out hunting'.

All of the modern languages contain an optional device for overtly marking nominalization, although, interestingly, the device is not cognate in all of them. In Tuscarora, an optional emphatic particle *ha'* can precede such clauses, marking them as arguments rather than predicates.

    (3) Tuscarora: *Nγθwa'nvnurʋ́hkhwek* ha'
    so-will-you-all-one another-love

    neθwa'nvtyákhv'
    you-all-each-other-are-married
    'Love one another, you married couples'.

In the other languages, an optional particle **ne* (> Wyandot (*n*)*de*) can mark clauses as dependent arguements.

    (4) Wyandot: *E:jará'se'*   *enǫ̀:ndaǫ́' skát*
    they two are cousins their home one the-he-

    deyǫ̀mihae'   ka'dé'ca'
    devours humans and-the-other
    de:jará'se'.
    the-they-are cousins.
    'Two cousins, one of whom was a cannibal, lived together'.

    (5) Mohawk: *Yah tha'tyesehshakowvnará:ni* ne
    not   did-he-to-them-word-speak the

rawvhé:yu   rutv́:ro
he-is-dead   they-are-friends
'Not a word did the dead man speak to his
friends'.

(6) Oneida: *Na'akoyá:tawv'*   n
so-it-to-her-body-   the

kheyv́ha.
I-to-her-parent-am happened
'It happened to my daughter'.

(7) Cayuga: *Shaǫwati'nya:'kę́'s*   ne'   *hǫwátǐfre:'*
they-them-escaped-again the   they-them-chased
'they escaped from those who were chasing
them'.

(8) S.   *Ta: o:nę saęnǫhtę:ti'*   ne   *hęnǫto:wæ:s.*
and then back-they-went the   they-hunt
'Then the hunters went home'.

Although the Tuscarora particle is not cognate to those in the Lake languages, its nominalizing function is the same. The arrangement of propositions into predicates and arguments, that is, the choice of what is to be the main predication and what is to be nominal (usually identificational) constituents, is determined in large part by the speaker's assessment of the shared knowledge of the hearer. New information is generally put into a main clause, while identifying or understood information is more likely to be presupposed and thus subordinate. Note the differences between the pairs of sentences below.

3a. You who are married should love one another.
3b. You who should love one another are married.

5a. The dead man did not say a word to his friends.
5b. The man who did not say a word to his friends was dead.

7a. They were chasing those who escaped.
7b. They escaped from those who were chasing them.

8a. The ones who were hunting went home.
8b. The ones who went home were hunting.

The languages exploit their nominalization processes in essentially the same way throughout the family.

A third syntactic device which enters into effective arrangement of information is that of noun incorporation, whereby a noun stem referring to the semantic patient of a predication may occur with a verb.[4]

(9) T.   *nekaku'*tikvh*kà:rv́hrv*
         ne+ka+ku+́ tikvh-*karvhr-v*
         DU-pl-them- *mind* — bother +STATIVE
         'they were depressed'

(10) W.   *ahàⁿǫmajá'kǫ'*
         *a+ha+*nǫma+*ja'k+ǫ'*
         PAST+he/it+ head + strike +PUNCTUAL
         'he hit her on the *head'*

(11) M.   *tyote*nyeht*ó:ru*
         *t+yo+te+*nyeht*+or+u*
         there+it+self+*snow*+cover+STATIVE
         'it was snow covered'

12) Oe.   *loya'takéhte'*
         *lo+*ya'*t+ʉ+keht+e'*
         he+ *body* +∅+ carry over the shoulders
         +STATIVE
         'he was carrying a corpse over his shoulders'

(13) C.   *w'ęnikʉa:ní:yo:t*
         *w+ę'*nikah+*ʉ+niyo:t*
         it+ *hoop* +∅+ hang
         'the hoop hangs there'

(14) S.   *o'thatiyeǫyen*
         *o'+t+ha+ti+*ye+ǫye+*ht*
         PAST+DU+masc+pl+ *bag* + slam +CAUSATIVE
         'they slammed the bags down'

The languages all share this device, although idiosyncratic restrictions on specific lexical items vary slightly from language to language. Some verbs must incorporate, some cannot, and others appear both ways. Some noun stems appear only incorporated, others never, and others both ways. Certain combinations yield unpredictable idiomatic meanings. Where there is a choice, however, the choice is governed, again, by the individual importance of the noun stem to the discourse. Focussed noun stems appear independently, unincorporated.

The Cayuga speaker opened a telephone conversation with the following statement.

(15) C.   *Ní: ké: thóne:'   ǫkahtǫ́:' ne'*
            say then you-know I-lost-have the

            akétkw'ęta'.
            my-wallet
            'Say, you know, I've lost my wallet'.

He closed it, after much discussion of the circumstances surrounding the mishap and possible solutions, with the request:

(16) C.   *Kyę́:kwa' ki'kyę:' ęka:she:ké'   sǫká:'a,*
            if   just   you-will-see-them someone

            ękasheho:wí'   shę ǫketkwęahto:'.
            you-will-tell-them how I-wallet-lost-have
            'Anyway, if you should see anyone, tell them
            that I have lost my wallet'.

The speaker's estimation of the knowledge and interest of the hearer, that is, of what is new, unexpected, and pertinent, is the main factor in incorporation. The process was clearly present in Proto-Northern Iroquoian and has changed very little in the modern languages.

Focus fronting, nominalization, and noun incorporation are, thus, three syntactic devices, shared by all of the Northern Iroquoian languages, which are triggered primarily by the speaker's estimation of the knowledge of the hearer. New and/or controversial information is put into focus by equivalent means in each of the languages, and given, agreed upon, or predictable information is backgrounded by other equivalent devices across the languages.

2   Morphological devices

All of the Northern Iroquoian languages share a cognate tense-aspect system. Two of the tenses in particular distinguish the speaker's certainty about a predication: the future and the optative. The future, PNI *ę (T. v, W. e, M., Oe. v) indicates that an event is certain to happen. The optative, PNI *a:/ *aǫ, indicates that an event might, should, could, or would occur. Compare the pairs of verbs below.

(17) T.   *vhratshù:ri'* 'he will eat'
         ahratshù:ri' 'he might/should/would eat'

(18) W.   *e:ja:jú'* 'he will kill you'
         aujàjú' 'he might kill you'

(19) M.   *vkatá:wv* 'I will take a bath'
                        a:katá:wv 'I should take a bath'

(20) Oe.   *vkatolátha'* 'I'll go hunting'
                        a:katolátha' 'I should/might/would go hunting'

(21) C.   *ękatekhǫ́:ni'* 'I will eat'
                        a:kate:khǫ́:ni' 'I should/might/would eat'

(22) S.   *ękhnǫhkwe'tsi:sakha'* 'I will go look for
                                        medicine'
                        a:khnǫhkwá'ysisa:kha' 'I should go look for
                                          medicine'

The future prefix also occurs with habitual events which are considered predictable because they happen so often or because they are the effect of a cause.

(23) T.   *vθhráhrku' àrv́h vkheyatkáhri'θ*
                        he-will-go-back if I-will-tell-him
                        'he will go home if I tell him'

(24) W.   *tehstǫt ndayémęh eyǫ̀:nǫ́ht wá'ja'*
                        you-will-return the-mine will-I-thee-give a-little
                        'If you go back, I will give you a little of mine'.

(25) M.   *Awvhniserakwé:ku vkutihú:take'*
                        all-day   they-will-eat-grass

                        ná:ku ne kwá:ti
                        under the side
                        'All day long (the cows) would graze on the east side'.

(26) M.   *Kvkwité'stsi' akhsótha vyahè:ru,*
                        early-spring my-grandmother she-will-say

                        "O:nv yeyóhe' a:hyati'tarakarhátho'".
                      now it carries   they should turn over clay
                        'In the early spring, my grandmother would say,
                        "It is now time to plow" '.

(27) M.   *Toka' vtéhsya'ke' sanúhkwis*
                        if   you-will-cut your-hair

> *nó:nv   oráhkwase'*
> the-when   moon-is-new
>
> *svha yohsnó:re'   vsewatehyá:ru'*
> more it-is-fast   it-will-grow-back
> 'If you cut your hair during the new moon,
> it will grow back much faster'.

(28) C. *Kanǫhskǫ́ ękhné:sek   kyę:kwa' ęyustáǫtih*
house-in we-will-stay if   it-will-rain
'We'll stay indoors if it rains'.

(29) S. *Ka:nyo' ęwokatkanǫní 'he't o:nę́ wa:é*
when   I will be rich   now before

ęké'sehta:ni:nǫ'
I-will-car-buy
'When I'm rich, I'll buy a car'.

The optative is used with irrealis constructions.

(30) T. *Arvh arvkwatsú'khu:k aknvhsá:tya't.*
if   I-would-be-rich I-would-house-buy
'If I were rich, I would buy a house'.

(31) M. *Toka' a:yetshiwvnará:'u, kati'   nú:wa'*
if   you-would-address- perhaps maybe
a-word-to-her-have

a:yetshiyatera'swá:wi'
she-might-have-given-you-good-luck
'If you had spoken to her, she might have
given you good luck'.

(32) C. *A:kate:khǫ:ní' kyę:kwa'*
I-would-eat   if

a:yǫkéhwanǫ:t
she-would-offer-it-to-me
'I would eat if she offered me something'.

(33) S. *A:kǫyęnowó's neh á:ke'ha:ste:'*
I-would-help-you when I-would-be-strong
'I would help you if I were strong'.

Another morpheme which reflects the speaker's knowledge about the truth of a predication is the contrastive prefix, PNI *th-*. It can indicate that an event or state is unexpected or contrary to normal procedure or fact. It replaces the optative in irrealis states.

(34) T.   tha*ka'nyè:rvh* a*yuté:nv:'*
I-would-do-so it-would-be-sunny
'I wish it were sunny'.

(35) C.   *I:' a:kẹfrọ:ni' kyẹ:kwá'* tha*'ak'yatahní:yọh*
I I-would-build if   my-body-were strong
'I would build it if I were strong'.

(36) S.   Tha*'a:katkọ:ni' a:ke'séhta:ni:nọ' næ:*
I-were-rich   I-would-car-buy emphatic
'If I were rich, I would buy a car'.

(37) M.   (What are we going to do about this hole in the pipe?)
Th*vkkohò:roke'*
'I'll *just* plug it up. (contrary to all you might expect me to go through, like calling a plumber or replacing the pipe)'

Th*vyókka'*
'It will *just* leak . (contrary to your expectation that it will be fixed)'

The contrastive is also used to hedge the degree of truth. In Cayuga, it cooccurs with the diminutive *-hah/-'ah* in this function.

(38) M.   *tsi ne* thi*ha'shátse'* 'he is sort of strong'
(*ra'shátste'* 'he is strong')

(39) M.   *tsi ne* thi*hahnv́:yes* 'he is sort of tall'
(*rahnv́:yes* 'he is tall')

(40) C.   thi*haks'ako:wá*hah 'he is sort of handsome'
(*haksa'kó:wah* 'he is handsome')

(41) C.   thi*ha'sasté:'*ah 'he is sort of strong'
(*ha'sáste'* 'he is strong')

(42) C.   thi*hawayẹhọ́:*hah 'he is sort of good at it'
(*hawáyẹhọ:* 'he knows how')

(43) C.   *họkwe'tɟetkẹ́:'*ah 'he is a little mean'
(*họkwe'tɟetkẹ'* 'he is mean')

(44) C.   *ohsno:we:ʾá ǫtríhoʾta:*   'she works sort of fast'
                  (*ohsnóːweʾ* 'it is fast')

(45) S.   *kakęːtʾah ʾit is* whitish'
                  (*kakęːęt* 'it is white')

(46) S.   *hotyanǫtʾah* 'he is kind of funny'
                  (*hotyaːnǫt* 'he is funny')

Finally, the plural suffix -*shǫːʾǫ,* which is cognate within the Inner languages, is exploited in one of them, Cayuga, to hedge numbers.

(47) C.   *Haːwakyǫhǫːk .kyęː' ǫ hneː' tekrǫʾshǫːʾǫh*
                  I-would-arrive it-is I-guess eight-ish
                  'I guess I would get there by around eight
                  o'clock'.
                  (*tekrǫʾ* 'eight')

The morphological markers which qualify the knowledge of speaker and hearer have remained stable in form and relatively stable in function across all of the languages. The future and optative tenses, which indicate the degree of certainty on the part of the speaker about coming events, have remained unchanged. The contrastive, which indicates the relation of the information to the hearer's knowledge and thus expectation, has also remained unchanged. Mohawk and Cayuga further exploit the contrastive as a qualifier of the degree of truth of the predication. Another Proto-Northern-Iroquoian morpheme has been extended in the Western languages to qualify the degree of truth: Cayuga and Seneca use the diminutive as a hedge, 'a little'. Finally the pluralizer, cognate among the Inner languages, has been extended semantically in Cayuga to hedge numbers.

3 Predicates

By far the richest sets of evidential devices are lexical. One group of lexical evidentials consists of overt predicates which specify the source or reliability of the information communicated.

(48) T.   Kyèːrih *úːʾy vθakaʾθv̀ːyaʾt*
                  I-think other I-will-hang-again
                  'I think I'll hang another drape'.

(49) T.   V'nehúːʾnv' *héːsnv:* wehrvhv̀ːweh
                  it-proved-it this it-is-true

> *hè:ní:kv: tyuyè:rvh*
> that   so-it-happened
> 'This proved that it had truly happened'.

(50) W. *Tiwà'yé:'a' a'yèhąǫ'*
much-likely she-said

de hudú'mę' daę' nǫ: yawáhtsih
the his-mother perhaps it-is-good
'His mother said that it was likely that it would
be good'.

(51) W. *Yatù:yýh   tę' unǫ'tó:'ndi'*
it-is-certain   not to-her-is-it-long
'She certainly did not find it long'.

(52) W. *Iréhe'   ca'awá'tat   da:anǫ:nę'*
he-thought they-were-same the-bear
'He thought he was a bear'.

(53) W. *Kari:wáyǫht   esǫmá'turè:ha'*
matter-is-sure   he-will-find-us
'He is sure to find us'.

(54) W. *Ude'kwa' kahę trǫ^{n}di' ahukwe^{n}dihahtę'*
very much there greatly she-him-scolded
'She scolded him very badly'.

(55) M. *Khè:rv kv   tá:'a   tehayv́kya'ks*
I-think this maybe he-is-chopping-wood
'I believe he is out chopping wood'.

(56) M. *Tkayé:ri   nahò:tv   we'è:ru*
it-is-correct what   she-said
'What she said is correct'.

(57) M. *Tsi ní:yot tsi   yukhihró:ri   yáh*
so so-it-is that we-are-told not

úhka' ne wv́:tu
anyone the ever

teyotú:'u a:yakothró:ri' ne   oh
it-happens they-would-tell the what

nihaya'tò:tv'
so-his-kind of body-is
'And so, we are told, no one was ever able to
tell what kind of body he had'.

(58) M.   *Wé:ne' ki' wáhe' tsi vske'sà:ni'*
it-is-evident   of course that you-will-beat-me
'It is evident that you will get the best of me'.

(59) Oe.   *Wé:ne' wi: ni: ji'   vske'shv́:hni*
it-is-evident   very so   you-will-beat-me
'it is evident that you will get the best of me'.

(60) Oe.   . . . wahv́:lu *ne'n   ohkwa:lí*
he-said   the-one bear

. . . *"kwáh olihwi:yó:*
just thing-good

ji'   yukhi'shvnyú:ne'"
that they-will-beat-us
' . . . The bear said, "It is a sure thing that we're
going to get cleaned up".

(61) Oe.   *Ta: tkaye:lí: thó   yahá:yuhwe*
and it-is-true   there there-she-arrived
'And, in fact, she did arrive there'.

(62) C.   *Kǫ:tǫ́ 'ǫ hne:' takwáe kye'trǫ'*
I-mean inf this this-side there-she-lives
'I suppose it is the lady over there'.

(63) C.   *Ne:' ne' tkaí:'   nę:kyę honǫ́htǫ'*
this the it-is-correct this   he-knows
'It is true that he knows'.

(64) C.   Akęnǫtǫ́ *shę honíhęh*
I-know   how he-borrowed-it
'I know that he borrowed it'.

(65) C.   Tka:kǫ́:t *hne:' tęthá:yę'*
it-is-certain this he-will-bring-it-back
'He is certain to bring it back'.

(66) C.   Thihę:né:' *tshǫ́: n'ethó ǫ   niyáw'ęǫh*
they-assume just the   there so-it-fell

'They just assume that this is the way it happened'.

(67) C.   *Tekekⱥné:*   a:yé:'   *onahtokȩhȩkyé'*
I-am-looking   it-seems   they-are-growing

kayȩ́thwahshǫ'
they are planted
'I see your plants are growing'.

(68) C.   Hȩna:tǫ́   *honíhȩh*
they-say   he-borrowed-it
'They say he borrowed it'.

(69) S.   Okwe:nyǫ́:   *nǽ'kwá*   *e:yænǫ́tkȩ:ni'*
it-is-possible   just-really   I-will-beat-him
'I just might beat him'.

(70) S.   Ha:wȩ́: *ȩthe'*
he-said   he-will-come
'He said he would come'.

(71) S.   Akenǫhtó' *ȩthe'*
I-know   he-will-come
'I know he is coming'.

A majority of these evidential predicates ('think', 'say', 'tell', 'certain', 'true', etc.) are cognate across the languages. As throughout the rest of the lexicon, the most closely related languages share the most cognates, the most distantly related languages slightly fewer.

4 Particles

Another type of lexical device which can modify the speaker's and hearer's knowledge consists of particles, morphologically unanalyzable words usually consisting of only one or two syllables. Such particles can incicate the speaker's assessment of the reliability of information presented, marking its source (hearsay, appearance, deduction), its probability (certain, probable, possible), its degree of truth or appropriateness (exactly, sort of, slightly). They can also indicate its correspondence or contrast with the hearer's expectations (indeed, you know, sure enough, surprisingly).

In Tuscarora discourse, such particles are conspicuously rarer than in the other languages. Some indicate the probability of an event, others the degree of truth. Some serve both functions.

(72) T.   Kwetí′ v′nyuríhvh   atsi′áh
            maybe it-will-boil   a-little

(73) T.   arv́h   tetsíhv′   ahsíhrv:′   25
            about   maybe   you-would-say   25
            tiwaristá:kye:
            so-metal-numbers
            'Perhaps you'd say about 25 minutes'.

(74) T.   arv́h   hv́′tahk   tiwakwv′strá:kye:
            about   four   so-pounds-number
            'About four pounds'.

(75) T.   Arv́h   há′ne′   úhya′k   tiwakwv′tsrá:kye:
            about   about   six   so-pounds-number
            tiwahwísne′
            so-it-is-heavy
            'It weighs around about six pounds'.

(76) T.   *Yahwahv́′ni′*   u′tésnakw ha′   kv́
            there-she-threw-is   behind   the   right
            thru′na′níhrv′
            there-he-was-standing
            'She threw it right back where he was standing'.

Wyandot also seems to have had relatively few such particles in comparison with the rest of the family. Since all of our knowledge comes from texts recorded longhand, a process which often serves to eliminate particles as speakers slow down and transcribers speed up, we can only speculate on their frequency. An experiential particle *a:yę′* indicates that the source of the evidence is observation.

(77) W.   *de ya^nguyomę*   à:yę́′   uskú′taye′
            the it-was-bloody   it-appears   its-head-on
            'His head looked bloody'.

(78) W.   *A′atijúh*   tehatáka   dà:yé′ dahstę′
            not-it-looks   he-talks   as if   that
            ta′úh   hu′diyọ:rą́cę′
            something   'his-mind-is-troubled'
            'He remained silent. He seemed to be troubled'.

(79) W.   *Nę ha:rǫt* *d*a:*yę́* *du tà:yuwáskaǫ'te*
now he-hears it-seems that someone-is-walking
'It sounds as if someone is walking around'.

An inferential particle *nǫ*: indicates that the source of information is a deduction from the evidence available.

(80) W.   (some hunters have just found some large,
unusual claw marks on a tree.)
Tą'ą nǫ: *te'yawahsti de: kwaka:jatǫ'*
no   maybe not-is-it-safe that we-trouble-it
'Maybe we had better not disturb it'.

(81) W.   (A friend has just informed the speaker that
horses do not hatch, but rather bring forth
their young.)
Nę tu i'*hsę ne* nǫ: *ahaye'diyǫha'tę'*
now there sure the inf he-cheated-me
'Then he must have cheated me! (when I bought
the horse egg)'

Other particles indicate the probability of the proposition.

(82) W.   *Nę ská'   etsikwaté'wah*
now surely we-will-again-run-away
'Now, surely, must we run away again'.

(83) W.   *Eja:ju'*   skamę̀ntáh
he-will-kill-you must-be

ska'mętaá:ska *eja:jú'*
must-be-sure he-will-kill-you
'He is sure to kill you'.

(84) W.   *Nę* hí   *a'yatenę^{n}díhcę   a:rijú'*
now surely I-have-accomplished I-killed-it
'Now I have surely killed it'.

Some indicate the degree to which the assertion is true or category assignment appropriate.

(85) W.   *Dę* kwa *wá'tanęsti*
greatly she-is-small-and-pretty
'She is really small and pretty'.

(86) W.   *Daę' kahę' keahtíhcahs*
            that   really   I-seek-it
            'That is really what I am looking for'.

(87) W.   *Kę $e^n dí'$ ahátǫmę'*
            very   much   he-is-tired
            'He is very tired'.

(88) W.   *$Cę^n$dar nę' ahteugadi' te'skę'nę...*
            really   now not-long   not-it-lapses
            'Very little time passed . . . . . '

(89) W.   *Nę kuskę:nę'   eha'de:ega'de'*
            now almost he/her overtakes
            'He almost caught her'.

Another particle contrasts the proposition with expectation.

(90) W.   *Haká'tra' ihcę́'   hu'diyǫ̀:ruwá:nę*
            he-ventures it-is-so his-mind-is-great

Mohawk speakers tend to make more frequent use of evidential particles
in discourse than Tuscarora and Wyandot speakers, although there is considerable variation among Mohawks themselves. The particles distinguish both
source and reliability of information, which are, of course, closely related.

One frequently occurring particle, both in conversation and in story telling,
is a quotative particle, *yá:kv'*, which indicates that the speaker does not take
full responsibility for the information.

       yá:kv' 'it is said'

(91) M.   *Wa'thohv̀:rehte'*   *yá:kv'*
            he-burst-out-laughing it-is-said

            kí:kv rake'níha
            this   he-is-father-to-me
            'They say my father burst out laughing'.

(92) M.   *Karhá:ku thati'terú:tahkwe'*
            woods-in there-they-used-to-live

            yá:kv' kí:kv' kahwá:tsire'
            it-is-said this   it-family
            'It seems there used to be a family which lived
            in the forest'.

Other particles are inferential. The information communicated is considered a reasonable deduction but not necessarily established fact. In 92, the speaker infers the bridge between remembered events. (Since they are particles, they do not contain pronouns.)

> *ki'ná:'a* 'I guess'

> (93) M.   *Ne kí' ki:kv Ahkwesahshró:nu:*
>   the just this   St.-Regis-resident
>
>   *thé:nv*   ki ná:'a
>   something I-guess
>
>   *yahori'wanù:tohse'*   *autahó:yu'*   *ne*
>   he-asked-for   he-would-give-him   the
>
>   *rahù:tsi*
>   he-is-black
>   'I guess the St. Regis man must have asked the
>   Black fellow to hand him something'.

The inference may be based on observation.

> *ta'/ta:'a* 'I suppose' (I have deduced the possibility)

> (94) M.   *Oskvnú:tu ta'*   *yotohétstu*
>   deer   possibly   it-has-passed
>   'A deer must have passed by here'. (I see tracks.)

> (95) M.   *Khé:rv kv tá:'a   oskvnú:tu o'wà:ru*
>   I believe that possibly deer   meat
>
>   *ýtewake'   vyò:karahwe'*
>   we will eat   it-will-evening-be
>   'I think we must be having venison tonight'.
>   (I smelled it as we walked in.)

> (96) M.   *Khè:rv kv tá:'a   tehayv́kya'ks*
>   I-think this possibly   he-is-chopping-wood
>   'He must be chopping wood'. (He usually chops
>   wood at this hour, and he is not here.)

Other particles indicate the degree of certainty on the part of the speaker.

> *to:ske'* 'truly'

> (97) M.   *Kí:kv oká:ra' nè:ne tó:ske kwáh e' thó*
>   this   it-story which truly   really   there

niyawv́:'v
so-it-happened
'This is a true story'.

(98) M.   *O:nv ni* tó:ske *tsi   tehoti'nikuhrahrí:'u*
now so truly   that their-minds-were-broken
'Now they were truly desperate'.

(99) M.   *Rawé:ras* úhte' *thí:kv ró:ne'*
he-thunders perhaps that   his-wife

wa'etshí:kv'
you-saw-her
'Perhaps you saw the Thunderer's wife'.

(100) M.   *Tá:ni'ts*   úhte'   *tho yá:yv*
might-as-well perhaps there there-she-should-go
'Well, maybe she *should* go'.

toka' 'maybe'

(101) M.   tóka' *yà:ya'k yawv̀:re'*
maybe six   teen

sha'tewakohseriyà:ku
as-I-winters-had-crossed
'When I was about sixteen years old. . . '

(102) M.   Toka' *ó:nv ki'* ne *okú:kwara*
maybe now   just the O Face

shakoyenáhsere'
he-is-going-to-catch-her
'O Face might just catch her'.

tó:wa' 'maybe'

(103) M.   *Tsyahyà:kshera* tó:wa' *vtóhetste' kí:kv*
one-week   maybe it-passed   this
'About one week went by'.

nu:wa' 'maybe'

(104) M.   *Kati'* nù:wa' *a:yetshyatera'swá:wi'*
perhaps maybe she-might-have-given-you-luck
'She might have given you good luck'.

kati' 'perhaps'

(105) M.   *Khè:rv* kati'   *kv*   *nekwá:*
I-think perhaps there side

yà:ke'
I-might-go-there
'I might just as well go over there'.

(106) M.   Kati'   *né*   *wa'è:ru*
perhaps that she-said
'Is that what she said?'

Some emphatic particles indicate greater commitment or certainty. The speaker is willing to take responsibility for greater intensity or precision.

kwah 'really, just, very'

(107) M.   *Ka'nyuhsákta*   *nú:we*   *nvhatikwè:tarv'*
near-the-nose   place   where-they-will-cut

kwáh *se's*
just   then

yá:kv'   *nè:ne*   *a:yohnatirúhthake'*
it-is-said   which   it-would-be-like-rubber
'Near the nose, they say, is a place which is just like rubber'.

(108) M.   Kwáh *í:kv* tsi   *rotiháhes*
really it-is that their-road-is-long
'Their road was truly long'.

ki' emphatic, 'just'

(109) M.   *E'*   *thó*   ki'   *na'á:wv'ne'*
there   just   so-it-happened
'And that is just what happened'.

(110) M.   *Nv*   ki'   *vkahtv́:ti'*
now   just   I-will-go
'Now, I think, I'll just start out'.

Some particles point out the correspondence of the truth with expectation.

(111) M.   *Tó:ske*
'It sure is'. (as response to a tag, such as "It's nice, isn't it")

wáhe'/wáhi' 'really, in fact, sure enough'

(112) M. *O:nv* wáhi' *wa wa'utkáhtho' ne   rawvhé:yu*
          then   in fact she she-saw   the he-is-dead
          'Then in fact she did look at the dead man'.

(113) M. *Ne ken* wáhe' *wa'è:ru'*
          the ?   indeed she-said
          'Is that what she said'?

(114) M. *Nyo:* ki' wáhe' *suke'nikúhrhv*
          gosh in fact I forgot
          'Oh gosh, as a matter of fact, I forgot about it'.

Oneida speakers use largely the same set of evidential particles as Mohawk speakers. The quotative particle is the same. A quotative particle is quite frequent.

(115) Oe. *Okhna'* yakv' *wí:* w *a wa'thatawvli'*,
           and-so   they-say   he-travelled-around
           'And, so they say, he travelled around'.

(116) Oe. *Wahawisakahlv:tú* yákv'   *thikv*
           he-ice-made-hole they-say that

           skvhnáksv;   nv
           one-it-skin-bad now

           yákv'   *thikv ohkwa:lí   tho*
           they-say that bear   there

           yahanitáhsowe
           away-he-put-his-tail
           'He made a hole in the ice, they say that fox did; and they say that bear put his tail in the water'.

(117) Oe. *Khale'* onv́ uhne   *wahv́:lu'* skvhnáksv,
           and   now it-seems he-said   one-it-skin-bad

           "Tutahsanítskwak. . . "
           'jump-up'
           'Finally said the fox, it seems, "jump up now"'.

(118) Oe. *Nv* uhne   *lotnuhtú:tu ka'ikv́*
           now it-seems he-wait   this

> *skvhnáksv*   *kwatokvu*
> one-is-skin-bad   really
>
> *akwai:sátvste'*   *lvtákne*
> it-would-ice-become-thick
> 'And so it seems the fox waited for the ice to
> become really thick'.

Some particles specify the probability of the information.

(119) Oe.   *Ký:tho ki'* uhte   *wi:a:kláthv'*   *kaluta:ke*
            this   just perhaps I-should-climb   tree-on
            'I guess I will climb this tree here'.

(120) Oe.   Ta:t   *núwa'*   *ne: tyoyánle'*
            perhaps maybe that it-is-good
            'Maybe it would be best'.

(121) Oe.   *Nv*   kati'   *vtkatáhsawv'*   *vkahtahkú:ni:*
            now maybe I-will-begin   I-will-shoe-make
            'Now, I guess, I'll start to make some shoes'.

Some particles specify the degree of truth or appropriateness.

(122) Oe.   *Nv*   se'   kwah   *kv'*   *nihv:náhse:*
            now just   really   so   they-are-large
            'Now they are quite big'.

(123) Oe.   Kwah *ok*   *tho*   *thahaláthv'*
            just   only   there   he-climbed-there
            'He just climbed right up'.

(124) Oe.   *Yah thau:tú:* ki' *wi: a:yako:tá:we'*
            not   possible just   could-she-go-to-sleep
            'She just could not go to sleep'.

(125) Oe.   *Yáh* se'   *tha:yekwe:ní:*
            not   just   could-she-tell
            'She just could not tell'.

Some particles indicate that not only is the statement true, but either in
accord with expectation or in contrast.

(126) Oe.   to:kýske'
            'yes, that is true' (in response to a tag, such as
            'isn't it'?)

(127) Oe.   *I:* wahe
'Yes, in fact I *am*'.

(128) Oe.   *Nv kwi wa' thoya:tahkwe'*
now just he-body-picked-up
vhatnehwahni:nu:te' ki*'*   wahe
he-will-skin-sell   just   infact
'And sure enough, he did pick him up to sell his hide'.

(129) Oe.   Yats   *tho wá:lawe'*
sure-enough there he-arrived
'Sure enough, he arrived there'.

Cayuga speakers draw from an extremely rich repertoire of evidential particles. A quotative particle distinguishes hearsay, as in Mohawk and Oneida, although it is not cognate.

akę' 'they-say'

(130) C.   *Akǫnohyá'k*   akę'
she-got-hurt   it-is-said
'I heard that she got hurt'.

(131) C.   *Thayękya'khǫhá'*   akę'
he-went-to-chop-wood it-is-said
'They say he went to chop wood'.

An experiential particle indicates that one saw, tasted, smelled, etc. the evidence.

a:yę:' 'it appears'

(132) C.   A:yę́:*'*   *wahe' ǫtshǫ́: otǫkǿtǫ́*
it-appears just   seems it-passed
tewáhǫhte:s
two-ears-are-long
'A deer must have just passed by here'. (I see the tracks.)

(133) C.   A:yę́:*'*   *tewahǫhté:s*   *'ǫ*
it-appears two-ears-are-long perhaps
ętwá:wɖa:k
we-will-eat
'We must be having venison for supper'. (I can smell it.)

(134) C.   A:yę́:   *sǫ́só:kha'*
                  it-appears you-limp
                  'You seem to be limping'.

An inferential particle, *'ǫ,* indicates that the information is a tentative conclusion deduced from the evidence available.

(135) C.   *Tętha:yę́:'*   ǫ   *hne:'*
                  he-will-bring-it-back I-guess this
                  'He'll bring it back, I guess'.

(136) C.   *Thę́'* ǫ   *hné:'* *t'eshé:'*
                  not I-guess this not-you-want

                  kaya'thá'   *há:se:'*
                  it-body-sets there-you-would-go
                  'You don't want to go to the movies then, do you'?

(137) C.   *Thihę:né:*   *'tshǫ: n'ethó:*
                  contr-they-think only the-there

                  'ǫ   *niyáw'ęǫh*
                  -guess so-it-fell
                  'They assume that that is how it must have happened'.

Some specify the probability of the proposition.

(138) C.   *Tętha:yę́:'*   *k'ishęh*
                  he-will-bring-it-back perhaps
                  'He might bring it back'.

(139) C.   *Thę́'* *k'ishę́* *hwá'* *t'á:ǫ*
                  not perhaps contr possible
                  taǫthá:yę:'
                  not-he-would-bring-it-back
                  'He might not bring it back'.

(140) C.   *Kyę:kwá'* *hné:'* *hwa'* *tęthá:yę:'*
                  maybe   contr this he-will-bring-it-back
                  'He might bring it back'.

Others indicate the degree to which the proposition is true or category assignment appropriate.

(141) C.　　　　Kwahs *wahe'* tshǫ́:　*akaky'ataháesi'*
　　　　　　　　really　now　only　I-body-wash-finished
　　　　　　　　'I just now finished taking a bath'.

(142) C.　　　　*Thę'* kwáhs *t'eǫkhniwayęnę́t'aǫ'*
　　　　　　　　not　really　we-two-did-not-finish
　　　　　　　　'We didn't quite finish'.

(143) C.　　　　*Thę'* kwáhs ǫ́:we　*t'ekǫyętéi:*
　　　　　　　　not　just　really　not-do-I-know-you
　　　　　　　　'I don't really know you'.

(144) C.　　　　*Thę'* akwáhs *tho　ni:yǫ:*
　　　　　　　　not　really　there so-much

　　　　　　　　t'eakhwistáę'
　　　　　　　　not-do-I-have-money
　　　　　　　　'No, I don't have quite enough money'.

(145) C.　　　　*O:nę́ hne:'* tho:há　hękahé:'
　　　　　　　　now　this　there-dim　there-will-I-take

　　　　　　　　ękyahtę́:ti'
　　　　　　　　we-two-will-leave
　　　　　　　　'It is almost time for us to leave'.

(146) C.　　　　*Tatsihá　kę:s*　tshǫ:
　　　　　　　　short-time　customarily　just

　　　　　　　　i:só'　atkhehtowé:nye:
　　　　　　　　much　I-stir-field
　　　　　　　　'In just a little while I can work up the dirt'
　　　　　　　　(plough).

Some evidentials indicate that the proposition is both true and either in accord with or contrary to expectation.

(147) C.　　　　To:kę́hs *kyę:'　nę:kyę́ a'éyętho'*
　　　　　　　　in-fact　this　this　she-planted
　　　　　　　　'And, in fact, this is what she planted'. (as predicted)

(148) C.　　　　To:kę́hs　*a'akowi:yáęta'*
　　　　　　　　in-fact　she-had-a-baby
　　　　　　　　'And indeed she did have a baby'.

(149) C.   *Aǫsta:ǫtí*   nǫ́ne:'
    it-rained   in-fact
    'It did *too* rain'. (contrary to what you said)'

(150) C.   *Tewakatǫhwętso:ní*   nǫ́ne:'
    I-want
    'I do *too* want some'.

(151) C.   *Thę' kyę:'* nǫ́ne:'   *ní:' kwa'yǫ́' t'é:kę:*
    not   this   you-know I   rabbit   not-is-it
    'I'm no rabbit, you know'. (so stop trying to
    feed me lettuce, as if you thought I were)

(152) C.   *Kenhohfrothá'*   sé'
    I-pile-it-up
    'I *am* piling it up'. (so your command was
    unnecessary)

Seneca speakers exploit a wide variety of evidentials with great frequency
in all types of discourse. A quotative particle indicates that the evidence is
hearsay. It is especially frequent in legends and other tales.

(153) S.   *Sǫ:ká:'* kyǫ'ǫ   *te:niksa'á:*   *hotiya'tahtǫ'ǫ́*
    someone they-say two-children they-are-lost

    so:te'.   *Berrino* kyǫ'ǫ *hiya:sǫh. Chickchick*
    last-night.   they-say their-names

    kyǫ'ǫ   *koksa'ta'shǫ́:'ǫh*
    they-say   her-children
    'I heard that two kids were lost last night.
    Berrino I guess their names were. Must be
    Chickchick's children'. (from a conversation)

(154) S.   *Ta: o:nę́ nœ:* kyǫ'ǫ   *sę nǫ'o:tá' o:nę́*
    and then really they-say 3   so-days then

    kyǫ'ǫ   *wa:ayǫ'*   *né   hǫ:kweh*
    they-say   he-arrived   the   man
    'And then, it seems, after about three days, it
    seems, a man appeared'. (from a legend)

An experiential particle, *a:yẹ:'* indicates that the evidence is appearance.

(155) S.   A:yẹ́:'   te'o:yai   ne   kæ:né'   ahsọh
it-appears it-is-not-ripe   the cherry yet
'The cherries don't look ripe yet'.

It is sometimes used somewhat as a quotative or inferential (not unlike English 'it seems' or 'it appears').

(156) S.   Ta: o:nẹ næ: kyọ'ọ   ne   haksá'tase:'a
and then really they-say the he-is-a-new-child

wæẹ'   kyọ'ọ   a:yẹ:',   "Waeyajẹọskọ:'".
he-said they-say it-seems I-got-the-best-of-him
'Now, then, it seems, the young man said, "I got the best of him" '.

(157) S.   "Tọta:eyọ́'   shọ: a:yẹ́:'   kwa   i:'
I-should-give-   really   it-seems really   us

a:yọkwaya'takéha'
it-should-help-us it-back-to-him
'It looks like it would help us for me to give it back to him'.

The inferential particle *nọ* appears to be cognate to the Wyandot *nọ:*.

(158) S.   Nọ: te'o:yái   ne   kæ:ne'
I-guess not-it-is-ripe   the   cherry
'The cherries must not be ripe' (because the strawberries are still out).

(159) S.   A:yẹ́:'   ni:' i:wí: hotkọ́' nọ:,   æ:htá'k
it-seems I   I-think wizard I-guess too-much

ha'te:yọ́:   hayẹte:ih
different things   he-knows
'He seems to be some kind of a wizard; he knows too much'.

Some particles indicate the degree of precision, truth, or appropriateness.

(160) S.   Næ:'   kwa   hi:kẹ́:   hoyá'tasha:yẹh
just   really   this   his-body-was-slow
'He was really moving very slowly'.

(161) S.   Akwás   *ne' hoh   niyáwę'ǫh*
               really   that   so-it-happened
               'This is how it really happened'.

(162) S.   *"Sę:nǫ shǫ:h" kyǫ'ǫ   waę',   "ta'a:ǫ*
               don't   just   they-say he-said not-could

               a:yǫkhni:nya:k".
               we-two-should-marry
               ' "We certainly cannot get married", he said'.

(163) S.   *"Hętsheyá   shǫ:h"*.
               you-will-take-her-back   just
               ' "You just take her right back" '.

(164) S.   *O:nę   tho:há   ękaniya:yę'*
               now   there-dim   it-will-snow
               'It was about to snow'.

Other evidential particles indicate not only the reliability of statements but also expectation concerning their truth.

(165) S.   *To:kęs   akekwe:nyǫ: ękǫ:kę's*
               it-is-certain   it-is-possible-for-me I-will-find-
               ne   yeksá'ko:wa:h   for-you
               the   she-child-large
               'Yes, I will certainly be able to find a beautiful girl for you' (as you suggested).

(166) S.   *Ta: o:nę nœ: kyǫ'ǫ'   to:kęs*
               and   then   really   they-say it-is-certain

               sa:htę:tí'
               he-went-back

               skęnǫ'ǫ́   kyǫ'ǫ   hatha:ine'
               slowly   they-say   he-follows-the-path
               'Then indeed, he made his way back slowly'.

Due to their brevity, tracing the source of particles can be only highly speculative. A comparison of evidentials across languages, however, indicates that the particles mirror most dramatically the varying degrees of genetic relationship among the languages in the family. Only one particle, the *kv'* of Tuscarora and Wyandot, appears remotely possibly traceable to Proto-Northern-Iroquoian, and in this case the sound correspondence is not regular. ($*k > ∅/\# \_V$ in Wyandot).

A few particles can perhaps be traced to Proto-Lake-Iroquoian: possibly the experiential W. *a:ye'*/S. *a:yę:'*/C. *a:yę:'*, the inferential W. *nǫ:*/S. *nǫ:*, perhaps /C. *ǫ:*/M. (*ki'*) *ná:'a*, the emphatic W., S., C., Oe., M. *kwah*(*s*). Again, the sound correspondences are not regular, since *y > ∅/V _ V and *k > ∅/ # _ wV in Wyandot.

More particles can be attributed to Proto-Inner-Iroquois. Not only the experiential, inferential, and emphatic particles cited above, but also the quotative C. *akę'*/M., Oe. *ya:kv'* and the certainty of expectation S., C. *to:kęhs*/ Oe. *tó:kvske'*/M. *tó:ske'* and S. *wai*/Oe., M. *wáhe'*/*wáhi'*. The Western languages share additionally the qualifiers *tho:ha* and S. *shǫ:*/C. *tshǫ:*. The Eastern languages, the most closely related, share additionally the probability markers *úhte'*, *nú:wa'*, and *kati'* and the precision marker *ki'*. (The cognate marker in Cayuga has developed a slightly different function). Each of the languages does contain unique evidential particles which appear in none of the others, however.

The relatively rapid historical change which yields this distribution of particles in the modern languages can be observed in operation in the modern languages in a number of cases. Different clusters of two or more particles have often taken on various idiomatic senses which vary from one language to the next. Languages with different internal and external sandhi rules show wavering treatment of such clusters. In Cayuga, for example, glottal stops metathesize to the left in all odd-numbered syllables except final ones. A monosyllabic particle like *ki'*, for example, retains its glottal stop word-finally because the first syllable is also the last. When combined with *shę*, however, the particle retains its individual form in slow speech but exhibits metathesis in fast speech: *k'ishęh* 'perhaps'. Speakers are unsure of word boundaries in such clusters, although they tend to feel strong bonds between the elements and favor joining them in writing. Equivalent ambivalent status of incipient clusters is apparent in the other languages as well. In a number of cases, clitic particles such as Cayuga *tshǫ:* ('just') and *ǫ* ('presumably') appear to be becoming ever more closely bound phonologically to the predicates they modify, pointing toward incipient morphologization.

At the same time, all of the languages exhibit synchronic loss of syllables from verbs to form particles and from disyllabic particles to form monosyllabic ones. In some cases speakers are aware of both long and short forms, while in others, speakers are no longer aware of the longer ones. Such a loss can be seen in the set W. *yatù:yę́h* 'it is certain', S. *to:kęs*, C. *tó:kęhs*, Oe. *to:kvske'*, M. *tó:ske* 'in fact', 'indeed'. The Inner languages have lost the pronominal prefix **ka-* (W. *ya-*) and aspect markers from the verb based on the root *-tokę-* 'certain', yielding unanalyzable particles. (The root remains otherwise in *-tokehti* 'holy').

The frequent combination of evidential particles into long strings suggests that they must perform a function beyond simply specifying the degree of reliability of an utterance, which could often be neatly accomplished with a single, well-chosen verb or particle. People credited with reputations as eloquent speakers tend to use more such particles more frequently than less admired speakers. There is enormous speaker variation in the choice and frequency of use of them. Furthermore, the particles seem in some ways to have less salience to speakers. If a speaker slows down for clarity or dictation, or writes out a text longhand, the particles tend to disappear. Teachers tend to omit them when teaching these languages to children or adults whose first language is English. Speakers are almost uniformly at a loss to translate them.

The distribution of these particles in discourse is also quite interesting. As might be expected, they tend to cluster around specific statements which speakers would like to hedge, such as direct quotations or measurements. They tend to occur in very long strings particularly before shifts in topic or around elements of high communicative value to the discourse. Their effect on the rhythm of information transmission is striking; they allow the speaker time to collect thoughts at moments of the greatest choice. In addition to facilitating the performance of the speaker, they contribute to the effectiveness of the communication. They allow the speaker to regulate the flow of information so as to be most easily and readily understood by the hearer. If too many short, highly important units of information were to occur in rapid succession, a hearer might not be able to take them in all at once with their proper force. Strings of particles permit the speaker to arrange important information such that it arrives at proper intervals.

In addition to making it easier for the hearer to take in information, proper rhythm can affect the hearer's willingness to listen. Plunging into a sentence can be considered brusque. The particles can soften the force of a communication. Consider the utterance below.

> (169) Mohawk *Khè:rv kati' kv nekwá: yà:ke'*
> I-think I-might there side there-will-I-go
> 'Well, I might as well go on over there, I think.'

The first two words are optional as far as propositional content goes. Speakers report, however, that if the particle *kati'* were removed, the sentence would indicate disgust and dissatisfaction.

Now in most cases, strings of evidential particles tend to be mixed with deictic particles. The deictic particles occur, in fact, much more frequently than is necessary to keep reference straight. Interestingly, Tuscarora, which exhibits fewer and rarer evidential particles than the other languages, exhibits correspondingly more deictic particles in discourse.

(170) Tuscarora   *U:nv́ha' kayetá:kre', vkwehv̀:weh,* kyè:ní:kv:
                  long-ago they-dwell people-real   this

                            kyè:ní:kv: kv̀:ne' *kwè:ni', kayetá:kre'* hè:ní:kv:
                            this   here   near   they-dwell that

                            nekaku'tikvkà:rv́hrv
                            their-minds-were-down
                            'Long ago, the Indians living near here were de-
                            pressed.'

The deictic particles in all of the languages have the same secondary effect as the evidential particles. They allow the speaker to adjust the flow of information so that the hearer can process it most effectively in terms of the information he or she already possesses.

4 The comparative diachronic behavior of syntax, morphology, predicates, and particles

A comparison of these two, interrelated sets of devices across related languages does, in fact, yield insight into the relative stability of functionally similar mechanisms on different levels of linguistic structure.

One set of devices, triggered by the speaker's assessment of the hearer's knowledge in large part, contains syntactic rules (constitutent ordering, nominalization, and noun incorporation), a morphological marker (the contrastive prefix), and lexical items of low salience, which allow the speaker to regulate the flow of information. These have changed at quite different rates in the Northern Iroquoian languages. While the syntactic rules and the morphological marker have remained stable, the lexical items have not.

The second set of devices, triggered primarily by the speaker's assessment of his or her own knowledge (the reliability of the information presented), exhibit exactly the same pattern. The morphological tense markers which indicate the probability of a proposed event, have remained completely unchanged in all of the languages. This is not surprising, since they are part of a closed, obligatory set. The contrastive prefix has remained formally stable in all of the languages, but has an added hedging function in Mohawk and Cayuga. The diminutive and plural suffixes can be traced to Proto-Inner-Iroquois, but they carry special hedging functions in the Western languages. Lexical evidentials have been much less stable. While many evidential verbs have been retained, such as PNI *-*ihrǫ* 'say' and PNI *-*ehr* 'think', 'believe', many others have been replaced. Evidential particles have been especially volatile. Tuscarora shares almost none with the Lake languages. Wyandot shares few with the Inner languages. Cayuga and Seneca, which are relatively closely related, share perhaps half of their particles. Even their quotatives and inferentials are different. Mohawk and Oneida, which are quite closely related, share most evidentials, although even here there are some differences. The same hierarchy of stability is apparent in this set of devices as in the other. Grammar is more stable than the lexicon. With grammar, syntax is functionally more stable than morphology, and within the lexicon, predicates are more stable than particles.

The resulting hierarchy of stability of functionally comparable but formally different devices in these two interlocking domain is, then, as follows, arranged in order of increasing volatility from left to right.

syntax ⟶ morphology ⟶ predicates ⟶ particles

Notes

1. I am grateful to Wallace Chafe and Hanni Woodbury for many helpful comments on this paper.
2. For clarity, this diagram shows only those languages considered in this paper. Another Five Nations language, Onondaga, is well documented, but, because of its relationship to the other languages, its inclusion here would not contribute to the argument made. Other Northern Iroquoian languages, Susquehannock, Huron, Erie, Wenro, Petun, Neutral, and Nottoway, are not sufficiently well documented to shed light on the issues considered here.
   Wallace Chafe and Michael Foster (1981), have proposed that the actual relationship between Seneca and Cayuga is more complex, as below, involving multiple separations and recontacts.

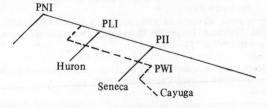

Since this issue does not affect the argument presented here, the representation of the relationship has been schematically simplified.
Wyandot is actually the descendant of a set of probably closely related languages, including dialects of Huron, Petun, and perhaps Neutral, Wenro, and Erie. The exact status of these last languages is unclear, due to a lack of documentation. Schematically, this situation could be represented as follows.

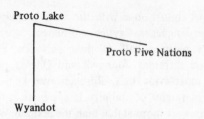

Proto Lake

Proto Five Nations

Wyandot

3. The data throughout the paper are from the following sources. The Tuscarora, abbreviated T., is from the late Edith Jonathan and the late Elton Green, of Lewiston, New York. The Wyandot, (W.), now extinct, is drawn from texts recorded by Marius Barbeau in 1911–1912 and published in 1960. The Mohawk (M.) is from Annette Jacobs, Rita Phillips, Josephine Horne, and Carolee Jacobs, of Caughnawaga, Quebec, and from Mary McDonald of Ahkwesahsne, New York. The Oneida (Oe.) is from Richard Chrisjohn of Red Hook, New York, Winnie Jacobs, of Oneida, New York, Georgina Nicholas of Southwold, Ontario, from a text published by Floyd Lounsbury (1953), and from a text published by Clifford Abbott and Lawrence Johns (1980). The Cayuga (C.) is from Reginald Henry and Jim Skye of Six Nations, Ontario. The Seneca (S.) is from Hazel Thompson, from Steamburg, New York, Sandy Crouse, of Salamanca, New York, and especially Myrtle Peterson, of Steamburg. I am grateful to all of these people who so patiently and generously contributed their time and expertise.

4. For a detailed discussion of the process of noun incorporation, see Hanni Woodbury (1975).

References

Abbott, Clifford – Lawrence Johns
   1980   "Two stories: Oneida", *International journal of American linguistics, Native American text series 4:67–76.*

Barbeau, Marius
   1960   "Huron-Wyandot traditional narratives" National Museum of Canada, Bulletin No. 165, (Ottawa: National Museum of Canada).

Chafe, Wallace – Michael Foster
   1981   "Prehistoric divergences and recontacts between Cayuga, Seneca and the other Northern Iroquoian languages", *International journal of American linguistics*, 47.2:121–143.

Lounsbury, Floyd
   1953   *Oneida verb morphology* (Yale University Publications in Anthropology No. 48), (New Haven: Yale University Press).

Woodbury, Hanni
   1975   "Noun incorporation in Onondaga", *International journal of American linguistics*, 41.1:10–21.

PAMELA MUNRO

Auxiliaries and auxiliarization in Western Muskogean[1]

Most languages seem to display a special syntactic category of "auxiliaries", extra words or parts of words which combine with "main verbs" to create complex verbal phrases more specified as to aspect, modality, and such qualifying elements as negation. Since auxiliaries often have the shape of elements like *have* or *be*, which may be main verbs themselves, sentences with main verbs and auxiliaries often share some structural traits with normal two-clause complement sentences. However, auxiliaries have many syntactic characteristics which set them apart from the matrix verbs of two clause complement sentences, as has frequently been noted for English, and has also been demonstrated for more exotic languages (among recent studies, cf. e.g. Akmajian, Steele, and Wasow 1979; Marchese 1979 (for Kru languages); and Hardy 1979 and Gordon 1980 (for Yuman languages)).

Many surface clauses in the Western Muskogean language Chickasaw are characterized by the presence of one or more of a wide range of auxiliary elements, a number of which can be shown to have derived historically from full verbs through various types of clause reduction. I will show in this paper that current developments in the modern Chickasaw auxiliary system thus parallel remote historical developments argued to have occurred in Muskogean by Haass (1977), and I will demonstrate how the different auxiliary structures in Chickasaw are changing gradually and in individual ways.

An extremely strong hypothesis concerning the origin of auxiliaries, whether in Muskogean or cross-linguistically, would be that all of them derive from full-fledged main verbs. The difficulty of proving such a hypothesis would vary, of course, according to how broad or restricted a definition of "auxiliary" was proposed. Although I find myself in sympathy with the strongest form of this hypothesis, I will propose (for Chickasaw) a relatively broad definition of auxiliary, which will guarantee that the hypothesis cannot be proven correct on the basis of the data available. However, I will show below many ways in which a great number of Chickasaw auxiliary constructions retain relic two-clause behavior, and I will present comparative data from the closely related language Choctaw (the other member of the Western branch of the Muskogean family) which adds further support to the basic claim. Because there are many auxiliaries in Chickasaw, and because auxiliarization begins at different times and occurs at different rates with different source constructions, the Chickasaw data present a wide range of auxiliary construction types, showing a number of different degrees of auxiliarization.

1. Haas (1977) has noted that certain Eastern Muskogean languages preserve relic auxiliaries in various inflectional patterns, some of which resemble synchronically occurring Chickasaw auxiliary structures. For instance, the Koasati paradigm of the verb *chew* in (la) originated as a MAIN VERB plus inflected AUXILIARY string in pre-Koasati, as diagrammed in (lb) (Haass 1977:532):

(1a)	*yaskali*	(1sg.)	(1b)	YAS	KA-li
	yasiska	(2sg.)		YAS-is-KA	
	yaska	(3sg.)		YAS	KA
	yasilka	(1pl.)		YAS-il-KA	
	yasaska	(2pl.)		YAS-as-KA	

Haass argues that this system derives from an old Proto-Muskogean periphrastic conjugation, with KA a reconstructable intransitive auxiliary. The inflections on the auxiliary KA in the pre-Koasati are cognate to those used for inflecting main verbs with active subjects in Chickasaw, such as *ishko* 'drink', in (2):[2]

(2)	*ishko-li*	'I drink'
	ish-ishko	'you drink'
	ishko	'he drinks', 'they drink'
	(k)il-ishko	'we drink'
	hash-ishko	'you (pl.) drink'

The first-person singular active affix is the only suffixed agreement marker in this system. These inflectional markers are not "pronominal" in the sense that they substitute for omitted independent pronouns; they appear in agreement with the person and number of the (semantic) subject (independent pronouns are used only rarely, generally in emphatic contexts). (The "active" subject agreement markers used in (2) are one of three sets of morphological affixes which can indicate agreement with the syntactic subject of a Chickasaw verb — cf. Munro and Gordon, forthcoming.)

So far, the Koasati example suggests that auxiliaries rather than main verbs are inflected. But Haas argues that the neat pattern in (1) has been reanalyzed by Koasati speakers as follows, with the newly perceived inflections again in lower case:

(3) YASKA-*li*
YAS -*iska*
YASKA
YAS -*ilka*
YAS -*aska*

The completion of the reanalysis is shown by the fact that the inflections in (3) may be used on any Koasati verb ending in *k* plus a vowel, such as 'drink', in (4):

(4) ISKO-*li*
IS -*iska*
ISKO
IS -*ilka*
IS -*aska*

There are a number of current Chickasaw auxiliaries which participate in paradigmatic alternations like those Haas describes for Koasati, despite the fact that simple conjugation of Chickasaw main verbs, as in (2), is what Haas calls "direct" (1977:528) or non-periphrastic.

Given third-person forms with $\emptyset$ subject marking, as in (5a), where MAIN VERB precedes AUXILIARY, there are three possible conjugational patterns that might occur in those forms which need to be marked for non-third-person subjects, as outlined in (5b-d):

(5a)   MAIN VERB   AUXILIARY
        (third-person pattern)
b)   PM – MAIN VERB   AUXILIARY
        (non-third-person patterns)
c)   MAIN VERB   PM – AUXILIARY
d)   PM – MAIN VERB   PM – AUXILIARY

Thus, if person markers (represented as prefixed PM's here, which I intend to represent the suffixed 1sg. -*li* as well) are to be applied to the string in (5a), they might logically show up on the main verb only, the auxiliary only (as in pre-Koasati's periphrastic pattern), or on both (in (5d), the two PM's have the same referent). Chickasaw displays all three auxiliary patterns in (5b-d) — but as I will argue in section 3.2 below, (5d) should not properly be considered an auxiliary configuration, since strings in this pattern lack other auxiliary characteristics.

As a working definition of "auxiliary" (at this point, for Chickasaw only), I will say that an auxiliary element is one which follows a main lexical verb and which is not perceived as having a different subject from that main verb.

(Note that in the third person-marking pattern above, (5d), the question of whether these two elements have the same subject is scarcely in doubt, since both elements are explicitly marked for the same subject. This means that the (5d) pattern is more like an ordinary two-clause complement construction than like a verb plus auxiliary phrase.) In addition, auxiliaries occur in "fixed constructions" − in particular, the order of the main verb and the auxiliary (whether they are separate words or not) never varies, and nothing other than morphological affixes of various sorts may be inserted between a main verb and following auxiliary. There are no such restrictions on other two-clause constructions in Chickasaw, so it is these features which distinguish auxiliary pattern (5d) from other such constructions.

The requirement that auxiliaries be perceived as having the same subjects as the main verbs which precede them means that one additional process must logically precede auxiliarization. Many − perhaps most − auxiliary elements logically take a clause (a fact or occurrence, if you will) as their subject. The logical form of the negation of some statement like 'I will go', for example, might be something like NOT (I-will-go) or 'It is not the case that I will go'. A verbal negative is a likely candidate for auxiliarization, but before such an auxiliary candidate can begin the auxiliarization process, a restructuring must occur such that the speaker perceives the subject of the auxiliary candidate to be the same as that of the main verb, often, but not always with an accompanying change in the syntax of the verb-plus-auxiliary candidate construction. (I discuss this pre-auxiliarization process of "subject copying" in some detail in Munro 1976.) The question of the same subject relationship which must hold between main verbs and their auxiliaries is related to syntactic issues involving the switch-reference morphology of Chickasaw to which I will return in section 3 below.

2. Chickasaw has a large number of different types of auxiliary constructions ranging semantically from tense/aspect and modal elements to degree "adverbials" and elements indicating speaker attitude. Syntactically, these elements range from suffixes, which seem hardly worth considering as auxiliaries at all (clearly, these occur in the most fixed of constructions), to verb plus inflected auxiliary constructions like those of pre-Koasati. Several syntactic features help to subclassify the set of Chickasaw auxiliaries, and to demonstrate how they illustrate different degrees of auxiliarization.

2.1 I recognize two groups of suffixal auxiliaries in Chickasaw. In the first group are +a'chi (irrealis), +aa'ni (modal), +aõ'si 'almost', and +tok (recent past). The second group includes #o (negative), #a'hibii'ka (potential),[3] #banka 'from the first', and #ttook (remote past). These auxiliary suffixes are cited with initial + or # boundaries according to the phonological effect they have on preceding elements. Suffixes joined to a verb by a + boundary do not impede the operation of a rhythmic rule by which the vowel of every second light syllable is lengthened (as indicated here with the macron):

> (6a) *halīli-lī-tok*
>   touch-1sI-past   'I touched it'
>
> b) *chi-hālilī-li-tok*
>   2sII-touch-1sI-past   'I touched you'
>
> (7a) *halīl-a'chi*
>   touch-irr   'He will touch it'
>
> b) *halīli-l-a'chi*
>   touch-1sI-irr   'I will touch it'
>
> c) *chi-hālilī-l-a'chi*
>   2sII-touch-1sI-irr   'I will touch you'

In (6b) and (7c) pronominal objects are marked on the verb with prefixes – the same set of prefixes also is used in Chickasaw to specify the subjects of verbs which may be broadly characterized as non-active, as in

> (8) *chi-chokma*
>   2sII-good   'You are good'

(cf. Munro and Gordon, forthcoming). Affixes from the first ("active") set are glossed here as 'I', while affixes from the second ("patient") set are glossed as 'II'.

In contrast to the situation with the + suffixes, those separated from the verb by # cause the gemination of any preceding single consonant which follows an odd-numbered light syllable:

> (9a) *halīli-ttook*
>   touch-rem   'He touched it (long ago)'
>
> b) *halīli-lī-ttook*
>   touch-1sI-rem   'I touched it (long ago)'
>
> c) *chi-hālili-lī-ttook*
>   2sII-touch-1sI-rem   'I touched you (long ago)'
>
> (10a) *halīl-a'hibü'ka*
>   touch-pot   'He can touch it'
>
> b) *halīli-l-a'hibü'ka*
>   touch-1sI-pot   'I can touch it'

All these suffixes are shown to be part of the same phonological word as the main verb by the obligatory deletion of any preceding vowel, and by other phonological rules which do not operate across word boundaries.[4] Another feature all these auxiliary suffixes have in common is their behavior after a negated main verb.

When a Chickasaw verb is negated, one of a special set of negative person markers substitutes for the usual I (active) person marker.[5] Also, in verbs which end in a single consonant plus a vowel, a glottal stop (') appears before this consonant in the negative:

> (11) *ak-hali'l-o*
>   1sN-touch-neg   'I'm not touching it'

When an auxiliary suffix[6] follows a negative expression like (11), the negative augment *ki* appears after negative *o*:

> (12) *ak-hali'l-o-ki-tok*
>   1sN-touch-neg-aug-past 'I didn't touch it'
>
> (13) *ak-hali'l-o-k-a'chi*
>   1sN-touch-neg-aug-irr   'I won't touch it'
>
> (14) *ak-hali'l-o-ki-ttook*
>   1sN-touch-neg-aug-rem 'I didn't touch it (long ago)'
>
> (15) *ik-ayo'b-o-k-a'hibii'ka*[7]
>   3sN-good-neg-aug-pot   'He can be bad'

Another auxiliary suffix, +*chayni*, which shows that the speaker was not aware of the performance of some action at the time of its occurrance, must always be preceded by +*tok* or #*ttook*:

> (16a) *holiss-ã ã-honkopa-tok-chayni*
>   book-obl 1sIII-steal-past-evid 'Someone stole a book from me'
>
>   b) *sa-nos-tok-chayni*
>   1sII-sleep-past-evid   'I went to sleep without knowing it'
>
>   c) *ishi-li-ttook-chayni*
>   take-1sI-rem-evid   'I took it (long ago) by accident'

((16a) shows one use of the Chickasaw "dative" prefixes (glossed III) — like the I and II affixes, these may also be used to show agreement with the syntactic subject of certain verbs (Munro and Gordon, forthcoming). The phonological form of the nasalized III prefixes varies with the following sound.) Essentially, then, +*chayni* shares the phonological features of the preceding suffix.

2.2 Several other types of auxiliary elements are also separated from the preceding main verb by #, but show more formal independence from that word than do the suffixes just considered.

Examples of this group include auxiliaries like #*biiyi'ka* 'all the time' and #*billi'ya* 'always' (and variants of these), which are often used with a preceding main verb inflected for what we may call iterative aspect. For instance, corresponding to *impa* 'eat [intransitive]' is the iterative form

      (17) *ihimpa-li-biiyi'ka*
           eat=itr-1sI-all=the=time 'I eat all the time'

Two other such auxiliary elements are #*hchaa* and #*finna*, each of which is subject to fairly severe selectional restrictions:

      (18) *pisa-li-hchaa-tok*
           see-1sI-perf-past   'I have seen it'

      (19) *chaaha-finna ki'yo*
           tall-too   not   'He's not too tall'

#*hchaa* (perfect) must always be followed by some past element, while #*finna* 'too' must always be negated. (The independent or periphrastic negative word *ki'yo* seen in (19) is, of course, related to the negative augment *ki*.) None of the verbs in this group requires the augment after a preceding negative verb:

      (20) *ak-pi's-o-hchaa-tok*
           1sN-see-neg-perf-past   'I haven't seen it'

I know of no phonological rules other than gemination which operate between the main verb and an auxiliary element like #*finna* or #*hchaa*.

As (20) shows, auxiliary suffixes of the first group (section 2.1) above may be attached to the last element of any verbal phrase, whether or not that element is a lexical main verb.[8]

An additional piece of evidence for the independence of #*finna ki'yo* is that this auxiliary element — unlike the others discussed here — may also show direct negation, as in

      (21) *chaaha ik-finn-o*[9]
           tall   3N-too-neg   'He's not too tall'

Here there is a definite word boundary between the two elements, since nei-

ther of the two contiguous vowels deletes (and *ik-finn-o* has no other phonological effects on the preceding word). My Chickasaw teacher is quite willing
to pronounce *ik-finn-o* in isolation, although it is apparently still hard for her
to gloss this element. Note though that none of the other auxiliary elements
considered so far may appear as separate words in alternative constructions.

An important fact about *ik-finn-o* is that it does not inflect for person.
(21) does not show this, because the verb *chaaha* 'tall' in that sentence has an
unmarked third-person II subject. However, (22) shows that the form of this
auxiliary does not change even with a marked I subject, as with the verb *hopoo*
'jealous':

> (22) *hopoo-li*   *ik-finn-o*
>   jealous-1sI   3N-too-neg 'I'm not too jealous'

2.3 Several other auxiliaries are phonologically separate words which follow
the inflected verb. One of these, *mina* (habitual) is clearly somewhat more
closely bound to the preceding verb than are the others to be discussed in the
next section, because it does require the augment *ki* on a preceding negated
verb, as (23b) shows:

> (23a) *yamm-akō aa-ishko   min-a'chi*
>   that-con   loc-drink   hab-irr
>   'She will (always) drink from that one'
>
> b) *ik-ayopp-o-ki   mina-ttook*
>   3N-happy-neg-aug hab-rem   'She used to be unhappy'

However, *mina* is a separate word, because it neither causes the gemination of
the *k* of *-ki* in (23b) nor has its *i* rhythmically lengthened following the single
final light syllable in (23a).[10]

2.4 Most of the uninflected auxiliaries which directly follow main verbs as
separate words, however, do not take the *-ki* augment following a negative.
These auxiliaries include *binka* 'each of two', *ma'polla* 'really'. *chommi/
chohmi* 'kind of', and the independent negative *ki'yo*. Of all these, only *ki'yo*
is acceptable uttered in isolation (it usually means 'no' or 'it's not so'). Here
are a few examples:

> (24) *sa-ssikopa chommi*
>   1sII-mean kind=of   'I'm kind of mean'
>
> (25) *i-hollo-li   ma'polla*
>   3III-love-1sI really   'I really love him'

(26) *ik-im-iksh-o   binka*
    3N-3III-exist-neg each=2 'They don't each have one'

(26) gives another example of the use of a III ("dative") prefix, here showing agreement with the subject.

Perhaps because of the fact that nothing is ever prefixed to auxiliaries of this group, some of them are being incorporated onto the preceding verb with only an intervening # boundary. This process seems to happen most often with *ma'polla*:

(27) *losa ma'polla / loša-ma'polla*
    black really   black-really 'It's really black'

2.5 The independent negative *ki'yo* and one other normally uninflected auxiliary, *salami* 'too much', occur in a slightly different construction, with the main verb obligatorily followed by the suffix #'. In this construction (in contrast to that described in 2.4) *ki'yo* is used to mean 'never':

(28a) *ishko-'   ki'yo*
     drink-nom not   'He never drinks'

  b) *ishko-li-'   ky'yo*
     drink-1sI-nom not   'I never drink'

(29a) *ishko-'   salami*
     drink-nom too=much 'He drinks too much'

  b) *ishko-li-'   salami*
     drink-1sI-nom too=much 'I drink too much'

  c) *ak-ishk-o-'   salami*
     1sN-drink-neg-nom too=much
     'I drink too little' (i.e., 'I don't=drink too much')

As (29c) shows, no *ki* augment follows a negated verb before #'.

The normal use of the suffix #' is as a nominalizer, forming deverbal nouns like those in (30).

(30a) *ishko-'*
     drink-nom 'drink (noun)'

  b) *hilha-'*
     dance-nom 'dance (noun)', 'dancer'

Like *#finna* (section2.2), *salami* can be inflected for negation:

(31a) *impa-'   ik-sala'm-o*
     eat-nom 3N-too=much-neg
     'He doesn't eat too much' (i.e., 'He doesn't eat=too=much')

  b) *impa-li-'   ik-sala'm-o*
     eat-1sI-nom 3N-too=much-neg 'I don't eat too much'

Unlike *#finna*, however (perhaps because it is always an independent word), *salami* can take personal negative prefixes. The more common way to say (31b), in fact, is as in (32):

(32) *impa-'   ak-sala'm-o*
     eat-nom 1sN-too=much-neg 'I don't eat too much'

  salami, then, is the auxiliary most like an independent verb of those we have examined so far, since it may inflect for the person of its subject. However, since this inflection is restricted to the negative, *salami* is still in a separate syntactic category. No lexical main verb inflects for a personal subject only in the negative.

2.6 The case of *#finna* (section 2.2), which has one alternant linked to the preceding verb by #, and another (negated) which is a separate word, and that of *salami* (section 2.5), which may inflect for a personal subject, parallel the case of two other auxiliaries, *taha* and *tahli*. Both of these are used to indicate a completed or totally effected aspectual reading, with *taha* selected for verbs whose subjects are marked with affixes from the II and III sets, and *tahli* used with verbs whose subjects are marked with I affixes.[11] In contrast with the other auxiliaries discussed so far, both of these may be used as independent verbs, *taha* meaning 'be all gone' and *tahli* meaning 'finish' or 'complete'. When used independently, both take personal inflections, *taha* marking its subject with II affixes and *tahli* with I.

(33a) *tikahbi-taha*
     tired-done   'She's all tired out'   (II subject)

  b) *im-alhkaniya-taha*
     3III-forget-done   'He completely forgot' (III subject)

(34) *apa-tahli*[12]
     eat-complete   'He ate it all up'   (I subject)

In each of these cases the cited form is treated as a single phonological word, with the auxiliary linked to the preceding verb by a # boundary, the effect of which can be seen in examples like (34). The presence of II object prefixes or the I suffix *-li* does not affect the word status of a *tahli* auxiliary phrase:

> (35a) *chi-pa-tahli-l-a'chi*
> 2sII-eat-complete-1sI-irr 'I'm going to eat you up'

However, there are alternative ways to express sentences like (35a):

> (35b) *apa-t chi-tahli-l-a'chi*
> eat-ss 2sII-complete-1sI-irr

Here, the object marker appears on the auxiliary verb (now a fully separate word), and a suffix, *#t*, follows the main verb. The same construction is used with III objects:

> (36) *im-apa-tahli-li* / *apa-t in-tahli-li*
> 3III-eat-complete-1sI eat-ss 3III-complete-1sI
> 'I ate it up for him'

(*#t* is discussed further in section 3 below.)

When the subject requires a I prefix, only the second of these two constructions is possible:

> (37) *apa-t ii-tahli* / **il-apa-tahli*
> eat-ss 1pI-complete 1pI-eat-complete 'We ate it up'

although the object may still be marked on either verb:

> (38) *chi-pa-t ii-tahli* / *apa-t ii-chi-tahli*
> 2sII-eat-ss 1pI-complete eat-ss 1pI-2sII-complete
> / **ii-chi-apa-tahli*
> 1pI-2sII-eat-complete 'We ate you all up'

I affixes must appear on the auxiliary verb, *tahli*, while II and III affixes optionally may occur on either the main verb or the auxiliary. When there are no prefixes on *tahli*, the suffixed *-t* which is a feature of the extended form of this construction appears to combine with the initial *t* of *tahli* to form a sequence which reduces phonologically to *#t*.

Despite the fact that II and III prefixes may occur on either the main or the auxiliary verb when they mark objects of a *tahli* phrase, the same markers cannot be prefixed to *taha* when they mark subjects, as shown in:[13]

> (39) *sa-tikahbi-taha* / **??tikahbi-t sa-taha*
> 1sII-tired-done tired-ss 1sII-done
> 'I'm all tired out'

(40) *im-alhkaniya-taha* / **(im)-alhkaniya-t in-taha*[14]
      3III-forget-done   3III-forget-ss 3III-done
      'He completely forgot'

When *taha* follows a negated verb, the augment *ki* must intervene:[15]

(41) *ik-im-alhpi's-o-ki-taha*
      3N-3III-sad-neg-aug-done   'He's completely sad'

ik-im-alhpi's-o is a negative verb which means literally 'it's not sufficient for him' but which is often used to translate 'sad'. *taha* generally may only follow negative verbs like *ik-im-alhpi's-o* which have lexicalized in a unitary non-negative meaning. Since there appear to be no such lexicalized negative active verbs, I have been unable to discover any instances of *tahli* following a negative.

Both *taha* and *tahli* may themselves be negated, in which case the preceding verb is always marked with the suffix *#t*:

(42) *sa-tikahbi-t ik-ta'h-o*
      1sII-tired-ss 3N-done-neg   'I'm not all tired out'

(43) *apa-t ak-tahl-o*
      eat-ss 1sN-complete-neg   'I didn't eat it all up'

Thus, *taha* and *tahli* share some semantic features and a few distributional traits (combination of the bare auxiliary with a preceding element with an intervening # boundary, occurrence when prefixed with the preceding verb marked with *#t*), but *tahli* acts much more like an independent lexical verb than does *taha*, since *taha* may not freely mark its subject with prefixes (despite the fact that the homophonous independent verb *taha* may be so marked).

2.7 A number of auxiliaries share with *taha* and *tahli* the property of having their main verbs marked with *#t*. In general, these follow similar distributional rules: different auxiliaries, or forms of auxiliaries, are selected for main verbs whose subjects are marked with I affixes than for those whose subjects are marked with II or III affixes, and no subject marking appears on the auxiliary in the latter case.

maa and *ishmaa*[16] 'get' (inchoative) and *aatapa* 'be too much' are two axiliaries used only with verbs taking II and III subjects:

(44) *sa-lhinko-t   maa*
      1sII-fat-nom get   'I'm getting fat'

(45) *sa-sipokni-t aatapa*[17]
    1sII-old-ss be=too   'I'm too old'

aatapa can be used (and translated) independently, but *(ish)maa* cannot.

aatabli 'do too much', *issa* 'finish', and *aalhoppolli* 'get through with' all are used only with main verbs taking I subject marking, as in (46) and (47). All three of these auxiliaries may be used and translated independently, without a preceding verb-plus-*t*.

(46) *impa-t aatabli-li-tok*
    eat-ss do=too-1sI-past 'I ate too much'

(47) *impa-t ish-issa-tok*
    eat-ss 2sI-finish-past   'You finished eating'

The phonological relationship of *aatapa* and *aatabli*, and their distribution according to the morphological treatment of the preceding verb, is similar to that of *taha* and *tahli* (section 2.6), but there is no comparable variation between separate word and suffixed auxiliary for *aatapa* and *aatabli*.

While both *issa* and *aatabli* inflect for the person of the subject of the main verb, the main verb itself is unmarked for person, as the preceding examples show. With *aalhoppolli*, however, the main verb may be inflected for person:

(48) *anompoli-t ish-aalhoppolli-ta* /
    talk-ss   2sI-be=through-Q

    ish-anompoli-t ish-aalhoppolli-ta[18]
    2sI-talk-ss   2sI-be=through-Q
    'Are you through talking?'

aalhoppolli is the first auxiliary we have considered which inflects for subject itself and which may be preceded by an inflected main verb (the person marking configuration schematized in (5d) above). Actually, only the first of these variants should properly be considered an auxiliary construction, since in it but not in the second is the order of the two verbs fixed (cf. section 3.2 below).

2.8 In two auxiliary constructions, person marking works just as with pairs of auxiliaries like *taha/tahli* and *aatapa/aatabli*, with II or III subjects marked on the main verb only and I subjects marked on the auxiliary only. But the form of the auxiliary remains the same in both of these patterns.

The first auxiliary which works this way is *isht-aya* 'begin', which is composed of the instrumental proclitic *isht* plus the verb *aya* 'go' (whose inflection, as the examples below will reveal, is somewhat irregular). In the following examples, main verbs marked for II or III subjects are suffixed with #*t* and followed by an uninflected *isht-aya* (49), while main verbs taking I subjects are unmarked, with the I subject marking appearing only on the auxiliary (50):

> (49a) *sa-ssikopa-t isht-aya*
> 1sII-mean-ss inst-go   'I'm starting to be mean'
>
> b) *an-takho'bi-t isht-aya*
> 1sIII-lazy-ss inst-go   'I'm starting to feel lazy'
>
> (50a) *impa-t isht-ish-iyya-ta*
> eat-ss inst-2sI-go-Q   'Are you starting to eat?'
>
> b) *im-issikopa-t isht-aya-li*
> 3III-mean-ss inst-go-1sI 'I'm starting to be mean to him'

Notice that the same lexical verb may be treated differently, as in (49a) and (50b), when it takes different morphological subject marking. Due to a cooccurrence restriction between the II and III affix sets, when a Chickasaw verb like 'mean' which normally takes II subject marking, as in (51a), is used with an added III ("dative") argument, as in (51b), its subject must be marked with a I affix:

> (51a) *sa-ssikopa*
> 1sII-mean   'I am mean', 'I act mean'
>
> b) *im-issikopa-li*   /   **i̅-sa-ssikopa*
> 3III-mean-1sI   3III-1sII-mean
> 'I'm mean to him',   'I act mean to him'

Thus, the restrictions on the form of the *isht-aya* auxiliary construction are not semantic, but are related to the morphological marking of the main verb (cf. Munro and Gordon, forthcoming).

2.9 The inchoative *(ish)maa* 'get' described in section 2.7 is most likely related to a motion verb *maa* 'be going along'. Another *maa* auxiliary which occurs with a preceding *t*-marked main verb is probably related to *maa*,[19] a plural locational verb. This *maa* auxiliary is used with plural positional verbs (which have separate singular, dual, and plural subject stems), resulting in paradigms like

> (52a) *hikki'ya-li* /   *ii-hii'li*   /   *hiyyoh-t   ii-maa*
> stand=1-1sI   1pI-stand=2   stand=pl-ss 1pI-pl=aux
> 'I stand'   'We (2) stand'   'We (3 or more) stand'

   b) *ish-binni'li* / *hash-chii'ya*/ *binnoh-t hash-maa*
     2sI-sit=1   2pI-sit=2   sit=pl-ss 2pI-pl=aux
     'You sit'   'You (2) sit'   'You (3 or more) sit'

As with the *maa* in section 2.7 speakers are reluxtant to gloss this *maa* auxiliary separately or to use it without a preceding *t*-marked positional verb. (*ii-maa*, then, cannot mean 'We (3 or more) were in that position'.)

The basic forms of the plural positionals shown in (52a) and (52b) are *hiyyohli* and *binnohli*, but these verbs are almost invariably cited with the *maa* auxiliary. The final *li*'s in these words delete because of an independently motivated rule deleting *li*'s (other than the 1sI suffix) which form odd-numbered light syllables when they precede suffixes beginning with a single non-continuant coronal consonant. The suffix *#t* always has this effect on any preceding *li* in an odd-numbered light syllable, as (53) shows:

  (53a) *anompoli-t isht-aya-li*
      talk-ss   inst-go-1sI   'I'm starting to talk'

    b) *anomphõ-t isht-aya-li*
       talk=itr-ss inst-go-1sI   'I'm starting to talk all the time'

The *li* of *anompoli* 'talk' is in an even-numbered light syllable, but the *li* of the corresponding iterative aspect verb *anompohõli* is in an odd-numbered light syllable, so it is deleted before *#t*.

Unlike other examples we have seen of prefixed auxiliaries which follow uninflected *t*-marked main verbs, however (cf. sections 2.6–2.8), plural positional verbs like those in (52) have two variant forms, in one of which the positional verb, and not the auxiliary, is marked for the I subject:

  (54a) *hiyyoh-t ii-maa*   *ii-hiyyoh-maa*
      stand=pl-ss 1pI-pl=aux   1pI-stand=pl-pl=aux
      'We (3 or more) stand'

    b) *binnoh-t hash-maa* / *hash-binnoh-maa*
       sit=pl-ss 2pI-pl=aus   2pI-sit=pl-pl=aux
       'You (3 or more) sit'

When the unprefixed auxiliary comes to stand in front of the *t*-marked verb, some sort of incorporation results (probably with a # boundary). This should result in an *h-t-m* consonant cluster in the verbs exemplified above, but there is a fairly general rule in Chickasaw by which the middle consonant of certain three-consonant clusters is deleted. Note that the *t* probably has to be assumed to be present, at some level, in forms like *ii-hiyyoh-maa*, since the lexical verb is *hiyyohli* and there is no independent justification for deletion of *li* before *m*.

The positional *maa* is the only Chickasaw auxiliary which allows a I prefix either on the lexical verb or on the auxiliary, but not on both. This is a very restricted usage, however — it is strictly limited to members of the closed class of position verbs with different stems for different numbers of subject. With other intransitive verbs, such as *hilha* 'dance', *maa* cannot be used to indicate a plural subject:

> (55) **ii-hilha-t maa   /   *hilha-t ii-maa*
>   1pI-dance-ss pl=aux   dance-ss 1pI-pl=aux 'We dance'

2.10 Several auxiliaries occur in a construction similar to that used with *issa*, *aatapa*, and *(ish)maa* (section 2.7), with the inflected main verb followed by the subordinator *#kat* rather than by *#t*. Auxiliaries of this class include *ishtayya'ma*,[20] *immo'ma*, and *i'ma*, all of which mean 'still' or 'again', according to whether the associated lexical verb is used in a stative or active sense; *alhpi'sa* 'enough'; and *ik-o'n-o* 'not enough'. Unlike the auxiliaries described in 2.7, however, the lexical verbs used with the auxiliaries of this group may take all varieties of subject person marking. In particular, although the auxiliary itself is uninflected this construction may be used with main verbs marked for I subjects.

> (56a) *illi-kat   immo'ma*
>   die-sbr=ss still   'He's still dead'   (II subject, stative)
>
> b) *illi-kat   ishtayya'ma*
>   die-sbr=ss again   'He died again'   (II subject, active)
>
> c) *hikki'ya-kat   immo'ma*
>   stand=1-sbr=ss still   'It's still standing'   (I subject, stative)
>
> d) *chokoshkomo-li-kat   i'ma*
>   play-1sI-sbr=ss again   'I'm playing again'   (I subject, active)
>
> (57) *impa-li-kat   ik-o'n-o*
>   eat-1sI-sbr=ss   3N-reach-neg   'I don't eat enough'

ik-o'n-o is the negative of the verb *ona* 'get there'.

The subordinator *-kat* is never preceded by the negative augment *-ki*:

> (58) *ik-sa-kappass-o-kat   i'ma*
>   3N-1sII-cold-neg-sbr=ss still 'I'm not cold yet'

The auxiliary *ishtayya'ma* has an interesting alternate form, as shown in examples like

 (59) *ak-í'p-o-kat* *ishtayya'ma* / *ak-í'p-o-ka-shtayya'ma*
    1sN-eat-neg-sbr=ss still   1sN-eat-neg-sbr-still
    'I'm still not eating'

This variant construction seems to be possible with any *ishtayya'ma* sentence. It is quite unparalleled in that it involves two deletions (of the *#t* of the first verb and of the initial *i* of the second) neither of which seems unusual if the other has occurred, but both of which ought to be impossible in the environment at hand. What this deletion results in, of course, is another incorporated one-word auxiliary construction derived from a two-clause structure.

3. Clearly the crucial elements in the syntax of the last few auxiliary elements considered here are the suffixes *#t* and *#kat* which appear before the main verb in the full form of the *tahli* construction (section 2.6) and in sentences with the other auxiliaries discussed in sections 2.7–2.10. These suffixes are "switch-reference" markers (Jacobsen 1967) which reflect the same-subject relationship between the main verb and its auxiliary.

3.1 The *#t* suffix is reminiscent of two other Chickasaw morphemes, the subject case marker and the same-subject marker. In each of these cases, however, the *t* morpheme is formally opposed to a morpheme ending in a nasalized vowel, which indicates oblique case on nouns and different-subject on verbs. (60) and (61), for instance, show two instances of the subject-oblique opposition on nominal constituents:

 (60a) *hattak-at isso-tok*
    person-su hit-past 'The man hit him' (normal subject)

  b) *hattak-ā*[21] *isso-tok*
    person-obl hit-past 'He hit the man' (normal oblique)

 (61a) *hattak-akot isso-tok*
    man-con=su hit-past 'It was the man that hit him'
             (contrastive subject)

  b) *hattak-akō isso-tok*
    man-con=obl hit-past 'It was the man that he hit'
             (contrastive oblique)

(62) and (63), on the other hand, show examples of two different pairs of opposing switch-reference markers, the first of which is the -*kat* which was seen in 2.10:[22]

(62a) *aya-l-a'chi-kat*   *ithaana-li*
    go-1sI-irr-sbr=ss   know-1sI   'I know I'm going'
                           (same-subject subordination)

  b) *ay-a'chi-kã*   *ithaana-li*
    go-irr-sbr=ds   know-1sI   'I know he's going'
                           (different-subject subordination)

(63a) *aya-li-hootokot*   *sa-nokhanglo*
    go-1sI-because=ss   1sII-sorry   'I'm sad because I'm going'
                           (same-subject 'because' subordination)

  b) *aya-hootokõ*   *sa-nokhanglo*
    go-because=ds   1sII-sorry   'I'm sad because he's going'
                           (different-subject 'because' subordination)

The Chickasaw switch-reference system (Payne 1980) is in most respects quite comparable to other such systems in American Indian languages and elsewhere that are described in Jacobsen (1967) and more recent studies. Note that two verbs linked by a same-subject marker may have their subjects marked with different affix sets, as (63a) above shows; Munro and Gordon (forthcoming) further show that sameness of subject in Chickasaw means sameness of derived syntactic subjects, not the sameness of semantic subjects. But for each set of normal switch-reference markers there is a same-subject member and a different-subject member, just as in (62) and (63). Although the element *#t* which appears before the auxiliary in the examples in sections 2.6–2.9 above appears to signal the same kind of information as the same-subject subordinators in (62a) and (63a) above, it is not part of a binary set – there is no comparable device of simply nasalizing the last vowel of a verb stem to show some sort of different-subject relationship (cf. Munro, forthcoming).

#t verb are used productively in Chickasaw sentences like

    (64a) *binni'-t impa-li*[23]
          sit-ss   eat-1sI   'I'm sitting eating'

     b) *binni'li-li-t impa-li*
        sit-1sI-ss   eat-1sI 'I'm sitting and (I'm) eating'

Payne (1980) argues that the double person-marking in (64b) shows greater conceptual distance between the two verbal ideas. Person marking only on the final verb, as in (64a) and all the *#t* auxiliary constructions, shows greater conceptual closeness, Payne claims.

3.2 Normally switch-reference constructions allow extraposition of the first verb, as in the following variants of the sentences in (62)–(64):

(65a) *ithaana-li aya-l-a'chi-kat* (= 62a)
   b) *ithaana-li ay-a'chi-kä* (= 62b)

(66a) *sa-nokhanglo aya-li-hootokot* (= 63a)
   b) *sa-nokhanglo aya-hootokõ* (= 63b)

(67) *impa-li binni'li-li-t* (= 64b)

However, #*t* and #*kat* clauses in two-verb constructions where only one verb is person-marked (like (64a) and the switch-reference auxiliary constructions described above) show fixed word order, as shown by

(68a) **impa-li binni'-t* (cf. 64b)
   b) **isht-aya-li anompoli-t* (cf. 53a)
   c) **i'ma chokoshkomo-.i-kat* (cf. 56d)

We may incorporate this fact into our definiton of auxiliary for Chickasaw, and note that when a same-subject marker is used in a Chickasaw auxiliary construction, only one of the two verbs may be person-marked, but not both.

3.3 Several other verbs which seem reminiscent of the auxiliaries already discussed use #*kat* marking on the first verb and generally inflect both verbs for person. One such example is *aaissachi* 'quit':

(69) *ish-impa-kat*   *ish-aaissach-aa'ni*
   2sI-eat-sbr=ss   2sI-quit-mod '(You should) quit eating'

Aside from its semantic resemblance to auxiliaries like *issa*, there is nothing particularly auxiliary-like about the behavior of *aaissachi*, however, since the order of the two verbs in (69) is not fixed.

Two other auxiliary-like verbs used with a preceding *kat*-verb show some degree of optionality of person marking. With *aatampa* 'be too much for' the first verb is only optionally marked for person; with *immayya* 'be more than' (the comparative auxiliary; cf. Scott 1980), the construction shows the full range of person-marking options outlined in (5b) above.

(70) *(sa-)sipongni-kat im-aatampa-li*
   1sII-older-sbr=ss 3III-be=too=for-1sI 'I'm too old for him'

(71) *sa-sipokni-kat im-mayya* / *sa-sipokni-kat im-mayya-li* /
   1sII-old-sbr=ss 3III-more   1sII-old-sbr=ss 3III-more-1sI
   sipokni-kat im-mayya
   old-sbr=ss 3III-more   'I'm older (than him)'

The syntax of these verbs seems more auxiliary-like than that of *aaissachi* (word order is generally fixed, especially when the auxiliary is not marked for the person of the subject), but the fact that both of them introduce additional arguments (marked in each case with III) in the "auxiliary" clause makes them quite different from the auxiliaries described in section 2. These verbs seem less like separate clauses than, say, *ithaana* 'know' (sentence (62) above), but much more independent than the other auxiliaries. The characteristic use of additional clauses and switch-reference constructions to express added arguments in Chickasaw is disscussed in Munro and Gordon (forthcoming).

3.4 In section 2 I characterized Chickasaw auxiliaries as being perceived as having the same subject as the preceding lexical main verb (or, perhaps better, as not having a different subject from it). The switch-reference system provides the appropriate test, for it allows us to see whether a main-verb-plus-auxiliary phrase will be marked as same or different relative to another clause with the same subject as the main verb. Potentially, we could examine either the case where the auxiliary phrase was the main clause, with another verb subordinated to it, or that in which the auxiliary phrase was itself subordinated, as schematized in (72a–b):

(72a) PM-VERB-SR (PM)-VERB (PM)-AUXILIARY
   b) (PM)-VERB (PM)-AUXILIARY-SR PM-VERB

Here (PM)-VERB (PM)-AUXILIARY represents the various configurations of the auxiliary phrase, and SR indicates some sort of switch-reference marking. In both cases, all the auxiliary constructions discussed in this section and section 2 result in same-subject switch-reference marking, regardless of the morphological form of the person marking on any of the verbs involved. Cases of the form (72b) seem to me to provide a more crucial test of this principle, since in the case of (72a) one might argue that the auxiliary was irrelevant to the perception of sameness between the two lexical verbs. Here are a few examples of cases in the (72b) pattern, illustrating that Chickasaw auxiliaries are not perceived as having different subjects from their main verbs:

(73) *sa-kaylimpi-finna ki'yo-kat*   *ik-sam-alhpi's-o*
    1sII-strong-too not-sbr=ss 3N-1sIII-sad-neg
    'I'm sad that I'm not too strong'

(74) *Lynn-at Jan tawwa'-at kar-at ï-wayya'a binka-kat*   *ayoppa*[24]
    Lynn-su Jan both-su car-su 3III-have each=2-sbr=ss happy
    'Lynn and Jan are happy that they each have a car'

(75) *sa-nokhanglo-hõ holiss-ā   ishi-li-tok-chayni-kat*
      1sII-sorry-excl book-obl take-1sI-past-evid-sbr=ss
      'I'm sorry that I accidentally took the book'

(75) is another example of the extraposition of a switch-reference marked subordinate clause, still illustrating the (72b) pattern.

(76) *il-impa-'*   *salami-tokot*   *a=po-bika*
      1pI-eat-nom   too=much-cause=ss   1pII-sick
      'We're sick because we ate too much'

(77) *talowa-t issa-li-t*   *chokka'*   *aya-li-tok*
      sing-ss finish-1sI-ss   home   go-1sI-past
      'I finished singing and went home'

(78) *yaa-l-a'chi-kat*   *ĩ'ma-kat*   *ithaana-li*
      cry-1sI-irr-sbr=ss   again-sbr=ss   know-1sI
      'I know I'm going to cry again'

3.5 Although switch-reference is indicated between most pairs of Chickasaw clauses in construction with each other, there are a number of verbs which take associated clauses (complements?) with no switch-reference or subordination marking. With *banna* 'want', for instance, an unmarked "complement" clause is interpreted as having the same subject as 'want', while a clause with a different subject is marked with the modal suffix *-aa'ni*:

(79a) *aya sa-banna*
       go 1sII-want   'I want to go'

   b) *ay-aa'ni sa-banna*
       go-mod 1sII-want 'I want him to go'

   c) *ish-iyy-aa'ni sa-banna*
       2sI-go-mod 1sII-want 'I want you to go'

A different means is used to show that the subject of a "complement" of 'say' is the same as or different from the say-er. Chickasaw has two different verb stems for 'say', *aachi*, used in most contexts, and *miha*,[25] used to mean 'say of oneself'. Neither verb's complement is overtly marked:

(80a) *hilha aachi*
       dance say   'He says he (someone else) is dancing'

b) *hilha miha*
   dance say=self   'He says he (himself) is dancing'

In this 'say' use, person marking on the first verb follows normal expectations:

(82) *hilha miha-li*
     dance say=self-1sI   'I'm trying to dance'

(Thus, (80b) above can also mean 'He's trying to dance'.)

This 'try' construction and the same-subject 'want' construction seem to share many features with the auxiliary constructions described in section 2. The lack of inflection on the unmarked first verb seems similar to the situation with many auxiliaries, and the word order in sentences like (79a) and (82) is not free. Once again, these seem to be constructions in which there are some auxiliary and some main-verb characteristics.

4. In this section I will present further data both from Chickasaw and from the closely related language Choctaw in support of the conclusions I have drawn regarding the verbal origin of certain Chickasaw auxiliaries. By all accounts (e.g. Pulte 1975) Chickasaw and Choctaw are very closely related, but the two languages treat a number of these auxiliary constructions very differently, at least as shown by a comparison of my Chickasaw data with e.g. Nicklas (1972, 1979) and Byington (1915). Choctaw provides additional data regarding the complex origin of auxiliary structures which are unanalyzable on the basis of Chickasaw data alone.

4.1 Nicklas (1979:53) claims that the Choctaw remote past suffix *-ttook* (I have adapted the orthography of forms in the text) is actually a separate element *took* preceded by a *t*-verb. Unfortunately, he presents no phonological or distributional evidence in support of this intriguing claim, and since he follows standard Choctaw orthographic practice of writing almost all morphemes as separate words it is difficult to evaluate the merits of this suggestion.

4.2 Byington (1915) glosses Choctaw *fiihna* as 'do intensely', suggesting an active use not readily apparent from the Chickasaw 'not too' construction with a negated *finna*. I have not seen an example of this verb with active person marking, however. Note, though, that Choctaw examples like (83) show that *fiihna* can have a positive use not possible in Chickasaw:

(83) *...an   tishu   hvt palsi isht abeka hosh issikkopa fehna*
     ...1sIII servant su palsy inst sick su   miserable too?

> kvt   chuka   ya   itonlv-shke...[26]
> sbr=ss house   obl   lie-hort
> '...my servant lieth at home sick of the palsy, grievously
> tormented' (Matthew 8:6, Choctaw Testament)

4.3 The origin of the *chommi/chohmi* 'kind of' auxiliary may well be a word
for 'like, similar', which is *chohmi* or *chiyohmi* in Choctaw but *chümi* or
chiymi in Chickasaw. All these words, in both languages, inflect for a I subject, and the semantic connection seems quite likely.

4.4 Byington (1915) gives an example of how *binka* 'each of two' may be inflected for person:

> (84) *hatak   sa-binka*
>   person   1sII-each=2   'a man who is like me'

It would be good to have more details about this construction – clearly *binka*
is not serving as an auxiliary in (84), since it does not follow a verb, but the
example does not make it clear whether *binka* may be a main verb itself. However, (84) shows that *binka*'s status as a (historically) separate verb-like element is not in doubt.

4.5 *billi'ya* 'always' has a cognate in Choctaw *bilia*, and this Choctaw verb
could inflect for person during the nineteenth century, when the first translations of the Bible into Choctaw were made. Byington (1915) cites (85a) as an
old translation of the verse which appears in the current translation as (85b):

> (85a) *vno   yokvt   hvchi-apehv-t   ayv-t   bilia-li*
>   I   su   2pII-be=with-ss go-ss   always-1sI
>   ("old translation")
>
> b) *vno   vt   hvchi   awan-t   aya   li   billia   ho*
>   I   su   2pII   go=with-ss go   1sI   always   excl
>   '...lo, I am with you alway...'
>   (Matthew 28:20, Choctaw Testament)

It appears that Choctaw may be moving in the same direction as Chickasaw in
losing personal inflection on this word.

A similar sort of situation appears to exist for *biiyi'ka* 'all the time'. The
Choctaw cognate *biika* ordinarily does not inflect (Nicklas 1972:192), but
Byington (1915) cites *sa-biika* (inflected for a 1sII) and *ish-biika* (inflected
for 2sI), glossed 'be alone' or 'be totally'. Thus *bii'ka* also seems likely to be
a grammaticized form of an older full verb.

4.6 According to Nicklas (1972, 1979), of the set *taha, tahli, issa, isht ia* (Chickasaw *isht-aya*), and *aalhoppolli* only *taha* may be used with verbs taking II (or, it seems reasonable to assume, III) subjects. As we have seen, Chickasaw has loosened this restriction in the case of *isht-aya* 'begin', which may be used with verbs taking all three types of subjects.

4.7 Nicklas (1979) cites the normal form of all plural position verbs with the suffix *-maya*, which exists as an independent stem related to Chickasaw *maa*. He does not suggest the existence of the alternate forms with *-t* which occur in Chickasaw.

4.8 Byington (1915) translates *imoma*, a cognate to Chickasaw *immo'ma* as either 'dure' or 'do thus', and he gives one example marked for a 1sI subject.

4.9 The differences between auxiliary constructions in Chickasaw and Choctaw seem remarkable. One Choctaw auxiliary construction which Nicklas (1979) regards as extremely common, the use of positional auxiliaries marked with *#t* to indicate the progressive, is relatively rare in Chickasaw. While Nicklas writes that I marking may be optionally omitted from a main verb followed by an auxiliary in this construction, my Chickasaw data do not support such a generalization. In fact, in Chickasaw sentences like (86) the positional verb seems (except for its position) less auxiliary-like than in sentences like (64a) above:

> (86) *holisso holissochi-li-t binni'li-li-tok ish-la-ka*
>   letter   write-1sI-ss   sit-1sI-past   2sI-arrive-sbr=ds
>   'I was writing a letter when you came'

However, just as in Choctaw, it is apparently the positional verb which adds the progressive sense to the 'write' clause.

5. The hypothesis presented in section 1 concerning the origin of many auxiliary constructions in Chickasaw — that they are fixed, grammaticized structures which have developed out of older productive two-clause structures — has been supported at a number of points in the course of the synchronic and comparative description in sections 2–4. In cases where the main verb and auxiliary are linked by a switch-reference morpheme (sections 2.7–2.8, 2.10, 3), the two-clause origin of the structure is clear, and in other cases it has often been possible to argue that the same-subject suffix *#t* has been deleted between main verb and auxiliary (*taha* and *tahli*, section 2.6; *maa*,

section 2.9). A similar piece of evidence in favor of a two-clause origin for many auxiliary structures in provided by the possibility of marking the auxiliary for person in certain constructions, and by comparative evidence suggesting that the auxiliary may occur as a main verb in other constructions.

Constraints on and distribution of person marking and morphological restrictions on the marking of the main verb, while varying from auxiliary to auxiliary, indicate ways in which these constructions are more limited than ordinary complement-taking verbs, and the fixed word order of all the auxiliary constructions described sets them apart from other two-verb constructions.

Although I presented the true suffixes of sections 2.1 and 2.2 as members of the class of auxiliaries, it is clearly less easy to argue a two-clause origin for them. Some of these (e.g. *-tok* (past) and *-aa'ni* (modal)) must be reconstructed as auxiliaries, probably already suffixes, for Proto-Muskogean,[27] so any claims we make about these must be based on more comprehensive comparative data than are available to me at present. Clearly, these are "old auxiliaries", in contrast to the newly developing auxiliaries whose more transparent origins were investigated in later sections. If such elements were themselves "newer" at the time of Proto-Muskogean, it is quite likely that Proto-Muskogean itself had some old auxiliaries which by now may have vanished without trace. I belabor this point only to avoid giving the implication that I believe that since complex synchronic one-clause constructions may derive historically from two-clause constructions, the proto-language was conceptually "simpler" and may have lacked auxiliary structures. Despite some recent suggestions along this line (e.g. Givón 1980), I see no justification for any such claims.

Another interesting question which I cannot treat in detail here concerns the process by which the auxiliary comes to function syntactically as though its subject were the same as that of the main verb, which I have argued (section 1 above) is part of the general phenomenon of auxiliarization. Certainly, some of the auxiliaries discussed here must be seen as having logical subjects at some underlying or original level which are different from the subjects of their preceding main verbs — for instance, consider *ik-o'n-o* 'not enough' (section 2.10), literally 'it doesn't reach'. Fairly clearly what doesn't reach (suffice) must be the whole preceding event or state, not simply its subject. Yet in sentences like the following *ik-o'n-o* is clearly treated as having the same subject as the preceding main verb 'eat':

(87) *impa-li-kat*   *ik-o'n-o-kat*   *ithaana-li*
      eat-1sI-sbr=ss   3N-reach-neg-sbr=ss   know-1sI
      'I know I don't eat enough'

Munro and Gordon (forthcoming) discuss several related processes by which semantic nonsubjects may become derived syntactic subjects capable of controlling such processes as switch-reference, but the mechanisms described there do not suggest a reason why the subject of the clausal semantic subject of *ik-o'n-o* would have been reinterpreted as its subject. Such a change must occur, however, before auxiliarization can take place.

A more detailed consideration of the syntactic differences among the various Chickasaw auxiliary structures must await a future study. A few facts can be noted here, however, concerning the rate of the auxiliarization process. Let us assume that the less separation (syntactic or phonological) there is between main verb and auxiliary, the greater the degree of formal auxiliarization.

One generalization to be noted concerns the rate of auxiliarization with different sorts of subjects. Sections 2.6–2.8 above show that auxiliarization proceeds more rapidly with II and III subjects than with I subjects – with main verbs whose subjects are marked with II and III prefixes, there is less variation in the form of auxiliaries and a greater chance of auxiliary incorporation.[28] Since the choice of II–III versus I marking is often based on lexical marking and syntactic criteria rather than on any semantic factors (Munro and Gordon, forthcoming; cf. also section 2.8 above), it is not immediately clear why a development in this direction would occur. However, despite the increase in the number of nonsemantic factors conditioning the choice of II–III versus I subject marking, it is nonetheless the case that most subjects marked with II and III affixes are non-active, while most subjects marked with I affixes are active. The effect of many Chickasaw auxiliaries (modals, negation and other modifiers of degree, many aspectuals) is to increase the apparent stativity of many inherently active or punctual predications (thus 'I might run', 'I am running', 'I ran enough', and 'I didn't run' all seem more stative than 'I ran'). Perhaps some basic conflict between an active verb (marked with a I affix) and a stative auxiliary can slow down the auxiliarization process.

A second general observation concerns the speed of auxiliarization in negative versus nonnegative sentences. The evidence of *finna* (section 2.2) and *salami* (section 2.5), suggests that auxiliarization proceeds more quickly in nonnegative sentences – *finna* is suffixed (fully auxiliarized) only when it is not directly negated; *salami* can be person-marked (showing less auxiliarization) only in the negative. Since negative sentences are generally syntactically conservative, we would expect them to show less rapid auxiliarization than nonnegative sentences.

The range of auxiliary structures in Chickasaw, and what can be seen of their historical origins, bears comparison to those described for the Yuman languages (Munro 1976, Langdon 1978, Hardy 1979, Gordon 1980). Like Chickasaw, Yuman has an extensive and active switch-reference system. Some auxiliary structures are linked to their main verbs by same-subject markers, others have no explicit indication of their relationship, and still others are incorporated as suffixes onto the main verb (Yuman, like Chickasaw, is verb-final). Through the examination of comparative data it is possible to see that original full verbs, many of which must be assumed to have once taken sentential (i.e., nonpersonal) subjects, have often been reanalyzed as having as their subject the subject of their subject clause (Munro 1976). Often this kind of change is the prerequisite to further reanalysis and, frequently, eventual incorporation or compounding of the main verb and auxiliary (Munro 1976, Gordon 1980). As more comparative Muskogean data come to be available similar arguments will come to be made in more detail than is now possible for Chickasaw and Choctaw.

Notes

1. My great thanks go to Catherine Willmond, my principal Chickasaw teacher. I would also like to thank Lynn Gordon, Bonnie Glover, Doris Payne, and other members of two UCLA Chickasaw classes for their contributions to my understanding of Chickasaw grammar and for their suggestions regarding this paper. In addition, I am grateful to the speakers of Chickasaw and Choctaw in Oklahoma who have extended my knowledge of their languages. While this paper primarily reflects Mrs. Willmond's usage, the description is generally correct for the other varieties of Chickasaw with which I am familiar. (I will not indicate here all the variations from Mrs. Willmond's usage that I have observed, however.)

2. Chickasaw is cited in practical orthography. Doubled vowels are underlyingly long, doubled consonants are underlyingly geminated, ch = č, lh = ɬ, ' = ?. The orthography used here is roughly equivalent to standard orthographies for Choctaw (particularly for consonants), especially the modified form used by Nicklas (1972).

   The abbreviations I use in the glosses in this paper include aug = (negative) augment, aux = auxiliary, con = contrastive, ds = different subject, evid = evidential, excl = exclamation, hab = habitual, hort = hortatory, inst = instrumental, irr = irrealis, itr = iterative aspect, mod = modal, neg = negative, nom = nominalizer, obl = oblique, pl = plural, perf = perfect, pot = potential, Q = question, rem = remote past, s = singular, sbr = subordinator, ss = same subject, su = subject. Pronominal affixes are glossed with I, II, III, or N(egative) for the affix set (as described in the text); 1, 2, or 3 for person; and s or p for number. An equals sign (=) is used to separate parts of a complex element or gloss.

3. *#a'hibii'ka* is doubtless segmentable into some element *a'hi* and the independently occuring *#biiyi'ka* (secton 2.2). *a'hi* does not occure elsewhere in Chickasaw, but is cognate to the Choctaw potential suffix (e.g. Nicklas 1979:100).

4. Other rules which can apply between a lexical verb and these suffixes include the *li* deletion process described in section 3 below and a process which deletes a non-lengthened vowel between a strident consonant and a single coronal consonant.

5. The negatives of verbs whose subjects are indicated with II or III affixes all begin with the prefix *ik-* (examples in the text). Thus, it is probably best to think of *ik-* as a neutral negative prefix rather than as being specifically associated with a third-person I argument. However, I will continue to gloss *ik-* here as '3N'. (Cf. also fn. 29 below.)

6. These positional statements do not apply to the negative suffix (auxiliary) *-o*.
7. No nonnegative version of *ik-ayo'b-o* 'bad' exists, but the root is evidently related to *ayoppa* 'good'.
8. Many of the auxiliaries described here may occur in combination, although it is beyond the scope of the present study to explore this in detail. There are a number of examples in the text of sentences with more than one auxiliary.
9. The *ik-* prefix here need not reflect a third-person argument − cf. fn. 5.
10. Another auxiliary-like element whose behavior is like that of *mina*'s is *mankō*. This word has a pragmatic function and can never occur in a subordinate clause, so it does not fit my basic definition of auxiliary (section 2), since to test for same-subject status of an auxiliary the auxiliary must be embeddable (section 3).
11. There are some indications that the strictly syntactic criteria for selecting *taha* vs. *tahli* presented here may be subject to some modification. While *taha* is never used with a positive verb taking I subject marking, it may follow the negative version of a verb taking I marking in rare instances like

    (i) *naafka   ak-fokh-o-ki--taha*
       dress   1sN-put=on-neg-aug-done   'I'm (completely) naked'

fokha 'put on' takes I subject marking, which explains the *ak-* prefix on the negated verb. Yet clearly the meaning of the negative expression in (i) is quite stative (as indeed many negative existential statements are). It is possible that the statement about the distribution of *taha* and *tahli* must be modified to fully specify what happens with negative main verbs.
12. *apa* 'eat' is transitive; *impa* 'eat' is intransitive.
13. II subject markers may appear on the Choctaw auxiliary *taha*, according to Nicklas (1979:47).
14. Normally III marking is not deletable even in cases where II marking would be. But neither version of this variant is correct.
15. Occasionally *ki* may be deleted before *taha* when it follows a negative verb which seems to have been lexicalized with a unitary meaning.
16. It seems likely that *ishmaa* is segmentable into *maa* with a proclitic *ish(t)* (cf., e.g., *isht-aya* 'begin', section 2.8 below), but I know of no way to prove this since *ishmaa* is never marked with any verbal prefix which might intervene between *isht-* and *maa-*. Cf. fn. 23 below.
17. Sometimes the main verb preceding *aatapa* is marked with the suffix #*kat*, discussed in the next section.
18. The *-ta* question suffix in this sentence and in sentence (50a) below would seem to be an auxiliary by the definition which I presented above. However, this seems counterintuitive. *-ta* is unique among Chickasaw suffixes I know of in carrying no stress and in failing to participate in the rhythmic alternations described in section 2.1. Perhaps the definition of auxiliary should be expanded to require that auxiliary elements be stressed, which would then exclude *-ta* from the class of Chickasaw auxiliaries. Another point, however, is that *-ta* like the suffix *-mankō* (fn. 10), cannot occur on embedded clauses, and so its same-subject status cannot be tested.

    Perhaps also we should require that auxiliary elements be able to occur in main as well as subordinate clauses (just as we require that they be able to occur in subordinate as well as main clauses). This would free us from having to decide, for instance, whether the same-subject subordinator *-kat* (section 2.10 below) and other such affixes which occur only in subordinate (non-final) clauses are auxiliaries, which again seems counterintuitive.
19. Cf. Nicklas (1979:69−70), for the comparative Choctaw data which helps support this claim.
20. Like *ishmaa* (fn. 16), *ishtayya'ma* probably contains the proclitic *isht-*.

21. The simple oblique suffix -*ā* is optional, or rather, its occurrence has a discourse value.
22. There is also a set of switch-reference markers for coordinate clauses, same-subject *-cha* and different-subject *-na*.
23. The form *binni'-t* has been reduced from underlying *binni'li-t* by the process of *li* deletion described in the text below. The same rule has operated on *mali(li)-t* in (64).
24. The Chickasaw 'have' construction is described in more detail in Munro and Gordon, to appear.
25. Often *miha* is pronounced as *miya*.
26. I have replaced the *ą*'s of Byington (1915) (apparently the addition of the editor, John Swanton) with the *v*'s more standard in Choctaw orthography. Both represent the equivalent of Chickasaw (short) *a*. Although I have left word boundaries as in the source, I have added hyphens and glosses.
27. Speculations about Proto-Muskogean not attributed to Haas are based on my informal observations of Creek and Alabama and comparisons of these languages to Chickasaw.
28. As noted in fn. 5 above, the direct (nonperiphrastic) negative prefix is *ik-* for all verbs with II and III subjects, regardless of person, but the negative prefix varies for person and number for verbs whose nonnegative subjects would be marked with I affixes. Thus, the *#o* negative auxiliary suffix is another which shows more auxiliarization (no variation for person) with verbs taking II−III affixes than with verbs taking I affixes.

References

Akmajian, Adrian – Susan Steele – Thomas Wasow
    1979   "The category AUX in universal grammar", *Linguistic inquiry* 10:1–64.
Byington, Cyrus
    1915   *A dictionary of the Choctaw language* (= *Bureau of American Ethnology Bulletin* 46), edited by J. R. Swanton and H. S. Halbert. [Reissued by Central Choctaw Council, Inc., Oklahoma City 1978]
Choctaw testament (no date; American Bible Society).
Givón, Talmy
    1980   *On understanding grammar* (New York: Academic Press).
Gordon, Lynn
    1980   *Maricopa morphology and syntax* (unpublished Ph. D. dissertation, U.C.L.A.).
Haas, Mary R.
    1977   "From auxiliary verb phrase to inflectional suffix", *Mechanisms of syntactic change,* edited by C.N.Li (Austin: University of Texas Press), 525–537.
Hardy, Heather
    1979   *Tolkapaya syntax: tense, aspect and adverbial modification in a Yavapai dialect* (unpublished Ph. D. dissertation, U.C.L.A.).
Jacobsen, William H., Jr.
    1967   "Switch-reference in Hokan-Coahuiltecan", *Studies in Southwestern ethnolinguistics,* edited by D. Hymes and W. Bittle (The Hague-Paris: Mouton), 238–263.

Langdon, Margaret
   1978   "Auxiliary verb constructions in Yuman", *Journal of California Anthropology publications in linguistics* 1:93–130.
Marchese, Lynell
   1979   *Tense/aspect and the development of auxiliaries in the Kru language family* (unpublished Ph. D. dissertation, U.C.L.A.).
Munro, Pamela
   1976   "Subject copying, predicate raising, and auxiliarization: the Mojave evidence", *IJAL* 42:99–112.
   forth-   "On the special status of certain same-subject constructions in Chickasaw",
   coming *Switch-reference: papers from the 1981 symposium on switch-reference and universal grammar*, edited by J. M. Haiman and P. Munro.
Munro, Pamela – Lynn Gordon
   forth-   *Syntactic relations in Western Muskogean: A typological perspective.*
   coming
Nicklas, T. Dale
   1972   *The elements of Choctaw* (unpublished Ph. D. dissertation, University of Michigan).
   1979   *Reference grammar of the Choctaw language* (Durant, OK: Choctaw bilingual education program).
Payne, Doris
   1980   "Switch-reference in Chickasaw", *Studies in switch-reference*, edited by P. Munro (=*UCLA Papers in syntax* 8), 89–118.
Pulte, William
   1975   "The position of Chickasaw in Western Muskogean", *Studies in Southeastern Indian languages*, edited by J. M. Crawford (Athens: University of Georgia Press), 251–256.
Scott, Janet
   1980   "Chickasaw comparatives", MS.

RUTA NAGUCKA

Explorations into syntactic obsoleteness: English *a-X-ing* and *X-ing*

1 "Mexico. Carter Goes A-Wooing"

This is a headline of an article which appeared in U. S. News and World Report magazine (February 19, 1979). Although stylistically marked (a joke?) and certainly not to be understood in its literal sense, an obsolete construction of the type

(1) *Carter goes a-wooing*

does not seem to have gone out of usage. Examples most frequently recorded by ModE dictionaries are as follows:

(2) *The ship was still a-building* (Webster)

(3) *Daddy's gone a-hunting* (Webster)

(4) *They set the bells a-ringing* (Hornby *et al.*)

in which *a-X-ing* appears with *be, go, set* to express either the purpose or result of the motion, or to denote some act, action, process not yet finished. The superficial form is conveniently explained as being derived from an OE preposition *on, an* 'on', possibly *æt* 'at' contracted into *a-* and a verbal form in *ing*, called the gerund by lexicographers. The first part of this statement is justified historically, but the information about the gerund is established from the ModE point of view; probably this is how the construction is apprehended by a contemporary speaker of English. Historically, however, the structure is wrongly construed: *a-X-ing* is not a relic of the OE gerund. To make this point clear let us take a quick look over the OE gerund and the infinitive.

According to a generally accepted hypothesis OE gerund and OE infinitive "are merely different cases of what was originally a neuter verbal substantive in Indo-European" (Kispert 1971:91). The infinitive goes back to the accusative singular, while the gerund, always preceded by the preposition *to* 'to', derives from the dative singular. Thus, OE *beran* 'bear' — the infinitive and OE *to beranne* (*berenne*) 'bearing' — the gerund, originally belong to the same category, that of a verbal noun. In Old English the relationship between these two forms is of a different nature: the infinitive seems to function as an 'independent' category, the gerund being its inflected form used to express only some special relations, the most common of which is that of purpose. Sentences (5) and (6) show this contrast:

(5) *Se forbead slean þa heorotas and þa baras* (Maxim) 'He forbade men to kill the harts and the boars, / He forbade the harts and the boars to be killed' (Reszkiewicz 1971:36)

(6) *Gif feorcund man oþþe fremde butan wege geond wudu gange and ne hrieme ne horn blawe, for þeof he biþ to profianne oþþe to sleanne oþþe to aliesanne* (Reszkiewicz 1971:82) 'If a farcome man, or a stranger, journey through a wood out of the highway and neither shout nor blow his horn he is to be held for a thief either to be slain or redeemed'

The boundary between these two is not always so clearly demarcated and often becomes too thin to differentiate the functions:

(7) . . . *ða ongan ic . . . ða boc wendan on Englisc* (Onions 6/73) 'then I began to translate the book into English'

(8) *ongann ða Augustinus mid his munecum to geefenlœcenne þœra apostola lif* (Kispert 1971:91) 'then Augustine with his monks commenced to imitate (the imitating) the life of the apostles'

Note that in (7) and (8) both the infinitive proper (*wendan* 'turn') and its inflected form, i.e. the gerund (*to geefenlœcenne* 'imitating') occur after the same verb *onginnan* 'begin'. Thus the OE gerund functions as a variant of the infinitive to which it is genetically akin, besides it is invariably accompanied by *to* and typically characterized by the *-enne/-anne* ending. All this shows that the OE gerund has formally nothing but the name in common with the ModE gerund, i.e. the *-ing* form.

The structure under discussion *a-X-ing* is a direct continuation of a different OE form, namely the OE abstract noun. It is also closely associated with the verb in the sense that it derives from it, but it is not treated as a gerund but as a noun with fully-fledged inflectional endings. The derivative suffix is *-ung* and the noun is inflected according to a pattern of a feminine $\bar{o}$-declension, e.g.

(9) *eal seo gesomnung brcðra ⁊ sweostra* (Bede 320/32) 'all the congregation of brethren and sisters'   Nominative sg.

(10) *seo modor þære gesomnunge* (Bede 282/29) 'the mother of
the society' Genitive sg.

(11) *þætte hwylchugu hraðe of þære gesomnunge sweltende wære*
(Bede 288/19) 'that someone of the society should soon die'
Dative sg.

(12) *ꝥ micle cirican ꝥ gesomnunge Drihtne gestryndon ꝥ begeaton*
(Bede 226/12) 'and acquired and won over a large church and
congregation to the Lord' Accusative sg.

and so on. Of the various functions the abstract *-ung* noun is used for, the one
expressed by the preposition *on* and the appropriate form of the noun is of
the greatest interest. It is worth noting that the preposition *on* requires either
accusative, or dative, or even instrumental cases, meaning 'on', 'in', 'into', 'on
to', 'to', 'among' (Wright 1948:178). The constraint on using *on* in any of the
three functions is of a semantic nature: when "implying movement or destina-
tion in space or time" (Quirk and Wrenn 1958:61) it is used with the accusative; when there is no motion but rest, position or temporal relations it is the
dative that is used (these relations are also expressed by the instrumental, e.g.

on þyssum geare 'in this year'

or with the instrumental form

þys geare 'in this year'

(cf. Quirk and Wrenn 1958:66)). With feminine nouns it is not always possible
to distinguish the proper function because of the structural syncretism of the
dative (instrumental) and the accusative singular unless they are preceded by
demonstrative pronouns or adjectives. This forces the interpreter to take into
account both the context and the meaning, e.g.

(13) *on his þenunge* (Bede 466/31)

can express either position or direction, 'in his service', 'to his service', respectively; however, when regarded contextually

(13a) *ꝥ eall his yldo ꝥ lif on his þenunge gefylde* 'and passed all his
years and life in his service'

it is the temporal/positional (?) interpretation rather than the motional/
directional one that seems appropriate for the understanding of the whole
sentence. In sentence

(14) *þa asprungan gedwolmenn on Godes gelaðunge* (Onions 63/

212) 'then the heretics rose against God's church (congregation)'

on Godes gelaðunge 'on God's church' is accusative with its directional implications because of the motion verb *aspringan* 'spring up'.

Even a cursory glance at the OE usage of the *-ung* noun provides enough evidence for treating this abstract noun within the same framework as any other noun. Its derivational affinity to the verb from which it originates is looser than that of the OE gerund. First, the *-ung* form can be used to express various relations, whereas the *-enne/-anne* form is restricted to the relation associated with the preposition *to*. Secondly, the *-ung* form is fully inflected, whereas the *-enne/-anne* is not. Thirdly, the *-ung* form is lexically defined and definable independently of its verbal origin (cf. *gelaðung* 'church', 'congregation' vs. *gelaþian* 'invite', 'summon', 'ask') whereas the *-enne/-anne* form is lexically governed by its verbal root. Fourthly, since the *-ung* form belongs to the category of the noun it undergoes the rules which the noun imposes, whereas the *-enne/-anne* form is sensitive to the verb requirements, cf.

> *mid þa leornunge þyssa boca* (Bede 448/2) 'by the reading of these books'

vs.

> *ꝥ ealle geornesse ic sealde to leornienne ꝥ to smeagenne halige gewritu* (Bede 480/29) 'and I gave all zeal to study and meditate on Holy Scripture'

þyssa boca 'of these books' is a genitive modifier to *leornunge* 'learning', while *halige gewritu* 'Holy Scripture' is a direct object to *to leornienne* 'learning'. Or take another pair of sentences:

> *þæt ðis wæs riht weorðung soðra Eastrana* (Bede 470/10) 'that this was the right celebration of the true Easter'

vs.

> *ꝥ to weorðianne þa rihtgesettan tide* (Bede 468/7) 'and honour the rightly-determined time'

and some others. This different distribution of properties constitutes a sufficient criterion to distinguish the abstract noun in *-ung* from the gerund in *-enne/-anne*. In this respect I do not fully agree with Lightfoot (1979:4.2) who claims that "*to* infinitives were once nouns and only later became verbal forms, losing their nominal status" (167).

Being different from the verbal forms the OE *-ung* noun occurred freely, of course in accordance with the rules which the OE noun was subjected to. The prepositional phrase *on + X-ung* was one of many other prepositional constructions, and there was nothing strange, or exceptional about its usage, function or meaning. It was only much later that the structure in question ceased to be transparent (using Lightfoot's concept), due to the fact that the OE *-ung* noun changed its categorial membership. By virtue of quite complicated processes which I am not going to discuss just here this class of nominal abstracts became verbal nouns, i.e. gerunds, or at least became indistinguishable from them. However, a small number of the original *-ung* nouns retained their nominal status in the construction under analysis, but only under strictly defined conditions. These rather severe restrictions refer to the semantic environment: the preposition *on* indicates rather direction than position, or time mingled with the idea of being engaged in the action/event expressed by the noun. The verb with which the *on + X-ing* occurs is a verb of motion such as *go*, *fall*, *come*, action like *set*, it can also appear with *be*.

Before I make an attempt at accounting for syntactic and semantic peculiarities of this construction as I understand it I should like to present briefly Visser's views (1973). Examples with the *a-X-ing* form are considered with regard to the main verb or *be* with which it occurs and "the first verb is mainly employed to qualify or modify aspectually or modally the action expressed by the second verb" (1888). While not diminishing the value of Visser's excellent collection of language data amply supplied, one has to admit that his classification of textual material is far from being satisfactory and often seems to be based on purely superficial characteristics. *a* before *X-ing* which is a weakened form of *on* has different functions and meanings depending on the function and meaning of the original *on*. The *a* in the following sentence

(15) *he keeps a puffing and a blowing* (Visser 1973:1899)

does not seem to have much in common with *a* in (16)

(16) *the people fall a hooting* (Visser 1973:1893)

although both *a*'s are used with *X-ing* and are identical phonologically. Secondly, the *X-ing* form is interpreted either as 'primarily verbal' e.g.

lie on (a) – lie a begging (1914)

or as a 'real noun', e.g.

be on (a) hunting (1993).

Thirdly, the division of verbs into verbs of inchoation, continuation, termination, motion, rest and modality is not sharply marked structurally, and even semantically is not always convincing: compare *fall*[1] – a verb of inchoation with *come* – (simply) a verb of motion, *keep* a verb of continuation while *lie* is a verb of rest. In connection with these critical remarks I should like to clarify the following point: not all the English constructions consisting of *on/at* (optionally used) and *X-ing* form are functionally identical. The super-ficial similarity is by definition rejected here; the sentences, although structur-ally the same, such as

> (17) *He goes on reading*

> (18) *He goes on hunting*

are semantically different in practically each lexical item except *he*. In my considerations and reflections on *a-X-ing* I shall be concerned only with the type illustrated by (1) through (4), (16) and (18).

In the sections that follow a hypothesis about some formal and semantic interpretation of these ModE (relic) sentences will be claimed and evaluated. A grammatical rule, which will make all the necessary predictions concerning the relevant data, is expected to correctly account for the form *(a)-X-ing*. Usually the *X-ing* form is assumed to be the surface product of gerundivization, i.e. the surface gerund. Such a hypothesis would disagree with the observations and the hypothesis about the OE formal origin of this construction (cf. the beginning of this paper); it would also be difficult to defend it in the light of the ModE standard data, as scanty and obsolete as they may be.[2] The simplest way out of this rather troublesome situation it would seem, is to assign the category of N(oun) to the *X-ing* form, as in Old English. The *-ing* suffix would mark abstract derivational nouns, not gerunds, generated through some lexical rule, not some transformational rule. Thus, there are two distinct one-place predications in an *a-X-ing* structure, if, of course, we follow the line of argu-mentation presented above. In this manner sentence (1)

> *Carter goes a-wooing*

is understood as two predications:

> (a) There will be a certain event of wooing
> (b) That event is connected with Carter's going (to Mexico)

By saying that 'wooing' is an event I do not mean it to be either factive or actional. "Events and their kin are primarily temporal entities" says Vendler (1967:144); their relation to space is indirect. Very roughly speaking this is exactly what I mean by 'event';[3] more specifically, however, it appears that a semantic characterization of the type of event I am discussing would involve manner-like specification intermingled with some sort of a social act, practice or an instance of a special mode of behaving. At this point a sociolinguist might have something interesting to say, as for instance to what extent a social behaviour imposes requirements on language, or whether a grammatical construction is limited to a given event only, etc.

The two one-place predications analysis can be successfully applied to other uses of *a-X-ing* as well, i.e. with *be*. The sentence

> *The house is a-building*[4]

is here understood as

    (a) There is a certain event of building
    (b) This event is connected with the house

Contrast between gerundal and nongerundal uses of *X-ing* form points up tough problems facing a grammarian of English, chiefly because of the structural syncretism, i.e. the morphemic identity. In Polish,[5] however, the distinction is clear in the following, semantically equivalent structures:

> *chodzić (jeździć, puszczać się) w zaloty* 'go a-wooing'
> *zalecanie się* 'wooing'   gerund
> *zalecać się* 'woo'   infinitive

or

> *iść (chodzić) na budowę* 'go a-building'   NP
> *budowanie* 'building'   gerund
> *budować* 'build'   infinitive

although the formal sameness can also be found:

> *iść (chodzić) na polowanie* 'go a-hunting'   NP
> *polowanie* 'hunting'   gerund
> *polować* 'hunt'   infinitive

cf. also

> *być w budowie* 'be a-building'   NP
> *budowanie* 'building'   gerund
> *budować* 'build'   infinitive

or

> *być w naprawie* 'being repaired', 'under repair'   NP
> *naprawianie* 'repairing'   gerund
> *naprawiać* 'repair'   infinitive

That the NP in Polish examples differs formally from the gerund is obvious; the difference goes even deeper and the forms in question are not interchangeable:

Janek chodzi w zaloty 'John goes a-wooing'   NP
Dom jest w budowie 'The house is a-building'   NP

are good, acceptable, idiomatic in a sense, sentences, while

*Janek chodzi w zalecanie się   gerund
*Dom jest w budowaniu   gerund

are far from being correct.

At this point I should like to find answers to some semantic problems, the first being whether it is possible to validate a claim that the idea of event predication relates the meaning of the finite verb to the meaning of the *a-X-ing*. The difficulties are added to by the fact that the verbs in question also respond semantically to the infinitive or some other prepositional phrases. But I do think that these do not refer to social, professional, cultural or the like, events. Rather they indicate purpose or direction as in the following:

(19) *He has gone to see his sister*   purpose

(20) *He has gone for a walk*   purpose

(21) *This road goes to London*   direction

apart from a great number of idiomatic uses. One might argue, and quite rightly, that the idea of event-like situation is also indirectly expressed in (19) and (20). However, it seems to me that the main concept is that of purpose and then something additional is implied, while in the case of such sentences as (1)

Carter goes a-wooing

the main concept is that of event (indirectly implying something additional like purpose). Thus, *hunting, wooing, building,* etc. are expressions of events in which a participant or participants either takes (take) part, or intends (intend) to participate. To express this the speaker uses *be* if he means the actual involvement of the participant in a given event, or one of the verbs of movement if the participation of some object in this event will take place in the future. The semantic relationship between the finite verb and the *a-X-ing* structure, their mutual compatibility, interdependence or cooccurrence allow some important generalization to arise: in order to adequately account for the meaning of the construction in question one has to go very deep and far beyond the explanation of the *X-ing* form. Since the event is chiefly temporal in character verbs like *go, fall, set* and even *be* can most successfully indicate the present or future involvement and participation of an object in this event. What is very significant for this statement is the lack of instances containing verbs expressing accomplishments, achievements, or states; none of the following sentences seems possible

(22) *He attended (a) wooing   accomplishment

(23) *He stopped (a) wooing   achievement

(24) *He likes (a) wooing   state,

neither do their Polish equivalents sound correct:

(22a) *Uczęszczał w zaloty

(23a) *?Skończył zaloty

(24a) *?Lubi zaloty

Here I am following Vendler's time schemata (1967:97 ff.) assuming that they are most appropriate for the discussion of the concept of event, which itself calls for a very careful characterization of temporal relations. Since events stretch over a period of time they are activities above all, constituting a subset of actions. And they have to be those activities which can very successfully fulfill the requirements I suggested earlier (cf. p. 368).

The next point worth considering is the question whether the construction *a-X-ing* is semantically unique like an idiom or a proverb. Within the scope of this rather limited discussion there is not enough ground to cover the problem in a fully satisfactory manner; however, I should like to draw the reader's attention to profusion and productivity of this structure in some English dialects,[6] which by itself denies any uniqueness. Take for instance any of the following examples:

(25) *it's right to go amowin'* (Lowell, *The Biglow Papers* 88)

(26) *w'ile de Hyener wur a laughin' ter hisse'f* (Harris, *Uncle Remus* 38)

(27) *an' she come a-wringin' her hands an' cryin' an' carryin' on!* (Haley, *Roots* 528)

in which the *a-X-ing* is used in the same function and for the same purpose as in a literary, educated variant of the language. To say only that the construction in question is obsolete or archaic is to my mind surely a simplification;[7] none of the dictionary definitions or explanations I have come across succeeds in bringing out to the full the intricacies and complexities both of its origin and of its usage.

In connection with this criticism I feel somehow compelled to assess the validity of Lightfoot's hypothesis and its reliability and applicability to the *a-X-ing* data. Does one have to admit that *a-X-ing* has undergone a categorial shift from the noun to the gerund? The answer to this question is negative: the whole discussion and argumentation presented to the reader so far were aimed at showing that for the reasons of proper semantic interpretation, supported by historical and comparative evidence, the *a-X-ing* construction is a prepositional phrase with an abstract noun. That this noun is derived from a corresponding verb does not invalidate the conclusion. It is up to a lexical rule, not a transformational one to explain the origin of *X-ing* and possibly also its meaning affinity to a verb. With this rather modest and cautious conclusion I should like to pass on to another *X-ing* construction which also poses many problems, these problems, however, being of a different type.

2   X-ing
"Trust and confidence are building slowly"

Although the construction in the above sense can be easily generated from the *a-X-ing* its production and usage potentials appear limited. Some verbs like *build*, *do*, *make*, cooking words can unhesitatingly enter into these grammatical relations which per se shows that the structure is still more than tolerable and that it manages surprisingly well to live in the language. The following textual evidence does not suggest at all that this *be X-ing* is on the way to disappear:

(28) *Trust and confidence are building slowly* (U. S. News and World Report August 27, 1979)

(29) *While the lobsters are steaming, stew the mushrooms* (Child *et al.* 1967:221)

(30) *While the rice is blanching, melt the butter with the seasonings* (Child *et al.* 1967:531)

(31) *While the brains are marinating, prepare the sauce* (Child *et al.* 1967:414)

(32) *as soon as fish is simmering* (Child *et al.* 1967:220)

The questions at issue range from the task to describe adequately the construction and its origin to the proper interpretation of the meaning.

Most grammarians, especially those concerned with historical aspects of the language, agree that *be X-ing* "originated (or to a great extent originated) from combinations with *on* (*a*) with the verbal substantive, in which *a* was later dropped through aphesis" (Jespersen 1949,iv:205). The *X-ing*, as they see it, is the verbal substantive (cf. Jespersen above), or a "nominalized form of the verb expressing manner" (Traugott 1972:143), or simply a present participle of a transitive verb which "may occur in the progressive in an intransitive or passive sense" (Zandvoort 1972:41).[8] Whatever the significance, these are statements which we encounter in linguistic literature. It will appear, however, that these statements are less significant when one considers *X-ing* in the light of its immediate origin, i.e. *a-X-ing* as understood in the previous section. And this is exactly the assumption on which I am going to analyze the structure in question. This being so that *be X-ing* comes from *be a-X-ing* the sentence (28) would be derivable from

(28a) *Trust and confidence are a-building slowly*

It is rather unlikely that (28a) would be used nowadays, neither would sentences (29a), (30a), etc. sound correct to the native speaker:

(29a) *While the lobsters are a-steaming, stew the mushrooms*

(30a) *While the rice is a-blanching, melt the butter with the seasonings*, etc.

In the past, however, the structures *be a-X-ing* and *be X-ing* were used side by side which is attested by the following examples:

(33) *it be so long a playing* (Tourner, *The Revenger's Tragedy* III, iii)

(34) *the whilst this play is playing* (Shakespeare, *Hamlet* III, ii, 83)

(35) *while the ark was a preparing* (Bible Auth. Version I Peter 3, 20)

(36) *while the arcke was preparing* (Bible I Peter 3, 20)

There are numerous instances[9] of this sort which strongly confirm the claim that the *X-ing* construction under analysis is ultimately traced back to the OE prepositional phrase (the issue was discussed at the beginning of this paper). Following this line of argument *X-ing* originated as an abstract noun, and functioned as a noun as long as it cooccurred with a preposition, even in its reduced form *a-*. But, can we argue that no matter how this *X-ing* behaves today it is categorially the same *X-ing* as before when used in a prepositional phrase? I have my strong doubts about this being the case and will try to justify these doubts.

The first observation to be made is that the structure of *be X-ing* is formally multiambiguous since *X-ing* can function either as a noun (cf. *understanding*), or an adjective (cf. *interesting*), or a gerund (cf. *John's driving*), or present participle (cf. *John is driving*). Now, if *be X-ing* were but a structural variant of *be a-X-ing*, the *X-ing* of the former would be treated and understood in the same manner as the *X-ing* of the latter, i.e. as an abstract noun. Further, if it were a noun it would be impossible to modify it with a manner adverbial which is the case in (28). To show this point more clearly take the sentence (37)

(37)   *There is a monetary understanding between two countries*

in which *understanding* is a noun modified by an adjective (*monetary*), not by an adverb; *understanding* modified by an adverb *monetarily*, e.g.

(37a)   **There is an understanding monetarily between two countries*

is decidedly ungrammatical (unless *monetarily* is a sentence modifier).[10] Therefore it seems that *X-ing* in *be X-ing* cannot be treated as a noun. To carry on the comparison further, one notices that *be X-ing* is paraphrasable into a passive, while *a-X-ing* is not, e.g.

(28b)   *Trust and confidence are being built slowly*

is grammatical and acceptable, which we cannot say about

(1a)   **Carter is being gone a-wooing*

nor about

(1c)   *?Carter goes being a-wooed*

(even if (1c) were understood as a meaningful sentence it would express a different message from the one expressed by (1)). Now the next test: *X-ing* changed into a past participle can have a modifying function, e.g.

(28c)   *Trust and confidence built slowly*

(38)   *Lobster steamed in wine with herb sauce* (Child *et al.* 1967: 223) (cf. 29)

a-X-ing cannot undergo such a transformation without destroying the relations which exist among the elements of a sentence, e.g.

(1d)   *?Carter goes a-wooed*

Finally, taking Polish semantic equivalents into consideration the discrepancy between *X-ing* and *a-X-ing* is convincingly evident: *be X-ing* is most frequently rendered by an impersonal construction with *się*, e.g.

(28d)   *Wiarę i zaufanie wyrabia się (buduje się, zyskuje się) powoli*

(29a) *Gdy homary gotują się na parze* . . .

but not by a nominal phrase, which is the case with *a-X-ing* (cf. p.   )

(28e) **Wiara i zaufanie są w budowie powoli*

(29e) **Gdy homary są w gotowaniu na parze* . . .

All these tests have failed to show that *X-ing* and *a-X-ing* are only variants and possess the same structural characteristics. On the contrary, the *X-ing* of *be X-ing* does not behave as a nominal any more, it is categorially different, perhaps still opaque to a great extent. Is this, then one more instance to support the Transparency Principle? It appears to be exactly the situation discussed by Lightfoot (1979). To simplify the explanation one may say that once *a-X-ing* was weakened to *X-ing* in the structure with *be*, the nominal character of *X-ing* became opaque. *Be X-ing* indistinguishable now from the progressive in its superficial structure has been gradually replaced by *be being X-ed*, as its closest semantic variant.[11] But the older *be X-ing* still lingering in the usage was restructured into the 'progressive' *X-ing* with all its verbal characteristics. In this way the nominal in the past *X-ing* changed into the verbal at present *X-ing*; hence its capability for being transformed into a past participle and for being accompanied by a manner adverbial. The most tricky aspect of the process which remains still to be accounted for is the question of how it is that *be X-ing* typically active in form is typically passive in meaning.

As far as I know there have been no investigations conducted to show the size and the complexities of the problem, although a considerable attention to this structure has been given by Jespersen and Visser. Let us hear what they say: "the substantive in *-ing* like all other verbal substantives (*construction*, *completion*, *conquest*, *discovery*, *punishment*, etc.) is in itself neither active nor passive: *is on (a) building* therefore may mean both 'is engaged in the act of building' (active) and 'is being built', as we say now (passive)" (Jespersen 1949, iv:205). Why it is just the passive that is assigned to *is building* remains unanswered. Visser (1973:2004—5) is more careful in his explanation when he says:

In this type of pattern [i.e. 'The house *is building*'] the action denoted by the form in *-ing* is not performed by the person or thing indicated by the subject, in this instance *the house*. In several grammars this kind of *-ing* is called 'passive', which is inacceptable, and often confusing, since the passive form is normally defined as consisting of a form of *to be* + past participle. To express the semantic difference between *building* in 'the house is building' and *building* in 'my uncle is building', the former had better been called 'passival', implying (not representing) as it does the passive construction. Structurally it seems simple to call 'the house is building' a passive transform of 'they are building', but in doing so, no light whatever is shed on its origin and development.

Leaving aside the formal aspect of this *be X-ing* as being of little help to explain its passival implication let us turn back to an immediate source of the structure to see whether it can provide any support for a notion of passivity expressed by this construction. For Jespersen an abstract noun *building* in *a-building* is unspecified with respect to activeness or passiveness. Perhaps this is a right approach in doubtful cases; in my opinion, however, the examples under analysis are not obscure to that extent. The nouns considered in a wider context express events viewed as predominantly active or predominantly passive depending on the meaning of the finite verb. It seems that the passive meaning is inherent in *be a-X-ing* when a nonanimate participant is involved in the event. Thus sentence (2)

The ship was still a-building

means that

There was a certain event of building which event was connected with the ship

In other words, the ship is involved (passively) in the event of building. It is not surprising that there is some sort of restriction imposed on the participant and its active/passive involvement in the event/activity. If the participant is a human or an animate object it actively participates in the event which is ren-dered by a non-*be* verb, usually a verb of movement, to indicate future in-volvement in the event, or by *be* to indicate present involvement in the event (future and present refer to the participant's actual involvement in the event with regard to the meaning of the finite verb). If, on the other hand, the participant has a feature of nonanimateness it is passively involved in the event, and these relations are expressed by *be*. The semantic interpretation suggested above is claimed to be valid for a *be X-ing* structure as well. Put it differently: *be X-ing* is passive in meaning because its immediate source *be a-X-ing* expressed mainly passive relations. There is some discrepancy between structural and semantic developments: formally *be X-ing* is not transparent any more and can be understood as an active progressive of an intransitive verb, semantically it continues the earlier stage, i.e. it implies passivity.

In conclusion I should like to mention two points: one point refers to the *X-ing* and its categorial membership, the other is connected with a lexical specification of the *X(-ing?)*. I have mentioned earlier that *be X-ing* is felt to be progressive because it behaves similarly to other progressive structures. For example, sentence (28)

> *Trust and confidence are building slowly*

is very close to

> (39) *John and Mary are going slowly*

which is unquestionably progressive (active in meaning though). To show this let me apply some tests to (28) which would eliminate the possibility of assigning X-*ing*[12] (i.e. *building*) to the category of

(a) the adjective

(28f) **Trust and confidence are very building*

(39a) **John and Mary are very going*

(b) the gerund

(28g) **Trust and confidence are his building of happiness*

(39b) **John and Mary are their going home*

(c) the noun

(28h) **Trust and confidence are slow buildings*

(39c) **John and Mary are slow goings*

These tests support a hypothesis that X-*ing* in (28) and sentences of this type functions as a progressive form of a verb. Since X-*ing* is structurally progressive then it is the lexical information of the item (the verb) itself that is supposed to convey the passive meaning; in this way we would have to treat this 'new' intransitive verb (derived from a transitive one) as an independent lexical item. In my opinion this is a wrong conclusion: the fact that a transitive verb changes into an intransitive one (or is used intransitively) does not necessarily mean that an independent item has originated and possesses all characteristic features of the intransitive verb. I would rather assume that the change is more superficial and has not gone deep enough to completely restructure the word semantically and syntactically as well. Notice that this 'new intransitive' verb is used under strictly defined conditions; one can say (28) but not

> (28i) **Trust and confidence built last year*

nor

(28j) *Trust and confidence will build in the future,* etc.[13]

To hypothesize on these observations one could postulate the following rule for present-day English: a transitive verb which regularly takes an animate noun for its subject can function as an intransitive one if the subject noun is nonanimate and the verb is used in the progressive form; these conditions being present the structure has passive implications. Thus, it seems that there is only one lexical item, e.g. *build* provided with all necessary information of various kinds and that it can be used either as a transitive verb or as an intransitive verb according to the context and more specifically, according to the features of the subject noun. To recapitulate the speculations about a possible historical development of the structure, active in form and passive in meaning, I should like to suggest the following stages:

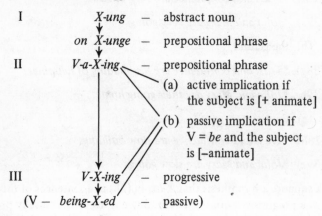

I	X-*ung*	—	abstract noun
	on X-*unge*	—	prepositional phrase
II	V-*a*-X-*ing*	—	prepositional phrase
		(a)	active implication if the subject is [+ animate]
		(b)	passive implication if V = *be* and the subject is [−animate]
III	V-X-*ing*	—	progressive
	(V — *being*-X-*ed*	—	passive)

Examples:

I   *þenung* 'service'
     on his þenunge 'in his service' (13)

II(a)   *he had been on a day a huntynge* (Froissart IV 147)
         Euery-on . . . went haukyng by þe ryuer (Orfeo 28, 293)
         Brzezinski goes a-purging (U. S. News and World Report November 5, 1979)

(b)   *it be so long a playing* (33)
       the whilst this play is playing (34)

III   *Trust and confidence are building slowly* (28)
       (There was no immediate explanation why the other women and blacks — more than a dozen in all — were not being freed (Newsweek November 26, 1979))

Notes

1. To do justice to Visser I must admit that the verb *fall* among many other meanings can express inchoation which is duly recorded by Webster: "to set about usu. heartily or actively: BEGIN — often used with an infinitive of action ⟨*fell* to work⟩ or a verbal noun after the prefix *a-* ⟨*fell* a-laughing⟩."
2. Compare Stockwell 1977:193–6.
3. For a slightly different understanding of the term event see Lyons (1977:483); for him, if a dynamic situation is momentary, it is an event.
4. According to a native informant whom I have consulted this sentence is very obsolete and would not be used ever nowadays in nondialect English.
5. Modern Polish thanks to its highly inflectional system serves for a good point of reference: it is structurally similar to Old English on the one hand, and structurally dissimilar to Modern English on the other.
6. By saying that the construction in question is used in dialects I do not mean that it is stylistically marked.
7. I do not quite argee with a British native speaker for whom the appearance of (1) as a newspaper headline shows that a joke is intended, either because it is obsolete, or dialect, or child language.
8. Most commonly in educated N. West (Northern) English. The southern speaker intuitively feels this to be a dialectical crotchet and tries vaguely to give it an active (intransitive) interpretation: *a new estate is building on the outskirts* (I owe this information to Professor E. C. McGahan; personal communication).
9. For different examples taken from various periods see Visser.
10. But *There is an understanding monetarywise between two countries* might be acceptable.
11. For the rise of the *The house is being built* type and its development see Visser (1973:2426 ff.). He is of the opinion that

> That, nonetheless, the substitution of 'the house is being built' for 'the house is building' was a matter of instinct or subconscious awareness, rather than of ratiocination is manifested by the fact that properly speaking it was by no means necessary, since the word serving as subject in the older type hardly ever referred to a human being capable of performing the action denoted by the *-ing*, and consequently misunderstanding was nearly always precluded.

> To my understanding whatever the validity of 'instinct or subconscious awareness' the structure was doomed to disappear because it became opaque and structurally multiply ambiguous.

12. *Slowly* is disregarded because as a manner adverb is used mainly with a verb; it can also be used with a noun formed from a verb, e.g. *his driving slowly* (Francis 1958: 305).
13. However, I can say *Trust and confidence will build up in the future*.

Sources

Bede — *The Old English Version of Bede's Ecclesiastical History of the English People*, edited by Thomas Miller. Part I, 1,2. E.E.T.S. O.S.95, 96. 1959.

Bible Auth. Version — *The Holy Bible Commonly Known as the Authorized (King James) Version* (Chicago: The Gideons International), 1959.

Bible – after F. Th. Visser. *An Historical Syntax of the English Language.* Part three. Second half: syntactical units with two and with more verbs (Leiden: E. J. Brill), 1973.

Child *et al.* – *Mastering the Art of French Cooking* by Julia Child, Louisette Bertholle, Simone Beck (New York: Alfred A. Knopf), 1967.

Froissart – after F. Th. Visser. *An Historical Syntax of the English Language.* Part three. Second half: syntactical units with two and with more verbs (Leiden: E. J. Brill), 1973.

Haley, *Roots* – Alex Haley. *Roots* (Garden City, N. Y.: Doubleday and Company), 1976.

Harris, *Uncle Remus* – from *An American English Reader.* Texts selected and provided with notes and glossary by Ruta Nagucka (Warszawa: PWN), 1975.

Hornby *et al.* – *The Advanced Learner's Dictionary of Current English* by A. S. Hornby, E. V. Gatenby, H. Wakefield. Second edition (London: Oxford University Press), 1963.

Kispert – Robert J. Kispert. *Old English: An Introduction* (New York: Holt, Rinehart and Winston), 1971.

Lowell, *The Biglow Papers* – from *An American English Reader.* Texts selected and provided with notes and glossary by Ruta Nagucka (Warszawa: PWN), 1975.

Onions – *Sweet's Anglo-Saxon Reader in Prose and Verse,* revised by C. T. Onions. Fourteenth edition (Oxford: At the Clarendon Press), 1959.

Orfeo – *Sir Orfeo,* edited by A. J. Bliss. Second edition (Oxford: At the Clarendon Press), 1966.

Reszkiewicz 1971 – *Synchronic Essentials of Old English.* West-Saxon, by Alfred Reszkiewicz (Warszawa: PWN), 1971.

Shakespeare, *Hamlet* – *Hamlet,* edited by Horace Howard Furness. *vol. I. A New Variorum Edition of Shakespeare* (New York: Dover Publications, Inc.), 1963.

Tourner, *The Revenger's Tragedy* – *Tourner,* edited by John Addington Symonds (The Mermaid Series) (London: T. Fisher Unwin Ltd), n.d.

Visser 1973 – F. Th. Visser. *An Historical Syntax of the English Language.* Part three. Second half: syntactical units with two and with more verbs (Leiden: E. J. Brill), 1973.

Webster – *Webster's Third New International Dictionary of the English Language.* Unabridged (Springfield, Mass.: G. and C. Merriam Company), 1971.

References

Francis, W. Nelson
    1958   *The structure of American English* (New York: The Ronald Press).
Jespersen, Otto
    1949   *A modern English grammar on historical principles.* Part IV. Syntax. 3rd vol. (London: George Allen and Unwin).
Kispert, Robert J.
    1971   *Old English: An introduction* (New York: Holt, Rinehart and Winston).
Lightfoot, David W.
    1979   *Principles of diachronic syntax* (Cambridge: Cambridge University Press).

Lyons, John
  1977   *Semantics* (Cambridge: Cambridge University Press).
Quirk, Randolph – C. L. Wrenn
  1958   *An Old English grammar* (London: Methuen).
Stockwell, Robert P.
  1977   *Foundations of syntactic theory* (Englewood Cliffs, N. J.: Prentice-Hall, Inc.).
Traugott, Elizabeth Closs
  1972   *A history of English syntax. A transformational approach to the history of English sentence structure* (New York: Holt, Rinehart and Winston).
Vendler, Zeno
  1967   *Linguistics in philosophy* (Ithaca, N. Y.: Cornell University Press).
Visser, F. Th.
  1973   *An historical syntax of the English language.* Part three. Second half: syntactical units with two and with more verbs (Leiden: E. J. Brill).
Wright, Joseph – Elizabeth Mary Wright
  1948   *An elementary Old English grammar* (Oxford: At the Clarendon Press).
Zandvoort, R. W.
  1972   *A handbook of English grammar* (London: Longman).

HERBERT PILCH

Syntactic reconstruction

1 The shortcomings of historical syntax

Historical and comparative linguistics devotes so much effort to phonology and accidence (inflexion), but so little, comparatively speaking, to syntax. We all know this and complain of it. Still, we have not done much to mend matters. Even the monumental Comparative Germanic Grammar of the Soviet Academy (for which we entertain the highest possible regard) has four volumes devoted to phonology and morphology, only one to syntax. Those first four volumes appeared between 1962 and 1966. We are still waiting for volume 5 on syntax.

We see two major reasons for this lamentable situation:

(i) Inductive generalization has, by this time, become a routine matter in historical phonology. The specific type of generalization from word shape change (OE. *stān* > MnE. *stone*) to sound law (OE. /ā/ > MnE. /ou/) has been practised for more than a hundred years. The further generalization from sound law to restructuring of the phoneme system (Martinet 1955) constitutes a more recent achievement and still causes surprise when it appears in a handbook (Pilch 1970a, Rix 1976). On the other hand, it is precisely the latter type of advance-level generalization that has made historical phonology rewarding once more, since all the major sound laws were discovered a long time ago.

(ii) Is there one universal phoneme system for all languages? Most of us probably reject this proposition, holding that every language has a phoneme system *sui generis* (not just a selection from some universal phonetic alphabet). Only on the basis of this assumption (which is, ultimately, axiomatic) can we even begin to study advanced-level historical phonology. On the other hand, if there were indeed just one universal phoneme system for all languages, then *a fortiori* there would be just one phoneme system for the different historical periods of any single language. The only historical changes that could be recognized under these circumstances would consist in a redistribution of entities within the universal set. In other words, we would then (if we did assume the universal sound system) be back on the well-trodden paths of the old sound law, which (for the reasons stated above) hold no promise of major discoveries these days.

Now in historical syntax there appears to be no analogue even to the elementary step of inductive generalization, namely the sound law, let alone an analogue to the advance-level restructuring of systems. The reason is that the very notion of system (as an analogue of the phoneme system) is not very widely accepted in syntax, not even by those who do accept the phoneme system (as a notion). Indeed, the time-hallowed idea that there is just one universal system of grammar for all languages has recently been re-enforced by generativist linguistics. Notions like the sentence, the noun phrase, verb phrase, relative clause, accusative case are once again widely believed to be "universal". At the same time, inductive generalization has been replaced by neuropsychological speculation about the grammar which is (or is not) "stored in the human brain".

This is, essentially, a revival of Latin school grammar dressed up in some (ostensibly) scientific trappings. Once we believe that there is just one system of syntax "underlying" all languages, the only type of syntactic change that can be recognized is the re-distribution of entities within this one system. For instance, the verb *bide* governs the genitive in Old English (*Grendles . . . bīdan* 'wait for Grendel', Bwf 527), but the accusative in Modern English (as in *he is biding his time*). Or *like* was construed impersonally down to Early Modern English (as in *the music likes me not* (*Two Gentlemen of Verona* 4.2.54)), but it has changed to the personal construction (*I do not like the music*) today. Such statements necessarily concern individual words, but they do not lend themselves to inductive generalization (even if we do not reject such generalization a priori).

This is the "parts-of-speech syntax" we find in historical treatises like Mossé's, Visser's, Mustanoja's, Carstensen's. We do entertain the highest possible regard for these books. On the other hand, we feel it is significant that Mustanoja's second volume ("which will deal with word order and the structure of the complex sentence", Preface to vol. I) has never come out. Once we assume that there is a "universal" list of parts of speech and clause types with "the sentence" at the top of the hierarchy, there is not much room left for "the structure of the complex sentence" to change. Similarly, if the "word order" we recognize is exhausted by VSO and its permutations, we are bound to find examples of all possible word orders in most languages and, *a fortiori*, in different historical stages of any given language. So again there is little scope for historical change.

To sum up: The reason why historical syntax has received so little attention is (we suggest) not in the absence of syntactic change in languages (we

all somehow know that it is present), but in the inadequacy of our preliminary assumptions. Assuming a "universal grammar", we have, in effect,
axiomatically denied syntactic change other than change of a few details.
Consequently, we are unable to lay our hands on it for all we "feel" that it
is there.

2 A new set of assumptions

In order to mend matters, we need (so we believe) a more adequate theory.
Specifically, let us recognize that:
   (i) Inductive generalization is a tool of knowledge — provided it operates
within (not apart from) an axiomatic-deductive theory (Mulder-Hervey
1980: ch. 3). The first step of inductive generalization is from protocolizing
given examples to a description of these examples in terms of analytical
categories. For instance, the advertisement *more house for your money* can
be described in terms of count nouns (such as *house*) being transferred to
the category of mass nouns. This inductive generalization covers ("gener-
ates") an unlimited number of further examples not yet observed. It has
to be validated by the future observation of such examples, such as *the most
car you can buy*.
   The second step is from one specific change as described (such as count
noun to mass noun) to a class of structurally similar changes. For instance,
in the passive construction of English, Old English used only single transitive
verbs as nuclei. Since then, this class has expanded to compound verbs, such
as *put down, run off* (as in *the rebellion was put down, the copies were run
off*), even to whole transitive predicates, such as *give a goingover* (as in *he
was given a goingover*). Analogous expansion has occurred in the group
genitive (Jespersen 1961: VI ch. 17; Quirk 1970: section 13.64). Only single
substantives appear in the genitive in Old English, but today whole nominal
groups do (as in *the Wife of Bath's Tale*), even relative constructions (as in
a man I know's car).
   We can generalize on these two specific changes, inferring that expansion
of the nuclear commutation class is one way in which syntactic constructions
change. This second step of inductive generalization thus produces types of
change (rather than merely specific instances).
   (ii) Every language has a syntactic system *sui generis*, not just a selection
from a set list of parts of speech and clause types with "the sentence" at the
top of the hierarchy. In fact, the set of "universal" syntactic notions with
which we operate is necessarily incomplete and of limited applicability. Even

for the wellknown European languages, the notion of *sentence* is applicable only to certain highly standardized written texts, but breaks down as soon as we consider spontaneous speech (Pilch 1979) or texts written prior to the standardization, say Old English poetry (Pilch 1970b). Once we try a language like Chinese, our parts of speech and clause types become very hard to operate with, and indeed we have no reason to expect that Chinese should conform to the traditional European notions of linguistic structure.

Consequently, we need a syntactic theory which operates with well-defined formal notions, not those traditional, substantive notions of European grammar. The most adequate theory we know of is Mulder's (Mulder-Hervey 1980: ch.s 4, 10, 11, 12). It is the only one which satisfies both the formal requirements of epistemology and the empirical requirements of linguistics. In other words, it is both impeccable theoretically and applicable empirically. We reserve the right, of course, to modify or add to Mulder's framework, as our empirical object requires.

(iii) The syntactic structure is in the "constructional meaning" of specific constructions, witness the semantic difference between *I found her an entertaining partner* construed as di-transitive 'I found a partner for her' and complex-predicative 'I found she was entertaining' (Quirk 1970: section 7.7). The converse of this assumption is that the constructional meaning is (wholly) in the syntactic structure. The two are, we take it, synonymous expressions denoting the same phenomena. It follows that the syntactic analysis of any protocolized expression is materially adequate, if and only if it exhaustively describes its constructional meaning.

Consequently, constructions are (we think) the major concern of historical syntax. By contrast, the choice of particular functional particles (say *and* rather than *if* in the conditional clauses of Early Modern English) is only a minor concern. It is a matter not of syntactic structure, but of its realisation on the lexical or allomorphic level, and so is the choice of word order, say SVO rather than SOV or *one the wisest prince* in Early Modern English (Franz 1939: section 365; Mustanoja 1960: 297–299) rather than *the one wisest prince* in Present-Day English:

> Syntactic analysis can, then, be said to be the account — for a given language — of syntactic relations between syntagmatic entities, ultimately pleremes. As these entities are "signa", not "allomorphs", let alone "phonological forms", etc., we can dispense with statements of "variance" or "realisation", and even the linear aspect of the latter becomes irrelevant. We must, of course, be able to add statements of realisation to our structural, analytical statements, but this is not part of the actual establishment of syntactic relations. This, of course, is

not to say that "allomorphic variance" may not be a *pointer* to syntactic relations.
(Mulder-Hervey 1980: 162 f.).

(iv) Those functional particles do not carry meaning in the same manner as do lexemes like *bird, insidious* or *write*. To take one example, what does the particle *yet* mean? Surely, it does not denote any phenomenon in the extra-linguistic world, but it functions as a cue of discourse structure (Pike–Becker–Young 1970: ch. 14), specifically of the reservation in the rhetorical pattern *concession : reservation*. This cue value is present in the concessive syntagm *though* a *yet* b, but it is not limited to this syntagm, nor is it limited to any specific set of syntactic structures. It works even regardless of any particular syntactic structure. For instance, an antique dealer from Ontario stated that he felt unable to distinguish between antiques of Canadian and United States provenience, adding the reservation: "And yet . . ." (Forum discussion on Radio Canada, stored on tape).

Cues are often ambiguous. For instance, *because* is used not only to suggest a causal connection, but equally to suggest almost any factual connection. For instance, the late Senator John F. Kennedy used it speaking of "Nikita Khrushchev is in New York right now, and he pursues the Communist offensive throughout the world, *because* of the productive power of the Soviet Union itself" (Pre-election TV debate with Mr. Richard M. Nixon, stored on tape). Colloquially, *'cause* is very often heard as a final tag, similar to *like, though*. The cue value of such particles is so ambiguous that they can "mean" almost anything – which is tantamount to nothing, as in: "It (this College) has its troubles-like athleticwise" (Spontaneous conversation of Californian speaker, stored on tape). As we all know from experience, the vagueness of such cues defies both lexical description and grammar rules.

(v) The cue value of functional particles is, strictly speaking, not part of the constructional meaning. For instance, comparing the meaning of the conditional syntagm *if* a *then* b and the concessive syntagm *though* a *yet* b, we see that the construction of both syntagms is the same. Both are, in fact, interordinate syntagms, i.e. *if x* is dependent on *then y*, and also inversely. By the same token, *though x* is dependent on *yet y*, and also inversely (Mulder-Hervey 1980: 173). It follows that the meaning difference between these two syntagms is not in the syntactic structure, but in the cue value of the particles *if . . . then* for the conditional, *though . . . yet* for the concessive. The labels *conditional* and *concessive* thus refer not to syntactic structure, but to discourse structure. As we have already noted, neither the functional particles concerned nor their cue values are necessarily tied to specific syntactic constructions.

Or let us check on the *do*-expansion of verbs. In Middle English, it is causative, as *do peynte* 'cause to paint' (Chaucer, *Book of the Duchess* 259; Mustanoja 1960: 601). In Modern English, it is periphrastic. The semantic difference between the causative *do* and the periphrastic *do* is apparently a case of multiple cue value, not of multiple syntactic structure.

3 The historical syntax of English

Looking at the history of English from the vantage point of our assumptions, we find at least three different types of change. The two former are a minor concern, only the third hinges on the syntactic structure:

(i) Cue value of functional particle remains the same, but functional particle is different linguistic sign. For instance, the disjunctive negative discourse structure was *no* a *ne* b in Old English (Pilch 1970: 190), *neither* a *ne* b in Middle English (as in "neither drye ne deed", *Merchant's Tale* 1463), and it is *neither* a *nor* b today. What has happened is that the functional particles concerned have been replaced by other particles with a similar cue value.

Lüdtke (1980: 205) has analysed this type of change in terms of the model *attrition* : *enrichment*. The model envisages that the functional particles are reduced phonetically to near-zero in actual speech. As they become progressively more difficult to perceive for their cue value, they are replaced by phonetically bulkier functionals which are easier to hear (as *no* by *neither*). But, eventually, the latter are reduced in turn, and so on.

There are, however, some remarkable instances in the history of English which do not fit Lüdtke's predictions. For instance, many functional particles were expanded by *that* in Middle English, such as *when that* 'when', *which that* 'which', e.g. in the first line of the *Canterbury Tales*: "Whan that Aprill ... hath perced to the roote". Such expansion is one way of making a reduced functional bulkier, and it constitutes an irreversible historical process according to Lüdtke. The fact is those *that*-expansions have been reversed, as *that* is no longer inserted after these functional particles today.

In certain other instances, the functional particle has been lost without replacement, and the construction as a whole has been lost with it. Instances are the Old English elliptic dual (as in *uncer Grendles* 'Grendel and myself', Bwf 2002; Pilch 1970a: 196) and the Old English sociative instrumental (as in *hē lȳtle werede* 'he and a small crowd', *Anglo Saxon Chronicle* 74.28; Pilch 1970a: 221). As the dual pronouns and the instrumental case endings were lost, so were the constructions concerned.

(ii) Functional particle remains the same linguistic sign, but its ambiguity as a cue is reduced. For instance, the periphrastic syntagms *have*-past participle, *be*-present participle are well evidenced throughout the history of the English language. Their modern cue values are labelled "present perfect" and "imperfective aspect" respectively. However, the cue values concerned were much less precise in the earlier stages of the language. In Old and Middle English those cues were sometimes used in situations where they would also be used today, but often enough in others, as in *hæbbe ic mærða fela ongunnen on geoguþe* 'I undertook many valiant deeds in my youth' (Bwf 408), *æglæca ehtende wæs* 'the monster persecuted' (Bwf 159). Inversely, the two syntagms concerned were not used in many situations where they are found in good usage today.

The relatively rare, but apparently erratic use of these syntagms has puzzled investigators who were looking for some "rule of grammar". They expected modern usage to be somehow foreshadowed by earlier usage, but these expectations have remained unfulfilled. On the other hand, the evidence fits our expectations perfectly. The cue value of *have*-past participle, *be*-present participle was at one time vague and ambiguous (as the cue value of *like*, *because* is today, see above), but it has been progressively disambiguated since the 18th century. Some ambiguity remains even today, so the "rules of grammar" which are believed to govern those syntagms have never been fully discovered even for modern usage, though no end of books have been written about them. This is the reason why we have limited our observation above to "good usage" only. Apart from "good usage", the present perfect and the imperfective aspect are indeed still used quite erratically even today.

(iii) Construction remains the same, but commutation class expands in the nuclear slot. At least three relevant instances have already been noted above, namely the compound passive, the group genitive and the syntagm *more*-mass noun. Such constructions are PRODUCTIVE. Productivity is at least one way in which syntactic innovations are brought about. In fact, a new construction arises, by definition, as soon as some commutation class starts expanding from one to two and ever more members – witness the *more house*-construction mentioned above. Another witness is the medio-passive construction (Jespersen 1961: III, 351; Jarceva 1961: 57–63). It started in advertising diction, e.g. *these apartments are now renting,* and is now being carried over into general diction, as in *money is wasting, support is building* (these two examples are found in the *Christian Science Monitor* May 6, 1966, p.1a; November 9, 1979, p.26c). The nuclear commutation class is indeed expanding.

The converse of productivity is SHRINKAGE, i.e. the nuclear commutation class contracts (rather than expands). For instance, of the large number of impersonal verbs of Middle English, very few remained in Early Modern English, such as *me likes* (in the example above), *me thinks, me rather had, it skills not*. This means that the impersonal verb construction was RESIDUAL in Early Modern English. The construction has lost every one of its nuclear members by this time, so the construction itself has "shrunk to zero", i.e. it has ceased to exist. However, in many instances, the nuclear commutation class contracts without therefore becoming residual. For instance, the combination of a possessive with a demonstrative pronoun has disappeared today, as in OE. *mīn þæt lēofe bearn* 'my dear child' (*Guthlac* 1076). We take these two pronouns to be in a co-ordinate construction. The co-ordinate syntagm *mīn þæt* is, we take it, in the same commutation class as any single possessive or demonstrative pronoun, as in *mīn lēofe bearn, þæt lēofe bearn*. Those co-ordinates have disappeared from the commutation class, but there is no indication the commutation class is shrinking to zero (We take the modern syntagm *this my child* to be a carryover from bureaucratic diction, not the historical continuation of *mīn þæt lēofe bearn*).

An even clearer instance of contraction (but not shrinkage) is the relative construction. Early Modern English still has prepositional groups as antecedents, as in *in that dimension which I did participate* (*Twelfth Night* 5.1.236). Even subsidiary clauses are found as relative transforms, as *your grievances which since I know* (*Two Gentlemen of Verona* 4.3.38). The relative construction is narrower in scope today, but it does not appear to be headed for extinction.

Can we carry generalization one step further from syntagm to restructuring of syntactic systems — on the analogy of the restructuring of phoneme systems noted above (Pike 1962)? We have at least attempted to do so. Like phonological systems, we take syntactic systems to be systems of recurrent distinctions. For instance, the elementary predicates of Old English are either verbal (e.g. *gomban gyldan,* Bwf 11) or equational (e.g. *þæt wæs gōd cyning,* ib.), and they are either personal or impersonal, as in this table:

ps. vb.   ps. equ.
ips. vb.   ips. equ.

Presenting them as a quadrilateral (on the analogy of vowels systems like $\begin{smallmatrix} i & u \\ æ & a \end{smallmatrix}$), we find the distinction *ps.* $\neq$ *ips.* recurs in the two columns, the distinction *vb.* $\neq$ *equ.* recurs in the two rows. The major change which this system has undergone is the loss of the second row, and this loss is bound up with the shrinkage of the nuclear commutation class, as explained above.

The passive transforms of Old English (Pilch 1970a: 199–203) also form a syntactic system (Kholodovič 1974). These transforms involve either changing the verb from active to passive or changing the object into the subject, or both or neither:

active vb./unch. obj. active vb./obj. → sbj.
passive vb./unch. obj. passive vb./obj. → sbj.

The top-left syntagm is the ordinary active transitive predicate. The bottom-left syntagm is the impersonal passive (e.g. *swā me gifeðe wæs*, Bwf 2491). The top-right syntagm is the medial transform (as in *ecghete ēoweð* 'hostility shows', Bwf 1738). The bottom-right syntagm is the ordinary passive transform (as in *ða wæs hord rāsod*, Bwf 2283). One major change which this system has undergone is the expansion of the passive as described above. Another major change is the expansion of the medial transform to the imperfective aspect, as in *these apartments are now renting*. Otherwise there has been remarkably little change. Even the celebrated construction *John is easy to please* goes back to the compound passive of Old English, as in *ofost is sēlest to gecȳpanne* (Bwf 256), *he biþ . . . egeslīc to gesēonne* (Chr 918).

There has, indeed, been a fair amount of syntactic restructuring in the history of English, even apart from those minor matters such as functional particles and word order. There have been major changes of syntactic structure, as certain constructions have been expanding, others contracting, and as such expansions have been carried over into general diction from specific styles and inversely. Contrary to traditional "universal grammar", our approach has enabled us to get hold of, and systematically describe the changes that we "felt" all the time were there.

References

Carstensen, Broder
  1959   *Studien zur Syntax des Nomens, Pronomens und der Negation in den Paston Letters* (Bochum: Pöppinghaus).
Cholodovič, A. A., ed.
  1974   *Tipologija passivnych konstrukcij* [Typology of Passive Constructions] (Leningrad: Nauka).
Franz, Wilhelm
  1939   *Die Sprache Shakespeares* (Halle a.S.: Niemeyer).
Jarceva, V. N.
  1961   *Istoričeckij sintaksis anglijskogo jazyka* [Historical Syntax of the English language] (Moscow: Akademija Nauk).
Jespersen, Otto
  1961   *Modern English Grammar* (London and Copenhagen: Munksgaard), reprint.
Lüdtke, Helmut
  1980   *Kommunikationstheoretische Grundlagen des Sprachwandels* (Berlin: de Gruyter).

Martinet, André
   1955   *Economie des changements phonétiques* (Bern: Francke).
Mossé, Fernand
   1959   *Manuel de l'anglais du Moyen-âge* 2nd ed. (Paris: Aubier).
Mulder, Jan – Sándor Hervey
   1980   *The Strategy of Linguistics* (Edinburgh: The Scottish Academy Press).
Mustanoja, Tauno
   1960   *Middle English Syntax I* (Helsinki: Société néophilologique).
Pike, Kenneth L.
   1962   "Dimensions of Grammatical Constructions", *Language* 38:221–244.
Pike, Kenneth L. – Alton L. Becker – Richard E. Young
   1970   *Rhetoric: Discovery and Change* (New York: Harcourt, Brace and World).
Pilch, Herbert
   1970a   *Altenglische Grammatik* (Munich: Hueber).
   1970b   "Syntactic Prerequisites for the Study of Old English Poetry", *Language and
            style* 3:51–61.
   1970c   "Matrix der altenglischen Satztypen", *Hommage à Eric Buyssens*, ed. Jean
            Dierick and Yvan Lebrun (Brussels: Institut de Sociologie de l'Université
            Libre), 161–167.
   1979   "Pour une syntaxe de la langue parlée: La construction anglaise à redouble-
            ment", *Festschrift Oswald Szemerényi*, ed. B. Brogyanyi (Amsterdam:
            John Benjamins), 655–661.
Quirk, Randolph et al.
   1970   *A Grammar of Contemporary English* (London: Longman).
Rix, Helmut
   1976   *Historische Grammatik des Griechischen: Laut- und Formenlehre* (Darm-
          stadt: Wissenschaftliche Buchgesellschaft).
Sravnitel'naja grammatika germanskich jazykov
   1962–   [Comparative Grammar of the Germanic Languages], 4 vol.s (Moscow:
   66   Akademija Nauk).
Visser, F. Th.
   1963   *An historical syntax of the English language I* (Leiden: Brill).
   1966   *An historical syntax of the English language II* (Leiden: Brill).
   1969   *An historical syntax of the English language III,1* (Leiden: Brill).
   1973   *An historical syntax of the English language III,2* (Leiden: Brill).

PAOLO RAMAT

"Es war ein König in Thule (...), Dem sterbend seine Buhle...": on the rise and transformation(s) of morphosyntactic categories*

0. In a well-known article of 1968 Emile Benveniste gave clear evidence for conservative mutations serving to replace old morphemic categories by new ones with the same function, as, e.g., the periphrastic development of perfectum and future in the Romance domain (Benveniste 1968).

The converse case is represented by innovating mutations introducing new morphological categories. The genesis of the definite and indefinite articles in the Germanic languages (Gmc.lg.s) is a good case for this type.

1. The rise of the article was caused by the need to have a new category to fill a functional gap opened by a typological shift the Gmc.lg.s underwent in the course of their history – though not all at the same moment.

The traditional explanation of the rise of the article is not satisfactory. Since we find articles coexisting with declension (as in German) the wear and tear of the endings caused by stress accent on the root syllable cannot be made responsible for the rise of articles: morphological changes are not caused by phonetic accidents alone. Recourse should be made to concomitant causes both of phonetic and morphosyntactic nature: endings of the inflectional synthetic type had been weakened by the strong stress accent on the root syllable and as a result a fixed order (SVO, with grammatical subject before the verb) became necessary; conversely the endings distinguishing, say, nominative and accusative were no longer strictly necessary since the position in the sentence was sufficient to distinguish between subject and object.

The new category ART, thus, did not rise to cope with any grammatical need. Theoretically, as I have said, the bare position in the sentence was sufficient to differentiate among the function of the NPs (and it is indeed! Cp. *The hunter killed the wolf* vs. *The wolf killed the hunter*). We shall see below that the origin of ART as morphological category has to be sought in a process of grammaticalization of pragmatic strategies of focusing and topicalizing, with the semantic feature [± definite] becoming morphologically compulsory.

2. On the basis of many typological features like nominal compounds showing a Determinans+Determinatum Structure (e.g. *hlewa-gastiR* lit. "famous guest") we can fairly assume Proto-Germanic (PGmc.) to have been a (predominantly) SOV-language (see Ramat 1980: chap. VII).

Gmc.lg.s show in the course of their history the tendency ('drift' in sapirian terms) to move towards an SVO-type. Also the most conservative language of the family, Modern Icelandic, is now undergoing changes which English underwent in its middle period: see, for instance, the use of 'dummy subject' pronouns like *það* "it" in sentences like

(1) *það leit   enginn við þessu drasli áður*
    it   looked nobody at this   trash before

"Nobody paid any attention to this trash before" (Kossuth 1978:449), comparable to the shift ME *me semeth* → ModE *it seems to me* (see Butler 1977).

Such a trend is consistent with a weakening of the inflectional principle — i.e. of the synthetic type — in favour of analytic features like the increasing usage of Prepositional Phrases in place of declension cases (*domi bellique*, locative, → *in pace et in bello*).

In other words, the shifting SOV → SVO is consistent with a tendency synthetic → analytic.

SVO-languages usually have preposed determinations: articles before nouns, personal pronouns and prepositions before verbs, whereas rigid SOV-languages show postpositions (among them also endings) to determine morphologically and syntactically nouns and verbs: cp. *the work~to work~I work* vs. OE *weorc~wyrcan~wyrce*. Moreover, it should be noticed that consistent OV-languages do not have ART. s; on the other hand "a language which uses word order to signal grammatical relations will tend to develop articles" (Thompson 1978:26).

3. This is the well-known typological frame which the rise of the new morphological category ART in Gmc.lg.s must be made to square with. Now, what means did Gmc.lg.s have at their disposal to elaborate the new category? It is well-known that articles can originate from deictic elements. As Greenberg rightly puts it, "the most common origin of the definite article is the demonstrative, a development of which there are numerous and well-attested examples ... It develops from a purely deictic element which has come to identify an element as previously mentioned in discourse" (Greenberg 1978:61).

We can thus introduce for such a deictic element the semantic feature [+ known].

In PGmc. the deictic element was $*sa$-, $þa$-, having the possibility of agreement with the head noun it referred to: $*sa, sō, þat$.

It is the thesis of the present paper that this deictic element, which we can simply call DET(erminer), gave rise not only to the definite article but also, by a split of a previously undifferentiated function, to postposed relative clauses (RCs). This is peculiar to the Gmc.lg.s; other language families – e.g. Romance – offer two different forms for def.art. and relative pronoun (*ille* or *ipse* vs. *qui*). The coincidence is not casual; on the contrary it is the trace of an earlier profound unity which can still be observed in the old Gmc. texts.

3.1 Two kinds of RC will be shown to have been possible in PGmc.: the cataphoric *wh*-type preposed to its head noun, and the anaphoric type introduced by the deictic DET. The profound difference formerly existing between the two types has progressively been cancelled by analogical processes of grammatical standardization so that we can now say

(2a) *I bought a volume* that *costs four pounds*

as well as

(2b) *I bought a volume* which *costs four pounds*

(See further § 5.2. For the purpose of the present paper it is rather pointless to discuss whether the 'relative particles' (Goth. *ei*, Engl. *the, that,* Ital. *che,* MGreek *poú,* etc.) historically preceed the relat. pron. or not (see for details Ramat 1981:105). The 'relative particles' are derived from the same deictic basis as the relat. pron.s so that the problem of the rise of the relative function remains the same.)

The preposed RC refers to a concept not previously introduced in the sentence, thus indefinite ([– known]):

(3) Lat. *Qui eorum non ita iuraverit* (...) *pro eo argentum nemo dabit* (Cat., *agr.* 144.2) "Whoever of them did not swear in this way (...) no one will give him money";

(4) Hitt.: *takku* İRaš   *hūwai*   *n-aš ANA* KUR ^{uru}*Luwija*
       if   (a) slave runs away ptc.-he to land   Luwian

kuiš-an appa uwatezzi nu-šše   6 GÍN   KUBABBAR *pāi*
who-him back brings   ptc.-him 6 shekels silver   gives
"If a slave runs away, goes to the land of the Luwians, one gives 6 shekels of silver to who (ever) brings him back" (see Justus 1978:116);

(5) Umbr.: *Pisi panupei fratrexs fratrus   atiersier   fust*
Whoever whenever 'fratricus' of the Brothers At. (shall) be,

erec (. . . .) portaia   seuacne   (Tab.Eug. VIIb 1)
he   has to bring (the cows) without imperfection.

And in Gmc. too (see Behaghel 1923: I 369):

(6) *thaz so wer so fon themo selben*
so that whoever of it   self

ezze, ni sterbe . . .   So wer so   izzit fon thesemo
eats (he) does not die. Whoever eats of this

brote lebet   in ewidu   (*Tat.* 82.10)
bread (he) shall live for ever;

(7) *sō hue sō ōgon   genimid ōδres mannes . . . . that he it*
Whoever (an) eye   takes of another man (I say) that he it

eft mid is selbes scal sān antgelden mid
after with of himself shall soon pay   with

gelīcun   liδion   (*Hel.* 1529ff.)
(the) same limb;

(8) *swā hwā swā sylδ   ānne drync cealdes wæteres. . . .*
whoever has given a   glass of cold water

ne amyrδ   he hys mēde   (Mth. 10.42)
not will spoil he his meed;

(9) *eal swā hwaet swā wē to gōde doþ. . .*
all whatsoever   we of good do

ealle   þās god · cumaþ of. . .   (Blikl. Hom.).
all   these goods come   from. . .

All the examples (except (6)) exhibit the anaphoric 'reprise' through a
deictic form (: *pro eo, -an, erec, he*) or through repetition as in (9) (:*ealle
þās god*) of the indefinite person/thing meant in the preposed RC: this per-
son/thing has now been determined through the RC and can be alluded to
via an anaphoric deixis:

(10) Wer *einmal lügt*, dem *glaubt man nicht* (≅ Der Lügner
[Topic and focus: see fn.2], dem glaubt man nicht);

(11) Qui *patriam defendit*, is *fortis vocatur* (≅ defensor patriae,
is. . .)[1] ; for conditional value of (10), (11) see fn. 5.

More generally we can say that a preposed RC can build up a concept that has not been previously lexicalized nor introduced in the sentence: *What John did was unbelievable* ≡ *John's action was unbelievable* (Chr. Lehmann 1979:348). Hence the use of the IE indef. pron. *$*K^wO$-/K^wI-* in many languages of the family (see Ex.s (3)–(8))[2].

3.2 The other type of RC, which forms the subject of this paper, has a quite different origin.

Postposed RCs refer to an already introduced head noun (i.e. [+ known]) and serve to give more information about it; they are an attribution of it:

(12) *Ándra   moi   énnepe, Moûsa, polýtropon,* hòs
    The man to me tell, thou M.,   skilful,   *who*

    mála pollà/   plágchthē   (*Od.* 1,1f.)
    very   many things   suffered

(13) OPers. *martiya* hya *āgariya āha   avam*
    the man *who* loyal   was, him

    ubartam   abaram   (DB 1.21f.)
    esteemed   I lifted up

(i.e. "... I rewarded him well");

(14) Osc. *eítiuvam*   paam (...) *deded*
    the money *which*   he gave,

    eísak   eítiuvad etc.   (Planta, N. 29)
    with   that money ...

(15) Lat. ... *paries* qui *est propter viam* etc. (see fn. 1).

In many cases the pronoun introducing the second clause is a deictic form from the IE basis *$*SO$-/TO-* which furnishes demonstratives in several IE lg.s:

(16) Gk. *autíka   d' égnō /   oulēn   tēn*
    and soon ptc. she recognised/(the) scar that/which

    poté min   sŷs   élase   (*Od.* 19,392f.)
    once to him a wild boar had done;

(17) *all' hó ge Talthýbión te kaì Eyrybátēn proséeipen/*
    but he ptc. (to) T.   and   E.   addressed

    tṓ   hoi   ésan kēruke   (*Il.* 1.320f.)
    those/who both to him were heralds.

Notice that such RCs introduced by *SO-/TO- never precede in Homer their head nouns. They can be embedded after the head noun, but they never occur in sentence-first position (Monteil 1963:38):

> (18) *ktḗmata   mén, tà*   *moí   esti, komizémen*
>   the goods ptc.,   these/which   to me   are,   to recover
>
>   *en   megároisi*   (*Od.* 23.355).
>   in   the hall

In (16) and (17) there is no sign of subordination of the second clause whose function is to individualize the head noun among the elements of the class to which it belongs (:restrictive function as in (16)³) or to give more information about a previously individualized head noun (: attributive function as in (14)⁴).

This is precisely the construction we find in old Gmc. texts:

> (19) *se   mon-dryhten se   ēow ðā   maðmas   geaf*
>   the   lord   *this/who* you the   treasures   gave
>   (cp.Campbell 1961:291)

> (20) ...*gi gilōbian sculun / endi gihuggian   thero*
>   you believe   must   and   remember   of the
>
>   *wordo*   the   *hie iu ... sagda*   (*Hel.* 5853)
>   words   *those/which*   he before said;

> (21) *gatauhun ina du Annin   frumist   sa   was   auk*
>   they brought him to A.   first,   *this/who* was   also
>
>   *swaihra   Kajafin*   (Joh. 18.13)
>   father-in-law   of K.;

> (22) *ains þan   ize   gawandida sik* (. . .)
>   one   then   of them turned back   (and)
>
>   sah *was Samareites*   (Lc. 17.15f.)
>   *this/who* was (a) S.⁵

> (23) *qaþ sums þize   skalke* (. . .) sah   *niþjis   was*
>   said one   of the servants (and) *this/who* relative was
>
>   *þammei   afmaimait Paitrus auso*   (Joh. 18.26)
>   of the one to whom had cut   P.   (his) ear.

From the point of view of the ancient Gmc. it is rather pointless to discuss whether the deictic form $^+$*sa, sō, þat* which we can simply call DET is a true relat. pronoun or not. The question makes sense only from the viewpoint of the languages that, like the modern Gmc.lg.s., have developed a full system of relative pronouns and compulsory articles. Note finally that the oldest Gmc. texts never show embedded RCs but almost always have "RCs" at the margin, in extraposition, so that it is really difficult to distinguish them formally from (adjoined) main clauses (see § 4).

4. The function of relat. pron. cannot with certainty be ascribed to a particular PIE form, as is proved by the different forms the relat. pron. has assumed in the languages of the IE family — and it might also be asked whether PIE did really know a relat. pron. as modern IE languages do. There was probably a generic deictic function of demonstrative stems, and a specification of this function will have been what we call the relative function. This is in keeping with the OV-character of PIE (see W.P. Lehmann 1974:66; 1980). Consistent OV-lg.s do not have markers to introduce RCs; of course the NP of the main clause must be identical with the NP of the RC, coreferentiality of the NPs enabling the deletion or the pronominalization of an NP — usually that of the RC, but sometimes the deletion/pronominalization can occur in the main clause.[6] But if a general feature to characterize RCs cross-linguistically is that the sequence manifesting a RC must include some characteristics marking it as a non-main clause (Antinucci—Duranti—Gebert 1979:146), then neither (16) and (17) nor (19)—(23) can be called RCs. Such clauses show only a textual, logical connection with the whole sentence and their syntactical relation is more one of juxtaposition[7] or coordination[8] than of subordination.[9] Interpretation of such clauses as relative is largely a pragmatic matter (see S. Romaine, this volume).

5. It is precisely at this point that considerations of the article (ART) must be inserted into the frame.

As I said above, OV-lg.s do not have markers to introduce RCs. RCs are simply preposed to their head nouns. More generally OV-lg.s show a tendency towards coordination rather than subordination. Repetition of the NP in both clauses or pronominalization of one occurrence of the NP through deictic forms is a good device to exhibit the coreferentiality of the two coordinated clauses.

To enhance the coreferentiality deictic forms can be reinforced by particles having deictic value (cp. French *ce → ce-lui → celui-ci*); or they can be repeated in both clauses. This is the origin of, e.g., the Gothic relat.pron. *sa-ei,* of the Nordic forms with *er* or of the WGmc. *dar, thar:*

(24) *sa   ist Helias* saei *skulda qiman*   (Mth. 11.14)
      this is H.   *who* shall   come

with definite head noun (:Helias), or

(25) *saei   habai ausona hausjandona gahausjai* (Mth. 11.15)
      who(ever) has ears   to hear   must hear

with preposed non-definite value;

(26) *inti sagata   den Judeon   daz der heilant was,*
      and he said   to the Jews that the saviour was

       der dar *tēta inan heilan*   (Tat. 88.5)
       who did him   heal.

On the other hand (26) already shows repetition of deictic *der* in both clauses. Cp., for this type,

(27) *alle* thie *knehta* thie thar *wārun in Bethleem* (Tat. 10.1)
      all   *the* children   *that* were   in B.

(28) sē   *ellen-gǣst* (. . . .) sē *þe in þȳstrum*
      the mighty spirit   *which* in the darkness
      bād   (Beow. 86f.)
      waited;

(29) *var   þar alt traust*   *þeira konunga eþa   iarla*
      (it) was there all (the) trust *of the* kings   and   earls
      þeira er   fyrer lande   rēþo
      who (Genit.attraction) over (the) country ruled.

                                              (Heusler 1962:162)

At this stage, having an NP in the main clause formed by a deictic form (= DET)+N, we are faced by a real article: *thie knehta, sē ellengǣst*, etc.

But such an NP is not usual in the oldest Gmc. texts: see, e.g., *runoR writu* (Järsberg) "I wrote (the) runes", *wurte runoR* (Tjurkø) "he made (the) runes", etc. The tendency to avoid DET before N is particularly clear when N is already determined being a proper name or being specified by some other element such as genitive,[10] possessive,[11] adjective[12] — and in certain temporal and locative constructions.[13] All this confirms the individualizing deictic function of DET ([+ known]: see Ramat 1981:85ff.).

5.1 The construction N_1 +DET+ADJ/N_2 is, on the contrary, old:

(30) Goth. *ik im hairdeis sa goda*   (Joh. 10.14)
            I   am shepherd the good

(the adjective exhibits weak declension with individualizing function: cp. Lat. *Marcus Porcius Cato* "M.P. the clever");

(31) *iþ   saei   nu   gatairiþ aina   anabusne*
But who (ever) now destroys one of commandments

þizo   minnistono...   (Mth. 5.19)
of the smallest. . .
i.e. ". . . (even) one of the smallest commandments";

(32) *. . . sea scoldin ahebbean. . . godspell that guoda (Hel. 24f.)*
      they had to begin   gospel   the   good

(33) *kallaði   þā   Knēfrǫðr, . . . seggr inn*
      said   then Kn.   man the

      suðrœ ni   (*Atlakv.* 2.5f.)
      from the South

(34) *māgas   wāron . . . on sele þām hean*   (*Beow.* 1015f.)
      (the) relatives were ˙   in hall the high

This pattern is very common, especially with personal nouns: OIc. *Eirīkr enn rauðe*, OE *Judith seō œčele* down to the modern forms *Alfred the Great, Karl der Große* etc. so that it is difficult to accept for (30) and (31) a mechanical derivation from a Greek model (:*egṓ eimi ho poimḕn ho kalós; mían tôn entolôn toútōn tôn elachístōn* do not completely correspond to the Goth. translation).

Extra-Gmc. parallels prove that this type is of IE origin: Gk. (*ho*) *dêmos ho tôn Athēnaíōn, Sokrátēs ho philósophos*, OPers. *Gaumātam tyam magum* (accus.) "G. the Magian", OBulg. *jego slovo-to pravoje* "his word the true", etc. Cp. Vulg.Lat. *vitulum illum saginatum* = Gk. *tòn móschon tòn siteutón* = Goth. *stiur þana alidan* (Lc. 15.27) "(the) calf the well fattened" (accus.), and also the Romance constructions like OFr. *Flore la belle*, Rum. *omul cel bun* lit. "man-the the good" (see Heinrichs 1954:30ff.).

This type is also known in non-IE lg.s (Tagalog, Javanese, Hebrew, Gurma, etc.: see Heinrichs 1954:32f.; Greenberg 1978:55).

The traditional explanation saw in the DET of this construction a 'Gelenkpartikel' (Gk. *árthron* "articulus") joining a noun to its attributive determination (see, e.g., Heinrichs 1954:30).

But it should be noticed that nominal clauses did not present the copula in PIE so that *hairdeis sa goda* can readily be interpreted as *hairdeis sa god ist:* we have to do with a relative-like construction. This is particularly evident when the clause has the form N+DET+PART (where PART is functionally equivalent to ADJ or N$_2$). See for instance

> (35) *rums   wigs   sa   brigganda in   fralustai*
>   wide (is the) way that/which leading   to   perdition;
>   (Mth. 7.13)

> (36) *dher   dhritto   heit   ist selbes   druhtīnes   Christ*
>   the   third   person is of [the] self   lord   Christ
>
>   *dhes   chisendidin*   (Js. 4.7)
>   the/who sent (Lat: *qui mittitur*)

and, with repetition of DET as in (19) and (20):

> (37) *sa   hundafaþs   sa   atstandands*
>   the centurion that/who standing
>
>   *in   andwairþja is*   (Mc. 15.39)
>   before   him.[14]

Thus, DET refers anaphorically to a previously given N ([+ known]) with the function of giving more information concerning it or of specifying it: *hairdeis sa goda* specifies which shepherd it is we are speaking of and individualizes this special shepherd within the class of shepherds.

Other languages of the IE family use in the same position and with the same function a pronominal form which developed to real relat.pron.:

> (38) *víśve marúto   yé sahásah*   (RV VII 34.24)
>   all (the) Marutaḥ who powerful (are);

> (39) *naracit   yōi taxma*   (Yt. 5.86)
>   (the) men-part.   who valiant (are)

(see Longobardi 1980; Ramat 1981: 96; see also Haider–Zwanziger, this volume).

The relative forms Skt. *ye* Avest. *yōi* refer anaphorically to the preceding head noun and the nominal RC does not have the copula: it is really no different from the type *hairdeis sa goda* or *Alfred the Great!*

The Gmc. DET **sa, sō, þat* developed by functional splitting both the function of relat.pron. and of ART (see below[15]).

5.2   At the same time the relative-like construction with anaphoric DET offers a reasonable answer to the question why and how a language, essentially still of the OV-type like PGmc. (and other IE lg.s as well), shifted from preposed to postposed RCs.

The evidence from the oldest Gmc. texts clearly shows that postposed

RCs already represent the normal order. It has even been suggested from a general typological point of view that the shift from preposition to postposition of the RC might have been a primary factor in activating the typological change (Antinucci 1977:176; Antinucci-Duranti-Gebert 1979:170) owing to the pressure that the processing mechanism of the hearer exerts on the structure constituted by prenominal RC towards a reorganization leading to a perceptually more favorable postnominal position.

Actually, what we find in many ancient IE lg.s (including PGmc.) is the coexistence of postposed RCs with many OV-features, whereas examples from Hittite and Vedic Sanskrit give evidence for intermediate forms of RCs (see W.P. Lehmann 1974:68), as, e.g., repetition of the head noun both in the main clause and in RC (cp. ex. s (14) (15) and fn. 6).[16]

When speaking of a shift from preposed to postposed RC we are not of course thinking of a mechanical transposition of linguistic material from prenominal to postnominal position, but rather of the assumption of the relative *function* by a different morphological category (namely the DET category), which for a certain time certainly coexisted with the old preposed RC as in (6), (7) and finally substituted the old $*K^wI\text{-}/K^wO\text{-}$ form of RC even when RC remained in prenominal position[17]:

(40) ter   *demo dīenōt,* ter *ist follūn*   *vrī*
      who (ever) him serves *he* is completely free
                                          (Notk. 3.30)

with indef. value and repetition of DET in both clauses as in

(41) der *ie* *gewesen wære ein tōtriuwesære,* des
      who ever would have been a repentant, of this

      herze   *wære da gevreut*   (*Iw.* 609f.)
      (the) heart would then have rejoiced;

or also with definite reference:

(42) *fon* thémo *er unsih rétita, in*
      from *that one* he us   rescued in

      héllu   nan *gistréwita*   (Otfr. 5.16.3)
      (the) hell *him* banished.

5.3 We can tentatively venture the following interpretation of the rise and successful spread of the new postposed RC.

As has already been pointed at the postposed DET, not yet specified as relat.pron. or ART, refers anaphorically to an already introduced N(P) which it serves to clarify via attribution or to specify via restriction (Ex.s (12)–(23)). We have also seen that in many cases there was no mark of subordination. This type of construction strongly resembles what Hyman 1975:120 has called the 'pattern of the afterthought': under particular pragmatic conditions – he writes – "the speaker may forget to say something in the course of his utterance; or he may find that it is necessary to add something, because his interlocutor has not understood; or he may realize that the sentence he has just uttered is unclear or ambiguous. In all of these cases (and doubtless others) he may wish to add something after the verb-final utterance". In German, for instance, a strictly SOV-language in subordinate clauses, the speaker will say:

(43) *Der Mann, den ich gesehen habe . . . gestern abend*

with a pause after the verb.

Hyman goes then on to point out that this pattern predicts that "there will be intermediate stages between SOV and SVO, i.e. the verb does not zap into the second position in one step, as it were" (ibid.:121): once again this is in keeping with what we have observed on the progressive rise of the Gmc. postposed RC.

This kind of asynthetic coordination is particularly evident in cases like those illustrated above (fn. 7 and 8). Such 'relative clauses' do really give new information about something that has already been introduced in the discourse – or is looked on as known to the hearer (cp. Hyman 1975:126), i.e. about the *topic* or *theme*.

Characteristic of the theme, as it is well-known, is the fact that it usually comes in discourse first position – or at the beginning of the sentence. The theme creates the frame of reference for the following text which will take it up again, expanding, clarifying or specifying it (see Chr.Lehmann 1979: 439). In colloquial American English:

(44) *Ol' George Creech, his son just wrecked his new Chevy*

as well as in colloquial French (of Paris)

(45) *Jean, son frère repare les mobylettes*

or in German 'Umgangssprache'

(46) *Ich habe eine Schwester – sie hat sich ein Fahrrad gekauft*

Ol' George Creech, Jean and the Schwester are what the sentence is about; they provide the theme of the sentence (Noonan 1977:380) which comes first to the mind of the speaker, who is thus obliged to add information later on as an afterthought. A. Culioli (1976:131) speaks of Jean in (45) as a 'point de repère': it is from this point that the sentence is constructed, if not grammatically, as for Engl., French or German, certainly from the viewpoint of pragmatic strategy.

In the first verse of the *Odyssey* (=(12)) "the man" (*ándra*) is the theme of the sentence and of the whole poem: as such it is focused at the very beginning and what is said about him ("skilful"+RC) comes after, when the attention of the hearer has already been pointed to the topic/theme.[18]

Now, we have seen that the structure of the Gmc. examples (19)–(23) is precisely the same as that of *Odyssey* 1.1 (and as (13)–(18)).

Pragmatic reasons of topicalization and topic focusing[19] can thus explain via the pattern of the afterthought the rise of an order which is clearly disharmonic with the OV-type we can reconstruct for PGmc. and for PIE. The rise of postposed RCs and of the ART can readily be thought of as a process of grammaticalization of previously marked forms, i.e. of the 'afterthought forms'.[20]

Let us take as an example the famous Margarete's Lied in Goethe's *Faust* which has been chosen as a paradigm case in the title of this paper because it clearly shows both features (afterthought and RC) we are concerned with:

> (47) *Es war ein König in Thule, / gar treu bis in das Grab, / dem sterbend seine Buhle / einen goldnen Becher gab.*

First the theme is given, to which in the second verse an apposition is added without verb — a nominal clause typical of the afterthought expansion, which could easily be understood as a relative-like construction. Once the frame of reference has been established, the third verse refers anaphorically to it via a DET whose translation could easily be a paratactic one, after a short pause: "to this king. . ." as well as " . . . to whom. . . " without pause (i.e. hypotactic) (see Johansen 1935:37).

The use of *ein* in the theme deserves further consideration (see § 6).

5.4 Actually the oldest pattern was to use **sa, sō, þat* only when referring to a noun previously introduced into the sentence or considered as known to the hearer:

> (48) ahma   ina ustauh in auþida   , jah was
> (the) spirit him brought into (the) desert, and (he) remained
>
> in þizai   auþidai dage fidwor tiguns   (Mc. 1.12f.)
> in that/the desert of days four   ten   (= forty days);
>
> (49) *ther man was reht. . . inti heilag geist was in*
> the man was right and (the) holy ghost was in

imo. *Inphieng   tho antwurti   fon themo*
him. He received then (the) answer from that/the

heilagen geiste   (*Tat.* 7.4f.)
holy   ghost;

(50) *griþungr stakk hornonom ī   sīþo hestenom. . .*
      (the) bull stake with horns in (the) side of the horse.

Konungs menn drōpo   griþungenn   (Heusler 1962:125)
King's   men killed   bull-the.

This anaphoric use of DET represents the first step towards the definite article.

5.4.1 Greenberg 1978 has convincingly sketched the typological evolution of the morphosyntactic category ART:

Stage I. No markers; definiteness is not expressed by morphological means (cp. Run. *wurte runoR* (already mentioned), *horna tawido* (Gallehus) "I made (the) horn", whereby the runes, the horn alluded to are under the reader's eyes, and thus clearly definite; *hali hino* (accus.) "stone this" of the Strøm whetstone or *runAR þAiAR* (accus.) "runes these" of the Istaby inscription show a particularly emphatic effect which can even achieve pronominal substitution of the understood noun: *sA þAt bAriutiþ* (Stentoften stone) "who (ever) this (= this stone) breaks"). In Pre- and Proto-Germanic the semantic feature [± definite], both in its particularizing and anaphoric function, was expressed by combining other grammatical features such as case declension, demonstratives (DET.s), personal pronouns, marked word orders etc.

Stage II.1. Definite articles develop from purely deictic elements (our DET.s) which have come to identify an element as previously mentioned in the discourse (the type *hairdeis sa goda*, a relative-like construction).

Stage II.2. The point at which the discourse DET becomes a defin. art. is the point at which it becomes compulsory. The way towards stage II.2. was the repetition of DET as in (19), (20), and (37) which originally served to enhance coreferentiality. The ART has now spread via grammaticalization, applying even to nouns which, having the semantic feature [+ unique], do not need specification (attribution or restriction) and are supposed to be already known:

(51) sēo *sunne is micle ufor þonne* se *mōna sȳ*
    the sun   is much above than   *the* moon be (=is)
                                               (*Leechdoms* iii 262.10)

This usage is not yet completely grammaticalized in Old English nor in Old High German so that we find *sunne* and *sēo sunne, sunna* and *diu sunna* (see Ramat 1981:86). Greenberg speaks of languages being on the borderline between two stages and quotes examples like Engl. *by hand, on foot, at home, at night* vs. *the hand, the foot* etc. (loc.cit.:67): "the whole development [of defin.art.s and gender markers:P. R.] is to be viewed as a single continuous process marked by certain decisive turning points" (Greenberg 1978:61).

Stage II. 3. Non-generic articles. At this stage we have an art. which includes, along with other possible uses, both defin. determination and non-defin. specific uses. The art. is used in contexts where it has gone well-beyond its anaphoric function and applies to a specific but as yet unidentified item. Engl. *I am looking for a book* is ambiguous as between specific reference to a certain book and a not specified book.

Stage III. Class prefixes. The former article has become a pure marker for nouns or for NPs. It can serve to subdivide nouns in gender classes (e.g. in Germ. *der Mond, die Sonne, das Weib*) or to signal nominality as such: Engl. *the work* vs. *to work,* with analytic marking of morphological determinations − consistent with an SVO type (see § 2). As for the ART marking an NP as a unity see the German type$_{NP}$ [*die zwei schönen, hölzernen Häuser*]$_{NP}$ [*des reichen Mannes*], $_{RC}$ [*der neben mir wohnt*]: the two NPs are clearly individualized as Immediate Constituents by the two articles and opposed to the RC by the different function of the third DET. In *the ups and downs* or in

(52) *Das* gnôthi seautón *von Delphi ist ein Befehlssatz*

the and *das* function as nominalizers, signs of nominality (Heinrichs 1954: 24; Greenberg 1978:71; Ultan 1978:252). In (52) the article even has a metalinguistic function.

We cannot say that the class prefixes are meaningless: their function is on another level with respect to the earlier one.

6. Lastly, a few words about the *a-the/this* opposition as found in (47) *ein* . . . *dem*.

The main function of the indef.art. is to introduce into the discourse an item not previously known (: [– known]), singled out in its class (: [+ unique]) but not specified (: [– specific]):

> (53) *A woman drew her long black hair out tight* (Eliot).

An indef.art. as such was unknown to PGmc., so that we can in this frame neglect to discuss the use of an NP with indef. art. as representative of the whole class ([+ generic]; see Hawkins 1978:214ff.):

> (54) *A rose is a flower* (= The rose is a flower = Roses are flowers)

and the use of indef.art.s with the feature [– generic] (≠ [+ definite] !):

> (55) *I have a rose on my table.*

Gothic used the adjectival indefinite *sums* with nouns:

> (56) *gamotida imma* wair *sums*   *us*   *baurg,*
>   met   him   *man certain* from (the) town
>
>   *saei* ...
>   who ...   (Lc.8.27)

In the Greek original *anḗr tis* "a man"; note the RC following the indef.!
   Also in Old English, Old Frisian, Old Saxon, Old High German, and Old Norse Gmc.* *sumaz* has not the meaning of its modern continuant *same* but that of indef.art.:

> (57) *þā* sume dæge *rād sē cyng ūp*
>   and one   day   rode the king. (Parker Chron., a.895)

The numeral *ān* "one" progressively ousted *sum* in the course of the 12th century. For the original equivalence of *sum* and *ān* cp.

> (58) *sum man hæfde twegen suna*   (Lc.15.11)
>   a   man   had   two   sons
>   (in Gothic: *manne* [partitive genit.] *sums aihta twans sununs*)

and

> (59) *ān man hæfde twegen suna*   (Mth.21.28).

The other Gmc.lg.s went the same way expanding the use of "one" as indef.art. (and as pronoun).[21] However it should be noted that indefiniteness was not expressed by an overt mark. We find in Old English texts clear evidence of this state of affairs:

(60) *hē   ār ǣrde   mǣre   mynster*
       he   builded   up   (a) large   monastery
                                             (Pet.Chron., a.1087)

(61) *hē   wæs   swȳðe   spedig   man*
       he   was   (a) very   rich   man   (Alfr., *Oros*.1.1.)

The use of *ān* seems to have been introduced first in translations where it was suggested by the original text:

(62) *ð ā   clipode   hē   ænne   ðēow*   (Lc.15.26)
       and   called   he   *one*   servant
                                          (*vocavit* unum *de servis*)

(63) *cume*   ān   *spearwa*   (Alfr., *Beda* 2.13 [1367])
       came   *a*   sparrow   (*adveniens* unus *passerum*)

See Ramat 1981:89. I think that an accurate philological analysis of the evidence will confirm the hypothesis that the rise of the indef.art. is contemporary with and complementary to, that of the defin.art., when the semantic feature [± definite] was on the way to becoming compulsory, and had, as a result, to be expressed by morphological means.

7. To sum up: ART is a new morphosyntactic category that took its rise in the Gmc.lg.s from the splitting of a DET, postposed to the N it referred to by an afterthought pattern. From the originally paratactic pattern *hairdeis sa goda* there developed both the indexical function of ART (*der gute Hirt*) and the attributive/restrictive RC postposed to its head noun (*der Hirt, der gut ist*). Both developments are consistent with the shifting from SOV to SVO which is the most salient development in the history of the Gmc.lg.s.

This shifting made it necessary to mark overtly the opposition definiteness ~ indefiniteness which earlier remained unexpressed being signified instead by pragmatic discourse strategies.

Neither in PGmc nor in PIE do we find a unitary form for relative pronouns — to say nothing of the articles. What we positively observe in Gmc.lg.s as well as in other IE lg.s is the rise of both categories, realized with different means but typologically showing the same tendency.

Since my aim was to sketch briefly a typological development I have used examples which derive from different linguistic traditions and from different periods and I have not distinguished quite usual forms from uncommon examples, like (29). This procedure would have been incorrect if the aim had been to describe the speech situation of a given language at a given moment; it is, on the contrary, perfectly legitimate in order to show the typological drift a language family followed during its evolution.

A diachronic consideration is the only way of explaining the present synchronic situation of the Gmc.lg.s with their double function of determinative forms like Germ. *der, die, das* Engl. *that*. Typological parallels prove the development sketched above to be the most likely.[22]

Notes

* A preliminary version of this paper was presented at the 2nd Meeting of the East-West Group on Typology (Budapest, Sept. 1980). For comments and valuable suggestions I am indebted to the participants in the Meeting. The research has been carried out within the framework of the Italian Research Program CNR CT 79.00285.08

1. Starting from this point of anaphoric coreference we can well understand the so called nucleus anticipation in the RC: *ab arbore abs terra* pulli qui *nascentur, eos in terram deprimito* (Cat. *agr*.51) "the sprouts which grow up from a tree out from the earth must be driven into the ground" (instead of . . . *abs terra qui nascentur, eos pullos*. . .). Down to the repetition of the head noun both in RC and in the main clause as in (9). See, e.g. *in area trans viam* paries qui (: [+ known]!) *est propter viam*, in eo pariete *medio ostiei lumen aperito* (CIL I² 698, I, 9–11) "*The wall* which is near the street on the area beyond the street – *on that wall* an opening must be made for a gate" (cp. Chr. Lehmann 1979:440; 1979a:9; W. P. Lehmann 1980:135). The function of the anticipation of the head noun in the preposed RC is to focus it, and to posit it as the theme of the whole sentence: see § 5.3.

2. C. Justus 1978 has convincingly shown that the *K^WO-/K^WI-* construction had originally the function of marking focus, and that the topic-focus feature of this pronoun is basic to relative, interrogative and indefinite usage. For the development in Gmc., however, this PIE reconstruction is not of primary importance, though completely in keeping with what we can observe in the ancient Gmc.lg.s, the point being here that interrogative-indefinite pronouns can give rise to relative forms, or – better – that interr.-indef. and relat. pronouns have the same origin.

3. Among the scars forming the class of the scars the wet-nurse recognizes a specific scar – that one a wild bore had caused to Ulysses. Cp. *Il.* 1. 138 f.

4. Cp. also . . . *phílos óleth'hetaîros,/ Pátroklos*, tòn egò perì
   . . .my   died friend P.   whom I above
   pántōn tîon hetaírōn (*Il.* 18. 80 f.)
   all   loved of the friends.

5. Goth. *sah* from *sa*, demonstrative pron.+*uh* "and" (< IE *-K^WE). This form clearly shows the original paratactic nature of the secondary clause: "and this. . .".

6. For coreferentiality expressed by NP repetition cp. . . *paries.* . . *in eo pariete* (see fn. 1); *erant omnino* itinera *duo, quibus* itineribus *domo exire possent* (Caes. *d.b.G.*, 1.6.1) "there were but two ways by which they could leave their country". For NP pronominalization in the main clause see, e.g., *quam quisque norit* artem, in hac *se exerceat* (Cic. *Tusc.* 1.41) "everyone must practice the art he knows"; . . *ut quae apud legionem* vota *vovi* (. . .) ea *ego exsolvam omnia* (Pl. *Amph.* 947 f.) ". . .so that I can fulfil all the vows I vowed in the army": it is the so-called attraction of the head noun into the RC (see Touraties 1980: 147f.). It is worth noticing that in many cases of 'attraction' the value of the preposed RC is (still) indefinite: *Ut in tabellis* quos *consignavi hic heri | latrones, ibus dinumerem stipendium* (Pl. *Mil.* 73 f.) "so that I can pay their money to the soldiers I enrolled yesterday" (Kroll 1912: 11 "ich habe einige Söldner in die Liste aufgenommen, denen will ich ihren Lohn auszahlen"; cp. Touratier 1980:162); qui *ager frigidior et macrior erit,* ibi *oleam Licinium seri oportet* (Cat. *agr.* 6.2) "and in the colder and leaner earth, there must be planted the Licinian olive tree". (For the possible conditional value of this RC: "if there is a colder and leaner earth. . .", see Chr. Lehmann 1979:392 ff.).

7. E.g. *þa cwæð heora ān his nama wæs quirion* (Aelfr. *Vitae* Xl. 67)
   then said of them one—his name was Q.

   M Dutch *enen ridder, was doot, vonden si*
      a   rider, (he) was dead, found they;
      quamen tere stat, hiet Babilone
   (they) arrived to the town, was called B. (Franck 1910:186).

8. Cp. sentences bound by "and" where we would now insert "which" or "that":
   hann sā at maðr stōð at baki Qlvi ok var hǫfði
   he saw that (a) man was at (the) back of O. and was (an) head
   hæri en aðrir menn (Egils S. 25.11)
   higher than other men (i.e. ". . .who was higher than. . . ");

   M Dutch *ene stat ende hiet Babilone*
      a town *and* was called B. (i.e. ". . .*which* was called B.");

   MHG *für dize zit* und [="at which, when"] *dize urteil ist geschehen* (see Behaghel 1923: III 739; Ramat 1981:102).

9. "Also steht der *hó*-R(elativ)S(atz) des homerischen Griechisch zwischen dem angeschlossenen RS und einem selbständigen Satz, der bloß durch textuelle Beziehungen implizit attributiv [bzw. restriktiv: P. R.] wirkt. Der kontinuierliche Charakter der Phänomene hat zur Folge, daß es auch keine binären Entscheidungskriterien für die Zugehörigkeit einer Konstruktion zur 'Kategorie RS' gibt. Strukturen, die ambivalent sind zwischen RS (. . .) und anderen Satztypen (. . .), sind das synchrone Erscheinungsbild dessen, was sich diachron als Genese oder Verfall des RSes in einer Sprache darstellt", Chr. Lehmann 1979:221.

10. E.g. *flōh her Ōtachres nid (Hild.*18) "he tried to escape (the) hatred of O."

11. E.g. *mit dīnem wortun (Hild.* 40) "with your words"

12. E.g. *Her furlaet in lante. . . prut in bure (Hild.* 20 f.) "he deserted at home (the/his) wife in (the) house".

13. E.g. Goth. *du maurgina* = Engl. *to morrow,* Goth. *himma daga* = Germ. *heute* "today", etc.

14. in the Greek original *ho kentyrión ho parestēkós;* but this construction is older than New Testament Greek: see e.g. *éphasan tèn pyramída oikodomēthénai tèn en mésōi tôn tríōn hestēkyîan* (Hdt. 2.126) "they said that the pyramid had been build up — that (which) was in the middle of the three".

15. The close relationship of the functions is proved not only by examples like (16)–(18). In Old Persian, for instance, the relat. pron. *hya* m., *hyā* f., and *tya* nt. is formed by an amalgamation of the demonstrative **sa, sā, tad* with the relative **yas, yā, yad.*

16. Gmc. ex.s of NP repetition

412   *Paolo Ramat*

> *Feng* Carl   *tō ðām westrīce. . .   Se*   Carl   was Louis'
> Got Charles   the west kingdom. This Ch.   *wæs Hlōþowīges*
> *sunu* (Erl. 84.10)
> son   (i.e. "Ch., who was the son of L., got. . .").

> *gengr þar inn*   maþr. . . . *sā* maþr *mælte*   (Heusler 1962:122)
> went there into (a) man this man said. . . . (i.e. "a man entered there who said. . ."). Notice in these examples that DET refers to a previously introduced noun [+ known]. See (48)–(50).

17. See, for a similar extension, the *wh-* postposed relat. pron. in Engl. *A man* who *was in the army*. . . ., whereas **KʷO-/KʷI-* was originally cataphoric (Justus 1978). Analogical processes of grammaticalization have cancelled the original difference between pre- and postposition. As for *that* vs. *which* in the English linguistic tradition cp. Rissanen, this vol.

18. W. P. Lehmann (1972:991) has very interestingly noticed that if we assume, according to Vedic evidence, that the PIE verse consisted of eight syllables, *Odyssey* 1.1 et sim. can be regarded as expansion over the shorter original line through apposition of *polýtropon*, i.e. an 'afterthought' after the theme has been announced at the very beginning. Such afterthought expansions may consist of appositions, absolute constructions, complements and also 'RCs', i.e. ₁NPs anaphorically related through DETs.

19. It is worth noticing that the **KʷO-/KʷI-* construction can also be traced back to a (cataphoric) focusing strategy (cp. fn. 2).

20. Japanese too, a strictly OV-language, shows examples of afterthought in colloquial speech:
> *kimi (wa)*   *yonda* ↗ *kono hon (o)* ↘   (Kuno 1978:60 ff.)
> you thematic part.   read   this book Obj. part.
> ↗ and ↘ mark rising and falling intonation.

21. Also *sum* and related forms could, of course, occur as indef. pron., and not only in preposed position as ARTs – thus underlining once more the close connection between ART and pronoun:
> *ond hira   scipu   sumu   genāmon*   (Parker Chr., a. 894)
> and of their ships   some (they) captured;
> *sum mann thann midfiri*   *mēn*   *forlātid*   (*Hel.* 3476)
> someone   then at the middle of his age the nastiness will abandon.

Hel. 3476 is a good example of the transition from adjectival use to pronominal function: we cannot translate "a man" as in (56), (58), and (59).

22. The most striking parallel is of course offered by the Romance languages (see Harris 1980a, and 1980b). The parallelism is so striking that – as is well known – it has been suggested that the Gmc. article might be viewed as a syntactic loan from (Vulg.) Latin, which on its turn would have derived this usage from Greek (see for references Ramat 1981:87 fn. 42). In Finnish, too, we find an anaphoric 3rd pers. pron. (≡ Lat. *ille*) used in deictic processes:
> *Annoin* sille *tytölle* se *kirja*
> I gave   the   girl   the book
> alongside the formal variety
> *Annoin tytölle kirja*-n
> I gave   the girl book-accus.

see Ultan 1978:256 f., who rightly underlines the correlations between definiteness, topicalization, word order and the loss of case contrast as important marker of definiteness. Other parallels have been illustrated by Greenberg 1978, Harris 1980 (Bulgarian) and already by Heinrichs (1954:30 ff., 46 ff.).

References

Antinucci, Fr.
 1977 *Fondamenti di una teoria tipologica del linguaggio.* (= *'Studi Linguistici e Semiologici'*, 7) (Bologna: Il Mulino).
Antinucci, Fr. et al.
 1979 "Relative clause structure, relative clause perception, and the change from SOV to SVO", *Cognition* 7:145–76.
Behaghel, O.
 1923 *Deutsche Syntax,* I (II 1924; III 1928; IV 1932) (Heidelberg: C. Winter).
Benveniste, É.
 1968 "Mutations of linguistic categories", *Directions for historical linguistics,* ed. by W. P. Lehmann and Y. Malkiel (Austin and London: Univ. of Texas Press), 85–94.
Butler, M. C.
 1977 "Grammaticalization of topical elements in Middle English", *Berkeley Linguistic Society* 3:626–636.
Campbell, A.
 1962 *Old English grammar* (Oxford: University Press).
Culioli, A.
 1976 Transcription séminaire de D.E.A., Univers. Paris 7, Octobre 1976 (mimeo).
Franck, J.
 1967 *Mittelniederländische Grammatik,* 2. Aufl. (Arnhem: Gysbers en van Loon).
Greenberg, J. H.
 1978 "How does a language acquire gender markers?", *Universals of human language,* ed. by J. H. Greenberg et al. (Stanford: Univ. Press), vol. 3, 47–82.
Haider, H. – R. Zwanziger
 this volume "Relative attribute: the 'ezāfe-construction' from Old Iranian to Modern Persian".
Harris, M. B.
 1980a "The marking of definiteness in Romance", *Historical morphology,* ed. by J. Fisiak (The Hague-Paris: Mouton).
 1980b "The marking of definiteness: a diachronic perspective", *Papers from the Fourth Intern. Confer. on Historical Linguistics,* ed. by E. Closs Traugott et al. (Amsterdam: Benjamins), 75–86.
Hawkins, J. A.
 1978 *Definiteness and indefiniteness. A study in reference and grammaticality prediction* (London: Croom Helm).
Heinrichs, H. M.
 1954 *Studien zum bestimmten Artikel in den germanischen Sprachen* (= *Beitr. zur dt. Philol., I*) (Giessen: W. Schmitz).
Heusler, A.
 1962 *Altisländisches Elementarbuch (= German. Bibliothek, 1. Reihe)* 5. Aufl. (Heidelberg: Winter).
Hyman, L. M.
 1975 "On the change from SOV to SVO: Evidence from Niger-Congo", *Word order and word order change,* ed. by Ch. N. Li (Austin and London: Univ. of Texas Press), 113–47.

Johansen, H.
1935   *Zur Entwicklungsgeschichte der altgermanischen Relativkonstruktionen* (Kopenhagen: Levin and Munksgaard).
Justus, C. F.
1978   "Syntactic change: evidence for restructuring among coexistent variants", *Journal of Indo-European studies* 6:107–132.
Kossuth, K. C.
1978   "Icelandic word order: in support of drift as a diachronic principle specific to language families", *Berkeley Linguistic Society* 4:446–456.
Kroll, W.
1912   "Der lateinische Relativsatz", *Glotta* 3:1–18.
Kuno, S.
1978   "Japanese: a characteristic OV language", *Syntactic typology: studies in the phenomenology of language*, ed. by W. P. Lehmann (Austin and London: Texas Univ. Press), 57–138.
Lehmann, C.
1979   *Der Relativsatz. Typologie seiner Strukturen, Theorie seiner Funktionen, Kompendium seiner Grammatik (Arbeiten des Kölner Universalien-Projekts* 36).
1979a   "Der Relativsatz vom Indogermanischen bis zum Italienischen", *Sprache* 25:1–25.
1980   "Der indogermanische *kwi-/kwo*-Relativsatz im typologischen Vergleich", *Linguistic reconstruction and Indo-European syntax*, edited by P. Ramat (Amsterdam: Benjamins), 155–169.
Lehmann, W. P.
1972   "Contemporary linguistics and Indo-European studies", *Publications of the Modern Language Association of America* 87:976–993.
1974   *Proto-Indo-European syntax* (Austin and London: Univ. of Texas Press).
1980   "The reconstruction of non-simple sentences in Proto-Indo-European", *Linguistic reconstruction and Indo-European syntax*, edited by P. Ramat (Amsterdam: Benjamins), 113–144.
Longobardi, G.
"Les relatives nominales indo-européens", *Linguistic reconstruction and Indo-European syntax*, edited by P. Ramat (Amsterdam: Benjamins), 171–182.
Monteil, P.
1963   *La phrase relative en grec ancien*. Sa formation, son développement, sa structure dès origines à la fin du Vme siècle (Paris: Klincksieck).
Noonan, M.
1977   "On subjects and topics", *Berkeley Linguistic Society* 3:372–385.
Ramat, P.
1981   *Einführung in das Germanische* (= *Linguist. Arbeiten 95*) (Tübingen: Niemeyer).
Ramat, P., et al.
1980(ed.) *Linguistic reconstruction and Indo-European syntax* (= Proceed. of the Colloquium of the Indogerm. Gesellschaft ...) (Amsterdam: Benjamins).
Rissanen, M.
this volume "The choice of relative pronouns in seventeenth century American English".

Romaine, S.
this volume "Towards a typology of relative clause formation strategies in Germanic".
Thompson, S. A.
1978 "Modern English from a typological point of view: Some implications of the function of word order", *Linguistische Berichte* 56: 19–35.
Touratier, C.
1980 *La relative.* Essai de théorie syntaxique (Paris: Klincksieck).
Ultan, R.
1978 "On the development of a definite article", *Language Universals* (= Papers from the Conference held at Gummersbach . . .), ed. by H. Seiler (Tübingen: G. Narr).

MATTI RISSANEN

The choice of relative pronouns in 17th century American English

1 Introduction

In recent years, the variational approach has gained a prominent position, not only in sociolinguistic studies focusing on present-day language but also in studies of diachrony.[1] This approach has been applied mainly to phonological and morphological questions, but it would also seem to give a clearer picture of the syntactic development of a language. In actual practice the variational study of syntactic development means a detailed recording of the variant forms of expressing a concept or a relationship, and an analysis of the changes in time of the distribution patterns formed by these variants. This method enhances the importance of the corpus; it also places the emphasis on the types and categories of the texts forming the corpus because contextual-situational factors play an important role in the choice of the variant.[2]

One aim of the present study is to find out to what extent a comparison of the distribution of syntactic variants in texts representing different types of formality will help us to outline the process of development. If we assume that text A represents a language form which is closer to the spoken idiom than that of the contemporary text B, we can, by comparing the distribution patterns of variants in these two texts, build up hypotheses concerning the occurrence of the variants in the spoken language of the same period. In other words, we can make an attempt to reconstruct the variation pattern at the level of spoken language (or, less ambitiously, to label the high, or low, frequency of certain variants as typical of spoken language) on the basis of a varying written corpus.[3]

Surprisingly few studies have been made of the language of seventeenth century Americans, except from the point of view of vocabulary.[4] Yet the special interest of this language variety should be obvious to all students of linguistic variation. The English spoken by the first, second and third generation inhabitants of the earliest colonies is of interest not only in the search for the roots of American English expression; it also offers an excellent opportunity, with a sufficient perspective in time, for the study of linguistic change in a colonial environment, with simultaneous pressures accelerating and retarding that development. It can be assumed that the literary, formal expression, which leant heavily on the British tradition, would show conservative features, whereas the colloquial spoken idiom would develop rapidly, owing to the effects of contact and the mixing of various native dialect groups. One can also assume a period of heterogeneity of language in the first decades of the settlement, with the ensuing development into relative uniformity of educated expression in the eighteenth century.

The study of syntactic development based on a comparison of texts representing different levels of formality poses problems familiar to all corpus researchers. The most obvious complication is the labelling of texts on the basis of their degree of formality – the danger of circular reasoning is evident. Furthermore, one has to keep in mind that the formula: written = formal/spoken = colloquial, does not hold true without modifications. Not all texts reflecting the spoken idiom are colloquial; conversely, there is great variation in the degree of formality among the texts representing the written language.

One way of categorizing texts, which will take into account their level of formality and their relationship to spoken language can be illustrated by the following diagram:

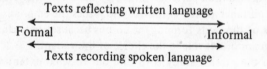

The categories appearing in this way are, of course, nondiscrete. What is meant by the texts reflecting written language is self-evident; at the informal end of this category we have private letters, diaries, journals, etc. The texts recording spoken language are represented by transcripts of sermons, notes of meetings, witness depositions in court records, recorded dialogue in chronicles and other narrative texts, etc. Texts of this type do not, of course, record spoken language faithfully; it is only through a comparison of their language with that of the texts reflecting written language that we can expect to get some information of the spoken idiom. The formal end of this text category is represented by sermons, the least formal perhaps by dialogue in informal narrative texts and by the quotations given by witnesses in depositions of other people's speech.

For this paper, New England texts from two periods, a generation or two apart, were sampled. The first set of texts dates from c. 1640; these texts should illustrate the starting point of the development of American English. The people producing these texts had spent their youth and acquired their education in England, but they had lived in America for a number of years — in the case of William Bradford, as many as twenty. The second set of texts comes from the last decades of the seventeenth century. The writers of these texts — and the people whose speech is quoted in them — are mostly second and third generation Americans; a comparison of their language with that of the 1640s should show not only development in time but also some special features of a colonial variety of the English language.

The corpus of the 1640s consists of extracts from four texts: William Bradford's *History of Plymouth Plantation*, years 1637—40 and 1643—44; John Winthrop's *Journal*, years 1640—41; Robert Keayne's collection of John Cotton's sermons (Keayne, *Serm*.); and the same author's notes of the meetings following the services, from 1639 and 1640 (Keayne, *Busin*.).[5] Bradford and Winthrop represent plain, non-rhetorical narrative style which could be described as formal, unmarked; Keayne, *Serm*. represents markedly formal, slightly archaic sermon style with some features characteristic of speech, and Keayne, *Busin*., a more colloquial style, which seems to approach the spoken idiom.

A slightly more varied selection of texts was sampled from the last decades of the seventeenth century. The written formal style is exemplified by a sample consisting of extracts from Cotton Mather's and John Hale's witchcraft accounts and from Mary Rowlandson's *Captivity*. This material was supplemented by a sample from Increase Mather's *Remarkable Providences* and by a number of formal letters (i.e., letters not addressed to friends or family members) from the Saltonstall collection.

Informal written prose is represented by the letters of the Saltonstalls to other family members. An interesting, and slightly unexpected, source of informal writing is offered by many of the appeals and answers issued in the 1670s and printed in the *Suffolk County Court Records*.[6] The witness depositions in the same records echo the spoken idiom, with varying degrees of formality. Finally, an extract from Sarah Kemble Knight's *Journal* was sampled for information on usage in informal narrative prose in the early 18th century. The length of the samples enumerated above varies between c. 7500 and 9000 words. The slight difference in length is due to an attempt to collect a sufficient number of cases of the main types of relative pronoun usage from each text.

The closed Puritan society produced few literary masterpieces, but it left behind a large amount of documentary material of various kinds, which should give a fair picture of the English language of the settlers. The personal history and family background of many members of this society are easily traceable, both in England and in America. The selection of texts outlined above could easily be made more many-sided and representative. Yet even the results based on this selection will give evidence of variation which seems relevant from the point of view of the development of English relative pronoun usage.

2 Factors influencing the choice of relative pronoun in early American English

In Old English, *which* and *who* (*hwilc*, *hwa*) were used as relative pronouns mainly in generalizing contexts, often combined with *swa*. In EME, these forms came to be used as non-generalizing relative pronouns along with *that* and *the* (the last-mentioned pronoun became obsolete in the course of the thirteenth century).[7] The growing popularity of the *wh-* forms in relative pronoun use is best accounted for through the growing load of functions given to *that*,[8] which increased the risk of ambiguity. If this assumption is accepted, it is only natural that the basic factor influencing the choice of the relative pronoun at the early stages of development was the tightness of the link between the head and the post-modifying clause: the tighter the link, the less risk of ambiguity there was, and, consequently, the less need to use the newer and more emphatic *wh-* forms.[9] Most other factors can be derived from this basic principle. The inherent demonstrative force of *that* and the more indefinite implication of the *wh-* forms are in accordance with this trend.

In previous studies of the relative pronoun distribution in early Modern English texts it has been shown that the *wh-* forms were favoured in non-restrictive and *that* in restrictive relative clauses. It has also been suggested that the growing popularity of the *wh-* forms was due to Latin influence and that those forms were characteristic of formal expression while *that* was favoured in colloquial style. Due attention has been called to the variation depending on the author and the type of text.[10] In most studies, however, no detailed survey of the possible effects of the syntactic and semantic contexts on the choice of relative pronoun has been attempted: the figures for the occurrence of each pronoun in the texts of individual authors have been given more or less *en masse*.[11]

In this paper, an attempt is made to show how the spread and establishment of the *wh-* forms follow the loose-link/tight-link axis both in formal and colloquial styles. The question of the tightness of the link can be approached both through semantic and syntactic criteria. The traditional classification of relative clauses into restrictive and non-restrictive reflects a basic semantic division, but it is also possible to make more delicate distinctions based on the quality of the antecedent. It seems, for instance, that the relative clause is more closely linked with a pronoun (indefinite or personal) antecedent than with a noun antecedent, possibly because of the vague semantic content of the pronouns. On the other hand, the link seems to be particularly loose when the antecedent is a clause or a VP. Of the purely syntactic factors relevant to the tightness or looseness of the link, the separation of the relative clause from its antecedent is the most obvious.

In most discussions of relative pronoun distribution, attention has been called to the function of the relative pronoun in the subordinate clause. While it is easy to find a statistical correspondence between the pronominal form and the function of the pronoun, it seems that this correspondence is subordinate to the more general aspect of the quality of the link described above.

2.1 *That* vs. *which*

2.1.1 Usage in the 1640s

A survey of the distribution of the relative pronouns in the American English corpus dating from the 1640s shows, first of all, that *which* and *who* were well established in non-restrictive clauses (Table 1):[12]

Table 1. Distribution of relative pronouns in four texts of c. 1640

	$that_r$	$which_r$	who_r	$zero_r$	Total
Keayne, *Busin.*	38 (56)	19 (28)	2 (3)	9 (13)	68 (100)
Keayne, *Serm.*	54 (84)	3 (5)	–	7 (11)	64 (100)
Bradford	26 (59)	10 (23)	3 (7)	5 (11)	44 (100)
Winthrop	2 (9)	10 (43)	5 (22)	6 (26)	23 (100)
Total	120 (60)	42 (21)	10 (5)	27 (14)	199 (100)

	$that_{nr}$	$which_{nr}$	who_{nr}		Total
Keayne, *Busin.*	10 (15)	45 (70)	10 (15)		65 (100)
Keayne, *Serm.*	4 (17)	16 (70)	3 (13)		23 (100)
Bradford	–	31 (65)	17 (35)		48 (100)
Winthrop	–	41 (73)	15 (27)		56 (100)
Total	14 (7)	133 (69)	45 (24)		192 (100)
$Total_{r+nr}$	134 (34)	175 (45)	55 (14)	27 (7)	391 (100)

The tendency to limit the use of *that* to restrictive clauses can be clearly seen in the texts representing written language (Bradford and Winthrop). As might be expected, the texts recording spoken language, Keayne, *Serm*. and

Keayne, *Busin.*, show more variation in the choice of pronoun. In both texts *that*$_{nr}$ can be found in variation with the *wh-* pronouns; in the more colloquial text (*Busin.*) the number of occurrences is relatively high (10).

If the relative pronoun distribution in these two texts is compared at a low level of delicacy, a somewhat surprising result will appear: in the more formal text *that* prevails (54 + 4 occurrences, or 67%); in the more colloquial, *which* (19 + 45 occurrences, or 48%, as against 36% of *that*, 9% of *who*, and 7% of zero). A division of the occurrences into restrictive/non-restrictive solves part of the problem: in his sermons, John Cotton no doubt follows the traditional style of the biblical expression, avoiding *which*$_r$. At the same time the number of non-restrictive clauses in his text is conspicuously low.

Giving simple percentages might also imply that *that*$_{nr}$ is less common in the colloquial text than in the formal one (15% and 17% of all non-restrictive clauses). These figures can be easily explained by the observation that if the antecedent is a clause or a VP, only *which* occurs as a relative pronoun in the material studied.[13] This type of loose relative linking is very common in Keayne, *Busin.* (22 cases) but is avoided in Keayne, *Serm.* (4 cases). If the examples with this "knockout" context are eliminated, the distribution is that shown in Table 2.

Table 2. Distribution of relative pronouns, noun or pronoun antecedent

	that	*which*	*who*	Total
Keayne, *Serm.*	4 (21)	12 (63)	3 (16)	19 (100)
Keayne, *Busin.*	10 (24.5)	21 (51)	10 (24.5)	41 (100)

These figures are, of course, too low to be statistically significant, but they show how important it is to take favoured and unfavoured environments into consideration before conclusions are drawn from the distribution of the variant forms in texts of different types. The figures would be even more revealing if the so-called progressive or continuative relative clauses were eliminated.[14] Because of problems of classification — there are no reliable criteria for determining whether a relative clause is progressive or non-progressive — no figures of the results of this elimination can be given; by a rough count, about half the remaining cases of *which*$_{nr}$ could be classified as progressive in Keayne, *Busin.*, while Keayne, *Serm.* avoids clauses of that type in the same way that it avoids relative clauses with clause or VP antecedent.

It seems, indeed, that the rather confused picture resulting from many studies of relative pronouns in early Modern English is partly due to a failure to observe the varying popularity of certain environments favouring one or another pronominal form in texts of different kinds. That the avoidance of some types of relative clauses is a characteristic of sermon style rather than of John Cotton's idiolect is proved by a survey of Cotton's speech as recorded in Keayne, *Busin*. In the relatively few lines attributed to Cotton in Keayne's notes, the relative pronoun *which* occurs five times, three times with a clause as the antecedent.

It is also obvious that at this stage of development a high frequency of *which* as such is not a sign of Latinate style. In view of the early establishment of *which* in progressive clauses and in clauses with a clause or VP antecedent, the following comment by Rydén on 16th century usage seems highly perceptive:

> The influence of Latin and latinized prose is chiefly discernible in the high frequency of relative clauses and in the sentence-structure: long sentences containing a number of relative clauses, loosely appended clause (often with wide distancing of antecedent and relative), concatenations, and non-finite constructions. The extended use of non-restrictive clauses strengthened the position of the *wh*-relatives. . .
>
> (Rydén 1966:356)

This implies that the general structure of the text rather than straightforward Latin imitation was responsible for the growing popularity of the *wh*- pronouns in the 16th and early 17th centuries. We can assume that all texts characterized by loose sentence structure, with an abundance of non-restrictive clauses, show a high frequency of *which* — not only those imitating Latin sentence structure.

A more detailed study of the environments favouring each relative pronoun confirms the pattern of development according to which the *wh*- pronouns spread from contexts of loose link in non-restrictive clauses towards tighter combinations of postmodification. The early establishment of *which* with clause and VP antecedents and in progressive relative clauses was noted above. In addition *which* is favoured when the relative pronoun connects an adverbial clause to the main clause. From the present-day point of view, the construction is often anacoluthic, with an iterative pronoun:

(1) *and soe was a partner with him in his wickedness, which if I had reaveled it might have tended much to Gods glory, and to the discovery of his wickedness in such revelations* (Keayne, *Busin*. 316)

(2) *yet it stirred me up to give satisfaction, which whan privat frendes was not soe ready to accept as I expected, I had then a temptation to remoove owt of this place* (Keayne, *Busin*. 301)

From these types the use of *which*$_{nr}$ seems to spread to the other constructions of fairly loose relative link. An obvious type is the one in which the relative clause is separated from the antecedent by heavy elements. If the separating element is another NP, allowing ambiguity as to the antecedent, *which*$_{nr}$ is invariably used. In these contexts, *that* would mark the immediately preceding NP as the antecedent.[15] Rydén (1966:309) points out that even in sixteenth century texts *that*$_{nr}$ is "exceedingly uncommon" in distanced relative clauses. In Keayne, *Busin.* there is only one instance of *that*$_{nr}$ in this context, as against six with *which*:

> (3)   *and thear was one, that meet us in the way, that came from Cohannet* (246)

(Attention is called to the second *that*.)

> (4)   *Sister Waight, I pray helpe yor Husband if yow Cane in bringinge this to his minde, which he remembers not* (318)

> (5)   *and many gratious admonitions thay gave to me, which I did not regard ase I ought to doe* (301)

Example (3) is, of course, a rather special case with two consecutive, coreferential relative clauses.

Another special type which, for obvious reasons, favours *which* is the one in which the relative link is formed by a preposition and the pronoun. The arrangement with *that* + a postposed preposition was not uncommon in sixteenth and seventeenth century texts (cf. Rydén, 1966:279 ff.), but in many cases the structure or the sheer length of the relative clause prevents postposition:

> (6)   *The next day, in which by the good mercy of God, and the helpe of yor prayers, God did accompany us with seasonable weather* (Keayne, *Busin.* 246)

If the antecedent is an *of*-phrase, *which*$_{nr}$ is favoured because the relative pronoun in many cases refers to the head NP rather than to the modifying NP, which is adjacent to the relative pronoun:

> (7)   *The last Lords day God did not let me see the sinfulness of my former protestations, which since he hath helped me to see* (Keayne, *Busin.* 316)

> (8)   *the 3 part of the Repentance, which is Satisfaction or restitution, which God reqwiers for all things that yow have wronged any in* (Keayne, *Busin.* 303)

There is a related type in which the antecedent consists of two noun phrases coordinated by a conjunction. The use of *that* might restrict the reference to the adjacent member of the pair:

> (9) *and we delivered owr message and the churches letter, which they read and gave us satisfactory answers* (Keayne, *Busin.* 248)

(See also the second *which* in (8) above.)

Outside these environments, there are only three examples of $which_{nr}$ in Keayne, *Busin*. Table 3 shows how the distribution of $that_{nr}$ and $which_{nr}$ is conditioned by the factors described above.

Table 3. The distribution of $that_{nr}$ *and* $which_{nr}$ *in various syntactic environments*

	Keayne, *Busin.*		Keayne, *Serm.*	
	that	*which*	*that*	*which*
Antecedent clause or VP	–	24	–	4
Rel. pron. + adv. cl.	–	4	–	–
Distanced rel. clause	1	6	–	4
Rel. pron. with prep., or antec. *of*-phrase or two coord. NPs	3	8	2	3
Others	6	3	2	5
Total	10	45	4	16

A semantic analysis of the examples in the environments in which both *that* and *which* occur would probably reveal more distinctions, but even the syntactic classification given above should show the role played by the tightness of the link in the choice of the relative pronoun.[16]

In restrictive clauses, the discussion of the distribution of *that* and *which* can also be based on texts reflecting written expression (Bradford and Winthrop). Rydén (1966: Appendix, Tables III, X, XV) shows that $which_r$ was fairly common in the 16th century, though it normally does not exceed *that* in frequency.

Keayne, *Busin*. shows, again, a clear-cut pattern of distribution: $that_r$ prevails while $which_r$ is used mainly in contexts in which *that* would cause awkward repetition (Table 4). Typical combinations are *that which* and *that* (+ adj.) + N + *which*:

> (10) *and his repentance that now he houlds owt is that which gives me satisfaction* (321)

(11) *I desier to knowe what yow thinke of that revelation which yor selfe professed to have whan yow wear cast owt of the church* (317)

Table 4. Distribution of that$_r$ and which$_r$ with various types of antecedent

Antecedent	Keayne Busin. that	which	Keayne Serm. that	which	Bradford that	which	Winthrop that	which	Total that	which
that	—	5	—	3	—	3	—	—	—	11
that + N	1	6	1	—	—	1	—	1	2	8
the + N	6	2	6	—	3	4	—	2	15	8
Other premod.+N[a]	17	1	15	—	8	2	—	7	40	10
Other pronoun[b]	11	4	15	—	9	—	2	—	37	4
Personal pronoun	3	1	17	—	6	—	—	—	26	1
Total	38	19	54	3	26	10	2	10	120	42

a) I.e., nouns preceded by *all*, *many*, *such*, *no*, indef. art., zero, etc.
b) I.e., indefinite pronouns or demonstrative pronouns other than *that*.

In Keayne, *Serm.* the only occurrences of *which* are of the combination *that which*. The distribution in Bradford is similar to that in Keayne, *Busin.*, but Winthrop shows an interesting deviation from the pattern by clearly favouring *which*$_r$.[17] The low frequency of restrictive relative clauses in this text is also worth noting. In Winthrop's usage, *which*$_r$ seems to have spread into the cases in which the antecedent is a noun preceded either by the definite article or some other premodifier. In the two cases in which the antecedent is an indefinite pronoun (*all that*), and the link between the head and the postmodifying clause is thus very close, *that* is used even by Winthrop.

The question why there is so much difference between Bradford's and Winthrop's choice of the relative pronoun in restrictive clauses is of interest though difficult to answer. We could assume that the low number of restrictive relative clauses and the high number of non-restrictive ones in Winthrop's text has some bearing on the favouring of *which*. Another possible solution might be that Winthrop, an educated man with a Cambridge background, was accustomed (and perhaps even advised) to use the *wh*- forms as relative pronouns whenever possible. Stylistic variation is certainly not a decisive factor here; the subject-matter of both texts is the same, and, intuitively, Winthrop's text sounds less formal than Bradford's. It can be mentioned in passing that the same tendency to favour *which* is also traceable in Winthrop's private letters to his wife, written in the early 1630s.

2.1.2 Usage at the end of the seventeenth century

The above survey has given us some indications of the relative pronoun distribution in the English language spoken in New England around 1640. Variation is possible both in restrictive and non-restrictive clauses, particularly in spoken language, though the trend towards establishing *which* in cases of loose link is obvious.

In later seventeenth century texts, *that*$_{nr}$ occurs only sporadically: there are two examples in witness depositions, four in the letters and two in Cotton Mather's writing (see Table 5). As the number of non-restrictive relative clauses in this corpus is over 300, it can be said that the regularizing tendency

Table 5. Distribution of relative pronouns in late seventeenth century texts

	that$_r$	*which*$_r$	*who*$_r$	zero	Total
CM, JH, MR[a]	45 (72)	6 (10)	8 (13)	3 (5)	62 (100)
Letters, formal	22 (54)	3 (7)	4 (10)	12 (29)	41 (100)
Letters, pers.	15 (31)	9 (19)	1 (2)	23 (48)	48 (100)
Appeals	10 (38)	8 (31)	–	8 (31)	26 (100)
Depositions	20 (62)	6 (19)	–	6 (19)	32 (100)
Total$_r$	112 (54)	32 (15)	13 (6)	52 (25)	209 (100)

	that$_{nr}$	*which*$_{nr}$	*who*$_{nr}$	Total
CM, JH, MR[a]	2 (3)	37 (53)	31 (44)	70 (100)
Letters, formal	3 (6)	39 (75)	10 (19)	52 (100)
Letters, pers.	1 (1)	50 (58)	35 (41)	86 (100)
Appeals	–	59 (88)	8 (12)	67 (100)
Depositions	2 (4)	31 (63)	16 (33)	49 (100)
Total$_{nr}$	8 (2)	216 (67)	100 (31)	324 (100)
Total$_{r+nr}$	120 (23)	248 (47)	113 (21) 52 (9)	533 (100)

a) Cotton Mather, John Hale, Mary Rowlandson.

of limiting the use of *that* to restrictive clauses was established in written American English by the end of the seventeenth century. This regularization can be seen even in texts which represent informal style and in those that record uneducated speech.

It is of interest that, according to Krüger (1929:34 ff.), *that*$_{nr}$ is amply recorded in British English texts of the late 17th and early 18th century. Krüger does not give any figures but he quotes a number of examples from Evelyn, Dryden, Temple, Addison, Steele, etc. It may not be too rash to assume that the early tendency in colonial written English towards fairly rigid rules of relative pronoun selection is a sign of a particular concern about the purity and elegance of the language. A detailed quantitative analysis of the distribution of the pronouns in late 17th century British English texts would either confirm or disprove this suggestion.

The development of the relative pronoun distribution in restrictive relative clauses shows some interesting features, too. The situation in 1640 would seem to imply that *which*$_r$ was gaining ground at the cost of *that*$_r$, though the shift was less radical than in non-restrictive clauses. Only the sermon style shows a systematic use of *that*$_r$ (except in the combination *that which*); in Bradford and Keayne, *Busin.*, *which*$_r$ is used in about 25% of the cases, and in Winthrop this form clearly prevails (see Table 1, above).

Towards the end of the century, in texts representing informal style and the spoken idiom (i.e., in personal letters, appeals and witness depositions), *which*$_r$ retains its position (23 out of 106 cases, or c. 22%), but in the texts representing the formal written style (Cotton Mather, *et al.*, formal letters), it is only used nine times, or 9% of the cases. These texts show a tendency to regularize the use of *that*$_r$, parallel to the earlier regularization of *which*$_{nr}$. (The growing popularity of *who*$_r$ in these texts will be discussed below). The question whether this tendency is earlier in American English texts than in British English, and thus typical of the colonial language form, can be answered by a detailed study of British English texts of the same period. Addison's famous *Humble Petition of Who and Which* may well have been directed towards this tendency of making *that* the sole pronoun introducing restrictive relative clauses rather than towards the use of *that*$_r$ in general.

It is of interest that Increase Mather clearly favours *which*$_r$ in *Remarkable Providences* (c. 33% of all restrictive relative clauses). In this respect his language is closer to Winthrop's than to Cotton Mather's, though the texts of both the father and the son were published, and probably written, in the same decade, the 1680s.

The few instances of *which*$_r$ in formal writings occur with antecedents which favour *which*$_r$ even in the earlier corpus and in the informal texts of the later corpus, as shown by Table 6 (cf. Table 4 above).

Table 6. *Distribution of* that$_r$ *and* which$_r$ *with various types of antecedent*[18]

Antecedent	C. Mather & al., Letters, formal		Appeals, depos., Letters, pers.		Total	
	that$_r$	which$_r$	that$_r$	which$_r$	that$_r$	which$_r$
that	–	2	2	3	2	5
that + N	–	1	1	2	1	3
the + N	16	3	9	6	25	9
Other premod.+N[a]	19	1	18	11	37	12
Other pronoun[b]	25	2	8	1	33	3
Personal pronoun	7	–	7	–	14	–
Total	67	9	45	23	112	32

a) I.e., nouns preceded by *all*, *many*, *such*, *no*, indef. art., zero, etc.
b) I.e., indefinite pronous or demonstrative pronouns other than *that*.

2.2 Other relative links

The use of *as* and *what* as relative pronouns in the period under discussion is of minor interest; a few observations on the use of *who* and the zero link may add some details to the development described above.

2.2.1 *Who*

It is only natural that the use of *who* was first established in non-restrictive clauses, where *which* superseded *that* in the course of the seventeenth century. Even *who$_r$* can be found in the 1640 corpus, though *that* prevails in all texts except Winthrop. But it is of interest that in the course of the seventeenth century the distribution pattern of *that$_r$* and *who$_r$* does not change in a manner similar to *that$_r$* and *which$_r$*. While *which$_r$* is scantily evidenced in the formal style in the late seventeenth century corpus, owing to the regularizing tendency favouring *that$_r$*, *who$_r$* is clearly more popular in these texts than in the ones representing a more colloquial style. Counting cases with personal antecedent only, the ratio between *who$_r$* and *that$_r$* is 12:33 in formal texts and 1:17 in the informal ones. It would seem that the regularizing tendency evidenced by the texts of formal style works in two ways. The first relevant distinction is between restrictive and non-restrictive clauses, the second between personal and non-personal reference. In polite and formal style, the use of a form expressing the latter distinction is natural; colloquial language is less sensitive in this respect.[19]

Which can be found with personal antecedents in seventeenth century texts, but the number of cases is low and decreases towards the end of the century. In the earlier corpus there are fifteen cases of *which* out of the total of 134 cases with personal antecedent, in the later twelve out of 169.

2.2.2 Zero

In the period under discussion the subject zero link was still possible but it seems to be rapidly disappearing in written texts of all types. In our corpus there are only five scattered instances of the zero subject.[20] In other functions the zero relative is fairly common: the total number of occurrences is 79, c. 19% of all restrictive clauses (see Tables 1 and 5). The zero relative is mainly used in short clauses with a pronominal subject and a noun antecedent. The subject pronoun is not normally separated from the verb of the relative clause.[21] This very specific environment (Antecedent$_{noun}$ + $\emptyset$ + Subject$_{pron.}$ + V) is probably the result of the principle of minimum ambiguity, although rhythmic considerations should also be taken into account.

It has been suggested that the zero relative is particularly favoured in informal style and in spoken language. Rydén (1966:266) points out, however, that in his sixteenth century material there is "no general difference between literary and popular texts" in the use of the zero relative (cf. also Visser 1963: 538). This is also the case in our corpus of the 1640s: the figures for the four texts are roughly equal (Table 1, above). In all examples the relative clause is short; with one exception, the subject is a pronoun. It seems that in the general regularizing process of the seventeenth century, the zero relative became less acceptable in formal writing — only isolated examples can be found in Cotton Mather, Rowlandson and Hale (Table 5, above).

In informal prose, the zero relative becomes increasingly popular; a comparison of the formal and personal letters of the Saltonstalls is revealing (Table 5). Furthermore, the environment favouring the use of the zero relative is no longer as closely defined as in the texts of the 1640s; there are instances of the zero relative in longer relative clauses and in clauses with a noun subject. It may be mentioned, in passing, that in Sarah Kemble Knight's *Journal*, which offers a good example of the colloquial narrative prose of the early eighteenth century, there are nineteen occurrences of the zero relative, as against eight instances of *that*$_r$, two of *which*$_r$ and three of *who*$_r$, in a sample of some 8000 words.

According to Krüger (1929:73) the difference in the occurrence of the zero relative in formal and colloquial texts written in England can only be seen in the second half of the eighteenth century. On the other hand, Strang (1970: 142) reminds us of Dryden's revisions of his own work as early as the 1680s.

Krüger's statistics show clearly that in British English texts the zero relative was common even in the "literary prose" of the period under discussion; thus it is not unlikely that even in this respect American English formal expression shows an early tendency toward regularization.

3 Final remarks

The main purpose of this paper has been to show that the seemingly incoherent and disorganized picture of relative pronoun distribution in seventeenth century English becomes more understandable through close scrutiny based on a variational approach and a simple classification and grouping of the texts forming the corpus. The growing popularity of the *wh-* forms along the loose-link/tight-link axis seems obvious. These forms were probably first introduced into the language through formal written expression, possibly due to the influence of Latin. They were soon established in certain environments characterized by loose linking, popular in the colloquial language. From these environments, the *wh-* forms spread to environments with tighter link, causing considerable variation both in the formal written and (at least in some varieties of) informal written and spoken language, first in non-restrictive and soon also in restrictive clauses. In American English, formal written expression seems to react against this variation by the end of the seventeenth century with a tendency to establish a system in which *that* and *who* were the pronouns of tight link and *which* and *who* those of loose link, dropping *which*$_r$, zero and *that*$_{nr}$. The colloquial language was more reluctant to accept *who*$_r$ to the system, perhaps because it retained *that*, *which* and zero as the pronouns of tight link, dropping only *that*$_{nr}$. The early regularization and rigid rule formation in formal writing in seventeenth century New England is probably in accordance with the general language behaviour of an immigrant population possessing a strong literary tradition.

Notes

1. Weinreich, Labov and Herzog (1968) gave much stimulus to the systematic application of the variational approach to diachronic study. Samuels (1972) is an excellent elucidation of the theory at a more practical level. A good concise survey of the present state of the art in historical syntax is Rydén (1979). See also Jeffers and Lehiste (1979).
2. See, for instance, Rydén (1979:12−13).
3. The model of description is of minor relevance in variation-based diachronic studies of syntax. The discussion most naturally concentrates on the inferences drawn from the comparison of synchronic surface level descriptions of the variation patterns dating from different periods. It also seems that no very theoretical approach to the

concept of variation is necessary for the type of study reported in this paper. It is obvious that the more adequately the model brings forth the dynamic character of language, the more usable it is for the purposes of diachronic study. The basic principles of Bailey's (1973) wave model, as expounded, for instance, by Fasold (1975), might offer a good starting point for analysis.

Owing to the pilot study character of this paper, based on a fairly restricted corpus, the results of the quantitative analysis are not presented in the form, or with the statistical accuracy, usually characterizing the studies of variation. For the same reason, no attention is paid to the combined effect of the conditioning factors.

4. The standard general works, such as Mencken (1963), Krapp (1925), Marckwardt (1958) and Laird (1970), give little systematic information on questions of syntax. Of the monographs discussing special syntactic problems of 17th century American English, Abbott's (1953) doctoral dissertation on verb syntax is worth mentioning. Miss Merja Kytö of the University of Helsinki is preparing a dissertation on the expression of modality in the earliest American English. I am indebted to Miss Kytö for valuable bibliographical help.

5. *Robert Keayne His Book*, which contains transcriptions of John Cotton's sermons and notes on the "Business of the Island", from the years 1639–42 is a highly interesting text from the point of view of the study of the earliest English spoken in Boston. It enables us to compare the language of John Cotton's sermons with his utterances in the discussions following the service, and gives us samples of the speech of people with varying educational background. Keayne seems to be a reliable "recorder of voices", who did not level out the individual modes of expression of the speakers according to his own stylistic ideals. It seems, however, that Keayne's text is a clean copy written by him on the basis of a draft made in the meeting.

6. Though these documents are formal by nature, their level of formality depends largely on the educational background of the writer. The basic assumption here is that an uneducated person possesses only a restricted selection of stylistic variants and is thus likely to write in an informal way even in formal contexts. A rather extreme example is offered by one William Obbinson's appeal:

> ... becavs yovar apellant was sentanced to pay twenty pownds in mony or leathear at mony price when as gilbird [Gilbert] shved for nether mony nor leathear: but for pols of ware which can not be undar stood ane othar but the faces of Skins from the ears to the nos: and the damedg prised bvt fowar pounds: Yovar apellant thinks it tis not vsall for a man to shv for a henn and recovar a hors and all thoe gillbird ses I disstroyed them by pvlling them ovt of the pits yet that mvst not pas all ways for a trvth: for the trvth is thay wear disstroyd before thay came into the pitt . . . (Suffolk Records I 740)

7. Mustanoja (1960:188–92).

8. Cf., however, Lass's (1980) recent doubts about the functional explanations of language change.

9. This is just another way of explaining Alphonse Smith's oft-quoted statement about "the greater carrying power of *which*"; see Jespersen (1927:III 103).

10. See, for instance, Rydén (1966:362–4); Caldwell (1974:79–80); Romaine (1980).

11. E.g. Steinki (1932), Krüger (1929), Winkler (1933). Rydén (1966) is a notable exception. Quirk's (1957) discussion of the choice of relative pronouns in present-day English, based on a variety of conditioning factors, can be regarded as a classic.

12. The attributive use of *which* is not included. There are sporadic examples of this type in most 17th century American English texts, but it is common only in formal letters and in the formal language of law.

The abbreviations *pron.*$_r$ and *pron.*$_{nr}$ are used to indicate the pronouns in restrictive and non-restrictive clauses.

The percentages are given in brackets.

13. Even in the sixteenth century *that* was uncommon in these contexts (Rydén, 1966: 204).

14. I.e., non-restrictive clauses with a very low descriptive force and loose link with the antecedent. The verb of these relative clauses is normally dynamic, and the interest is focused on action rather than on the description of the antecedent (Rydén, 1966: xlviii-xlix; Jespersen, 1927:105–6). According to Rydén (1966:163, 172, 188), *that* is only exceptionally used in progressive relative clauses in 16th century prose; in the present corpus, no examples with *that* can be found in contexts of that kind.

15. In restrictive clauses *that* can be used even if the clause is separated from the antecedent. But there are few cases of this type, and it seems that the risk of ambiguity is always very small.

16. The cases with who_{nr} do not change the picture. In these two texts *who* occurs as a relative pronoun only in oblique cases or with a proper name as the antecedent.

17. The few occurrences of who_r in Bradford and Winthrop are evenly distributed between the various types and do not change the total picture.

18. Who_r does not change the picture essentially. Of the twelve occurrences of who_r in the formal texts, six have "other pronoun" as the antecedent, five "other pronoun + N", and one "*the* + N". The sole occurrence of who_r in informal texts has "other pronoun" (*those*) as its antecedent.

19. Cf. the Finnish pronominal form *se* 'it', the prevailing pronoun with personal reference in colloquial spoken language but impossible in formal or polite expression.

20. One in Keayne, *Busin.*, one in Winthrop, one in Hale and two in the Appeals. According to Rydén (1966:267), this type was infrequent even in 16th century texts. Krüger (1929:66) quotes a number of instances of varying types from late 17th and early 18th century British English texts.

21. These principles are in accordance with Rydén's observations on the environments favouring the zero relative in sixteenth century texts.

References

1. Texts

Bradford, William
    1908   *Bradford's history of Plymouth Plantation, 1606–1646* (= *Original narratives of early American history* 2), edited by William T. Davis (New York: Barnes & Noble).

Burr, George Lincoln (ed.)
    1914   *Narratives of the witchcraft cases, 1648–1706* (= *Original narratives of early American history* 17) (New York: Barnes & Noble).

Hale, John
    1914   "A modest inquiry into the nature of witchcraft," in Burr (ed.), 399–432.

Keayne, Robert
    1974   *Notes of sermons by John Cotton and proceedings of the First Church of Boston from 23 November 1639 to 1 June 1640*, edited by Helle M. Alpert (Tufts University diss.).

Knight, Sarah Kemble
    1939   "The Journal of Madam Knight," Theodore Dwight (1825), in *The Puritans*, edited by Perry Miller and Thomas H. Johnson (New York: American Book Company), 425–447.

Mather, Cotton
    1914   "Memorable providences, related to witchcrafts and possessions," in Burr (ed.), 94–143.

Mather, Increase
    1890   *Remarkable providences illustrative of the earlier days of American colonisa-
            tion*, with introductory preface by George Offor (London).
    1914   "An essay for the recording of illustrious providences," in Burr (ed.) 8–38.
Moody, Robert E. (ed.)
    1972   *The Saltonstall papers, 1607–1815*, I (1607–1789) (= *Collections of the
            Massachusetts Historical Society* 80) (Boston: Massachusetts Historical
            Society).
Morison, Samuel Eliot (ed.)
    1933   *Records of the Suffolk County Court, 1671–80*, I–II (= *Publications of the
            Colonial Society of Massachusetts: Collections* 29–30) (Boston: The Co-
            lonial Society).
Rowlandson, Mary
    1913   "Narrative of the captivity of Mrs Mary Rowlandson," *Narratives of the In-
            dian wars, 1675–1699*, edited by Charles H. Lincoln (= *Original narratives of
            early American history* 13) (New York: Barnes & Noble), 112–167.
Winthrop, John
    1908   *Winthrop's Journal: History of New England, 1630–49*, I, James Kendall
            Hosmer (= *Original narratives of early American history* 3:1) (New York:
            Barnes & Noble).

2. Studies

Abbott, Orville Lawrence
    1953   *A study of verb form and verb uses in certain American writings of the sev-
            enteeth century* (Michigan State College diss.).
Bailey, Charles-James N.
    1973   *Variation and linguistic theory* (Arlington: Center for Applied Linguistics).
Caldwell, Sarah J. G.
    1974   *The relative pronoun in early Scots* (= *Mémoires de la Société Néophilolo-
            gique de Helsinki* 42) (Helsinki: Société Néophilologique).
Fasold, Ralph W.
    1975   "The Bailey wave model: a dynamic quantitative paradigm", *Analyzing var-
            iation in language,* edited by Ralph W. Fasold and Roger W. Shuy (Washing-
            ton, D. C.: Georgetown University Press), 27–58.
Jeffers, Robert J. – Ilse Lehiste
    1979   *Principles and methods for historical linguistics* (Cambridge, Mass. & London:
            The MIT Press).
Jespersen, Otto
    1927   *A modern English grammar* III (London: Allen & Unwin).
Krapp, George Philip
    1925   *The English language in America* I–II (New York: Ungar).
Krüger, Alfred
    1929   *Studien über die Syntax des englischen Relativpronomens zu Beginn der
            spätneuenglischen Zeit* (Diss., Giessen).
Laird, Charles
    1970   *Language in America* (New York and Cleveland: The World Publishing Com-
            pany).
Lass, Roger
    1980   *On explaining language change* (London: Cambridge University Press).
Marckwardt, Albert H.
    1958   *American English* (New York: Oxford University Press).

Mencken, H. L.
1963   *The American language, the fourth edition and the two supplements, abridged, with annotations and new material*, edited by Raven I. McDavid, Jr. (London: Routledge & Kegan Paul).
Mustanoja, Tauno F.
1960   *A Middle English syntax* I (= *Mémoires de la Société Néophilologique de Helsinki* 23) (Helsinki: Société Néophilologique).
Quirk, Randolph
1957   "Relative clauses in educated spoken English", *English Studies* 38:94–108.
Romaine, Suzanne
1980   "The relative clause marker in Scots English: diffusion, complexity and style as dimensions of syntactic change", *Language in Society* 9:221–47.
Rydén, Mats
1966   *Relative constructions in early sixteenth century English, with special reference to Sir Thomas Elyot* (Uppsala: Almqvist & Wiksell).
1979   *An introduction to the historical study of English syntax* (Stockholm: Almqvist & Wiksell).
Samuels, M. L.
1972   *Linguistic evolution, with special reference to English* (London: Cambridge University Press).
Steinki, Johannes
1932   *Die Entwicklung der englischen Relativpronomina in spätmittelenglischer und frühneuenglischer Zeit* (Diss., Breslau).
Strang, Barbara
1970   *A history of English* (London: Methuen).
Visser, F. Th.
1963   *An historical syntax of the English language* I (Leiden: E. J. Brill).
Weinreich, Uriel – William Labov – Marvin I. Herzog
1968   "Empirical foundations for a theory of language change", *Directions for historical linguistics: a symposium*, edited by W. P. Lehmann and Yakov Malkiel (Austin & London: University of Texas Press), 97–188.
Winkler, Gerda
1933   *Das Relativum bei Caxton und seine Entwicklung von Chaucer bis Spenser* (Diss., Berlin).

SUZANNE ROMAINE

Towards a typology of relative-clause formation strategies in Germanic

Introduction[1]

It has been suggested that there were no relative clauses in the early pre-literate stages of Germanic. Although there are no relative pronouns or particles common to the modern Germanic languages (i.e. inherited from a common ancestor), the extension of demonstrative and interrogative pronouns as relative markers in early stages of some of the languages, e.g. English and Dutch, can be seen as a 'Germanic strategy' for creating relativizers.[2] Although the Germanic languages have arrived at similar means for marking relative clauses which cannot be related to a common historical relative pronoun or marker, it is evident that the similarities are functional. That is, they have to do with the syntactic task of relativizing. This becomes clear if we examine other cases in which relativization is not a distinct syntactic category, e.g. pidgins and creoles.

I will suggest here that the process of creolization, which involves, among other things, the development of greater distinctiveness in marking relative clauses, may shed light on Germanic events (and in particular, the history of English). I will argue that there do seem to be universal principles governing the process of creating relativizers and strategies of relativization. The facts about the development of relative clause formation strategies in Germanic which I will present here are best interpretable, in my opinion, within a panchronic framework. At a theoretical level then, what I propose to do here is to show how synchronic typology can offer important insight into syntactic change. In fact, I will argue that in this case, it is the input from diachronic change in the Germanic languages which makes the synchronic typology interesting.

1 Synchronic typologies of relative clause formation strategies

Like most syntactic typologies, those which have been proposed to account for relative clause formation strategies have been synchronic. I will argue here that Keenan and Comrie's views (with some modification) on NP accessibility and its relation to relative clause formation strategies provide a useful and insightful scheme for typing languages. They have, however, made no claims about the diachronic implications or validity of the NP hierarchy. The kinds of strategies available to natural languages represent synchronic 'states', but the precise nature of the routes between them remains unexplored.

After investigating relative clause formation strategies in a number of different languages Keenan and Comrie (1977; 1979 a,b) concluded that languages did not vary randomly with respect to the relativizability of NPs in certain syntactic positions. They have postulated the existence of the following case (or accessibility) hierarchy, which they have used to predict certain constraints on relative clause formation in universal grammar.[3]

Case hierarchy

Subject > Direct Object > Indirect Object > Oblique > Genitive > Object of Comparison

The case hierarchy has been used to predict the following:

1. the frequency with which NPs in certain syntactic positions are relativized in a language, i.e. subject NPs are most frequently relativized and objects of comparison are least frequently relativized.
2. the accessibility of NPs in various syntactic positions to a particular strategy of relative clause formation, i.e. if a given relative clause formation strategy works on two possible NP positions, then it must work on all intermediate positions between the two.

Some languages may have more than one relative clause formation strategy. The manner in which alternative strategies distribute themselves over the positions in the case hierarchy likewise does not seem to be random (but I will be making more specific claims about this later). For example, in Welsh, the primary strategy applies only to the subject and direct object positions. The other syntactic positions are relativized by means of a different strategy in which a clause is introduced by a relative particle and a personal pronoun is retained in the place of the shared nominal. As the case hierarchy is descended, there seems to be a greater tendency to use pronoun-retaining relative clause formation strategies; and where a clearly available option exists for promoting a relative clause to a position further up the hierarchy it is utilized.

Typologically speaking, the modern Germanic languages/dialects can be divided into three groups on the basis of their relative clause formation strategies (cf. Romaine 1982 and 1980):

1. those which use an invariant relativizing particle;
   e.g. Norwegian, which uses the particle *som*; and Zurich German, which uses the locative adverb *wo*.
2. those which use a 'mixed' system;

e.g. English, which uses the subordinator/complementizer *that* and the interrogatives, *who, which* etc.; and Swedish, which uses the invariant particle *som* and the interrogatives *vilken, vars* etc.

3. those which use 'true relative pronouns', i.e. case-coding pronouns;

e.g. modern German, which uses the demonstratives *der*, etc. as relative pronouns; and standard Dutch, which uses both demonstrative pronouns, *die* etc. and interrogative pronouns *wie, wier*, etc.

I am assuming for the moment that the most relevant typological distinction is not between languages which have mixed or unmixed strategies, but rather that the relevant criterion for the grouping is the use (or, as we shall see, the diachronic development) of true relative pronouns. I will propose that these synchronic states may be seen as different points along a diachronic continuum which extends from those types which use invariant relativizing particles to those which use pronominalization, even if the latter strategy is not available for use in all syntactic positions. Thus I take it that a language like Dutch is an instance of a 'mixed' type only in the sense that it uses both interrogative and demonstrative pronouns rather than one or the other set exclusively. Otherwise, Dutch can be regarded as having one strategy for relativization, namely, pronominalization.

Figure 1 shows how some of the Germanic languages/dialects fit into these typological groupings and how the strategies apply to various syntactic positions in the case hierarchy.[4]

It should be clear from this diagram that it would not be quite accurate to group whole languages under one basic type. There are dialects of English (like Scots) and of German (like Zurich German), which 'violate' typological norms. I will return to this interesting fact later.

Figure 1

Syntactic position in the case hierarchy   SU   DO   IO   OBL   GEN

1. invariant particle   Norwegian (*som*) ——————————————————

                           Frisian (*wat*)   ———————————————

                           Yiddish (*vos*)   ————————————

                           Zurich G. (*wo*)   ————————————

                           Scots E. (*that*)   ———————————

2. mixed   St. (standard) English TH

	SU	DO	IO	OBL	GEN

WH

Swedish *som*

vilken, vars

3. pronominalization   St. German *der*

St. Dutch *die*

wie

In a more recent discussion of data on relative clause formation Keenan and Comrie (1979b) refer to a distinction between case-coding and non-case-coding strategies. On this basic we can make a further refinement in the typology proposed so far. The languages/dialects I have grouped under the invariant type do make use of a case-coding strategy. Yiddish and Zurich German, for example, retain pronouns in oblique and genitive positions. Except in the case of Scottish English (which is, as far as I know, unique among English dialects in this respect), the coding of case in those languages/dialects with invariant relative markers is realized as invariant relative marker + personal pronoun. Although Scots possesses this option, it also allows the case-coding of otherwise invariant *that* (cf. Romaine 1980).

E.g.   *the man* [that's *wife I ken*]
    the man [that *I ken* his *wife*]
    the man [whose *wife I know*] (standard English)

The use of pronoun-retaining strategies permits the case-marking of the lower positions of the hierarchy.

Languages like Swedish and English, which are mixed types, differ in the way in which their strategies are distributed over the syntactic positions of the case hierarchy. The use of *who* etc. in English allows the full range to be case-marked (at least in those dialects which retain *whom* for direct and indirect objects). In Swedish the case-marking strategy is confined to the oblique and genitive positions.

In German and Dutch, which have one strategy in my typology, i.e. pronominalization, the situation with respect to case-marking is somewhat different. In Dutch the subject and direct object relative pronouns are identical, so the grammatical role of the head NP in the relative clause is not unequivocally coded in these cases.

E.g. *de man* [die *Marie aanviel*]
'the man [who attacked Mary/whom Mary attacked]'

For the other positions, indirect object, oblique and genitive, the relative pronoun codes the grammatical function of the head NP in the restricting clause (cf. the discussion and examples in Keenan and Comrie 1979a:335).

E.g. *De vrouw* [van wie *de man in het ziekenhuis ligt*]
'the woman [of whom the husband in the hospital lies]'

Dutch thus bears some similarity to English in this respect. If the WH strategy of relativization in English were to oust completely the TH one (which is non-case-coding), then English, like Dutch, could be characterized as a language which used a pronominalizing strategy. Alternatively, in Keenan and Comrie's terms, both Dutch and English could be thought of as possessing secondary strategies of relativization. The English one is capable of applying to the full range of syntactic positions, while the Dutch one marks the case of the relativized NP in indirect object, oblique and genitive (but not subject and direct object) positions.[5]

Such a development in English would not be entirely unexpected, and certainly not without precedent elsewhere in the history of the Germanic languages. If a relative pronoun loses its inflectional case distinctions, it may evolve historically into a relative marker. This appears to have happened already to a large extent in Germanic and it may be an on-going process in English and German. Modern German makes no distinction between nominative and accusative relative pronouns except when the head NP is masculine singular. Although the relative pronoun agrees with the head NP in gender (and number), if the head NP is feminine or neuter, the pronoun does not code the case of the NP. Thus in subject and direct object positions a case-coding and a non-case-coding strategy are in complementary distribution; the conditioning factor is the gender of the head NP (cf. Maxwell 1979:357).

Following Givón (1975), Maxwell (1979) has suggested some modifications to Keenan and Comrie's hypotheses about strategies of relativization. I would like to discuss three of the types Maxwell has defined.

1. WO-S (*word order strategy*)

The distinguishing characteristic of this strategy is the absence of an NP_{rel} (i.e. relativized NP) in the restricting clause; the clause may be post- or prenominal.

There may also be an invariant relative marker separating the head from the restricting clause. This strategy is very common in the higher positions (i.e. subject and direct object) of the case hierarchy. In this instance it corresponds to Keenan and Comrie's [-case] strategy. When the NP_{rel} is in oblique position, however, its function will be signalled by a stranded preposition, and thus is [+case]. Of all the relative clause formation strategies the WO-S is the least perspicuous in the sense that it is the most likely to fail to code unequivocally the case of the NP $_{rel}$ (cf. Maxwell 1979:357).

2. *Rel-S*

This strategy is distinguished by the presence within the restricting clause of a relative pronoun, or the combination of a relative pronoun and preposition as the only case-coding morpheme(s) for the NP$_{rel}$. In the Dutch, English and German cases I cited earlier, where subject and direct object positions are not unequivocally distinguished by case-marking on the relative pronoun, Maxwell (1979:356–7) would claim that we have examples of WO-S strategies. Thus, in the following English sentence, *who* does not code the case of the oblique NP$_{rel}$ any more than *that* does (although it does, of course, code animacy). The function of case-marking is carried out by the stranded preposition.

E.g.   the girl $\left[\begin{Bmatrix} \text{who} \\ \text{that} \\ \emptyset \end{Bmatrix} \right.$ John bought flowers for.]

3. *Pro-S*

In this strategy an anaphoric pronoun co-referential to the head NP occurs within the restricting clause, usually in the underlying position of the NP$_{rel}$. The Pro-S strategy may also occur pre- or post-nominally.

In Keenan and Comrie's classification both the Rel-S and Pro-S strategies are conflated into the category of [+ case]. This captures the generalization that in these two strategies one or more morphemes are used to code the case of the NP $_{rel}$ in the restricting clause. The WO-S strategy is a [-case] one in Keenan and Comrie's terms. The common ground between Maxwell's and Keenan/Comrie's typologies is that all the strategies may be thought of as case-coding in one sense; namely, they all usually make the case of the NP$_{rel}$ recoverable (though in some cases recovery is dependent on the operation of pragmatic rather than syntactic constraints). The opposition between the WO-S and the other two strategies, Rel-S and Pro-S, draws attention to word order and morphology as alternative ways of indicating the relationships between different parts of a sentence.

Maxwell (1979:361) has objected to Keenan and Comrie's classification because it makes no claims about *how* case is coded. Therefore, the difference between their system and Maxwell's centers on the importance of *form* vs. syntactic *position*. Maxwell's distinction between Rel-S and Pro-S makes the form of the case-coding morpheme the critical parameter. Keenan and Comrie's hierarchy, on the other hand, emphasizes the position of the relativizer. If strategies which use a combination of invariant relative plus personal pronoun in the position where a variable relative pronoun is expected are classified according to their form, they must be considered specimens of Pro-S; if they are classified according to their position, they are Rel-S.

I will now suggest how the incorporation of a diachronic perspective sheds some light on the classification of this type of strategy. It very often happens that borderline cases cause difficulties in synchronic typology; one solution to the problem is to 'dynamicize' typology. I have given a summary in Figure 2 of the strategies available in some of the modern Germanic languages in terms of the syntactic positions they apply to using Maxwell's framework.

Figure 2

Syntactic position in the case hierarchy		SU	DO	IO	OBL	GEN
Dutch	WO-S	+	+	−	−	−
	Rel-S [+ case]	−	−	+	+	+
English	WO-S	+	+	+	+	−
	Rel-S [+ case]	+	+	+	+	+
German	WO-S	+/−	+/−	−	−	−
	Rel-S [+ case]	−/+	−/+	+	+	+
Swedish	WO-S	+	+	+	+	−
	Rel-S [+ case]	−	−	+	+	+
Zurich German	WO-S	+	+	−	−	−
	Pro-S [+ case]	−	−	+	+	+
Frisian	WO-S	+	+	+	−	−
Scots	WO-S	+	+	+	+	−
	Pro-S [+ case]	−	−	−	−	+
	Rel-S [+ case]	−	−	−	−	+

(A plus indicates that the strategy applies; a minus indicates the strategy does not apply; the notation +/−, −/+ indicates that the strategies are in complementary distribution).

2 Diachronic typology: where do relative markers/clauses come from and where do they go?

The connections between synchronic typology and diachronic change are by no means clear. Although typology is generally conceived to be synchronic, it has become increasingly recongnized that diachrony has close connections with language typology and linguistic universals. Greenberg (1978), for example, has tried to formulate generalizations about diachronic processes by interrelating them with cross-linguistic regularities arising from synchronic typological investigations. And Vincent (1980) has discussed some of the ways in which typology (in particular, one which can provide an inventory of grammatical categories and possible construction types) may serve as the input to a method of syntactic reconstruction. What I would like to do here is establish a diachronically-oriented typology of relative clause formation strategies which will yield some insight into syntactic change and diachronic universals. There are of course trivial typologies and boring universals. That is, one can construct typologies which establish no significant or interesting connections among facts, but merely order a collection of facts without providing an interpretative framework for them. The goal of diachronic typology will be to illuminate the synchronic facts.

I think most linguists would accept that one goal of synchronic typology is to define a possible human language. Thus, each of the logically possible types within a typology which finds empirical exemplification represents a type or state. Synchronic generalizations can be considered as specifications of constraints on synchronic states through the delimitation of logically possible but empirically non-occurring (or non-demonstrable) types (cf. Greenberg 1978:65–7). In a similar fashion, the goal of a diachronically-oriented typology will be to define what can/cannot be a pair of languages whose speakers are time-sequentially related in a particular way. We assume in every case where there are two defined states or types that there is some way a language can move in and out of them, i.e. each state must have an arrow going towards and away from it. The task for diachronic typology with regard to any two states (or range of types) is to discover the process by which a language in one state can change into another and vice versa (cf. again Greenberg 1978:65–7). In other words, the problem is to define the possible routes in and out of the various types or typological states. Labov et al. (1972) have attempted something of this kind with regard to patterns of vowel shifting in phonetic space. Very simply speaking then, the relationship between synchronic typology and diachronic universals is this: typology provides/defines the targets (or states), and diachronic universals, the routes and modes of implementation of typological shift.

The establishment of a relationship between these two areas depends on several working assumptions. Firstly, one must accept that there are limitations on synchronic types; secondly, that change must proceed from lawful type to lawful type; and thirdly, that there is always ingress to and egress from a state. Unless we accept the truth of the third assumption, if there is one state with no egress and which is connected directly or indirectly with every other state, then everything must ultimately end up in that state. Thus, directionality becomes a non-issue. Alternatively, if there are no connections between two states, then these would represent two eternal properties of language which were universal. Thus, one has to accept that every type must ultimately be able to change into every other type, even if not directly. The first and second assumptions have been amply and fully discussed by a number of linguists under the rubric of the 'Uniformitarian Principle' (cf. for example, Lass 1980 and also Lightfoot 1979) and 'universal grammar' (cf. Greenberg 1978). I won't bother to discuss these two assumptions further here since most would probably now agree, pace Joos, that languages do not vary without limit.

I am hypothesizing here that we can view the synchronic typology of relative clause formation strategies which I set up in the last section as a continuum with at least three well-defined points. (The points in this case are defined morpho-syntactically in the first instance). One end is characterized by the marking of relative clauses with invariant relative particles and the other by relativization strategies involving pronominalization. These strategies represent a cycle or continuum whose precise nature is not yet known. Movement along the continuum may take place via a stage in which two strategies co-exist. Thus, from a diachronic point of view, the process of change may itself constitute a type, e.g. my so-called 'mixed' or 'transitional' type as exemplified in languages like Swedish and English.

My problem here will be to define pertinent patterns in the sequence of shift along the continuum and to identify implicational relationships which hold among the types and the nature of the constraints on change. This raises the following questions:

1. Can a language which uses an invariant relativizing strategy change directly into a type which uses pronominalization?
2. Must implementation of typological shift be gradual?
3. Are the constraints governing syntactic change purely syntactic?
4. What are the typological correlates of a language at any given position along the continuum of relative clause formation strategies?

My results to date (cf. in particular, Romaine 1980) provide a negative answer to the first and third of these questions, but an affirmative one to the second.

With regard to the fourth question, I will try to show that the continuum of relative clause formation strategies can be thought of as parallel to or coincident with two other continua. The first of these is a continuum ranging from adjunction to embedding and deals with syntactic process, while the second ranges from pragmatic to syntactic/grammatical and specifies the nature of the constraints which apply to relative clause formation strategies at various points along the first two continua. These are sketched out in Figure 3.

Figure 3

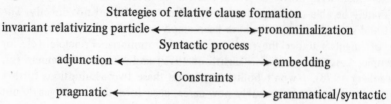

Strategies of relative clause formation

invariant relativizing particle ←——————————→ pronominalization

Syntactic process

adjunction ←——————————————→ embedding

Constraints

pragmatic ←——————————————→ grammatical/syntactic

I will introduce next some evidence from the history of relative clauses/ markers in Germanic to elucidate some of the connections among these continua. Later I will bring in some additional data, in particular from several English-based creoles, child language acquisition, and a non-Germanic language which has undergone typological shift with regard to relative clause formation strategy to show that these continua may reveal universal principles governing the process of creating relativizers and strategies of relativization.

I will begin my discussion of the historical evidence from Germanic by referring to the adjunction/embedding continuum. It has been suggested that there were no relative clauses at all in the early pre-literate stages of Germanic (cf. O'Neil 1976). Curme (1912), for example, and a number of other historical grammarians have commented that one can distinguish two basic types of sentence structure or relations between structures: *parataxis* and *hypotaxis*. These terms represent relative notions which have been used somewhat vaguely. In both paratactic and hypotactic constructions successive clauses may occur in sequence with no formal connecting link between them. Some have claimed that parataxis is a property of 'primitive' languages and is the simpler construction of the two because of its presence in the early stages of many languages. Jespersen (1926:103) has observed, however, that parataxis is more frequently found in the spoken language, while hypotaxis is more often employed in the written, literary language.

From this premise, i.e. that parataxis is a property of primitive languages, it is only a short step to the hypothesis that there is a transition from paratactic to hypotactic constructions which takes place in the evolution of a language; thus, hypotaxis represents a high stage of development which 'more highly evolved' languages like Greek and Latin were alleged to have attained, and to which other languages in the course of their development aspired.

In fact, it seems to be largely under the influence of Greek and Latin tradition that the use of complex syntactic structures has come to be taken as an important, if not indeed the most significant, means by which ability in language is displayed and evaluated. Such notions about syntactic complexity figure prominently more recently in the work of Bernstein (1973), who cites syntactic complexity as one important hallmark of the elaborated code.[6]

What has not been accepted or recognized by all scholars who have made a distinction between parataxis and hypotaxis is the fact that there are clues to the relationship between two successive clauses other than the presence or absence of certain grammatical items. For example, differences in rhythm, intonation, stress and context are used in the spoken language today, and presumably always were. The presence of a subordinating marker is perhaps the most obvious of the forms of hypotaxis, but it does not follow from this that the absence of such a marker proves a construction to be paratactic (unless, of course, we take this as the defining characteristic of the distinction).

The distinction between parataxis and hypotaxis is a difficult one to apply in the case of the development of the relative clause in English, as in other Germanic (and indeed non-Germanic) languages. This is so because when the relative pronouns do make their appearance, they are often not new linguistic devices, but have the same formal marks as other elements already in use in the language. Historical grammarians have differed in their opinions as to whether or not a word introducing a clause was being used with 'subordinative force', or if it belonged to the second or first of two successive clauses. The latter question is connected with the depth of linguistic analysis one assumes. For example, it would be possible to analyze relative clauses as having an underlying paratactic structure (cf. Thompson 1971).

Curme (1912:13) is one of the few earlier Germanic scholars writing about the relative pronouns who accepts that the distinction between parataxis and hypotaxis is not purely formal, since in each case two propositions may lie side by side. However, when the first formal attempts to connect two clauses more closely begin to appear, some have claimed that this is the origin of clear-cut relativization. In Old English, for example, either the demonstrative pronoun or the place adverb *þe, þær*, were used in a relative pronoun function. There is however the possibility that the second occurrence of the demonstrative in two successive clauses might have been used for repetition or emphasis as a stylistic device. This, Curme has suggested, is an instance of *asyndetic hypotaxis* and does not really involve the use of true relative pronouns at all. It is better to consider this a transitional stage in the development of the relative pronoun system.

There are really two issues at stake here: what is a *true* relative clause and what is a *true* relative pronoun? The early Middle English relative pronouns which are the ancestors of the modern English relatives originate in certain uses of the Old English demonstrative and interrogative pronouns. In the first instance the Old English demonstrative and article *se, seo, þæt*, either with or without a substantive in the initial clause, was repeated at the end of the clause to focus on some particular referent and point forward to some additional information which followed in the next clause, and thus in some way elaborated or restricted the referent in the first clause. Such an example is given in (1).[7]

(1) *pæt is se A braham [se him engla god naman niwan asceop]*
    'That is Abraham that to him angels' God name new made.'
    (Exodus 380–1; cited by Visser 1963:522)

It has been common practice among some of the traditional Germanic grammarians to call this extended use of the demonstrative an early instance of the relative. In examples such as these they explained that the demonstrative agreed with the case of the first demonstrative by 'attraction', instead of taking on the case marking that would indicate its position in the relative clause, which is what happens at a later stage. Curme (1912) maintains that the case of the extended demonstrative can be used as a criterion to indicate whether one is dealing with a true instance of a relative. He says that once the demonstrative began to be felt as part of the second clause it no longer took the case required by the verb of the initial sentence or clause, but took the case required by the second. This criterion cannot work of course in nominatives since the case form would be the same.

There was also the possibility in Old English of placing *pe*, an indeclinable particle, or *pær*, the locative adverb meaning 'there', after a substantive or pronominal element, which could serve the same function as the demonstrative. Curme (1912) again feels that these instances cannot be taken as examples of 'true' relatives; and in this case there are no formal signs of agreement since these markers were indeclinable particles. He cites the fact that *pe* was carefully avoided by the glossarists after a noun where the Latin version used a relative pronoun; here they used instead *se* or the combination form *sepe*, where *se* took the case of the verb of the relative clause and was therefore a true relative pronoun (compare Gothic which used the demonstrative pronouns plus an invariant particle *ei*). Both *se* and *sepe*, Curme says, became extended by this time into true relative pronouns. An example of a *sepe* relative construction is given in (2).

(2) *pa com he on morgenne to pam tungerefan [se pe his ealdormon wæs.]*
    'Then came he in morning to that steward that one that his superior was.'
    (cited by Mitchell 1965:74)

This extraposed relative clause structure is derived from conjunct or adjoined clauses introduced by either a general subordinating particle, i.e. what I am calling a 'relative marker' or an invariant particle, or a form of the demonstrative pronoun. The distinguishing criterion for a relative marker (as opposed to a pronoun) is that it does not vary according to some feature of the co-referential NP, e.g. case, animacy, gender etc., and is not felt to be derived from it via a process of pronominalization. It seems clear that *þe* has the status of a relative marker and may be thought of as a complementizer. However, even if the marking of concord is essential to the status of true relative pronoun, there can still be true relative clauses which are not introduced by relative pronouns. That is, if the clause shows any marks of subordination, then there is very little reason to take constructions such as (1) with characteristic OV word order as 'pre-relatives' or anything other than true relative clauses. In other words, non-pronominal relativizers can introduce genuine relative clauses. Relativization by *se* involves movement of the relative pronoun; if this were not the case, then we would expect the pronoun to have its case determined by the upper clause instead of the case expected by the relativized NP (cf. also Allen 1977:91).

In fact, O'Neil (1976) has claimed that relativization was introduced into the Germanic languages as an adjunctive process. He argues, for example, that there is little evidence in Old English to support the view of relative clauses as being embedded Ss under an NP. It makes more sense, he says, to speak of 'clause adjunction', because the most striking characteristic of the relative clause (and in fact of all subordinate clauses) in Old English is the fact that such clauses are almost always at the margins of the main clause (and almost never flanked by material from the main clause). Thus, Old English has no relatives of the following type, S O_{rel} V, where O_{rel} represents the syntactic position of the relativized NP in the relative clause, though it does have object relatives such as S V O O_{rel}.

In late Old English, and vertainly by the early Middle English period, relative clauses are found flanked by the major constituents of the main clause; so at some point it becomes necessary to postulate a change from adjunction, i.e. [$_S$ ... NP ...S], to actual embedding under an NP, i.e. [$_{NP}$ NP S] (assuming the latter analysis is justified for modern English). I will return to these facts after I have discussed some more evidence from Middle English.

During the Middle English period *þe* and *þæt* (the neuter form of the Old English demonstrative pronoun) were used to introduce relative clauses until *þat* (from OE *þæt*) gradually replaced *þe*. It is at this stage that the interrogative pronouns, the ancestors of modern English *who, which*, etc. began to be used as relatives. Mustanoja (1960: 191) says that the transition from interrogative to relative pronoun began in types of indirect questions where the interrogative character of the pronoun became weakened, and the pronouns so used were generalizing relatives. The final stage in this development occurred when the pronoun referred to a clearly definable antecedent and was used with a strictly relative function. Mustanoja (1960) also believes that the use of the interrogative pronouns as relatives may have been prompted by

Latin influence originally and became strengthened in Middle English under French influence.

We can summarize the major events in the development of relativization in English as follows:

1. expansion and use of demonstrative pronouns and place adverbs as relatives in OE.
2. replacement of *þe*, a relative particle, by the subordinator *that* in ME
3. replacement of the demonstrative pronouns by the interrogative pronouns in ME.

I will now look briefly at events in some of the other Germanic languages, in particular, German, where tendencies were similar to those in Old English, but resulted in a different typological state. In the oldest Old High German texts, especially in Otfrid, *the* is used as an invariant relative particle. However, asyndetic hypotaxis was frequent in Old High German, but rare afterwards. The demonstrative pronouns then began to be used as relatives. During the Old High German period the simple interrogatives, *hwer* 'who' and *hwelîh* 'which', also appear as relatives, particularly in connection with *-sô* in the function of indefinite relative pronouns. A similar development took place in Middle English (cf. Mustanoja 1960:192), but in German the usage did not spread. The interrogative adjective/pronoun *welcher* was also used as a relativizer in Middle High German about the same time as *which* was being used in Middle English, but the Middle High German usage was largely a feature of the written language and never really gained ground.[8]

The neuter interrogative *was* ousted the older relative *das* in a number of positions, e.g. when the antecedent in the main clause was a pronoun with indefinite reference. In modern spoken non-standard (and also to a certain extent standard) German *was* has replaced *das* in all positions, i.e. regardless of the gender and number of the antecedent.

E.g.   Leute *was* viel Geld haben
       (Compare non-standard English: 'People *what* have a lot of money.')

Similarly, the demonstrative adverb *dâr* 'there', developed into a relative adverb (meaning 'where') in Old High German. The locative adverb *wo* encroached upon *dâr* (*da* in the modern language) in a way similar to the replacement of *das* by *was*. In Alemannic dialects in particular (e.g. Zurich German), *wo* is used uniformly as the relative marker.

E.g.   Leute *wo* viel Geld haben
       (cf. the discussion and examples in Lockwood 1968: 242–255).[9]

Old Dutch, like Old English and Old High German, used demonstrative pronouns as relativizers. In Middle Dutch however, the interrogative pronouns (i.e. *wiens* and *wier*) began to be used along with the demonstratives. The former are however still limited to the genitive and oblique positions. At this time the inflections of the Dutch demonstratives were exactly parallel to those of the interrogatives (cf. Winkel 1898); thus loss of inflections does not seem to have been a motivating factor in the introduction and spread of interrogatives in relative clauses in Dutch. I mention this fact because Curme (1912) has attributed the adoption of the interrogatives as relative pronouns in English to the decline in inflectional marking in the determiner system. Clearly this isn't a sufficient factor for change as the evidence from Dutch indicates.

O'Neil (1976:207) has suggested that what we can see happening between the Old and Middle English periods (and more generally in the history of Germanic) is the working out of a syntactic strategy for the incorporation of sentences into sentences, i.e. a change from adjunction to embedding. His 'explanation' for this phenomenon is the advent of literacy among the Germanic peoples, which forced a change in adjunction. And he links the change specifically to performance strategies and perceptual factors. That is, adjunction poses a burden by allowing the build-up of perceptually difficult sentences. Heavy modifiers in a sentence are delayed to the end and not allowed to break up the integrity of the sentence. Once the process of subordination or embedding was well developed, it was utilized to reduce the perceptual burden of adjunction.

At this stage of my argument we can see a connection between the adjunction/embedding continuum and relativization strategy types. The development of a strategy involving pronominalization is coincident with the marking of relativization as a syntactic category distinct from subordination. We can now also provisionally link this continuum with Maxwell's typology of relative clause formation strategies by giving a formal characterization of these in transformational terms. The WO-S strategy involves deletion; thus, in the older stages of the Germanic languages, e.g. Old English and Old High German, we can have relativization by deletion, or so-called asyndetic hypotaxis. Relativization by means of *se* in OE involves movement of the relative pronoun, whereas relativization by *þe* or deletion does not. The Pro-S strategy involves pronominalization; and the Rel-S strategy involves both movement and pronominalization. The typological split between those Germanic languages which have invariant relative particles and those which do not also coincides with the incidence of preposition stranding. It appears that an indeclinable relative particle is a necessary precondition for preposition stranding in relative clauses. Preposition stranding occurs, for example, in Old English and Old Norse in those constructions where there is no surface evidence of movement. Since relative pronouns like English *who* etc. and Dutch *wie* etc. do not require stranding, the adoption of these interrogative pronouns as relativizers must be seen as motivated in part by purely syntactic principles.

Allen (1977:355–6) has suggested that these facts about the incidence of preposition stranding and strategies of relativization can be accounted for by assuming that some languages have relativization by deletion or movement and that others have only relativization by movement. If we postulate that wherever there is no surface evidence for movement in relatives, then deletion is involved, it follows that languages with no invariable relative particle have only movement. The languages which have only pronominal relatives, like Dutch and German, have no pronoun deletion rule, but the languages which have an invariable relative particle, e.g. English and Swedish, do. Relatives like, *He is the man ∅ I saw,* are assumed to be the result of the deletion (or non-insertion) of only the complementizer rather than deletion of both a complementizer and a pronoun. Since deletion of a pronoun under the complementizer node is assumed not to exist, and there is no relative complementizer in the languages having only pronominal relatives, there are no relatives without overt markers. Nevertheless, even though an indeclinable relative particle may be a necessary condition for stranding, it isn't sufficient. Yiddish, for example, which has an indeclinable relative, *vos,* doesn't allow stranding.[10]

We can also speculate at this point about the connection between the adjunction/embedding and relativization stategies continua and the pragmatic/grammatical-syntactic constraints continuum. If relative clauses in the early stages of Germanic are never found truly embedded under an NP, but almost always at the clause margins, then unless the extraposed clauses have some distinctive marking that results from a process of relativization, the only properties which distinguish such clauses from independent ones are the result of general anaphoric properties and more general subordination marking. Thus at this stage the interpretation of such a clause as relative, i.e. when a relativizing particle is not present, is largely a semantic or pragmatic matter (cf. for example, Downing 1978:409 for a discussion of languages that have no embedded relative clauses and Hale 1976 on the adjoined relative clause in Australia).[11]

I will hypothesize that shift/drift along this continuum from adjunction to embedding represents a typological change in the discourse-pragmatic strategies used by the language (cf. Givón 1977 for discussion of a similar shift along a syntactic continuum from VS/SV to SV word order). Thus, pragmatic constraints are operative at the lower end of the continuum, whereas at the upper end, grammatical and syntactic constraints apply, viz. overt case-marking on pronouns and implicational order of syntactic position in the case hierarchy.

3 Evidence from creolization and other developmental continua

Although the Germanic languages have arrived at similar means for marking
relative clauses, which cannot be related to a common historical relative marker or pronoun, it is evident that the similarities are functional, i.e. they have
to do with the syntactic task of relativizing. This becomes clear if we examine
other cases in which relativization is not a syntactically distinct category, e.g.
pidgins, creoles and dying languages. I would like now to look more specifically at what happens in the process of creolization, which involves, among
other things, the development of greater distinctiveness in marking relativization. Generally speaking, in pidgins and creoles there are no formal markings
to indicate that one part of an utterance is subordinate to another. Distinctive marking of relative clauses come later, i.e. after the development of coordinate structures, if at all. I hope to show how the creation of relative markers/
clauses in two English-based creoles supports the continua I have set up here
and also sheds light on events in natural languages such as the Germanic group
under discussion.

Sankoff and Brown (1976) have recently studied the process of how speakers of Tok Pisin, a New Guinea English-based pidgin, have created a relativizer from the place adverbial *ia* meaning 'there' (also spelled *hia*). In previous
grammatical descriptions of Tok Pisin *ia* has been treated as a place adverbial
derived from English *here*; and it is fairly clear from what others have said
that it had not been used as a relativizer or relative particle throughout the
history of Tok Pisin. So far the English WH forms seem to be used only in
indirect questions; and from what Sankoff and Brown report, it does not
seem likely that they will expand to create a full system of relatives in the
way that *who*, *which* etc. did in Middle English.

Instead, what is happening in Tok Pisin is that the lexical item *ia*, which
originated as a place adverbial, has been extended to a demonstrative or generalized deictic function in discourse. The authors (1976:632) give this
example:

> *Meri ia [em i yangpela meri, draipela meri ia] em harim istap*
> 'This girl, who was a young girl, big girl, was listening.'

In this sentence *ia* is being used to bracket an embedded clause from a matrix
S by virtue of its placement after both the head noun and the embedded
clause.

Sankoff and Brown suggest that *ia*, while preserving its deictic function,
has been extended to another structural possibility; namely, it has become a
focussing particle which is backward-looking, i.e. it alerts listeners to a previous item in discourse or focusses on a particular referent and marks it as

different from another one. But at the same time *ia* has taken on a more general deictic function; it is also forward-looking in that it points to the slot where new material will be inserted. In Tok Pisin then, we have a nice illustration of how an original place adverbial becomes extended as a postposed deictic and then eventually used for general bracketing in relativization. Sankoff and Brown claim that one must look for the origins of syntax in discourse, i.e. the creation of relativization is motivated by speaker organization of discourse.

A chain of events similar to those which Sankoff and Brown have presented for Tok Pisin is represented synchronically in Buang, where the deictic particle *ken* is used as a place adverbial, post-posed demonstrative and relativizer. Hence they have rejected a strictly syntactic view of relativization in favor of a functional one which shows some of the properties which relative clauses share with other constructions. It appears that so-called natural languages create relativizers in similar ways to pidgins and creoles (ruling out borrowing from the superstrate, of course). That is, there are certain kinds of categories or syntagms in languages which can become relative markers/pronouns, e.g. deictics such as demonstrative pronouns and place adverbials, interrogative pronouns, etc., and thus come to perform the syntactic work of separating an NP from an embedded sentence.

I would argue then that what happened in Tok Pisin has a great deal of relevance to relativization in the Germanic languages. To take Old English as an example, in the case of the extension of *se* in a relativizing function and the use of the locative adverb *þær* to mark relative clauses, we can note a trend similar to Tok Pisin. This should not of course be surprising since Tok Pisin is an English-based pidgin; but Tok Pisin did not just borrow the superstrate system of relativization. I would claim that this suggests there are universal principles governing the process of creating relativization.[12]

There seems to be additional support for my claim in a recent study by Dreyfuss (1977), which compared the relative clause formation strategies used by four creoles (Haitian Creole, Tok Pisin, Sango and Sranan). She found that all four languages used the order NP-S (with SVO word order), and that three of the languages used a deictic marker as a relativizer. The choice of the deictic in a relativizing function is, according to Dreyfuss (1977:150), an independent innovation, i.e. the languages have not borrowed from the superstrate (though there has been considerable influence from French in the case of Haitian Creole). The fact that the languages are creoles does not seem to have influenced the kind of marker; none uses true relative pronouns that vary with case, animacy or other characteristics of their antecedents.[13]

Resumptive pronouns (i.e. a Pro-S strategy of relativization) occur in all four languages, but there are differences in the positions in which these occur.

However, all the languages use them in oblique and genitive relatives. Drey-fuss (1977:170) suggests that this may be evidence that pronominalization is the most favored mechanism of the three possible choices available for marking the case of a co-referential NP. The other possibilities would be marking the case on the relative pronoun (i.e. Rel-S) or deletion (WO-S). Where the relativized NP is a subject or direct object however, the languages use a variety of means for encoding case. I have summarized these possibilities in Figure 4.

Figure 4.

Case marking in four creoles (from Dreyfuss 1977:170)

Creole	HC	TP	SG	SN	ENG
Subject	1	2,3	2,3	2	1 (2)
Dir. Obj.	2	2,3	2,3	2	1,2
Obl. & Gen.	3	3	3	3	1 (2)

(1 = coding on relative marker; 2 = deletion; 3 = pronominalization)

I have included modern English here for comparison. If we just consider the WH relatives, then English can be thought of as using only the first two strategies for coding case, namely either by marking case on the pronoun or by deletion. I have put parentheses around the deletion strategy to indicate that it is not always possible to delete relatives in subject, genitive and oblique positions in modern English; I will have more to say about constraints on deletion later. The use of resumptive pronouns in modern English is very limited, at least in standard English, but it does occur in some dialects, such as Scots. This permits the relativization of NPs which are otherwise in inaccessible positions.[14] Resumptive pronouns do not seem to be in frequent use with WH relatives in standard spoken English; but they may occur in certain registers of the written language, e.g. legal language.

We might expect further changes to take place in the newer creoles (e.g. Tok Pisin and Sango), as they come to be more widely spoken. The first thing we might predict is that the use of resumptive pronouns in subject and object position would die out. This may represent a first step on the way to developing relativization as a distinct syntactic category. In all four creoles relativization sometimes merges with conjunction (or adjunction), especially when there is no relative marker, i.e. deletion. Thus, we would also expect some constraints on deletion to be imposed as time went on.

It is also difficult to tell in the case of Hawaiian Pidgin English and Creole whether embedding or merely a conjoining process has taken place. The surface marker which may eventually be used in a relativizing function is not a specialized relative pronoun, but a simple pronoun. Bickerton (1977:126) for example, cites the following sentence:

> *Da boi jas wawk aut fram hia, hiz a fishamæn*
> 'The boy who just walked out of here is a fisherman.'

Bickerton (1977:274) suggests that the pronouns are an intermediate stage between zero forms and the full range of English relative pronouns. Maxwell (1979:368) has independently speculated that anaphoric pronouns in a position next to relative markers may be a step away from becoming relative markers. Thus, the Pro-S strategy, where an NP_{rel} is expressed by a personal pronoun may be thought of as an intermediate stage between a WO-S and a Rel-S strategy of relative clause formation.

From the evidence I have considered so far it is apparent that progression along the continuum from adjunction to embedding on the one hand, and relativization by delection and invariant particles to relativization by case-coding pronouns on the other, is not Germanic-specific, even though Germanic has dialects/languages which occur at various points along these continua, both synchronically and diachronically, i.e. panchronically. The mapping of languages/dialects along a panchronic continuum will show us where a particular language, dialect or even style of a language in question is along the continuum of change.

The position of a language/dialect along the continuum of relative clause formation strategies and development of relative pronouns/markers may also have a perceptual correlate. In other words it may be useful to postulate the existence of an additional continuum of perceptual saliency which correlates with relativization strategy. Keenan and Comrie (1979b:653) have in fact suggested that the case hierarchy represents a semantically or cognitively based characterization of relative clause formation strategies.[15] There is evidence from psycholinguistic testing that the positions in the case hierarchy are correlated with relative difficulty in comprehension, i.e. the lower positions of the hierarchy do appear to be perceptually more difficult to decode. It has been argued that in addition to perceptual difficulty there is a trend of developmental complexity as well, and the following hierarchy has been proposed (cf. for example, Sheldon 1973 and Offir 1973):

OS > SS > OO > SO

In this hierarchy S represents the position occupied by a subject and O that occupied by a direct object; the first letter in each pair refers to the syntactic position of the head NP in the matrix sentence and the second to the syntactic position of the relativized NP in the relative clause. Thus, the hierarchy indicates that OS relatives are more easily decoded than SS, and SS more so than OO, and OO more so than SO.

It is illuminating to compare this perceptual continuum with the developmental continuum resulting from the process of creolization. Bickerton and Odo (1976:274–9) have observed that the few Hawaiian Pidgin English speakers who do produce relative clauses, relativize on the object noun of the matrix sentence far oftener than on the subject noun. We can see that in both the OS and OO types the head NP is closer to the relative marker than in the SO type, if we look at the following examples:

OS *The dog bit the man* who *lives next door.*
OO *The dog bit the cat* that *the man next door owns.*
SO *The cat* that *the dog bit belonged to the man next door.*

They speculate that relativization on the object noun is easier than subject relativization because it still entails (in terms of surface structure) only paratactic conjunction of sentences, rather than the insertion of one within the other, i.e. embedding, as in the case of subject relativization, e.g. SS and SO.

SS *The man* who *owns the cat lives next door.*

I assume that these types of relative clauses have the following phrase markers.

1. NP_1 V $[NP_2]$ – $[NP_3]$ V NP_4 (OS)
               object   subject

2. NP_1 V $[NP_2]$ – NP_3 V $[NP_4]$ (OO)
               object   object

3. $[NP_1]$ V NP_2 – NP_3 V $[NP_4]$ (SO)
   subject   object

4. $[NP_1]$ V NP_2 – $[NP_3]$ V NP_4 (SS)
   subject   subject

It is worth reiterating an earlier point I made about Old English relatives; namely, that Old English had no relatives of the SO type, though it did have OO relatives.

Bever and Langendoen (1972) have viewed the loss of inflectional endings with the concomitant fixing of word order and the appearance of restrictions on the absence/deletion of relative markers as related trends in the history of English. They claim that modern English no longer permits deletion of subject relatives (which, in effect, restricts the application of the WO-S strategy to lower positions of the case hierarchy), because these relative clauses became perceptually complex. Thus, they argue that the constraints governing deletion of relatives have changed by dint of the demands of perceptual or cognitive strategies of decoding.

We can see then two (to some extent competing) changes at work in the history of the relativization system in English. One is the adoption ('borrowing'?) of the WH strategy (possibly under the influence of Latin and French syntax). I have discussed the gradual diffusion of WH pronouns in a differentially sensitive manner with respect to syntactic position in the case hierarchy in Romaine (1980). Using a measure of syntactic complexity based on the frequency with which NPs in certain syntactic positions are relativized, I found that the WH relativization strategy entered one variety of English, namely Middle Scots, in the most complex styles and least frequently relativized syntactic positions, until it eventually spread throughout the system.

The second change concerns rate of deletion of relative pronouns. It is generally accepted that in Old and Middle English subject deletion is frequent, while object deletion is rare. The direction of spread of deletion is however opposite to that of the WH relativization strategy, i.e. it goes from left to right through the syntactic positions in the case hierarchy (cf. Romaine 1980 and also Dekeyser, this volume).

I have described both changes as instances of 'syntactic diffusion', a term I have taken from Naro and Lemle (1977). They have proposed a principle of perceptual saliency as a universal constraint governing the implementation of syntactic change. Their claim is that syntactic change manifests itself first and most frequently in those environments where it is least noticeable or salient. Syntactic change actuated by hypercorrection, however, would work in the opposite way, i.e. it would manifest itself first in the most salient environments. The distinction made between natural change and change by hypercorrection can also be characterized in terms of Bailey's (1973) opposition between natural and unnatural change. The direction of natural change is from the heaviest weighted (or most marked) environment to the lightest (or least marked); in creolization this order is reversed.

What is the connection then between these two changes? Certainly in the history of English-based creoles (and more generally in the process of creolization) one should more appropriately speak of the insertion (rather than deletion) of relative markers; or alternatively, as I have done in connection with the history of English, of the spread of the inhibition of zero marking of relative clauses (i.e. the restriction of the WO-S strategy). Bickerton (1977: 270–1) has argued (and I would agree) that it is counter-intuitive to assume an underlying structure for features that never appear on the surface level. That is, there must be some evidence at some level (in either a synchronic or diachronic derivation of a feature), before one is justified in speaking of deletion. In Hawaiian English Creole relativization is being built up from scratch; pidgin speakers begin first with zero marking, then subsequently insert pronouns and finally the relative pronouns of standard English. This sequence of stages in the surface marking of relativization follows in a strict implicational order.

Although a plausible explanation for the high percentage of object relatives (i.e. OO) in both Old English and Hawaiian English Creole (rather than subject relatives, as one would predict from the case hierarchy), can be based on perceptual factors, it may actually be more reasonable to refer to the influence of discourse. That is, new information nouns tend to be located in object position. Thus, the high percentage of object relatives is a reflection of this fact. During the course of acquisition it may be that speakers switch from a discourse-oriented system to a purely syntactically-motivated one; this notion is perhaps behind Sankoff and Brown's hypothesis concerning the origins of Tok Pisin relatives in certain discourse functions. This change-over may help to explain their finding that the case hierarchy does not work, i.e. account for the frequency of distribution of relative clauses in various syntactic positions.

Bickerton (1977:284) also finds that in Hawaiian English Creole the rate of insertion of relative markers in OS sentences is at least twice that for OO types. This appears to fit in well with Bever and Langendoen's hypothesis about perceptual strategies governing deletion. However, we would then expect the same constraints to apply to SS sentences; but Bickerton finds a considerably lower rate of insertion. There is no marking in 70% of SS sentences, while half the OO types are marked. This may indicate a crucial discrepancy between developmental (i.e. acquisitional) and synchronic/diachronic continua with respect to relativization. That is, the case hierarchy may apply just in case a language has relative clauses already and is not in the process of developing them. A similar interpretation based on a switch from discourse to grammatical strategies may also not be too far-fetched in the history of English, where data on the deletion of relative markers indicate there was an increase in the deletion of object relatives in the late Middle English period, but a decrease in subject deletion (cf. Romaine 1981a and 1982). In other words the differential change in rates of deletion (or more appropriately, absence) of relative markers is concomitant with this change-over from discourse-pragmatic to grammatical-syntactic constraints on strategies of relative clause formation. This view fits in well with O'Neil's (1976:207) opinion that a change from adjunction to embedding (i.e. a syntactic strategy for the incorporation of sentences into sentences) took place between the Old and Middle English periods. In this way loose paratactic structures were condensed or syntacticized into tight hypotactic structures.

4 More evidence for a panchronic typology of relative clause formation strategies

I would like now to bring in some additional support for the diachronic typology I have set up for the Germanic languages. The evidence comes from syntactic change in certain varieties of Konkani, which is an Indo-European language related most closely to Marathi and Gujerati. For the past 400 years Konkani speakers in certain areas have been fluent bilinguals in Kannada (a Dravidian language). Nadkarni (1975) provides an account of the impact of Kannada influence on Konkani relative clause formation. Contact has been pervasive, so that now a Kannada or Dravidian strategy of relative clause formation is in the process of ousting the native (Indo-European) Konkani one. The Konkani case is furthermore interesting in that it has some parallels with Middle Scots and English. The Kannada strategy of relativization was itself originally borrowed from Indo-European, so in adopting the Kannada type strategy, Konkani is actually 'borrowing a borrowing'. In effect then, "the borrowing of a borrowing replaces an original which was the model for the first type" (Nadkarni 1975:674).

We know that the changes in relative clause formation have come about by dint of contact because there are other dialects of Konkani which retain the native Indo-European strategy. The examples below (from Nadkarni 1975) show patterns of relative clause formation in Kannada and two varieties of Konkani. In each case the relative clause is bracketed and the relative markers are in roman type.[16]

Kannada   [yāva *mudukanu pēpar ōdutta iddān-ō*] *avanu ḍākṭaranu iddāne*
Konkani   [khanco *mhāntāro pēpar vāccat āssā*-kī] *to ḍākṭaru āssā* (+ contact)
Konkani   [jo *mhāntāro pēpar vāccat āssā*] *to ḍākṭar āssā*   (– contact)
[which old man paper reading is] that doctor is
'The old man who is reading the paper is a doctor.'

Varieties of Konkani which have come into contact with Kannada have two relative clause formation strategies: the Dravidian type illustrated in the second sentence marked (+ contact), which makes use of the native Konkani interrogative pronoun *which* (Kannada makes use of *yāva*, which is also an interrogative pronoun), and the native Indo-European type, illustrated in the third sentence. The native type makes use of a relative pronoun, *jo*, to introduce the relative clause.

Varieties of Konkani which are not in contact with Dravidian have only the third type of relative clause; the type which makes use of an interrogative pronoun is ungrammatical. In addition, the Kannada relative clause attaches the relative particle *-ō* to the verb of the relative clause (e.g. *iddāne* + *ō* =

iddānō). Only the varieties of Konkani in contact with Kannada make use of a particle on the basis of analogy with the Dravidian strategy (e.g. *āssā-kī̃*). Thus the two types of relative clause formation strategy in 'Dravidianized Konkani' differ not only in the choice of the relativizer (i.e. *jo* vs. *khanco*), but also in the optional vs. obligatory presence of the particle *-kī* on the verb of the relative clause. The particle *-kī* serves a double function in Konkani as a relative clause or bracketing particle and as an interrogative particle in yes/ no questions. (It is also used as a complementizer.) Similarly, *khanco* is used as both a relative and interrogative pronoun. The relativizer *jo* has no other function in the language. The particle *-kī* must co-occur with *khanco*; it may optionally be present with *jo*, but only in those varieties of Konkani in contact with Kannada.

One further shared structural characteristic is relevant; namely, that the Kannada type relative clause formation strategy must immediately precede its head. The native Konkani type need not obey this constraint.

E.g. *to ḍākṭaru āssā* [jo *mhã̄ntāro pēpar vāccat āssā-*(kī̃)]
      that doctor is [which old man paper reading is]

Thus, Konkani has borrowed the Kannada order pattern along with the relative clause formation strategy. The difference between the Kannada and the native relative clause formation strategies lies in the grammatical morpheme used as relative marker and in a rule of extraposition which allows the relative clause to be post-nominal in the latter case but not in the former.

I have discussed the Konkani case in such detail because it raises a number of theoretical issues and has important implications for the relationship between diachronic universals and synchronic typology. The most important questions raised are these:

1. What is the *direction* of development of relative clause formation strategies? I.e. Has there been any typological change in Konkani?

2. If so, what is the mechanism of change? I.e. How is it implemented and how is it to be accounted for?

Within the synchronic typological framework I have introduced here, the Dravidian relative clause formation strategy is a Rel-S (pre-nominal) type or a case-coding one (involving pronominalization and movement). The crucial (and indeed, most interesting) factor in this case is that Konkani hasn't borrowed the actual Dravidian pronoun (i.e. *yāva*), but only the strategy or basic pattern for relative clause formation. Konkani uses its own interrogative pronouns and particle in a relativizing function. The native Konkani type, on the other hand, is an instance of a complementizer type or invariant relative particle strategy (or in Maxwell's terms a WO-S, which may be either pre- or post -

nominal). This strategy itself however is an instance of typological change when seen within the larger context of comparative Indo-European developments. The relativizer *jo* is a 'true relative pronoun' in Hindi, Marathi, Gujerati, and most importantly, in varieties of Konkani not in contact with Dravidian; that is, the relativizer may be marked for case in all these languages/varieties, but not in 'Dravidianized Konkani'. Thus, in the latter case we have an instance of typological shift from a Rel-S (pronominalizing) strategy to one of WO-S. The relativizer *jo* then is no longer a relative pronoun, but is instead a relative marker. The native strategy is no longer a case-coding one. We can summarize these developments in Figure 5, which can then be compared with the Germanic data in Figure 2.

Figure 5

Syntactic position in the case hierarchy	SU	DO	IO	OBL	GEN
Konkani (+ contact) WO-S (*jo*)	+	–	–	–	–
Rel-S (*khanco*)	–	+	+	+	+
Konkani (– contact) Rel-S (*jo*) (also Marathi, Hindi, Gujerati)	+	+	+	+	+

Now there is a striking similarity between developments in Konkani and certain of the Germanic languages and dialects I have been discussing here. Some varieties of Konkani can be viewed as 'transitional types' in much the same way I suggested was the case for English within the context of the Germanic languages. Konkani is in the process of losing one of its strategies of relative clause formation, which is now restricted to subject position NPs. The Kannada type has taken over the other positions in the case hierarchy. This change has the effect of bringing Konkani back in line, so to speak, with its original typological class, namely, Rel-S.

To employ a functional metaphor, syntactic change is operating as a regulatory or homeostatic device. (Incidentally, this would be a good example of Lightfoot's 1979:149 principle that grammars practice therapy, not prophylaxis.) There are then arguably two typological changes which must be distinguished here, although Nadkarni (1975:697) has noted only one, i.e. the adoption of the Dravidian type strategy. The latter in any event is still a case-coding one, as was the original Konkani strategy. Perhaps it is better to see these two processes, i.e. restriction of the *jo* strategy to subject position and the entrance of the *khanco* strategy as two aspects of the same phenomenon, i.e. a syntactic change which is leading to a greater distinctiveness in relative clause formation. There is probably not much point in arguing which came first, i.e. the restriction on *jo* or the entrance of *khanco*, and hence 'triggered' the other. They are probably better regarded as competing changes. Lightfoot's distinction between prophylaxis and therapy is a moot one anyway (cf. Romaine 1981 c). Oddly enough, from a typological point of view, it is as if there had been no change: the starting point is the same as the ending point, a Rel-S language.

It is interesting that Moravcsik (1978:107) has cited this particular instance of contact-induced change as a counter-instance to a proposed hypothesis about universal constraints on borrowing. The hypothesis predicts that the ordering of syntactic constituents can be borrowed only if the phonetic form of at least some members of the constituent class is also borrowed. If the hypothesis were correct, then Konkani should have borrowed entire relative clauses and head constituents in their phonetic manifestations from Kannada. Konkani hasn't borrowed the Dravidian pronoun, *yāva*, but only the strategy or basic pattern for relative clause formation. And this is of course precisely what is intriguing in this case; I have demonstrated that similar events take place in the history of natural Germanic languages like English and German, and in English-based creoles. Konkani, like many of the other languages I have mentioned here, has created a Rel-S, or pronominalizing relative clause formation strategy for itself through the use of its native interrogative pronouns as relativizers.

Nadkarni (1975:675) maintains that the borrowing is structurally unmotivated and cannot be explained in terms of purely linguistic factors. The native mode of relativization is more versatile in that it allows extraposition. The Konkani borrowings are also difficult to account for in terms of social factors. That is, it is not the case that the structure was borrowed under the influence of prestige, as one might reasonably argue in the history of English with respect to the adoption of the WH strategy. Kannada, according to Nadkarni, has *no* social prestige. In fact, the Kannada-speaking community is *less* socially prestigious.

I think Nadkarni is wrong in his conclusion that the change has no explanation in pure linguistic terms. The change and the mechanism of its implementation can be accounted for in terms of the framework I have set up here which embeds diachronic directionality in synchronic typology. The direction of the change fits one prediction my typology would make; namely, the trend in natural languages if from invariant relativizing particle to a strategy employing pronominalization.[17] The constraints governing implementation are largely syntactic. That is, new strategies of relativization will enter a language in 'reverse' order on the Keenan-Comrie accessibility hierarchy. In other words, the change 'sneaks in the back door' via the least frequently relativized positions, and spreads out from there. Interestingly, the mechanism of implementation can be described as one of 'syntactic diffusion', i.e. gradual syntactic change in which one construction gives way to another via periods and syntactic environments where both overlap or are used variably (cf. Romaine 1980 for a more detailed discussion of syntactic diffusion in the history of English). The net result is the creation of a relativization strategy which permits maximum distinctive use of the full range of syntactic positions in the case hierarchy. While the implementation phase appears to be governed largely by purely syntactic constraints, it is clear that functional considerations must be important in a wider context. The loss of a distinct, i.e. case-coding, strategy of relativization capable of working at the lower end of the hierarchy presumably yields a language which is in some sense less easily able to cope with complex modes of discourse.

Conclusion

I have argued here that the connection between typology and language universals becomes even more interesting when seen in a diachronic perspective. I have discussed the part typology plays in establishing diachronic universals. Queries concerning typological shift and mechanisms of syntactic change by reanalysis can be illuminated by the notions 'syntactic diffusion' and 'transitional type'. These can be thought of as micro- and macro-dimensions of diachronic change. That is, once we acknowledge that syntactic change may take place by gradual and variable diffusion, we have a means of understanding how a language can get from one analysis of a construction to another different one and thus undergo typological change. The shift may take place via a stage in which the language may alternate between two analyses/constructions at the same time. The diffusion of characteristic patterns and construction types from one language to another under language contact or in purely internal change may give rise to synchronic typological inconsistency.

Although the Keenan-Comrie hierarchy has connections with both relational and (to some extent with) transformational grammar and has been used primarily in synchronic typology, it allows the formulation of a number of empirically testable hypotheses. I have concentrated here on the diachronic implications of typology in order to show how these contribute to our understanding of hierarchy phenomena and relative clause formation. As it turns out, the implications of my initial diachronic investigations with the case hierarchy (cf. Romaine 1982) are even more far-reaching than I originally thought. It remains to be seen however just to what extent my findings reflect the specific facts of Germanic (in particular, English) or are more widely applicable. I would very much like to have comparative-historical data on varieties of Dutch (especially non-standard) and Dutch-based creoles. The data I have presented from Konkani however do support a number of the claims I have made on the basis of the Germanic data.

Many questions about the possible connections between literacy (and stylistic expansion) and developments in relative clause formation strategies await further investigation. This will perhaps explain why it is we find dialects/ styles within the same language at different points along the continuum of change. Is it the case that we are seeing primarily a dichotomy between spoken and written language reflected in the preference for paratactic as opposed to hypotactic structures?

Although one can try to account for the kinds of changes in relativization I have discussed here in terms of purely syntactic principles (as Lightfoot 1979:333—6 has done in the history of English), or social and stylistic factors (as I have done in the case of Middle Scots in Romaine 1980 and 1981a), or perceptual mechanisms (as Bever and Langendoen 1972 have done), it may actually be more profitable within a panchronic framework to refer to the intersection and interaction of various continua. What makes a language easy to understand, e.g. case-coding of the syntactic position of relatives by unequivocal marking of the pronoun, may also make it difficult to learn. That is, inflectional endings, allomorphy etc. are among the linguistic devices which are left out in child and second language acquisition, and in pidginization.

One needn't get carried away with the similarities between the development of relativization in the post-creole continuum in Hawaii and in Old English and thus conclude on the basis of such parallelisms that Old English (or Middle English) was a creole. It would be futile, in my opinion, to launch a debate about the prospect of uncovering creole origins for Old and Middle English (or for that matter, proto-Germanic). Bailey (1973) and no doubt others would wish to push these similarities farther than I would. When referring to pidginization/creolization (and pidgins/creoles), we must be careful not to confuse the process with the entities which result from them. Hence the term 'creolization' should be reserved for a situation in which a creole results. There are however cases where conditions are conducive to simplification, reduction etc. (e.g. second language acquisition), but which do not give rise to a pidgin or creole.

As I have already indicated, I think the similarities in the development and expansion of relative markers and relativization strategies in natural languages like Old English, modern Dutch, Konkani, etc., and creoles like Tok Pisin and Hawaiian English Creole are functional and need to be seen within a panchronic framework. Then it isn't surprising, I would claim, to find that the creation of relativization in Hawaiian English creole (and in other creoles) and natural languages follows a very similar course and displays certain developmental pathmarks, i.e. it begins with adjunction and a WO-S strategy of relativization, whose interpretation is governed largely by pragmatic rules. The functional similarities are crucial in understanding the connections between natural languages and pidgins and creoles. One outcome of the cross-fertilization of synchronic typology with diachronic universals will be the construction of panchronic grammars which will offer insight into the relationship between various developmental and historical continua.

Notes

1. I am grateful to Peter Matthews for comments on an earlier version of this paper, some of which I have incorporated here.
2. This is of course not a purely Germanic problem. The derivation of the relative pronoun in Indo-European and many of its daughter languages creates difficulties since two separate bases, **yo* and **k^wo*, function as relative markers. The latter of these has a dual function as an indefinite and an interrogative (cf. also the discussion in Justus 1978).
3. A separate issue, which I will not deal with here, is whether there is a single set of syntactic-semantic properties by means of which relative clauses and notions like 'subject', 'object' etc., can be identified as universal syntactic-semantic categories (cf. however, Downing 1978 and Keenan and Comrie 1979b:650).
4. I have omitted object of comparison here because relativization on NPs in this syntactic position is rare in many languages. This classification is also somewhat controversial (cf. the discussion in Maxwell 1979:367). I am also omitting discussion of so-called 'free relatives'.
5. I am not using 'secondary' in exactly the same sense as Keenan and Comrie do. They (1979b:653) say that a given strategy is primary in a language just in case the strategy can be used to form relative clauses on subjects. Although all languages have a primary strategy, some may have only primary (and no secondary) strategies. The strategies which apply to subject position are the most basic relative clause formation strategies in natural languages. Keenan and Comrie claim that in its strongest form the accessibility hierarchy makes generalizations which apply only to primary strategies. Of all languages which may relativize subjects by whatever strategies, some languages may relativize no other NP in those ways (or indeed in any other way). In referring to the WH strategy in English as 'secondary' (which is derived historically from the extended use of interrogative pronouns as relativizers), I am using the term in a diachronic sense.
6. The controversial issue is whether the observed differences between syntactic complexity in relation to social class are related to referential meaning and cognitive abilities. Schulz (1972:101), for example, has concluded that in colloquial German the particles *ja, doch, da* etc. (so-called *Füllwörter*) are just as capable of serving as logical connectives as the causal conjunctions, *weil, daher*, etc., of the standard language, which require subordinate clauses with transposed word order. What Schulz is claiming is that particles and conjunctions are to be understood as functionally equivalent variables in the expression of discourse cohesion. Traugott (1979:18) has however questioned whether a relatively paratactic stage of a language is only syntactically and pragmatically different from a more hypotactic stage, or if it is also different semantically (cf. also Romaine 1981b).
7. Traugott (1972:86–7) says that *se* + proper noun complexes seemed to be used as

a 'singling out' construction in Old English, and that *se* also indicated previous mention. Thus, modern English *the* grew out of such uses of *se* through the weakening of the dual sense of 'specific' and 'previous mention' to just previous mention.

8. The terms 'middle', 'early' etc. are of course relative.

9. I have cited the following example of relativization with the locative adverb in English (cf. Romaine 1982):

These two (children), *where* the father had died.

Interestingly, a possible alternative construction to the relative clause introduced by *where*, would be a possessive relative, as indicated below: These two (children) *whose* father had died. In first referring to this example I did not attribute this pattern of relativization to substratum influence from Pennsylvania Dutch (i.e. a variety of German). The speaker in this case was an elderly woman from Birdsboro, Pennsylvania, who did display other syntactic oddities, such as the following 'what for dishes' (compare German *was für* NP- 'what kind of . . .'), which can be accounted for in terms of influence from Pennsylvania Dutch. If I am right, then this provides yet another case in which an alternative strategy of relativization is adopted which makes possible the relativization of NPs on the lower, i.e. more complex, portion of the case hierarchy. This construction with *where* as an invariant relative marker doesn't appear in other syntactic positions in this speaker's usage.

10. Old English *þe* shared many of the characteristics of modern English *that*, despite the latter's formal resemblance to Old English *þæt*. For example, relativization both by *þe* and *that* involves movement of the noun which they pronominalize to the left of the clause and stranding any preposition in construction with that noun in its original position. In some cases *þe* also appeared at the beginning of the relative clause while the underlying noun was pronominalized as a personal pronoun. *Se*, on the other hand, does not appear to occur with the personal pronoun form of the relativized underlying noun; furthermore, if the relativized NP has a preposition associated with it, the preposition is shifted with the relative pronoun to the beginning of the relative clause. In modern English, however, the preposition may retain its original position. In this respect, *se* resembles modern English *who*, *which*, etc. Traugott (1972:153) has argued on the basis of the functional similarities between *se* and *who* on the one hand, and *þe* and *that* on the other, for the origin of the modern English *that* in the complementizer *that*, which in Middle English became generalized to all subordinate structures, and was used in conjunction with any other subordinator, e.g. *if that*, *whether that*, etc. (Cf. also Lightfoot 1979:314 for arguments that modern English *that* in relative clauses is not a pronoun).

11. In the Australian languages a continuum is represented from adjoined to embedded relative clauses via languages which have both types. The continuum may also be reflected in a single language, such as Yidiṅ, where the relative clause combines features of both types in a single construction, thus representing an adjoined-embedded 'squish' (Hale 1976).

12. It is perhaps premature to argue that there are universal principles at work here; at the risk of overstating my case, I think my results are interesting even if they turn out to hold just within Germanic.

13. Pidgins and creoles of course characteristically lack case-marking and thus have no special markers for relatives, i.e. the marker for relative clauses and verb complements is quite often the same. This may happen in natural languages too. When a language has no case-marking, then the distinction I have made between relative markers and pronouns on the basis of invariance vs. case-coded pronouns wouldn't arise. The criterion for a relative marker would be simply that of complementizer status.

14. Some dialects of Danish apparently have a strategy of relative clause formation with a resumptive pronoun which is similar to the Scots one. I am grateful to Niels Davidsen-Nielsen for giving me the following example:

Konen at hendes sØn du kender
'the woman that her son you know.'
(Compare standard Danish: Konen hvis sØn du kender.)

15. In fact, both semantic prominence (in terms of distribution of NPs in discourse) and the accessibility of syntactic positions are reflected in the hierarchy. Accessibility however is not only a matter of NP distribution in English (and, I would also argue, in other languages); it also correlates well with syntactic complexity (cf. Romaine 1980 and 1981b, and also Dekeyser, this volume).

16. I am excluding here the so-called 'participial relative' in Kannada and Konkani (cf. Nadkarni 1975:674).

17. I am not claiming that all the Germanic languages are going through such a progression now. I am suggesting that if a language is 'aiming at' the creation of relativization as a distinct syntactic category, this is one possible route it might take. Although this route is in fact a rather frequent one, it is not unidirectional. For example, Norwegian used to employ interrogatives in a relative function in certain syntactic positions (i.e. indirect object, oblique and genitive) as modern Swedish and Danish do today. The usage survives now however only in older written Norwegian (cf. Haugen and Chapman 1964).

References

Allen, C.
1977   *Topics in diachronic English syntax* (unpublished Ph.D. dissertation, University of Massachusetts).

Bailey, C.-J.
1973   *Variation and linguistic theory* (Washington, D. C.: Center for Applied Linguistics).

Bernstein, B.
1973   *Class, codes and control* Vol. II. (London: Routledge and Kegan Paul).

Bever, T. G. – D. T. Langendoen
1972   "The interaction of speech perception and grammatical structure in the evolution of language", *Linguistic change and generative theory*, edited by R. P. Stockwell and R.K.S. Macaulay (Bloomington: Indiana University Press), 32–95.

Bickerton, D.
1977   *Change and variation in Hawaiian English*. Vol. II: *Creole syntax* (Social Sciences and Linguistics Institute: University of Hawaii).

Bickerton, D. – C. Odo
1976   *Change and variation in Hawaiian English*. Vol. I: *General phonology and pidgin syntax* (Social Sciences and Linguistics Institute: University of Hawaii).

Curme, G.
1912   "A history of the English relative constructions", *Journal of English and Germanic philology* 11:10–29, 180–204, 355–80.

Dekeyser, X.
this volume "Relativizers in early modern English".

Downing, B. T.
1978   "Some universals of relative clause structure", *Universals of human language*. Vol. 4: *Syntax*, edited by J. Greenberg (Stanford: University of Stanford Press), 375–419.

Dreyfuss, G.
1977　*Relative clause structure in four creole languages* (unpublished Ph.D. dissertation, University of Michigan).
Givón, T.
1975　"Promotion, NP accessibility, and case-marking: toward understanding grammars", *Working papers on language universals* 19:55–125.
1977　"The drift from VSO to SVO in Biblical Hebrew: the pragmatics of tense-aspect", *Mechanisms of syntactic change* edited by C. Li (Austin: University of Texas Press), 181–255.
Greenberg, J.
1978　"Diachrony, synchrony and language universals", *Universals of human language*, Vol. I: *Method and theory*, edited by J. Greenberg (Stanford: Stanford University Press), 61–93.
Hale, K.
1976　"The adjoined relative clause in Australia", *Grammatical categories in Australian languages*, edited by R. W. Dixon (Canberra: Australian Institute of Aboriginal Studies), 78–105.
Haugen, E. – K. Chapman
1964　*Spoken Norwegian* (New York: Holt, Rinehart and Winston).
Jespersen, O.
1926　"Notes on relative clauses", *Society for Pure English. Tract* No. 24 (London: Oxford University Press).
Justus, C.
1978　"Syntactic change: evidence for restructuring among co-existent variants", *Journal of Indo-European studies* 6:107–32.
Keenan, E. L. – B. Comrie
1977　"Noun phrase accessibility and universal grammar", *Linguistic inquiry* 8: 63–99.
1979a　"Data on the noun phrase accessibility hierarchy", *Language* 55:332–352.
1979b　"Noun phrase accessibility revisited", *Language* 55:649–655.
Labov, W. – M. Yaeger – R. Steiner
1972　*A quantitative study of sound change in progress* (= Final report on NSF contract 3287) (Philadelphia: U. S. Regional survey).
Lass, R.
1980　*On explaining language change* (Cambridge University Press).
Lightfoot, D.
1979　*Principles of diachronic syntax* (Cambridge University Press).
Lockwood, W. B.
1968　*Historical German syntax* (Oxford: Clarendon Press).
Maxwell, D.
1979　"Strategies of relativization and NP accessibility", *Language* 55:352–372.
Mitchell, B.
1965　*A guide to Old English* (Oxford: Basil Blackwell).
Moravcsik, E.
1978　"Language contact", *Universals of human language,* Vol. I: *Method and theory*, edited by J. Greenberg (Stanford: Stanford University Press), 93–123.
Mustanoja, T.
1960　*A Middle English syntax* (Helsinki: Mémoires de la Société Néophilologique 23).
Nadkarni, M.
1975　"Bilingualism and syntactic change in Konkani", *Language* 51:672–683.
Naro, A. – M. Lemle
1977　"Syntactic diffusion", *Ciencia e cultura* 29. 3:259–268.

Offir, C.
   1973   "Recognition memory for relative clauses", *Journal of verbal learning and behavior* 12:636–643.
O'Neil, W.
   1976   "Clause adjunction in Old English", *General linguistics* 17:199–211.
Romaine, S.
   1980   "The relative clause marker in Scots English: diffusion, complexity and style as dimensions of syntactic change", *Language in society* 9:221–49.
   1982   *Socio-historical linguistics. Its status and methodology* (Cambridge University Press).
   1981a   "Syntactic complexity, relativization and stylistic levels in Middle Scots", *Folia Linguistica Historica* 1:56–77.
   1981b   "On the problem of syntactic variation", *Working papers in sociolinguistics* (Austin, Texas: Southwest Educational Development Laboratory).
   1981c   "The transparency principle: what it is and why it doesn't work", *Lingua* 55:93–116.
Sankoff, G., – P. Brown
   1976   "The origins of syntax in discourse. A case study of Tok Pisin relatives", *Language* 52:631–666.
Schulz, G.
   1972   "Über die dürftige Syntax im restringierten Kode", *Zeitschrift für Literaturwissenschaft und Linguistik* 7:97–116.
Sheldon, A.
   1973   "The role of parallel function in the acquisition of relative clauses in English", *Dissertation Abstracts International A – The Humanities and Social Sciences* 34 (Michigan: Ann Arbor).
Thompson, S. A.
   1971   "The deep structure of relative clauses", *Studies in linguistic semantics*, edited by C. Fillmore and D. T. Langendoen (New York: Holt, Rinehart and Winston), 79–97.
Traugott, E. C.
   1972   *The history of English syntax* (New York: Holt, Rinehart and Winston).
   1979   "From propositional to textual and expressive meanings; some semantic-pragmatic aspects of grammaticalization", Paper given at the First International Conference on Historical Linguistics, Durham.
Vincent, N.
   1980   "Iconic and symbolic aspects of syntax: prospects for reconstruction", *Linguistic reconstruction and Indo-European syntax*, edited by P. Ramat (Amsterdam: John Benjamins B. V.), 47–68.
Visser, F.
   1963–   *An historical syntax of the English language* (Leiden: Brill).
   1973
Winkel, Jan te
   1898   *Geschichte der Niederländischen Sprache* (Strassburg: Karl J. Trübner).

BLAIR A. RUDES

Reconstructing word order in a polysynthetic language:
From SOV to SVO in Iroquoian[1]

1 Introduction

A relatively common working principle in the historical reconstruction of word order has been that the relative ordering of morphemes in the words of a language in some way correlates with an earlier syntactic order of words. While this idea has been around linguistics for some time, the most systematic presentation of the principle was that provided in Givón (1971). Since that time, a number of articles have appeared which have seriously challenged the reliability of synchronic morpheme ordering as an indicator of earlier word ordering.[2] In particular, Comrie (1980) has made a strong case for the unreliability of such evidence. However, Comrie allows of one exception where the morphological ordering of certain morphemes usually does reflect an earlier word order. This exception is the relative order of incorporated nouns with respect to verbs in languages possessing such morphemes. The present work seeks to explore the implications of relying on this principle in reconstructing the earlier word order of a family of languages in which noun incorporation is a highly productive and widespread phenomenon, the Iroquoian family. As a preface to this investigation it must be pointed out that it is impossible to prove in any scientific way that noun incorporation is or is not a reliable indicator of an earlier word order, particularly with languages such as those of the Iroquoian family where the parent language is unattested. The best that can be hoped for is to show that the use of such evidence provides for a reconstruction which accounts for the disparate features of the attested languages by providing a reasonable starting point for their development. This I believe to be able to show for the Iroquoian languages.

In order to illustrate the relationship of the Iroquoian languages to one another, a family tree is provided below. Languages at the bottom of the tree are still spoken in North America, while those at the next row up are attested, but no longer spoken.

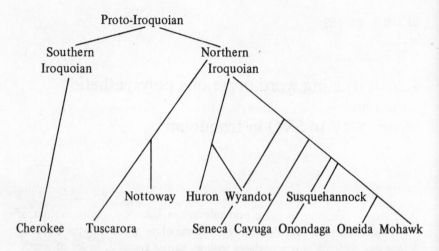

In addition to the languages given above, there are five extinct Iroquoian languages known from a few isolated glosses or placenames: Erie, Meherrin, Neutral, Tionontate, and Wenro. The earliest attested Iroquoian is provided in two vocabularies recorded during Cartier's voyages to Canada in the sixteenth century. The two hundred or so forms recorded are not from a single Iroquoian language, but represent a mixture of Northern Iroquoian languages, including at least one which has since become extinct without leaving any further trace of its prior existence (Mithun 1980). The language of these vocabularies is generally referred to as Laurentian Iroquoian.

This family tree, however, is somewhat deceptive in its representation of the relationship of the Iroquoian languages to one another. While the phonological and morphological isoglosses which separate Cherokee from the other Iroquoian languages are numerous, there are at the same time a significant number of other isoglosses which cut across the division into Cherokee versus the Northern Iroquoian languages. Lounsbury (1961) presents examples which necessitate a distinction between a peripheral, conservative group of languages (Cherokee, Tuscarora, Huron, Wyandot and Laurentian) and a central, innovating group (Seneca, Cayuga, Onondaga, Oneida, and Mohawk). Nottoway was shown to also belong to the conservative peripheral group in Rudes (1981), while Huron and Wyandot appear to be in fact ambiguous with respect to this peripheral/central division, occasionally agreeing with the peripheral group (e.g., in showing a reflex of *hą́?nahk* 'four' rather than the central *kayé:rih* 'four') and at other times agreeing with the central group (e.g., in showing a reflex of *karáhkwa?* 'sun, moon' rather than the peripheral *híhne?* 'sun'). The family tree diagram is, however, appropriate for illustrating the important isogloss which divides those Iroquoian languages with productive noun incorporation (the Northern Iroquoian languages) from the one Iroquoian language where the process of noun incorporation has atrophied with only relics of the original process remaining (Cherokee).

While comparative work on the Iroquoian languages dates back to the work of Thomas Jefferson and Pierre DuPonceau in the early nineteenth century, very little other than determining the subgroup relationships of these languages was accomplished until the work of Marius Barbeau in the early twentieth century (Barbeau 1915). The first truly rigorous comparative-historical reconstruction of the Iroquoian languages was carried out by Floyd Lounsbury in the mid-twentieth century, some of the results of which appeared in Lounsbury (1961). While significant progress has been made in the reconstruction of Proto-Iroquoian phonology and morphology, very little has been done in the way of reconstructing Proto-Iroquoian syntax and word order. Aside from incidental comments in various recent works, the only published material on Proto-Iroquoian syntax appears in Chafe (1978). The present work seeks to broaden our knowledge of the origins of the syntactic structures of the modern Iroquoian languages by investigating a central aspect of Proto-Iroquoian syntax, its basic word order.

2 Overview of the proposal

The hypothesis to be discussed here on the evolution of word order in the Iroquoian languages may be summarized as below.

1) The word order of Proto-Iroquoian was basically SOV, an hypothesis based primarily on the relative ordering of pronominal subjects and objects, classificatory nouns, and verb roots within the predicate complex of the modern and well attested Iroquoian languages.
2) Four partially overlapping stages were involved in the shift in word order from the earlier SOV pattern to the modern "free" SVO word order:
   a) phonological fusion within clauses (SOV → SO-V → S-O-V),
   b) the loss of the ability to modify nouns by direct juxtaposition of modifiers (e.g., adjectives, articles, possessives, etc.) due to the phonological fusion in a), and the resulting rise in the frequency of relative clauses to compensate for this loss ([S-O-V [S_{obj}-O-V]]),
   c) continued fusion affecting subordinate as well as main clauses ([S-O-V [S_{obj}OV]] → [S-O-V [S_{obj}-O-V]]).
   d) reinterpretation of original objects as classifiers of the object, and the relative clauses as the true objects ([S-O-V [S_{obj}-O-V]] → [S-Class.-VO]).

2.1 Proto-Iroquoian word order

Although the word order of the modern Iroquoian languages, as well as the extinct ones for which we have sufficient data, has been shown to be what might best be called "free" SVO (Mithun-Williams 1973, 1974) – that is, if the subject and object may be clearly distinguished from one another by separate pronominal markers on the verb, any order is permitted, but if not, the subject must precede the object, the object must follow the verb, and the subject must precede the verb – there is good reason for believing that the word order at an earlier stage (which shall hereafter be referred to as Proto-Iroquoian) was SOV.[3] The evidence for this comes principally from the morphological structure of the predicate complex in the modern Iroquoian languages.

The predicate complex of the Northern Iroquoian languages consists minimally of a pronominal prefix, a verb root, and an aspect marker. An example of such a structure is (examples here from Tuscarora (= T)):[4]

> (1) T *rá:kęh*
> *ra + kę + h*
> he/see/perfect aspect
> 'he sees (it)'

The pronominal prefix may be preceded by certain prepronominal prefixes having adverbial meanings. For example:

> (2) T *θhrá:kęh* 'he sees it again'
> (*θ+* 'repetitive morpheme')
>
> (3) T *thrá:kęh* 'he sees it there'
> (*t+* 'cislocative morpheme')

Modes are also marked by prepronominal prefixes:

> (4) T *wahrá:kę?* 'he saw it'
> (*wa+* 'aorist')
>
> (5) T *ęhrá:kę?* 'he will see it'
> (*ę+* 'future')

The verb root may be followed by certain morphemes marking such distinctions as intensive, causative, dative, inchoative, instrumental, as well as tense and aspect. For example:

> (6) T *wahrakę́:či?* 'he did! see it'
> (*+či+* 'intensive')

(7) T   *wahrá:kkę?θ* 'he saw it for me'
                (+?θ 'dative' (+*hrak*+ 'he . . . me'))

The final, and for our purposes most important aspect of the structure of the predicate complex is the position of incorporated nouns. Noun roots may be infixed – incorporated – inside of the predicate complex under specific conditions. When this occurs, the noun shows up between the pronominal prefix and the verb root.

(8) T   *wahranę́hsakę?*
                wa + hra + nęhs (a) + kę + ?
                aorist/he/house/see/punctual aspect
                'he saw (a kind of) house'

Though the above is only a summary presentation of the structure of the predicate complex in the Northern Iroquoian languages, the basic order of elements within the complex remains the same, regardless of the specific morphemes present. That is, the morphemes occur in the order: prepronominal prefixes, pronominal prefixes, incorporated nouns, verb roots, derivational suffixes, and tense/aspect suffixes. The incorporated noun is a classifier of the patient of the verb, and as such generally refers to the object of transitive verbs or the subject of intransitive verbs (see Chafe 1970, Woodbury 1975). In fact, if the patient of the verb is identical to the incorporated noun and is not modified by adjectives, possessives, articles, etc., the incorporated noun is the only overt realization of the patient. Thus we find sentences such as the following in Tuscarora (see Section 2.8 for further discussion and examples).

(9) T   *wahranę́hsakę?* 'He saw a (kind of) house'.

But not:

(10) T   **wahranę́hsakę? unę́hseh*

where the patient is stated twice, once in the incorporated noun +*nęhs*+ 'house' and once in the free word *unę́hseh* 'house'. In cases such as this, it becomes clear that the morphological order of elements is S (the pronominal subject +*hra*+ 'he') – O (the incorporated object +*nęhs*+ 'house') – V (the verb root +*kę*+ 'see'). The same is true when the subject and object are marked pronominally in the predicate complex. The Iroquoian languages possess thre classes of pronominal prefixes which may occur within the predicate complex: (1) the agent set, used to mark the subject of non-perfective transitive verbs and certain intransitive verbs; (2) the patient set, used to mark the object of non-perfective transitive verbs when the subject is neuter third person singular, the subject of perfective verbs, and the subject of certain intransitive verbs; and (3) the transitive set, used to mark simultaneously both the subject and object of transitive verbs when neither is neuter third singular. These may illustrated by the following examples.

(11) *Agent* T   *rá:kęh*
ra + kę + h
he (agent)/see/perfect
'he sees it'

(12) *Agent* T   *rahę́sči*
ra + hęsč + i
he (agent)/be black/perfect
'he is black'/'he is a negro'

(13) *Patient* T   *rú:kęh*
ru + kę + h
he (patient)/see/perfect
'it sees him'

(14) *Patient* T   *rú:kę:*
ru + kę +:
he (patient)/see/perfect
'he has seen it'

(15) *Patient* T   *rúhuhr*
ru + hur + h
he (patient)/be old man/perfect .
'he is old/old man'

(16) *Transitive* T *rá:kkęh*
rak + kę + h
he (agent) – me (patient)/see/perfect
'he sees me'

Again, in the case of transitive pronominal prefixes, the morphological order is seen to be SOV when both the subject and the object are marked pronominally: S (*ra-* 'he') – O (*-k+* 'me') – V (*+kę+* 'see'). Based on this, for the most part consistent,[5] morphological order of SOV, regardless of whether the object is marked pronominally by a transitive pronominal prefix or nominally by an incorporated noun, I reconstruct the word order for Proto-Iroquoian to have been SOV. In the following sections, the changes which resulted in this earlier SOV word order appearing as "free" SVO order in the modern languages will be discussed. First, however, we will briefly examine the word order possibilities in the modern languages.

2.2 Northern Iroquoian word order

The observable word order in all of the documented and/or still spoken Northern Iroquoian languages is what has traditionally been labeled "free" word order. That is, subjects, verbs, and objects may, with certain restrictions to be discussed later on, occur in any order with respect to one another; the orders SOV, SVO, OSV, VOS, VSO, and OVS may all occur, although certain of these word orders are very rare, and the individual languages show considerable difference as regards the frequency of each of these. We may illustrate the word order possibilities with examples from Tuscarora (Rudes, forthcoming) and Huron (Fraser 1920).[6]

(17) *SVO*

Huron: *Isa ichien sateienondi de Ka ondechen, din de Ka ǫronhiaę* . . . (Fraser 1920:717)
/*i:sa? íhšęh sate?yęǫ^{n}di: ^{n}dé:kha? o^{n}déhšę? ^{n}din ^{n}dé:kha? xarǫ́hya?xe*/
2nd pers. that-is you sg. (patient)-reflexive-dummy noun-make-perfect this it (patient)-land and this it (agent)-sky-in
'C'est toi qui as fait cette terre que voilà, et ce ciel que voilà'. ('It is you who (you!) have made this earth and this sky'.)

Tuscarora: *Ę́:či raturá:the? wahrá:kę? rá:ku:?y raturá:the?* . . .
one he-hunt-purposive-perfect aorist-he-see-punctual he (patient)-dummy noun-other he-hunt-purposive-perfect
'One hunter saw another hunter . . .'

(18) *VSO*

Huron: *Te saǫXaska ies8s d'aǫrih8anderaskon d'etsik8atonnhont, ondechon n'ondaie esaǫataonti.* (Fraser 1920:271)
/*tesaxokháska? yé:sus ^{n}d-a?xorihwa^{n}deráskǫ ^{n}d-ecikwatǫ́nhǫht, o^{n}déhšǫ n-ǫ^{n}dá:yeh esaxoa? tǫ́:ti*/
duplicative-he=them-separate-punctual Jesus the-aorist-one-(patient)-matter-mistake-distributive the-future-repetitive-we inclusive plural-reciprocal-be alive-causative it-hell the-these future-he=them-precipitate-perfect

'Jésus séparera les pécheurs quand nous res-
susciterons, il les précipitera en enfer'. ('Jesus
will separate the sinners when we are resurrect-
ed, he will send them to Hell')

Tuscarora: *Wahrá:kę? Rutrę̀:we ha? u?thnęhstéhu?y*
aorist-he-see-punctual he (patient)-Akutrę̀:we
the it (patient)-ball-augmentative
'Akutrę:we saw the big ball'.

(19) *VOS*

Huron: *I8erhe ason8ariskonten n'on8e de di8.* (Fraser
1920:173)
/iwérhe? asǫxwariskǫ́htę? n-ǫ́:weh ^{n}de ^{n}dí:uh/
it-believe-serial optative-he=us inclusive plural-
suffer-dative-punctual the-person the-God
(No translation given) ('Is it to be believed
that God suffered for us humans?')

Tuscarora: *Kę:θ wahra?nehá?ne? ha? uté?wahraht ha?*
Akutrę̀:we.
customarily   aorist-he-cause-punctual   the   it
(patient)-terror-causative the Akutrę̀:we
'It is usually Akutrę:we who does these terrible
things'.

(20) *OVS*

Huron: *Steñiesθa θa son8atatindiX n'ondechonronnon*
i8erhe a^{ñ}ionskand aierih8anderaj. (Fraser 1920:
362)
/stęyéstha?tha? sǫxwatatí:^{n}dihk n-o^{n}dehšǫhró:-
nǫ? iwérhe? a(ñ)yǫ́ska^{n}d ayerihwa^{n}dé:rax/
not-one-use-serial contrastive he=us inclusive
plural-present the-it-hell-populative it-believe-
serial optative-one-desire-punctual optative-one-
matter-mistake-punctual
'Le démon nous présent q. image, q. fantôme
pour nous la faire désirer et pécher'. ('The devil
presents to us all sorts of things so that we will
want them and sin'.)

Tuscarora: *Áhsę tikęhraksá:kye: wahrá:ryu? ha? ratù:rač.*
three partitive-it-mountain lion-be in number

aorist-he-kill-punctual the he-hunt-serial
'Three mountain lions were killed by the hunter'.

(21) *OSV*

Huron: ... *isa aak ǫtoǫn aat endi ǫnnonh8e,* ... (Fraser 1920:310)
/í:sa? á:a?k xató:xęh á:at eⁿdi xǫnǫ́hweh/
you for-that it-be special much I I=you-love-perfect
'... mais je t'aime beaucoup, ...' ('but I love you very much')

Tuscarora: *Uθrà:yę? uhè:reh í:?i: nękha?w.*
it (patient)-be raw it (patient)-be green I cislo-cative-future-I-bring-punctual
'I'll bring a salad'.

(22) *SOV*

Huron: *Onné d'aïsten d'eǫ haha8i.* (Fraser 1920:256)
/ó?ne ⁿd-aístę ⁿd-éxa? hahá:wi:/
just the-my father the-water he-bring-perfect
(No translation given) ('My father is bringing the water'.)

Tuscarora: *Í:θ ha? uhčíhrę? wáhskę?.*
you the it (patient)-bear aorist-you (sg.)-see-punctual
'You saw the bear'.

(23) *OVS*

Huron: ... *n'on8e ǫnaǫnndra ǫronhiaęr̂8nnon* ...
(Fraser 1920:610)
/n-ǫ́:weh xǫaxá?ⁿdrah xarǫhyaxehrú:nǫ?/
the-human they=one-watch-perfect it-sky-external locative-populative
(No translation given) ('Man is watched by the angels'.)

Tuscarora: *Tkęhwènuhkę́ha?nę? wa?khé:kę? í:?i:.*
panther-distributive aorist-I=them-see-punctual I
'I saw the panthers (implication: although I was not supposed to)'.

The relative freedom of word order in the Northern Iroquoian languages is, however, more apparent than real. Mithun-Williams (1974 [1976]) has shown that there is a basic, unmarked word order in these languages which is clearly SVO. For example, the freedom of word order breaks down in these languages whenever the subject and the object of the verb cannot be clearly distinguished from one another by gender/number/case prefixes on the verb, unless the subject and object may be distinguished on other grounds such as the subcategorization requirements of the particular verb (e.g., Seneca *Nyahkwai? o?ka:kę? onęǫ?* (bear aorist-it-eat-punctual corn) 'A bear ate the corn' may also be said as *Onęǫ?nyahkwai?o?ka:kę?*, etc., since logically only the bear (*nyahkwai?*) can be the subject of this sentence). As was noted elsewhere, the Northern Iroquoian languages possess transitive prefixes which mark the gender/number/person/case of both the subject and object of transitive verbs. However, for various reasons outside our present concern, not all possible combinations of subject and object have distinctive transitive prefixes. For example, in Tuscarora the prefix *+?na?n(e)+* marks 'he=her', 'he=him', 'she= her', 'she=him'. Thus, if both the subject and the object of a verb are third person singular animate, there is no way to distinguish which is the subject and which is the object by this prefix (cf. *+(h)sk(w)(e)+* which means only 'you (sg.)=me'). In such a case, word order becomes crucial; the subject must precede the object.

(24) a. T   *Wì:ręn wa?ná:tkę? Mè:rih.* 'William saw Mary'.
     b. T   *Wì:ręn Mè:rih wa?ná:tkę?.* 'id.'
     c. T   *Wa?ná:tkę? Wì:ręn Mè:rih.* 'id.'

(25) a. T   *Mè:rih wa?ná:tkę? Wì:ręn.* 'Mary saw William'.
     b. T   *Mè:rih Wì:ręn wa?ná:tkę?.* 'id.'
     c. T   *Wa?nátkę? Me:rih Wì:ręn.* 'id.'

We might note further that, of the above sentences, only (24a) and (25a) are considered by native speakers of Tuscarora to be semantically neutral statements. Both of the b. 's carry the extra meaning that the object is being seen as opposed to someone else (e.g., (24b) 'William saw Mary (as opposed to Joan or Sue).'). The c. 's carry the meaning that the seeing is being done despite a prohibition against it (e.g., (25c) 'Mary saw John (although she was told not to).'). For this among other reasons, the Northern Iroquoian languages are better characterized as incipient SVO languages where, however, topicalization and fronting are common.

This incipient SVO word order of the modern languages is claimed here to have arisen from an earlier SOV word order in Proto-Iroquoian. The next sections are devoted to illustrating how this change was accomplished. In particular it will be pointed out that the change was not a simple reordering of S's, O's and V's, but a complex set of phonological, morphological and semantic changes which led to syntactic reanalysis.

2.3 Synthesis and fusion

There is overwhelming evidence showing that Proto-Iroquoian was far less synthetic than are the modern languages. This evidence consists in differences in the pronominal, prepronominal, aspect, tense, and derivational morphemes, and differences in the application of morphophonological alternations at different types of morpheme boundaries, and points to a weakly agglutinating, almost isolating type of morphology for the protolanguage.[7] The rise in the morphological complexity of words in the Iroquoian languages appears to have resulted from waves of phonological fusion of unstressed or weakly stressed pronouns and particles to the predicate complex, creating the polysynthetic and highly fusional modern Iroquoian languages. This fusion continues to this day, and may be illustrated by the behavior of the sentence particle **ne* 'the' in Mohawk, Seneca and Wyandot. In Mohawk, the reflex of Proto-Iroquoian **ne* appears consistently as an independent word as for example in the sentence: *Wahrá:kp? ne kahyatúhsera?* 'He saw the book'. In Seneca, **ne* appears as an independent word in normal and careful speech. As an independent word it is affected by the general Seneca (and Cayuga) phonological rule which inserts an /h/ after word final vowels. Thus, in Seneca we find the sentence: *Waha:kę? neh ka:yatǫshæ?* 'He saw the book'. However, in casual speech, **ne* becomes a proclitic on the following noun. This is marked phonologically by loss of the final /h/ as well as by certain changes in stress, intonation, and rhythm too complex to go into here. The above sentence then becomes *Waha:kę? neka:yatǫshæ?*. In Wyandot, the process went beyond cliticization to the point where **ne* appears as a true prefix on nouns (and occasionally verbs). In this language, the sentence 'He saw the book' appears as: *ahà:yę?* ^{n}*duhyatǫ́hša?*, where the prefix $^{n}d+$ is the Wyandot reflex of **ne*.

Historic layers of phonological fusion are responsible for much of the apparent complexity of Iroquoian morphology. For example, the forms for 'I fought', 'you (sg.) fought', 'it fought' in Mohawk are:

> *wa?katateri:yo?*   'I fought'
> *wahsatateri:yo?*   'you (sg.) fought'   ɔught'
> *ụtateri:yo?*   'it fought'

The verb stem is composed of {*+atate+*} 'reflexive' with {*+riyo+*} 'kill.' To this are added the punctual aspect suffix {+?}, the aorist modal prefix {wa?+}, and the person/number/case markers {+k+} 'first person singular agent', {+hs+} 'second person singular agent', and {+w+} 'neuter third singular agent'. The formation of 'I fought' is straightforward enough since the constituent morphemes are simply put in sequential order with no further change: *wa?katateri:yo?* except for the automatic stressing of the penultimate vowel and its lengthening in the open syllable. With 'you (sg.) fought', the constituent morphemes are sequentially ordered, then the general Iroquoian sound change which deletes the first of two laryngeal consonants in a row applies to link the aorist morpheme to the second person singular agent morpheme thus producing *wahsatateri:yo?*. The Mohawk form for 'it fought' is the most interesting here because it shows a change which is perhaps the oldest morphophonological alternation in the Iroquoian languages. The sequential ordering of the constituent morphemes of this item gives: {wa? +w+atate+riyo+?} (cf. *watateri:yoh* 'it fights'). This sequence is then affected by the Iroquoian sound change which causes sequences of *(w)a(?)wa* to coalesce into the nasal vowel /o̧/ which in Mohawk raises to /u̧/. This very archaic alternation serves to fuse three separate morphemes in the form above into a single phonological unit, giving *u̧tateri:yo?* for 'it fought'. Such dramatic fusion as a result of morphophonological changes is not at all uncommon in the Iroquoian languages, particularly in the pronominal and prepronominal morphemes. It was this kind of phonological fusion in Proto-Iroquoian which was responsible for initiating the series of changes which altered the SOV structure of Proto-Iroquoian and produced the "free" SVO structure of the modern languages.

2.4 The impact of fusion

One inevitable result of extensive fusion is boundary downgrading (see Langacker 1977:65 ff. for detailed discussion of this phenomenon). In Iroquoian, this meant the change of word boundary (##) to clitic boundary (#) to morpheme boundary (+). The first wave of fusion resulted in the changes which may be represented graphically in the following rule.

(26)   ## X (## X ##)* X ## Y ## VERB (## Z ##)* Z ##
    ↓   ↓
   (+ X +)*   (+ Z +)*

  where: X is any prepronominal or pronominal element, Y is
  a noun, noun phrase or other constituent functioning as ob-

ject of the verb, and Z is any verbal derivational or tense/
aspect element.

Up to this point, Proto-Iroquoian was still SOV. The next wave of fusion,
however, marks the beginning of the end for this syntactic pattern. We may
illustrate this second wave of fusion by the following rule.

$$(27) \quad \#\# X (+ X +)^* X \#\# Y^1 \#\# VERB (+ Z +)^* Z \#\#$$
$$\downarrow$$
$$+ \ Y^1 \ +$$

where: Y^1 is a single noun functioning as object of the verb.

Note that at this stage, the entire clause, including adverbial and modal
markers, subject and object pronominals, nominal object, verb, and tense/
aspect and derivational markers, has become a single morphological and phonological word. This fact has manifold implications for Proto-Iroquoian.

Principal among these implications was the fact that the object of the verb
could no longer be modified by the direct juxtaposition of such elements as
articles, adjectives, possessive pronouns, relative clauses, etc. That is, since the
object was now fused on one side to the pronominal complex and on the
other side to the verb, no other element could be inserted next to the object
to modify it. Clearly this is an intolerable situation for a language. It appears
that the Iroquoian resolution to this problem consisted of recourse to relative
clauses off of the object. In order to see this more clearly, we must now examine the structure of simple nouns in the modern Northern Iroquoian
languages.

2.5 Simple nouns

Simple nouns in the Northern Iroquoian languages are, with few exceptions,
morphologically complex. Their basic structure is given below and illustrated
with examples from Tuscarora, Seneca and Huron.

(28)

pronominal prefix	noun root	noun suffix

Tuscarora:	$u + tákn + eh$	'bed'
	$u + táhskw + eh$	'domestic animal'
	$u + ?tik\acute{e}hr + eh$	'mind'
Seneca:	$ka + n\varrho kt + a?$	'bed'

	ka + nǫ:skw + a?	'domestic animal'
	ka + ?nikǫ́ + ę?	'mind'
Huron:	*xa + ⁿdá:t + a?*	'bed'
	xa + ⁿdáskw + a?	'domestic animal'
	xa + ?ⁿdixǫ́hr + a?	'mind'

Tuscarora *u +* is a reflex of the neuter singular patient pronominal prefix (Proto-Northern Iroquoian **yo+* <Proto-Iroquoian **ya+u+*), while Seneca *ka +* and Huron *xa +* are reflexes of the neuter singular agent prefix (Proto-Northern Iroquoian **ka+*).[8] Simple nouns may also occur in certain cases with masculine, feminine/indefinite, or plural pronominal prefixes, e.g., *ré:kweh* 'man' < {*hra +*} 'masculine singular agent' plus {*+ękw+*} 'human being' plus {*+eh*} 'noun suffix' (cf. *é:kweh* 'human being').

While the presence of the neuter singular pronominal prefixes might at first seem somewhat odd since they serve no function in the modern languages, the presence of the noun suffix is even more perplexing. It has no meaning whatsoever; it does not appear to be related to any other morphemes in the languages; and yet it is obligatory on most nouns. While the modern languages show a number of different simple noun suffixes, two of them seem to be the most common and the basic ones reconstructable for Proto-Iroquoian **+a?* and **+eh*.

Since as was shown in Keenan and Comrie (1974), if a language has relative clauses off of the object, it must also have such clauses off of the subject, and since we are assuming that Proto-Iroquoian had relative clauses off of the object, the language must have had some way of distinguishing between these two kinds of relative clauses. Normally, a language can distinguish such relative clauses by simple juxtaposition of the clause next to the noun it refers to (e.g., English 'The man who I saw yesterday met the girl': 'The man met the girl who(m) I saw yesterday'). This option would not, however, have been available in Proto-Iroquoian once fusion had occurred since there would have been no way to juxtapose a relative clause next to the object fused between the pronominal prefixes and the verb. Therefore, there must have been some other mechanism for distinguishing such clauses. The evidence seems to point to the use of pronominal prefixes inflected for case in this function. That is, relative clauses off of the object were introduced by a patient pronominal element while those off of the subject were introduced by an agent pronominal.

The evidence for this may be stated as follows. As noted above, nouns in the Northern Iroquoian languages, with rare exceptions, require pronominal prefixes. In most of these languages, it would appear to be arbitrary whether a given noun occurs in its elicitation form with an agent or a patient pronominal prefix, and there may be variation in the choice with a given noun among the languages, although the patient prefixes are by far the most common overall on simple nouns.

	Seneca	Onondaga	Mohawk	Huron
'eye'	*ka-ka:?*	*o-káhæ?*	*o-kâ:ra?*	*xa-xáhra?*
'sand'	*o-?néhsa?*	*o-?néhsa?*	–	*xa-?ⁿdéhša?*
'fire'	*ka-ci:sta?*	*o-císta?*	–	*o-císta?*
'leg'	–	*o-?nǫ:ta?*	–	*xa-?nǫ:ta?*
'root'	–	–	*o-htê:ra?*	*xa-hté?ra?*

In Tuscarora (and apparently also in Nottoway), however, the situation was not so arbitrary. In Tuscarora, the only simple nouns which occur with the agent prefixes are either recent borrowings from other Northern Iroquoian languages or a few unincorporable nouns, e.g., *ká:-ryu:?* 'wild animal', *ká:-tkę?* 'blood' (cf. Nottoway *gātkum* 'blood'). *All* other simple nouns occur solely with the patient prefixes in their elicitation form.[9]

Among complex nouns we may distinguish those which are unincorporable and which derive from the nominalization of descriptive verb phrases from those created by the suffixation of derivational affixes. The former group may occur with either agent or patient prefixes, the choice depending on the syntactic and semantic requirements of the original subject/object/verb combination of the verb phrase.

Agent	Patient
wat?ęhrę?ytha? 'aspen tree'	*yuyękwérhar* 'mold (botanical)'
w + at + ?ęhr + ę?yt + ha?	*y + u + yękwer + har*
it/reciprocal/leaf/shake/serial	it/patient/smoke/hang
(lit. 'it shakes its leaves')	(lit. 'hanging smoke')
kačíhkwna:ks 'monkey'	*čuhne?ré:θ?u?y* 'sarsaparilla'
ka+čihkwn + (a) +:k +s	*č + u + hne?r + e:θ + ?u?y*
it/louse/eat/serial	repetitive/patient/root/be long/
(lit. 'it eats lice')	augment
	(lit. 'its large root is long')

Included within this group are nouns which consist of a simple noun root attached to an adjectival or classificatory verb root, e.g., *kanęhse:θ* 'longhouse' (cf. *unęhseh* 'house'), *kaha?θì:yu:* 'graceful neck' (cf. *uhá?θeh* 'neck').

The second group consists of nouns created by the addition of one of the following derivational morphemes: the nominalizers {*+hčr+*}, {*+hst+*},

{+*hθr*+}; the causatives {+*ʔ*+}, {+*hkw*+}; or the instrumentals {+*ht*+}, {+*hkw*+}. Those created by the affixation of a causative or instrumental, though they may be incorporable (but usually are not), take an agent or a patient prefix based on the syntactic and semantic subcategorization requirements of the verb base from which the item is formed, e.g., *neyeʔnę?-θáhkhwa?* 'pencil' (*ne* + *ʔnę?θ*+ 'to write' + *ye*+ 'feminine/indefinite agent' + +*hkw*+ 'instrumental' + +*ha?* 'serial' (lit. "one writes with it"). Nouns created by the affixation of one of the nominalizers, on the other hand, behave essentially like simple nouns in that they are often incorporable and take patient prefixes in their elicitation form. For example: *uʔθréhčreh* 'vehicle' from the root of *waʔkíʔθre:?* 'I rode'; *uʔęhsteh* 'maternity, motherhood' from the root of *θá:ʔę* 'your (sg.) mother'; *uhihtéʔčreh* 'month' from *híhte?* 'sun/moon'.

In summary, simple nouns and complex nouns derived by the addition of a nominalizer are marked by a patient prefix if they may be incorporated. In those few cases where they cannot be, they are marked by an agent prefix. The appearance of agent or patient prefixes on descriptive nouns and nouns derived via the suffixation of an instrumental or causative morpheme is related not to the incorporability of the noun, but to the syntactic and semantic requirements of the verb stem from which the noun is derived.

The appearance of agent prefixes only on those inherited nouns which may not be incorporated provides significant support for the hypothesis that these nouns derive from earlier relative clauses. If the noun root could never be incorporated, i.e., could not originally have appeared as the object of the verb, then the only time when a relative clause containing this noun root would be needed would have been when the relative clause modified the subject. As such, the clause would have been introduced by an agent pronominal marker, and would never have occurred with a patient pronominal. After fusion and reinterpretation, the relative clause would appear as a noun with an obligatory agent prefix. The majority of nouns in the language, however, must have been able to serve as the object of transitive verbs as reflected by the fact that majority of nouns may be incorporated in the modern languages. Thus, one would have expected there to have been relative clauses modifying both the object and the subject containing these nouns. However, once fusion of the object to the preceding pronominal elements and following verb had occurred and the object could no longer be modified by direct juxtaposition of modifiers, the frequency of relative clauses off the object and marked by patient pronominal prefixes would have significantly increased to carry this load. Since there would have been no corresponding increase in the frequency of relative clauses off the subject, however, since direct juxtaposition of modifiers was still possible, relative clauses marked by patient pronominal prefixes would have become more frequent than those marked by agent prefixes. This, I believe, accounts for the fact that after fusion and reinterpretation of relative clauses as nouns, the majority of incorporable nouns (in Tuscarora, all incorporable nouns) appear with the patient prefix. The reconstructed Proto-Iroquoian and modern Tuscarora situations are illustrated below.

(29) Formation of simple nouns from relative clauses[10]

a. Proto-Iroquoian   *ka nıkǫ a? ka yę h*
    it/blood/X aspect it/lay/aspect
    'It is blood which is there
    (e.g., in a pool on the ground)'

   Tuscarora   *ká:tkę? kà:yęh*
    blood it/lay/ perfect aspect
    'Blood is there'.

b. Proto-Iroquoian   *ya u hucr a? ıkı rǫt kę h*
    it/patient/basswood/X aspect I/tree/see/aspect
    'I see a basswood tree (I see a tree which is a
    basswood)'.

   Tuscarora   *uhúhsteh krę́:?akęh*
    patient/basswood/noun suffix I/tree/see/perfect
    'I see a basswood tree'.

While sentences like (29a) could have been paraphrased in Proto-Iroquoian without the use of relative clauses (e.g., *nıkǫ yę ·h* 'blood lays/there is blood') as reflected by the number of unincorporable nouns which take no pronominal prefix whatsoever, sentences such as (29b) would not have been so able to be paraphrased, the reason being that once fusion had occurred, *-rǫt-* 'tree', the object, could not have been modified by the noun *-hucr-* 'basswood' without recourse to a relative clause (i.e., **ıkıhucrarǫtakęh* with both *-hucr-* and *-rǫt-* fused in object position would not have been a possibility because fusion only occurred if a single noun was in object position). As stated above, the result was a high frequency of relative clauses off of the object, but a much lower frequency of relative clauses off of the subject, a situation which is accurately reflected in the greater number of simple nouns beginning with a patient prefix in the modern languages than nouns beginning with an agent prefix or no prefix at all.

2.6 Nouns from relative clauses

In the preceding section it was argued that the presence of pronominal prefixes on simple and complex nouns in the modern Iroquoian languages can
best be explained if one assumes these nouns to be derived from relative
clauses. Further, a reason for the frequent use of relative clauses in Proto-
Iroquoian was suggested. One problem, however, remains in relating the
structure of simple and complex nouns in the modern Iroquoian languages to
the structure of relative clauses which must be reconstructed for Proto-Iroquoian. This concerns the apparent absence of a verb in these clauses.

Main clauses in Proto-Iroquoian are reconstructed with the structure SOV;
the relative clauses which were posited in the preceding section appear to
have the structure S (pronominal) O (noun) plus an aspect marker. It is unlikely that relative clauses in Proto-Iroquoian contained no verb, and highly
improbable that, if they indeed had no verb, there would have been an overt
aspect marker. However, one feature of nouns in the modern Iroquoian
languages which has not yet been discussed in detail may help to resolve this
difficulty, namely, the nature of the simple noun suffix. All nouns, with the
exception of descriptive nouns and recent borrowings, require a simple noun
suffix after the noun root or noun root plus nominalizer combination.

While as noted previously, this suffix may take many forms, two are by far
the most frequent: *+eh* (the "normal" noun suffix in Tuscarora, relatively
infrequent in the other languages) and *+a?* (the "normal" noun suffix in all of
the languages except Tuscarora). While these suffixes in their entirety do not
appear to be related to any other morphemes in the language, their final
laryngeal consonants bear suspicious resemblance to two common aspect
markers, *+h* 'perfect aspect' and *+?* 'punctual aspect'. This leaves the vowels
of these suffixes. The Northern Iroquoian languages (i.e., all of the Iroquoian
languages except Cherokee) lack both a copula and a substantive verb 'to be';
however, there are forms — particles — which appear to reflect fossilized
forms of a verb 'to be'. For example, in Tuscarora and other Northern Iroquoian languages, we find the particle *í:kę:* 'it is'.[11] Since the Cherokee substantive verb is *+i+*, it is tempting to analyse this particle as coming from
*ka + ı 'it/be', 'it is', with regular change of *a + i* to *ę* and a predictable pro-
thetic *i*. However, the verb *+i+* 'to be' does not exist in the modern languages
and thus, if this is the correct etymology for *í:kę:*, it must have been formed
at some earlier date prior to an apparent loss of the verb 'to be' in the
Northern Iroquoian languages. In this connection it should be noted that
there is a regular correspondence between Cherokee and the Northern Iroquoian languages of Cherokee *i*: Northern Iroquoian *e*, in addition to a correspondence Cherokee *i*: Northern Iroquoian *i* (cf. Cherokee *yɣwi* 'human':

Tuscarora *ę́:kweh*; Cherokee *hi:skí* 'five': Tuscarora *wísk*). The former correspondence I reconstruct to a Proto-Iroquoian *ι (e.g., Proto-Iroquoian *$yǫ́k^w\iota h$ 'human'), the latter to a Proto-Iroquoian *i (e.g., Proto-Iroquoian *$hwísk$ 'five').

Returning to the simple noun suffix, it may be noted that the *e* of the suffix +*eh* would correspond perfectly with the Cherokee substantive verb +*i*+ and reconstruct to a Proto-Iroquoian *ι 'to be'. Since both *$a + i$ and *$a + \iota$ may yield *ę*, this verb could also have formed the basis of particles such as Tuscarora *í:kę:*. Thus I would claim that the simple noun suffix +*eh* is the fossilized reflex of the Proto-Iroquoian substantive verb *+*ι+ followed by the descriptive aspect marker +*h*. Given this analysis, relative clauses may be said to have the same structure in Proto-Iroquoian as do main clauses, SOV, where S is a relative pronoun and V is the substantive verb followed by an aspect marker, which gives -*eh* in the modern languages. I assume a similar origin for the simple noun suffix +*a?*, although in this case, one can only speculate about the verbal origin of +*a*+. One possiblity is that it might reflect an otherwise unattested copula.

2.7 Descriptive nouns, adjectivals and possession

In the preceding section it was suggested that simple nouns in the modern Iroquoian languages derive historically from relative clauses having the structure SOV where V is hypothesized to have been a copula or substantive verb. Supporting evidence for this reconstruction comes from the structure of other types of nouns and noun phrases in these languages, in particular, descriptive nouns, adjectivals and possessed nouns.

Descriptive nouns derive from a verb phrase which has been nominalized by a zero nominalization marker, i.e., descriptive nouns are identical in structure to the verb phrases from which they derive. Given their origin, it is not surprising that descriptive nouns share all of the structural characteristics of verb phrases as to possible constituent morphemes except that descriptive nouns occur only in the perfect or serial aspect. Thus, structurally, descriptive nouns are all SOV as illustrated in (30) with forms from Tuscarora.

(30)   *čuhyé:θ?ú?y*
    č + u + hy + e:θ + ?u?y
    repetitive/patient/fruit/be long/augment
    'mulberry'
    (lit. 'it is a long large fruit')

> *wa?wnę?ythá?u?y*
> *w + a?wn + ę?yt + há? + ?u?y*
> it/earth/shake/serial/augment
> 'earthquake'
> (lit. 'it shakes the earth a lot')

Similar in form to descriptive nouns are adjectivally modified nouns. The Iroquoian languages have no adjectives proper, adjectival notions being expressed by clitics (such as the augmentative morpheme in the examples above), by stative verbs, or by what may be called adjectival verbs. The principal difference between stative verbs and what I have called adjectival verbs is that the latter may incorporate the modified noun while the former may not. Examples of stative verbs are given in (31) below.

(31)   *ré:kweh   rásθę:*
        he/human   he/be fat/perfect
        'fat man'
        (*rękwásθę:*)

        ukyerhúhčreh   kahésči:
patient/body/cover/nominalizer/noun suffix
                            it/be black/perfect
        'black coat'
        (*kakyerhuhčrahésči:*)

In contrast to stative verbs, adjectival verbs are characterized by their ability to incorporate the noun which they modify, and the above average frequency with which they do this. That is, while the majority of non-stative verbs in the modern Northern Iroquoian languages allow for noun incorporation, adjectival verbs incorporate the noun more often than any other type of verb. Examples of adjectival verbs are given in (32).

(32) a.   {*+akwast+*}   'be good'
           wákwast   'it is good'
           wę́:?nakwast   'good day/good weather'
           (*wę́:?neh* 'day/weather')

     b.   {*+iyu+*}   'be great/beautiful'
           wì:yu?   'it is great/beautiful'
           kanęhsì:yu: 'great/beautiful house'
           (*unę́hseh* 'house')

For both the examples given in (32) the unincorporated equivalents (i.e., *wę́:?neh wákwast*, and *unę́hseh wì:yu?*) would be highly marked stylistically, and very unlikely to occur in normal discourse. For some other adjectival verbs, the difference between the incorporated and unincorporated forms is not so great. This is true, for example, of the adjectival verb meaning 'to be white' where the forms given in (33) are nearly synonymous and equally neutral stylistically.

(33) $\{+hwaryak\ę+\}$ 'be white'
         unę́hseh uhwaryá:kę?   'white house'
         unę hsahwaryá:kę?   'white house'

The absence of adjectives as a category morphologically and syntactically distinct from verbs, and the frequency with which adjectival verbs incorporate suggests that words in the modern Northern Iroquoian languages which contain adjectival verbs also reflect Proto-Iroquoian relative clauses. The difference between these and simple nouns is that the verbal element in the word remains analyzable as such in the modern languages, whereas the verbal element in the relative clauses from which simple nouns derive has fossilized into the simple noun suffix. The origin of such words in relative clauses would explain the frequency with which they incorporate their head noun, while their analyzability into SOV structures would explain why they may also occur at times with the head noun not incorporated.

The assumption that words containing adjectival verbs reflect older relative clause structures also correlates with the assumption that relative clauses were used in Proto-Iroquoian whenever it was necessary to modify the object of the main clause. The appearance of a double of the object noun in the adjectival relative clause would parallel English sentences such as, *he was housesitting Mary's house* or *she is streetwalking 32nd Street* where the double may optionally be deleted (see Section 2.8 for a more detailed discussion of syntactic doubling in Iroquoian).

The structure of possessed nouns in the Iroquoian languages is also similar to that of simple, complex, descriptive and adjectivally modified nouns. Possession is marked by changing the neuter pronominal prefix on the noun to a first, second, or third person prefix which marks the person, gender and number of the possessor(s). For inalienable nouns, most body parts and some kinship terms, an agent pronominal is used to mark the possessor; for alienable nouns, the possessor is marked by a patient pronominal prefix (e.g., Tuscarora *khę́hneh* 'my ear': *akhę́hneh* 'my interpreter', both from the root $\{+hęhn+\}$ 'ear'). Additionally, inalienably possessed nouns may be marked by the occurrence of the external locative suffix at the end of the noun (e.g., Tuscarora *kta?rá?kye* 'my head' (cf. *utá?reh* 'head')). Alienable nouns, on the other hand, may additionally be marked for possession by the replacement of the simple noun suffix with the verb $\{+aw\ę+\}$ 'to have, possess' (e.g., *runę́hsawę h* 'his house' (cf. *unę́hseh* 'house')). In possessed alienable nouns such as *runę́hsawęh* (*ru* 'he (patient)' + *nęhs* 'house' + *awę* 'have, possess' + *h* 'aspect') we see clearly the SOV morphological structure of possession. Based on the hypothesis that the simple noun suffix represents a fossilization of Proto-Iroquoian combination's of the verb 'to be' with an aspect marker, it is possible to say that all possessed nouns are derived from original relative clauses which were introduced by a pronominal element which agreed in person, gender and number with the possessor. In order to clarify the reason why possession would have marked in this way, it is necessary to look at a phenomenon in the Iroquoian languages known as *syntactic doubling*.

2.8 Syntactic doubling

Syntactic doubling consists of repeating the object noun of a verb with a separate word in certain cases when the object is already marked by an incorporated noun within the predicate complex. As Woodbury (1975: 98a—99) states it:

> Such doubling — a term Postal (private communication) uses for the phenomenon — can only happen, however, when the noun that occurs outside of the main verb is qualified in some way, for example by demonstratives, possessive pronouns, relative clauses, etc. Thus we had example 2.29 *wa?tha?ahsǽhkwa? ne? ko?áhsæ?*, literally, 'he picked up a (kind of) basket, her basket' in which the separate occurrence of the noun is qualified by the possessive pronoun. This doubling of the noun is impossible when the separate noun is not qualified in some way, so that **wa?tha?ahsǽhkwa? ne? ka?áhsæ?* literally, 'he picked up a (kind of) basket, the basket' is completely unacceptable. This fact is extremely suggestive, given the 'kind of' hypothesis. In such a sentence the specifying phrase, the one which would make overt the subcategory to which the incorporated noun makes reference, is *more' general* than is the incorporated noun which is to be specified. The 'kind of' hypothesis predicts that sentences with doubling in which the separate noun is not qualified will be unacceptable.

Doubling is strong evidence in favor of the hypothesis that simple, complex, possessed, and adjectivally modified nouns in the modern Iroquoian languages arose from earlier relative clauses. I have claimed that incorporated nouns represent original objects which became "trapped" within the predicate complex as a result of phonological fusion, and that because of this, modifiers could not reach them. In order to compensate for this situation, relative clauses off of the object came into play. According to this hypothesis, these relative clauses also underwent fusion with subsequent reinterpretation (see Section 2.9) as the new objects of the verb, and reinterpretation of the original objects as classifiers of the new objects. If this was the case, doubling is precisely what one would expect. That is, the double appears *only* when the object noun is in some way modified, just as relative clauses off of the object would have been necessary in Proto-Iroquoian only when it was necessary to modify the object. Syntactic doubling in the modern languages may be illustrated with examples from Mohawk, Onondaga and Seneca taken from the *Iroquois Cosmology* (Hewitt 1903 [1974]).

Sentence (34) illustrates the appearance of a double when the object is modified by an adjectival notion. Here, and in the following examples, the incorporated noun and its double(s) are given in roman type.

(34)   Mohawk (Hewitt 1903 [1974]: 276, lines 3–4)

E?thó:ne?   yá:kʏ?   nʏ   yahahrá:thʏ?
at-that-time   it-is-said now   translocative-aorist-he(agent)-
                                   climb-punctual aspect

ê:nekʏh   taha?wahɾaníhserʏhte?   né
high (place)   cislocative-aorist-he(agent)-meat-fall down-   the
                causative-punctual aspect

yo?wahɾáthʏh.
it (patient)-meat-be dry-perfect aspect
'Thereupon, it is said, he climbed up above and drew down quarters of meat that had been dried'.

In sentence (35) a double is used for the purpose of stating the specificity or "definiteness" of the object.

(35)   Mohawk (Hewitt 1903 [1974]:282, lines 2–3)

Í:kerhe?   ʏ́hteh
I(agent)-believe-serial aspect   perhaps

aʏsakye?wʏ́:ta?ne?   tó:ka?
optative-repetitive-I(agent)-recover-punctual aspect   if

aesewaɾʏtotá:ko?   ne
optative-you plural-tree-take out-punctual aspect   the

akwatʏnohserâ:keh   í:kʏh   kérhite? , . . .
I(patient)-yard-external locative   it-is   standing tree
'I am thinking that, perhaps I should recover from my illness if ye would uproot the tree standing in my backyard . . .'

(note: the unincorporated form of the word for 'standing tree/the tree' *kérhite?* is suppletive with the incorporated root *-ryt-* in most of the Northern Iroquoian languages)

In sentence (36) is found the same use of doubling for definiteness, this time with a non-suppletive root in Seneca.

(36)   Seneca (Hewitt 1903 [1974]:247, line 6)

O:nęh   waé:ih   wa?enǫ?cotá:ko?
now   of course   aorist-one(agent)-pot-take down-punctual
                       aspect

neh   kanǫ?co:t . . .
the   it(agent)-pot-set up
'Now, of course, she took the pot from the fire . . .'

(note: "definiteness" as such is marked, if at all, in the Northern Iroquoian languages primarily by "classificatory" verbal suffixes on nouns which specify their "normal" positions (e.g., 'be upright', 'be lying', 'be standing', etc.) and is only secondarily reinforced by particles such as the backgrounding particle (Seneca *neh*, Mohawk *ne*, Tuscarora *ha?*, etc.)

Sentence (37) shows the use of doubling when the object noun is possessed.

(37)   Onondaga (Hewitt 1903 [1974]:211, lines 8—10)

Ó:nęh   né?tho   wa?thaté:ni?
now   there   aorist-cislocative-he(agent)-reciprocal-change-
                      punctual

ne?   ohtéhka:?;   *ná:ye?   ne?*
the   patient-rib-noun suffix that is   the

é:hęh   *ako*htéhka:??   *ne?*
one(agent)-be female-perfect   one(patient)-rib-noun suffix   the

hací:nah   *wa?hohtehká:etę?* , . . .
he(agent)-be male-perfect   aorist-he (patient)-rib-put in-punctual
'And now, changing the ribs, he placed the rib of the woman-
being in the male human man-being , . . .'

(note: here, as is frequently the case, the modified noun *akohtéhka:?* precedes the incorporated noun since the reference is unambiguous)

Another kind of doubling occurs when the intended object is itself unincorporable. In this case, the incorporated noun is taken from a higher level of the taxonomic hierarchy of nominals for the language. The incorporated noun thus specifies the class of entities to which the object belongs. In such cases, the incorporated noun may be doubled if the object is definite, giving a sentence such as that in (38).

(38)   Mohawk (Hewitt 1903 [1974] :282, lines 5–7)
Tá, e?thó:ne?   *né*   *raųkwê:ta?*
so   at that time   the   he(patient)-human-specific

wahatirųtotá:ko?   *né* kérhite?
aorist-they(masculine agent)-tree-pull up-punctual   the standing
né   *cí*   *raotɣnohserâ:ke*   tree
the where he(patient)-yard-external locative

ohrâ:tųh   *nakarųtô:tɣ?*
patient-wild cherry-   partitive-aorist-it(agent)-tree-be kind of-
noun suffix   punctual

né kérhite?   *tyótkųh*
the standing tree   cislocative-it(patient)-continue-punctual

yocî:cųte? . . .
it(patient)-flower-contain-perfect
'So thereupon his people uprooted the tree that stood in his dooryard. This tree belonged to the species wild cherry . . . , and was constantly adorned with flowers'.

In the above phrase, *ohrâ:tųh* may mean either 'wild cherry (fruit)' or 'wild cherry (tree)'. The incorporated noun root *-rųt-* 'tree' specifies that the tree is meant. The noun *kérhite?* standing tree' is the suppletive double for *-rųt-* 'tree' discussed in the note to sentence (35).

If the object is unincorporable and indefinite, then no double is present as in sentence (39).

(39)   Onondaga (Hewitt 1903 [1974] :668, line 12)

. . . *ho*ya?*takéhte?*   *onhé?ta?*
he(patient)-body-bear away-punctual patient-porcupine-noun
                                     suffix
'. . . he carried a porcupine (on his back). . .'

After looking at the above examples, it should almost go without saying that if the object is not modified in any way, there is no double as illustrated by sentence (40).

(40)   Mohawk (Hewitt 1903 [1974] :314, line 9)
Akwáh   *ihserhe?*
very   you (singular agent)-believe-serial

a:yeruhyá:ky?ci?   *né cí*
optative-one(agent)-struggle-intensive-punctual   the where

yyenâ:tarake?
future-one(agent)-bread-eat-punctual
'Verily, they shall customarily be much wearied in getting bread
to eat'.

We should note that the details of syntactic doubling vary, but only slightly,
for the different modern Iroquoian languages.

2.9 Reinterpretation

Throughout the preceding discussion the words reinterpretation and reanalysis have been used in talking about changes in Proto-Iroquoian structures.
Mention has been made of the reinterpretation of objects as classifiers of
objects; relative clauses as simple nouns, possessed nouns or noun-adjective
combinations, etc. Such reinterpretations appear to have been crucial in the
evolution of word order in the Iroquoian languages. It would therefore seem
appropriate to state here more explicitly what is meant in this work by reinterpretation.

   Langacker (1977:64 and 82 ff.) discusses at some length the notion of
reinterpretation ("syntactic reanalysis") which he divides into two basic
types: "resegmentation" and "syntactic/semantic reformulation". It is the
latter type which encompasses the kinds of changes which have been posited
here for Iroquoian. Langacker presents a number of examples from the Uto-
Aztecan language family, some of which are quite similar to the changes in
syntactic category membership noted for Iroquoian. All of the Iroquoian
changes appear to have been in the direction of decreased syntactic complexity, i.e. independent nouns became dependent classifiers, polylexemic clauses
became polymorphemic words, etc. Langacker (1977:95) also noted that "a
reanalysis may have the effect of creating conditions that trigger another
reanalysis". This seems to be what happened when the reinterpretation of
relative clauses as simple noun or noun plus modifier resulted in the reinterpretation of the original object as a classifier.

   In discussing the causes of syntactic reanalysis, Langacker (1977:98 ff.)
goes to great lengths to show that such changes occur for the purpose of
"signal simplicity" and "optimality". While such was the effect of the
changes seen for Iroquoian as well, the actual motivation for the change
seems to have been more along the lines of necessity. That is, once phonological fusion had trapped the original object within the predicate complex and

effectively isolated it from potential modifiers, it was necessary for the language in order to preserve communication to come up with an alternative method of modifying the object. This it did with relative clauses. However, at this point, the relative clauses were doing all of the real work of explicitly distinguishing the object of the verb from the universe of possible objects. It thus naturally followed that these relative clauses came to be viewed as the true object of the verb. Since the original object now was doing little more than narrowing the range of possible objects of the verb, it followed that it came to be viewed as a classifier. Thus, these reinterpretations seem to have been the result of pragmatic considerations, and not due to notions of simplicity or optimality of the speech signal.

2.10 Why SVO

Earlier in this work it was noted that, although any of the possible word orders SOV, SVO, OSV, SOV, VSO, VOS may and do occur in the modern Iroquoian languages, the unmarked neutral word order is SVO. It is not immediately clear from what has been said so far, however, why this should be the case. Given that the word order which must be reconstructed for Proto-Iroquoian is SOV, and that relative clauses in an SOV language tend to precede the verb and the head noun to which they refer, one might reasonably expect that the Proto-Iroquoian order would have been the same. This would lead one to expect the unmarked word order in the modern languages to be either SOV or OSV. The reason for SVO having become the unmarked order would seem to be the following. Once reinterpretation of relative clauses off of the object as true objects had occurred, the pronominal prefix which served to mark the case agreement between the relative clause and its head became dysfunctional, i.e., there was no longer a referent for it to refer back to since the original object was now a classifier. Once these prefixes became dysfunctional, analogy seems to have occurred, with patient prefixes spreading to nouns used as subjects while agent prefixes spread to nouns used as objects. The result was the skewed and wholely arbitrary appearance of pronominal prefixes seen on nouns in most of the modern languages (see 2.4). While it is not clear why the Iroquoian languages did not reinterpret these pronominal prefixes as case markers on nouns, and, for example, use the agent prefixes to mark nominative case and the patient prefixes to mark accusative case, it is clear that they did not do this. One possible reason may have been that there was already case marking for subject and object on the verb. This took the form of the transitive pronominal prefixes discussed earlier (see 2.1). However, while these transitive prefixes could serve to distinguish the subject from the object in most cases, there remained some situations in which there was no such prefix to distinguish certain combinations of subject and object (e.g., when both were third person, singular, neuter) as illustrated by examples (24), (25). In such cases it became necessary to use word order to distinguish between the subject and the object. Given the earlier SOV word order, and the fact that pronominal prefixes referring to the subject precede those referring to the object on verbs, it follows naturally that the subject would be expected to precede the object when word order is used to distinguish between the two. However, this leaves SOV, SVO, and VSO all as possibilities. The deciding factor among these three alternatives seems to be that the greater the distance between the subject and the object, the more distinctive they are. That is, through separating the subject from the object by placing the verb between them, the nouns serving as subject and object are optimally distinctive in their roles.

3 Additional evidence

Three further aspects of the morphological and syntactic structure of the modern Iroquoian languages support the reconstruction outlined in the preceding pages. They are: (1) dummy incorporated nouns, (2) connectives on incorporated nouns, and (3) the structure of relative clauses in the modern languages. These will be briefly discussed below.

3.1 Dummy incorporated nouns

In each of the modern Northern Iroquoian languages, certain verb stems require that the pre-stem incorporated noun slot be filled at all times, even when there is no statable non-pronominal object. In such cases, a semantically empty form is incorporated into this slot. Such forms are called "dummy" incorporated nouns.

Tuscarora

    ktuhskwuhà:reh 'I am washing the animal'
    (*utáhskweh*   'domestic animal')
    ktuhà:reh   'I am washing it'
    (*-t-*   "dummy" noun)

Oneida (Lounsbury 1953:75)

    lotkųhsolų 'his face is covered/he has a mask on'

> (*kakuhsa?* 'face')
> *lote?lholu* 'he is covered up'
> (-*?lh*- "dummy" noun)

Dummy nouns such as these have no discernable meaning, and do not occur as unincorporated nouns. However, there is reason to believe that they derive historically from true nouns whose free forms, and meanings, have subsequently been lost. Evidence for this comes from the fact that there is not infrequent agreement across a number of the Northern Iroquoian languages as to the form of the dummy noun to be used with a specific verb root. For example,

> M   *wa?kenóhare?*   'I washed it'
> Oi *wa?knóhale?*
> C   *akhnóhae?*
> S   *o?khnowae?*
> T   *wa?ktuhà:re?*

all agree in having the dummy incorporated noun *-*n*- with the verb root *-*ohare*- 'wash' (cf. Oo *wa?kóhae?*, H *a?xóhare?*, W *a?yuharé:* 'I washed it' where there is no dummy incorporated noun). The most probable explanation for these dummy nouns is that they reflect old nouns which occurred frequently as the objects of certain verbs. Sometime subsequent to fusion, the free form of the noun was replaced by a borrowing or neologism, thus abandoning the incorporated form. The absence of the free form led to the loss of meaning for the incorporated form, resulting in its being viewed as but a stem extender on a given verb root (see Rudes 1980 for a similar situation in the Romance languages). This analysis is supported by the development of classificatory verbs in Cherokee (see Section 4). Thus, the existence of dummy incorporated nouns attests to the antiquity of the changes discussed in this work since such forms could not have come into existence in a short time.

3.2 Connectives on incorporated nouns

The incorporated nouns used as examples so far in this work have all consisted of the bare stem of the noun infixed immediately before the verb stem in the predicate complex. However, for a large number of incorporated nouns in the Northern Iroquoian languages, the bare noun stem must be accompanied by a connective element which intervenes between the noun root and the following verb stem.

T   *wa?kθahe?rá:tya?t*
                           wa? + k + θahe?-r (a) + tya?t
                           aorist/I/beans-connective/buy
                           'I bought beans'
                           (cf. *θáhe?* 'bean(s)')

T   *wa?ekhęhčrę:ti?*
                           wa? + e + khę-hčr + ęti + ?
                           aorist/feminine/soup-connective/make/punc-
                           tual
                           'she made soup'
                           (cf. *úkhęh* 'soup')

At least some of these connective elements appear to have originally been
part of the noun root, and to have disappeared through phonological change
everywhere except when the root was incorporated. Others of these connectives appear to be old modifying/classifying/derivational morphemes which
became trapped with the object nouns within the predicate complex as a
result of fusion. This assumption is based on the formal similarity between
these connective elements and elements which occur at the end of certain
unincorporated noun roots in the modern languages. These latter I call stem
increments. The nature of stem increments in the Iroquoian languages may
be illustrated by the following sets.

    Proto-Iroquoian *-kah-* 'eye':

    a. with stem increment *-t-*:   H *xaxáhta?*   'pupil'
                                     Ck *ikata*   'eye'
                                     L *hegata*   "yeux"

    b. with stem increment *-r-*:   T *ukáhreh*   'eye'
                                     M *okâ:ra?*   'eye'
                                     H *xaxáhrɑ?*   'eye'

    c. with stem increment *-hcr-*: T *ukáhθreh*   'tears'
                                     M *okáhserɪ?*   'tears'

    d. with stem increment *-k-*:   H *xaxáhka?*   'white of the eye'

These stem increments are not used productively to derive new noun roots.
Some of them appear related to verb roots. For example, the *-t-* increment
may well be the same as the verb 'to stand' *-t-* in the modern languages,
while the *-r-* increment appears related to the verb 'to be in' *-r-* . Verbs of
position are widely used in the Iroquois languages to signal definiteness and
to classify the noun root.

The presence of connectives on incorporated nouns and their apparent similarity to stem increments on unincorporated nouns strongly supports the assumption that incorporated nouns were originally more like free nouns, and that they arose from independent object nouns.

3.3 Modern relative clauses

A final piece of evidence in favor of the reconstructions given in the preceding pages involves the structure of relative clauses in the modern Iroquoian languages. It was stated earlier that Proto-Iroquoian relative clauses had come to be reinterpreted as simple, complex, possessed, or adjectivally modified nouns. If this were the case, one would expect new relative clauses structures to have evolved in the Iroquoian languages. What one in fact finds is that relative clauses as such are rather weakly developed in these languages, that there is significant diversity among the languages in how relative clauses as such are marked, and that it is frequently difficult if not impossible to tell the difference between subordinate and coordinate clauses in general (on this latter point, see Mithun-Williams 1973).

First we may note that the modern languages do not in general agree on the particle to be used as the neutral relative marker ('that' ~ $\emptyset$ in English). In Mohawk we find *ne* and *nê:ne*, in Oneida *ne?n* and *ci?*, in Onondaga *ne?*, in Cayuga *ne?* and *né?neh*, in Seneca *neh* and *ne?*, in Huron ^{n}*de* and *né:^{n}di*, and in Tuscarora *ha?*. All of these particles may be reconstructed for Proto-Iroquoian, each having other more or less determinable meanings, e.g., **ci?* 'where', **ne?* 'thus', **ha?* '(?)diminutive', **ne* '(?)deictic'. In each of these languages, the appearance of one of these particles to introduce a relative clause is for the most part optional. Further, most of them, in particular Tuscarora *ha?*, Seneca *neh*, and Mohawk *ne?* may be used much like the definite article in English to background a noun, e.g., T *wá?ktya?t ha? u?-nhéhseh* 'I bought the (aforementioned) eggs'.

The optionality of the neutral relative particles, the fact that they are not cognate across the languages (although they show cognates used for other purposes in some of the other languages), and the fact that they may be used to indicate "definiteness" on nouns suggests a late development of these relative clause structures. This also suggests a period during which the relative clause structures of Proto-Iroquoian were in the process of disappearing in that they were being used for something else. This would fit in well with the proposed reinterpretation of relative clauses as nouns. However, the evidence is for the most part only suggestive. It is possible that the optionality of the relative markers reflects an ongoing loss of such particles as is the case with English *that* in sentences such as 'I bought the book (that) I wanted.' Further, the fact that the languages do not all agree as to which particle to use to introduce a relative clause may be due to simple substitution of inherited particles for one another without any real change in the structure of relative clauses, paralleling the Indo-European situation where reflexes of **to-*, **kʷo-*, **so-* are all used in different languages to introduce relative clauses.

4 The influence of language contact

A number of authors have claimed that syntactic change, in particular changes in basic word order, come about solely or in part as a result to contact between languages of differing syntactic types. While due to the absence of written texts from the period when Iroquoian was changing its basic word order, and the fragmentary nature of our knowledge of the contact situations occurring at this time, it is impossible to show with any certitude that contact was not responsible for the changes which occurred, it can at least be shown that language contact was unlikely to have been the cause.

Historical records show that when first contacted by Europeans, the Northern Iroquois were neighbors of various New England, Eastern and Central Algonquian peoples. In addition, the Tuscarora, Nottoway and Meherrin were in contact with Eastern Siouan and Muskogean groups. The Cherokee were surrounded by Muskogean, Algonquian and Siouan peoples, as well as the Natchez and Yuchi. There is little reason to believe that the situation was very different at the time when the changes discussed herein were taking place.

The Iroquoian languages are, even today, generally resistant to borrowing from unrelated languages. Despite over two hundred years of contact with English, French, Dutch, German, and Swedish, they show only a handful of borrowed nouns. European influence on the phonological systems of these languages has been negligible, and non-existent with respect to the morphological systems (see, for example, Bonvillain 1978 for a discussion of European influence on the Mohawk language).

I mentioned earlier that the Northern Iroquoian languages are by far more synthetic than their southern relative Cherokee. The Algonquian neighbors of the Northern Iroquois, e.g. the Abnaki, Montagnais, Fox, Algonquin, Shawnee, Powhatan, etc., also spoke highly synthetic languages. The Siouan, Muskogean, Yuchean and Natchez neighbors of the Cherokee, on the other hand, spoke morphologically less synthetic languages. Thus, one might reasonably argue that the difference in degree of synthesis between the Northern Iroquoian languages and Cherokee is a result of contact. However, one cannot go further and extend the contact argument to syntactic changes which have occurred. Since none of the languages neighboring the Northern Iroquois or Cherokee showed a basic SVO word order, they could not be responsible for inducing the Iroquois languages to change in this direction. In fact, many of the neighboring languages (e.g. Yuchi, Muskogean, Natchez) show a predominantly SOV word order, the same as that which we have posited for Proto-Iroquoian. Thus, if anything, contact with these languages should have acted to maintain the SOV word order of Proto-Iroquoian and not to change it.

In addition to being highly synthetic, the languages surrounding the Northern Iroquois also show intricate fusion of bound morphemes to one another. This is also true of the languages surrounding Cherokee. In fact, all of the indigenous languages of the Eastern United States and Canada are fusional. It is possible, but not necessary, that Proto-Iroquoian acquired this characteristic of fusion from surrounding languages.

Another point should also be made here with regard to differences between Cherokee and the Northern Iroquoian languages which might be a result of language contact. As we have seen, noun incorporation is a highly productive process in the Northern Iroquoian languages with well over a thousand nouns being incorporable in each of the well attested or still spoken languages. Also, in these languages, the incorporated form of the noun is clearly relatable phonologically to its unincorporated form. This is not the case in Cherokee. Here incorporation has become totally unproductive, with only a handful of cases remaining. For a number of reasons, e.g. phonological change, replacement by borrowings, semantic divergence, etc. the few incorporated nouns which remain in Cherokee are not synchronically relatable to their unincorporated forms. In Cherokee, these few remaining relics of noun incorporation combine with selected verb roots to form classificatory verbs. Such verbs may classify a patient as flexible (F), round (R), long (L) or liquid (Q) (Reyburn 1953:50–1). The position of the classifier is the same as in the Northern Iroquoian languages, i.e. between the pronominal prefixes and the following verb root. These four types of classification may be illustrated with the verb root *-wathγ-* 'to find' (Reyburn 1953:50; I have changed Reyburn's phonemicization of stops to conform to the current practice of writing all voiceless stops rather than voiced ones for the stop consonants of the Iroquois languages).

(41)		
	ka-na-wathi-ha	'he is finding (F)'
	ka-ne-wathi-ha	'he is finding (Q)'
	ka-?-wathi-ha	'he is finding (R)'
	ka-γγ?-wathi-ha	'he is finding (L)'

The classifier *-ne-* is undoubtedly derived historically from the Proto-Iroquoian root *-hne-* 'drink, liquid' seen in Northern Iroquoian words such as

Mohawk *ohné:ka?* 'water, liquid, alcohol, drink', Onondaga *ohné:kanos* 'water, liquid, drink' — an incorporable noun in all of the languages. However, in Cherokee, this root is reflected only in the relic classifier given above; there is no free form of this root. When a free form for 'liquid' is required, the word *ama* 'water' from Proto-Iroquoian **áwę?* is used (cf. Mohawk *awý:ke* Tuscarora *à:wę?* 'water', etc.).

Returning to our discussion of the effects of contact on the Iroquoian languages, we may note that many of the languages surrounding Cherokee show systems of classificatory verbs (Haas 1948). The Algonquian languages surrounding the Northern Iroquoian languages, on the other hand, show a form of productive noun incorporation which, though differing considerably in detail, is more like that of the Northern Iroquoian languages than is noun incorporation in the latter like the classificatory verb system of Cherokee. In Algonquian, incorporated nouns — mainly body parts — appear post-verbally (the morphological order of elements is SVO) as illustrated by the following examples from Shawnee (Voegelin 1938–40).

(42)	*niθakaškitepeena*	'I grabbed him by his head hair'
	(-ški- 'hair')	
	nilel'kiškiše	'I have the side of my mouth torn'
	(-škiše- 'lips')	
	noolakwanowe	'I have fat cheeks'
	(-anowe- 'cheeks')	
	noočikawike	'I have my house leaking'
	(-w-ike- 'house')	

Thus, it would not be outside the realm of possibility that the difference between the Northern and Southern Iroquoian languages could be explained as due to contact. Cherokee, surrounded by languages possessing classificatory verbs, would then be assumed to have frozen and degenerated the process of noun incorporation developing in Proto-Iroquoian, while the Northern Iroquoian languages, surrounded by languages where incorporation was an active process, would have continued, developed and expanded the process into that which we find today. Whether or not contact was actually involved, it is clear that Cherokee reflects a petrified version of what the Northern Iroquoian languages have developed into a most complicated system of noun incorporation.

5 Conclusion

The principal goal of this work has been to test the hypothesis that the relative morphological ordering of incorporated nouns with respect to verbs is a reliable indicator of earlier syntactic object/verb order by applying it to the reconstruction of Proto-Iroquian basic word order. The result has been, in the opinion of the author, supportive of this hypothesis in that a series of diverse, seemingly unrelated features of the modern Iroquoian languages were shown to be the result of small sets of phonological, syntactic and semantic changes acting on an original SOV word order. As stated at the opening of this work, this analysis of Iroquoian word order does not "prove" the reliability of the above-stated hypothesis, since no such proof is possible when dealing with languages for which the reconstructed stage is unattested. While as such, numerous other analyses of the data are possible, it is highly unlikely that any of these would lead to as satisfactory an account of the complex morphological and syntactic structures of the Iroquoian languages as does the present analysis.

Notes

1. I would like to take this opportunity to thank the many people who have discussed the ideas presented in this work with me, and thus assisted me in my analysis. In particular I would like to thank Joan Bybee, Wallace Chafe, Hanni Feurer, Winfred Lehmann, Marianne Mithun, Sandra Thompson, and Roy Wright. I would also like to thank Lloyd Anderson, Floyd Lounsbury and Roy Wright for reading earlier versions of this manuscript and making valuable suggestions. None of the above named individuals necessarily agrees with the remarks made in this work, and any errors are of course my own.

2. See, for example, the discussion in Langacker 1977, Langdon 1977, and Campbell and Mithun 1978.

3. Whether the Proto-Iroquoian reconstructed here on the basis of morphology and syntax corresponds to the Proto-Iroquoian which has been reconstructed on the basis of phonological correspondences among the modern and attested languages in uncertain. It is quite possible that what I call here Proto-Iroquoian may correspond to some earlier stage in the history of these languages such as Proto-Iroquois-Caddoan or Proto-Macro-Siouan (see Chafe 1973, Rudes 1974).

4. I have used data from the Tuscarora language for the most part in illustrating the structure of the modern languages for the reasons that the morphological and syntactic structure of the modern Northern Iroquoian languages is essentially the same, with minor differences in detail only, and a plentiful supply of readily available data was on hand from my own fieldnotes.

Abbreviations used in this work are:

C	–	Cayuga	Oo	–	Onondaga
Ck	–	Cherokee	S	–	Seneca
H	–	Huron	T	–	Tuscarora
M	–	Mohawk	W	–	Wyandot
Oi	–	Oneida	L	–	Laurentian

The question mark *?* is used to represent the glottal stop.

5. The first person transitive and patient pronominals are an exception to this generalization with the object/patient normally preceding the agent.

6. Again, Tuscarora has been used here because of the availability of the data. Huron data have been used for two reasons. First, Huron was the earliest of the Iroquoian languages to be well documented. Second, Huron belongs to a subgroup of the Northern Iroquoian languages which shows significant differences in morphology and syntax from Tuscarora.

7. See also the discussion in Beatty 1980.

8. See Chafe 1978 for an excellent discussion of the development of third person pronominals in the Iroquoian languages.

9. The only consistent exception to this statement are *i*-stem nouns such as *kę:čeh* 'fish' (stem {-ičę- }) and *kę̀:yę?* 'grease' (stem {-iyę- }) which occur with the agent prefix (which becomes *kę-* with an *i*-stem). The reason for this is unknown.

10. The symbol *X* is used here to represent an element about which more will be said in a subsequent section of this work.

11. Other particles beside *i:kę:* 'it is' which may reflect a Proto-Iroquoian verb *-ı- 'to be' include: T *tí:kę:* 'as many are', *né:kę:* 'two are', H *cę:* 'that (feminine) is', Oi *thíkν*, etc. It should also be noted that there is recorded for Huron a verb *-i-* meaning 'be alone, be the only one' (Fraser 1920: 393) which may be descended from Proto-Iroquoian *-ı-*. This Huron verb occurs only with incorporated nouns. In the Tuscarora of the 19th century there was apparently a verb *-ę-* meaning 'to be', the conjugation of which was recorded and left in manuscripts in the National Anthropological Archives of the Smithsonian Institution by J.N.B. Hewitt. The form *-ę-* may have derived from the original feminine, neuter and masculine third person singulars of Proto-Iroquoian *-ı-* where the verb would have regularly contracted with the final /a/ of the pronominals to produce *iyę:* 'one is', *ikę:* 'it is', *ihrę:* 'he is'. This *-ę-* may then have generalized to other forms of this verb where *-e-/-i-* would have been the expected reflexes.

References

Ballard, W. L.
    1975   "Aspects of Yuchi morphophonology", *Studies in Southeastern Indian languages*, edited by J. M. Crawford (Athens: University of Georgia Press), 163–187.
Barbeau, Marius
    1915   *Classification of Iroquoian radicals with subjective pronominal prefixes* (Ottawa: Department of Mines. Geological Survey, Memoir 4, Anthropological Series no. 7).
Beatty, John
    1978   "Implications of some historical changes in Mohawk", Paper read at the International Conference on Historical Morphology, Boszkowo, Poland.
Bonvillain, Nancy
    1978   "Linguistic change in Akwesasne Mohawk: French and English influences", *International journal of American linguistics* 44. 1: 31–39.

Campbell, Lyle – Marianne Mithun
    1978   "Syntactic reconstruction: priorities and pitfalls", Paper read at the International Conference on Historical Morphology, Boszkowo, Poland.

Cartier, Jacques et al.
    1843   *Voyages de découverte au Canada, entre les années 1534 et 1542* (Québec: William Cowan et fils [reprinted 1921]).

Chafe, Wallace L.
    1973   "Siouan, Iroquoian and Caddoan", *Current trends in linguistics*, vol. 10, edited by T. Sebeok (The Hague: Mouton), 1164–1209.
    1978   "The evolution of third person agreement in Iroquoian", *Mechanisms of syntactic change*, edited by C.Li (Austin: University of Texas Press).
    forth-   "The Northern Iroquoian languages", *Handbook of North American Indians*, coming vol. 17 (Washington, D. C.: Smithsonian Institution).

Comrie, Bernard
    1980   "Morphology and syntactic reconstruction: problems and prospects", *Historical morphology*, edited by Jacek Fisiak (The Hague: Mouton), 83–96.

Foster, Michael (ed.)
    1974   *Linguistic papers from the 1972 conference on Iroquoian research* (Ottawa: National Museum of Man, National Museum of Canada).

Fraser, Alexander
    1920   *Huron manuscripts from the collection of Rev. Potier* (= 15th Report of the Bureau of Archives of the Province of Ontario, Toronto).

Givón, Talmy
    1971   "Historical syntax and synchronic morphology: an archaeologist's field trip", *Papers from the seventh regional Meeting of the Chicago Linguistic Society, April 16–18, 1971* (Chicago: Chicago Linguistic Society).

Haas, Mary
    1945   "Classificatory verbs in Muskogee (Creek)", *International journal of American linguistics* 14. 4: 244–6.

Hewitt, John N. B.
    1974   *Iroquoian cosmology* (New York: AMS Press [originally published in two parts: 1903. *Bureau of American Ethnology-Annual Report* 21,1926, *Bureau of American Ethnology-Annual Report* 43]).

Keenan, Edward – Bernard Comrie
    1972   "Noun phrase accessibility and universal grammar", Paper read at the Annual meeting of the Linguistic Society of America.

Langacker, Ronald
    1977   "Syntactic reanalysis", *Mechanisms of syntactic change*, edited by C.Li (Austin: University of Texas Press), 57–139.

Langdon, Margaret
    1977   "Syntactic change and SOV structure: the Yuman case", *Mechanisms of syntactic change*, edited by C.Li (Austin: University of Texas Press), 255–90.

Li, Charles (ed.)
    1977   *Mechanisms of syntactic change* (Austin: University of Texas Press).

Lounsbury, Floyd G.
    1953   *Oneida verb morphology* (=*Yale University Publications in Anthropology 48*) (New Haven: Yale University Press).
    1961   "Iroquois-Cherokee linguistic relations", *Symposium on Cherokee-Iroquois culture*, edited by W. Fenton (=*Bureau of American Ethnology Bulletin 180*), 1–20.
    1978   "Iroquoian languages", *Handbook of North American Indians* vol. 15 (Washington, D. C.: Smithsonian Institution), 334–343.

Mithun, Marianne Williams
    1973   "A case of unmarked subordination in Tuscarora", *Comparative syntax festival* (Chicago: Chicago Linguistic Society).

1974   "Word order in Tuscarora", *Linguistic papers from the 1972 conference on Iroquoian research*, edited by M. Foster (Ottawa: National Museum of Man, National Museums of Canada), 27–35.

1974   *A grammar of Tuscarora*, Ph.D. dissertation, Yale University (published version 1976, New York: Garland Press).

1980   "The mystery of the vanished Laurentians", Paper read at the Conference on Iroquoian Research, Renselaerville, New York.

1981   "Stalking the Susquehannock", *International journal of American linguistics* 47. 1: 1–27.

Reyburn, William D.

1954   "Cherokee verb morphology III", *International journal of American linguistics* 20. 1: 44–64.

Rudes, Blair A.

1974   "Sound changes separating Siouan-Yuchi from Iroquois-Caddoan", *International journal of American linguistics* 40. 2: 117–9.

1976   *Historical phonology and the development of the Tuscarora sound system*, Unpublished Ph.D. dissertation, State University of New York at Buffalo.

1980   "The functional development of the verbal suffix +esc+ in Romance", *Historical morphology*, edited by Jacek Fisiak (The Hague: Mouton), 327–348.

1981   "A sketch of the Nottoway language from a historical comparative perspective", *International journal of American linguistics* 47. 1: 28–51.

1982   *Yehsnahnę̨hkhwa? Nekayę̨?na?nenę̨?ya?r Uwę̨:teh Tíhsnę? Urihwakayę̨?kyę̨ha? Skarù:rę?: Materials for the study of the Tuscarora language and traditions* (Ottawa: National Museum of Man).

Voegelin, Charles F.

1938–40 *Shawnee stems and the Jacob P. Dunn Miami dictionary* (Indiana Historical Society, Prehistory Research Series).

Woodbury, Hanni

1974   "Noun incorporation and Onondaga relative constructions", *Linguistic papers from the 1972 conference on Iroquoian research*, edited by M. Foster (Ottawa: National Museum of Man, National Museums of Canada), 1–17.

1975   *Noun incorporation in Onondaga*, unpublished Ph.D. dissertation, Yale University.

1976   "Onondaga noun incorporation: some notes on the interdependence of syntax and semantics", *International journal of American linguistics* 42. 1: 10–20.

MATS RYDÉN

The study of eighteenth century English syntax

0 Introductory

The ultimate object of historical scholarship is to set events and ideas in a time-perspective and to help us understand the relation between the past and the present. The aim of the historical linguist is essentially twofold: (1) to find out the 'actual' uses of language in past times and (2) to account for language stability and language change, i.e. continuity and discontinuity in language development, including for instance typology and directionality of change.[1] 'State' and 'development' are closely interrelated and intertwined and in our analysis of the language (system) as used today history is important as an explanatory factor and, vice versa, "the highest peak from which we can survey the past is the present" (Erades 1943:87).[2]

Recent (theory-based) scholarship on historical English syntax − from the mid 1960s onwards − has focused on syntactic change as reflected in especially Old and Middle English texts and on synchronic analyses of early texts (see Rydén 1979:28−29). Particularly in more traditional research, special attention has also been paid to the early modern period (1450−1700), witness works like Ando (1976), Brorström (1965), Pennanen (1966), Rydén (1966) and (1970) and Weida (1975),[3] whereas the later modern era (1700−1900) has been rather neglected − by 'traditionalists' as well as by 'modernists'. Two notable exceptions here are Arnaud (1972) and Dekeyser (1975). It is symptomatic that we have recently been given two introductions to early Modern English (Barber 1976 and Görlach 1978), whereas nothing similar exists for the ensuing period.

1 Previous research on 18th century English syntax

In particular, the 18th century has been disregarded.[4] This also holds true in a wider time perspective: the sum total of the work done on 18th century English syntax during the past hundred years or so (i.e. since the beginning of the scholarly study of historical English syntax) is strikingly small. Naturally, the century has been covered in general histories of English and in histories of English syntax, or in treatises on special problems including the whole history of English or at least the whole of the Modern English period, for example Brorström (1963), Casparis (1975), Nehls (1974), Saito (1961) and Scheffer (1975), to name only a handful of recent studies.

The few books or articles devoted more specifically to 18th century English syntactic usage can be grouped as follows:

(a) themes: Franz 1892–95, Krüger 1929, Rohr 1929, Knorrek 1938 (socio-syntax), Charleston 1941 (the period 1710–60), Reinbold 1957 (unpublished diss.), Brorström 1979. More marginal treatments of the 18th century are given in for example Redin 1925 and Pelli 1976.

(b) individual writers: Uhrström 1907 (Richardson), Lannert 1910 (Defoe), Horten 1914 (Defoe), Huber 1951 (Goldsmith and Sheridan; unpublished diss.). Cf. also works like Klapperich 1892 (Sheridan), Sheldon 1956 (Boswell), Vallins 1957 (the Wesleys) and Ito 1962 (the *Spectator*).[5]

Matters of syntax (particularly "sentence-structure") are also included in some stylistic studies, as Bühler (1937), Zickgraf 1940 (Swift), Wimsatt 1941 (Dr. Johnson), Lannering 1951 (Addison) and Lawton 1962 (John Wesley).

As appears from the lists presented above, the last book-length study of 18th century English syntax (apart from a couple of unpublished dissertations) is B. M. Charleston's thesis from 1941. And none of the influential writers of the century has received a full modern syntactic treatment.

2 Attitudes to the study of 18th century English syntax

The main reason for this neglect of the study of 18th century English syntactic usage is the widespread view that little "happened" in the domain of syntax in that period (at least as compared with the preceding stages), a view reflecting, *inter alia*, the relatively little concern there is for syntactic continuity as against syntactic change. Syntactically, the 18th century has been taken to be a period of relative stability, and many (still current) syntactic paradigms are considered to have been "established" by the beginning of the 18th century. Consequently, 18th century syntactic usage has been assumed to deviate too little from modern practice to invite comparison. Attitudes like these are mirrored in a number of works on the history of the English language. A few quotations may be adduced:

"By about 1700 ... the language had reached a stage at which its differences from present-day English were very small" (Barber 1972:207)

"The eighteenth century was a settled age" (McLaughlin 1970:75)

"The eighteenth century . . . was a time of consolidation between two periods of change"; "a time of consolidation and relative stability" (Robertson-Cassidy 1954:375 and 327)

"The changes that took place in the writing and speaking of English between 1600 and 1850 were few compared to those of the preceding centuries" (Bloomfield-Newmark 1963:288)

"Since the year 1700 the English language has grown in a hundred ways. But its fundamental and structural features, the patterns of its sentences and the forms of its words, have not materially changed"; "all those complex changes and developments . . . had achieved in the year 1700 a certain balance or equilibrium" (Potter 1950:61 and 60).

"By 1700 the modern English system [underlying the use of the *do* periphrasis] was very largely established" and "by about 1700 *be* + *PrP* was restricted in Southern British roughly as it is now to the expression of ongoing activity at a moment of time" (Traugott 1972:176 and 178).[6]

In consequence of the general opinions (as illustrated above) of English syntactic development since the beginning of the late modern period, the 18th century has been barred *a priori* from syntactic examination. But did syntactic development come to a (temporary) standstill in the 18th century?[7] In many other respects the 18th century was a changing period — in literary taste and achievement, in philosophical thinking, in significant social developments and in attitudes to language use (cf. below) — features which must have set their marks (though less conspicuously) on the use of language, also in terms of syntactic variation and change, at least in matters of acceptability and of diffusion in various speech-communities. Clearly, the 18th century is "a period of transition to modern speech from the English of the seventeenth century" (Platt 1926:126), a period preparatory to later conditions of the language, to 'innovations' as attested at subsequent stages. It should however be emphasized here that a 'natural' systemic innovation (as distinct from prescribed uses) is a gradual phenomenon, a reflection and a product of processes which may have been going on for a long time. Such processes are not easily detectable in written material, but to recognize them is essential for our understanding of syntactic continuity. And the diachronic gaps found are probably in many cases only due to textual deficiencies and/or inadequate research.[8] Cf. Visser's discussion (Visser 1963–73, III:2426) of the forerunners of the type *The house is being built*, not attested until the very end of the 18th century. Cf. also, for example, the analytic type *to have a try/to take a look*, which "develops rapidly from about 1800" (Strang 1970:101), but which is only an extension of a usage (with zero-article) dating back to Old English (Visser 1963–73, I:138).

It is true that in many cases the main outlines of present-day usage were established by the 18th century and it is possible that differences between present-day English syntactic usage and that of the 18th century are primarily differences in variant-frequency, style and social stratification — few constructions current around 1780 would be impossible today in an overall perspective. But such issues need themselves investigation and the appreciation of syntactic variants as style markers presupposes an intimate knowledge of internal syntactic structure and patterning.

3 Strata and levels and the textual evidence

The statements in some histories of the English language cited above do not signal the heterogeneous or multi-layer character of 18th century syntactic usage in terms of social strata and levels of discourse, or the bearing of social, stylistic and situational variables on syntactic usage (but cf. here Knorrek (1938), Schlauch (1964), Strang (1970) and Tucker 1967).[9] On the whole, the diachronic dimension of social and stylistic variability in syntactic usage has received little attention. For the earliest periods, these parameters are difficult to apply due to lack of textual evidence. The 18th century is, in effect, the first century in the development of English where the extant texts allow us to view and evaluate syntactic usage in a reasonably full contextual light (stylistic, social or otherwise). Of course there are earlier records mirroring various strata and levels (cf. Romaine 1980), but the surviving written evidence of the 18th century is more extensive and more varied than for any other previous stage in the history of English. But, paradoxically enough, the disparity between the textual evidence available and the syntactic work done is greater for the 18th century than for any other period in the history of the English language.

The 18th century has rightly been designated as the "Age of Prose", a century when the English novel came to maturity, an art form which largely recorded the cultivated conversational speech of the time. But, as is well known, 18th century English prose also manifested itself in many other forms — in the periodical essay and in historical, philosophical and scientific prose. Further, there are the prose of the dramatic dialogue and the emotive ("romantic") prose of the closing decades of the century (see for example *The Oxford History of English Literature* (Vols. 7–9) and Gordon 1966). And finally we have a great number of collections of private letters and similar documents not intended for publication, mirroring less standardized and more genuinely colloquial idiom and unpremeditated speech, i.e. contemporary living ('non-edited') usage.[10] For collections and modern editions of such documents, see *The New Cambridge Bibliography of English Literature*, Vol.

2, columns 1569–1600, and Wyld (1936), and cf. (for the 17th century) Williamson (1929). This type of text has been comparatively little studied, but merits close attention, not least from historical syntacticians.[11] As emphasized by Wyld (1936:186), "we want minute studies of such documents as the Verney Letters and the Wentworth Papers, and also of similar letters and diaries of the same period, and if possible, of more recent collections covering the period from about 1740 to the first quarter of the nineteenth century".

Other texts presumably reflecting (to differing degrees) spontaneous language are reports from state trials and parliamentary debates, purporting to contain speech-like transcriptions (cf. Barber 1976:48, and Finkenstaedt 1963:10 and 288 f.). Plays must be used with special caution as reflexes of spontaneous, spoken diction (see Barber 1976:38 and 50, Page 1972:117, and Rydén 1979:23).[12] The invented dialogue in fiction is important as mirroring the interactional level of language production, for instance class variation, but not infrequently it transmits exaggerated and parodied rather than natural language. However, since the "satirical use of language presupposes the existence of a secure standard" (Strang 1967:1950), such language may give us, indirectly, a clue to actual, spoken usage.

In this connection it should be pointed out that 'natural' speech should not be confused with 'colloquial' or 'informal' idiom, since 'natural' is a wider concept encompassing all variants as used appropriately according to purpose and situation. Clearly, there are various types of spoken syntax, a fact not always recognized. And we should be wary of considering language colloquial merely because it is part of texts defined *a priori* as colloquial. Contrariwise, one of our objects when investigating past linguistic usage must be to find out what distinguishes the colloquial level from the non-colloquial ones, as manifested in the texts. This can only be done by way of systematic comparisons of different texts showing differences in styles and registers. On the problem of identifying colloquialisms, see Clark (1978).

In any study of syntactic usage a valid data base is crucial. And in order to measure degrees of optionality in usage and directionality of change we need as exact information as possible on variant-frequency. Statistics (properly evaluated) are of value both as indicating optionality (synchronically and diachronically) and as neutralizing conspicuous, but rare features and great individual variation in usage.

4 The problem of 'good' and 'bad' usage

One of the fundamental intellectual changes in post-Renaissance England was a change in attitude to language usage. The 18th century is the first century to evince a more massive interest in syntactic usage, albeit primarily from a prescriptive or proscriptive angle: the grammarian, not usage, became the official arbiter of language. Grammar came to be viewed essentially as the selection of 'proper' forms, or, as Dr. Johnson (1755) has it, "the art of using words properly". These prescriptive grammarians (for example Lowth and Murray), whose rules were largely a mixture of Latin grammar, "logic", "reason" and prejudice, were ignorant of or unwilling to accept the processes of linguistic change[13] and unaware of the fact that usage is essentially a matter of social convention (many of the issues discussed in those grammars are still a major concern in school-grammars). What was not realized was the basic fact that a proper evaluation of 'correct' or 'good' usage requires a knowledge of linguistic variability and a historical perspective. The attitudes of the prescriptive grammarians set a distance between written and spoken language and made the selection of syntactic variants a potential token of social distinction and discrimination. The categorical rules laid down in the grammars were welcomed by the rising middle class who were anxious to have norms in linguistic usage. We can say that in the 18th century we witness "the start of class warfare in the English language" (Nist 1966:272). The doctrine of correctness involved, on the one hand, the arrest of levelling tendencies such as the use of *was* in the second person singular (favouring paradigmatic complexity) and, on the other hand, the prescription of certain forms or constructions, to the exclusion of others, such as *it is I* and simple negation (favouring paradigmatic simplicity).

Another objective in our study of 18th century English syntax is to compare the results obtained from corpus-analyses with usage as described and prescribed by the grammarians and rhetoricians of the day. Cf. Leonard (1929), Charleston (1941) and Reinbold (1957) (including analyses of contemporary grammars) and Sundby (1980), emphasizing the need for "a (reasonably) complete listing of the various syntagmas and phrases, tokens as well as types, which were frowned upon by the early grammarians". Stability (non-variation) and regularity were the aims of most 18th century grammarians. Stability in actual usage has also been taken to be the hall-mark of the time by modern historians, a contention which however remains to be proved or refuted.

5 'Variation' and 'change' and the study of past syntax

Change presupposes variation (though variation does not necessarily entail change), and the study of diachronic variation or change presupposes the study of synchronic systemic variation (cf. Rydén 1980). In other words, the evaluation of variation (or non-variation) through time must be based on evaluations of successive 'synchronic' paradigms (cf. Rydén 1979:10).

Syntactic change is often measured in terms of variant-additions and variant-losses, i.e. in systemic amplification or reduction (two examples are the addition of anaphoric relative *who* in the 15th century and the loss of relative *the which* in standard 17th century English), but syntactic change is also 'merely' a matter of systemic redistribution or change in markedness (in the form of 'specification' or 'generalization') of the variants available, involving contextual refinements. Of interest here, not least to the investigator of 18th century English syntax with its both natural and prescribed rules and changes, is that it appears as if natural syntactic change manifests itself most frequently "under those circumstances in which it is least noticeable or salient", whereas syntactic change as actuated by learned reaction or hyper-correction seems to "manifest itself first in the most salient environments" (Romaine 1980:233).

The study of synonymy, including syntactic synonymy, is the study of the paradigmatic resources (potentiality) of a language at a given point of time. And in view of the inevitable textual gaps and of the analytical difficulties there are, the results of the study of earlier usages should be presented in terms of systemic potentiality as evidenced in the texts available rather than in terms of obligatory rules. Cf. here Weinstock (1975:347): "Evidence from script and print should be ascertained in the affirmative only; it will by no means entitle investigators to draw negative conclusions *ex silentio*".

An intimate knowledge of systemic redistributions is crucial for our understanding of syntactic continuity and of relative syntactic chronology. 18th century English syntactic usage may not include many systemic additions or losses (a fact contributing to its 'modern' appearance), but no doubt it involves a number of systemic refinements, communicatively essential, but subtle and small-scale and not easy to identify and formulate.

6 Conclusion

The greatest difficulty in analysing 18th century English syntax is in fact its modern or pseudo-modern character (cf. here for the vocabulary Tucker (1967) and Page 1972).[14] As noted earlier, little that was normal in 1780 would be entirely unacceptable today viewed in a multi-level perspective. As stated by Tucker (1967:8): "the eighteenth century is a period so near to us that we can read its writings without the apparatus needed for even the seventeenth, and yet it is far enough away to make us perpetually on the alert lest we fall into a sudden or routine pitfall. It is therefore an ideal training ground for observant students".

One obvious consequence of the modern appearance of 18th century English is that we are liable to overlook differences and distinctions between present-day usage and that of the 18th century. Crucial to our interpretations here is the co(n)textual analysis. In our analyses of non-contemporary syntax, intimate familiarity with the texts and close reading can (to some extent) substitute for introspection and for elicitation procedures and acceptability judgements as used in the study of contemporary usage. Syntactic analysis is not only a matter of ascertaining structural dependencies and paradigmatic variability but also of detecting and evaluating acceptability and diffusion (contextual and individual). And when probing linguistic history we must try to rid ourselves of any preconceived ideas as perpetuated in, for example, historical textbooks.

Notes

1. I.e. to determine why a language changed in the way it did, rather than in some other way, or why it did not change.
2. On the distinction between 'historical' and 'diachronic' linguistic research, see Rydén (1979:9).
3. For earlier works, see Rydén (1979).
4. A century is of course an arbitrarily delimited diachronic segment or stretch of time. The years 1700 and 1800 are chosen for convenience' sake, not necessarily reflecting any linguistic periodicity. And, evidently, "some developments will not be clearly established within a century" (Strang 1970:21).
5. See also Storm (1896:932–51). For syntactic-stylistic studies of the English of Jane Austen, who is usually classified as a 19th century writer (though she was deeply imbued with 18th century taste and though her lifetime belongs more to the 18th than to the 19th century), see Page (1972) and Phillipps (1970). A study of a specific syntactic feature in Austen's works is Raybould (1957).
6. Cf. here Charleston (1941:171) stating that "between about 1750 and the present day there was a rapid change in, and regulation of, the use of the verb".
7. Another matter, worthy of exploring in its own right, is that "some areas of grammar . . . have remained unchanged since our earliest records" (Strang 1970:59). Cf. also Rydén (1979:19).
8. An example of that may be the near-total gap in the use of the mandatory subjunctive in late 17th and 18th century English (as recorded by Visser 1963–73, II:843ff.).
9. Cf. also Wyld (1936:187) calling for analyses of "the precise extent and character of both Regional and Class dialect influence upon Received Standard during the seventeenth and eighteenth centuries". A socio-syntactic analysis of pre-18th century English is Finkenstaedt (1963).
10. "Personal Letters and Private Diaries . . . are our nearest approach to everyday speech as practised by those who wrote not for fame nor with any suspicion of the prying eyes of posterity, but from the necessity of finding straightforward expression for feelings, opinions, or daily happenings" (Williamson 1929:3). It should however be

noted that just because of their intimacy personal letters are exponents of idiosyncracies to a greater extent than more neutral prose.

'Innovations' (cf. above) are not surprisingly often first recorded in writings reflecting more advanced or spontaneous language. Two examples are anaphoric relative *who* (first found in letters of the 15th century) and the passive progressive (first found in a letter by Southey from 1795). Cf. also Visser's note (Visser 1963–73, III:2427) on Macaulay's use of the passive progressive (evidenced in some of his letters but not in his literary works).

11. A study largely based on letters and diaries is Reinbold (1957).
12. Studies entirely based on plays are e.g. Brorström (1979), Pelli (1976) and Saito (1961).
13. Cf. also Swift (1712): "I see no absolute Necessity why any Language should be perpetually changing". The textual revisions made by Swift and by other 18th century writers, e.g. the Shakespeare editors, are also indicative of the linguistic temper of the age.
14. Cf. the modernity of Dryden's style as against his (on the whole) conservative syntax (Söderlind 1958:218ff.). See here also Krüger (1929:134).

References

Ando, S.
   1976   *A descriptive syntax of Christopher Marlowe's language* (Tokyo: University of Tokyo Press).
Arnaud, R.
   1972   *La forme progressive en anglais du XIXe siècle* (Diss. Paris).
Barber, C.
   1972[5] *The story of language* (London: Pan Books).
   1976   *Early Modern English* (London: André Deutsch).
Bloomfield, M. W. – L. Newmark
   1963   *A linguistic introduction to the history of English* (New York: Knopf).
Brorström, S.
   1963   *The increasing frequency of the preposition About during the Modern English period. With special reference to the verbs Say, Tell, Talk, and Speak* (Stockholm: Almqvist & Wiksell).
   1965   *Studies on the use of the preposition Of in 15th century correspondence. With special reference to constructions differing from present-day usage* (Stockholm: Almqvist & Wiksell).
   1979   "A diachronic study of structures expressing the idea 'It's no good -ing, What's the good of . . .' ", *Studia Neophilologica* 51:3–16.
Bühler, W.
   1937   *Die 'erlebte Rede' im englischen Roman. Ihre Vorstufen und ihre Ausbildung im Werke Jane Austens* (Zürich-Leipzig: Niehans).
Casparis, C. P.
   1975   *Tense without time. The present tense in narration* (Bern: Francke).
Charleston, B. M.
   1941   *Studies on the syntax of the English verb* (Bern: Francke).
Clark, Cecily
   1978   " 'Wiþ scharpe sneateres': some aspects of colloquialism in 'Ancrene Wisse' ", *Neuphilologische Mitteilungen* 79:341–353.

518   *Mats Rydén*

Dekeyser, X.
    1975   *Number and case relations in 19th century British English. A comparative study of grammar and usage* (Antwerpen-Amsterdam: De Nederlandsche Boekhandel).
Erades, P. A.
    1943   Review of Visser 1941, *English Studies* 25:86–90.
Finkenstaedt, Th.
    1963   *You und Thou. Studien zur Anrede im Englischen* (Berlin: Walter de Gruyter).
Franz, W.
    1892–95 "Zur Syntax des älteren Neuenglisch", *Englische Studien* 17:200–225, 384–402, 18:191–219, 20:69–104.
Gordon, I. A.
    1966   *The movement of English prose* (London: Longman).
Görlach, M.
    1978   *Einführung ins Frühneuenglische* (Heidelberg: Quelle & Meyer).
Horten, F.
    1914   *Studien über die Sprache Defoes* (Bonn: Hanstein).
Huber, S.
    1951   *Syntaktische Studien zur Sprache Goldsmiths und Sheridans* (unpublished Ph. D. diss., University of Graz).
Ito, H.
    1962   "The language of 'the Spectator' ", *Anglica* 5:36–62.
Johnson, S.
    1755   "A grammar of the English tongue", in *A dictionary of the English language* (London).
Klapperich, J.
    1892   *Bemerkungen zur Sprache des Lustspieldichters Richard Brinsley Sheridan* (Elberfeld progr.).
Knorrek, Marianne
    1938   *Der Einfluss des Rationalismus auf die englische Sprache. Beiträge zur Entwicklungsgeschichte der englischen Syntax im 17. und 18. Jahrhundert* (Breslau: Priebatsch).
Krüger, A.
    1929   *Studien über die Syntax des englischen Relativpronomens zu Beginn der spätneuenglischen Zeit* (Giessen: J. Christ).
Lannering, J.
    1951   *Studies in the prose style of Joseph Addison* (Uppsala: Lundequistska Bokhandeln).
Lannert, G.L.
    1910   *An investigation into the language of Robinson Crusoe as compared with that of other 18th century works* (Uppsala: Almqvist & Wiksell).
Lawton, G.
    1962   *John Wesley's English. A study of his literary style* (London: Allen and Unwin).
Leonard, S. A.
    1929   *The doctrine of correctness in English usage, 1700–1800* (Madison: University of Wisconsin).
Lowth, R.
    1762   *A short introduction to English grammar* (London).
McLaughlin, J. C.
    1970   *Aspects of the history of English* (New York: Holt, Rinehart and Winston).
Murray, L.
    1795   *English grammar* (York).

Nehls, D.
1974 *Synchron-diachrone Untersuchungen zur expanded Form im Englischen* (München: Hueber).
Nist, J.
1966 *A structural history of English* (New York: St. Martin's Press).
Page, N.
1972 *The language of Jane Austen* (Oxford: Blackwell).
Pelli, M. G.
1976 *Verb-particle constructions in English: a study based on American plays from the end of the 18th century to the present* (Bern: Francke).
Pennanen, E. V.
1966 *Notes on the grammar in Ben Jonson's dramatic works* (Tampere: Yhteiskunnallinen Korkeakoulu).
Phillipps, K. C.
1970 *Jane Austen's English* (London: André Deutsch).
Platt, J.
1926 "The development of English colloquial idiom during the eighteenth century", *Review of English Studies* 2:70–81, 189–196.
Potter, S.
1950 *Our language* (London: Penguin).
Priestley, J.
1761 *The rudiments of English grammar* (London).
Raybould, Edith
1957 "Of Jane Austen's use of expanded verbal forms", *Studies in English language and literature presented to Professor Dr. Karl Brunner*, edited by S. Korninger (Wien: Braumüller). 175–190.
Redin, M.
1925 *Word-order in English verse from Pope to Sassoon* (Uppsala: Lundequistska Bokhandeln).
Reinbold, H.
1957 *Shall und Will. Der englische Sprachgebrauch 1750–1850* (unpublished Ph.D. diss., Heidelberg University).
Robertson, S. – F. G. Cassidy
1954[2] *The development of Modern English* (New York: Prentice-Hall).
Rohr, Anny
1929 *Die Steigerung des neuenglischen Eigenschaftswortes im 17. und 18. Jahrhundert mit Ausblicken auf den Sprachgebrauch der Gegenwart* (Giessen: Glagow).
Romaine, Suzanne
1980 "The relative clause marker in Scots English: diffusion, complexity, and style as dimensions of syntactic change", *Language in Society* 9:221–247.
Rydén, M.
1966 *Relative constructions in early sixteenth century English. With special reference to Sir Thomas Elyot* (Uppsala: Almqvist & Wiksell).
1970 *Coordination of relative clauses in sixteenth century English* (Uppsala: Almqvist & Wiksell).
1979 *An introduction to the historical study of English syntax* (Stockholm: Almqvist & Wiksell).
1980 "Syntactic variation in a historical perspective", *Papers from the Scandinavian symposium on syntactic variation,* edited by S. Jacobson (Stockholm: Almqvist & Wiksell), 37–45.
Saito, Toshio
1961 "The development of relative pronouns in Modern colloquial English", *The scientific reports of Mukogawa Women's University* 8:67–89.

Scheffer, J.
    1975   *The progressive in English* (Amsterdam: North-Holland).
Schlauch, Margaret
    1964²   *The English language in modern times (since 1400)* (Warsaw: Państwowe Wydawnictwo Naukowe).
Sheldon, E. K.
    1956   "Boswell's English in the *London Journal*", *PMLA* 71:1067–1093.
Söderlind, J.
    1951–58 *Verb syntax in John Dryden's prose* (I-II) (Uppsala: Lundequistska Bokhandeln).
Storm, J.
    1896²   *Englische Philologie* (I:2) (Leipzig: Reisland).
Strang, B.M.H.
    1967   "Swift and the English language. A study in principles and practice", *To Honor Roman Jakobson* (The Hague: Mouton), 1947–1959.
    1970   *A history of English* (London: Methuen).
Sundby, B.
    1980   DENG. *A dictionary of English normative grammar 1700–1800. A preliminary report* (Bergen University).
Swift, J.
    1712   *A proposal for correcting, improving and ascertaining the English tongue* (London).
Traugott, Elizabeth Closs
    1972   *A history of English syntax* (New York: Holt, Rinehart and Winston).
Tucker, S. I.
    1967   *Protean shape. A study in eighteenth-century vocabulary and usage* (London: The Athlone Press).
Uhrström, W.
    1907   *Studies on the language of Samuel Richardson* (Uppsala: Almqvist & Wiksell).
Vallins, G. H.
    1957   *The Wesleys and the English language* (London: The Epworth Press).
Visser, F.Th.
    1941   *A syntax of the English language of St. Thomas More* (Louvain: Uystpruyst).
    1963–73 *An historical syntax of the English language* (I-III) (Leiden: E. J. Brill).
Weida, Gudrun
    1975   *Der Gebrauch von shall/should und will/would in englischer Prosa am Ende des 16. Jahrhunderts* (I-II) (Augsburg: Blasaditsch).
Weinstock, H.
    1975   Review of Strang 1970, *Neuphilologische Mitteilungen* 76:342–348.
Williamson, Margaret
    1929   *Colloquial language of the Commonwealth and Restoration* (The English Association, pamphlet no. 73, Oxford).
Wimsatt, W. K. Jr
    1941   *The prose style of Samuel Johnson* (New Haven: Yale University Press).
Wyld, H. C.
    1936³   *A history of Modern colloquial English* (Oxford: Blackwell).
Zickgraf, Gertraud
    1940   *Jonathan Swifts Stilforderungen und Stil* (unpublished Ph.D. diss., Marburg University).

ARIANE VON SEEFRANZ-MONTAG

'Subjectless' constructions and syntactic change

0. It is not surprising that impersonal constructions of the type *me hun-greth* in Middle English, being an apparent exception to the usual Indo-European sentence pattern, as well as their historical change to personal constructions such as *I hunger/I am hungry* in Modern English have always been a favourite topic in historical syntax. What is surprising, however, is that up to now no attempts seem to have been made to find out whether this reanalysis of 'subjectless' sentences is idiosyncratic to English or a process which can be observed in a variety of related and unrelated languages. More specifically, no general explanation of the development of 'subjectless' sentences, referring to correlated (morpho)syntactic changes in the languages involved, has been given.

In this paper, I will argue that the decrease of impersonal constructions can be be explained as a natural consequence of 'typological' changes in Indo-European and other languages. After giving a brief outline of the development of grammatical relations in some Indo-European languages (1), I will try to characterize the typological status and origin of 'subjectless' expressions (2) and survey their development in four languages, English, French, German and Icelandic (3–6). In (7), some data from non-Indo-European languages will provide further evidence for the interpretation presented in this paper.*

1 The development of grammatical relations in Indo-European

Pre-Indo-European is generally reconstructed as a (group of) language(s) characterized by 'pragmatically' determined word order with predominant SXV-patterns and an elaborate system of case inflection (e.g. Lehmann 1974, 1976; cf. Friedrich 1975 and Miller 1975 for modified positions).

In prehistoric times, the selection of specific cases for verb arguments was determined exclusively by semantic considerations; therefore it was still relatively variable (Meillet 1909:145, 219, Lehmann 1974:110f., 1976:451). Depending on its lexical properties and certain discourse functions, a particular verb could be combined with a varying number and different kinds of syntactically equivalent arguments. Consequently, there was no verb-specific valence and government and no special functions of particular verb arguments in terms of uniformly coded syntactic relations like subject and object. This 'adverbial' character of verb arguments gave the verb a relatively high degree of semantic and syntactic independence, the status of a no-argument impersonal as *(there is) love from-me to-you* 'I love you' or *(there is) sight of-me to-you* 'you see me'. According to this view, recent studies have postulated for Pre-Proto-Indo-European sentence structure a kind of verbal noun with only loosely connected adphrases (cf. Velten 1931, Watkins 1969:49, Hartmann 1977:161ff., Wagner 1978).

One prerequisite for this kind of syntax is an efficient marking system to identify the semantic functions of adverbal constituents, e.g. a case system. The 8-case-systems attested for the earliest Proto-Indo-European languages still fulfill this function rather well. Since, however, the category of case is universally characterized by the economical tendency (in terms of encoding strategies) to comprise in each case a *combination* of semantic information, case systems historically tend towards optimization by melting a maximal number of case functions into a minimal number of case forms — as long as perceptual needs are fulfilled. In Indo-European, this process was supported by the growing complexity of sentence structure, i.e. the extension of paradigmatic classes and syntagmatic patterns, which decreased the efficiency of case markings as a means of distinguishing various kinds of verb arguments.

The reductive tendencies within case systems led early in the development of Indo-European languages to a *hierarchical ordering* of case forms and functions, making use of discourse functions typically correlated with particular kinds of verb arguments: depending on their relative frequency of being topicalized, specific kinds of verb arguments, in which (highly language-particular) combinations of semantic functions are melted, tend to acquire syntactic properties.[1] The increasing 'grammaticalization' of argument types connected with the loss of semantic specificness finally leads to the formation of a set of adverbal *grammatical relations* like subject, direct object etc., which are defined by their respective degree of syntactic 'closeness' to the verb.

The original semantic functions of verb arguments are now conveyed by means of syntactic functions, which reflect them only in a rather vague and arbitrary way. To compensate for the loss of distinctive marking of semantic argument functions, valence properties of verbs are incorporated into the lexical meaning of verb stems (cf. the semantic difference in verb meaning determined by the difference of syntactic valence in ME *me liketh sth.* versus

I like sth., MHG *mich verlanget eines dinges* versus *ich verlange ein dinc*; cf. below).

Early stages of documented Indo-European languages already have firmly established grammatical functions. Nevertheless even in later Indo-European dialects such as Old English, Old French and Old High German, the marking of verb arguments was still to a certain extent determined by semantic distinctions: the correlation of syntactic relations and particular cases still allowed for some variation.[2] Thus the relationship of syntactic functions and particular cases e.g. in Old English and Old High German can be outlined approximately by the following diagram (cf. Penhallurick 1975:12 for Old English):[3]

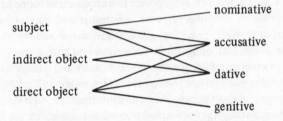

In most Indo-European languages, the system of grammatical relations and their encoding has historically been — or is in the process of being — stabilized by the reduction or elimination of synthetic nominal morphology, the functions of which were taken over by new analytic markings (adpositions) and the rigidification of word order.

The growing dysfunctionality of case morphology has recently been attributed partly to phonological reductions and analogical processes which made inflectional endings an increasingly intransparent and potentially ambiguous means of signalling grammatical functions (e.g. Vennemann 1974, 1975), partly to functionally motivated changes within case systems themselves (cf. Harris 1978a, b, Geisler 1982 for French). The compensating shift of word order regularities from primarily stylistic and discourse functions (SXV, TVX) to the primarily syntactic function of distinguishing subjects and various kinds of non-subjects (SVX) has as yet been explained only hypothetically, e.g. as a result of the extension of extraposition, originally restricted to 'heavy' non-topical constituents (clauses, adverbials), to all kinds of adverbal non-topics and finally to all constituents but the subject (plus topicalized adverbials) (TXV > V/2 > SVX; cf. Vennemann 1974, 1975, Stockwell 1977 and others).

A (preliminary) end-point of this development from a semantically and pragmatically determined sentence structure with quasi-adverbial verb arguments to a syntactically determined sentence structure with verb valence controlling the selection of hierarchically ordered types of arguments seems to have been reached by Modern English. This language represents an almost complete transition to an 'indirect' encoding of semantic argument functions by means of grammatical relations, which are marked by word order, adpositions and some residual case forms.

2 The typological status and origin of 'subjectless' constructions

In many languages, impersonal constructions with oblique experiencer arguments[4] are a productive syntactic device to encode expressions of a specific semantic class: verbs denoting physical, emotional and mental experiences (hunger, thirst, chill, heat, pain; joy, grief, anger, shame; doubt, recollection etc.), but also needs and obligations, possession and sometimes perceptions and abilities, existence and happenstance — processes and situations, in which a person is *unvolitionally/unselfcontrollably* (McCawley 1976:194) involved. In some languages, dative experiencer constructions are systematically correlated with nominative/ergative experiencer constructions of the same verbs denoting 'volitional' actions (cf. Tschenkéli 1958:450, 487f. for Georgian, Masica 1976:161 for Hindi-Urdu, Klaiman 1980 for Bengali, McCawley 1976:195f. for Russian and Japanese).

The overt marking of the experiencer (recipient) function by an oblique case trivially presupposes a language system in which adverbal complements are preferably marked according to semantic considerations, and in which an efficient morphological marking system is able to convey these semantic differentiations.

For Klimov 1973 (cf. Comrie 1976), 'affectional verbs' are therefore characteristic of active, and 'still' of ergative systems. Languages, on the other hand, in which semantic differentiations are limited in favour of greater uniformity of syntactic patterns, do not overtly mark this category of verbs by oblique experiencers.

'Subjectless' constructions in Indo-European languages can therefore be considered a *relic* from Pre-Proto-Indo-European syntax. In proportion to the gradual restriction of syntactic rules, this type of construction has become unacceptable in the individual Indo-European languages.

According to Velten 1931, impersonal verb constructions as (*it*) *grieves* (*within*) *me, me thinks, me likes you* etc. derive from the verbalization of nominal constructions of the type (*there is*) *grief-of-me*, (*there is*) *thought-mine*, (*there is*) *fatigue-in-me*, (*there is*) *like-of-me-to-you* etc. Within Indo-European, impersonal constructions with oblique experiencers had a wide range of distribution e.g. in Old Norse, Gothic, Old Saxon and Latin (Wagner 1959:54ff.); they are still common e.g. in Slavic, esp. in Russian (Scholz 1973), in Rumanian (Stimm 1980, Whalen 1978 (for Russian and Rumanian)), in Celtic (Wagner 1959:43ff., Hartmann 1977), in Icelandic (see below), in Indo-Iranian (Masica 1976:161, 164; cf. Klaiman 1980 for Bengali). Outside Indo-European, constructions with dative (or genitive, locative) experiencers occur in Finnougric (Masica 1976:164), in Hebrew (see below), in Kartvelian Caucasus languages (see below), in Dravidian (cf. Sridhar 1976 for Kannada), in Japanese (Kuno 1973:79ff., Shibatani 1977:799f.) and other languages.

Impersonal constructions seem to be distributed complementary to semantically equivalent or similar 'personal' types of verb constructions such as reflexive and (medio)passive. (In transitory stages of development between those alternatives, 'blended' constructions like impersonal passives or impersonal reflexives are a frequent phenomenon.) In late Latin, e.g., the loss of synthetic mediopassives led to a temporary increase in impersonal constructions. The reduction or loss of 'subjectless' sentences in the individual Indo-European languages, on the other hand, was brought about by the interaction of four processes (cf. Velten 1931):

1) the introduction of *formal subjects*, esp. in Germanic and French;
2) the *reanalysis* of oblique experiencers as nominative subjects, esp. in English;
3) the creation of a 'personal' *reflexive* in Germanic, Romance and Slavic;
4) the extension of a new (analytical) *passive*, esp. in English.

These changes have one characteristic in common: They all serve to make 'subjectless' sentences conform to the stricter syntactic constraints of an SVX language by providing a nominative subject constituent in the position before the verb.

3 The development of impersonal constructions in English

Probably every reader of Lightfoot 1979 is also familiar with the essentials of the development of impersonal constructions in Middle English (Lightfoot 1979:229–293; cf. also Gaaf 1904, Visser 1963:20–35, Fisiak 1976, McCawley 1976, Butler 1977). The facts concerning the loss of this type of construction in English can therefore be summarized and supplemented briefly in this paper.

Expressions of the type *me hungreth*, *me aileth* + patient NP/infinitive/ clause (for the differentiation of one- and two-place predicates see n. 4) were a productive syntactic pattern in Old English and early Middle English; the loss of about 40 of the lexemes involved, before or during Middle English (Visser 1963:29), was compensated by analogical extensions of the impersonal pattern to otherwise 'personal' verbs, e.g. *me nedeth, me lacketh, me wondreth, me irketh, me happeth* (+ patient), and even to loans from Old French and Old Norse, e.g. *me repenteth, me remembreth, me pleseth, me greveth* (+ patient); *me deyneth, me semeth, me dremeth, me wanteth* (+ patient). Except for some quasi-adverbial relics as *meseems, methinks,* 'subjectless' constructions were altogether eliminated from English syntax by the end of the 15th/mid-16th c. along three avenues:

1) further lexical obliteration (OE *þyncan,* ME *boot, rue*);
2) the introduction of a dummy subject (*h*)*it* and/or subjectivalization of a genitive, adpositional, sentential or infinitive complement (merger of impersonal construction types 3a and 3b, see n. 4), e.g. *it/sth. pleases me, it/sth. likes me, it/sth. ails me;*
3) the assignment of nominative case to oblique experiencer complements, producing forms such as *I need sth., I remember sth., I think sth., I like sth.*

The insertion of a dummy subject was structurally the most simple device to adapt 'subjectless' constructions to the rules of the new Old English TVX-syntax which required a preverbal, possibly already a nominative constituent for all sentences. This 'pseudo-subjectivalization', incurring no changes whatever in grammatical relations and their marking, was therefore applied earliest in those types of impersonal constructions which often occurred without a topicalizable constituent: no-argument verbs referring to weather, time of day or year and the like. While dummy-(*h*)*it* became mandatory with weather verbs already in Old English around the 9th c. (OED (1933) 1961:517) (1a) – as well as in Old French and in Old High German –, impersonal passives (1b) and one- or two-argument impersonal expressions (1c), which could easily fill the topic slot, introduced (*h*)*it* only in case of an empty initial position (*TVX-subject*), and not before the 11th c. (OED (1933) 1961:517). Postverbal dummy subjects became common during Middle English, esp. in the function of a correlate to extraposed subject clauses and infinitives (1d).

(1)   a. *hit sniwþ* (Aelfric, Gramm. 22)
           þa rinde hyt (O. E. Gosp., Mt. VII, 27)
       b. *me was toold* (c1386 Ch., C. T. D WB 9)
           but thus it was told me (1422–1509 P. L. 460, 112)
       c. *yet were me lever to dey* (1470 Winchester 128, 24)
           it were me leuer . . . to dye (1485 Caxton 121, 30–31)
       d. *nought nedeth it to yow . . . To axe at me* (Ch., T. C. III,
                                                      1681–1682)

Of course, impersonal constructions with TVX-subjects also satisfied SVX word order, which became predominant since the end of the 14th c. (Fries 1940:201–204). Therefore it seems strange that with impersonal expressions,

a) (*h*)*it*-constructions were almost without exception replaced by expressions with a nominative experiencer since the 13th to 15th c. (*it* survived only in those constructions which preserved a patient (infinitive or sentential) subject, e.g. in *it behoves me*, *it becomes me* (+ patient), and, as an alternative to the experiencer subject construction, in *it ails/smarts/grieves/happens/seems/pleases* (*to*) *me* (+ patient)),

b) the old 'subjectless' type coexisted side by side with the new nominative experiencer constructions for about 200 years *after* SVX was generalized.

This seems to indicate that oblique experiencers in impersonal expressions were *interpreted as subjects* on the basis of their syntactic (see below), semantic and pragmatic properties long before SVX became dominant. Therefore they could preserve their morphological form, which only now was becoming a sufficient characteristic of non-subjects, throughout TVX and during the transition to rigid SVX, while *it*-subjects, being only a provisory device to make impersonals conform to TVX-syntax, were given up in favour of *nominative experiencer* subjects, which gradually acquired the full range of syntactic and morphological subject properties characterizing the completely grammaticalized relation of subject in Modern English.

In this view, the development of impersonal constructions in English is a process in which topical oblique experiencer 'subjects' of impersonal verbs acquired those syntactic and morphological properties which became mandatory for subjects only in an advanced stage of the development from a 'synthetic' SXV-language to a largely 'analytic' SVX-syntax with an established system of uniformly coded syntactic functions. For according to the syntactic definition of 'subject' as the last complement to bind an argument place of the verb (Vennemann/Harlow 1977:245, cf. n. 3), impersonal constructions with oblique experiencers never were 'subjectless' in the documented stages of Indo-European. What was indeed exceptional with these expressions was not their lack of a subject constituent, but the way this constituent was morphologically marked. The semantically determined obliqueness of dative subjects became a syntactic problem only when case forms were no longer assigned to verb arguments on the basis of semantic relations but rather on the basis of their position. The resulting conflict in Middle English between a constituent marked by a growing number of syntactic subject properties ('last' verb argument, topic-position, later also control of subject raising, co-referential deletion etc.) and its — now definitely object-like — morphological form was finally solved in favour of the tendency towards uniform syntactic patterns: Irrespective of their semantic function, all subjects are marked by nominative case, control of verb agreement and preverbal position since early Modern English.

The development towards a syntax with preferably referential preverbal subjects with an obligatorily nominative case marking was largely accomplished during the 15th c. (cf. Fries 1940:201–204). In this process, *it*-subjectivalization of impersonal expressions marks a transitory stage in which

a) word order had not yet assumed distinctive function for verb arguments,

b) subjects had already become so 'prominent' in English syntax, that an empty topic-position had to be filled with a dummy subject (a TVX device conforming to SVX),

c) oblique experiencers were provisionally interpreted as 'objects' according to their case form, therefore they could be shifted to postverbal position and sometimes even be morphologically restored by adpositions.

During the intermediary stage between the 14th and 16th c., between a TVX- and a rigid SVX-syntax, the various structural alternatives for impersonal expressions coexisted as variants in a language in flux: 'subjectless' constructions (2a, 3a), *it*-constructions with oblique (2b, 3b) or adpositional experiencers (2c), and constructions with non-experiencer subjects (2d, 3d) and with nominative experiencers (2f, 3f), which finally won the day. With French loans like *repent* and *remember*, even the reflexive personal forms (3e) were abandoned.

> (2) a. *if thee like to be myn* (a1393 Gower CA i 950)
> b. *it lykede him to take flesch* (c1400 Mandeville I, 6)
> c. *it lyketh to youre fader and to me þat I yow wedde* (c1386 Ch., C. T. E 345)
> d. *this message lyketh me wel* (1485 Caxton 187, 19)
> f. *somewhat she likede hym the bet* (c1385 Ch., L. G. W. 1075–1076)

> (3) a. *certes, thee remembreth wel* (Ch., Boethius II, Prose VI, 11)
> b. *it ne remembreth me* (Boethius III, Prose III, 33)
> d. *and what his compleynt was, remembreth me* (Ch., Compl. Mars 150)
> e. *a man shal remembre hym of his synnes* (c1386 Ch., C. T. I, 133)
> f. *thou remembrest wel* (Boethius I, Prose IV, 236)

According to traditional hypotheses (Gaaf 1904, Jespersen 1927, Fries 1940, Visser 1963, Traugott 1972, Fisiak 1976), which were essentially adopted e.g. by Lightfoot 1979, impersonal constructions were lost in English primarily

a) due to morphosyntactic ambiguities caused by inflectional decay, which brought about the reanalysis of experiencer complements which had lost their distinctive case endings as subjects,
b) due to the rigidification of SVX word order, which required preverbal subjects and thereby supported the reanalysis, e.g.

> (4) *whan a wolf* (dative/nominative) *wanteþ his fode* (nominative/accusative) (Alex. & Dind. 860)
> *þat mani* (dative/nominative) *þoht gret ferli* (Curs. Mundi 16862 C)
>
> *who* (dative/nominative) *lykes to luke* (N. E. Leg. 29,9)

> (5) *him behofaþ, þam cyninge* (dative) *behofaþ* >
> *þe kyng* (dative/nominative) *behoveth* > *he behoveth;*
> *þam eorlum* (dative plural) *licode* (singular) >
> *þe erles* (dative/nominative plural) *likode* (singular/plural)
> > *they liked.*

However, the data provided by the above account of the development of impersonal constructions in English somewhat weaken both of these arguments.

First, concrete cases of subject-object-ambiguity of experiencer arguments cannot have more than supported and accelerated the reanalysis: When 'personalization' started around the 13th/14th c., 'subjectless' sentences had for the most part already been 'disambiguated' as oblique complements by dummy subjects, which had become common with one- and two-argument verbs not later than the 11th c., and partly even by using adpositional phrases for experiencers. On the other hand, case distinctions for nominative-accusative of nominals were already lost in early Middle English, for nominative-accusative-dative around the 10th to 13th/14th c. (Mustanoja 1960:67, 94f., Traugott 1972:110). Besides, ambiguous nominal experiencers were probably relatively rare with verbs denoting subjective experiences, compared to pronominal experiencers, which throughout their history remained subject-object-distinct for the 1st and 3rd person in English (McCawley 1976:198).

Second, while the productivity of the 'subjectless' pattern in the 14th and 15th c. (Gaaf 1904:143–152, Mustanoja 1960:436) – i.e. after SVX had become predominant in the second half of the 14th c. (Fries 1940:201–204) – might be accounted for by the usual time-lag of morphological changes compared to syntactic changes, the SVX-hypothesis cannot explain the loss of *it*-constructions with impersonal verbs since late Middle English, which did conform to the new SVX-syntax. It equally fails to explain why even constructions with non-personal nominative subjects were given up with many verbs in favour of nominative-experiencer constructions, e.g.

> (6) *anoþer drem dremede me yet* (Havelok 1304) >
>   *I dreamed another dream.*[5]

This means that an explanation of the change of impersonal constructions in Middle English presupposes an investigation of the syntactic, semantic and pragmatic properties of experiencer subjects, and an analysis of the development of grammatical relations in this language. In this view, the loss of impersonal expressions in English is a consequence primarily of changes in the morphosyntactic coding properties and the syntactic behavioural properties of subjects, which encode specific semantic and pragmatic information, in a language on its way towards SVX.

In proportion to the degree a language advances toward stricter rules for the encoding of grammatical relations, oblique experiencer subjects are incorporated into the system of properties defining these relations at the respective stage of syntactic development. In many languages, this is done by a *step-by-step acquisition first of syntactic, then of morphological subject-properties*, a tendency which is in keeping with Givón's (1971:413) slogan about the relative conservativism of morphology as compared to syntax (cf. also Cole et al. 1980).

E.g., dative subjects control reflexivization and coreferential subject deletion in Modern Icelandic (cf. below) and in Russian (Nichols 1979), these two and some kinds of causativization in Dravidian Kannada (Sridhar 1976: 142), impersonal verbs can govern an accusative object in Dravidian Malayalam (Masica 1976:163); dative experiencers trigger reflexivization, reciprocity and causative clause union in Georgian (Boeder 1979:455, Cole et al. 1980: 736f.) and reflexivization and subject honorification in Japanese (Shibatani 1977:739).

In Old English and early Middle English, long before the acquisition of subject coding properties (7d, 7e), the experiencers of impersonal constructions undergo subject raising (7a), deletion under identity with a nominative subject (7b), they acquire control of coreferential subject deletion (7c) and other syntactic subject properties (cf. Visser 1963:31, Butler 1977 and Cole et al. 1980: 729f., from where the examples are taken):

> (7) a. subject-to-subject raising
>   *þa ongan hine eft langian on his cȳþþe*
>   'then he began to long for his kith' (971 Blick. Hom. 113,
>   15)
>   b. coreferential deletion of experiencer arguments

lewed men leued hym well and liked his wordes
'ignorant men loved him well and his words pleased (them)'
(1362 Langland, Piers Plowman, Prol. 72)

c. coreferential deletion of nominative subjects
us sholde neyther lakken gold ne gere, but ben honured
while we dwelten there 'we should not lack gold nor gear,
but be honoured while we dwelt there' (Ch., T. C. IV,
1523)[6]

d. control of verb agreement
sum men . . . wondren what hem eilen (c1450 Chastising
of God's Children 103, 15)
me thynke they are syngyng of placebo (1533 Bale, King
John 30)

e. nominative case
whan hem bi-stode nede (a1375 Will. of Palerme 175) –
if he nede bestode (c1460 Towneley P. 340)

The change in verb valence connected with the process of 'personalization'
from DAT/ACC – verb – NOM/GEN/PP/inf/clause to NOM – verb – ACC/
PP as in

(8) *me* (DAT/ACC) *remembreth of the day of dome* (PP) (c1386
Ch., C. T., I, 159)>
I (NOM) *remember sth.* (ACC)

entailed in many cases characteristic morphosyntactic changes like transformations to periphrastic, often passive constructions (*I am hungry/thirsty/
angry, I am ashamed/annoyed/disgusted/horrified/amused* (+ PP)), or semantic modifications of the verbs involved. The reanalysis of two-argument verb
constructions according to the transitive pattern, which often contains an
agentive subject, brought about the reduction of 'causative' components in
the semantics of those verbs: *like* changed from 'please' to 'like', *need, lack,
want* lost their meaning of 'be lacking' when combined with a nominative
experiencer, *remember* its meaning of 'make so. think of sth.', etc.

If the development of 'subjectless' expressions in English is a model for
general tendencies in the historical change of syntactic relations, we might
expect other languages to change along the same lines. The validity of this
model is in fact proved by comparative evidence.

4 The development of impersonal constructions in French

In Old French, Middle French and early Modern French until the 16th c.

– and still in some South Romance languages –, the 'subjectless' type of construction with an oblique experiencer argument was as productive as in English. This becomes evident in analogical extensions of the Latin impersonal pattern to verbs such as OF *(de)plaist, covenist, grieve, besogne, semble, fait, avient, afiert, abelit, suffit, importe, fâche* and many others (cf. Horning 1879, Gebhardt 1895, Meyer-Lübke 1899:111f., Brunot 1913:226), e.g.

> (9) *morir le covint* (Yvain 4707)
> *quel chose vous est avenu* (Froissart, Poés. II, 225, 174)
> *moi n'est chaut* (Fabliaux 5, 9)
> *de mon seigneur Ivain li manbre* (Ch. Lyon 1260)
> *tei covenist helme e bronie a porter* (Alexius 411) ⟩

In quasi-adverbial expressions, this type of construction was still common in the 17th c. (Haase 1965:125), e.g. *suffit, peu importe, plût a Dieu, mieux vaut que, m'est avis que, reste à savoir, tant s'en faut que* and many others; some of these are still acceptable.

Around the 15th c., many of the lexical impersonals fell into disuse, e.g. *chaut, afiert, appert, apent, conste, loist, besoigne, abelit, atalente, monte, membre, espart, haite* (Kjellman 1919:8, Brunot/Bruneau 1949:315).

Parallel to the generalization of verb-second word order around the 12th c. (Wartburg 1971:12f., Price 1973:259ff.), TVX-subjects appeared with these constructions in initial position: Dummy-*il* occurred in the early 12th c., became frequent in the late 12th c. and appeared regularly since the 15th c. (Horning 1879:265). 'Subjectless' usage continued, however, until the end of the 16th or the 17th c. (Brunot/Bruneau 1933:384, 1949: 315; Haase 1965: 13, 15ff.).

> (10) *et se faut bien garder de dire 'Sisygambe'* (Vaugelas, *Remarques,* I, 149)
> *et ne seroit pas besoin de répéter le pronom* (ibid. II, 383.)
> *faut que j'y monte* (La Fontaine, Contes, II, 7, 172)

By the 15th/16th c., the preverbal position of topicalized non-pronominal objects was gradually abandoned, and during the 16th c., SVX word order became dominant (Lerch 1934:270, Crabb 1955:61, Price 1973:270, Harris 1978b:168; according to Gardner/Greene 1958, SVX was already predominant by the 14th c.). OVS continued in marked sentences, however, until the 17th c. (Haase 1965:412ff., Wartburg 1971:130): In those instances where the preverbal topic slot could otherwise be filled, (dummy) subject pronouns could still be omitted, e.g. (Haase 1965:16):

> (11) *de l'éprouver un jour me prit envie* (La Fontaine, *Ballades,*
> XII, 11)

The completely word-order-determined function of dummy-*il* is confirmed by Falk (1969:249): While referential subject pronouns increased in his 12th and 13th c. text corpus slowly from $68 \to 61 \to 88 \to 82 \to 73 \to 66 \to 71 \to 65 \to 72$ to 77 % of all instances, TVX-*il* increased from $20 \to 0 \to 38 \to 31 \to 42 \to 33 \to 23 \to 34 \to 33$ to 41 %. The usual omission of preverbal dummy subjects in impersonal sentences (which still holds for the 15th c. (Gardner/ Greene 1958:90)) as opposed to the frequency of referential subject pronouns points to the *topic-before-subject-preference* still valid in Old French and Middle French impersonal constructions: While in Old French and Middle French, any topical, even an oblique, constituent could meet the requirements of TVX-syntax, since the 16th/17th c. (Haase 1965:13, 15ff.), an overt subject, albeit sometimes 'empty', became mandatory to meet the rule of Modern French syntax that *the preverbal position must be filled with a nominative subject* (cf. Harris 1978a:112).[7]

The transition from TVX- to obligatory dummy subjects, even when some other element filled the topic position, was prepared already in Old French:

> (12) *et je prie Deu que, se li plest* (Yvain 2585) >
>   *. . . se il li plest* (FG),. . . *sil li plest* (H)
>   *quelle perdiction il nous est avenu* (Ch. Cygne 26346)

While in contemporary colloquial French, subject ellipsis occurs again in expressions such as *faut y aller, suffit que je lui ai dit, parait que nous sommes à l'arrière-garde* (Boer 1954:56), impersonal constructions with dummy-*il* and an extraposed subject constituent are still quite common with a few verbs (although their number has been reduced since the 17th c. (Haase 1965: 125)) in comparison to English, esp. for purposes of topicalization and focusing (Martin 1970, Gaatone 1970, Martinet 1975).[8]

> (13) *il importe de/que, il convient de/que, il me plaît de/que,*
>   *il appartient de, il se peut que, il s'agit de, il me faut de,*
>   *il m'intéresse de, il touche de, il me tarde de, il paraît que,*
>   *il répugne de, il sied de, il suffit de, il dépend de, il se trouve*
>   *que; il est bon/mauvais/temps . . . de, il est dit/permis/donné/*
>   *reconnu/convenu/exclu/envisagé de/que* etc.

On the whole, however, in present-day French, "the group of impersonal verbs not involving *être* (other than weather verbs) is in any case a shrinking group" (Harris 1978a:126 n. 24). According to the general tendency to require one of the nouns collocated with a particular verb to appear as surface subject (Harris 1978a:112), originally 'subjectless' constructions with dummy -*il* are on their way of being replaced by expressions with *referential nominative subjects*.

One way this is done is by substituting *il* by *ce* (when followed directly by the verb *être*) or *cela/ça* (elsewhere) (cf. Harris 1978a: 121):

> (14) *ça pleut, ça va*[9] ; *ça m'ennuie, ça me plait, ça me dégoute*[9] ; *c'est possible/vrai/intéressant* etc.

In other cases, the semantic content of 'unvolitional' experiences is transposed to constructions with nominative experiencer subjects by *reflexivization*, which became a productive syntactic device in French since the 14th c. (Horning 1879:254, Meyer-Lübke 1899:357, Boer 1954:57ff.) — in many instances as an alternative to passivization: *je m'ennuie, je me souviens, je me fâche, je me repentis, je me rappelle, je me trompe, je m'amuse, je me contente, je me plais, je m'étonne, je me passe* etc. A transitory phenomenon is the combination of impersonal and reflexive construction as in *il se faut, il se fait*, of impersonal, reflexive and passive as in *il s'est parlé*.

> (15) While impersonal *m'ennuie* is exemplified since 1135, reflexive personal *je m'ennuie* occurs since 1175. MF *il m'ennuie* is now restricted to archaic or literary usage in favour of *cela/ça m'ennuie* or the reflexive form (*Trésor de la langue française* 1971).

> (16) Since the 12th/13th c. (Roland), *je me remembre* is used besides OF *me/moi remembre* and MF *il me remembre de*. Afterwards, the verb is lost (Littré 1964, Wartburg 1946).

> (17) *Me sovient de* is the usual Old French form (1150–1330), while *il me souvient de* occurs from the 15th to the 17th c. with an infinitive, before Modern French with a *que*-clause; *je me souviens* is documented since 1636 (Wartburg 1946).

Around the 17th c., personal (reflexive) constructions became predominant with a great number of former impersonals; some have lost their reflexive pronoun again since the 17th c. (*je m'oublie* > *j'oublie*) (Brunot/Bruneau 1949:315f.).

Also around the 17th c., the old impersonal passives with (*y*) *a* or *être* such as

> (18) *n'i avra soné un mot* (Perceval 1688f.)
> *ainsi fut dit, ainsi fut fait* (La Fontaine, *Les Rieurs de Beau Richard,* Prol. 37)
> *il fut dansé, sauté* (La Fontaine, Contes, I, 1, 518)

fell into disuse (Brunot/Bruneau 1949:316). They were replaced since the 17th c. by reflexive constructions with nominative experiencers using *se voir* or *se faire* (Price 1973:236f., H. Martinet, p.c.):

(19) * *le père fut offert un livre*
      le père s'est vu offrir un livre

Instead of a 'direct' personalization of impersonal constructions (partly connected with passivization) as in English, French thus seems to make extensive use of reflexive constructions, which preserve an overt marking of the original semantic experiencer-verb-relation by subject-object coreference, in a way conforming to the rules of SVX-syntax.

A third device to provide referential preverbal subjects in former impersonal expressions used in French is the extension of periphrastic constructions with *avoir* (cf. German *haben*-periphrases, below). While since Vulgar Latin, dative-subject expressions such as Rumanian *mi-e frig* 'I am cold', *mi-e cald* 'I am hot', *mi-e foame* 'I am hungry', *mi-e sete* 'I am thirsty', *mi-e ruşine* 'I am ashamed' (which are still common in some South Romance languages) have been replaced in French by *j'ai froid, j'ai chaud, j'ai faim, j'ai soif, j'ai honte, j'ai peur, j'ai le vertige* etc., in Modern French this pattern has been extended not only to possessive constructions such as

(20) *le livre est à moi – j'ai un livre*
      (but *c'est un livre à moi*),
      Lat. *mihi sunt capelli nigri*, F *j'ai les cheveux noirs,*

but also to dative-experiencer constructions, e.g. (cf. Stimm 1980:637f.)

(21) **(il) me tourne la tête, j'ai la tête qui (me) tourne,*
      j'en ai eu le souffle coupé (avoir-passive),
      j'ai ma femme qui est très malade,
      elle a son cœur qui bat,

which preserve the topic-comment structure of the dative experiencer construction in a way conforming to SVX (non-nominative subjects can no longer be topicalized by simple fronting operations in Modern French).

To summarize, while in English 'subjectless' sentences were adapted to verb-second word order by using TVX-subjects in constructions with dative experiencers since the 11th c., and to SVX-syntax, requiring referential nominative subjects before the verb, by reanalysing dative experiencers as nominatives during the 13th to 15th/16th c., this process started much later in French and is still going on. It was only around the 15th to 17th c. that 'subjectless' expressions gradually fell into disuse in French, and only since the 17th c. there has been a tendency to introduce referential – possibly human – nominative subjects in all sentences at the expense of dummy subject constructions, which no longer correspond to the favoured sentence pattern of

Modern French. This time-lag may (tentatively) be explained by the fact that preverbal position has never become a *sufficient* characteristic of subjects in French as it did in English, due to the proclisis of oblique personal pronouns. Thus there was no strong 'pressure of position' (Fries 1940:203) to reanalyse preverbal arguments as nominative subjects. Only in present-day French, the tendency to *identify topical verb arguments with nominative subjects* seems to prevail.

5 The development of impersonal constructions in German

The recent development of 'subjectless' sentences in German offers a slow motion picture of syntactic change in progress. Like in Old English and early Middle English, in Old French and Middle French, impersonal constructions with a topical oblique experiencer argument were a highly productive pattern in Old High German and Middle High German (cf. Grimm 1898 IV:267ff., Behaghel 1932 II:128ff. for examples).
While 'subjectless' variants of otherwise personal verbs such as *mir wird/ist wohl/gut/übel/besser* etc. are still productive, a great deal of lexical impersonals became obliterated by Modern German, e.g.

> (22) *mir/mich gerinnet* 'I lack', *mir bâzet* 'I get better', *mir (gi)spuoet* 'I succeed', *mir gerîset* 'it befits me', *mich belanget* 'I long for', *mich betrâget* 'I am bothered', *mich bevilt* 'I have had enough of', *mir zoget* 'I am in a hurry', *mir gollet* 'I loathe' and many others.

Many impersonal expressions are still familiar to some speakers from literary texts dating from the 16th to early 20th c., but are now preferably used as stylistic archaisms, e.g.

> (23) *mich hungert, mich dürstet, mir/mich schaudert, mir/mich ekelt, mich juckt; mir bangt, mir träumt, mir zweifelt, mir denkt, mir ahnt* (+ patient).

They have been replaced by basically two kinds of constructions:
1) the construction with a dummy subject *es* (*es juckt mich, es schaudert mich*), or
2) the construction with a nominative experiencer subject (*ich bange, ich schaudere*).

TVX-*es* occupying an empty preverbal position became mandatory with no-argument weather verbs since Old High German, with oblique-experiencer verbs since late Middle High German (Brugmann 1917:22f., 29), when, around the 13th c., verb-second order was generalized (Maurer 1926:185–194).

'Subjectless' usage continues, however, even in Modern German in those types of construction which are best compatible with Modern German TVX-syntax:

a) with some verbs governing (usually topical) oblique experiencers, e.g. *mich friert, mir graut, mir schwindelt*,

b) with two-argument impersonals with an extraposed subject clause (restrictedly with subject infinitives) – which until Modern German usually did not function as subject complements (cf. n. 4) –, e.g.

> (24) *mich wundert, daß dein Auto den TÜV geschafft hat*
> *mir gefällt nicht, wie er mit seinen Kollegen umspringt*
> **mir gefällt, nachts im Meer zu baden,*

c) in constructions with predicative nouns or adjectives such as *mir ist/wird angst/bange/seltsam/schlecht/kalt/schwindlig* etc.

d) in impersonal passive constructions such as *hier wird hart gearbeitet, ihm ist nicht zu helfen, geredet wird darüber schon lange*, as well as in some Modern German passive variants: *hier läßt sich leben (?), ihm gehört gekündigt.*

In most of these expressions, dummy-*es* is (still?) restricted to its original TVX-function. Only in some of them, *es* is in the process of being inserted postverbally.

> (25) **hier wird es gearbeitet*
> **ihm gehört es gekündigt*
> *mir ist es komisch/schwindlig (?)*
> *hier arbeitet es sich gut*
> *hier läßt es sich leben/hier läßt sich's leben*

The constructions a) to d) usually contain more than one topicalizable constituent; this is probably why there is still no strong pressure to make *es*-subjects mandatory: The preverbal position is in most instances occupied, according to the verb-second rule of Modern German.

In constructions with one-argument verbs (26a) and recently also with two-argument verbs governing a subject clause or infinitive (26b), however, *es* is in the process of becoming *obligatory* even in postverbal position, especially in the spoken language.

> (26) a. *mir graut > es graut mir, mir graut (es)* 'I dread'
> *mir/mich schwindelt > es schwindelt mir, mir/mich schwindelt (es)* 'I am dizzy'

mich friert > es friert mich, mich friert (es) 'I am cold'
b. *mich wundert, daß > es wundert mich, daß; mich wundert*
(es), daß 'I am surprised at'
mir gelingt zu (?) > es gelingt mir zu; mir gelingt (es) zu
'I succeed'
mir gefällt, daß/*zu > es gefällt mir, daß/zu; mir gefällt es,
daß/zu 'I like'

In present-day German, *es*-constructions are the usual pattern for the majority of former 'subjectless' expressions: for those which have preserved their original meaning determined by their particular valence properties (cf. below).

As in early Modern French and early Middle English, dummy subject constructions are therefore very frequent in Modern German, compared to the almost exceptionless personalization of impersonal verbs in Modern English. Two kinds of arguments provide an explanation for this fact. First, in Modern German verb-second syntax there is still no urgent need to change preverbal topic-nominals to nominative subjects. Therefore the TVX-device of placing non-topical dummy-subjects in preverbal position still meets Modern German syntax rules fairly well, although — as I have shown above — nominative subjects, albeit dummy pronouns, are gradually becoming mandatory in all sentences irrespective of word order: The rule to provide a nominative subject for every verb is on its way to replace the less restricted rule which requires any kind of (possibly topical) constituent before the verb.

The second reason for the prevalence of dummy subjects in Modern German impersonal constructions is provided by Middle High German morphological changes. While morphological S-O-ambiguities of experiencer complements have been limited in German to accusative singular feminine and neuter experiencers (because of the singular verb ending) and therefore cannot be considered a decisive factor for the reanalysis of impersonal expressions in Modern German, another kind of case syncretism can — at least in part — account for the predominance of *es*-subjectivalization in German: Around the middle of the 13th c. (Grimm 1858:169), the distinction of nominative/ accusative versus genitive forms of the neuter personal pronoun *ez* versus *es* collapsed in Modern German *es*. In impersonal expressions, genitive complements were the most frequent kind of argument before Modern German (sometimes genitives were interchangeable with infinitives, *daß*-clauses or adpositional phrases, cf. n. 4), e.g.

(27) MHG   *mir/mich anet* + GEN, *mich jamert* + GEN/*in/*
nâch, mich verdriuzet + GEN, *mir/mich grûset*
+ GEN, *mich betrâget* + GEN/*umbe, mir ge-*

> *nüeget* + GEN/*an, mich gelustet* + GEN/*nâch,*
> *mir gebricht* + GEN/NOM/*an, mir gelinget* +
> GEN/*an, mich wundert* + GEN/AKK *über/von/in.*

Whenever these genitive complements were pronominalized by *es*, which became common since late Middle High German, especially with *es* functioning as a correlate to an extraposed constituent, they now were ambiguous as to their subject or object function. Since impersonal constructions had no nominative complements, which were about to be generalized in all sentences during Middle High German, an interpretation of these ambiguous *es*-complements as subjects must have seemed most plausible. Moreover, *es*-subjects had been common with impersonal weather verbs since Old High German, which may have supported the analogical reanalysis.

(28) OHG   *nu ist es* (GEN) *not* (Otfried IV, 30, 31) >
      ModG   *jetzt es es* (NOM) *nötig;*
      OHG   *so thih es* (GEN) *wola lustit* (Otfried I, 1, 14) >
      ModG   *es* (NOM) *gelüstet dich;*
      OHG   *thaz uns es* (GEN) *iamer si the baz* (Otfried
                                                 IV, 25, 14) >
      ModG   *es* (NOM) *jammert uns*[10]

While dummy subjects abound in Modern German to adapt 'subjectless' expressions to the requirements of TVX-syntax, constructions with *nominative experiencers* are still in the process of replacing the old impersonal and the younger *es*-constructions coexisting as variants in the language. Nevertheless, although present-day German is verb-second (with SVX being the predominant subtype), there is a strong tendency, especially in the spoken language, towards nominative experiencer subjects, however not necessarily in preverbal position.

(29) *mich hungert* (arch.) > *ich hungere, mich dürstet* (arch.) >
      ich dürste, mir/mich ahnt (arch.) > *ich ahne, mir zweifelt*
      (arch.) > *ich zweifle, mir beliebt* (arch.) > *ich beliebe* (arch.),
      mich begehrt (arch.) > *ich begehre, mir träumt* (arch.) >
      ich träume, mich friert > *ich friere, mich schaudert* > *ich
      schaudere*

Nominative experiencers are sparingly attested since Old High German (*(ich) hungere/dürste/wundere*), Middle High German (*ich ekle*) and early Modern German (*ich ahne, ich verdrieße*), but most of them do not occur before the 18th c. (Paul 1919:36f., Dal 1952:175).

The still relatively great relevance of semantic distinctions of verb-argument relations in Modern German is manifest in the fact that only a small proportion of verbs have directly undergone personalization together with the necessary semantic changes of verb meanings; most of them were subject to a variety of morphosyntactic modifications in order to bring the old semantics of 'subjectless' constructions in line with the syntax of nominative subject expressions:

The reanalysis of impersonal as nominative-experiencer constructions caused, in the case of a few verbs, as a consequence of the change of valence as e.g.

> (30)　a.　*mich* (ACC) *anet eines dinges* (GEN),
> 　　　　*mich* (ACC) *wundert über ein dinc* (PP),
> 　　　b.　*mir/mich* (DAT/ACC) *ahnt etwas* (NOM),
> 　　　　*mich* (ACC) *wundert etwas* (NOM),
> 　　　c.　*ich* (NOM) *ahne etwas* (ACC),
> 　　　　*ich* (NOM) *wundere mich über etwas* (PP),

characteristic *semantic changes* like in English, e.g. MHG *mir versmâhet* 'sth. is despisable to me, makes me despise' changed to *ich verschmähe* 'I despise', *mir beliebt* 'sth. pleases me, makes me like' changed to *ich beliebe zu* (arch.) 'I like', *mir zweifelt* 'sth. seems doubtful to me' changed to *ich zweifle* 'I doubt', *mich begehrt* 'sth. makes me desire' changed to *ich begehre* 'I desire', and others more.

The usual correlation of nominative arguments of transitive verbs with an agent role brought about the analogical interpretation of new nominative experiencer verbs as denoting volitional, intentional actions. 'Subjectless' one-argument expressions such as *mich hungert, mich friert* accordingly can be interpreted only as 'unvolitional' (31a), while the personal forms of these verbs can be understood both as volitional and unvolitional (31b).

> (31)　a.　*mich hungert (es), weil ich nichts im Magen habe*
> 　　　　*mich friert (es), weil ich Fieber habe*
> 　　　　**mich hungert, damit ich endlich abnehme*
> 　　　　**mich friert, um meine neuen Pelzstiefel zu schonen*
> 　　　b.　*ich hungere, weil ich nichts im Magen habe/um abzu-*
> 　　　　　　　　　　　　　　　　　　　　　　　*nehmen*
> 　　　　*ich friere, weil ich Fieber habe/um meine neuen Pelz-*
> 　　　　　　　　　　　　　　　　　　　*stiefel zu schonen*

Verbs which did *not* undergo the necessary semantic adaptation to their new valence properties, either (a) kept the old structural pattern with an additional dummy-subject, e.g. *es graut mir/mir graut (es),* or (b) they lexically fell into disuse (*geriset*) or, of several semantic variants, lost the one that had been realized by the 'subjectless' construction, e.g. *mich verlangt* 'I long for' was lost in favour of *ich verlange* 'I claim', *mich jammert* 'I pity' was lost in favour of *ich jammere* 'I lament', *mich leidet* 'I loathe' was lost in favour of *ich leide* 'I suffer', or (c) they *preserved the original semantic characteristics of impersonal expressions* in the nominative experiencer construction by means of (additional) morphosyntactic modifications:

1) substitution by periphrastic *haben-* or *sein-* constructions, e.g.

> (32) a. *mich hungert* > *ich habe Hunger, mich dürstet* > *ich habe Durst, mich gelüstet* > *ich habe Lust, mir genügt* > *ich habe genug von, mich ängstigt* > *ich habe Angst, mich friert* > *ich habe kalt, mir ahnt* > *ich habe eine Ahnung, daß, mir ekelt* > *ich habe einen Ekel vor, mir scheint* > *ich habe den Eindruck, daß* (cf. French *avoir-*constructions);
>
> b. *mich hungert* > *ich bin hungrig, mich dürstet* > *ich bin durstig, mir schwindelt* > *ich bin schwindlig, mich schläfert* (arch.) > *ich bin schläfrig* (cf. English *be-*periphrases);

2) substitution by reflexive constructions, e.g.

> (33) *mich wundert* > *ich wundere mich über, mich ekelt* > *ich ekle mich vor, mich sehnt* > *ich sehne mich nach, mich belanget* > *ich langweile mich, mich schämt* > *ich schäme mich, mich ängstigt* > *ich ängstige mich, mir graut* > *ich graule mich* (regional), *mich erinnert* > *ich erinnere mich, mich erbarmt* > *ich erbarme mich, mir ist gut/schlecht/komisch ...* > *ich fühle mich gut/schlecht/komisch ...* (cf. French)

Only a few relics of 'subjectless' constructions (with *es*-variants) are still unrestrictedly acceptable in contemporary standard German: *mich friert, mir graut, mich ekelt, mir schwindelt*. However, even these relics are in the process of being contextually restricted. They are increasingly confined to written elevated style, they are used mainly by elder speakers and only in some regional varieties of German.[11] In colloquial spoken German, on the other hand, and especially in substandard varieties of the language, 'subjectless' expressions are almost completely eliminated: Younger speakers prefer *ich friere, ich hab kalt* to *mich friert* and even to *mich friert es*, they would hardly use *mir graut* but *ich hab'n Horror vor*, not *mich gelüstet* (arch.) but *ich hab Lust auf*, not *mir schwindelt* but *ich bin schwindlig/ich hab'n Drehwurm*, not *mir gefällt das* but *ich finde das gut/da fahr ich drauf ab* and similar (slang) expressions with referential nominative subjects, which identify the topic and the subject constituents of the constructions involved.

The current usage of 'subjectless' expressions and alternative constructions in present-day German reflects a transitory stage of the morphosyntactic reorganization of the language. Considering the prevalence of dummy-subject constructions with impersonal verbs in standard German, which preserve the oblique marking of experiencer subjects and the original semantic properties of impersonal expressions, and the coexistence of a variety of structural patterns for the verbs involved, Modern German parallels approximately late Middle English of the 14th/15th c. and early Modern French of the 16th/17th c.

Considering, on the other hand, a) the degree of inflectional reduction, b) the degree of rigidification of word order and c) the form and function of grammatical relations in Modern German, it becomes evident that the tendency towards a uniform coding of the relation of subject (c) has *priority* over a) and b) in German: While nominative subjects have become mandatory in almost all sentences, in German verb-second syntax, there is still no strong pressure to place them in preverbal position. In French and English, on the other hand, the establishment of overt nominative subjects in all sentences was temporally and causally more closely related to the early loss of nominal inflection and the generalization of SVX word order.

The last step towards SVX-syntax, involving changes in a), b) and c), the homogeneous encoding of specific pragmatic (topicality) and semantic (agent, experiencer role) information in a morphologically and syntactically uniformly marked constituent 'subject' has been taken by English. French is rapidly approaching this stage, while German is still on its way, representing an advanced transitory stage between a synthetic and an analytic morphosyntax, between TVX and SVX, and between a type of language still allowing for some formal variation in the encoding of grammatical relations according to the semantic functions of verb arguments, and a type of language with completely grammaticalized syntactic relations.[12]

6 The development of impersonal constructions in Icelandic

Compared to German, Modern Icelandic is characterized by a more conservative syntax on its way from TVX/VSX to verb-second and SVX word order (Einarsson 1945:172, Kossuth 1976:24). Old Icelandic was particularly rich in 'subjectless' constructions (cf. Kossuth 1980:161–171). However, the dummy subject *það* 'it' (or *hann* 'he') was not introduced before the 13th c. (Heusler 1921:152). Even today, *það* is restricted to initial position (TVX-subject), where it is not yet consistently inserted. It occurs only rarely preverbally with no-argument verbs (34a); impersonal passives (34b) and verbs with an oblique experiencer argument (34c), which are still common in Modern Icelandic (though some have fallen into disuse) usually do not have a dummy subject (Einarsson 1945:105ff., 123, 167, 171, Kossuth 1976:14, 16, Kossuth 1980:164–169).

> (34) a. *það/hann dimmir* 'it is getting dark'
>   *nú snjóar* 'now it is snowing'
>   b. *þessa* (GEN) *verður minnzt* '(of) that is remembered'
>   c. *mig* (ACC) *þyrstir* 'I get thirsty'
>   *mig* (ACC) *dreymdi draum* (ACC) 'I dreamed a dream'
>   *mér* (DAT) *líkare-ð* (ACC) 'I like something'

Already in Old Icelandic, oblique *patient* arguments were subjectivalized in a few instances (*hann* (NOM) *líkar mér* (DAT)[13] ; cf. n. 4), whereas ambiguous accusative *experiencers*, on the other hand, tend to be transformed into dative terms (Kossuth 1976:26) as in late Middle High German, instead of being transformed into nominative subjects.

However, subjectivalization of experiencer arguments is already on its way in Modern Icelandic: While in Old Icelandic only one single verb triggered reflexivization, *þykkia* 'seem' (Cole et al. 1980:724), in present-day Icelandic oblique experiencers of impersonal constructions increasingly acquire syntactic subject properties like reflexivization and control of coreferential subject deletion (Kossuth 1976:30ff.) as well as subject-to-object raising (Cole et al. 1980:724).

In other North Germanic languages, the acquisition of subject properties by oblique experiencer complements has further proceeded from syntactic to morphosyntactic coding properties (Cole et al. 1980:725f.): In Faroese, dative subjects of impersonal passives can assume the nominative case. While e.g. in Old Swedish, dative experiencers could only trigger reflexivization, in Modern Swedish, Danish and Norwegian they have acquired nominative case and control of verb agreement.

In these languages as in English and others (see below), syntactic properties of subjects are acquired earlier than or simultaneously with subject coding properties. This has been noted among others by Keenan (1976) and Cole et al. (1980). Unfortunately, they have not provided an explanation of the various stages of subjectivalization in particular languages. It seems to be evident, however, that the acquisition of subject properties – whether occurring in steps as e.g. in English, or abruptly as apparently in German and French – is a symptom of the growing relevance of syntactic relations in a language and therefore tends to correlate with the degree of SVX-stabilization – at least in the languages treated in this paper.

According to this criterion, the Germanic languages investigated here could

be ordered along a scale of relative syntactic 'conservativism' versus 'progressivity':
Icelandic → German → North Germanic languages (other than Icelandic) → English.

7 Appendix: The development of impersonal constructions outside Indo-European

Modern Hebrew, an SVX/VSO language with a variety of fronting operations, also has a wide range of sentence types lacking an overt grammatical subject, e.g. no-argument and dative-experiencer constructions as well as subjectless existential sentences (Berman 1980). Most impersonal construction in Hebrew exhibit VSO-order (in predicative expressions often with deletion of the finite verb), e.g. (Berman 1980):

> (35) *nora kar/xam li* 'awful cold/hot to-me, I am very cold/hot'
>   *yeš lanu hamon pekanim* 'be to-us many pecans, we have lots of pecans'
>   *margiz oti še hu kolkax satum* '(it) annoys me that he is so dumb'

Like Old and Middle English, Old and Middle French, German, and Icelandic, Hebrew does not belong to those languages where the requirement that sentences have overt nominative subjects is a strong syntactic constraint. Accordingly, there are only few of those operations of subjectivalization which are typical of 'subject-prominent' languages such as passivization, subject raising, etc. The dummy-subject *ze* is only now being generalized as an antecedent before foregrounded sentential complements, e.g. (Berman 1980: 767):

> (36) *ze še hu kolkax satum margiz oti* 'it, that he is so dumb annoys me'

However, in colloquial spoken Hebrew, the oblique possessor nominals of possessive constructions are on their way towards being promoted to subjecthood, while the grammatical subjects of these expressions, the possessed nominals, are losing their subject properties: While the possessor arguments are placed immediately after the verb (VSO) like canonical subjects, definite possessed nominals are losing control of verb agreement, they are reanalysed as objects by the direct object marker *et*, they can be pronominalized only by accusative personal and relative pronouns and have lost control of subject raising (Ziv 1976:331).

(37) *haya*   *lahem*   *et*   *hamexonit*
was (3 *m.* sg.)   to-them   ACC   the car (*f.*)
hazot   *od*   *beyisrael*
the-this (f.)   still   in Israel
'they had this car back in Israel'

Word order in Hebrew is to a relatively high degree (still?) pragmatically determined. However, the data may indicate a beginning establishment of uniformly coded nominative subjects in all sentences as in many Indo-European languages on their way to SVX.

In Kartvelian Caucasus languages, e.g. in Georgian, 'subjectless' constructions with oblique experiencers are an equally productive structural pattern (Tschenkéli 1958:446ff.). In Georgian, a split ergative language, which has passed from ergative-absolutive to nominative-accusative encoding of verb arguments in the present tense series of verbs and is now on its way from SXV to SVX (Aronson 1970:295, Wagner 1978:43, 46, 71n. 145, Comrie 1976:255), dative subjects of impersonal verbs are likewise gradually acquiring subject properties.

While in Old Georgian, these arguments already displayed syntactic subject properties like control of reflexivization and reciprocity (Boeder 1979:455f.), in Modern Georgian they are also treated as subjects with respect to causative clause union and one kind of subject coding properties (Cole et al. 1980: 736ff.): In some impersonal expressions, grammatical third person nominative subjects are losing their verbal markers (38b), while third person dative subjects control plural agreement on verbs in opposition to third person dative objects (38c). In Old Georgian, however, the verb always agreed in number with the nominative argument irrespective of its semantic role (38a), as it still does with first and second person nominatives in standard Modern Georgian (Tschenkéli 1958:453f.; the following examples are taken from Cole et al. 1980:739f.).

(38) a. OGeorg.   *me*   /   *miqvaran*   *isini*
                 me (DAT)   me-love-*they*   they (NOM)
                 'I love them'

     b. Mod.   *mas*   *uqvars*   *is/isini*
       Georg.   him (DAT) him-loves-he/they   he/they (NOM)
                 'he loves him/them'

     c. Mod.   *mat*   *uqvart*   *is/isini*
       Georg.   them (DAT) them-love-he/they   he/they (NOM)
                 'they love him/them'

This shows that with respect to number agreement, third person dative experiencers have been treated like canonical subjects only recently in Modern Georgian. According to Tschenkéli (1958:453f., 460), this usage did not become common until present-day Georgian and is still rather inconsistent. However, while control of number agreement by dative experiencers is limited to their co-occurrence with third person nominatives in the standard language, in colloquial Georgian it has already been extended by some speakers to contexts with first and second person nominatives (Cole et al. 1980: 740).

In accordance with the current shift of Modern Georgian from ergative to nominative-accusative marking of verb arguments in the present verb series, the shift of subject properties like control of reflexivization and number agreement from nominative to topical dative subjects indicates a gradual change of the impersonal ('indirect') verb series towards the coding system of nominative-accusative languages, requiring preverbal, topical nominative subjects for every sentence at the expense of a differentiated marking of various semantic verb-argument relations: another step towards a nominative-accusative SVX-syntax.

8 Summary

The survey given in this paper of changes concerning the reanalysis of impersonal constructions has shown that this process cannot conclusively be explained by the loss of inflection or the rigidification of SVX word order in the languages involved.

These factors cannot account, e.g., for the time-lag of the reanalysis of oblique experiencer constructions with respect to the loss of nominal S-O-distinctions in English or French, nor for the extension of nominative subjects with impersonal verbs in verb-second Modern German, which still has a relatively efficient case morphology, nor for the early acquisition of syntactic subject properties by dative experiencers in comparatively 'synthetic' stages of particular languages such as Old English or Modern Icelandic, nor for the status of dummy-subjects in the development. The evidence provided in this paper indicates that the change of 'subjectless' constructions is a consequence of historical changes in the functional and coding properties of the grammatical relation 'subject': The gradual acquisition of syntactic and morphosyntactic subject properties by experiencer arguments of impersonal verbs is proportional to the establishment of grammatical relations in a language.

The generalization of uniform syntactic patterns at the expense of semantic distinctions, which characterizes the development of 'subjectless' expressions in the languages investigated in this paper, has proven the reanalysis of impersonal constructions in English a valid model of syntactic change. One may expect that other languages on their way towards SVX and a complete grammaticalization of subjects will develop along the same lines.

Notes

* This paper summarizes parts of my dissertation on the development of 'subjectless' constructions in Various languages (von Seefranz–Montag 1983). Some of the questions necessarily left open in the present paper will, I hope, have been answered by the more comprehensive analysis given there.

1. This hierarchical ordering of argument types partly determined the direction of early reductive processes in Indo-European case systems: It was the semantically relatively specific, low-ranking cases (locative, ablative, instrumental), the functions of which were earliest absorbed by higher ranking cases such as dative and genitive, while only later those two were reduced in favour of accusative and finally nominative. (Simultaneously, the most 'concrete' case functions were transposed to adpositions.) The resulting case syncretisms led to a gradual accumulation of heterogeneous functions in a decreasing number of polyfunctional cases, which were therefore increasingly subject to 'grammaticalization'.

2. E.g. in Old English, the choice of alternative object cases was correlated with many verbs with differences in meaning (cf. Plank 1980):
   hieran + ACC 'hear' vs. *hieran* + DAT 'listen to, obey'; *demennen* + ACC 'condemn' vs. *demennen* + DAT 'judge'; *hyrsumian* + ACC 'make obedient' vs. *hyrsumian* + DAT 'obey'.
   On the other hand, verbs occurred with different argument cases without entailing any recognizable difference in meaning since the earliest stages of Old English. This interchangeability of argument cases indicates the gradual functional decrease of the category of case, before any strong morphological reductions of the case endings concerned had taken place (cf. Penhallurick 1975:20f.):
   oft þone geþyldegestan (ACC) *scamaþ þaes siges* (GEN) 'often the most patient man is ashamed of the victory' (CP 226, 19);
   and him (DAT) *þaes* (GEN) *sceamode* 'and they were ashamed of that' (Aelfric, Homilies, I, 18, 12);
   oþþe hwa biþ gescended þaet ic (NOM) *eac þaes* (GEN) *ne scamige?* 'or who is shamed and I am not ashamed?' (CP 100, 5–6).

3. The definition of 'subject', 'indirect object' and 'direct object' underlying this diagram is the one given in Vennemann/Harlow 1977:245: "the subject of a verb is the last noun phrase to bind an argument place of the verb"; the indirect object is accordingly the noun phrase next to the last to bind an argument place of the verb; the direct object is the first argument to bind an argument place of the verb.

4. According to their valence properties, several kinds of 'subjectless' constructions (which were affected by different kinds of syntactic changes and at different times) have to be distinguished:
   1) constructions with no-argument verbs and analogous expressions with otherwise 'personal' verbs (E *it is raining*, G *es regnet*; F *il fait beau*, G *es klopft*);

2) constructions with one-argument verbs governing an oblique experiencer complement (ME *me hungreth*, G *mich hungert*);
3) constructions with two-argument verbs governing an oblique experiencer complement and a patient complement realized by

   a) a genitive, accusative or adpositional phrase (MHG *mich wundert eines dinges*, *mich wundert umbe ein dinc*) or by
   b) a nominative NP, an infinitive or sentential complement (G *mich wundert*, *daß du noch kommst*).

   E.g. in Middle English, Middle High German and Old Icelandic, however, the 'grammatical subjects' in 3b) were not consistently treated as subjects with respect to word order and verb agreement (cf. ME *me liketh wel his wordes* (Piers P. A I, 41)); therefore this type is treated here as 'subjectless', together with the expressions of 3a). With some verbs, on the other hand, groups 3a) and 3b) merged in the later reanalysis by reinterpreting oblique patients as nominatives.
4) No-argument (G *es wird gearbeitet*) and oblique-argument impersonal passives (Latin *mihi invidetur*).

   The present study focuses on types 2) and 3). Types 1) to 4) are more thoroughly treated in the dissertation mentioned in*.
5. For a refutation of the ambiguity thesis cf. also Butler 1977; Kovatcheva (forthcoming) referred to Marchand (1951:79), who comes to similar conclusions, however on the basis of rather speculative arguments. – For a psychological explanation of the reanalysis of impersonals in Middle English see Jespersen 1917:208.
6. Butler (1977:164) noted, however, that identity deletions of subjects may not have been restricted to subjects in Middle English, but rather that subjects could be deleted at that time on identity to any of a number of NPs in preceding conjoined sentences. If this is correct, (7b) and (7c) do not provide evidence for an interpretation of oblique experiencers as subjects. Instead, they would in this case indicate the priority of *referential* rather than purely syntactic properties of verb arguments with respect to control of syntactic operations in Middle English – i.e. the 'incomplete' establishment of subjects as a syntactic relation at that stage – a finding which is in accordance with the interpretation of the data given in the present paper.
7. For the time being, an attempt to account for the introduction of dummy-subjects in French on the basis of syntactic rather than extralinguistic, e.g. areallinguistic arguments, seems to be closer to a conclusive explanation of the data. (Cf. e.g. Kuen 1970, who attributes the upcoming of dummy-subjects in French to French-German contact; cf. also A. Danchev, this conference).
8. Cleft constructions with otherwise 'personal' verbs governing a nominal subject are – albeit quite common in Modern French – restricted by possible ambiguities arising from the syncretism of the masculine personal pronoun *il* and the neuter dummy-subject *il*, which are distinct in English (*he* vs. *it/there*) or German (*er* vs. *es*). E.g.: *il manque un train* (impersonal) vs. *il manque le train* (personal). I am grateful to H. Martinet for referring me to this problem; cf. also Martinet 1975.
9. *Ça va, ça me dégoute* are not synonymous to *il va, il me dégoute*, which suggest a 'personal' interpretation. I owe this information to H. Martinet, p.c.
10. In personal constructions, which already had a nominative complement, ambiguous former genitive-*es* was reinterpreted as accusative, e.g.

    ich habe/bin es (GEN ⟩ ACC) *satt*
    ich bin es (GEN ⟩ ACC) *leid/müde/zufrieden*
    ich will es (GEN ⟩ ACC) *nicht wahrhaben*
    laß es (GEN ⟩ ACC) *genug sein.*

    Old genitives have been preserved only in a handful of – now obliterate – *person-*

alized constructions, e.g. *ich gedenke seiner* (today *ich denke an ihn*), *ich freue mich dessen* (*darüber*), *ich erbarme mich seiner* (*über ihn*).

11. I am grateful to W. Abraham for drawing my attention to the question of interdialectal differences concerning the decrease of impersonal constructions in German. I am sure the relationship between the degree of case reduction and the inventory of 'subjectless' constructions in particular dialects could be a rewarding object of research. To give a few hints, H.-J. Sasse, Munich, informed me that in his Berlin idiolect, neither *mir friert* (syncretism of dative and accusative) nor *es friert mir* are (still) acceptable as compared to *ick frier*. Marchand (1951:70) notes that in his Low German (Krefeld) idiolect, the complete syncretism of dative and accusative forms brought about nominative-subject passives of verbs originally governing a dative argument, e.g. *ich werde geholfen* (standard German *mir wird geholfen*), *er ist gekündigt worden* (standard *ihm ist gekündigt worden*).

12. Therefore subjects in Modern German (still) cannot straightforwardly be identified with 'nominative NP', which is a position held by Reis (1982).

13. I am grateful to K. Kossuth for bringing this fact to my attention.

References

Aronson, H. L.
  1970   "Towards a semantic analysis of case and subject in Georgian", *Lingua* 25: 291–301.
Behaghel, O.
  1932   *Deutsche Syntax: Eine geschichtliche Darstellung* (II) (Heidelberg: Winter).
Berman, R. A.
  1980   "The case of an (S) VO language: subjectless constructions in Modern Hebrew", *Language* 56.4:759–776.
Boeder, W.
  1979   "Ergative syntax and morphology in language change: the South Caucasian languages", *Ergativity: towards a theory of grammatical relations*, edited by F. Plank (London: Academic Press), 435–480.
Boer, C. de
  1954   *Syntaxe du français moderne* (Leiden: Universitaire Pers.).
Brugmann, K.
  1917   *Der Ursprung des Scheinsubjekts 'es' in den germanischen und den romanischen Sprachen* (Leipzig: Teubner).
Brunot, F.
  1913   *Histoire de la langue francaise des origines à 1900* (I, III. 1). (Paris: Colin).
Brunot, F. – C. Bruneau
  1933   *Précis de grammaire historique de la langue française*, 1st edition, 3rd edition 1949 (Paris: Masson).
Butler, M.
  1977   "The reanalysis of object as subject in Middle English impersonal constructions", *Glossa* 11.2:155–170.
Cole, P. – W. Harbert – G. Hermon – S. N. Sridhar
  1980   "The acquisition of subjecthood", *Language* 56.4:719–743.
Comrie, B.
  1976   "Review of Klimov, G. A. 1973, *Očerk obščej teorii èrgativnosti* [Outline of a general theory of ergativity], *Lingua* 39:252–259.
Crabb, D.
  1955   *A comparative study of word order in Old French and Old Spanish prose works* (Washington: Cath. Univ. of America).

Dal, I.
1952   *Kurze deutsche Syntax* (Tübingen: Niemeyer).
Einarsson, S.
1945   *Icelandic grammar, texts, glossary* (Baltimore: Johns Hopkins).
Falk, P.
1969   "Particularisme des propositions impersonnelles en ancien français",   *Studia neophilologica* 41.1:235–252.
Fisiak, J.
1976   "Subjectless sentences in Middle English", *Kwartalnik neofilologiczny* 23.3: 263–270.
Foulet, L.
1968   *Petite syntaxe de l'ancien français* (Paris: Champion).
Friedrich, P.
1975   *Proto-Indo-European syntax*, Journal of Indo-European Studies, Monograph Series 1.
Fries, Ch.
1940   "On the development of the structural use of word-order in Modern English", *Language* 16:199–208.
Gaaf, W. v. d.
1904   *The transition from the impersonal to the personal construction in Middle English* (Heidelberg: Winter).
Gaatone, D.
1970   "La transformation impersonnelle en français", *Le français moderne*, 389–411.
Gardner, R. – M. A. Greene
1958   *A brief description of Middle French syntax* (Chapel Hill: University of N. C. Press).
Gebhardt, C.
1895   "Zur subjektlosen Konstruktion im Altfranzösischen", *Zeitschrift für romanische Philologie* 20:27–50.
Geisler, H.
1982   *Studien zur typologischen Entwicklung: Lateinisch-Altfranzösisch-Neufranzösisch* (München: Fink).
Givón, T.
1971   "Historical syntax and synchronic morphology: an archaeologist's field trip", *Papers from the 7th regional meeting, Chicago Linguistic Society* (Chicago: CLS), 394–415.
Grimm, J.
1898   *Deutsche Grammatik* (IV) (Gütersloh: Bertelsmann).
Grimm, J. – W. Grimm
1958   *Deutsches Wörterbuch* 1854–1963, vol. 3 (Leipzig: Hirzel).
Haase, A.
1965   *Syntaxe française du XVIIe siècle* (Paris: Delagrave and München: Hueber).
Harris, M.B.
1978a   *The evolution of French syntax: a comparative approach* (London/New York: Longman).
1978 b "The inter-relationship between phonological and grammatical change", *Recent development in historical phonology*, edited by J. Fisiak (The Hague: Mouton), 159–172.
Hartmann, H.
1977   "Das Impersonale im Keltischen und Indogermanischen", *Kolloquium der Indogermanischen Gesellschaft 1976* (Wiesbaden: Reichert), 159–203.

Heusler, A.
  1932   *Altisländisches Elementarbuch* (Heidelberg: Winter).
Horning, A.
  1879   "Le pronom *il* en langue d'oil. Son origine, son extension", *Romanische Studien* 4:229–272.
Jespersen. O.
  1927   *A modern English grammar on historical principles* (II) (Heidelberg: Winter).
Kattinger, G.
  1970   *Die Verwendung des Personalpronomens als Subjekt zum Verbum, dargestellt an "Erec und Enide" von Chrétien de Troyes* (diss. Erlangen-Nürnberg: Univ. Erlangen-Münster).
Keenan, E. L.
  1976   "Towards a universal definition of 'subject' ", *Subject and topic*, edited by Ch. N. Li (New York: Academic Press), 303–334.
Kjellman, H.
  1919   *La construction moderne de l'infinitif dit sujet logique en français* (Uppsala).
Klaiman, M. H.
  1980   "Bengali dative subjects", *Lingua* 51:275–295.
Klimov, C. A.
  1979   "On the position of the ergative type in typological classification", *Ergativity: towards a theory of grammatical relations*, edited by F. Plank (London: Academic Press), 327–332.
Kossuth, K. C.
  1976   "Subjectless sentences, word order change and non-nominative subjects in Icelandic" (MS Pomona College and the Westfälische Wilhelms-Universität Münster).
  1980   *Case grammar of verbal predicators in Old Icelandic* (Göppingen: Kümmerle).
Kuen, H.
  1970   "Die Gewohnheit der mehrfachen Bezeichnung des Subjekts in der Romania und die Gründe ihres Aufkommens", H. Kuen, *Romanistische Aufsätze* (Nürnberg: Carl), 154–184.
Kuno, S.
  1973   *The structure of the Japanese language* (Cambridge (Mass.)/London: M. I. T. Press).
Kuryłowicz, J.
  1964   *The inflectional categories of Indo-European* (Heidelberg: Winter).
Lehmann, W. P.
  1974   *Proto-Indo-European syntax* (Austin: Univ. of Texas Press).
  1976   "From topic to subject in Indo-European", *Subject and topic*, edited by Ch. N. Li (New York: Academic Press), 445–456.
Lightfoot, D. W.
  1979   *Principles of diachronic syntax* (Cambridge: University Press).
Littré, E.
  1964   *Dictionnaire de la langue française* (Paris: Editions Universitaires).
Marchand, H.
  1951   "The syntactical change from inflectional to word order system and some effects of this change on the relation 'verb/object' in English: a diachronic-synchronic interpretation", *Anglia* 70:70–89.
Martin, R.
  1970   "La transformation impersonnelle", *Revue de linguistique romane* 34:377–394.
Martinet, H.
  1975   "Les variantes impersonnelles d'énoncés en français", *La Linguistique* 11.1:75–86.

552 *Ariane von Seefranz-Montag*

Masica, C. P.
1976   *Defining a linguistic area: South Asia* (Chicago/London: Univ. of Chicago Press).
Maurer, F.
1926   *Untersuchungen über die deutsche Verbstellung in ihrer geschichtlichen Entwicklung* (Heidelberg: Winter).
McCawley, N.
1976   "From OE/ME 'impersonal' to 'personal' constructions: What is a 'subjectless' S?", *Papers from the Parasession on diachronic syntax, Chicago Linguistic Society* (Chicago: CLS), 192–204.
Meillet, A.
1909   *Einführung in die vergleichende Grammatik der indogermanischen Sprachen* (Leipzig/Berlin: Teubner).
Meyer-Lübke, W.
1899   *Grammatik der romanischen Sprachen* (III) (Leipzig: Winter).
Miklosich, F.
1865   *Die verba impersonalia im Slawischen* (Denkschrift der Kaiserl. Akad. der Wiss., Philos.-hist. Kl. XIV) (Wien).
Miller, D. G.
1975   "Indo-European: VSO, SOV, SVO, or all three?", *Lingua* 37:31–52.
Mustanoja, T.
1960   *Middle English syntax* (I) (Helsinki: Soc. néophilologique de Helsinki).
Nichols, J.
1979   "Subjects and controllers in Russian", *Papers from the 15th regional meeting, Chicago Linguistic Society* (Chicago: CLS), 256–266.
Paul, H.
1919   *Deutsche Grammatik* (III. iv. 1) (Halle: Niemeyer).
Penhallurick, J. M.
1975   "Old English case and grammatical theory", *Lingua* 36:1–29.
Plank, F.
1980   "About subjects, objects, and the history of English (preliminary version)" (MS).
Price, G.
1973   *The French language: present and past* (London: Arnold).
Reis, M.
1982   "Zum Subjektbegriff im Deutschen", *Satzglieder im Deutschen: Vorschläge zur syntaktischen, semantischen und pragmatischen Fundierung,* edited by W. Abraham (Tübingen: Narr), 171–211.
Scholz, F.
1973   *Russian impersonal expressions used with reference to a person* (Paris: Mouton).
Seefranz-Montag, A. von
1983   *Syntaktische Funktionen und Wortstellungsveränderung: Die Entwicklung "subjektloser" Konstruktionen in einigen Sprachen* (München: Fink).
Shibatani, M.
1977   "Grammatical relations and surface cases", *Language* 53.4:789–809.
Sridhar, S. N.
1976   "Dative subjects, rule government and relational grammar", *Studies in the linguistic sciences* 6.1:130–151.
Stimm, H.
1980   "Satz-Periphrasen mit *habere* im Bündnerromanischen (Surselvischen)", *Romanica Europaea et Americana: Festschrift für H. Meier,* edited by H. D. Bork, A. Greive and D. Well (Bonn: Bouvier), 628–638.

Stockwell, R. P.
1977 "Motivations for exbraciation in Old English", *Mechanisms of syntactic change*, edited by Ch. N. Li (Austin/London: University of Texas Press), 291–314.
Traugott, E. C.
1972 *A history of English syntax* (New York: Holt).
Tschenkéli, K.
1958 *Einführung in die georgische Sprache* (I) (Zürich: Amirani).
Velten, H. V.
1931 "On the origin of the categories of voice and aspect", *Language* 7.4:229–241.
Vennemann, Th.
1974 "Topics, subjects and word order: from SXV to SVX via TVX", *Historical linguistics: Proceedings of the first international conference on historical linguistic* (I), edited by J. Anderson and C. Jones (Amsterdam: North-Holland Publishing Co), 339–376.
1975 "An explanation of drift", *Word order and word order change*, edited by Ch. N. Li (Austin/London: University of Texas Press), 269–305.
Vennemann, Th. – R. Harlow
1977 "Categorial grammar and consistent basic *VX* – serialization", *Theoretical linguistics* 4.3:227–254.
Visser, F. Th.
1963 *An historical syntax of the English language* (I) (Leiden: Brill).
Wagner, H.
1959 *Das Verbum in den Sprachen der britischen Inseln* (Tübingen: Niemeyer).
1978 "The typological background of the ergative construction", *Proceedings of the Royal Irish Academy* 78.C.3:37–74.
Wartburg, W. v.
1946 *Französisches etymologisches Wörterbuch* (Basel: Zbinden).
1971 *Evolution et structure de la langue française* (Bern: Francke).
Watkins, C.
1969 *Indogermanische Grammatik* (III.1) (Heidelberg: Winter).
Whalen, S.
1978 "The impersonal sentence in Russian and Romanian", *Papers and studies in contrastive linguistics* 8:5-68.
Ziv, Y.
1976 "On the diachronic relevance of the promotion to subject hierarchy", *Studies in the linguistic sciences* 6.1:195–215.

CARMEN SILVA-CORVALÁN

Semantic and pragmatic factors in syntactic change

1 Introduction

This paper examines the factors that condition the use and diffusion of clitic pronouns coreferential with an object noun phrase in Spanish. These factors are shown to be related to the degree of topicality of the object noun phrase, i.e. to the likelihood of the noun phrase to qualify as the topic, where *topic* is defined, at the sentence or discourse level, as "what a speaker may be talking about at any given moment" (Hyman and Zimmer 1976:209). Thus, when the object noun phrase is in topic position, i.e. preverbal, the occurrence of the clitic is categorical in Spanish as well as in other Romance languages exemplified below:

French: *A Marie, il* lui *a donné un livre.*
Italian: *A Maria* le *ha dato un libro.*
Portuguese:*Para Maria* lhe *deu um livro.*
Rumanian: *Mariei* i-*a dat o carte.*
Spanish: *A María* le *dio un libro.*
            'To Mary he gave (her) a book'

On the other hand, we observe different patterns of diffusion of coreferential clitics, both within Spanish and comparatively in the four other Romance languages illustrated above, when the object noun phrases are postverbal.

This phenomenon is studied quantitatively in contemporary spoken Spanish[1] and in samples of written Spanish from the 12th to the 16th century. Both diachronically and synchronically, the occurrence of the clitic is shown to increase along a scale of increasing topicality of the object noun phrase. Thus, indirect objects (IOs) always require a coreferential dative clitic in the data from contemporary spoken Spanish (CSS) analyzed here, and over 90% of the IOs are definite and human, and 43% are preverbal, three features that correlate with topicality. Almost the opposite situation holds for non-pronominal[2] direct objects (DOs): only 15% are human,[3] 36% are definite, and a low 7% are preverbal. DOs, therefore, are the least likely topics and this is

reflected in the variable occurrence of coreferential accusative clitics, as illustrated in (1–7):

(1) *Y la verdura no, la verdura$_i$ te la$_i$ llevan de la zona central.*
'And not the vegetables, the vegetables$_i$ (they) take them$_i$ to
you from the central part'

(E, f, 34, *B*)[4]

(2) *A mí se me abrió el mundo cuando lo$_i$ conocí a Eugenio$_i$*
'The world changed for me when (I) met Eugenio$_i$.'

(E, f, 34, *B*)

(3) *Lo$_i$ hacen pasar vergüenza al hombre$_i$*
'(They) embarrass the man$_i$'

(M, m, 39, *A*)

(4) *Lo$_i$ adoraba a su perro$_i$*
'(She) adored her dog$_i$'

(M, f, 66, *B*)

(5) *Uno los$_i$ ve los problemas$_i$, digamos, reducidos en dimensión.*
'One sees the problems$_i$, say, in reduced dimension'

(P, m, 41, *B*)

The occurrence of the accusative clitics in sentences of the type illustrated
by (1) to (5) is variable, as shown by examples (6) and (7) where no coreferential clitic is expressed:

(6) *Pero el cobre se llevaban pues.*
'But the copper (they) took away'

(H, m, 33 *B*)

(7) *Yo cuando conocí a mi esposa le dije -----*
'When I met my wife (I) told her -----'

(R, m, 35, *A*)

This paper views the use of coreferential accusative clitics as a manifestation of object-verb (O-V) agreement sensitive to the relative topicality of the
dative and accusative noun phrases. The results of this study support Givón's
(1976) proposal that *grammatical agreement arises from topic-verb agreement*
and that object pronouns coreferential with object noun phrases should be
viewed as markers of object-verb agreement motivated by topicality.

Our analysis of coreferential clitics as markers of topicality allows us both
to explain the diffusion of coreferential object clitics from medieval Spanish,
when these clitics occurred with very low frequency, to contemporary Span-

ish, with its different patterns of occurrence of dative and accusative clitics, and to predict the direction of the process on its way to becoming a phenomenon of categorical O-V agreement, i.e. grammaticalized.

The variable occurrence of a clitic with a preverbal DO is discussed first.

2 Object-Verb agreement with direct objects

2.1 O-V agreement with preverbal DOs

It has been observed before (Hatcher 1956) that in contemporary Spanish the coreferential clitic is usually present when the preverbal object is definite. This is supported by our data. As shown by the results of Table 1, the tendency is clearly for the clitic to be present when the DO is definite and absent when it is indefinite.

Table 1. Percentage of object-verb agreement by definiteness of the preverbal DO in CSS.

Preverbal DO	lo[5]	
Total	233/303	77%
+ definite	220/241	91%
− definite	13/62	21%

The presence of a pronominal copy does not depend solely on definiteness. Even though this is an important factor, the data indicate that 21% of the indefinite preverbal DOs were marked for OV agreement and that agreement is not categorical for definite preverbal DOs. It is possible, on the other hand, that the occurrence of the clitic may respond to a scalar rather than a binary value for 'definiteness', as the examples below appear to suggest:

(8) *Hogar* $\left\{ {*\text{lo} \atop \emptyset} \right\}$ *necesitamos todos.*
   '(A) home (we) all need'

(9) *Un hogar* $\left\{ {?\text{lo} \atop \emptyset} \right\}$ *necesitamos todos.*
   'A home (we) all need'

(10) *Un hogar bien constituido* $\left\{ {\text{lo} \atop \emptyset} \right\}$ *necesitamos todos.*
   'A well founded home (we) all need it'

(11) *El hogar* $\left\{ {\text{lo} \atop ? \emptyset} \right\}$ *necesitamos todos.*
   'The home (we) all need it'

Chafe (1976:39) proposes that an item is given the status of definite by a speaker when he thinks that the listener knows and can identify the particular referent that he (the speaker) has in mind. On the basis of Chafe's definition, Li and Thompson (1976:461) consider generic nouns to be definite. It should be expected, therefore, that if generic nouns are definite, they would strongly favor O-V agreement. This is not so, however. Genericity is not sufficient to account for the acceptability of the clitic pronoun in the continuum illustrated by (8) to (11). *El hogar* in (11) may be generic as *hogar* in (8) but only in (11) is O-V agreement allowed. On the other hand, if the preverbal objects in (8) and (11) are generic, the speaker may assume that the listener knows the class of referents that may be categorized by the noun *hogar* so they are definite in Chafe's definition. We hypothesize, then, that the presence of the clitic may be sensitive to a syntactic rather than a pragmatic definition of definiteness. In order to investigate this possibility, four points in a continuum are identified with respect to the combination of two features, [± determiner] and [± definite]. The term 'specificity' is here used as a cover term for the combination of the two features, 'determiner' and 'definite'. A bare noun is less specific than a noun modified by a determiner, and a noun modified by an indefinite determiner is less specific than one modified by a definite determiner. The combinations of the features [± determiner] and [± definite] classify the DOs into four groups along a scale of increasing specificity, as shown in Figure 1 and illustrated by examples (12) to (15):

Figure 1. DO-Verb agreement continuum.

$$\emptyset \qquad \begin{Bmatrix} \emptyset \\ ? \text{ lo} \end{Bmatrix} \qquad \begin{Bmatrix} ? \emptyset \\ \text{lo} \end{Bmatrix} \qquad \text{lo}$$

$$\begin{bmatrix} - \text{ determiner} \\ - \text{ definite} \end{bmatrix} \begin{bmatrix} + \text{ determiner} \\ - \text{ definite} \end{bmatrix} \qquad \begin{bmatrix} - \text{ determiner} \\ + \text{ definite} \end{bmatrix} \begin{bmatrix} + \text{ determiner} \\ + \text{ definite} \end{bmatrix}$$

(12) [- determiner, - definite]
Padrastro tengo.
'Stepfather (I) have'

(G, m, 50, *A*)

(13) [+ determiner, - definite]
Un hogar mal constituido$_i$ no lo$_i$ necesita nadie.
'A poorly founded home$_i$ nobody needs it'

(E, f, 34, *B*)

(14) [- determiner, + definite]

Eso tomo de desayuno.
'That (I) have for breakfast'

$$(S, f, 62 \; A)$$

(15) [+ determiner, + definite]
Y a los pascuenses$_i$ los$_i$ amontonaron en la parte de pedregullo.
'And the Easter Islanders$_i$ (they) packed them$_i$ in the area with rocky ground'

$$(C, m, 69, B)$$

Based on the results displayed in Table 1 and on the discussion of examples (8) to (11), we expect that the two ends of the continuum, [- determiner, − definite] and [+ determiner, + definite] will correspond to absence and presence of a pronominal copy respectively, and that the intermediate points, [+ determiner, − definite] and [- determiner, + definite], will correspond to a lower versus a higher percentage of pronominal copies.

It is important to note here that definiteness is one of the parameters that correlate highly with topicality. As stated in the introduction, 'topicality' refers to the likelihood of a given constituent to qualify as the topic of a sentence or of a discourse passage, i.e. a constituent that has a series of features that are characteristic of the kinds of referents that people tend to talk about (cf. Chafe 1976; Duranti and Ochs 1979; Givón 1976; Hawkinson and Hyman 1975; Hyman and Zimmer 1976; Li and Thompson 1976). It has been observed (cf. Duranti and Ochs 1979; Givón 1976; Hawkinson and Hyman 1975; Moravcsik 1974; Wald 1979) that in many languages grammatical agreement between the verb and its arguments follows certain implicational hierarchies related to topicality, which Givón (1976:152) has summed up in schema (16):

(16) Indefinite Object ⊃ Human Object ⊃ Definite Object ⊃ Subject

where the implicational sign '⊃' is a one-way conditional. Based on an analysis of a large number of languages, Givón (1976:152) proposes that this implicational hierarchy of the likelihood of verb agreement is governed by a universal hierarchy of topicality, here reproduced in schema (17). *Grammatical agreement,* then, *arises from topic-verb agreement,* and as we stated above, object pronouns coreferential with object noun phrases should be viewed as markers of object-verb agreement.

(17) a. Human > Non-Human
  b. Definite > Indefinite

c. More Involved Participant > Less Involved Participant
d. First Person > Second Person > Third Person

(17c.) predicts the following case hierarchy with respect to topicality:

(18) Agent > Dative > Accusative

The data analyzed in this paper support Givón's analysis of verb agreement as controlled by topicality. The frequency with which the semantic function 'agent' and the discourse function 'topic' correspond to the syntactic function 'subject' is reflected in the categorical existence of subject-verb agreement in Spanish. Subject-verb agreement is signalled by the verb ending. IO and DO agreement is signalled by means of dative and accusative clitic pronouns respectively. The semantic function 'dative' corresponds to the grammatical relation 'indirect object' and in CSS IOs always require O-V agreement (v. ex. 19). On the other hand, only pronominal[6] DOs require categorical agreement (v. ex. 20) regardless of position.

(19) *Le$_i$ di el libro a María$_i$*
      '(I) gave the book to Mary$_i$'

(20) *La$_i$ vi a ella$_i$ en la playa.*
      '(I) saw her$_i$ at the beach'

The different patterns of occurrence of dative and accusative clitics is thus accounted for by our analysis of coreferential clitics as markers of topicality.

The results displayed in Table 2 partially bear out the hypothesis: DO-V agreement increases along a scale of increasing specificity of the DO in pre-

Table 2. Percentage of preverbal DO-Verb agreement by specificity of the DO.[7]

		lo	
1. [− determiner / − definite]		6/47	13%
2. [+ determiner / − definite]		6/14	43%
3. [− determiner / + definite]		68/81	84%
4. [+ determiner / + definite]		153/161	95%

verbal position. The two ends of the continuum, however, show a slight amount of variation.

DO-V agreement is almost categorical for the group [+ determiner, + definite], 95%. Conversely, the percentage of DO marking in the group [− determiner, − definite] is quite low, 13%. The areas of greater variation are the intermediate groups and, as predicted, [− determiner, + definite] corresponds to a higher percentage of DO-V agreement. The variability in the intermediate groups is not surprising. It has been shown (Cedergren 1973, Labov 1972, Poplack 1979, Silva-Corvalán 1979) that linguistic change proceeds gradually and that during the spread of the change the innovation displays different frequencies of occurrence in the various linguistic environments before reaching grammaticalization.

In medieval and renaissance Spanish (MRS), the frequency of occurrence of clitics coreferential with preverbal DOs is very low. We have studied the phenomenon in samples selected from four literary works: Cantar de Mio Cid,[8] El Conde Lucanor,[9] La Celestina,[10] and La Vida de Lazarillo de Tormes,[11] which illustrate written Spanish from the 12th, 14th, 15th, and 16th centuries respectively. It must be noted that any comparisons of the results obtained from the study of these written works, either among themselves or between them and CSS, must necessarily be only tentative given differences of style among the written works and differences of medium with contemporary spoken Spanish.

Some of the general properties of DOs from the 12th to the 16th century are displayed in Table 3.

Table 3. Percentage of definite, human, and preverbal DOs in 12th, 14th, 15th, and 16th century written Spanish.

	+ definite		+ human		preverbal		+ preverbal + definite	
Mio Cid (12th c.)	318/500	64%	94/500	19%	181/500	36%	117/181	65%
El Conde *Lucanor* (14th c.)	64/121	53%	18/121	15%	20/121	17%	15/20	75%
Celestina (15th c.)	98/147	67%	32/147	22%	19/147	13%	13/19	68%
Lazarillo (16th c.)	123/200	62%	16/200	8%	27/200	14%	10/27	37%

It is interesting to note that the percentage of preverbal DOs decreases through time from 36% in the 12th c. to 14% in the 16th c. to 7% in CSS (cf. p. 2). This correlates with a decrease in the percentage of definite DOs from an average of 62% in MRS to 36% in CSS. This correlation may be related to the development of a constraint on the preverbal placement of DOs, such that the most frequent position for [− definite], non-topical DOs is now postverbal. Indeed, Table 3 shows that an average of 62% preverbal DOs are [+ definite] in MRS while in CSS preverbal DOs are almost categorically definite, 80% without including personal pronouns (based on figures given in Table 1).

Given that preverbal DOs are not necessarily topics in MRS, it is not surprising that the overall percentage of coreferential clitics is low compared with CSS. In CSS, 77% of the preverbal DOs cooccur with a clitic (v. T. 1) while in 12th c. Spanish only 34% have a coreferential clitic and the percentages are much lower in the later works. The results are given in Table 4.

Table 4. Percentage of O-V agreement with a preverbal DO in 12th, 14th, 15th, and 16th century written Spanish.

	Preverbal DO		+ definite		− definite		[+ definite / + human]		[+ definite / − human]	
	lo		*lo*		*lo*		*lo*		*lo*	
Mio Cid (12th c.)	61/181	34%	56/117	48%	5/64	8%	27/37	73%	29/80	36%
Conde Lucanor (14th c.)	1/20	5%	1/15	7%	0/5[12]		0		1/15	7%
Celestina (15th c.)	0/19	0%	0		0		0		0	
Lazarillo (16th c.)	3/27	11%	1/10	10%	2/17	12%	0/2		1/6	

The results displayed in Table 4 appear to contradict our hypothesis about the diffusion of O-V agreement. Notice that coreferential clitics occur more frequently in the 12th c. (34%) than in the 16th c. (11%). However, the fact that in CSS they occur with a frequency of 77% leads us to conclude that the low frequency in the works of the 14th to the 16th c. reflects a stylistic difference with the language of the Mio Cid rather than a real decrease in the use of coreferential clitics in the Spanish spoken in those later centuries. In fact, the Mio Cid, created to be recited by bards, was transmitted orally before being put into writing and so it may be closer to the spoken language than El Conde Lucanor, La Celestina or Lazarillo de Tormes.[13] Therefore, we compare the percentages in Mio Cid only with CSS, and the percentages in the other three works with one another. This pattern of comparison shows a diachronic increase in the percentage of coreferential clitics which lends support to our hypothesis. In the Mio Cid, O-V agreement with preverbal DOs appears to be related to topicality: it occurs more frequently with [+ definite] DOs (48% vs. 8%) and with [+ human] DOs (73% vs. 36%). The total percentage of coreferential clitics in the Mio Cid, 34%, is low as compared with CSS, 77% (v. T. 1). It seems to us, then, that in medieval Spanish DO preverbal position was not yet strongly associated with topicness. As this position became a preferred topic position, O-V agreement motivated by topicality became more frequent, to the point of being almost grammaticalized with definite preverbal DOs (95%, v. T. 2) in CSS.

Table 4 also shows an increase in the use of coreferential clitics from the 14th (5%) to the 16th (11%) century, though the percentages are still quite low even in the 16th c.

Examples (21) to (26) illustrate the variation:

> *With coreferential clitic*
>
> (21) *El Cid a doña Ximena$_i$ ívala$_i$ abraçar.*   (*Mio Cid*, verse 368)
> 'The Cid was going to embrace doña Ximena'
>
> (22) *todo$_i$ lo$_i$ fazía por consejo de aquel su cativo.*
> (*Conde Lucanor*, p. 58)
> 'everything (he) did according to the advice of that poor wretch'
>
> (23) *Yo oro$_i$ ni plata no te lo$_i$ puedo dar.*   (*Lazarillo*, p. 91)
> 'I cannot give you gold nor silver'
>
> *Without coreferential clitic*
> (24) *a tí adoro e credo.*   (*Mio Cid*, verse 362)
> 'you (I) adore and believe'
>
> (25) *et que todo aquello le fiziera el rey por [le] provar.*
> (*Conde Lucanor*, p. 60)
> 'and all that the king did to him to test him'
>
> (26) *Al triste de mi padrastro açotaron.*   (*Lazarillo*, p. 86)
> 'My poor stepfather (they) whipped'

We proceed now to discuss verb agreement with postverbal DOs.

2.2 O-V agreement with postverbal DOs

Accusative clitics coreferential with a postverbal DO, exemplified by (2) to (5) on p. 2, have been observed to occur variably in CSS (v. Bordelois 1974, Marcos Marín 1978, Roldán 1971, Poston 1956, Silva-Corvalán 1979). This phenomenon, quite widespread in Argentinian Spanish (Barrenechea y Orecchia 1977), is not very frequent in our data. Of a total of 5,086 postverbal DOs only 65 cooccur with an accusative clitic *in the same sentence*. On the basis of the results obtained for preverbal DO-V agreement and the fact that DOs are frequently [– human] and [– definite], this low number is not surprising given that postverbal DOs are not expected to be high in topicality. We predict, therefore, that verb agreement will spread first to postverbal DOs that are likely to qualify as the topic of the sentence or discourse, i.e. to human specific DOs. The results confirm this prediction: the 65 DOs are definite and 27 of them are human. In order to compare percentages, only those DOs whose referent had been mentioned in either of the preceding 2 clauses were counted. This decision was based on the observation that most of the postverbal DOs with verb agreement, 35 out of 65, had been referred to also in one of the preceding 2 clauses.

Table 5 displays the results for all the speakers included in the study.

Table 5. Percentage of occurrence of O-V agreement for postverbal DOs whose referent has been mentioned in either of the preceding two clauses (CSS).

DO	lo	
$\begin{bmatrix} + \text{human} \\ + \text{definite} \end{bmatrix}$	17/59	29%
$\begin{bmatrix} - \text{human} \\ + \text{definite} \end{bmatrix}$	19/193	10%
Total $\begin{bmatrix} \pm \text{human} \\ + \text{definite} \end{bmatrix}$	36/252	14%

As predicted, the frequency of occurrence of the clitic correlates with the degree of topicality of the DO. Thus, 29% of the human definite DOs, higher in the hierarchy of topicality than [– human] definite DOs, are marked for verb agreement as compared to 10% marking for the [- human] definite DOs.

O-V agreement with postverbal DOs is much less frequent in MRS. The percentages are illustrated in Table 6.

Table 6. Percentage of O-V agreement with a postverbal DO in 12th, 14th, 15th, and 16th century written Spanish.

	Postverbal DO		$\begin{bmatrix} \text{+ definite} \\ \text{+ recent} \end{bmatrix}$[14]		*Personal pronoun DO*
Mio Cid (12th c.)	3/319	1%	2/22	9%	0/1
Conde Lucanor (14th c.)	0/101	0%	0/15	0%	0
Celestina (15th c.)	1/128	1%	1/7		1/3
Lazarillo (16th c.)	2/173	1%	2/18	11%	2/2

The data are scant and allow only some tentative comparisons. Of the definite postverbal DOs referred to in one of the preceding 7 clauses (see note 14), 9% cooccur with a clitic in the Mio Cid and 11% in Lazarillo. Table 5 indicates a frequency of 14% for CSS, but this percentage does not include personal pronouns, which now require agreement, so the diffusion is greater than it appears to be. The occurrence of DOs with the stressed form of the personal pronoun (e.g. *mí, tí, nosotros*, etc.) is rare from the 12th to the 16th century.[15] Of the occurrences quantified and included in table 6, we observe that one occurs with a coreferential clitic in La Celestina (ex. 29 below) and the only two occurrences in Lazarillo also have a coreferential clitic (one is given as ex. 30). This is evidence that the diffusion of coreferential clitics *has proceeded selectively*, affecting first postverbal DOs that are higher in the hierarchy of topicality. Examples (27) to (30) illustrate the variation:

> *Without a coreferential clitic*
> (27) *Oíd a mí*.   (*Mio Cid*, verse 616)
>   'Hear me'

(28) *é dexa a mí para siempre.*   (*Celestina*, p. 63)
      'and leaves me for ever'

With a coreferential clitic
(29) *Que ni la$_i$ quiero ver a ella$_i$ ni á muger nascida.*
                                               (*Celestina*, p. 63)
      'And (I) don't want to see her$_i$ nor any other woman'

(30) *tanto que me$_i$ mataba á mi$_i$ de hambre*   (*Lazarillo*, p. 94)
      'so much that (he) starved me$_i$'

In sum, we have shown that there are two major differences between MRS and CSS with respect to the use of clitics coreferential with a DO: 1. A diachronic increase in the percentage of clitics coreferential with preverbal DOs, and a reduction in the percentage of preverbal DOs. This appears to be a consequence of the fact that preverbal position has become constrained to NPs that are high in topicality. 2. The addition of a rule of categorical, i.e. grammaticalized O-V agreement with full pronoun DOs, the occurrence of which has become much more frequent in CSS. This fact appears to support the hypothesis that clitics are being reinterpreted as markers of O-V agreement and therefore full pronouns are more frequently called for to perform the anaphoric function.

It is possible that DO-V agreement will continue to spread. If this is so, our analysis predicts that the diffusion will follow the cline represented in Figure 2 (on p. 15) in such a manner that if agreement becomes categorical it will affect first [+ specific][16] preverbal DOs and last [- specific] postverbal DOs.

Figure 2. Percentage of DO-V agreement along a scale of topicality of the DO.

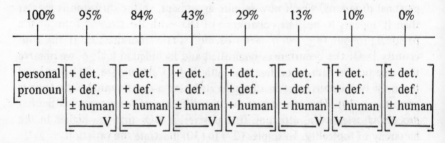

3 O-V agreement with IOs

The general properties of IOs have not changed through time: in MRS an

average of 94% are definite and human as compared to 90% in CSS, and an
average of 30% occur preverbally as compared to 43% in CSS. On the other
hand, while O-V agreement with IOs is grammaticalized in CSS, the situation
is far from being so in MRS. The variation is exemplified in (31) to (38):

> *Without a coreferential clitic*
> (31) *a mí dedes çient cavalleros*   (*Mio Cid*, verse 1129)
>   'give me one hundred knights'
>
> (32) *que esso mismo faré a ti*   (*Conde Lucanor*, p. 190)
>   'and the same (I) will do to you'
>
> (33) *que vendía las moças á los abades*   (*Celestina*, p. 160)
>   'who sold the young women to the abbots'
>
> (34) *pedi á Dios muchas vezes la muerte*   (*Lazarillo*, p. 178)
>   'many times (I) asked God to let me die'
>
> *With a coreferential clitic*
> (35) *a mí$_i$ non me$_i$ pesa, sabet, mucho me plaze*
>   (*Mio Cid*, verse 1480)
>   '(it) is not a nuisance to me$_i$, you know, (it) is much pleasing
>   to me'
>
> (36) *a mí$_i$ mucho me$_i$ plaze de la dar a vuestro fijo*
>   (*Conde Lucanor*, p. 189)
>   '(it) is much pleasing to me$_i$ to give her to your son'
>
> (37) *No le$_i$ dés parte de lo que passó a esse cauallero$_i$*
>   (*Celestina*, p. 189)
>   'Don't say what happened to that gentleman$_i$'
>
> (38) *Offressciendosele$_i$ á él$_i$ las gracias.*   (*Lazarillo*, p. 228)
>   'Giving him$_i$ thanks'

We observe that preverbal position favors the occurrence of the clitic in
all periods, and that from the 14th to the 16th c. there is a steady increase
in the percentage of coreferential clitics. This is particularly noticeable in the
pronominal group of IOs, which reaches 75% in the 16th century. This is
exactly what our hypothesis predicts: O-V agreement spread first to those
NPs that are higher in topicality, i.e. to pronominal IOs and to preverbal IOs,
and then to non-pronominal and to postverbal IOs.

Table 7. Percentage of O-V agreement with an IO in 12th, 14th, 15th, and 16th century written Spanish.

	Total	Preverbal IO		Postverbal IO		Nominal IO		Pronominal IO	
	le	*le*		*le*		*le*		*le*	
Mio Cid (12th c.)	28/100 28%	19/41	46%	9/59	15%	24/79	30%	4/21	19%
Conde Lucanor (14th c.)	6/35 17%	3/6		3/29	10%	2/26	8%	4/9	
Celestina (15th c.)	5/35 14%	3/12	25%	2/23	9%	3/5		2/5	
Lazarillo (16th c.)	16/77 21%	9/16	56%	7/61	11%	7/65	11%	9/12	75%

4 Conclusions

We have shown in this paper that a syntactic phenomenon which in CSS has become grammaticalized in certain environments and remains variable in others may be accounted for synchronically and diachronically within a flexible model that looks for explanations beyond autonomous syntax and the limit of the sentence. Thus, certain factors such as recency of reference in the discourse, animacy and definiteness, related to the likelihood of a given noun phrase to qualify as the topic of a sentence or a discourse passage, are shown to play a role in determining the occurrence of coreferential clitics. We have analyzed this phenomenon as a manifestation of O-V agreement in a process of diffusion which has spread first to NPs high in topicality and appears to be gradually extending to NPs which are lower in topicality,[17] i.e. to postverbal, non-human DOs (v. exs. 4,5).

A comparison with four other Romance languages, French, Italian, Portuguese and Rumanian, shows that O-V agreements is more common in Spanish.[18] All these languages allow verb agreement when the object is preverbal, as illustrated in the introduction, but the situation varies when the object is postverbal.

A clitic coreferential with a postverbal IO is possible in Italian and Rumanian but this agreement is not possible in Portuguese and French. Furthermore, Duranti and Ochs (1979) report that in Italian postverbal definite DOs may cooccur with a coreferential clitic pronoun, and the Rumanian Academy of the Language (1966) states that coreferential clitics are required with pronominal DOs and optional with postverbal definite human DOs. The facts related to the possibility of occurrence of O-V agreement in the Romance languages are summarized in Figure 3.

Figure 3. Possibilities of O-V agreement in five Romance languages. The symbol "+" means that O-V agreement is possible; the symbol "−" means that agreement is not possible.

	Preverbal object	Postverbal pronominal object	Postverbal IO	Postverbal definite human DO	Postverbal definite non-human DO
Spanish	+	+	+	+	+
Italian	+	+	+	+	−
Rumanian	+	+	+	+	−
French	+	−	−	−	−
Portuguese	+	−	−	−	−

Figure 3 shows that O-V agreement has spread to a larger number of contexts in Spanish, to include definite, non-human DOs. Note that across languages the diffusion of agreement follows a similar hierarchy of types of objects that tend to cooccur with a coreferential clitic pronoun to the one represented in Figure 2 for Spanish. It is likely, therefore, that the cline illustrated in Figure 2 is not language-specific but represents the direction that O-V agreement may follow in all the Romance languages.[19]

Notes

1. The data consist of recorded semi-directed conversations with 29 speakers from Santiago, Chile. The sample includes different ages and level of education (see note 4 below).
2. For the purposes of this paper, the pronominal category includes only personal pronouns (i.e. *mí, tí, él, ella, nosotros, ellos, ellas,* 'me, you, him, her, us, them'). DO personal pronouns are not included in the study of CSS because they always require a coreferential clitic.
3. The percentages of human and definite DOs correspond to a total number of 555 DOs counted in the data from two of the speakers only: R, m, 35, *A* and E, f, 34, *B* (see note 4 below).
4. Information about the speaker is presented within parentheses: first name initial, sex (f= female, m= male), age, level of education (*A*= 3 or fewer years of schooling; *B*=

more than 12 years of schooling). Examples with no information in parentheses are made up. A series of dashes (——) is used to indicate that some language material, irrelevant to the discussion, has been left out. A subscripted letter ($_i$) is used to mark coreferentiality between arguments. Subject pronouns that are not expressed in the Spanish examples are presented in parentheses in the English translations. A smooth English translation of the Spanish examples is given in each case.

5. *Lo* stands for any of the accusative clitic pronouns in Spanish. There is dialectal variation in the choice of the form for 3rd person but we are not concerned with this variation here. *Le* and *les* stand for the dative clitic pronouns *le*, *les*.

Person	Singular	Plural
1	*me*	*nos*
2	*te*	*os*
2 (formal) &		
3	*le, la*, fem.	*les, las*, fem.
	le, lo, masc.	*les, los*, masc.

6. See note 2.

7. The following decisions were made in the classification of nouns in one of the four groups:

   a. Proper nouns of animate reference were not included in the count. In spoken Chilean Spanish these nouns occur variably with a determiner and categorically trigger DO-V agreement when in topic position.

   b. Names of disciplines (e.g. medicine, chemistry, agronomy) and of products (e.g. Coca-Cola, Effortil, Tylenol) were classified in group 1 (– determiner, – definite) on the basis that they could have occurred with a determiner if they had, for instance, been mentioned before in the discourse. In this case, they would trigger verb agreement if in preverbal position.

   c. The noun *todo* ('everything') was classified as [+ definite] while *algo* and *nada* were classified as [– definite] on the basis that *todo* appears to have an implied definite determiner while *algo* and *nada* do not, as their paraphrases suggest:

$$todo \ = \ todas \ \begin{Bmatrix} las \\ * \emptyset \end{Bmatrix} cosas \quad \text{'all the things'}$$

$$algo \ = \ alguna \ \begin{Bmatrix} * la \\ \emptyset \end{Bmatrix} cosa \quad \text{'any thing'}$$

$$nada \ = \ ninguna \ \begin{Bmatrix} * la \\ \emptyset \end{Bmatrix} cosa \quad \text{'no thing'}$$

8. The Cantar de Mio Cid is believed to have been written for the first time around 1140. This study is based on the version prepared by R. Menéndez Pidal (see references) and includes the first 500 DOs in the Cantar, from verse 1 to verse 1615, and the first 100 IOs found from verse 1 to verse 1637.

9. El Conde Lucanor was written in the year 1335. We have used the edition introduced by José Manuel Blecua (see references) and have quantified the DOs in Exemplos 1 and 35, and the IOs in Exemplos 1, 35, 42, and 43.

10. La Celestina was written in the year 1499. The data for this study were selected from three parts of the book: the beginning, the middle and the end. Thus, we quantified the DOs from the following pages: 31–51, 60–70, and 153–162. The same pages were included for the selection of IOs, but due to their low frequency of occurrence, the count was continued up to page 229. The version used is introduced by Julio Cejador y Frauca.

11. La Vida de Lazarillo de Tormes was written in 1553. This study is based on the edi-

tion introduced by Julio Cejador y Frauca (see references) and includes the first 200 DOs, from pages 77–146, and the first 77 IOs, from pages 78–254.
12.When the number of cases is less than 10, no percentages are calculated.
13.In fact, according to the critics who introduce them, these works are latinized and learned, except perhaps Lazarillo, which is considered to be written in a less formal style. .
14. [+ recent] means that the DO has been referred to also in one of the preceding seven clauses.
15.In the sections of the works included in this study (see notes 8–11), we found 6 in Mio Cid, none in El Conde Lucanor, 3 in La Celestina, and 2 in Lazarillo.
16.See definition of specificity on p. 4.
17.We are not concerned here with the fact that DO-V agreement is not equally spread in all dialects of Spanish. What is of interest to us is the discussion of some of the principles of syntactic change and of a model of analysis that could account for both a synchronic system and the development of such a system.
18.Unfortunately, the data are not quite comparable since only the Spanish and Italian information is based on recordings of spontaneous or semi-directed conversations.
19.Duranti and Ochs (1979) offer evidence that supports this direction of the spreading in Italian.

References

Academia Republicii Socialiste România
  1966 *Gramatica limbii Romane* [Grammar of the Rumanian language], (Bucharest: Editura Republicii Socialiste România), Vol. I.
Barrenechea, A. M. – T. Orecchia
  1977 "La duplicación de objectos directos e indirectos en el español hablado en Buenos Aires" [The duplication of direct and indirect objects in the Spanish spoken in Buenos Aires], *Estudios sobre el español hablado en las principales ciudades de América* [Studies of the Spanish spoken in the main cities of America], edited by J. M. Lope Blanch (México: Universidad Nacional Autónoma de México), 351–381.
Bello, Andrés
  1925 *Gramática de la lengua castellana* [Grammar of the Castilian language], (París: Andrés Blot).
Bordelois, Ivonne
  1974 *The grammar of Spanish causative complements* (M.I.T., unpublished Ph.D. Dissertation).
Cedergren, Henrietta
  1973 *The interplay of social and linguistic factors in Panama* (Cornell, unpublished Ph.D. Dissertation).
Chafe, Wallace
  1976 "Givenness, contrastiveness, definiteness, subjects, topics and point of view", *Subject and topic*, edited by C. N. Li (New York: Academic Press), 25–56.
Contreras, Heles
  1976 *A theory of word order with special reference to Spanish* (North-Holland Linguistic Series 29) (Amsterdam: North-Holland).
Duranti, A. – E. Ochs
  1979 "Left-dislocation in Italian conversation", *Discourse and syntax*, edited by T. Givón (New York: Academic Press), 377–416.

Gili Gaya, Samuel
  1979   *Curso superior de sintaxis española* [Advanced course of Spanish syntax],
          (Barcelona: Biblograf).
Givón, Talmy
  1976   "Topic, pronoun, and grammatical agreement", *Subject and topic*, edited by
          C. N. Li (New York: Academic Press), 149–188.
Hatcher, Anna G.
  1956   "Theme and underlying question: two studies of Spanish word order",
          Word, Vol. 12, monograph No. 3.
Hawkinson, A. – L. Hyman
  1975   "Hierarchies of natural topic in Shona", *Studies in African Linguistics* 5:
          147–170.
Hyman, Larry – K. Zimmer
  1976   "Embedded topic in French", *Subject and topic*, edited by C. N. Li (New
          York: Academic Press), 189–212.
Klein, Flora
  1979   "Pragmatic and sociolinguistic bias in semantic change", paper presented at
          the IV International Congress of Historical Linguistics, Stanford University.
Labov, William
  1972   *Sociolinguistic patterns* (Philadelphia: University of Pennsylvania Press).
Li, Charles N. – S. Thompson
  1976   "Subject and topic: a new typology of language", *Subject and topic*, edited
          by C. N. Li (New York: Academic Press), 457–490.
Marcos Marín, Francisco
  1978   *Estudios sobre el pronombre* [Studies on the pronoun], (Madrid: Gredos).
Menéndez Pidal, Ramón
  1944   *Cantar de Mio Cid. Texto, gramática y vocabulario* [Song of Mio Cid. Text,
          grammar and vocabulary], (Madrid: Espasa Calpe) Vol. 1, 2, and 3.
Moravcsik, Edith
  1974   "Object-verb agreement", *Working Papers in Language Universals 15* (Stan-
          ford: Stanford University), 25–140.
Poplack, Shana
  1979   *Function and process in a variable phonology* (University of Pennsylvania,
          unpublished Ph.D. Dissertation).
Poston, Jr., Lawrence
  1953   "The redundant object pronoun in contemporary Spanish", *Hispania* 36:
          263–272.
Real Academia Española
  1973   *Esbozo de una nueva gramática de la lengua española* [Preliminaries to a new
          grammar of the Spanish language], (Madrid: Espasa-Calpe).
Roldán, Mercedes
  1971   "The double object constructions of Spanish", *Language Sciences* 15: 8–14.
Silva-Corvalán, Carmen
  1979   *An investigation of phonological and syntactic variation in spoken Chilean
          Spanish* (Los Angeles: University of California, unpublished Ph.D. Disserta-
          tion) (Ann Arbor: University Microfilms).
Wald, Benji
  1979   "The development of the Swahili object marker: a study of the interaction
          of syntax and discourse", *Discourse and syntax*, edited by T. Givón (New
          York: Academic Press), 505–524.

Literary works studied:

Cantar de Mio Cid
  1946   Edición Crítica de R. Menéndez Pidal (Madrid: Espasa-Calpe).

La Celestina
1972   Décima edición de Julio Cejador y Frauca (Madrid: Espasa-Calpe).
El Conde Lucanor
1971   Edición de José Manuel Blecua (España: Clásicos Castalia).
La vida de Lazarillo de Tormes
1914   Edición y notas de Julio Cejador y Frauca (Madrid: Ediciones de "La Lec-
tura").

ROBERT P. STOCKWELL

On the history of the verb-second rule in English

In historical phonology we talk about later reflexes of some earlier phoneme.
We may say that a certain phoneme has merely changed in its phonetic
manifestation, that it has been lost altogether by merger with something else,
that it has split into two or more phonemes at some stage, or that it still
exists in a different distribution. But we do not commonly talk about syntactic rules in these ways. As far as I know, I have never heard it said that the
SUBJ-AUX-INVERSION rule of Modern English is a reflex of a rule of Old
English called VERB-SECOND, the same rule that has been fully grammaticized in Modern Standard Dutch and German. There are some other V-2
constructions in Modern English which are *not* reflexes of that rule. They
appear to be innovations of a later date. It seems reasonable to me to talk
about the history of specific syntactic rules so long as we can identify some
property which the rule shares through time. A history of relativization in
English would concern itself with the different manifestations of relativization, a universal syntactic process, over the last 1200 years or so. Such a
history differs from the one I am here concerned with in that relativization
is necessarily present in a language and we only have to trace the differences
that its formal manifestation has undergone. A history of subject marking
would be of the same sort. Subjects are always marked in some way, but the
manifestation changes. But not all of syntax is of this sort: there are syntactic
types which *did* exist but do not now; and there are syntactic types which
come into existence out of altogether different earlier constructions. The rise
of the syntactic category MODAL AUXILIARY in the 16th century, following the Lightfoot (1979) scenario, is such a case. There were no syntactic
modals in Old English or Middle English. The creation of the new category
had far-reaching consequences throughout the grammar of English. There was
of course a *semantic* category of modality in Old English, expressed by main
verbs; but it is important to distinguish between the history of syntactic
codes and the semantic content of the codes.

The property that is constant through time in respect to the V-2 rule is
that the second constituent position of a main clause in declarative sentences

is, under definable contexts, restricted to the finite verb. What has changed through time is the set of contexts in which this restriction applies. V-2 is a totally language-specific rule, one which has no general semantic characterization of the type one might invent for relative clauses or subjecthood. In Late OE, I claim the rule characterized an optional norm, probably a rhetorical norm for the introduction of a new or surprising subject, and even more for 'heavy' subjects. I have speculated (Stockwell 1977) that it arose from Verb-First sentences introduced by a transitional adverb. In declarative main clauses of late OE prose, represented e.g. by the Homilies and Saints' Lives of Aelfric, the V-2 rule characterizes a word-order norm that is not fully grammaticized. By that, I mean that it is very common but not obligatory or fully categorical. The common violations of this norm in OE are of three types:

(i)   SUBJ-NP – PRO-OBJ – V – X
   (1)   Oswald him cōm tō. (St. Oswald, 11)
      Oswald him came to
      'Oswald came to him'
(ii) Absolute exceptions, about 10%
   (2)   Sē biscop þā ferde geond eall Norhymbraland. (St. Oswald 58)
      'The bishop then went throughout all Northumbria'
   (3)   Hwæt þā Oswold cyning his cynedome geheold hlīsfullice . . . (St. Oswald 120)
      Lo then Oswald King his kingdom held gloriously
      'Lo, then King Oswald ruled his kingdom gloriously'
(iii) Second Conjunct S
   (4)   and sē ādliga sōna on slǣpe wearþ gehǣled. (St. Oswald 30)
      and the sick (one) immediately in sleep became healed
      'And the sick man was straight away healed while sleeping'

The first class of exceptions is probably best explained as cliticization of the object pronoun in its earlier SOV order. The second class has no explanation except the hypothesis already stated that the V-2 rule was not fully grammaticized. The overwhelmingly dominant order of examples like (2) is

   (5)   þā ferde se biscop . .
      then went the bishop

Andrew (1934) speculates that *þā* in some exceptions like (3) was perhaps due to enclisis to the interjection, and unstressed, which would explain the non-inverted position of the verb on the hypothesis, which I think is correct, that only the stressed form of *þā* sufficed to fill first position and create what Andrew calls 'Demonstrative Order'. Demonstrative order refers simply to a proper subset of V-2 sentences, namely all of those in which the verb is second and the subject follows the verb. Andrew introduces some confusion into discussion of the V-2 rule by listing as examples of 'Neutral Order' the other proper subset of V-2 sentences, namely those in which the subject occupies first position immediately followed by the finite verb. If we keep track of this feature of his analysis, then Andrew's brilliant and to my mind much undervalued study fully confirms the view that OE prose was characterized by a word order norm that is best described by the V-2 rule. We have to accept Andrew's repunctuation of many crucial examples, but if we do, then his conclusion that a sentences like

(6) þā he ādrifen waes
     then he driven-away was

"is a solecism as incredible as the principle sentence 'da er fortgetrieben war' would be in modern German" (176) is, if not absolutely correct, at least correctly indicative of the direction in which OE prose style was moving. We have further confirmation of this direction in Bean's (1983) study, which correctly conflates the two types of V-2, and records V-2 as characterizing 70% to 80% of all main clauses after the earliest period. According to Bean, X S V O – the Modern English order – never was higher in prose than about 10% after the earliest period. It is only 2% in Wulfstan, as compared with 40% X V S, and 78% V-2 overall, which includes SVX. Aelfric, in the Preface to Genesis, has only 20% XVS (Andrew's Demonstrative order) but V-2 is 70% of the total of all main clauses.

The third class of exceptions is outside the domain where I claim the rule was nearly categorical, and though one might expect second conjuncts to behave like main clauses, it is a fact that they didn't. The facts are correctly characterized by Andrew (1934) as 'Conjunctive Order' under which he includes 'Subordinate Order'. Andrew calculates that in the Homilies on St. Cuthbert or St. Benedict the absolute exceptions, after repunctuating texts where the editors have assumed paratactic *þā* rather than hypotactic *þā*, come to only about one absolute exception in every thousand examples (173). Some of his proposed repunctuations have been challenged (e.g. by Hill, 1960). But even giving Hill the decision on the debatable cases, and raising the exception level to, say, 10%, I believe we have to agree that V-2 in OE was sufficiently frequent to be called a prose word order norm, characterizable by an optional rule. I shall henceforth speak of 'the V-2 rule' with the understanding that it was not fully grammaticized, as it is in German and

Dutch, but was apparently moving in that direction. The question is: what happened to it? To seek an answer, I turn now to Modern English.

In Georgia Green's effort to explain "Some Wherefores of English Inversions" (Green 1980), we find a splendid categorization of living V-2 examples in terms of pragmatic and functional parameters. She calls them all "inversions", resulting in surface X V S Y or X AUX S V Y. For the most part her examples also involve 'preposing' of some constituent to the front of the sentence. I prefer the term 'fronting' to 'preposing', since I include in the set of relevant examples such constructions as 'Neg-Fronting' and 'WH-fronting'. And though the term 'inversion' is perfectly suitable for the MnE examples, I will refer to these instances as 'V-2 placement', since it is clear that many of them are direct reflexes of the earlier V-2 rule. The formalism for stating the rule is of no great concern, in this context, but it deserves a word or two. Under the Chomskyan analysis in which *do* is supplied as a dummy carrier for tense, it is possible to state the V-2 rule as requiring Tense to move alone just in case it is followed by a main verb, but to carry forward the first Auxiliary with it otherwise. But it is neater to conceive of the *do*-forms as being present to serve as the moveable tense-marked constituent. The rule then has this simple form: 'Move into second position the tense marked constituent'. Without *do* in the base, the rule has a slightly more complex form: 'Into second position move Tense when followed by Main Verb, or move Tense + X where X is a single constituent not including Main Verb'. But of course the simpler formulation of the V-2 rule requires another rule or surface filter to delete *do* whenever at the end of a derivation the sequence *do* + MV turns up without stress (i.e. focus) on *do*. Nothing but the simplicity of rule formulation hinges on the choice between these alternatives.

To describe the relevant examples in MnE, then, we require two interacting rules, FRONTING and V-2. V-2 is obligatory with some frontings, optional with others, and disallowed with still others. Green, like me, is puzzled by these facts, though she notes that the inversion structures "may be semi-frozen relics of processes more productive in an earlier stage of the language" (598), and that the unevenness of applicability of V-2 "may have to be sought in a historical description rather than a synchronic one" (598). It is some insight into those historical sources that I shall seek to provide. I began looking for these long before I was aware of Green's interest in a functional explanation of the synchronic facts (Stockwell 1977), but I am pleased to have my task lightened by her excellent synchronic account, which I take to be as nearly correct as any functional account is likely to be.[1]

The V-2 rule is not triggered by a unified class of fronted constituents. And perhaps 'fronting' is not itself a single rule or a single class of constructions. Here are the classes of frontable constituents in relation to the V-2 rule:

I. Frontable constituents of a predicative content that trigger V-2 obligatorily:

1. Present Participle + $\begin{Bmatrix} \text{Complements} \\ \text{Modifiers} \end{Bmatrix}$ (i.e. all of Prog VP except *be*)

    (7) Sitting down is Kevin Jones. (Green 583)
    (8) *Sitting down Kevin Jones is.
    (9) Supporting merger were [A, B, C, and D]. (Green 586)
    (10) * Supporting merger A, B, C, and D were.
    (11) Developing offshore drilling in California are two Texas oil men.
    (12) *Developing offshore drilling in California two Texas oil men are.

2. Past Participle + $\begin{Bmatrix} \text{Complements} \\ \text{Modifiers} \end{Bmatrix}$ (i.e. all of Passive VP except *be*)

    (13) Scheduled to testify were representatives of A, B, and C. (Green 583)
    (14) *Scheduled to testify representatives of A, B, and C were.
    (15) Expected to draw considerable interest are the quilts made by women of the East Bend church. (597)
    (16) *Expected to draw considerable interest the quilts are.
    (17) Bought dear is the honey that is licked off the thorn.[2]
    (18) *Bought dear the honey is.

3. Adjective Phrase
    (19) Some of them are very beautiful, but most important are their fascinating detail and accuracy. (Green 596)
    (20) *...but most important their fascinating detail and accuracy are.[3]
    (21) ...but most important is their intricacy.
    (22) *...but most important their intricacy is.
    (23) Dead in the accident were the chauffeur and his passenger.[4]
    (24) *Dead in the accident the chauffeur and his passenger were.
    (25) Less known, save to students, is her husband. (Poutsma 406)

(26) *Less known, save to students, her husband is.

4. Predicative PP's (called 'Preposed Abstract Prepositional Phrases' by Green)

(27) At issue is Section 1401(a) of the Controlled Substances Act. (Green 586)

(28) *At issue Section 1401(a) of the Controlled Substances Act is.

(29) Under litigation are all the royalties paid out for Tetracycline.

(30) *Under litigation all the royalties paid out for Tetracycline are.

(31) To such straits was I reduced. (Sweet NEG 1871, quoted by Poutsma 406)

(32) ?*To such straits I was reduced.

II. Frontable constituents of a non-predicative content that trigger V-2 obligatorily:

1. Negative and Affective Adverbs

(33) Rarely have I encountered such beauty.

(34) *Rarely I have encountered such beauty.

(35) Only under special circumstances can you register for more than three courses.

(36) *Only under special circumstances you can register for more than three courses.[5]

2. WH-constituents:

(43) When can I leave?

(44) *When I can leave?

(45) Who did you know there?

(46) *Who you knew there?

3. Some Comparative markers

(47) No sooner was the door closed than the car leaped forward violently. (Green 597)

(48) *No sooner the door was closed than the car leaped forward violently.

(49) So little does that matter that if the verb is omitted no harm is done. (Green 597)

(50) *So little that matters that if the verb is omitted no harm is done.

III. Frontable constituents that trigger V-2 optionally

1. Directional Adverbs
   (51) Through the half-open windows drifted the mingled smell of wood smoke and freshmen. (Green 583)
   (52) Through the half-open windows the mingled smell of wood smoke and freshmen drifted.
   (53) Into the fray, fearless and snarling, dove the terrier.
   (54) Into the fray, fearless and snarling, the terrier dove.
   (55) Down the hill careened a wagon without brakes.
   (56) Down the hill a wagon careened without brakes.
   (57) Down the hill a wagon without brakes careened.

2. Locative Adverbs
   (58) Outside stood a little angel. (Green 596)
   (59) Outside a little angel stood.
   (60) On the third line above the second word in the manuscript appears a tiny smear.
   (61) On the third line above the second word in the manuscript a tiny smear appears.

3. Point Time Adverbs
   (62) In the year 1748 died one of the most powerful of the new masters of India. (Poutsma 397)
   (63) In the year 1748 one of the most powerful of the new masters of India died.
   (64) Soon after began the busy and important part of Swift's life. (Poutsma 397)
   (65) Soon after the busy and important part of Swift's life began.

4. Manner Adverbs
   (66) Most humbly do I take my leave. (Shakes. Ham. 1.3.83, in Poutsma 400)
   (67) Most humbly I (do) take my leave.
   (68) With very different impressions did the unfortunate lover regard the tidings. (Scott, in Poutsma 400)
   (69) ?*With very different impressions the unfortunate lover regarded the tidings.

5. Sequential Adverbs (very restricted verb selection)
   (70) Next came the middle-sized Billy Goat Gruff. (Green 583)
   (71) Next the middle-sized Billy Goat Gruff came.

(72)   Finally came the last day of school.
(73)   Finally the last day of school came.

6. Quotations

(74)   'We could have another fair,' suggested Arthur.
(75)   'We could have another fair,' Arthur suggested.

IV. Frontable constituents that disallow V-2

1. NP-fronting without copy *in situ*

(76)   Professors like him I can't stand to study with.
(77)   *Professors like him can't I stand to study with.
(78)   Terriers we have enough of; let's get a Chihuahua.
(79)   *Terriers have we enough of; let's get a Chihuahua.[6]

2. NP-fronting with copy *in situ*

(83)   People who eat that much garlic, I'd rather not be around them.
(84)   *People who eat that much garlic had I rather not be around them.
(85)   A hi-fi system as good as Dick's, you'd have to pay a fortune for it.
(86)   *A hi-fi system as good as Dick's have you to pay a fortune for it.

3. Bare Infinitives

(87)   Eat liver I'd rather not.
(88)   *Eat liver had/would I rather not.
(89)   Play the cello I wish that I could.
(90)   *Play the cello wish I that I could.

V. Some classes of V-2 not triggered by Fronting

1. Comparative Pro-Verb

(91)   I spend less than do nine out of ten people in my position. (Green 583)
(92)   I spend less than nine out of ten people in my position do.

2. *There*-insertion

(93)   There's a pen on the table.
(94)   A pen is on the table.
(95)   *There a pen is on the table.

3. *It*-insertion

(96)   It's obvious that he is wrong.

(97) That he is wrong is obvious.
(98) *It that he is wrong is obvious.

4. Rightward movement of heavy subjects
(99) All of a sudden was seen a thundering herd of angry elephants. (Richard Janda)
(100) In the distance appeared a light that gave hope of reaching civilization at last.

I've omitted none, have added four, and have merged only two types from Green's list. She claims "twenty-to-forty inversion structures" whereas I count seven obligatory, six optional, and a few unrelated to Fronting. Not that the numbers matter much.

The first question of interest is this: What, if anything, do classes I, II, and III share in contrast with IV? Except for WH-, all the members of I and II, the obligatory triggers, are predicative in a fairly clear sense. This claim might be argued to be false for II.1, the negative/affective adverbs, but I think it is no accident that sentential, clearly predicational, paraphrases exist (which have, indeed, sometimes been taken as underlying structures, and almost anyone's logic would set them up as superordinate propositions):

(101) It is rare that I have encountered such beauty.

(102) It is only under special circumstances that you can register for more than three courses.

On the other hand, the class IV frontings which disallow V-2 all apply to relation-bearing constituents of the main verb — subject, direct object, indirect object, infinitival complement. The class III triggers are not so clearly predicative, nor so clearly relation-bearing, and they go both ways optionally. The only example out of line with this distinction is the WH-constituent. The adverbial ones might be viewed as similar to class III. But the nominal ones fill argument places like any NP. I have to record them as an absolute exception to my preliminary generalization about the predicativity of fronted constituents that trigger V-2.

I turn now to Middle English to see what can be found in the course of the breakdown of the near-categoriality of the OE V-2 rule to give us some clue as to how predicativity comes to trigger V-2, and to determine which constructions are true fossils of OE V-2. Since there are at least 20 million words of ME text, it will be a while before my sampling can be deep enough to be secure, but here's how it looks now. My scenario for the loss of V-2 as a general rule is this:

(i) In late OE the rule represented an optional norm, probably a rhetorical norm for the introduction of a new or surprising subject. We have labeled it an ungrammaticized word order norm. Such a situation is commonly found in lexical and morphological norms. For instance, *as far as*: I can now document hundreds of examples like

(103) As far as complexity, I think inflation is in a class by itself.

This is a classical instance of Conjunction becoming Preposition, by dropping the predicate *is concerned*. It is common, but not yet a grammaticized norm. A similar case in MnE (American) is *gotta,* which is on its way to becoming the only modal predicate of necessity, to the exclusion of *must* and *hafta,* even in the epistemic reading:

(104) It's gotta be five o'clock by now.

Still another case of an ungrammaticized norm is the ϕ relative marker: Okay at all style levels for objects (*The boy ϕ I met*. . .), it is moving into wider use even for subjects, especially indefinites:

(104a) Anyone ϕ says I'm an idiot better be ready to fight.

(ii) Optional ungrammaticized norms can develop in three ways:

   a. They can become fully grammaticized, as V-2 did in Dutch and Standard German.
   b. They can become limited to narrow domains, fully grammaticized there.
   c. They can drop out of fashion altogether, usually being reanalyzed as something else and taking on a different function.

In English, both limiting and reanalysis occurred to V-2.

The primary reanalysis took the subject-first instances of V-2 as marking subjecthood: the position of NP before V was interpreted as subject-marking. Note that I did not say, 'NP in first-position was interpreted as subject-marking'. Basic SVO order is really XSVO, and subject-marking is a function of NP to the left of V-finite, not necessarily in first position, whereas V-2 necessarily entails only one constituent to the left of the finite verb.

The primary limiting came with initial negatives, affectives, and interrogatives, Class II. Throughout the history of English these have triggered V-2, and V-2 has become fully grammaticized in these environments, the only change being in the use of the auxiliary verb *do* to occupy that position when no other AUX is in the sentence. However, even this grammaticization was not absolute until some time after ME; in the Mercers' Petition of 1386 we find

(105) And not oonlich ushewed or hidde it hath be by man now, or before tyme the most profitable poyntes of trewe governaunce of the Citee. (Chambers and Daunt 35, lines 62–4)

Crucially, never in the history of English did V-2 serve to set off NP-topics, class IV, e.g. direct and indirect objects, as it does in Dutch and German. This topicalizing function simply did not exist commonly in OE (*pace* Vennemann). If it had, V-2 would probably have become grammaticized outside its limited domain.

(iii) The kind of predicative fronting with V-2 found in Class I is innovative some time after the ME period. It is found rarely if at all in OE, and very rarely in EME, increasing in frequency toward the end of the ME period.

(iv) The kind of predicative fronting with V-2 in Class III is common in OE and ME, but optional at all dates, as it is today.

To flesh out this history, we need empirical data to support the claims made above about what occurred when; and we need some move in the direction of explaining how Class I might have come into the language. My own speculation is that the Class I examples should really be thought of as equational sentences in which the new information in the equation is foregrounded, but still simply equational sentences. Most of the examples of these constructions cited here, and all of those cited by Green, except direct quotations, have the V-2nd *be*. This cannot be accidental. Consider what happens with other verbs which can occur in the domains appropriate to fronting:

(106)   Kevin Jones works sitting down.
(107)   *Sitting down works Kevin Jones.
(108)   A, B, C, and D left supporting the merger (but changed their minds).

(109) *Supporting the merger left A, B, C and D.
(110) Representatives of ABC came scheduled to testify.
(111) ?*Scheduled to testify came representatives of ABC.
(112) The quilts made by women of the East Bend church arrived, expected to draw considerable interest.
(113) *Expected to draw considerable interest, arrived the quilts made by women of the East Bend church.
(114) Their fascinating accuracy and detail seems most important.
(115) *Most important seems their fascinating accuracy and detail.
(116) A, B, C, and D turned up dead in the accident.
(117) *Dead in the accident turned up A, B, C, and D.
(118) All the royalties paid out for tetracycline continue under litigation.
(119) *Under litigation continue all the royalties paid out for tetracycline.

If *be* is present at all, the inversion is okay, because the verb with *be* as complement functions as a modality marker:

(120) At issue continue to be all the royalties paid out for tetracycline.
(121) Most important seems to be their fascinating accuracy and detail.

The Class I examples can be viewed simply as inverted equations, predicate-focused equations. The 'inversion' can be analyzed as flipping the subject and the predicate around the verb *be*, with *be* remaining untouched:

(122) Subj *be* Pred

or it can be derived by a sequence of two rules:

(123) (i) Subj *be* Pred (Canonical form)
       (ii) Pred Subj *be* (Fronting)
       (iii) Pred *be* Subj (V-2)

I will have a little more to say below about the question of whether the material after *be* is a single constituent. Clearly a single constituent is needed, though traditionally the predicate-minus-*be* is not taken as a single constituent in progressive and passive verb forms.

Unfortunately equational inversions are not entirely limited to *be*, though after mentioning them I shall ignore them:

(124) Blowing air furiously from his spout emerged the largest whale ever seen. (Richard Janda)

(125) Flanked by the royal guards entered the queen and her consort. (David Gil)

I can neither find nor construct examples with initial predicative expressions which do not have either *be* or a motion verb like *emerge, enter*; and as the examples with *leave, come,* and *arrive* above suggest, by no means can all motion verbs be twisted into grammaticality with fronted predicatives. The examples with *emerge, enter* are forced at best. Examples with *remain*, however, are quite good:

(126) Section 1401(a) of the Controlled Substances Act remains at issue.

(127) At issue remains Section 1401(a) of the Controlled Substances Act.

Remain acts like *be*; and like *be*, it must be inverted:

(128) *At issue Section 1401(a) of the Controlled Substances Act remains.

It appears, then, that the equational inversions of Class I may be viewed as convergence with the true V-2 fossils of Classes II and III. They are on the surface V-2 constructions, but not reflexes of the V-2 rule. I have no firm evidence yet about when this equational inversion comes into the language. The first clear ME example I have is from Lavynham's "Litil Tretys" of ca. 1380:

(129) Betere is a good name þan many rychessys. (van Zutphen 15.23)

From the Appeal of Thomas Usk, 1384, these examples of Class III.2, not of I.4:

(130) And ate euery conseyl was John More, Richard Norbury, & William Essex &, otherwhile, Adam Bame. (Chambers and Daunt 24.49)

(131) Also, atte thilk parlement was pursued a patent to the mair for to chastise vsurers. . . (Chambers and Daunt 26.104)

So far I have found no earlier examples of Class I in ME prose, nor have I found any in OE prose, though I'm reasonably confident that at least type I.3 must exist. Besides reading texts, I've checked the standard word order studies (see reference list below). I have no confidence in the negative state of this search at the moment, however. This is only an interim report. Of types II, III, and IV, there are of course numerous examples in any OE text — these represent the true V-2 norms of OE, type IV being the only one not surviving at all into MnE. In later ME, represented by the Sermons (Ross 1940), Świeczkowski (1962) cites two examples that can be analyzed as Class I.3:

> (132)   And therefore cursed is the child. (Ross 119, 37)
> (133)   Blynde was Adam when. . . (Ross 146 ,18)

This fronting is not obligatorily accompanied by V-2 in the Sermons, however:

> (134)   Defe he was when that he harde hym. (Ross 146.21)

Fronted objects (IV.1) are rare with V-2 but evidently still possible:

> (135)   Figure and ensampull of this goynge finde we in holy writte. (Ross 76.1)

The true V-2 types are vigorous in the Sermons:

> (136)   Than said Crist unto hym. (Ross 134.18)
> (137)   Than maketh God vs for to speke. (148.4)
> (138)   And so lese I my loue. (81.12)
> (139)   Here arn resceyved synners. (162.25)
> (140)   Therefore biddeth the prophete thise too together. (35.8)

Świeczkowski's hypothesis that "inversion takes place when a word of light semantic load stands at the beginning of the sentence" (1962:105) is in my opinion less explanatory than the assumption of V-2 fossilization. His own data is too heavily laden with counterexamples, like (135) above, to support his 'semantic weight' hypothesis, though there is no doubt that heavy subjects favor inversion in general. In his study of Piers Plowman, Świeczkowski points out several examples of Class I.3 — in fact they are common in Piers, but the fact that it is poetry, not prose, rules out any generalization about the sudden increase in frequency:

> (141)   Dredeles is Dobet. (A, XII, 191)
> (142)   Thus i-robed in russet romed I a-boute. (A, IX, 1)
> (143)   Worthi is the werkmon his hure to haus. (A. II. 91)
> (144)   Ne ryghte sori for my cynnes get was I neuere. (B, V, 406)
> (145)   Bygute was he neuere. (C, III, 144)

There are a very few examples of V-2 with topicalized direct objects, though the topicalized norm, vastly more frequent, is like MnE (NP NP V):

(146) The culorum of this clause kepe I not to schewe. (A. III. 264)

(147) And that seeth the saule. (C. II. 39)

(148) Al this saug I slepynge. (A. P. 109)

And of course the text is loaded with true V-2 reflexes of the OE type:

(149) Ther prechede a pardoner. (A. P. 65)

(150) Therinne wonieth a wighte. (B. I. 63)

(151) And thanne cam Coueytise. (B. V. 188)

(152) Thenne gon I meten a meruelous sweuene. (A. P. 11)

(153) In glotenye goth they to bedde. (C. I. 44)

Preliminary Conclusions:

A good deal of searching and counting remains to be done. But it seems clear that MnE has (i) surface V-2 constructions that are true reflexes of OE V-2; (ii) surface V-2 constructions that have been innovated and merged with true reflexes; and (iii) surface V-2 constructions that are not manifestations of V-2 except accidentally (e.g. Class V. 4).

It seems likely that the correct explanation of the innovated classes I. 1 – 2, the only ones that simply do not occur in OE or EME, is that past participles and present participles were at some point reanalyzed as Adjectives, i.e. as independent, predicative constituents, which would merge them with the earliest equational inversions (Classes I. 3 and I. 4) and bring them into line with this increasingly common fronting. I have yet to prove, however, that this reanalysis is the source of the innovation. I hope to be able to do so through research now in progress. The merger provides historical evidence that the grammar of EMnE, and perhaps of MnE, requires a node to dominate not only ADJ after *be* but also any verbal phrase preceded by *be*, since this is exactly the class of frontable constituents that trigger V-2. Both traditional and transformational grammars have taken the *be* of progressive and passive verb forms to be a different entity from the equational *be*, but it seems reasonable, on this evidence, to argue that there was a rule which reanalyzed progressive and passive constructions by moving progressive and passive *be* up into the Modal node, leaving the rest of the Predicate, whether it was Adjectival, Verbal, or Prepositional, as a separate constituent.

Notes

1. I don't mean to suggest any reservation about the correctness of her account in particular, only about functional, as distinct from historical, accounts in general. The problem with using a functional account to explain a historical change is that communicative functions, like the set of possible speech acts, must be presumed to be nearly constant through time. The functions may be served by different coding devices at different times, but one cannot safely assume that a function like maintaining topic continuity or highlighting new information was not served by some coding device at all times.

2. This example modified from "Dear is bought the honey that is licked off the thorn" (Poutsma 397). Poutsma argues that inversion "is hardly avoidable when the subject is qualified by an adnominal clause of some length", but as (18) shows, the inversion is obligatory whether the subject is short or long.

3. Again, contrary to the first conclusion one jumps to, the inversion is not a function of length; cf. (21).

4. Adapted from Green 586.

5. Although Poutsma (394) cites examples of non-inversion and claims that the V-2 rule 'is not so rigidly observed as we usually find it stated', I consider his examples to be violations of the norms of MnE: e.g.,
   (37) Never her sweet voice had sounded so exquisitely tender to him.
   (38) No sooner he comes into the cathedral, but a train of whispers runs buzzing round the congregation.
   (39) Never a serener saint had trod the ways of men.
   (40) Not once, but twice this performance took place.
   (41) Not seldom the process of mutual education has been to all appearance interrupted by the outbreak of hostilities.
   (42) Never a word he said. (Stevenson, *Kidnapped* 181).

6. The exceptions are clearly archaic:
   (80) Greater love hath no man than this . . . (John XV. 13).
   (81) The tongue can no man tame. (James III. 8).
   (82) Telescopes have they, and they see not; telephones have they, and they hear not. (Chesterton, in Poutsma 405).

References

Andrew, S. O.
  1934 "Some principles of Old English word-order", *Medium Aevum* 3: 167–88.
  1940 *Syntax and style in Old English* (Cambridge: C U P).
Barrett, Charles Robin
  1953 *Studies in the word-order of Aelfric's Catholic homilies and lives of the saints* (Cambridge University Press).
Bean, Marian C.
  1983 *The development of word-order patterns in relation to theories of word order change* (London and Canberra: Croom Helm).

Chambers, R. W. — Marjorie Daunt (eds.)
1931   *London English 1384–1425* (Oxford: Oxford University Press).
Dahlstedt, August
1903   *The Word-order of the Ancren Riwle* (Sundsvall: Rob. Sahlins).
Fries, Charles C.
1940   "On the development of the structural use of word-order in Modern English", *Language* 16:102–64.
Gardner, Faith F.
1971   *An analysis of syntactic patterns in Old English* (The Hague: Mouton).
Green, Georgia
1980   "Some wherefores of English inversions", *Language* 56:582–601.
Haiman, John
1974   *Targets and syntactic change* (The Hague: Mouton).
Heussler, F.
1888   *Die Stellung von Subjekt und Prädikat in den Erzählungen des Melibeus und des Pfarrers in Chaucer's Canterbury Tales* (Wesel).
Hill, L. A.
1960   "Diachronic study of word-order in the CCCC Ms A of the Anglo-Saxon Chronicle", *Zeitschrift für Phonetik und Allgemeine Sprachwissenschaft* 13:199–334.
Jacobsson, B.
1951   *Inversion in English with special reference to the Early Modern English period* (Uppsala: Almqvist and Wiksell).
Jansen, Frank (ed.)
1978   *Studies on fronting* (The Hague: Mouton).
Laeseke, B.
1917   *Ein Beitrag zur Stellung des Verbums im Orrmulum* (Berlin: Ebering).
Li, Charles (ed.)
1975   *Word order and word order change* (Austin: University of Texas Press).
1977   *Mechanisms of syntactic change* (Austin: University of Texas Press).
Lightfoot, David
1979   *Principles of diachronic syntax* (Cambridge: Cambridge University Press).
McKnight, G. H.
1897   "The primitive Teutonic order of words", *JGPh* 1:136–219.
Poutsma, H.
1928   *A grammar of Late Modern English*. Part I, First Half (Groningen: P. Noordhoff).
Reszkiewicz, Alfred
1962   *Main sentence elements in The Book of Margery Kempe* (Warsaw: Ossolineum).
1966   *Ordering of elements in Late Old English prose in terms of their size and structural complexity* (Warsaw: Ossolineum).
Ross, Woodburn O. (ed.)
1940   *Middle English sermons* (Oxford: Clarendon Press).
Rothstein, R.
1922   *Wortstellung in der Peterborough Chronicle* (Halle/S.: Niemeyer).
Shannon, Ann
1964   *A descriptive syntax of the Parker Manuscript of the Anglo-Saxon Chronicle from 734–891* (The Hague: Mouton).
Skeat, W. W. (ed.)
1886   *The vision of William concerning Piers the Plowman. In three parallel texts.* (Oxford: Clarendon Press).
Smith, C. A.
1893   "The order of words in Anglo-Saxon prose", *PMLA* 7:210–42.

Stockwell, Robert P.
1977   "Motivations for exbraciation in Old English", *Mechanisms of syntactic change*, edited by C. Li (Austin: University of Texas Press), 291–316.
Świeczkowski, Walerian
1962   *Word order patterning in Middle English* (The Hague: Mouton).
van Zutphen, J.P.W.M. (ed.)
1956   *Richard Lavynham's A Litil Tretys on the Seven Deadly Sins*. (Rome: Institutum Carmelitanum).

THEO VENNEMANN

Typology, universals and change of language

1. Invited to speak at the 1973 *Symposium on Typology* in Prague, I began my talk on "Language type and word order" with an apology. I said, "I
am not a typologist. I do not know much about typology. Furthermore,
while I can see the value of general statements about language, or language
universals, I am not at all sure if I understand what a typology is supposed to
achieve" (Vennemann 1974:219). Since then I have heard and read quite a
bit about typology, both in contemporary lectures and pronouncements such
as those of the Prague *Symposium* (published 1977 in Acta Universitatis Ca-
rolinae 1974), Sgall's 1979 introduction to Skalička's typological studies, and
Ineichen's 1979 survey, and in relevant passages of the classics such as August
Wilhelm Schlegel, Wilhelm von Humboldt, Nikolaus Finck, and Edward Sapir;
and I have even dabbled in typology myself, writing the word-order paper
mentioned as well as related articles, a chapter on language classification in a
book on the theory of language (Bartsch — Vennemann 1982) and a festschrift article "Isolation — Agglutination — Flexion" (1982). But I am
afraid matters have not improved much: I still have considerable problems
understanding precisely the nature of linguistic typology as others view it.
Things have not been made clearer, in my opinion, by recent attempts to
connect typology to — or in part identify it with — the study of linguistic
universals à la Greenberg, or global aspects of language change à la Lehmann.
On the contrary: It seems to me to be one of the few demonstrable things
about the concept of a typology of languages that if it is to have any value
at all, it has to remain completely distinct from both the study of linguistic
universals and the study of language change.

If this were a monograph on the nature of linguistic typology, I could
begin by wading through tons and tons of books and articles, quoting relevant passages of relevant authors and dissecting them one by one. Unfortunately, this is only a short paper, and not only about typology either. Therefore, I cannot even hope to begin quoting the authorities to the degree of
detail they deserve. I will, therefore, approach the subject matter from the
opposite end, tentatively developing my own questions and answers, and only

on a few occasions comparing them to views expressed in the literature. What I am really hoping for is that some merciful typologist, when hearing or reading this talk, will take pity on me and explain to me the true nature of typology.

2. I have fewer problems with universals than with typology. As I see them, they come in two varieties, belonging to two different parts of the theory of language, even though the dividing line may be hard to draw in individual cases. The first variety forms an important part of a general theory of language. It includes universals pertaining to language systems, universals of language use, and others (cf. Lieb 1978:77f., 183–186). Only universals pertaining to language systems – *grammatical universals*, as we may say for short – have played a role in the present context of discussion; so I will concentrate on this sort. The universals of this sort have the form 'for all L: $A(L)$', where L is a variable ranging over the set of all language systems, and A is a predicate – basic or defined, simple or complex – of the language of the theory of which these universals form a part. In particular, such a universal may be called 'implicational' if there exist predicates B and C of the same sort such that $A = \lambda x(B(x) \rightarrow C(x))$, which amounts to saying that implicational universals of this variety take the form 'for all L: if $B(L)$, then $C(L)$'.[1] Of course, B and C may themselves be complex predicates, $\lambda x(B_1(x)$ *and* $B_2(x)$ *and* . . . *and* $B_m(x))$ and $\lambda x(C_1(x)$ *or* $C_2(x)$ *or* . . . *or* $C_n(x))$, so that implicational universals of this variety may take forms such as 'for all L: if $B_1(L)$ and $B_2(L)$, then $C(L)$', and 'for all L: if $B(L)$, then $C_1(L)$ or $C_2(L)$', and 'for all L: if $B_1(L)$ and $B_2(L)$, then $C_1(L)$ or $C_2(L)$', etc.

Interesting examples of universals of this sort express empirical hypotheses about natural language systems, or are derived from such in the theory in which they occur. As the following examples show, such universals cannot meaningfully be stated outside an explicit general grammatical theory.[2] The lexicological part of a general grammatical theory may contain the axiom (or derived theorem) 'for all L: $\Lambda E \Xi (L)$ is finite'. Obviously this makes sense only in a theory in which a predicate $\lambda x (\Lambda E \Xi (x)$ is finite) is defined, i.e., a theory which specifies a function $\Lambda E \Xi$ ranging over the set of all language systems and whose language is rich enough to contain the mathematical predicate 'is finite' defined for sets. If $\Lambda E \Xi$ happens to be a function assigning every language system a set of items interpreted as stems, or paradigms, or words, or any of these plus idioms (in some standardized format), in short: lexical items, and if the idea is that $\Lambda E \Xi (L)$ is the totality of such items of L, so that $\Lambda E \Xi (L)$ may be understood as the lexicon of L, then the universal expresses that idea which may informally be worded as follows: 'the lexicon of every language system is finite'. Whether this hypothesis is true, or even plausible, depends on the theory as a whole; one cannot even begin testing it, or discussing it, unless one knows at least what is a language system in that theory, and how the theory relates lexical items to morphological regularities.

As a second example, consider Greenberg's universal No. 13: "If the nominal object always precedes the verb, then verb forms subordinate to the main verb also precede it" (Greenberg 1966:84). The context makes it clear that this is to be taken as a statement about all language systems, even though no quantified variable occurs in it. But then note how many predicates enter into the complex predicate predicated here of all language systems, all of which would have to be characterized in a comprehensive general grammatical theory before this universal would become a testable hypothesis: 'nominal', 'object' (or 'nominal object'), 'precedes', 'verb' (or 'the verb'), 'verb forms', 'subordinate', 'main verb'. I believe this to be easy in the case of 'precede', feasible in the case of 'subordinate'/'main (verb)', hopeful in the case of 'verb', impossible in the case of 'object' or 'nominal object'. ('Always' is, of course, simply a universal quantifier ranging over instances of the kind considered, as pointed out in Lewis 1975). Aside from such reservations, Greenberg's statement is a universal of the kind so far considered.

An example of a morphological universal of this kind is Greenberg's No. 26 (aside from the same kind of reservations): "If a language has discontinuous affixes, it always has either prefixing or suffixing or both" (Greenberg 1966:92). Examples of word-phonological universals occur in Vennemann 1979.

Clearly universals of this sort can only occur as part of a general grammatical theory.

The second variety of universals comprises what has been called 'generalization' (as opposed to 'universal'), 'near-universal', 'universal preference', 'unmarked case', 'natural case', and instances of 'more than chance frequency' that correlate with intuitive concepts of the preceding kind. As well-known examples, consider the 'universality' of place assimilation of nasals before obstruents; the universal preference for high-sonority speech sounds as syllable nuclei and for progressively increasing sonority in syllable onsets, progressively decreasing sonority in syllable offsets; the naturalness of basing the conceptually more complex form (such as the plural) on the conceptually less complex form (such as the singular), a universal morphological preference whose violation − e.g. as a consequence of sound change − may lead to rule inversion (cf. Vennemann 1972a, Mayerthaler 1981); "*Universal 17.* With overwhelmingly more than chance frequency, languages with dominant order VSO have the adjective after the noun" (Greenberg 1966:85). Such insights do not, in my opinion, belong to grammatical theory at all but should be accommodated in a separate theory, a theory of linguistic preferences including grammatical naturalness or markedness, as I have suggested for word-phonology some twelve years ago (cf. Vennemann 1972b) and would like to propose for all aspects of grammatical structure, or even languages in general, here. Such a theory would form the basis of, or actually be part of, a theory explaining why natural language is the way it is. As such it would naturally not be part of a general grammatical theory whose purpose it is to account for language systems the way they are (or: to describe language systems to the extent they share linguistic properties). Rather, such a theory would *presuppose* a general grammatical theory but nevertheless be a theory in its own right.

3. It seems to me that every linguistic typology has something to do, how-ever remotely or indirectly, with the goal of classifying languages or, put less sharply, arranging languages in some orderly system based on certain gram-matical properties. (Systems based on language use are not excluded in prin-ciple but have not in practice been proposed, as noted earlier.) Assuming that this is, in fact, true, it follows immediately that typologies cannot have any-thing to do with universals of the first variety discussed in section 2, because these hypothesize properties possessed by all languages and thus cannot possi-bly be made the basis of divisions, or distinctions, among languages. One may, of course, choose grammatical properties of languages as a basis for a typolo-gy in such a way that they are, or permit the derivation of, antecedents of implicational universals; in this case languages having the antecedent proper-ties will by necessity also have the consequent properties, unless a universal is false. This is trivial; it is merely a matter of the methodology of typologizing but is otherwise extrinsic to the resulting typology, which is still based on the antecedent properties (or those implying them). Since implicational univer-sals of this variety, as well as the linguistic predicates occurring in them, are nothing but parts of a general grammatical theory, maintaining a relationship between typologies and universals of language conceived along these lines amounts to no more than the position that a linguistic typology presupposes a general grammatical theory — a position which I am very happy to accept.

Skalička bases his typology not on properties that stand in an implicational relationship — this would be useless anyway because it would amount to nothing more than basing it on the antecedent properties alone — but rather on bundles of properties that stand in a 'favoring' relationship. Whether these favoring relationships are conceived of as essentially symmetric, as seems to be true of Skalička himself, or as essentially asymmetric (cf. Sgall 1979:8), they all seem to belong to the domain of linguistic preference, or naturalness or markedness: Types are characterized by bundles of preferentially (or natu-rally) cooccurring properties.[3] If this is so, then a linguistic typology of this sort presupposes a theory of linguistic preference (naturalness, markedness, etc.) as well as, by implication, a general grammatical theory.

In either case, linguistic typologies are not parts of the respective linguistic theories. Both a general grammatical theory and a theory of linguistic preference (naturalness, markedness, etc.) are formulated withoud any reference to typological concepts — or, at least, they can be, and in my opinion they should be, as they have nothing to gain from such an association. The converse is not true. Therefore, linguistic typologies, if conceived in agreement with the introductory remarks of this section, are applications of certain linguistic theories. As applications, they must be developed for some specific purpose. What precisely is this purpose?

4. As a succinct characterization of the goals of linguistic typology, let us consider the following quotation taken from a monograph on typology (Altmann — Lehfeldt 1973:15):

> Unter den Zielen einer *allgemeinen Sprachtypologie* werden wir im folgenden nur zwei Probleme verstehen:
> a) die *Sprachklassifikation*, d.h. den Aufbau eines Ordnungssystems für die natürlichen Sprachen aufgrund ihrer globalen Ähnlichkeit;
> b) die *Aufdeckung des Konstruktionsmechanismus* der Sprachen, d.h. den Aufbau eines Beziehungssystems, eines "Netzes", an dem man nicht allein die offensichtlichen, kategorischen, sondern auch die latenten Mechanismen der Sprache ablesen kann.

In order to understand these goals, one has to look at some other concepts and assumptions the authors use. They distinguish *partial typologies* (Teiltypologien, 1973:14) from the *general typology of languages* (die allgemeine Sprachtypologie). Partial typologies are based on one or a few properties of languages; they result in what they call *monothetic classifications* (1973:14f., 27). The general typology of languages, by contrast, is not based on one or a few selected properties but on as many properties as one can possibly get a hold of ("so viele Merkmale . . . , wie sich nur irgendwie erfassen lassen", 1973:26), or even all properties, if possible ("möglichst alle Merkmale sind zu berücksichtigen", 1973:29); this procedure leads to a *polythetic classification*. Altmann and Lehfeldt believe that the general typology of languages, conceived in this way, solves both of the cited goals (1973: 15). I will argue here that it solves neither because the idea of a general typology of this sort — the general typology of languages — is untenable.

How many properties that languages may or may not have are there? It should be obvious that there is no limit to the set of such properties, even if we restrict it to such properties that are linguistically relevant, or even grammatical. If Altmann and Lehfeldt wanted to begin their imagined task by listing 'as many properties as one can possibly get hold of', or even 'all properties', they would never come to an end with this, nor would they ever have time to attack their problems, or goals, (a) and (b).

But let us now look at these goals. First (a), the *classification of languages*. What is to be the purpose of such a classification if it is based on as many properties as one can possibly get hold of? What do the authors want to learn from it, or what theoretical or practical problem do they want to solve with it? That remains in the dark. The only purpose that I can see would be the preparation of an attack on problem, or goal, (b); but in this case (a) would not itself be a goal but only a means toward solving (b).

But what about (b), the *discovery of the construction mechanism* of languages? If I understand this at all, it must mean that a general typology of languages of the kind suggested by the authors – or, more likely, a classification of the languages of the world based on it – leads to a theory about the structure of languages. This idea is erroneous, for two reasons. First, the authors seem to believe that their method of classification automatically leads to insights into the grammatical structure of language, or to a theory of language systems. But there is nothing to warrant this idea, either in linguistics or, analogously, in any other science. Secondly, the entire imagined procedure is circular. What is and what is not a property of a certain language system is only determined within a theory of that language system (i.e. a grammar of that language system). What is and what is not a property such that we can decide whether it applies to any given language system is only determined within a general grammatical theory. In other words, a general typology of languages already presupposes that which the authors hope to discover with its help. Now, if they objected to this argument that the work does not have to begin from scratch, that certain 'construction mechanisms' are already known, and that the task is merely to find more, then I would reply that even for this revised job the proper answer is not a general typology, for even in the search for additional 'construction mechanisms' linguists do not look blindfolded, so to speak, but guided by more or less precise hunches, conjectures, hypotheses. To test a conjecture, however, one does not need a general typology but rather research into the distribution of just those properties the conjecture is about – in other words: at most a partial typology based on those selected properties, i.e. just that type of typology looked down upon by the authors. Therefore, a general typology of languages cannot serve as a heuristics for grammatical theory either. In short, I believe this idea of a general typology of languages to be nothing but a chimera, an outgrowth of metaphysical yearning. The metaphysical spirit in which the idea of a general typology of languages has been conceived and can thrive is also evident from the following quotation:

[Es] bleibt . . . das Hauptziel der Typologie, die *Zusammenhänge* zwischen den Sprachphänomenen zu erforschen (Skalička), alle latenten Mechanismen der Sprache, alle verborgenen und unterschwelligen Kräfte, die in der Sprache wirken, aufzudecken, m.a.W., die ganze Dynamik der Sprache, die sich mit den deterministischen Methoden der beschreibenden Linguistik allein nicht erfassen läßt (Altmann – Lehfeldt 1973: 15).

I do not know what the authors mean by 'deterministic methods' and descriptive linguistics', but if they are trying to suggest that the general typology of languages is outside the scope of linguistics, so be it.

5. What kinds of typologies of languages can there be? First of all, let me conclude from the preceding section that all reasonable typologies of languages are partial typologies, in the sense specified there; so we do not have to call them *partial*. All linguistic typologies of languages are based on a limited set of linguistically relevant properties of languages.

Now let us return to the question of the purposes of such typologies. Here I find it useful to begin with a traditional distinction usually associated with the typological ideas of A. W. Schlegel and W. von Humboldt, respectively: that between *classificatory typologies* and *ideal typologies* of languages.

The purpose of a *classificatory typology* of languages is a classification of all the natural languages of the world by means of a fixed set of linguistic, say: grammatical predicates. Which predicates does one choose for a classificatory typology? There is only one answer to this question: It depends on the purpose of the classification. One reasonable purpose is to discover the relative frequency of the cooccurrence of two properties. Another may be to discover correlations between grammatical properties of languages and properties of their users or their environment, e.g. cultural development (Jespersen!), race, climate, social origin, economic system (Marr!), and others. It is a necessary condition on classificatory typologies that they divide the totality of natural languages – or rather: language varieties, because the varieties of a language may be of different type – uniquely into disjoint non-empty classes; mathematically speaking: The set of types constituting a classificatory typology has to be a partition of the set of all natural language varieties. Here are two examples of classificatory typologies. (1) Let P be the predicate 'is consistently prespecifying' (= 'is a consistent XV language'). Then P divides the set Z of all language varieties into two sets M and M' such that M is the set of all members S of Z such that $P(S)$ is true, and M' is the set of all members S of Z such that $P(S)$ is false. $\{M, M'\}$ is a classificatory typology, as it is based on a set of grammatical predicates, $\{P\}$, and is a partition of Z. (2) Let P be as in (1), and let Q be the predicate 'permits only CV syllables'. Let M_1 be the set of all members S of Z such that $P(S)$ and $Q(S)$ are both true, M_2 the set of all members S of Z such that $P(S)$ is true and $Q(S)$ is false, M_3 the set of all members S of Z such that $P(S)$ is false and $Q(S)$ is true, and M_4 the set of all members of Z such that $P(S)$ and $Q(S)$ are both false. Assuming that the sets so defined are all non-empty, $\{M_1, M_2, M_3, M_4\}$ is a classificatory typology based on $\{P, Q\}$. (English varieties would all be members of M_4).

The purpose of an *ideal typology* of languages is the characterization of a fixed number of ideal linguistic types. An ideal type is represented as a set T of linguistic, say: grammatical predicates. This set may be such that there are language varieties S such that for every predicate P of T, $P(S)$ is true; but there need not be any such varieties. Let $\mathcal{T}$ be the set of ideal types defined by an ideal typology. Then it is a necessary condition that $\mathcal{T}$ be finite. (In fact, the number of elements of $\mathcal{T}$ is usually quite small, all the way down to two.) Let, for every T of $\mathcal{T}$, $\Sigma(T)$ be the set of all language varieties S such that for all predicates P of T, $P(S)$ is true. Then it is a necessary condition that there be at least one language variety S such that there is no T in $\mathcal{T}$ such that S is in $\Sigma(T)$. Indeed; for without this condition being fulfilled the typology would become classificatory. In general, ideal typologies are such that a great number of language varieties, or even all of them, are not 'ideal' according to the typology.[4] The following is a maximally simple, yet non-fictitious example: Let P be the predicate 'is consistently prespecifying' (= 'is a consistent XV language'), and let P' be the predicate 'is consistently postspecifying' (= 'is a consistent VX language'). Then $\{\{P\}, \{P'\}\}$ is a set of ideal types (and thus is, or constitutes, an ideal typology). Note that the two necessary conditions given are both fulfilled: The set of ideal types is finite, and there are language varieties S for which there are no ideal types T such that for all predicates Q of T, $Q(S)$ is true, e.g. all varieties of English. For let E be any variety of English (and there are some, of course). Then: $P(E)$ is false, and $P'(E)$ is also false.

What is the purpose of an ideal typology? My answer is: a purely practical one. To the extent that the ideal types are common knowledge, they allow linguists to briefly characterize any language variety S by locutions such as: S is like ideal type T of $\mathcal{T}$ except for ... . E.g., with reference to the above non-fictitious ideal typology $\{\{P\}, \{P'\}\}$: RP English is like $\{P'\}$, except that the nominative precedes the verb, simple adjectives precede the noun, grade adverbs precede the adjective, ... Ideal typologies are thus like Daniel Jones' system of cardinal vowels: They have a purely orientative function.

Graduating typologies, which at advanced levels of development may be *numerical*, share features with both ideal and classificatory typologies. W. von Humboldt's typology is ideal in that there are language varieties that are neither purely agglutinative nor purely flexional nor purely isolating nor purely incorporating (assuming that these properties have been defined by sets of predicates taken from a general grammatical theory — a contrary-to-fact assumption, but harmless for our discussion). However, one can imagine scales of agglutinativeness etc., on which languages may be ranked as more or less agglutinative etc., or be assigned a numerical agglutination value etc. One can see that such values, or ranges of values, could be made the basis of a classificatory typology. This is why I said that graduating (numerical) typologies share features with both other types of typologies.

What is the purpose of a graduating typology? The only purpose that I can see is the refinement of a given ideal typology: Instead of saying something like 'language variety S is somewhat like ideal type T of the ideal typology $\mathcal{T}$', given a graduating typology $\mathcal{G}$ associated with $\mathcal{T}$ one may be able to say 'S is more similar to T than S_1, but less so than S_2'. And if $\mathcal{G}$ is numerical, one may be able to say 'S has a distance d from T (d_1 from T_1, d_2 from T_2, etc.)'. One may object that there are other purposes of numerical scales than the measuring of distances from ideal types. I agree. But then I am trying to make sense of the notion of a numerical typology, not of numerical linguistics in general.

6. Is a typology of languages a theory? Is it a part of the theory of language? It should be evident by now that my answer to this question is no. Linguistic typology, as a discipline, is a part of applied theoretical linguistics. Applied theoretical linguistics applies (parts of) theories of language but — by definition — does not produce any.

Since typologies of languages are not theories, they cannot either be true or false but have to be evaluated by different criteria, criteria applicable to their specific purpose, e.g. 'useful', 'adequate', 'revealing'. The error of confusing typologies with theories is committed in Hawkins 1980. Hawkins refers to the ideal word order typology $\{\{P\}, \{P'\}\}$ cited in the preceding section and says, "Vennemann thus defines his two language types abstractly" (1980:198), which I take to mean that the typology is an ideal typology, especially since Hawkins continues, "He notes that not all languages are fully consistent with his schema, and hypothesizes that this is for historical reasons". Hawkins goes on to present some figures from Greenberg 1966 which show that quite a number of languages are not ideal according to this typology, and concludes still on the same page: "To have over 50 per cent counterexamples is unpalatable for any theory, even one which proposes a historical explanation for synchronic exceptions". Hawkins is free to believe to have shown all kinds of defects of the ideal typology under discussion: e.g., that it does not do the kinds of things Hawkins expects a typology to do, viz. that it "makes no predictions concerning the relative sizes of the other attested co-occurrence types" (1980:200), and that it should be replaced by a different one. But believing to have falsified it is committing a logical error: Ideal typologies are not the type of objects that can be falsified.[5]

While typologies are not theories, or parts of theories, they do presuppose theories, as I have noted in section 4. Typologies cannot be better than the theories they are based on. It follows from this that doing typology is not an alternative to doing theory of language, an alternative way of getting insights into the nature of languages. Typologies are not the type of objects that express insights into the nature of languages. This would be the job of theories, and typologies are not theories.

I will show with two examples the extent to which typologies depend on theories. As a first example, consider the following pet parameter of numerical typologists: degree of syntheticness, defined as average number of morpheme occurrences per word (whether across the lexicon or in running text — type or token — makes no difference for my discussion). This looks like a perfectly clear criterion, yet it is completely meaningless without a theory telling us what words are and what morphemes are. These terms cannot be defined in the vernacular language, just as the equally troublesome concept of a sentence, but only in a general grammatical theory, as Bierwisch (1962) has convincingly argued especially with reference to the morpheme. Consider the singular/plural pairs *cow/cows, mouse/mice, sheep/sheep*. What is the average number of morpheme occurrences in this sample? Let us assume that the singulars are all monomorphematic (an assumption to which some morphologists would undoubtedly object, claiming that a singular form consists of a stem morpheme and a singular morpheme, of which the latter happens to be zero). Let us further assume that *cows* is dimorphematic, consisting of a stem morpheme (or the singular morpheme?) plus (an allomorph of) a plural morpheme (or *the* plural morpheme). What about *mice*? Here some morphologists would say that *mice* is an allomorph of *mouse* and thus monomorphematic, while others would claim that it contains *mouse* plus an allomorph of a plural morpheme. The former group would most likely consider the plural *sheep* monomorphematic as well, but the latter could again be divided into those analyzing *sheep* as dimorphematic on the analogy of *cows* and *mice*, and those analyzing it as monomorphematic on the grounds that the plural is not formally distinct from the singular. So here we have three different degrees of syntheticness for a short corpus of six words (*only* three because we disregarded some theoretical possibilities at the beginning): 9/6,

8/6, and 7/6, i.e. – for those who like decimals better – 1.5, 1.33 ... , 1.166 ... . Of course, one can also assume a general grammatical theory that does not split words into morphemes at all (I happen to be rather sympathetic to such a theory). In this case there would not be any degree of syntheticness definable as average number of morpheme occurrences per word at all, and thus no typology based on it.

As a second example, consider once again the ideal word order typology $\{\{P\}, \{P'\}\}$, where P is the predicate 'is consistently prespecifying' (= 'is a consistent XV language'), and P' is the predicate 'is consistently postspecifying' (= 'is a consistent VX language'). I said in section 5 that, if E is a variety of English, say: of RP English, then $P(E)$ and $P'(E)$ are both false. But how can we know? The answer is that we can't unless we have a theory telling us what these predicates mean. Since the 'pre-' and 'post-' part is easy, what is needed is a theory of specification, i.e. a theory telling us for any given asymmetrical syntactic construction which part is specifier (operator, qualifier, modifier etc.) and which part is specified (operand, head, etc.). The closest thing to such a theory is that developed in Vennemann 1976b, Vennemann and Harlow 1977, with comparisons drawn to other theories, e.g. Leonard Bloomfield's and Lucien Tesnière's, in Vennemann 1977. This theory defines specification relative to a given categorial grammar of the language under study. Assume that α, of category h, and β, of category k, enter into an asymmetrical construction. If $h = k/k$, then α is an *attribute* of β; and if $k = g/h$ for some category g different from h, then α is a *complement* of β. In either case α is a *specifier* of β, and β is the *head* of the construction. This is a completely general and language-independent definition; but unfortunately it is dependent on the syntactic categorization of the expressions of a language in a given categorial grammar. I will give two examples of differences in categorization leading to differences in specification.

(1) Kasimir Ajdukiewicz assumed only two basic categories: s for sentences, and n for nouns (or nominals). Thus articles had to be categorized as taking nouns and yielding nouns:

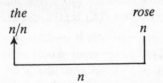

According to this categorial grammar, *articles are specifiers*, viz. attributes. David Lewis assumed three basic categories: s for sentences, n for noun phrases (terms), and c for common nouns. In one of the two analyses Lewis gives, the example would receive the following interpretation:

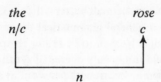

According to this categorial grammar, *articles are heads*, taking nouns as complements.

(2) In fragments of categorial syntaxes in the papers mentioned (where also references to the other authors cited may be found), noun phrases are categorized as *n* and intransitive verbs as *s/n*, e.g.:

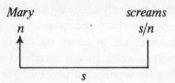

Thus, noun phrases in construction with intransitive verbs (i.e., nominatives, in English) are specifiers, viz. complements, of the verb; and since this is precisely the definition of 'subject' in this theory (cf. Vennemann and Harlow 1977:245), subjects are specifiers of their verbs, according to this theory.[6] However, many linguists following the lead of Richard Montague assume subject noun phrases to be of category *s/(s/n)*:

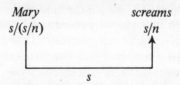

According to this categorization, subjects are heads, taking intransitive verbs as specifiers.— Since in the theory of the three papers mentioned noun phrases are categorized as *n*, and transitive verbs as *(s/n)/n*, the following graphic, properly interpreted, *proves* at once that *P(E)* is false and that *P'(E)* is false, *relative to that theory*:

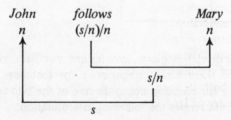

The analogous proof would not work relative to a theory in which noun phrases are categorized as $s/(s/n)$ and transitive verbs as $(s/n)/(s/(s/n))$:

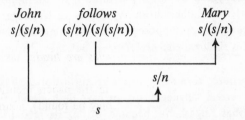

John $\quad$ follows $\qquad$ Mary
$s/(s/n)\quad (s/n)/(s/(s/n))\qquad s/(s/n)$

s/n

s

This analysis would be compatible with $P'(E)$. I happen to believe that this theory is false. I also happen to believe that the alternative theory is false, though in a less damaging way. I believe that the truth – i.e., a better theory – lies somewhere in the direction of my Japanese fragment (Vennemann 1976b: 627–630), but will not say more about it until I have worked it out.[7]

These examples should suffice to show that there can be no effective typologies without detailed and explicit (partial) theories of language. The converse is not true: Theories of language in no way depend on typologies of languages. In particular, theories of language do not contain typological concepts. If someone thinks this is not so, he can be certain to be confusing the study of typology with the study of universals.[8]

7. What is the relationship between a typology of languages and a theory of language change? My answer to this question should by now be obvious.

A theory of language change is a part of a general theory of language, though, of course, not of a general grammatical theory. Typologies are not parts of general theories of language but applications of parts of such theories. So there is no connection. The distinction is even clearer than in the case of general grammatical theories (or general theories of language use; let us say: general synchronic theories of language): Whereas a typology of languages at least presupposes a general synchronic theory of language, the same is not true with regard to general theories of language change. Typologies of languages do not presuppose theories of language change. The converse also holds: Theories of language change do not presuppose typologies of languages. Both of these statements are to be understood both in a methodological and in a heuristic sense: Typologies do not even have a heuristic function in the study of language change. Where things appear to be different, again one can be certain that the study of typologies and the study of universals are being confused, 'universals' in both of the senses explicated in section 2. Needless to say that a general theory of language change presupposes both a general synchronic theory of language and a general theory of linguistic preferences. But as we have seen earlier these do not presuppose typologies of languages but are themselves presupposed by them. So there is no presuppositional relationship by transitivity. Rather, both typologies of languages and general theories of language change presuppose general synchronic theories of language and general theories of linguistic preferences; but they do not presuppose each other.

What about locutions, abounding in the recent historical linguistic literature, such as that certain languages are, or have been, developing toward a certain type, e.g., that English has become, during its recorded history, an ever more consistent *SVO* language? In my opinion such statements have a purely orientative value; they illustrate once more the orientative function of typologies stressed in section 5. In particular, such statements have in my opinion no explanatory value whatsoever. Nothing is said by them about the individual steps taken by the language in its development, nor about their motivation. The explanation (or, more modestly: the plausibilification) still has to be given for every single step in the development, and therefore the global statement itself does not form a part of the actual account.

Why then do so many linguists believe that typology plays – or should play – a role in the theory of language change? The reason is simple enough: Ideal typologies implicitly or explicitly involve the notion of 'preferred (natural, unmarked, ...) linguistic states of affairs'. E.g., the idea behind the *OV/ VO* typology or its refined version, $\{\{P\}, \{P'\}\}$ of section 5,[9] is that everything else being equal, unidirectional serialization of constituents in the specifying relation is preferred to (more natural than, less marked than, ...) non-unidirectional serialization.[10] Language change likewise very frequently involves the notion of 'preferred (natural, unmarked, ...) linguistic states of affairs' inasmuch as certain recurring kinds of change may be interpreted as transitions from less to more preferred linguistic states of affairs. To the extent that such transitions increase the cooccurrence of properties that define an ideal type of some typology, they are liable to be interpreted as changes in the direction of that type; from there it is only a small step to the understanding that such changes are 'typologically motivated'. But this is, of course, a *non sequitur*.[11] – In short, theories of language change and ideal typologies, at least as they are presently understood, both involve the notion of 'preferred linguistic states of affairs' and therefore both presuppose a theory of linguistic preferences; but they do not presuppose each other.

What is the function of linguistic typologies in linguistic reconstruction? Here linguists say things such as that Proto-Indo-European was a *VSO* language (Greenberg's type I'), an *SVO* language ('type II'), or an *SOV* language ('type III'), with or without certain deviations from consistency within the alleged type. The purely orientative function of such typological characterizations seems to be most obvious.[12] A characterization of the reconstructed word order in purely syntactic terms, without reference to typologies, is, of course, possible and is in fact required. The typological labels merely serve as a shorthand, but have no theoretical or methodological significance. Also the idea that 'reconstructed languages have to be typologically possible' does not alter this relation between typologies and reconstruction. It is, as a matter of fact, a nonsensical idea. What is meant is that 'reconstructed languages have to be possible languages'; and what is and what is not a possible language is not expressed in typologies but in theories of language – this is indeed the one and only purpose of a general theory of language.

8. The words 'typology', 'typological', 'language type', etc. have become very popular and fashionable in our days, especially by association with other favorable epithets such as 'universals' and 'types of language change'. There is hardly a book or article on universals or language change anymore without 'typological' epithets applied in them as ornaments. In my opinion this behavior rests on a conceptual confusion. Typology is nothing grand or distinguishing. Typologies are not theories or alternatives to theories. The field of linguistic typology, as I see it, is nothing but a branch of applied theoretical linguistics. – I am happily looking forward to being taught by typologists that I am wrong.

Notes

1. Cf. van den Boom 1980 for an analysis of this special kind of universals.
2. Lieb (1978:176) relativizes universals to persons during periods of time: "A property F is universal in language relative to a person during a certain time, if that person during that time requires that F should be attributed to all languages by any theory of language". In my opinion universal properties are attributed to languages not by persons during a period of time but by theories of language. Of course, a relativization to persons during periods of time is implicit in my view inasmuch as theories of language are entertained by persons during periods of time. Thus, if a person during a certain period of time entertains a certain theory of language attributing a property F to all languages, he will naturally require during that period of time that F should be attributed to all languages by *any* theory of language – at least by any theory of language aiming to meet the same standards of correctness and completeness.
3. "Ein weiterer Stützpunkt unserer Theorie ist die Existenz eines Typus als eines Bündels von aufeinander abgestimmten Erscheinungen" (Skalička 1979:335). Literally this defines a language type as 'a bundle of phenomena tuned to each other', i.e., more succinctly, 'a bundle of harmonic properties'.
4. "Von den verschiedenen sprachtypologischen Konzeptionen wollen wir hier jene aufgreifen, die von selten oder nie realisierten Extremen ausgeht" (Skalička 1979: 335). Skalička calls these 'rarely or never realized extremes', i.e. the ideal types,

'typological constructs' (typologische Konstrukte). His typology consists of five typological constructs, each of them defined by a finite set of harmonic properties: (1) the agglutinative type, (2) the flective type, (3) the isolating type, (4) the polysynthetic type, and (5) the introflexive type. Skalička says, "Bekanntlich ist keine Sprache die Realisation eines einzigen Typs. Das wäre z.T. unmöglich oder mindestens unwahrscheinlich" (1979:341). We may conclude that in Skalička's view there is at least one language system such that no typological construct has the property that all of its defining properties apply to that system. Thus, Skalička's typology is conceived as an ideal typology as defined above. (Skalička himself employs the label 'deductive typology', for reasons that I do not recognize.)

5. Skalička calls his approach a theory (cf. the quotation in note 3 above), but it should be evident from my very brief and incomplete characterization that it is not. – In his discussion at the conference, Hénning Andersen has pointed out that in Coseriu's view of languages, typology becomes a part of the theory of language. Yes indeed. But then I do not understand this view, even after pondering such seemingly very clear and poignant passages as the following (Coseriu 1979:83f.):

Innerhalb der technischen Verfahren, die eine Sprache konstituieren, können nun drei funktionelle Ebenen unterschieden werden (die im Bereich der Grammatik auch 'Stufen der Grammatikalität' genannt werden dürfen): *Norm*, *System* und *Sprachtypus*. Die 'Norm' umfaßt die in der Sprache einer bestimmten Gemeinschaft historisch realisierte Technik, alles, was in dieser Sprache allgemein und traditionell verwirklicht ist, ohne dabei notwendig schon funktionelle zu sein. ... Das 'System' stellt die Gesamtheit der funktionellen (distinktiven) Oppositionen dar, die in einer und derselben Sprache festgestellt werden können, sowie die distinktiven Regeln, nach denen diese Sprache gesprochen wird, und, daraus folgend, die funktionellen Grenzen ihrer Variabilität; das System als solches geht schon über das historisch Verwirklichte hinaus, zumal es auch das nach den bestehenden (in der Norm teilweise angewandten) Regeln Realisierbare enthält. ... Der 'Sprachtypus' schließlich enthält die funktionellen Prinzipien, d.h. die Verfahrenstypen und die Oppositionskategorien des gesamten Systems, und stellt somit die zwischen den einzelnen Teilen des Systems feststellbare funktionelle Kohärenz dar. So verstanden, ist der Typus eine objektiv vorhandene sprachliche Struktur, eine funktionelle Ebene der Sprache: er ist einfach die höchste strukturelle Ebene der Sprachtechnik. ... Um noch einmal zusammenzufassen: die 'Norm' enthält das traditionell in einer Sprache Verwirklichte; das 'System' die dem Verwirklichten entsprechenden Regeln;, der 'Typus' die den Regeln des Systems zugrundeliegenden Prinzipien.

I do not understand this characterization (it is not a definition, of course), despite Andersen's attempt to interpret Coseriu's views (Andersen 1980:205–207). I believe that all these seemingly subtle distinctions will evaporate when Coseriu or someone supporting his ideas attempts to make precise the notions of 'functional level', 'structural level', 'steps [or 'levels'] of grammaticality', 'functional', 'distinctive rule', 'functional limits of [its] variability', 'functional principle', 'functional coherence', 'objectively existent linguistic structure', 'principle underlying the rules of the system', etc. As long as this methodological obligation is not fulfilled, there is no reason to take the idea of a language type as a 'functional level' of a language seriously.

6. Hawkins (1980:212) writes, without a reference, "Notice also that the distributional evidence of this section suggests, contra Vennemann, that subjects should also be regarded as operators on verbs as operands". He cannot have had the above three articles in mind but only earlier papers where I had exempted subjects from the specification relation altogether, as is also true, e.g., of Nicolai Trubetzkoy, but not, e.g., of Lucien Tesnière and other traditions.

7. Further examples of linguistic typologies, such as depend on theories of language in

a more immediate sense, can, of course, be given in abundance. To suggest the nature of such examples: (1) A typology of languages based on syllable structure presupposes a theory of language accomodating a theory of syllable structure. (2) A syntactic typology based on other levels than that of the most superficial structure, e.g. on 'deep structure' or some 'intermediate structure', presupposes a general syntactic theory providing for such structures, such as Transformational Grammar; cf. Birnbaum 1970, of which pages 9–48 have been reprinted, discussed, and compared to related accounts in Ramat 1976; cf. also Ramat 1978.

8. This is meant in a strict *methodological* sense. *Heuristically* typologies may serve as guidelines in the development of certain aspects of a theory of language. E.g., the intuitive typological concepts of a consistent *OV* language and a consistent *VO* language together with the classification of Japanese, Turkish, and other languages as members of the former, Maori, Arabic, and others as members of the latter type have guided me in developing my concept of specification, which is not a typological concept but a concept of a general theory of language, viz. a general syntactic theory. This concept, together with the concept of linear order, enters into the definition of a prespecifying and a postspecifying construction, and these serve to define the predicates 'is a consistently prespecifying language' (= 'is a consistent XV language') and 'is a consistently postspecifying language' (= 'is a consistent VX language'), which are still concepts of (viz. definable in) a general syntactic theory, i.e., by implication, of a theory of language. These predicates are then *used* in typology, viz. in the formulation of the ideal typology $\{\{P\}, \{P'\}\}$ (cf. section 5 above) which serves as a more precise version of the original OV/VO typology. But nowhere has a typological concept entered into the theory of language; the concepts mentioned could have been developed *in principle* without knowledge of the OV/VO typology.

9. Cf. also note 8.

10. Similarly, the frequent cooccurence of (several of) the defining properties of Skalička's five 'typological constructs' (cf. notes 3 and 4) is based on linguistic preference. It is, of course, the observation of such preferences which causes typologists to define their ideal types in the first place.

11. Coseriu (1979:77–78) criticizes the idea of 'tendencies' being responsible for the similarity of changes in similar languages and the oriented nature of change, and cautiously suggests that the type (or types) of a language may be responsible for such changes (1979:86–87). Andersen (1980:206) goes even further:

Coseriu's conception, in effect, provides a solution to the problem of drift (Sapir 1921) by assigning what appear to be 'metaconditions on change' a place in the structure of language – and hence in the internalized grammars of the bearers of any language, the only place where such 'metaconditions' can exist in reality. ... It implies in effect that language learners beyond forming hypotheses about the functional system of their language – hypotheses they apparently are able to maintain even in the face of counter-indications in the observable usage that serves as their raw data – form superordinate hypotheses about the ideal type of their language, which may be only imperfectly manifested in its functional system.

The suggestion, if I understand this passage correctly, amounts to the following. Children, on the evidence of supporting as well as counter-indicating data from language use, try to guess the true type of the language they do not yet master; then, under the guidance of the hypothesized type, they acquire (or may, or tend to acquire) a variety of the language whose system is in better harmony with that type than the system of the language they are actually exposed to. If this is the idea, then here we have a case of a theory of change which literally holds language types responsible for language change. But then Andersen continues, "One might question whether such a view of language acquisition [and, by implication, of language change, T. V.] can be confirmed or disconfirmed in any way". One might indeed.

12. Needless to say that the orientative value of such a characterization can be no better

than the typology it is based on, and thus in turn no better than those aspects of the theory of language the typology is based on. As a case in point, consider the suggestion in Friedrich 1976 that Proto-Indo-European may have been an *SVO* language (or 'type II' language) and thus a special case of a *VO* language. Since these types are only vaguely defined, Friedrich (1976:468–470) is in a position to cite as evidence the placement of 'locative auxiliaries' (i.e. adverbial particles with a locative meaning such as English *up, down, along*) both before the noun phrase (i.e., as prepositions) and before the finite verb (i.e., as 'preverbs') in the older European languages. This would not count as evidence in reference to the more precisely defined ideal typology $\{\!\{P\}, \{P'\}\!\}$ of section 5: Prepositions are heads of prepositional phrases, taking noun phrases as complements and thus as specifiers; they are thus indeed evidence for postspecification, or *VX* character. But preverbs are adverbial attributes, and thus specifiers, of finite verbs; they are thus evidence for prespecification, i.e. for *XV* character. See Vennemann 1976a: 34–38 for a more detailed analysis.

Note added in proof

This paper stresses the *conceptual differences* between universals, tendencies, principles of language change, and typologies, associating them with different subdisciplines of linguistics. By contrast, Bernard Comrie's recent book *Language universals and linguistic typology: Syntax and morphology* (Oxford: Basil Blackwell, 1981) emphasises and illustrates the *heuristic relations* among them, which I have mentioned only briefly in note 8 and *passim*. – I have further developed my conception of linguistic preferences in two recent papers, "Überlegungen zu einer Theorie der linguistischen Präferenzen", forthcoming in the Proceedings of the 9. Österreichische Linguistentagung (*Klagenfurter Beiträge zur Sprachwissenschaft*), edited by Willi Mayerthaler and Dieter Pohl, and "Causality and language change: Theories of linguistic preferences as a basis for linguistic explanations", forthcoming in *Folia Linguistica Historica* (June 1983). – My characterization of ideal linguistic typologies in section 5 above has been elaborated and in part corrected in two other recent papers, "What is a linguistic typology?", forthcoming in *Studies in Linguistics* 2 (1982): 3–44 (Taegu Linguistic Society of Korea), and "Universals, preferences, typologies: Definitions and delimitations", presented at the 15th Annual Meeting of the Societas Linguistica Europaea, Athens, September 8–11, 1982 and forthcoming in a festschrift for Werner Winter. All four papers may be obtained from the author.

References

Altmann, Gabriel – Werner Lehfeldt
    1973   *Allgemeine Sprachtypologie: Prinzipien und Meßverfahren* (Munich: Wilhelm Fink).
Andersen, Henning
    1980   "Introduction [of 'Summarizing discussion']", *Typology and genetics of language* (= *Travaux du cercle linguistique de Copenhague*, 20), edited by Torben Thrane et al. (Copenhagen: The Linguistic Circle of Copenhagen), 197–210.

Bartsch, Renate – Theo Vennemann
1982   *Grundzüge der Sprachtheorie: Eine linguistische Einführung* (Tübingen: Max Niemeyer).
Bierwisch, Manfred
1962   "Über den theoretischen Status des Morphems", *Studia Grammatica* 1: 51–89.
Birnbaum, Henrik
1970   "Deep structure and typological linguistics", in: Henrik Birnbaum, *Problems of typological and genetic linguistics framed in a generative framework* (= *Janua Linguarum*, Series minor, 106) (The Hague: Mouton), 9–70.
Boom, Holger van den
1980   "Zur Logik implikativer Universalien", *Wege zur Universalienforschung: Sprachwissenschaftliche Beiträge zum 60. Geburtstag von Hansjakob Seiler*, edited by Gunter Brettschneider and Christian Lehmann (Tübingen: Gunter Narr), 53–58.
Coseriu, Eugenio
1979   "Synchronie, Diachronie und Typologie", in: Eugenio Coseriu, *Sprache – Strukturen und Funktionen: 12 Aufsätze zur allgemeinen und romanischen Sprachwissenschaft* (= *Tübinger Beiträge zur Linguistik*, 2), 3rd edition [1st edition 1970], edited by Uwe Petersen (Tübingen: Max Niemeyer), 77–90.
Friedrich, Paul
1976   "The devil's case: PIE as type II", *Linguistic studies ...*, edited by A. Juilland (Saratoga: Anma Libri), 463–480.
Greenberg, Joseph H.
1966   "Some universals of grammar with particular reference to the order of meaningful elements", *Universals of language*, 2nd edition [1st edition 1963], edited by Joseph H. Greenberg (Cambridge, Mass.: M.I.T. Press), 73–113.
Hawkins, John A.
1980   "On implicational and distributional universals of word order", *Journal of Linguistics* 16: 193–235.
Ineichen, Gustav
1979   *Allgemeine Sprachtypologie: Ansätze und Methoden* (Darmstadt: Wissenschaftliche Buchgesellschaft).
Juilland, Alphonse (ed.)
1976   *Linguistic studies offered to Joseph Greenberg on the occasion of his sixtieth birthday* (Saratoga, California: Anma Libri).
Lewis, David
1975   "Adverbs of quantification", *Formal semantics of natural language*, edited by Edward L. Keenan (Cambridge: Cambridge University Press), 3–15.
Lieb, Hans-Heinrich
1978   "Universals and linguistic explanation", *Universals of human language*, vol. 1: *Method and theory*, edited by Joseph H. Greenberg (Stanford: Stanford University Press), 157–202.
Mayerthaler, Willi
1981   *Morphologische Natürlichkeit* (= *Linguistische Forschungen*, 28) (Wiesbaden: Athenaion).
Ramat, Paolo
1978   *Y a-t-il une typologie profonde? (Quelques considérations théoriques (et pratiques))* (= *Arbeiten des Kölner Universalienprojekts*, 33) (University of Cologne, Department of Linguistics).
Ramat, Paolo (ed.)
1976   *La tipologia linguistica* (Bologna: Il Mulino).
Sapir, Edward
1921   *Language: An introduction to the study of speech* (New York: Harcourt, Brace and World).

Sgall, Petr
  1979 "Die Sprachtypologie V. Skaličkas", *Typologische Studien*, edited by P.
         Hartmann (Braunschweig: Vieweg & Sohn), 1–20.
Skalička, Vladimir
  1979 *Typologische Studien: Mit einem Beitrag von Petr Sgall*, edited by Peter
         Hartmann (Braunschweig: Friedr. Vieweg & Sohn).
Vennemann, Theo
  1972a "Rule inversion", *Lingua* 29:209–242.
  1972b "Sound change and markedness theory: On the history of the German
          consonant system", *Linguistic change and generative theory: Essays from
          the UCLA Conference on Historical Linguistics in the Perspective of Trans-
          formational Theory*, edited by Robert P. Stockwell and Ronald K. S. Macau-
          lay (Bloomington: Indiana University Press), 230–274.
  1974   "Language type and word order", *Linguistica Generalia I: Studies in linguis-
          tic typology* (= *Acta Universitatis Carolinae* 1974, *Philologica* 5) (Prague:
          Charles University [1977]), 219–229.
  1976a "Beiträge der neueren Linguistik zur Sprachgeschichtsschreibung", *Sprach-
          wandel und Sprachgeschichtsschreibung im Deutschen* (= *Sprache der
          Gegenwart: Schriften des Instituts für deutsche Sprache*, 41) (Düsseldorf:
          Pädagogischer Verlag Schwann), 24–42.
  1976b "Categorial grammar and the order of meaningful elements", *Linguistic
          studies ...*, edited by A. Juilland (Saratoga: Anma Libri), 615–634.
  1977   "Konstituenz und Dependenz in einigen neueren Grammatiktheorien",
          Sprachwissenschaft 2: 259–301.
  MS   *An outline of universal phonology* (University of Munich, Department of
  1979   German Philology).
  1982   "Isolation – Agglutination – Flexion? Zur Stimmigkeit typologischer
          Parameter", *Fakten und Theorien: Beiträge zur romanischen und allgemeinen
          Sprachwissenschaft: Festschrift für Helmut Stimm zum 65. Geburtstag*,
          edited by Sieglinde Heinz and Ulrich Wandruszka (Tübingen: Gunter Narr),
          327–334.
Vennemann, Theo – Ray Harlow
  1977   "Categorial grammar and consistent basic *VX* serialization", *Theoretical
          linguistics* 4:227–254.

WERNER WINTER

Reconstructional comparative linguistics and the reconstruction of the syntax of undocumented stages in the development of languages and language families

0. In a recent article by W. P. Lehmann, originally a lecture presented to a fairly wide audience, the following remarks can be found (*Studies in Linguistics* 3.1979.67):

> Much as we reconstruct Proto-Indo-European phonology, or Proto-Semitic phonology, or Proto-Sino-Tibetan phonology, we must now proceed to the reconstruction of Proto-Indo-European syntax, Proto-Bantu syntax and so on. For scholars who explore the early interrelationships within such families or among them must have the same opportunities to deal with syntax as with phonology. In short, historical syntax must be pursued as has been done for historical phonology.
> To develop historical syntax in this way, the same methods are available as for historical phonology: the comparative method and the method of internal reconstruction. Both are relatively simple . . Both have been minutely described. And the use of both of them is well-known from historical phonology.

Some comments are called for.

The first of these may seem almost superfluous: Lehmann uses the term 'historical' in the loose way so commonly found in linguistic writings — that is, not with reference to the study of observable data found in actual documents, but rather to the domain of reconstruction, be it comparative or internal: 'historical' is supposed to mean 'pertaining to times prior to those of attested texts'. The confusion of 'historical' and 'prehistoric' (in the sense of 'pertaining to prehistoric times') is regrettable, but almost usual, and a change in terminology can hardly be hoped for.

The next comment is of greater weight. A traditionally-minded Indo-Europeanist, when faced with Lehmann's remarks, may well be tempted to ask: 'Why is it that Lehmann adduces phonology as a field supposedly neatly parallel to that of syntax, and not what would seem to be a much more likely candidate, viz., morphology?' The answer to this question is in all probability that Lehmann, along with many linguists of this day and age, prefers not to consider morphology a separate level of linguistic structure and of linguistic analysis, of equal standing with phonology and syntax — a decision which to the student of Proto-Indo-European is bound to appear highly questionable because of the paramount importance work on comparison and reconstruction in paradigmatic morphology had for the development of well-reasoned notions about the Proto-Indo-European proto-language (at various stages of its development) as well as about unattested links between Proto-Indo-European and directly observable daughter languages. One may indeed say that hardly anything in the entire field did as much to enhance the status of Indo-European studies as a viable discipline and of Proto-Indo-European as a well-reconstructed entity (or series of entities) as did the careful and painstaking comparative analysis of paradigmatic morphology.

Finally, Lehmann's remarks include a call for action: 'historical syntax must be pursued as has been done for historical phonology'. A comment like this, made more than a century and a half after the inception of Indo-European studies as a scientific endeavor, implies a repetition of a by now rather familiar view: When it became fashionable to consider syntax the area of principal concern for anyone who wanted to be counted among the ranks of linguists, it was only natural that those who had been working in the field of reconstructional comparative linguistics came to be accused of having neglected syntax to the detriment of progress in their field. To be sure, certain achievements of the past, such as Delbrück's, to a lesser extent also Havers' and Hirt's work, did receive credit, but on the whole the fact that comparativists preferred to concentrate on morphology, phonology, lexicon, but not on syntax, was considered a major shortcoming of the efforts of past generations. It is only fair to admit that the neglect of syntax in reconstructional comparative studies is a fact, not an invention of latter-day critics. Whether the conclusions drawn from this fact are also justified is, however, a different matter.

In order to reach a decision on this point, I shall, in the present paper, discuss a number of questions. They are as follows:

(1) Is reconstructional comparative study of syntax really comparable to reconstructional comparative work in phonology and morphology?

(2) Is reconstructional comparative syntax possible if the same data base is used as for reconstructional comparative phonology and morphology?

(3) Is reconstructional comparative syntax possible if the data base is improved?

(4) What possible strategies are conceivable for the establishment of such a data base?

1. It seems a sound approach to the first question to wonder whether the conspicuous neglect of reconstructional comparative syntax was due to some basic weakness in the decision procedures of the comparativists, or whether there was some deeper reason behind what now appeared to be a fault. It probably has to be admitted as a fact that very many comparativists of the past were practitioners rather than theoreticians, that their epistemological

appraisal of their work was perhaps not well reasoned, often maybe not even felt worth considering; but the question remains: why, if they refrained from philosophizing about the necessity of work on syntax, did they not at the very least do it? This is a vexing question: After all, not much time and effort went into certain theoretical aspects of comparative phonology, but work continued to be done all the time. And while there was even less of a theoretical base for comparative morphology, the achievements in the realm of paradigmatic morphology were most impressive. Why, then, was there so little work on syntax?

At first glance, an easy answer seems to be available: There were no adequate models of analysis and presentation at the disposal of comparativists; so they had no way of handling their data in a satisfactory manner.

However, no matter how pleasing this simple answer would be to the hearts and minds of modern linguists, it does not appear to be quite right. To be sure, prestructuralist comparative phonology left much to be desired with respect to an inclusion of units in systems and to an evaluation of units postulated in terms of systems reconstructed from and along with the units, but in one way or other, the units tended to be there, presented perhaps in an atomistic fashion, but nevertheless available as it were as building blocks to work with. Comparative morphology, for all weakness in theory, was handled in an even more satisfactory way: units were always viewed as parts of paradigms, and structuralism was practiced in fact, if not in terminology. Why should it be that comparative syntax did not get a better treatment at the hands of our scholarly forebears?

Perhaps things are after all not as easy as Lehmann and others with him seem to think when it is claimed that reconstructional comparative syntax is a field neatly parallel to that of reconstructional comparative phonology, and that the two should be subjected to the same methods of investigation. It seems that Lehmann, and again numerous other linguists trying their hand at reconstructional comparative syntax, failed to notice the fundamental difference between work in comparative syntax on the one hand and comparative phonology and morphology on the other: Although both types of work share the goal of reconstructing earlier conditions in the development of a language or a language family, phonological and morphological reconstruction deal with manifestations of structures and only through them, all the while retaining the information about the manifestations, with the structures themselves, whereas syntactic reconstruction of the type advocated and practiced by Lehmann is concerned only with generalized patterns (although patterns reconstructed from patterns may secondarily be enriched with illustrative material, as in Lehmann's and Zgusta's rewriting of Schleicher's tale in *Festschrift for Oswald Szemerényi* . . , Amsterdam 1979, 455—

466, but this procedure is diametrically opposed to that followed in 'normal' comparative reconstruction — normally, generalizations are made on the basis of data, here 'data' are invented on the basis of previous generalizations).

Put in a nutshell, it can be said that reconstructional comparative linguistics as practiced in the fields of phonology and morphology (to some extent also in that of lexicology) is a discipline concerned with both substance and form (with substance taking precedence), while comparative syntax à la Lehmann is limited to a comparison of form. Or, to use a different terminology, comparative phonology and morphology are interested in tokens and, through them, in types, whereas the domain of comparative syntax as practiced in recent years is exclusively that of types.

These observations, if correct (and I think they are correct), force me to conclude (as has been done by others) that comparative syntax along Lehmann's lines is not part of reconstructional comparative linguistics in the traditional sense; if anything, it is typology applied diachronically — and we all should know that a diachronical application of typological findings is of highly dubious value, to put it mildly.

I shall return to this point later. Meanwhile, let me take up an argument which Lehmann (following Dressler) gives in favor of his comparison of patterns and not of manifestations of patterns (*Studies in Language* 3.1979.85):

> The syntactician . . is interested in the reconstruction of the *langue,* in what Dressler calls the immanent system of Indo-European syntax, its structures (Baupläne) and rules.

Obviously, this is not an argument, but a statement of preference to which scholars should, of course, be entitled like other human beings, provided there is a rational basis for the statement. All of us would, I think, agree with the expression of an opinion to the effect that a linguist not aiming at a grasp of a particular *langue* would be on the wrong track. But how many of us would seriously claim that access to a *langue* can be gained independently of a painstaking study of the *parole* associated with the *langue* in question, in particular if the shortcuts a native speaker may believe to be able to use are not available to the investigator? The seeming strength of Lehmann's approach to reconstructional comparative syntax, its direct access to patterns of Proto-Indo-European, to Proto-Indo-European *langue,* is indeed its very weakness, a weakness which must be considered fatal if one wants comparative syntax to be part of 'normal' comparative linguistics, a discipline whose principal purpose is reconstruction: Only through a reconstructed Proto-Indo-European *parole* could Proto-Indo-European *langue* become a goal toward which one could work in the field of syntax, too.

To underline this argument, it may not be pointless to enumerate briefly what reconstruction-oriented comparativists actually do.

From data available in several languages known or suspected to be genetically related, say from sounds found in specific environments (such as words with comparable meanings) in several Germanic languages, provided these sounds are similar, they reconstruct hypothetical items that explain the attested phenomena optimally, that is with a minimum of auxiliary hypotheses required. They juxtapose the reconstructed items and others arrived at by the same procedures and study the possibilities of combining the reconstructed items in patterns, in this case sound patterns; they try to select, as the best approximation of the sound system of the reconstructed language, a pattern that is both natural, that is, not improbable in terms of what is known about the typology of sound systems, and maximally explanatory, that is, minimally different, in its constituent members, from the items actually included in the input, in this case then, actually observed. If need be, they adjust the original reconstructions so as to obtain a more reasonable pattern. Reconstructed items and patterns derived from the controlled combination of reconstructed items are then ascribed to a particular stage in the prehistory of the language group under consideration, say Proto-Germanic. Along with the items that were extracted as particles from longer forms, the longer forms, to the extent that they agree with one another in the languages compared, are also ascribed, rewritten in terms of the reconstructed items, to the reconstructed language: the proto-language, say Proto-Germanic, is thus endowed with items, with systems derived from the combination of items, and with strings of items reflecting the existence of comparable strings in the languages compared.

In moving from a later reconstructed stage in the prehistory of a language group to an earlier one, the comparativist repeats what he has done before: he compares items from the reconstructed language with items from other languages or language groups, or from other reconstructed languages, and reconstructs an item that can be ascribed to the earlier stage here under consideration, say, Proto-Indo-European. The item so reconstructed is juxtaposed again with other reconstructed items, patterns are studied, and details of the reconstruction of an item may be revised in the light of the pattern obtained. Again, strings of items, to the extent that they agree in the (proto-)languages compared, are ascribed to the earlier proto-language, say Proto-Indo-European.

Thus, like all languages directly observable, proto-languages are endowed with items that are combined into systems and systems that are derived from the combination of items. Likewise, like all observable languages, proto-languages are claimed to contain strings in which items occur.

A crucially important point should be noted: Nowhere in reconstructional comparative linguistics do we find a direct comparison of patterns or systems. This may at first seem an incredible assertion, but it is easily enough to illustrate the point: If we were to compare the vowel systems of Middle High German and of Modern High German, we would come up with a statement that the systems are identical for short and long (or lax and tense) vowels. This observation, though doubtless correct, is also utterly trivial: it fails to provide information about the changes that have affected the items in the Middle High German vowel system (diphthongization of long vowels, lengthening of short vowels in open syllables), changes which made relatable Modern High German strings differ significantly from their Middle High German counterparts. Or, if we were to compare the system of Proto-Indo-European stops with its three sets of voiceless, voiced, and aspirated items, and were to compare this system with that of Proto-Germanic, which, using Grimm terms, contained a contrast of tenuis, media, and aspirata, we would have to conclude, from the comparison of systems, that there never was a consonant shift setting off Proto-Germanic from Proto-Indo-European. Both proto-languages would belong to the same typological class, no doubt; but from the point of view of diachronic research that is of very little importance — one is almost tempted to say: of none.

The fact that patterns and systems are of no immediate significance for reconstructive work (which does not at all mean denying their vast importance for synchronic linguistics and for the characterization of reconstructed languages) explains very easily why Indo-European (and other reconstrutional-comparative) studies could be so successful in the fields of phonology and morphology. Insights to be gained from systems serve a corrective, not a constitutive, purpose; the role of the evaluation of reconstructed items in terms of systems is by no means to be despised, but that does not mean that a system or pattern as such is part of the reconstructional-comparative process.

If 'historical syntax', as advocated by Lehmann and others, proposes to compare patterns and not realizations of patterns, it cannot be considered part of 'normal' reconstructional-comparative linguistics. This does not imply that it is without value in itself; but there is no basis for an accusation of comparativists of the past and of the present for having neglected to include syntax in their studies to the proper extent and along the lines practiced by Lehmann and others. Once one realizes that traditional comparative phonology and morphology on the one hand and 'historical syntax' as advocated by Lehmann on the other, are not birds of one feather, one senses why our predecessors, perhaps by sheer instinct, shied away from all-out efforts to reconstruct Proto-Indo-European syntax: such all-out efforts would have meant abandoning tested and cherished (and one may add: necessarily required) methods, and since results could not possibly be viewed as independent of the methods chosen to achieve them, the results of the two types of comparison would not have been commensurable.

The reaction on their part should, I think, be applauded and not deplored: reluctance to tackle syntax other than piece-meal led to the result that comparative linguistics aimed at reconstruction remained a unified discipline.

2. The first question I raised has thus been answered if it is interpreted in a narrow sense: 'Historical syntax' as practiced by Lehmann and others is indeed not a peer of reconstructional comparative phonology and morphology; if reconstructional comparative phonology and morphology with their goals and, more important, methods are used to define 'comparative linguistics', then 'historical syntax' is not part of it.

My second question in a way requires the introduction of an even more general query: If Lehmann's 'historical syntax' is no candidate for inclusion in one group with reconstructional-comparative phonology and morphology, what type of syntax, if any, could be included under the common heading 'reconstructional comparative linguistics'?

If the source of comparative reconstruction can only be surface strings and items within such surface strings, then reconstructional comparative syntax can only be based on surface texts, surface sentences, or parts of surface sentences such as surface phrases. Any recourse to generalized patterns, underlying forms, deep structure is out of the question. The data for reconstructional comparative syntax must be matching strings — matching texts, matching sentences, matching phrases. Matching, in turn, must be interpreted in a very strict sense: matching strings on the level of syntax must show the same degree of similarity as matching strings, say, in word formation — the elements making up the surface string must show a regularily recurrent correspondence with the elements constituting a surface string in the language compared. Only by applying these extremely rigid criteria will it be possible to reconstruct syntactic strings of the proto-language, and since generalizations about patterns in a specific language can be considered legitimate only if they have been based on observational data from this very language, generalized statements about the syntax of a proto-language will be legitimate, in the context of reconstructional comparative grammar, only to the extent that they have been based on the comparison of syntactic strings properly reconstructed for this proto-language. It should be noted that I insist on these criteria only for a syntax that is to be part of reconstructional comparative linguistics, it goes without saying that for other types of syntax other rules may be acceptable — but this question is of no immediate concern to me right now.

If the criteria just spelled out are accepted and we now approach my second question ('Can our usual data base, so successfully utilized in work on phonology and morphology, also be used for the reconstruction of syntactic strings?'), we find ourselves faced with a perturbing set of facts. Matching texts can, but need not, be produced in response to matching situative or linguistic stimuli. The likelihood for a matching is much greater in the case of a linguistic triggering — a text in L_1 is more likely to show a close resemblance to a text in L_2, if one is a translation of the other than if both are independent responses to nonlinguistic stimuli. Thus, the most adequate source for matching strings would seem to be translations. However, before we can use translated texts, we have to determine whether they are genuine in the sense that strings found in L_2 are not there only because matching strings in L_1 caused an imitation to be used in L_2, but that the L_2 strings were also found in sufficient number in untranslated L_2 texts. It is immediately obvious that the requirement just introduced (a very natural requirement, by the way) creates very major difficulties in our work with dead languages. What do we do if our early sources are all or at least almost all translations in some of the languages we want to use as a basis for reconstructive work, as is the case in Gothic, Old Church Slavic, Armenian? The irony of the situation is that precisely those properties which we can safely ascribe to the respective syntax of these languages, viz., properties not shared with the Greek texts translated, cannot be used for comparative purposes since they do not meat the matching condition. (An exception to this statement would be in order only if, say, Armenian and Gothic shared a property not found in Greek, but such a case is of a very low rank of probability, and one cannot base a method on it.)

We find then that translations are likely to provide matching strings, but that these strings can only be used for our purposes if they have been proved to be genuine from other, untranslated texts. The condition can be met in relatively few cases: thus, the total corpus of postclassical Latin is in all probability large enough to check out the genuineness of Latin strings in the Vulgate matching their Greek counterparts; for the Gothic Bible translation, the task cannot be fulfilled; for Armenian texts translated from Greek, a certain control is possible by translations from other sources and some original material.

Other texts in early Indo-European languages can be used with utmost caution only for another reason — they are not prose texts. Here the rule must be that strings to be used for interlanguage comparison have first to be proved to be natural by showing that they recur in other than poetically reshaped texts. This makes us exclude Homeric Greek as well as Avestan and most of Old Indic. As a matter of principle, we cannot adopt an eclectic attitude, using some preconceived idea we may have as to what is natural and what deformed in a poetic text, and then introduce what we have ruled to be natural in our reconstructive work. It is precisely this approach (combined with the failure to distinguish typology from comparative linguistics) that detracts so much from the value of Lehmann's *Proto-Indo-European syntax*.

Our answer to my second question has to be: To our great regret, no.

3. The third and fourth question are closely related.

Obviously, some weaknesses of current approaches can be eliminated. A careful study of surface phenomena would benefit not only typological syntax, but also comparative syntax directed toward reconstruction. However, the results would in all probability be marginal.

One possible change in our attitudes may, however, be worth considering. I pointed out that the study of translated texts might prove useful in cases like that of the Latin Bible translation where enough data seem to be available to confirm the nativeness of a Latin string matching a Greek one, or to disconfirm it. In similar ways, translations could be used for analysis in other languages where sufficient indigenous data are at our disposal. The facts of history force us, if we choose to consider this approach, to give up a time-honored principle of comparative linguistics, viz., that the possible effects of change should be minimized by working with the earliest material at our disposal in any given language or language group. If we want to work with a satisfactory data base, we will have to utilize languages with ample texts and preferably languages for which texts can be produced at will, that is, living languages. It is immediately obvious that we would find ourselves confronted with the fact that change has done away with much of what we would have liked to use in reconstructive work. Still, it seems that it would be possible to reconstruct interesting fragments of a Proto-Germanic, a Proto-Slavic, an Indo-Iranian syntax or even a Proto-Indo-European one on the basis of a comparison of living languages of the subgroups or of the entire family. The whole effort might not yield very satisfactory results − we may end up with little more than the reconstruction of a few fragments of sentences, perhaps little more than what has already been suggested on the basis of a study of Indo-European compounds, of poetic collocations, and of legal expressions. The effort needed would be tremendous, the yield possibly very limited, although we might feel a certain sense of satisfaction at having brought comparative syntax, at long last, back to the fold of reconstructional comparative linguistics.

4. But we should not end our line of argument here. There is the fifth question still to be asked: 'Or is reconstructional comparative work impossible in the field of syntax, and if so, why?'

Reconstructional comparative linguistics is concerned with what is 'inherited'. The term, itself inherited, is grossly misleading. What is really meant, is this: What I have called items and strings of items is acquired through a learning process within a single speech community. (Note that this definition does not exclude entities borrowed at an earlier time; this fact seems to pose no problem.) The strings referred to here include morphemes and some combinations of morphemes, but, for instance, only a fraction of words formed by productive derivational processes or by composition, and a very limited number of phrases and clauses. Along with the acquisition of items and some strings goes the development of the learner's ability to recognize relationships among strings and within complex strings and to put this recognition to use by producing new strings rather than having to acquire them by a learning process. The longer and the more complex the strings are, the less likely becomes an acquisition by mere learning. If 'to acquire by learning' is another way of saying 'to inherit', then it is immediately clear why we should have so much trouble with reconstructional comparative syntax: The area of concern of reconstructional comparative linguistics is, as I said, that which was 'inherited'. For sentences, even for most phrases, let alone for texts, acquisition by learning is most unusual (oral literature notwithstanding — it is probably no accident that two of the three areas I mentioned as showing some promise for syntactic reconstructability were poetic and legal diction). Sentences are formed, not learned; morphemes and simple lexemes are learned, not formed. Only for learned entities is there a connection between the use in the speech of an earlier and a later generation, at an earlier and a later stage in the development of a language, in a proto-language and a daughter language. Syntax deals almost exclusively with entities not learned, but constructed — or generated, if we want to use that term. Word formation is a transitional area — some complex forms are learned, others constructed on the basis of patterns extracted from the forms learned. Paradigmatic morphology is even more slanted toward learning, but its productive aspects are covered by constructive processes. (It is interesting to note that the areas of difficulty for reconstructional comparative linguistics and for generative grammar are in complementary distribution — the former is strong in areas where learning, or 'inheritance', counts, the latter, where productive processes have to be accounted for. I shall refrain from a tempting excursus into the question why some comparativists have so little use for generativists, and vice-versa; however, I tend to think that the differences alluded to in this paper have something to do with the more rational aspects of the mutual aversion.)

By its very nature, acquisition by learning can only be applied to a limited number of phenomena. Therefore, phonemes and grammatical morphemes, forming totally or nearly closed sets, are apt to be 'inherited' and therefore eminently suitable for inclusion in the domain of reconstructional comparative work. The same applies to simple lexemes; although it is unlikely that any speaker of a language will ever master all the simple lexemes of this language, the only way open to him for acquiring them is through a learning process. Sentences, on the other hand, form an open-ended set; it is impossible to learn them all, and very few indeed will be learned − most of them are constructed from entities learned and rules abstracted, not acquired by learning in the sense of imitating an entity provided by the extraneous source.

If a learner is able to extract rules from data he incurs, it cannot be said that he 'inherits' rules. Rules, therefore, cannot be subjected to a type of research concerned exclusively with properties of language acquired by imitative learning. This in turn means that there cannot be a reconstructional comparative syntax except for the marginal area of strings transmitted with the intent that they be learned as such (as in oral literature or in the case of complex idioms).

As for morphology, there will always be difficulties when one has to decide whether two forms in related languages with matching constituents and a matching structure should be considered 'inherited' (and thereby subject to comparative reconstruction) or 'generated' from 'inherited' constituents by the application of independently extracted rules. Here one will want to introduce probability criteria: If a complex form can be interpreted as reflecting a pattern very common in the language under consideration, the odds are in favor of language-internal generation unless arguments can be adduced that make this particular form likely to have been acquired as an entity by learning (so that this form, possibly along with others, could have been the raw material from which the speaker extracted the rule that became productive). The more widespread a particular complex form turns out to be among related languages without contact in time and space, the stronger the argument for 'inheritance' becomes. Unproductivity of a pattern found in a complex form, on the other hand, makes it likely that this complex form was learned along with simple ones and could therefore be used for purposes of comparative reconstruction.

The interference of language-internal processes seems to be least in phonology. Here assimilation and dissimilation phenomena, even if found in matching strings, can still be parallel innovations rather than 'inherited' properties; but such considerations will affect the reconstructed lexicon, not the phonology.

5. My claim in this paper has been that reconstructional comparative linguistics can operate only in the area of what has been acquired by learning, that

is, 'inherited'. Anything that is outside the range of direct imitation by the learner, is also outside the domain of this type of linguistics. This fact shows up limitations of our discipline which one may regret to encounter; whatever we reconstruct is bound to be incomplete as a statement of the grammar of a proto-language, incomplete in particular with respect to levels of language which syntax-oriented and semantics-oriented linguists will consider of paramount importance. I have tried to show why we have to live with this situation, whether we like it or not. Typology does not offer a way out; it is not patterns that are transmitted and imitated, but manifestations of patterns which may be interpreted in analogy to the interpretation of the transmitter and be put to productive use, but which may also be subjected to a novel interpretation, which in turn may be used to generate strings different from the ones the transmitter produces (although as a rule the grammar of the transmitter and of the recipient will coincide, or that of the recipient will be made to coincide — the explanation of grammar change is not all that easy). In any case, we know that genetically closely related languages differ greatly in matters typological; it is a mistake to use typological characterizations as an input for reconstructional comparative work. If syntax is only concerned with structures and rules, syntacticians have no chance for succeeding in comparative reconstruction; syntactic rules can be derived only from generalizations based on texts, and if texts cannot be reconstructed beyond some modest phrasal expressions (if these are texts), there can be no Proto-Bantu, Proto-Sino-Tibetan, Proto-Indo-European syntax that is a peer of Proto-Bantu, Proto-Sino-Tibetan, Proto-Indo-European phonology and morphology. One may regret this state of affairs, but I think it is time to reemphasize again the truly great achievements of reconstructional comparative phonology and morphology: they, and to a lesser extent reconstructional comparative lexicology, are the basis for the identification of language groups for which a common origin can be safely assumed; they have proved to be the only reliable access we have to human communication prior to the use of writing. They, and only they, are the branches of 'prehistorical linguistics' accessible to us, and, being that, the only way for us to know anything in a falsifiable, and therefore scientific, way about prehistoric language. This is no mean feat. Those who feel that our failure to reconstruct the syntax of a proto-language (or, for that matter, all aspects of its word formation or of its lexicon) seriously detracts from the importance of the results achieved by reconstructional comparative linguistics should keep in mind that incomplete reconstruction is found wherever the data input is incomplete; only inventions of the human mind may appear perfect — though usually just for a while, as the example of quite a few linguistic theories should show. So I do not feel it necessary to apologize for the imperfections of the reconstructional comparative method; what I was interested in was to show some of its limitations and the reasons for them.

THEO VENNEMANN

Verb-second, verb late, and the brace construction comments on some papers

This discussion does not precisely comment on any of the papers of the Conference. Rather it takes up a number of themes that have been developed in several papers, e.g. in Gerritsen's, Ramat's, Romaine's, and Stockwell's. As the idea is not a presentation of new material but rather a new arrangement of some well-known themes, with some variation, and the new piece has to be short, no time will be wasted on complete citations of any kind.

1 The distinction between verb-early and verb-late placement in Germanic: Speculations on its origin

Disregarding clauses marked for special moods such as interrogatives and imperatives, and concentrating on declarative sentences ('main clauses') and on subordinate clauses introduced by subjunctions (conjunctions and relativizers), we find as a common pattern in the early Germanic dialects that the finite verb is placed later in a subordinate clause than it would be in the corresponding main clause — provided, of course, that there is enough material in the clause to allow for this distinction. Let us call this the verb-earlier / verb-later, or simply the *verb-early* / *verb-late*, distinction. How did this distinction arise?

I take up the following two traditional themes: First, the ancestral language of Germanic was a prespecifying (*XV, OV, SOV*) language. Secondly, noun-specifying clauses, i.e. clausal noun attributes and complements, and verb-specifying clauses, i.e. clausal verb attributes and complements, arose in very early Germanic from loosely adjoined explicative main clauses with demonstrative anaphora; these clauses in time superseded and in part ousted such earlier specifier constructions as are harmonious with prespecifying syntax. Let us see what follows when we combine these two themes.

In a consistently prespecifying language, a sentence has the structure *XV*, where *V* is the finite verb. If the language is not entirely consistent, some constituents may be allowed to follow the finite verb; this may be indicated by the notation *XVx*. A typical explicative sentence with demonstrative anaphora (*d*) has the form *dYV*, or *dYVy*, in such a language. Let us now consider a sequence of two sentences, S_1 and S_2, in which the second stands in the explicative relation to the first, i.e.: $S_1 = XV_1$, $S_2 = dYV_2$, or: $S_1 = XV_1x$, $S_2 = dYV_2y$; and let us assume a gradual process of unisententiation whereby the sequence of S_1 and S_2 becomes a sequence of a main clause and a subordinate clause, the latter introduced by a subjunction *d*, in a new sentence *S:*

$$\underbrace{\underbrace{X \ V_1,}_{S_1} \quad \underbrace{d \ Y \ V_2}_{S_2}}_{S} \qquad \underbrace{\underbrace{X \ V_1 \ x,}_{S_1} \quad \underbrace{d \ Y \ V_2 \ y}_{S_2}}_{S}$$

Here are the consequences: First, subordinate clauses of the resulting kind, viz. clausal specifiers of nouns and verbs, follow the main clause, since this used to be the position of the explicative sentences from which they developed. Secondly, the subjunction of this kind of subordinate clause have a demonstrative etymology, because such is the etymology of the anaphoric elements from which they developed. Thirdly, the subjunctions occupy the initial position within the subordinate clause, because this, according to Behaghel's Second Law, used to be the position of the anaphoric elements from which they developed. Now all of this is well known to be true for the early Germanic languages. But there is yet another consequence: Fourth, the finite verb stands earlier in the resultant sentence *S*, a declarative sentence, than in its subordinate clause S_2, because the verb of *S*, viz. V_1, is followed by the subordinate clause S_2, whereas no such subordinate clause follows the verb V_2 of S_2 (except in the rare event of further subordination). My hypothesis is that postspecifying expansion of verbs by subordinate clauses set up a model for postspecification with sub-clausal constituents, and that postverbal clausal specifiers of nouns exerted a rightward pull on their head nouns according to Behaghel's First Law — but, of course, only in main clauses, because only main clauses would normally be expanded by subordinate clauses. Other developments of a later period, such as the mutual contamination of the rightward expanding subordinate clauses with 'demonstrative' subjunctions and the leftward expanding subordinate clauses with 'interrogative' subjunctions, or the attraction of subordinate clauses to their referential heads according to Behaghel's First Law, are outside the scope of this discussion.

2 Verb-second syntax: Speculations on its origin

During the early period when the new unisententiation device was first available, the difference in verb position was the only feature marking the distinction between parataxis and hypotaxis. The development of demonstrative cataphora signaling subordination of following clauses, in particular the rise of the definite article, had hardly begun and was to take centuries to develop into a new norm. There may have been intonational clues, as is true of other languages. But certainly the most conspicuous and most widely used device to mark the difference was not available at this stage: the distinction between anaphoric demonstratives and subjunctions, e.g. coordinating and subordinating conjunctions. The difference between coordination and subordination may not have mattered a whole lot because the semantic impact is slight in many instances, but it is there nevertheless, cf. the following pair of German sentences, the only difference of which is in the position of the finite verb, at least in the written language:

(a)   Paula nimmt die Pille, trotzdem IST sie schwanger.
(b)   Paula nimmt die Pille, trotzdem sie schwanger IST.
(a')   Paula takes the pill, NEVERTHELESS she is pregnant.
(b')   Paula takes the pill, EVEN THOUGH she is pregnant.

When the Germanic languages were first used in writing, the position of the finite verb in many constructions became the only means of marking the difference in question; e.g., the device of the correlating conjunctions in Old English writing depends on it entirely. Since grammatical markers have to be clear if they are to work, the difference between verb-early and verb-late clauses came to be stressed by placing the finite verb more and more early in main clauses. This development came into conflict with Behaghel's Second Law concerning the early placement of anaphoric constituents: This is the stage of *TVX* main clause structure where several 'thematic' constituents before the finite verb are quite normal. But the development continued until the conflict was resolved with a compromise: the finite verb in second position in main clauses, or *verb-second* syntax. This development is reflected in all the Germanic languages, even in Gothic.

3 The clausal brace: A consequence of verb-second plus verb-late syntax

The finite verb of a Germanic clause is the center — the innermost head — of the clause. All the other clause-level constituents are specifiers of ever more complex finite verbs; the most complex finite verb of a clause is the clause itself. In the ancestral language of Germanic, the position of the finite verb was at or near the end of the clause, according to the traditional hypothesis mentioned; the specifiers appeared mostly before the verb, from right to left in the order of their specificational application. This state of affairs was preserved in subordinate clauses. It may be illustrated with an example from Contemporary Standard German:

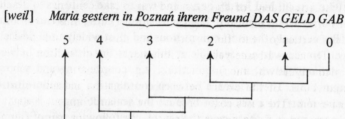

The numbers indicate the order of specificational application. In particular, the constituent with the number 1 is the immediate specifier of the verb with the number 0; they have both been capitalized for perspicuity.

When the finite verb moved to the second position in main clauses, there arose two main possibilities concerning the specifiers of the verb: They could either obey Behaghel's First Law and reorient themselves in relation to the shifted verb position, cf. the Contemporary English main clause analog of the German subordinate clause:

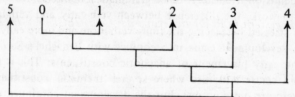

Or they could maintain their old position, letting the finite verb move all by itself, cf. the German main clause analog of the German subordinate clause:

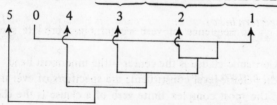

The first solution would result in complete mirror image verb syntax for main and subordinate clauses. Though this is a logical and graphical possibility, I am not certain whether it is a syntactic possibility in natural languages. The second solution is the attested one. Note that this solution by necessity leads to the brace construction: The finite verb and its immediate specifier form a *clausal brace* around the remaining verb specifiers, except for the first constituent of the clause. (This picture retains its essential features even if we realistically assume a slight foward movement of the immediate specifier of the finite verb under the pressure of Behaghel's First Law. The clausal brace persists as long as this specifier has not moved all the way to reunite with the finite verb).

The second part of the clausal brace may be of any category admitted by the finite verb. The cases commonly cited are those where it is an adverbial prefix or a non-finite deverbal derivate (participle or infinitive); they are examples of the *verbal brace:*

(a) [*weil*] *Maria gestern in Poznań ihrem Freund das Geld HERAUSGAB*
$\qquad$ 6 $\quad$ 5 $\quad$ 4 $\qquad$ 3 $\qquad$ 2 $\quad$ 1 $\quad$ 0

(a') *Maria GAB gestern in Poznań ihrem Freund das Geld HERAUS*
$\qquad$ 6 $\quad$ 0 $\quad$ 5 $\qquad$ 4 $\qquad$ 3 $\qquad$ 2 $\quad$ 1

(a") *Mary HANDED OVER the money to her friend in Poznań yesterday*
$\qquad$ 6 $\quad$ 0 $\quad$ 1 $\qquad$ 2 $\qquad$ 3 $\qquad$ 4 $\qquad$ 5

(b) [*weil*] *Maria gestern in P. ihrem Freund das Geld GEGEBEN HATTE*
$\qquad$ 6 $\quad$ 5 $\quad$ 4 $\qquad$ 3 $\qquad$ 2 $\quad$ 1 $\qquad$ 0

(b') *Maria HATTE gestern in Poznań ihrem Freund das Geld GEGEBEN*
$\qquad$ 6 $\quad$ 0 $\quad$ 5 $\qquad$ 4 $\qquad$ 3 $\qquad$ 2 $\quad$ 1

(b") *Mary HAD GIVEN the money to her friend in Poznań yesterday*
$\qquad$ 6 $\quad$ 0 $\quad$ 1 $\qquad$ 2 $\qquad$ 3 $\qquad$ 4 $\qquad$ 5

(c) [*weil*] *Maria gestern in Poznań ihrem Freund das Geld GEBEN SOLLTE*
$\qquad$ 6 $\quad$ 5 $\quad$ 4 $\qquad$ 3 $\qquad$ 2 $\quad$ 1 $\quad$ 0

(c') *Maria SOLLTE gestern in Poznań ihrem Freund das Geld GEBEN*
$\qquad$ 6 $\quad$ 0 $\quad$ 5 $\qquad$ 4 $\qquad$ 3 $\qquad$ 2 $\quad$ 1

(c'') *Mary WAS-TO GIVE the money to her friend in Poznań yesterday*

  6   0   1   2   3   4   5

The brace vs. mirror image construction of the complex verb may even span over all of these constituents at once:

(d) [*weil*] *Maria gestern in Poznań ihrem Freund das Geld*

  8   7   6   5   4

herausgegeben HABEN SOLLTE

  3–2   1   0

(d') *Maria SOLLTE gestern in Poznań ihrem Freund das Geld*

  8   0   7   6   5   4

herausgegeben HABEN

  3–2   1

(d'') *Mary WAS-TO HAVE handed over the money*

  8   0   1   2   3   4

to her friend in Poznań yesterday

  5   6   7

These examples have been taken from Contemporary German for ease of exposition, but analogous examples abound in all of the older Germanic languages. They illustrate my hypothesis that the clausal brace is a consequence of a verb-second plus verb-late syntax.

4 Lengthening or reduction of the clausal brace: A consequence of verb-late development

Verb-second syntax is a stable device, easily formulated in a rule and generalizable. It has been preserved as the basic main clause syntax in all the Germanic languages except English, and as a subsidiary syntax even there. By contrast, verb-late syntax is inherently vague: How late is late enough? Furthermore there is the inevitable analogical pressure of a split syntactic system: Pressure to remodel the subordinate clause syntax upon the main clause syntax. This opens two scenarios for the development of subordinate clause syntax in the Germanic languages: Strengthening or loss of the verb-late device.

The verb-late syntax of subordinate clauses has been preserved in all the German dialects, the languages descended from them, and neighboring Frisian. It has been strengthened in Literary Standard German, possibly owing to the spread of literacy together with the printed book after 1450, to the degree that one can say, with little exaggeration, that Standard German subordinate clauses have *verb-last* syntax, even though rightward transposition beyond the finite verb is a common stylistic device, equivalent to exbraciation from main clauses. The development of verb-last syntax in Standard German may in turn have influenced the dialects, even though these have never gone quite as far. Thus German exemplifies the first scenario.

The second scenario is exemplified by the remaining Germanic languages, viz. English and the Scandinavian languages. This process presupposes the development of a separate category of subjunctions; such a development is indeed more advanced in English and Scandinavian than it is in German. German teachers have made heroic efforts to get their students to understand the difference between *trotzdem* 'nevertheless' and *trotzdem* 'even though'; nevertheless an entire army of substitutes – *obgleich, wenngleich, obschon, obzwar, wenn . . . auch* – have not managed to oust *trotzdem* from its use in subordinate clauses. Likewise earlier attempts to substitute interrogative pronouns for the demonstratives in relative clauses have met with little success: The normal relative pronoun in Standard German is simply the demonstrative. The same is true of earlier attempts to distinguish the subordinators by means of identifying markers such as *daß, was, wo:* They never became general enough to establish a distinct category of subjunctions. The opposite seems to have occurred in the Scandinavian languages and in English – a development which deserves an investigation of its own. – Once a category of subjunctions had been established, the analogical remodeling of subordinate clauses after main clauses was innocuous, even in cases where the subjunction was still homophonous with some coordinating constituent: Main clause word order, i.e. verb-second, amounts to *verb-third* after a subjunction, and thus main clause word order itself became a new mark of subordination, viz. after subjunctions, e.g. in Icelandic:

(a)	*honum batnaði*	'he got well'
(a')	*þegar batnaði honum*	'already he got well'
(a'')	*þegar honum batnaði*	'when he got well'
(b)	*kaffið var hitað*	'the coffee was made'
(b')	*á meðan var kaffið hitað*	'meanwhile the coffee was made'
(b'')	*á meðan kaffið var hitað*	'while the coffee was (being) made'

One may note that the generalization crucially depends on verb-second syntax. It would not work with subject-verb syntax: Generalized subject-verb syntax not only requires a category of subjunctions but a clear division between subjunctions and anaphorical elements:

(a)   *he got well*
(a')   *then he got well*
(a")   *when he got well*

As I have pointed out in the preceding section, the clausal brace owes its existence to the coexistence of verb-second and verb-late syntax. Since this coexistence continues in German, enhanced by the strengthening of verb-late syntax to verb-last syntax in subordinate clauses, the clausal brace has always thrived and even gained length in German. Contrariwise, since verb-late syntax was given up in Scandinavian and, for an intermediate period, in English in favor of generalized verb-second syntax, the clausal brace lost its support, Behaghel's First Law made its power felt, and the brace has been on the decline for centuries, with *exbraciation,* i.e. rightward transposition from the brace, as the mechanism of brace reduction. In English, where the assimilation of subordinate clauses to main clauses was executed with the greatest thoroughness, the reduction of the clausal brace has been carried to the greatest extreme of all of the Germanic languages, with only traces surviving in pronominal object embracing, unmarked indirect object placement, and simple adverb embraciation:

(a)   *I looked it up (*I looked up it)*
(b)   *I gave John a book* (alongside *I gave a book to John*)
(c)   *I have often asked myself this question (*I have more often than seems reasonable asked myself this question)*

Thus, in my theory, the preservation or loss of the clausal brace is not an independent variable but is contingent upon the preservation or loss of the verb-second / verb-late distinction.

5 From theme-marking verb placement to subject-marking verb placement: The new order

The most common constituent before the finite verb in verb-second syntax is the subject, even in Standard German which is still very remote from subject-verb order (more than 60 % *TVX = SVX* in running text). It is this state of affairs which prompts the idea of *inversion:* While not yet applicable to German which is simply a verb-second language, in Scandinavian and Middle English *TVX = SVX* has progressed so far that any *TVX* pattern other than this is felt to be a deviation from *SVX* order, i.e. an inversion. I do not want to speculate on the factors that have furthered it: Accelerated loss of inflection may be a factor, and a linguistically mixed population (Danish / English, Norman-French / English) trying to find a common linguistic ground may be one too; and one may simply be the cause of the other. But one thing seems to me to be an indispensable prerequisite for the development of verb-second into *subject-verb* syntax: A new systematic way of distinguishing between main clauses and subordinate clauses. This has been achieved in English: Subordinate clauses are distinguished from main declarative clauses by a set of nearly unambiguous subjunctions. They are furthermore distinguished rather consistently from main interrogative clauses by their very subject-verb order, whereas interrogatives continue the old verb-first or verb-second order in the guise of auxiliary placement:

(a) *John sang loudly.*
(b) *Why (what, which, that) John sang loudly.*
(c) *Did John sing loudly?*
(d) *Why (what) did John sing loudly?*

(a') *Hans SANG laut.*
(b') *Warum (was, das, daß) Hans laut SANG.*
(c') *SANG Hans laut?*
(d') *Warum (was) SANG Hans laut?*

These examples show that whereas German still relies on finite verb placement to differentiate clause types, English has developed a new complex system for this purpose; and since the difference between finite and non-finite verb forms has largely been eroded by the elimination of flexion, English has gone almost all the way toward an immutable subject-verb complex (*John . . . sing*).

5 Conclusion

I have tried in this discussion to give a unified account of the development of a number of seemingly disparate phenomena in the Germanic languages: verb-early / verb-late; verb-second / verb-late and verb-last; verb-second / verb-third; the brace construction and its loss; inversion; subject-verb syntax. In my account they are all consequences of a single process: the unisententiation of sentences with following explicative sentences and the ensuing exigencies of distinguishing between coordinate and subordinate structure. Needless to say that the present arrangement is hardly more than a piano-score of a piece still to be written. Full orchestration requires an in-depth comparative investigation of coordination and subordination techniques in all the Germanic languages — a task most formidable but most promising.